THE
IMPOSSIBLE
STATE

THE
IMPOSSIBLE
STATE

NORTH KOREA,
PAST AND FUTURE

VICTOR CHA

ecco

An Imprint of HarperCollins Publishers

HarperCollins books may be purchased for educational, business, or sales promotional use. For information please write: Special Markets Department, HarperCollins Publishers, 10 East 53rd Street, New York, NY 10022.

FIRST EDITION

Designed by Suet Yee Chong

Library of Congress Cataloging-in-Publication Data has been applied for.

ISBN 978-0-06-199850-8

12 13 14 15 16   OV/RRD   10 9 8 7 6 5 4 3 2 1

For my mother, Soon Ock, and my wife, Hyun Jung

CONTENTS

A NOTE ON THE KOREAN TEXT   ix

GLOSSARY OF ACRONYMS AND ABBREVIATIONS   xi

ONE   CONTRADICTIONS   1

TWO   THE BEST DAYS   19

THREE   ALL IN THE FAMILY   64

FOUR   FIVE BAD DECISIONS   110

FIVE   THE WORST PLACE ON EARTH   162

SIX   THE LOGIC OF DETERRENCE   212

SEVEN   COMPLETE, VERIFIABLE, AND IRREVERSIBLE DISMANTLEMENT (CVID)   247

EIGHT   NEIGHBORS   315

NINE   APPROACHING UNIFICATION   386

TEN   THE END IS NEAR   427

ACKNOWLEDGMENTS   465

NOTES   469

INDEX   507

A NOTE ON THE KOREAN TEXT

Romanization of the Korean language has long suffered from a lack of a single, agreed-upon standard for spelling, which is why you will variously see "Kim Jong Il," "Kim Jong-Il," "Kim Jong-il," and "Kim Chŏng-il" in the press and academic publications. The book at hand uses something of a mishmash of different standardized Romanization techniques. For names and places that will be familiar to many readers, such as "Kim Il-sung," "Kim Dae-jung," and "Pyongyang," Revised Romanization is used. For names of people and places less familiar to the casual observer, McCune-Reischauer Romanization is used. And for those who aren't acquainted with Korean, Chinese, or Japanese names, it bears pointing out that in nearly all cases (with the exception of a few, whose names are widely known and/or used in the reverse order, such as Syngman Rhee), Korean, Chinese, and Japanese names are written in their traditional order, with the surname first and the given name last.

GLOSSARY OF ACRONYMS AND ABBREVIATIONS

BDA	Banco Delta Asia
BTWC	Biological and Toxin Weapons Convention
CCP	Chinese Communist Party
CMEA	Council for Mutual Economic Assistance (Comecon)
CSIS	Center for Strategic and International Studies
CWC	Chemical Weapons Convention
DMZ	Demilitarized Zone
DNI	Director of National Intelligence (U.S.)
DPJ	Democratic Party of Japan
DPMO	Defense Prisoner of War/Missing Personnel Office
DPRK	Democratic People's Republic of Korea (North Korea)
EEZ	Exclusive Economic Zone
EIU	Economist Intelligence Unit
FAO	Food and Agriculture Organization (U.N.)
FDR	Flight Data Recorder
FROG	Free-Rocket-Over-Ground
GDR	German Democratic Republic (East Germany)
HEU	Highly Enriched Uranium
HFO	Heavy Fuel Oil
IAEA	International Atomic Energy Agency
ICAO	International Civil Aviation Organization
ICBM	Intercontinental Ballistic Missile
ICC	International Criminal Court
IED	Improvised Explosive Device
IOC	International Olympic Committee
JFA	Joint Field Activity
JRA	Japanese Red Army
JSP	Japan Socialist Party
KAL	Korean Air Lines
KCIA	Korean Central Intelligence Agency (South)
KCNA	Korean Central News Agency (North)
KDI	Korea Development Institute (South)
KEDO	Korean Peninsula Energy Development Organization
KINU	Korea Institute for National Unification (South)
KOTRA	Korea Trade-Investment Promotion Agency (South)
KPA	Korean People's Army (North)

KWP	Korean Workers' Party (North)
LDP	Liberal Democratic Party (Japan)
LWR	Light-Water Reactor
MAC	Military Armistice Commission
MTCR	Missile Technology Control Regime
NAM	Non-Aligned Movement
NBA	National Basketball Association
NCAFP	National Committee on American Foreign Policy
NDC	National Defense Commission (North Korea)
NEACD	Northeast Asian Cooperation Dialogue
NPT	Nuclear Non-Proliferation Treaty
NSA	National Security Agency (North Korea)
NSC	National Security Council (U.S.)
NWFZ	Nuclear Weapons–Free Zone
ODA	Official Development Assistance
OECD	Organisation for Economic Co-operation and Development
POW/MIA	Prisoners of War/Missing in Action
PUST	Pyongyang University of Science and Technology
PRC	People's Republic of China
PSI	Proliferation Security Initiative
ROK	Republic of Korea (South Korea)
SAM	Surface-to-Air Missile
SDF	Self-Defense Forces (Japan)
SEZ	Special Economic Zone
STU	Secure Telephone Unit
TD-I	Taep'odong-I
TD-II	Taep'odong-II
UNHCR	United Nations High Commissioner for Refugees
UNSCR	United Nations Security Council Resolution
USAID	United States Agency for International Development
WHO	World Health Organization
WMD	Weapons of Mass Destruction

THE
IMPOSSIBLE
STATE

CHAPTER ONE

CONTRADICTIONS

WE PASSED OVER BARREN AND GRAY FIELDS AS THE GULFSTREAM VI TOUCHED DOWN on the empty runway of the airport. As the plane taxied on the tarmac, there was no flight traffic to be seen. No baggage carts or fuel trucks shuttling about. It looked as though we were the only arrival or departure of the day. We cruised past two passenger planes with propeller engines, the kind you would see in a 1940s Humphrey Bogart movie. Then the plane turned right and the main terminal came into view, a small 1960s-era building about one-tenth the size of today's international air terminals. Scrawled across the top of the edifice with large, red block letters was PYONGYANG, written in English and in *Han'gŭl* (Korean characters). Hanging atop the center of the Sunan international air terminal's façade was an oversize portrait of the first leader of the Democratic People's Republic of Korea (DPRK, North Korea), Kim Il-sung.

We prepared to deplane into the cool spring air, after the long flight from Elmendorf Air Base in Alaska. It was dusk with an orange glow to the sky, and it was eerily silent: no street sounds, no car horns, no birds. We disembarked one by one, following established security protocol, while two security officers, known as "ravens," checked each of our names off the passenger manifest. The ravens then escorted us to a receiving party of North Korean airport staff and foreign ministry officials, who were standing on the tarmac in front of the Kim Il-sung portrait. It was at that point that our security detail turned around and headed back to the plane. I blurted out, "Hey, aren't you guys coming with us?" The agent, looking puzzled at my naive question through his dark sunglasses, responded, "No sir, we stay with the plane. Too much sensitive comms equipment aboard to stay overnight in enemy territory. We will transport southbound to Osan [air base in South Korea]. See you on the other side in a few days, sir." The Gulfstream VI was a military plane that the White House provided at the request of New Mexico's then-governor Bill Richardson who had pressed the George W. Bush administration to allow him to visit North Korea. The plane was capable of confidential communications (and probably a whole host of other things I was unaware of). I then remembered that the ravens, who were fully armed, always checked us on and off the plane at our various stops along the way, but the only time they ever separated from the plane was when we overnighted at Elmendorf Air Force Base, a secure facility. I thought to myself, "U.S. military plane, invaluable; U.S. government officials, expendable."

My job on this trip as National Security Council (NSC) staff was to accompany the governor and make sure he did not make any nuclear deals outside of the ones we were then trying to negotiate through the Six-Party Talks. Our specific mission was to negotiate the successful return of a set of POW/MIA (Prisoners of War/Missing in Action) remains from the Korean War that was held by the Korean People's Army (KPA). Two experts from the Defense Department were detailed for the trip. One was a forensics expert. The other was a Central Asia policy expert, who also was a Ph.D. candidate at Georgetown University, and on whose dissertation committee I later served. Richardson, then about to announce his candidacy for president on the Democratic ticket, was the media highlight of the trip (he had brought with him Andrea Mitchell of NBC News and an Associated Press correspondent, to ensure adequate publicity), but this was the first time U.S. officials from the second term of the Bush administration had entered North Korea. The last time had been in 2002, when the United States confronted North Korea about a clandestine second nuclear program that was in violation of standing agreements. This sparked a major crisis that led to ballistic missile tests and, ultimately, a nuclear test by Pyongyang. So no one knew exactly what to expect.

As we walked up a small set of steps to meet the receiving party in front of the VIP entrance, the only recognizable face was that of Mats Foyer, the Swedish ambassador to Pyongyang, who I later found out had insisted on being at the airport to greet us, since Sweden was the protecting power for American interests in North Korea. This arrangement with Sweden exists because the United States has no embassy in Pyongyang, as it remains technically at war with the country. A cease-fire, not a peace treaty, ended hostilities in 1953. I looked over my shoulder to see our plane departing down the runway, and mumbled to the two Pentagon officials standing next to me, "The three of us should stay together, and not get separated during this trip." Once inside the terminal, we were offered some refreshments and exchanged some diplomatic pleasantries. We were asked to pay an entry fee in cash. (Credit cards don't work in North Korea.) We were given our schedules by the hosts, which under normal circumstances would be something handled by our embassy and for which every detail would have been painstakingly ironed out in advance of the trip. In this case, however, the North Koreans provided no details in advance, preferring to maintain total control of the itinerary; hence, we were literally flying blind into the country, unclear of what we would do.

As we headed out to the transportation vehicles, I looked at the departure board for flights. The long, black board had only one entry for the day, a flight to Beijing. The Sunan Airport parking lot was empty except for our awaiting convoy. The North Koreans directed Governor Richardson to one car, an old 1970s Cadillac sedan, and indicated for me to get into a separate car, a brand-new Volkswagen Passat. They told everyone else to get into the vans. The two Defense Department personnel immediately tried to rectify the situation, claiming that I needed to travel with the other members of the official detail, but we really did not have much choice in the matter unless we wanted to create a scene. I made eye contact with them saying that it was okay. I sat in the backseat of the car and watched as the rest of the traveling party filed onto the van. I peered over at the odometer and noticed that the car had less than one hundred kilometers (60 mi) on it. I induced that the Chinese must have provided a fleet of these new Passats in contravention of standing U.N. sanctions against the North. At that moment, the thought crossed my mind that I was alone in an enemy country with White House security clearances of the highest order, no diplomatic or security protection, and sitting in the back of a sedan with no idea where the driver and his companion in the front seat might be instructed to take me. I sat back and closed my eyes. Normally, one would use the car ride on official trips to work on the BlackBerry or field calls from Washington. But there was no BlackBerry service and no global cell service. I had no U.S. embassy control officer passing me cables and intelligence traffic to review. I could not even ask the driver what the score of the previous evening's Yankees–Red Sox game was. (I was born in New York City.)

I dozed off and awoke thirty minutes later to see our convoy speeding down wide and empty thoroughfares as I got my first look at Pyongyang. As an academic, I had studied the country for decades, and as a U.S. official, I had negotiated with their diplomats, but I had never set foot in the country until this trip. We sped past what appeared to be a work unit of hundreds of school-age children walking twelve-wide and thirty-deep with the first student carrying a numbered placard. We whizzed past the gates of Kim Il-sung University, where book-toting college students were pouring onto the sidewalks after their day's study. The car then slowed as we passed a large, white, gated structure on my right side. This used to be the official residence of Kim Il-sung, but after his death in 1994, it was turned into a mausoleum, an $8.9 billion, 115,000-square-foot structure surrounded by moats and complete with marble floors, kilometer-long (0.6 mi) halls, moving walkways, escalators, air-purification systems, and automatic shoe-cleaners, where the Great Leader's embalmed body is housed in a clear sarcophagus.[1] Our car then turned right down a secluded dirt road with barbed-wire fencing. I could see farmers in the distance tilling the land with an ox. (I saw only one tractor on the whole trip despite passing hundreds of acres of farmland.) We drove past a guarded checkpost and entered the Paekhwawŏn State Guesthouse, a lush green compound with a private lake and many pheasants wandering about. The manager greeted us and escorted us to our rooms.

The high-ceilinged, tastefully appointed European-style rooms had an inner door and an outer door with traditional keyholes, but no keys. I flipped on the television to see what service was available. A black screen came to life momentarily with the BBC logo in the bottom right corner, but then a graphic appeared, saying SERVICE NOT AVAILABLE. I turned to another channel, with the CNN logo at the bottom, but after a few seconds the same notice showed up. I flipped through all the channels to find only two that came through. One was a broadcast of the Supreme People's Assembly—DPRK rubber-stamp legislature—hearing in progress. The other was a documentary about the exploits of Great Leader Kim Il-sung as an anti-Japanese guerrilla fighter. The only phone service available in the room was two white phones sitting atop the writing desk. Written on a thin strip of white paper underneath one of them was LOCAL CALLS, and the other INTERNATIONAL CALLS. I thought about dialing a random number on the local phone to see whom I would get, but then picked up the international phone, dialed 9 to get an outside line, and then called the White House Situation Room, knowing full well that there were probably about ten people listening in on the call from a room somewhere in the guesthouse. The Sit Room patched me through to Steve Hadley, the national security adviser. I said, "Mr. Hadley, I just wanted to let you know that the party has safely arrived in Pyongyang." "Good," he responded. I then said, "Mr. Hadley, we are staying at the Paekhwawŏn Guesthouse, where I am calling you from a phone designated for international calls in my room." There was a brief pause on the other end of the line, after which Hadley, fully aware of the lack of any secure communications, responded, "Okay, got it." Every call after that was a one-way conversation in which I would report on the day's events, but the White House would be in receive mode only, not giving the North the benefit of any insights into our position.

I could not sleep very well that night, a combination of jet lag and restlessness at what the trip might have in store. As I stared at the ceiling in my room, I was thinking that I had never imagined myself to be in this position. As a professor of international relations at Georgetown University, I had written about U.S. policy in Asia, and was interested in studying policy, but did not intend to practice it. Friends in the Bush administration, such as Dr. Michael Green, had liked some of what I had written, and during two postdoctoral stints at Stanford University's Hoover Institution (where I was the Edward Teller National Security Fellow) and the Center for International Security and Cooperation, I had gotten to know Dr. Condoleezza Rice, then a professor of political science and university provost. When they asked if I would be willing to serve on the NSC, it was hard to say no—both out of a sense of public duty and because of my substantive interests in the area. Three years later, another sleepless night was not unusual except that it was without the incessant humming of a BlackBerry, which was now basically an overpriced paperweight in service-absent North Korea.

At dawn, I walked downstairs and onto the grounds. There were no birds chirping, as the country suffered deforestation because of floods and energy shortages that forced the people to cut down trees for firewood. Distant military marching-band music could be heard piped from loudspeakers in the center of the city. Small pheasants ran about, making shrieking sounds I had never heard before. (I think they may have been served at dinner that night.) On the contained compound, there were no ubiquitous North Korean guides normally accompanying foreigners every minute, so I wandered around the grounds by a pond. I caught glimpses of armed soldiers quietly standing guard every two hundred yards or so on the other side of the fence. The contrast between this blissfully peaceful moment and the larger strategic context of the trip was stark. Here we were in the midst of a nuclear crisis with North Korea—the worst since 1994, when the United States contemplated a preemptive strike on the Yongbyon nuclear complex. The Kim regime had only months earlier carried out an unprecedented nuclear test, which led to the severest U.N. Security Council (UNSC) sanctions since the Korean War. Additional financial sanctions were targeting the leadership's personal assets held in overseas bank accounts. Pyongyang threatened to turn the Republic of Korea (ROK, South Korea) into a "sea of fire," and declared that it was unafraid of war with the United States. I returned to the guesthouse to see the manager standing outside the entrance puffing on a cigarette. He was a middle-age man with a friendly smile, wearing a gray overcoat, dark glasses, slippers, and the ubiquitous Kim Il-sung lapel badge. He asked if there was enough heat and hot water last night. I told him that there was more than enough. We chatted about the weather in Washington and Pyongyang, and I complimented him on the beauty of the Paekhwawŏn grounds. He then said quietly to me in Korean that I was the first White House official to stay in the guesthouse since former president Jimmy Carter in 1994. I laughed uncomfortably, since this fellow did not know that I was just a lowly NSC staff director of Asian affairs. Then, as he extinguished his cigarette and exhaled his last puff, he murmured quietly that he wished us well in trying to bring peace between our two countries. It was the last thing I had expected to hear, given the poor state of our relations.

NORTH KOREA IS the Impossible State. The regime, created in 1948 out of the division of the Korean Peninsula by U.S. and Soviet occupation forces at the beginning of the Cold War, has outlasted anyone's expectations. Even after the mighty Soviet Union and other communist regimes collapsed some two decades ago, this enigmatic Asian nation continues to hang on. Today, we witness an Arab Spring, where dictators in Egypt, Tunisia, Yemen, and Libya, ensconced in power much longer than North Korea's leadership, have been ousted, and yet the Dear Leader Kim Jong-il (as he is referred to within the DPRK), until his death in late 2011, and his son, Kim Jong-un (the so-called Great Successor), sit happily in Pyongyang declaring 2012 as the year of a "powerful and prosperous nation" (*kangsŏng tae'guk*). The regime remains intact despite famine, global economic sanctions, a collapsed economy, and almost complete isolation from the rest of the world. By any metric, this poor, backward, and isolated place should have been relegated to history's graveyard. It is a hermetically sealed Cold War anachronism.

North Korea is a land of contradictions. North Korean schoolchildren learn grammatical conjugations of past, present, and future by reciting "We killed Americans," "We are killing Americans," "We will kill Americans." They learn elementary school math with word problems that subtract or divide the number of dead American soldiers to get the solution. Yet, at the same time, since 1994 the school curriculum has made English, not Russian, the mandatory foreign language of study. In terms of economics, the facts are even more bewildering. North Korea sits at the heart of the most vibrant economic region of the world. It has the globe's second largest economy on its border (China), the third largest economy across the sea (Japan), and the fifteenth largest economy contiguous to it, with which it shares a common language (South Korea). It has a young, literate, and inexpensive labor force. The U.S. Geological Survey assesses North Korea to have some of the world's largest untapped reserves of coal, iron ore, limestone, magnesite, and other minerals akin to rare earth reserves (tungsten, molybdenum, and niobium-tantalum). A Goldman Sachs report estimated the value of North Korea's mineral deposits at 140 times the country's GDP.[2] Yet the economy has been in freefall for the past two decades. Per capita gross national income has contracted from $1,160 in 1990 to $960 in 2009. Life expectancy rates are 67.4 years, down from 70.2 years in 1990. Rather than engage in commerce with the world, the North Korean regime engages in self-sustaining illicit activities. It is one of the world's biggest counterfeiters of U.S. currency. North Korea's fake $100 bill is so authentic-looking that U.S. law enforcement agencies refer to it as the "supernote," because it is based on printing technology and a specialized ink that is better than the original bills produced by the U.S. government. North Korea is also one of the world's biggest producers of counterfeit cigarettes and medications, including Viagra.

Along with this colossal economic mismanagement, the people of North Korea endure some of the worst human rights abuses in the world. North Korea ranks seventh out of seven (lowest possible) on Freedom House's Freedom in the World index, and is therefore one of just nine countries to be given the ignominious title "the Worst of the Worst."[3] It is in the 0th percentile for the World Bank's Voice and Accountability index and ranks dead-last in the Freedom of the Press index. In North Korea, you can get thrown into a gulag for six months of hard labor for watching a DVD of Jackie Chan's *Twin Dragons*[4] or for humming South Korean pop songs. If the portraits of Kim Il-sung and Kim Jong-il in your home or office are not properly dusted or are hung off-center, you could be sent to jail. Even if you do everything right, one evening the secret police can knock on your door, strip you and your entire family of your worldly possessions, and throw you into a gulag because it was discovered that someone in your family from a previous generation was a collaborator with Japanese colonial authorities.

A recent CNN report with Wolf Blitzer and Alina Cho showed North Koreans in Pyongyang using cell phones and enjoying themselves at amusement parks. The impression given was that the world knows very little about what happens behind Kim's iron curtain (this is true) but that when we peer behind it, things are not all that bad (this is false). A few neatly dressed elites playing games on their cell phones, which do not have cell service outside the country, does not represent North Korea. Public executions more than tripled in the past year. The numbers of prisoners in North Korea's infamous *kwalliso* (prison camps)—a system as bad as Stalin's gulags—is reportedly on the rise. Shoot-to-kill orders are in effect for North Korean refugees seeking to cross the Yalu or Tumen Rivers into China. When international news reporters broadcast that cell phones are a sign of the North's willingness to reform, they must have missed the public bulletin boards in Korean, which forbid the use of Chinese-made mobile phones (which, with a prepaid SIM card, can dial outside of the country) and the use of foreign currency as a crime punishable by death. Three North Koreans in ninety thousand today own their own car. About ten out of a hundred own a refrigerator in their apartments. The DPRK is one of the few industrialized societies in the history of the modern nation-state system to have suffered a famine that killed as much as 10 percent of the population. Most everyone is a vegetarian, but not by choice. The average meal is a small bowl of boiled corn with a sprinkling of pickles. Beef is so scarce that for the average North Korean, it is a delicacy eaten only once per year. NGO groups that visited rural areas in February 2011 had a question on their nutritional surveys that asked, "When was the last time you had protein?" Virtually every respondent could remember the exact date when they last had an egg or a piece of meat, revealing the state of undernourishment. The government's public distribution system (PDS) provides about 1,500 calories per day, which is less than the U.N. requirement for minimum need. The effects of this systemic malnourishment will be evident for generations: the average seven-year-old boy in North Korea is twenty centimeters (8 in) shorter and ten kilograms (22 lb) lighter than in South Korea. In spite of all this, when the world tries to help the people of North Korea with food, the regime blatantly violates the four basic norms of humanitarian aid: access, transparency, nondiscrimination, and a focus on the most vulnerable.

Yet the North Korean people, despite all of their hardship, believe that they are the chosen people. They consider themselves fortunate to have been born of the purest race, and in the most innocent, virginal, and virtuous society in the world. They followed the direction of their Dear Leader Kim Jong-il until his death because they believe that they need a strong leader to protect them from the evils of the world. Even those who defect from the country do so not out of political dissension but because of economic hardship. Nearly nine out of ten defectors today, many of whom settle in South Korea, where there are now over 21,000,[5] still self-identify as "North Korean" rather than as a "Korean" or "South Korean." And 75 percent of them say that they still retain affection for the Great Leader Kim Il-sung, Dear Leader Kim Jong-il, and the Great Successor Kim Jong-un.[6]

For decades, North Korea has demanded face-to-face negotiations with the United States over Pyongyang's nuclear programs. It has called for the United States to treat it with respect and to declare nonhostile intent if it wants the North to sit down for serious denuclearization negotiations. Pyongyang has said countless times that if the U.S. did not threaten it, there would be no need for nuclear weapons. They claim that ridding the Korean Peninsula of nuclear weapons was the dying wish of the Great Leader, Kim Il-sung. Yet when President Barack Obama extended an open hand to the regime, it was slapped away definitively. In his inaugural speech, President Obama promised to engage with isolated regimes in all corners of the globe if others would be willing to unclench their fist. As an initial gesture of his commitment, the new American president appointed four ambassadorial-rank special envoys for North Korea. The administration sent its top envoy, Ambassador Stephen Bosworth, dean of the Fletcher School of Law and Diplomacy at Tufts University and former U.S. ambassador to South Korea, to Pyongyang in December 2009 with a personal letter from President Obama for the North Korean leader, explaining the U.S.'s sincere intent to improve relations. Despite the most forward-leaning start to any U.S. administration's efforts at engagement with the DPRK, Pyongyang did not allow Bosworth to deliver the letter to the leader. It reciprocated instead in April 2009 by conducting a ballistic missile test that overflew Japan in the direction of the United States. In May 2009, it conducted a second nuclear test. In March 2010, DPRK submarines torpedoed a South Korean naval vessel, killing forty-six young men. In November 2010, it fired artillery at a South Korean island, killing four, injuring scores, and forcing an evacuation of the island's civilians. And in that same month, it revealed that it was pursuing a second nuclear program based on uranium enrichment, which it had denied it was doing for the previous seven years.

North Korean behavior is offensive not only to the United States. Its second nuclear test, at 9:54 A.M. local time on May 25, 2009, took place at an underground facility only seventy kilometers (44 mi) from the Chinese border. By any metric, this is a very dangerous action, threatening to Chinese interests. The test took place on Memorial Day in the United States, a national holiday, and ballistic missile tests in 2006 took place on Independence Day (July 4). Pyongyang has also called for sessions of the Six-Party Talks, which China hosts, to extend through Chinese Lunar New Year festivities. With each of these "in-your-face" actions by the North, international pressure mounts on China, as the only country with real material leverage on the North. Yet Beijing countenances an extraordinary amount of bad DPRK behavior, continues to feed the country with about 1 million tons of food assistance annually, and makes rote calls for a return to dialogue among all the parties. For Kim Jong-il's seventieth birthday in February 2011, Beijing presented him with a large porcelain peach, which symbolizes longevity. The complexity of this relationship is profound.

Pyongyang claims it pursues nuclear weapons out of self-defense against a U.S. invasion, and Kim Jong-il said he was willing to give these up in exchange for security assurances and economic benefits. Yet the only monument to the late leader—in a land of thousands of statues to his father—sits in front of the Yongbyon nuclear complex, where they make plutonium for nuclear weapons. It is a fifty-foot (15 m) structure with a likeness of Kim standing with a group of scientists and soldiers urging them to work in the nation's defense. North Korean propaganda warns their citizens to be on 24/7 alert for aggression from American imperialists. On several occasions, I have said to North Korean interlocutors that this is about the craziest assertion they could make. The United States has no intention of invading North Korea. The one administration that they were probably the most concerned about, under George W. Bush, even put in writing in the 2005 Six-Party Joint Statement that the United States had no intent to attack North Korea with nuclear or conventional weapons. I asked my North Korean interlocutors, "Why would we possibly want to invade you? Even if we were the revisionist imperialists that your propaganda spouts we are, what do you have of value that we could possibly want?" The North maintains its need for a powerful nuclear deterrent nonetheless. Yet thirteen thousand pieces of

North Korean artillery can rain millions of shells, both conventionally and chemically armed, on the population of Seoul in one day. The warning time for a North Korean artillery shell hitting South Korea is forty-five seconds. Seventy percent of North Korea's 1.1-million-man army sits forward-deployed on the Demilitarized Zone (DMZ), ready to attack at a moment's notice. That is a powerful deterrent to any American or South Korean contemplation of invasion. So why the nukes?

North Korea has undergone extraordinary hardships for a country that emerged at the end of World War II with one of the most developed economic infrastructures in Asia. Japanese colonial authorities had built a network of heavy and chemical industries, railroad and telecommunications systems that were state-of-the-art at the time. Today, North Korea's industrial capacity is worn down and its economy has contracted, if not collapsed. It continues to have massive food shortages of over 1 million metric tons annually. While neighboring South Korea boasts the most online subscribers and smart-phone users per household in the world, North Korean city-dwellers still line up on the street thirty-deep to use a public phone, and less than one hundredth of 1 percent of the population has access to a computer (which itself is restricted from access to the Internet). Yet in spite of this all, there are signs throughout the city of Pyongyang that carry revolutionary slogans about the strength of the nation, the most ironic of which reads, WE HAVE NOTHING TO ENVY.

THE ARGUMENT

How did North Korea become the Impossible State? How has it survived when many others of its ilk have long since collapsed, and as revolutions in the Middle East and North Africa spell the demise of the few remaining ones like it? How could the leadership have made so many poor decisions? Why don't the people rise up against the injustice? How can one trash an economy as bad as the North has? What do they want to achieve with their nuclear threats? Why won't they accept help from others? And what does the leadership ultimately want?

In one sense, the answers to these questions are simple. North Korea has survived as the Impossible State because no one on the inside is empowered to overthrow it, and no one on the outside cares enough to risk the costs of changing it. But the answers are also quite complex. I believe that without looking at the history of the Kim family, its over-the-top personality cult, and its ideology, we cannot explain why the North Korean people, even those who have defected, still harbor affection for the leadership. We cannot understand the nuclear weapons threats without understanding some of the bad economic choices the regime has made over its sixty-plus-year history. We cannot understand the human rights abuses without understanding the intense paranoia of the regime. And I don't think we can begin to understand the regime's bizarrely professed self-confidence without understanding how it views its own history, ideology, and mission.

I believe that the forty-fifth president of the United States will contend with a major crisis of governance in North Korea before he or she leaves office. The regime has survived for this long due to a unique confluence of factors that include geography, humanitarian assistance, a temporarily generous South Korean government, Chinese support, and some dumb luck. But this confluence is dissipating. The core argument of this book is that a growing space between the state and the people will cause a crisis of governance and uproot the foundations of the regime. This gap derives from state ideologies and political institutions that are becoming even more rigid and controlling, on the one hand, while society is moving in the direction of greater marketization and economic entrepreneurship, on the other. The crisis of governance is being accelerated by Kim Jong-il's sudden death in December 2011, which forced an abbreviated and rushed dynastic succession process to the inexperienced and not-yet-thirty-year-old son, Kim Jong-un. (We don't know his exact age.) The state is becoming more rigid because a new leadership in North Korea must be accompanied by a new ideology. The old ideology of a "Powerful and Prosperous nation" or "rich nation, strong army" (*kangsŏng tae'guk*) under Kim Jong-il will not suffice, because it was an utter failure in terms of the state's performance, with the one exception of building nuclear weapons. The new ideology that accompanies this leadership change is what I call "*neojuche* revivalism." This is a return to a harder-line, more orthodox *juche* ideology (defined as self-reliance) of the 1950s and 1960s, when North Korea saw its best days. *Neojuche* revivalism, moreover, denigrates as a mistake and as ideological pollution the failed period of experimentation and reform that was attempted at the end of the Cold War. The problem the regime encounters is that this hard-line ideological shift is occurring at a time when fledgling markets have become a permanent fixture of North Korean society. Government-authorized markets, but more important, black markets have emerged all over the country in response to the economic failures in the early 2000s and in response to the government's suspension of the public distribution system. Once the state stopped providing rations of food and other goods to the people, they were forced to find their own means of survival through barter and trade to avoid starvation. The government's failure, in this regard, led to society's marketization. The government has since cracked down, but the change is unmistakable and unstoppable. Recent defectors from North Korea admit that they purchased as much as 75 percent of their food from the market, as opposed to receiving it through government rations. Thus, a gap, not unlike the ones witnessed in the Arab Spring, is emerging where political institutions cannot keep apace of societal changes. This combustible situation is taking place amid a shaky and unprecedented third Communist dynastic succession. This is an untenable situation. North Korea is not capable of circumventing this crisis of governance, because in the end, Chinese-style economic modernization is not possible. China had Deng Xiaoping, a charismatic leader, to push for reform. There is no Deng in North Korea. Chinese leaders espoused the virtue "To get rich is glorious." But in North Korea, political control is still more important than money. We do not know what spark will cause the crisis of governance, just as no one predicted that the self-immolation of Mohamed Bouazizi, a frustrated and humiliated twenty-six-year-old vegetable vendor in Tunisia, would set off the greatest movements for political change the Middle East has seen since the fall of the Ottoman Empire some ninety years ago. But it is coming.

In this book, I will also look at U.S. relations with North Korea. In November 2007, a North Korean merchant vessel was attacked by Somali pirates. The twenty-two-member crew was beaten as the ship was overtaken. The USS *James E. Williams* responded, freed the ship, and provided medical treatment to the North Korean crew. Both the U.S. State Department and the North Korean news media referred favorably to the operation. In the long history of U.S.-DPRK relations, this was one of the rare positive moments in a deep sea of acrimony. For North Korea, the relationship with the United States is personal. Pyongyang expresses its hostility by doing ballistic missile and nuclear tests on American national holidays like July 4 and Memorial Day, and in one instance, within a day of a sitting president's birthday. North Korean children to this day do not know that a man has landed on the moon, since this would suggest some respect for the United States.[7] They have never heard of Elvis Presley or Michael Jackson, but they do know of Michael Jordan and can recite passages from the movie classic *Gone with the Wind,*[8] because these were personal favorites of the Dear Leader. There are anti-American billboards on the streets of Pyongyang just as there are movie billboards on Sunset Boulevard. One hears a great deal about the close relationship between China and North Korea. Indeed, China may be the one country that has consistently kept North Korea afloat despite the regime's many mistakes, by giving it food and energy assistance. But the only country that can solve the security problem that North Korea poses is the United States. Pyongyang wants diplomatic relations with the world's superpower, and it wants to be recognized as a normal state without the plethora of U.S. sanctions levied against it. It wants a peace treaty ending the Korean War, and it seeks to be accepted in the community of nations. The key country that can provide these benefits is the United States. The problem for Washington is that after three decades of negotiation through successive administrations starting with Ronald Reagan through to the current one, it is becoming increasingly clear that Pyongyang wants all of these things while it keeps a portion of its current nuclear arsenal, not in exchange for complete denuclearization. In surveying the history of American diplomatic efforts to stop the nuclear program, I will try to answer critical questions about how the United States should deal with North Korea. What alternatives are there to denuclearizing North Korea, if any? Does the death of Kim Jong-il and a change of regime in Pyongyang make the challenges for the United States greater or not?

IN THE PAGES that follow, I will try to unpack this enigma of a country. The world knows very little about North Korea. There is probably no society more closed off from the world today; not even Burma or Syria rival the level of control found in this country. From a government perspective as well, North Korea presents one of the hardest intelligence targets to penetrate. Very few are allowed to enter the country. Even fewer are allowed to exit. What can be seen from satellites, moreover, is probably only a portion of that which is buried deep underground in eleven thousand tunnels and caves.

Though the treatment I offer in this book is not flattering to the regime, I attempt to offer a corrective to some of the punditry, misconceptions, and caricatures in the news and entertainment media about the place. Most Americans know little more about North Korea than the comical portrayal of Kim Jong-il in the movie *Team America*.[9] Numerous editorials in newspapers have referred to him as a "plutonium madman" with a penchant for fine cognac and Swedish models. It is also widely known that most North Koreans are told that the first time Kim Jong-il played golf, he got eleven of eighteen holes-in-one. Even serious news periodicals like the *Economist* could not resist, once putting Kim Jong-il on the cover with the caption "Greetings Earthlings."[10] If little is known about Kim Jong-il, far less is known about the heir apparent, Kim Jong-un, the third and youngest son of the Dear Leader. Up until September 2010, the only picture that existed of him in the world was one from when he was in elementary school. At the North Korean Workers' Party (KWP) conference in October 2010, party officials declared to foreign journalists amid the massive displays of military hardware and goose-stepping soldiers that "Our people are honored to serve great president Kim Il Sung and the great leader Kim Jong Il. Now we have the honor of serving young general Kim Jong Un . . . [our country] is blessed with great leaders from generation to generation."[11] A *Washington Post* front-page story interviewed former classmates at an international school in Switzerland, where Kim Jong-un reportedly studied. From these interviews, we learned that he was a big fan of the National Basketball Association (NBA), and especially idolized Michael Jordan and Kobe Bryant, but not much else.[12] Again, this is all very amusing and mysterious, but the lack of information about North Korea is deadly serious. Here is a country that is the newest nuclear-weapons state. It has violated every nonproliferation and human rights norm, and has sold every weapons system it has ever produced to regimes in the Middle East, South Asia, and Africa that are unfriendly to U.S. interests, including Iraq, Iran, Pakistan, and Syria. And with the sudden death of its dictator, the state is in the process of handing power over to an inexperienced young man of whom we did not even have a picture until late 2010. We knew far more about Mahmoud Ahmadinejad in Iran, the late Osama Bin Laden, the late Saddam Hussein, the late Muammar Qaddafi, and General Than Shwe in Burma than we know about Kim Jong-un, who is about to lead the world's worst renegade nuclear state.

In order to understand North Korea, one must begin with a look at the way they view their own history. Chapter 2 will consider international relations and the Cold War through the eyes of North Korea, when the regime truly saw its best days. In chapter 3, I will offer the reader a fairly close look at the bizarre personality-cult leadership of North Korea with particular focus on the only three leaders the country has ever known: Kim Il-sung; his son Kim Jong-il; and the grandson, Kim Jong-un. I will also delineate the leadership dilemmas the young Kim faces. After studying the leadership, chapter 4 will regard the North Korean economy in the context of five historic, bad decisions made by the regime. These decisions are largely responsible for the current economic collapse of the country. Books about North Korea give too little attention to the human rights abuses. I chronicle some of the horrific stories of defectors, famine survivors, and gulag prisoners in chapter 5, which is not for the faint of heart. With this understanding of the history, leadership, economics, and society, I move to the security issues that matter most for Americans: deterrence and the nuclear program. Chapter 6 looks at the military balances that have maintained the peace on the Korean Peninsula since 1953. Chapter 7 studies the history of how Pyongyang got into the nuclear business, and the history of U.S. diplomacy to denuclearize North Korea. Chapter 8 provides the reader with an understanding of the complex relationships the DPRK has had with countries in the region, including China, Russia, and Japan. With China in particular, I argue that the relationship is not nearly as chummy as the popular press believe. The two countries in actuality dislike each other quite intensely, but they are caught in a mutual hostage relationship—the North needs Chinese help for their survival, and the Chinese need the North not to collapse. No discussion of North

Korea would be complete without a discussion of inter-Korean relations and unification. Chapter 9 looks at how the two Koreas historically have thought about unification and what the prospects are for it today. I conclude the book by looking at the meaning of Kim Jong-il's death and the Arab Spring for North Korea. As events unfolded in the Middle East and North Africa, Pyongyang banned all news stories of the demonstrations. To the extent that there were reports in the North Korean media, the demonstrations were portrayed as anti-American. The regime has banned all public gatherings and has even gone so far as to remove booths and partitions in public places like restaurants to discourage people from meeting. Hosni Mubarak reportedly was a friend of Kim Jong-il's, and the DPRK leader must have watched with empathetic unease as Mubarak and his son, Gamal, lost control of the country amid the protests. I believe the events in the Middle East and North Africa, in conjunction with a shaky leadership transition following Kim's death, have tremendous implications for the future of the country.

I am not the first author nor the last to write about North Korea. And I do not profess to know the truth about what happens inside this country. My analysis is based on years of study of North Korea and the East Asian region as a scholar. It is also based on my brief period of public service in the White House dealing with these issues, and interacting with the North Koreans in different places around the world, including in Pyongyang. The discussion in the pages that follow is based on facts and history, but it is also based on hunches, guesses, and gut instincts derived from these personal experiences.

THE BEST DAYS

WHEN I WAS NATIONAL SECURITY COUNCIL STAFF TO THE PRESIDENT, ONE OF MY many tasks was to draft everything that the president and his national security adviser might read or say about Korea. What the staff writes, of course, goes through an editing and clearance process, whether by speechwriters or by other directorates at the NSC that have interests in Korea, or even by the president himself. This was a position of tremendous honor and responsibility, and I treasured every opportunity to write for the president. One of the themes that then–senior director for Asia Michael Green and I used to emphasize in President Bush's speeches and statements was the common values and ideals that underlay the military alliance between the United States and the Republic of Korea. This was an alliance born out of the Cold War, between peoples who knew nothing about one another, literally at opposite ends of the earth. There was nothing intrinsically valuable about Korea to the United States. It was merely a patch of earth that had strategic value only because Washington did not want the Communists to own it, and for which 33,692 Americans died in a terrible war.[1]

But the alliance blossomed from these early days. South Korea went from an economy that USAID (United States Agency for International Development) specialists predicted would not amount to more than an agriculturally based and light-manufacturing economy to a global ranking as high as the eighth largest economy in the world (now ranked fifteenth), and one of the world's most technologically sophisticated societies. While at the end of the Korean War telephone usage was virtually nil, today South Korea has the highest cell phone and Internet usage per population of any country in the world. Korean companies like Samsung Electronics have higher revenues today than Sony, Panasonic, and Toshiba combined. In politics, South Korea went from a Cold War anti-Communist military dictatorship to a full-fledged, vibrant democracy. During these early days, America had mixed views about South Korea. It was a bulwark against Communism and the front line of defense to protect Japan, but its authoritarian leaders were human rights abusers who trampled freedom of speech. In this regard, South Korea's democratic transition and vibrant civil society today stands as one of the most successful cases of peaceful political transition in the history of the modern state system.

President Bush understood this evolution well. In his speeches, he would constantly refer to Korea as a model of an advanced industrialized society that emerged from the ashes of the war, and would describe the alliance between the countries as built upon a foundation of democratic values and an agenda of helping provide for the global common good. South Koreans received help from the United States in the past, but once it developed, it gave back, sending troops to Afghanistan and Iraq, participating in peacekeeping missions in Lebanon and East Timor, and donating to earthquake victims in Haiti. (The latter held special sentimental value for Koreans, since Haiti once donated supplies to a struggling Korea in the 1950s.) South Korea went from being a recipient of international development assistance to a provider of this assistance to poorer countries around the world. Seoul's hosting of the G-20 summit in November 2010 was a watershed moment in Korea's odyssey, as it became the first non-G8 country to host this global governance event. As both Presidents Bush and Obama have stated publicly, South Korea today represents the quintessential successful example of what the United States fought the Cold War to achieve.

The Cold War was integral to South Korean history, but for North Korea, the Cold War is not only its past, it is also its present and future. The country still lives in the siege mentality of those bygone days even as the rest of the region has long since moved on. The Soviet Union made peace with South Korea and normalized political relations in 1990. Communist China followed suit in 1992. But for the Kim regime, there still is no peace settlement with the United States, Japan, or South Korea. While South Korea remembers the Cold War as the distant past, the North is constantly reliving it, spewing threats about American imperialists and South Korean puppet regimes. The rote political science explanation for this clinging to the past is that the leadership needs external threats in order to justify its iron grip on the people and build its military capabilities. But I think there is more to this yearning for the Cold War. It is shaping up to be an integral part of the ideology being created for the post–Kim Jong-il era in North Korea. This ideology does not look forward; instead it seeks to revive the images and terminology of the Cold War, and shuns reform and openness. Why this fixation on the Cold War?

The answer, I believe, lies in the fact that the Cold War era has been and will continue to be the best days of the North Korean nation-state. It was during a period of about three and a half decades beginning in 1945 that the North Korean leadership and its people saw history on its side. By most metrics, the North was doing better than its rival regime in the South. There was a confidence in Pyongyang that their system was better and that unification, the ultimate Korean prize, would eventually be its destiny. Despite the failed attempt to unify the peninsula through war in 1950, events after the war bolstered North Korean confidence. Aid from two Communist patrons, political turmoil in the rival South, and the American entanglement in Vietnam were all perceived as trends that favored Pyongyang. If you travel to Pyongyang today, you would see neat eight-lane-wide thoroughfares, carefully manicured public spaces, and a city planned around iconography and monuments dedicated to Kim Il-sung, the first leader of North Korea. But you would also notice that almost everything looks retro—in the sense that it was all built in the 1950s and 1960s—when the North had the resources and capacity to govern as a fairly well-to-do Communist state. The Cold War represents history, but it also represents an aspiration point for North Korean ideology. This history and narrative continues to inform North Korea's "back-to-the-future" thinking today. It is to this history that I now turn.

THE NORMAL NARRATIVE for North Korea that we see used on CNN or in *Time* magazine goes like this: weak, desperate, and starving country. No money, no friends. An outlaw state. Kooky and isolated leader. But what we fail to understand is that this is largely a two-decades-old, post–Cold

War narrative about North Korea that coincided with the first revelations of its pursuit of nuclear weapons in the late 1980s, early 1990s. The media then drew links between the country's relative deprivation and the leadership's gambit to shift all remaining resources to becoming a nuclear weapons state.

But in North Korean minds, for ninety years before the collapse of the Soviet Union, North Korea was hardly a basket case. It was a well-endowed and well-supported country, which was a model example for communism in the developing world. Looking at the country today though, few people could imagine that North Korea was the most industrialized and urbanized Asian country to emerge from World War II. This was because Japan's occupation of Korea from 1910 to 1945 left massive industries in northern Korea. Colonial authorities built mines and processing plants for deposits of coal, iron, magnesium, and zinc, which were more plentiful in the north than in the south. The Japanese constructed large nitrogen fertilizer plants, and scores of reservoirs and hundreds of pumping stations, which allowed the North to fully fertilize and irrigate its lands. By 1945, when Korea was liberated by Soviet and U.S. troops, the northern half possessed 76 percent of the peninsula's mining production, 80 percent of its heavy industrial capacity, and 92 percent of its electricity-generation capabilities.[2] The North Korean government found itself in 1945 inheriting and nationalizing state-of-the-art factories and technology. By contrast, in South Korea, which the Japanese treated as the "bread basket" of the Korean colony, there was no industry to nationalize and only scorched rice paddies.

I was reminded of North Korea's superior position in these early years at a dinner hosted by the Chinese at the state guesthouse during a round of Six-Party Talks in 2005. I sat with my North and South Korean counterparts as we continued the day's negotiations on what sorts of energy assistance could be provided to the North in exchange for their denuclearization. The North insisted on light water reactor (LWR) technology (civilian nuclear energy), because that was the deal they were promised by the Clinton administration in an earlier agreement made in 1994. The South Koreans, knowing the Bush administration's reluctance to give any form of nuclear capacity to the North (and the administration's allergy to this element of the Clinton-era agreement), instead offered the

North 2 million kilowatts of conventional electricity annually as a substitute. This was objectively a better offer, because the power would be immediately usable, whereas a light water reactor–based civilian nuclear energy grid would take over ten years to build. The South Korean delegate said his country could provide this to the North through existing power stations and the laying of power lines northward across the thirty-eighth parallel. The North Korean delegate refused the idea outright, remembering clearly what the then-richer North had done some fifty years earlier to the electricity-deprived South. In 1945, the North had inherited the largest collection of hydroelectric power plants in Asia from the Japanese occupation, which enabled them to produce electricity for the whole peninsula. When the peninsula was divided at the thirty-eighth parallel by U.S. and Soviet occupying forces, one of the main power plants in Korea was located on the northern side of the dividing line with power distributed through lines southward. Once the division became permanent, however, the North cut off all electricity to the South, creating tremendous hardship. Though the South Korean delegate promised that his country would never cut off power in the same way, the North refused to even consider the idea.

The Korean War from 1950 to 1953 leveled a lot of the North's inherited advantages. Kim Il-sung's mistaken calculation to invade the South led, among other things, to U.S. carpet-bombing of the country, which essentially wiped out all Japanese-built industries. (In defending the South, the United States dropped more bombs on the North than they had done in all air campaigns in World War II.) China and the Soviet Union, however, worked hard to rebuild the country. The North benefited immensely from this. Only two weeks after the August 1953 armistice ending the war, Kim Il-sung gave a speech titled "Everything for the Postwar Rehabilitation and Development for the People." The first Three-Year Plan's (1954–1956) focus was on reconstruction and expansion of heavy industry as the basis of national power. Kim Il-sung received heavy industrial equipment, power plants, hydroelectric dams, electrified railroads, and irrigation systems from Soviet benefactors. China offered crude oil, food, and fertilizer. North Korea gained additional currency by exporting gold, zinc, steel, and minerals to both Moscow and Beijing. The names of the major facilities give a sense of the heavy industry push: Hwanghae and Kimch'aek Iron Works; Ch'ŏngjin and Kangsŏn Steel Works; Hŭich'ŏn, Nagwŏn, and Pukch'ang Machine Factories; Sŏngch'ŏn Lead Mine; Hŭngnam Chemical Fertilizer Plant; Korea-Soviet Oil Company; Aoki Synthetic Oil Plant; and Namp'o Glass Factory. The pace of this development was rapid, spanning a decade before any South Korean heavy industry took root in the economy. The results soon became clear: the DPRK was producing exponentially more of everything than the South, including coal, fertilizer, ferrous metals, cement, steel, and machine equipment. Industrial production grew at an average 15 percent annually in the North, far ahead of that of the South. Indeed, for the first thirty years after the establishment of the two Koreas, the U.S. Central Intelligence Agency estimated that North Korean GNP per capita outstripped that of the South.

Though difficult to imagine today, when buildings outside of Pyongyang have no windows or heating, the North was a well-heated and well-lit society during the Cold War. With Soviet help, the North rebuilt large hydroelectric power plants after the Korean War so that by 1963, the country had reached 71 percent electrification, and by 1970 all households and villages were covered, outpacing the South in metrics of both coverage and energy consumption. In 1971, energy consumption in the North (1,326 kW) was more than twice that of the South (521 kW) on a per capita basis. North Korea retained its dominance in energy use right up until 1988, but since then the South has pulled ahead rapidly. Today, South Korea's per capita energy consumption (4,856 kW) is more than six times that of the North (774 kW), which has been on a steady decline since 1985.[3]

The North Koreans were also the better-fed lot on the peninsula. From the 1950s to the late 1970s, the DPRK embarked upon a massive modernization program of its irrigation, rural electrification, agricultural mechanization, and chemical fertilization programs. With Soviet help, they built scores of reservoirs and over five hundred pumping stations for irrigation. While in 1954 irrigated land totaled only 227,000 hectares, by the 1980s the North had over 1,700 reservoirs running water through a 40,000-kilometer (24,855 mi) irrigation network to feed 1.4 million hectares of cropland.[4] The average calorie intake of North

Koreans (3,000 calories/day) was higher than that of South Korea. Mechanized agriculture also exploded during these years, with rural electrification going from just 47 percent in 1953 up to 92 percent of all towns and villages in 1961.[5] While the DPRK was using high-technology chemical fertilizers in its fields, the South Koreans were using manure. Though North Koreans suffered through a famine in the mid-1990s, during the Cold War they enjoyed bumper crop years and produced enough food that Chinese, during their great famine in the late 1950s, were migrating across the Yalu River border into the North for sustenance. Beyond agriculture, the North had large cattle, sheep, goat, pig, and poultry (which it is said to have been particularly proud of) farms that annually produced millions of tons of meat and eggs. And in the 1960s and 1970s, North Korea rapidly expanded its fisheries industry, going from 465,000 tons of fisheries equipment in 1960 to 1.14 million just a decade later, enabling the harvesting of large volumes of pollack, squid, herring, mackerel, and pike.[6]

Though hard to imagine today, given its autarchic state, North Korea was a fairly high-tech economy in the 1960s and 1970s. It engaged mightily in trade with Soviet bloc countries, selling iron and steel, cement, minerals such as gold and magnesite, and textiles and clothing, importing foodstuffs, energy, light machinery and equipment, and electronic goods to fill up its department stores. North Korean trade with non–Soviet bloc countries, including West Germany and Japan, was also significant, allowing them to import the latest hospital equipment and light and heavy construction equipment. While in the 1950s Communist countries comprised 90 percent of North Korean trade, by 1974 these countries totaled only 51 percent as the North diversified toward the West and other OECD (Organisation for Economic Co-operation and Development) countries.[7] Its trade relationship with Japan during this time is estimated to have been especially robust, comprising as much as one-third of all of the North's international trade.[8] Visiting in 1972, the Pulitzer Prize–winning American journalist Harrison Salisbury called North Korea "a tremendous technical and industrial achievement," and even claimed that it was "on a per capita basis . . . the most intensively industrialized country in Asia, with the exception of Japan."[9]

By comparison, the South's struggling agrarian economy could barely get off the ground despite large amounts of foreign-development assistance, mostly from the United States. The relative advantages of the North at the time were not lost on the South. When then–South Korean intelligence director Yi Hu-rak traveled to North Korea for the first time in 1972 for secret negotiations that eventually led to the signing of an inter-Korean joint communiqué (see chapter 9), he could not help but admire the city of Pyongyang with its manicured thoroughfares, tall buildings, and massive monuments. When he returned home to Seoul, he told President Park Chung-hee (1961–1979) about the North's high level of development and construction, and both men worried that their own countrymen might see the socialist model on display in the North as more appealing. Park's and Lee's concern was that Marxist-Leninism remained quite popular among university students in the South, since the defeat of colonizer Japan was depicted as the defeat of imperialism on the peninsula. Indeed, many Koreans-in-exile who returned to the country after 1945 joined the Korean Communist Party in the South as nationalists and patriots. (There were actually a higher number of communists and socialists in the South at the end of World War II than in the North.) The material well-being of the North at this time only added to its ideological appeal: here was a government that was fulfilling the social contract, providing for its people, and anti-imperialist/nationalist (meaning anti-Japan) in its political stance.

In the early Cold War years, the North Korean military grew rapidly. At its outset, the DPRK military started out with about 135,000 men, with many of the officer corps battle-hardened from experiences fighting as anti-Japanese guerrillas during the war. Soviet troops left the peninsula in 1948, but 350 military advisers stayed behind to train the KPA in how to use state-of-the-art Soviet T-34 tanks, artillery, automatic weapons, fighter planes, and bombers. In 1958, the Korean People's Army attained a level of readiness that permitted the complete withdrawal of all Chinese forces that had been stationed in the country since the end of the Korean War, despite the U.S.'s stationing of between 50,000 and 75,000 troops in the South in the few preceding years.[10] In the 1970s, the regime also started acquiring Scud missiles from Egypt and began to reverse-engineer these to create their own. The Korean People's Army underwent massive reorganization and modernization, likely based on their perceptions of the U.S.'s struggles in the Vietnam War and tactics employed in Arab-Israeli wars of the time, emphasizing speed, surprise, and unconventional warfare.[11] North Korea's military leadership developed an operational doctrine that they referred to as "Two-front War." This basically entailed their very large conventional forces, supported by artillery, armor, and mechanized infantry units, employing shock, speed, and surprise to overrun the DMZ, envelop the South Korean forces, and take the entire peninsula (the first front). The second front would be composed of their elite special forces units, who would infiltrate deep into South Korean territory to destroy, disrupt, or neutralize U.S. and South Korean operations and lines of communication.[12] By the end of the decade, North Korean forces primed to carry out such plans numbered over 720,000,[13] with approximately 60,000 of these being elite special forces units. By contrast, the South Korean military was terribly weak. It had nine army divisions, but they were poorly trained and equipped. The United States at the time did not provide a lot of arms, for fear that South Korean president Syngman Rhee (1948–1960) might use them to provoke a war with the North, thereby drawing the United States into his reunification plans. Moreover, the U.S. military sent half as many tanks to the South as existed in the North, because they believed that tanks could not operate in rice paddies.

Geopolitics during the Cold War favored the North. This might sound strange, given the steadfast alliance between the United States and South Korea. However, one need only scratch beneath the surface to find the alliance as one constant source of anxiety in a world of political and economic uncertainties for South Korea. Meanwhile, the North was strongly supported by its two big power patrons, was politically stable, and was seen as a model of socialist development. In July of 1961, Kim Il-sung succeeded in persuading Nikita Khrushchev to sign a "Treaty of Friendship, Cooperation, and Mutual Assistance." This treaty bound the two parties to extend military assistance if either suffered an attack, to not enter into any alliance directed against the other, to not interfere in the internal affairs of the other, and to consult together on important international issues of mutual interest. Just a few days later, Kim inked an alliance bearing the same name with the People's Republic of China

(PRC, China). The treaty with the Chinese had identical terms: namely, mutual defense, a mutual agreement not to ally against each other, non-interference, and mutual consultation. The two treaties not only provided security guarantees to Pyongyang, but they also showered Kim with large amounts of patron aid and trade. During this period, the Soviet Union, China, and other Council for Mutual Economic Assistance (CMEA, Comecon) countries provided food, machinery, equipment, and even built entire industrial enterprises in North Korea. While estimates vary widely, it is believed that as much as $4.75 billion worth of aid was delivered to the North between the end of World War II and 1984. Nearly half of this aid was put forth by the Soviet Union, almost 20 percent by the Chinese, and the remainder by other Soviet bloc countries. The Soviets helped the North Koreans build or rehabilitate approximately 170 large industrial plants in the power, mining, chemical, construction, and heavy machinery industries. These plants reportedly produced about 40 percent of North Korean steel and iron ore, 50 percent of its oil products, and 60 percent of all the North's electric power.[14] In the late 1970s, the Chinese, too, reportedly had ten thousand workers in the DPRK, working on the construction of a number of hydroelectric power plants.[15] While, officially, the majority of this aid was given in the form of "loans," as the years went by, the Chinese and Soviets likely understood well that they would not be seeing their money again.

One of the primary causes for the mutual courting of the North was the emerging tensions within the Communist bloc between Moscow and Beijing. Brewing since the 1940s, the roots of the Sino-Soviet split generally lie in their divergent applications of Marxism and competition for power within the Communist bloc. The Soviets followed traditional Marxist-Leninist theory of an urban or worker-based revolution. But the Chinese found this impossible, given their demographics and geography, and therefore modified Marxist theory and incorporated a peasant-based revolutionary doctrine. The added fact that the Soviets were so happy to sit on the sidelines during the Korean War further created a culture of resentment and mistrust among Chinese Communist Party (CCP) elites. Then, when Nikita Khrushchev came to power in 1956, he gave a Communist-world-shattering speech at the Twentieth Party Congress of the Communist Party, which became known as the "Secret Speech."

In this address to the Communist bloc, Khrushchev denounced Stalin's "extreme methods and mass repressions," and derided "his intolerance, his brutality, and his abuse of power." He referred to Stalin's leadership as a "vile provocation of odious falsification and of criminal violation of revolutionary legality," and described Stalin himself as "capricious, irritable, and brutal."[16] This policy of "de-Stalinization" and Khrushchev's subsequent embarkation upon "peaceful coexistence" between Communist and capitalist worlds led Chairman Mao and the Chinese leadership to further distance themselves from their Soviet Communist comrades. While in the early years of Sino-Soviet tensions mutual hostility was largely subdued, by 1960 it had lost all subtlety, with Khrushchev publicly referring to Mao as "an ultra-leftist, an ultra-dogmatist, and a left revisionist . . . oblivious of any interests but his own, spinning theories detached from the modern world." The Chinese responded in kind, claiming Khrushchev's rule was "patriarchal, arbitrary, and tyrannical."[17] These divisions, while unnoticed by many in the West until border clashes started between the two countries in 1969, were certainly not lost on the North Koreans, and they positioned themselves to take full advantage.

The Sino-Soviet split had the effect of increasing the strategic value of North Korea to both countries. Neither believed that it could afford to let the North's allegiances fall fully to the other camp. This belief especially rang true after the Korean War, which made the peninsula a front line of the Cold War confrontation. The shame of allowing the other to claim the sole mantle of supporting the North in the cause of the Revolution was too much for either Communist power to bear. Kim Il-sung benefited immensely from this competition, alternating loyalties between the two sides while maximizing assistance from each. The North swung ever so slightly, back and forth between the two camps, not so far as to lose the support of either one but far enough so that they noticed the distance and would vie for its loyalty. After Khrushchev's "de-Stalinization" speech, Kim leaned slightly in the direction of Mao, as the denunciation of Stalin's personality cult threatened Kim's own rule. Once the Cultural Revolution (1966–1969) took hold in China though, Kim tilted back toward the Soviets, and it is said that during this period posters of Kim could be found in Beijing depicting him as a "fat revisionist" and a "disciple of Khrushchev."[18] During the 1970s, once Chinese politics stabilized, Sino-DPRK relations warmed once again, and those with the Soviets cooled, evinced by the fact that not a single Soviet Politburo member visited the North between 1971 and 1978.[19] And after Deng Xiaoping's rise to power in 1978, and the initiation of the reform era in China, Kim and the North would once again primarily return to Soviet patronage, until the collapse of the Soviet Union a decade later.

Kim Il-sung's country was popular in both the Communist movement and in the Non-Aligned Movement (NAM). The North Korean leader was good friends with the likes of East Germany's party secretary-general Erich Honecker and Romania's president Nicolae Ceausescu. According to recently released archives at the Woodrow Wilson Center, on a visit by Ceausescu with his wife in 1971, the Romanian leader marveled at the city of Pyongyang, its development, and its efficiency. In the Non-Aligned Movement, the North was recognized as a model socialist state, with an ideology of self-reliance and independence that fit well, at least rhetorically, with the political stance of the movement. By contrast, the South tried in 1975 and failed to become a member of the Non-Aligned Movement. Non-aligned members rejected the South because of the presence of foreign (U.S.) troops on its soil. Of course, North Korea was not without its problems, but the point to emphasize is that if the country today seeks to build an ideology for its future leadership that harkens back to the past, it is not surprising that they look back to the Cold War years. The picture of South Korea, by contrast, was quite different at the time. If the North was being courted by its two patrons, the ROK was not exactly a capitalist paradise. It was a domestically distraught country that was having more than its share of problems with its patron ally, the United States.

The ROK was dealing with very ambivalent U.S. governments that were offering highly qualified security commitments. The United States sought to defend the first government of the ROK under Syngman Rhee as a bulwark against communism, and to develop its economy, but unlike that of the North's patrons, Washington's support was highly conditional. Both Truman and Eisenhower saw Rhee's rule as dictatorial and corrupt, and neither trusted the South Korean very much. Relations at the outset were badly bruised when the ROK president, defiant at U.S. attempts to end hostilities on the peninsula, tried to sabotage Korean War armistice talks by unilaterally releasing thousands of captured North Koreans, the return of which was a key issue in the negotiations. Both Truman and Eisenhower were concerned that Rhee was trying to draw the U.S. back into a second war on the peninsula to fulfill his dream of unification, and therefore were wary of offering him too much in military assistance. The United States even had secret plans to overthrow Rhee if he overstepped the bounds of the alliance. The plan, known as EVERREADY, was devised in 1952 and called for the arrest of Rhee and the declaration of martial law in the name of the United Nations if he got too far out of line.[20] In the end, the Princeton-educated Korean was ousted from power by a student-led revolution in April 1960, after corrupt elections, with little opposition from Washington.

The Kennedy administration initially opposed a military coup by General Park Chung-hee in 1961 that overthrew a transitional government in the South after Rhee. Park ran the country with an iron fist, which he deemed necessary to counter the communist threat. The United States helped to broker deals with Japan that enabled Park to gain much-needed capital and technology to develop heavy industries in Korea, but his authoritarian style and martial-law rule embarrassed the United States and caused Washington to distance itself politically from Seoul. In 1969, the Nixon administration declared the Guam (or Nixon) Doctrine, which, in case of war, called for "the nation directly threatened to assume the primary responsibility of providing the manpower for its defense."[21] This doctrine, highly influenced by the quagmire in Vietnam, called for fewer U.S. troops and more Asian commitments to fighting ground wars in Asia, while the U.S. continued to provide the nuclear umbrella. The Nixon doctrine instilled acute fears of abandonment in Park, who felt betrayed after sending two divisions of his ground troops to fight in Vietnam with the United States. Two years later, as North Korea was consolidating its military ties with China and the Soviet Union, Nixon pulled twenty thousand troops out of Korea (the Seventh Infantry division), which constituted the single largest withdrawal of troops since the end of the Korean War. Moreover, Nixon began withdrawals from Vietnam, and with his national security adviser Henry Kissinger secretly negotiated a rapprochement with Communist China. On July 15, 1971, Nixon shocked the world with this decision in a televised announcement that he would visit China. Seoul had been given no advance notice.

The level of distrust between South Korea and its ally was palpable. An insecure President Park told reporters at the Blue House (the South Korean presidential mansion as it is known to foreigners) in 1969: "How long can we trust the United States?" He wrote letters to Nixon demanding security assurances and essentially accused the American president of selling out South Korea. Park's letters went unanswered, and when he demanded a summit in Washington before Nixon's historic trip to China, Washington's answer was an emphatic no. Archives suggest that the North was also surprised by the secret Sino-American diplomacy. (Indeed, Kissinger was in China for secret meetings with Zhou Enlai the very same week in July 1969 that a high-level DPRK Workers' Party delegation of officials were in Beijing for a week of Sino–North Korean friendship celebrations.) The difference was that after the secret meetings with Kissinger, Zhou went immediately to brief the Vietnamese and North Koreans ahead of Nixon's announcement.[22] And after the February 1972 Nixon-Mao meetings, Beijing assuaged its ally's fears of abandonment by sending a high-ranking envoy to Pyongyang to debrief the meetings. The Chinese also provided a new economic aid package and signed the first military assistance agreement with the North in fifteen years. Two months later, Beijing delivered new tanks and new fighter planes to Kim Il-sung as his birthday present. It is no small wonder that North Korea felt, in these heady days, that it was getting an upper hand in its inter-Korean competition.

The fall of Saigon and the American defeat in Vietnam only inflated North Korean confidences that geopolitics in Asia were working to its advantage. The Vietnam syndrome undercut American public support for further engagements in wars on the Asian mainland. When Saigon fell in April 1975, only 14 percent of Americans responded positively to a Louis Harris poll favoring U.S. involvement if North Korea attacked South Korea. Sixty-five percent said they would oppose American involvement. Matters for South Korea were only made worse when, in 1974 and 1975, a scandal emerged in which the Park regime was caught trying to bribe American congressmen. The "Koreagate" scandal led to the arrest and indictment of Congressmen Otto Passman (D-LA) and Richard Hanna

(D-CA), with Hanna serving a year in prison. President Jimmy Carter took alliance relations to a historic low when he proposed, as a campaign pledge in 1976, to withdraw all U.S. troops from Korea. Carter's phased withdrawal plan called for the immediate removal of one combat brigade (six thousand troops) by 1978, a second brigade and nine thousand additional noncombat personnel by mid-1980, and the removal of remaining troops, U.S. headquarters, and nuclear weapons by 1982. Carter viewed the U.S. troop presence as part of the security problem on the peninsula rather than as the solution. He believed their removal would spur the South Koreans to pursue autonomous self-defense capabilities, and would incentivize the two Koreas to sign a peace treaty. His conviction was in no small way fueled by his utter disgust with the authoritarian nature of the Park regime. In a June 1976 speech, President Carter explicitly stated, "It should be made clear to the South Korean government that its internal oppression is repugnant to our people and undermines the support of our commitment there."[23] Park had by this time implemented the *"Yusin"* system of draconian suppression of all civil rights in the name of anticommunism, which drew widespread criticism in the West. Hundreds of senators and congressmen wrote letters of protest to the White House as well as to President Park, condemning political repression. Koreagate in combination with *Yusin,* coupled with political needs for Congress to show distance from Seoul after the damaging bribery revelations, created a negative spiral in relations. Park clamped down at home out of insecurity against the North, thereby alienating American supporters who sought to distance themselves from the regime. This caused Park to clamp down even harder and undertake deviant actions, such as bribery. Park's insecurities were so intense that he even tried on two occasions to develop a covert nuclear weapons program. In the mid-1970s, Park sought to secretly acquire the reprocessing technology from France necessary to make weapons-grade plutonium for nuclear bombs from civilian nuclear fuel. These actions were outside of the civilian nuclear power plant agreements with the United States. Then–secretary of defense Donald Rumsfeld bluntly threatened in 1976 that Washington would consider severing the entire relationship unless Seoul canceled the contract with France. If, by the late 1970s, North Korea was still a model of socialism for the developing Communist world, South Korea was a rogue ally in the eyes of the North, rapidly losing the support of its great power ally and its people.

THE AUTHENTIC KOREAN

In Pyongyang's eyes, the volatility in South Korean politics, which scholars today associate with the country's trials and tribulations of democratization, were an asset in the North-South struggle. Its rival's first four leaders were forced out of office by extralegal means, military coup, or assassination.[24] Meanwhile, the North had one leader for almost five decades, who ruled with undisputed control. North Korean confidence in Kim as the superior leader of Koreans on the peninsula was augmented by his physical appearance. A large man by Korean standards, nearly six feet tall, he represented youth and vitality over the geriatric first leader of the South, Syngman Rhee. Kim also towered over the physically diminutive Park Chung-hee. Only about five feet two inches tall (157 cm), Park was reportedly conscious of his height difference with other world leaders. During his meeting with Lyndon Johnson, Park's aides fumed when the two presidents were pictured walking Johnson's dogs on the White House compound. Johnson, a large Texan standing at six feet four inches tall (193 cm), walked a Great Dane and towered over Park, who was given a poodle to walk. When Park's aides complained, they were asked whether they would have preferred it if Park was made to look even smaller by walking next to the Great Dane. Similarly, when the North and South engaged in secret negotiations in 1972, Korea Central Intelligence Agency (KCIA) director and negotiator Yi Hu-rak asked Park whether he wished to have a summit with Kim. Park reportedly expressed little interest, in part because of a summit photo optic that would not work to his advantage.

More important than pictures, however, was the North's genuine belief at this time that they owned the nationalist narrative between leaders on the Korean Peninsula. Kim Il-sung was the authentic Korean patriot. He was born in Man'gyŏngdae, a small farm village only one-half mile from where the Koreans heroically burned the USS *General Sherman* in 1866. The American side-wheel steamer was in Korea with the intention of opening up the "Hermit Kingdom" to trade, but conflict arose and the steamer saw its end when the Koreans set it alight and killed its crew as they scrambled desperately for shore. Kim Ŭng-u, the hero who led the defeat of the American "barbarians," was allegedly Kim Il-sung's great-grandfather (though Yi dynasty records do not record the names of the combatants). Kim later became an anti-Japanese guerrilla in the hills of Manchuria, a true independence fighter. The Japanese police put a price on his head, which was a badge of honor by Korean standards. By contrast, Syngman Rhee was an American-bred expatriate and a puppet of the American imperialists who had spent nearly fifty years outside of the country. Park, moreover, was a Japanese lackey. A man of humble origins in class-stratified precolonial Korea, Park volunteered for the Japanese army as his ticket to success. He became a model student and was sent to the top Japanese military academy in Manchuria. He even took on a Japanese name as a lieutenant in the army, Takagi Masao. For many Koreans, including progressives in the South who hated the authoritarian government's rule, Park was a stooge of both the Japanese and the American foreign occupiers.

North Korean propaganda further emphasized that their part of the country was the true historic seat of Korean ethnicity. Koreans on both sides are an extremely nationalistic people. Emphasizing the unique ethnic homogeneity of the people, Korean nationalism borders at times on xenophobia, which stems from its history and place as a "shrimp among whales," a small country constantly put upon by surrounding great powers in the region. Any Korean will defiantly talk about how their country has been invaded by foreign powers more than nine hundred times over two thousand years of recorded history. For a people with this sense of nationalism and ethnic identity, myths and history become very important. The North Koreans did all they could to own the historical nationalist narrative with the claim that everything that Korea is proud of in its history took place in the northern portion of the peninsula. The myth of Tan'gun, for example, informs the Korean people's birth five thousand years ago. Tan'gun is said to have created the first dynasty, Chosŏn, in 2333 B.C. Tan'gun's father was Hwanung, the Supreme Divine Regent and son of the emperor of heaven, and his mother was a bear-turned-woman, Ungnyŏ. The regent and the bear-woman created Tan'gun at Mount Paektu, which is a huge extinct volcano on the Sino–

North Korean border. Tan'gun made his capital near the current North Korean capital city of Pyongyang. When Tan'gun died, he was buried in the mountains about one hour southeast of Pyongyang. The South Korean public holiday Kaech'ŏnjŏl (Festival of the Opening of Heaven or National Foundation Day) falls on October 3 and has been celebrated annually for over two thousand years as marking Tan'gun's founding of the Korean nation. Kim Il-sung in the 1990s claimed that he had found the remains of Tan'gun.

Similarly, the Koguryŏ dynasty, situated in northern Korea, dominated the peninsula for several centuries after they expelled the Chinese (37 B.C. to A.D. 668). The largest and most powerful of the three kingdoms in Korean history, Koguryŏ (Silla and Paekche were the other two) extended its rule into parts of Manchuria so that the large contingent of ethnic Koreans in today's Jilin Province in China are said to be remnants of Koguryŏ rule. Many North and South Koreans see the Koguryŏ kingdom as the primary precursor of the modern Korean nation. This era produced illustrious scholars, revered Buddhist ecclesiastics, and its elaborately decorated and constructed royal tombs were recognized in 2001 as North Korea's first UNESCO World Heritage Site. Kim Il-sung identified himself with Koguryŏ and its monarchs. He claimed credit for ending Japan's colonization of Korea (there is no mention of Hiroshima and Nagasaki), just as Koguryŏ ended Chinese influence on the peninsula. The North Koreans emphasize how the Koguryŏ kingdom's capital was not Seoul but Pyongyang. Kim Il-sung rebuilt the walls and gates of the ancient city after the Korean War, all as part of an effort to own the nationalist narrative.

North Koreans even claim to use the authentic "Chosŏn" to refer to their country. Meaning "Land of Morning Calm," Chosŏn was the original name for Korea as referred to by Chinese records dating back to 100 B.C., which the North uses today. South Koreans, on the other hand, use the term "Korea," given it by Portuguese explorers in the sixteenth century, and now "Han'gŭk" or "Nation of Han," which was used from the end of the nineteenth century. Furthermore, choices made by the Soviet and American occupiers at the end of World War II also aided North Korea's owning of the nationalist narrative. The Soviets allowed former Korean anti-Japanese guerrilla fighters, like Kim Il-sung, to run the country and comprise its military. But in the South, the United States was utterly unprepared for a military occupation of Korea, and therefore relied on existing structures and personnel. Among these was the use of the Japanese colonial headquarters as the U.S. headquarters. (The building was later turned into a museum and then torn down in 1995.) U.S. occupation forces also employed former Korean collaborators with the Japanese imperial army to staff the new Korean police force and military. This was done out of expediency, because these individuals were already trained, but the propaganda effect for Pyongyang was clear. The West was replacing one colonizer with another. Moreover, it was allowing hated former Korean colonial police to run the South, while the "patriotic" North was shooting and imprisoning them as traitors to the nation.

JUCHE IDEOLOGY

During the Cold War, nothing epitomized the North Koreans' view that they were the true defenders of Korean ethnic identity and nationalism more than Kim Il-sung's ideology of *juche*. Translated into English, *juche* means "self-determination," but not in the way that Woodrow Wilson thought of it. Self-determination in the North Korean context meant that as a small country surrounded by ravenous large powers, it had to practice *juche,* or "self-reliance" and independence, in its internal and external policies. Under *juche,* North Korea could not rely on the good graces of others, it had to fend for itself and preserve true Korean identity. In an ideological context, *juche* consisted of four formal tenets: (1) man is the master of his fate; (2) the master of the Revolution is the people; (3) the Revolution must be pursued in a self-reliant manner; and (4) the key to Revolution is loyalty to the supreme leader, or *Suryŏng,* Kim Il-sung. It was communist in that it constituted a partial adoption of Marxism and Leninism. It accepted, for example, that capitalists and imperialists were the enemy and that the Revolution would be won in a class struggle by laborers over their oppressors. But it placed less emphasis on a scientific view of history as an evolutionary, deterministic process, ultimately reaching a point of capitalist contradiction and socialist utopia. Instead of this sort of Marxist-Leninist universalism, it stressed the role of man's efforts as the primary mover of history. This revision, in part, justified the need to use the ideology as a form of both nationalism and control over the people. For *juche,* the priority was on man making his own history by showing complete loyalty to the leader so that Korea could be non-subservient to outside powers and could progress to the final phase of human development, which was defined as unification of the peninsula under Kim Il-sung.

In this regard, *juche* greatly differed from Marxism-Leninism in its privileging of the state and sovereignty. For Marx, the nation-state would eventually "wither away" as workers united against capitalism. An egalitarian utopia without governments would emerge in the socialist phase of history, in which all social and economic classes would disappear. *Juche,* by contrast, was all about the Korean state, Korean sovereignty, and Korean identity and independence. University of Georgia professor and *juche* expert Park Han-shik classified as xenophobic *juche*'s claim of Korea as a chosen land from which human civilization emerged, but the prizing of Korean ethnic identity as part of a political ideology was something that resonated with all Koreans.[25] Any Korean will tell a foreigner about how Koreans are the most ethnically homogeneous race in Asia and even in the cosmopolitan South today, interracial marriages are socially frowned upon. As B. R. Myers has written eloquently, the *juche* ideology's insistence on Koreans as a unique race was in this sense more fascist than it was communist.[26] And at the top of it all, Kim Il-sung was the embodiment of everything good about this race, its fierce defender against external impure forces, and its trailblazing leader to utopia.

Juche first emerged in 1955 in a speech by Kim Il-sung titled "On Eliminating Dogmatism and Formalism and Establishing *Juche* in Ideological Work," and was subsequently adopted by the state. I met the creator of the ideology, a North Korean professor and party official Hwang Chang-yŏp, in 2009, when the Center for Strategic and International Studies (CSIS) in Washington, D.C., hosted him to give his first public speech before an American audience. By then a frail man who could barely hear, Hwang had defected to South Korea in 1997. Over my dinner with him in 2009, he explained to me how the ideology was written into history as created in 1930, when Kim was barely eighteen years old. He recalled that in the 1955 speech, Kim talked about how *juche* was Korea's revolution, which Hwang then worked into an ideology. At the Fifth

Party Congress in 1970, *juche* was formally adopted as the sole guiding principle of the state. It evolved over time, largely through the work of Kim Jong-il, from a political ideology to a cult of personality in which Kim Il-sung came to have godlike qualities as the embodiment and savior of the Korean race. (This is discussed in detail in the next chapter.) In case anyone doubts that an atheist country like North Korea could turn its political leadership into its own distorted version of a god, one need only look at a North Korean calendar. In 1997 (following a three-year mourning period after Kim Il-sung's death), North Korea officially withdrew from the Christian calendar and put itself on "*juche* time," which marks the beginning of history as 1912—the year of Kim Il-sung's birth.

While *juche* served as the primary instrument of control internally, it also served as a way for North Korea to stake out a middle position between the two feuding Communist powers, both of whom were patrons supporting Pyongyang. Kim Il-sung needed Soviet aid, but at the same time did not fully support the de-Stalinization that took place in Moscow after the Soviet leader's death. Similarly, the Cultural Revolution in China in the 1960s pushed in a radical direction that not even Kim was comfortable with. *Juche* enabled a path that was rhetorically "independent," while continuing to rely on both for help.

There have been many books written by political scientists about this bizarre ideology. Many first-time observers of North Korea cannot fathom how citizens can blindly follow a leadership that serves its own needs before those of the people, and in such extravagant ways, building $150 million luxury villas while the nation starves. They presume that the ideology is merely a nameplate, and that the leadership gets away with what it does through a combination of brute terror and ruthless suppression. While the latter is certainly true, in North Korea the ideology runs much deeper than we might believe. It forms the backbone of the state's control. Without the ideology, the state could not survive. So how did the ideology become such a source of strength for the regime during the Cold War and make the people so obedient?

First, *juche* claimed its legitimacy as the antithesis of what was practiced by the corrupt leadership in South Korea. *Juche*'s "self-reliance" did not mean autarky, but independence and freedom from the pressures and influence of external powers. The North Korean version of self-determination meant fighting against foreign predators, which was the complete opposite of how they framed what was happening in South Korea at the time. This they termed *"sadaejuŭi,"* which meant being a slave or servant to another big power. According to the *juche* narrative, South Korea was a foreign-occupied country, allowing U.S. and Japanese imperialists to use it to aggress against the North, and allowing foreign military troops to rape and pillage Korean society. The Soviets had troops stationed in the North as well (who did much more raping and pillaging in their short stay than any U.S. troops), but they left the peninsula long before the ideology's emergence. You can imagine how this independence narrative associated with *juche* might have been appealing to all Koreans, particularly at a time when the North was still economically better off than the South. Students in the South were banned from studying the ideology, which, of course, only made it more intriguing. This banning led to an underground radicalism in the South among students and laborers, which borrowed heavily from the North Korean critical narrative of the Seoul government. Rather than viewing the North as the aggressor in the Korean War, Pyongyang now became the heroic defender of Korean patriotism, which tried to unify the Korean people in 1950 only to be undermined by the United States. (There is minimal mention of China's role in the war.) Seoul subsequently became a corrupt toady of the Americans, and allowed the United States to station military forces and nuclear weapons that put all Koreans at risk. The most damning criticism of this narrative was that the United States sought to impede unification and prevent the Korean race from realizing its full potential. Students then used this ideology to protest against authoritarian governments and U.S. troops. This was why, during the Cold War years, Kim held many conversations with Communist leaders like Erich Honecker of East Germany and Nicolae Ceausescu of Romania, expressing confidence that the masses would rise up in the South and seek unification under Kim's terms.

The ideology also became a source of strength and control for the regime because it borrowed Korean notions of Confucianism. Concepts of respect and hierarchy as the basis of order and social harmony worked very well for the control motives of the government. *Juche* also defined collectivism in a Confucian rather than Marxist context. Marx saw collectivism as the equal sharing of obligations and benefits of the masses. But Kim revised collectivism as a Confucian concept. The masses would serve the state leader just as children would show filial piety to their parents. The father of the country, Kim, would then distribute the benefits accordingly. The language of *juche* teachings and propaganda played heavily on this filial-piety context. There were many references to masses yearning for the "bosom" of the leader's wisdom just as a child feels comfort in the bosom of his mother. In 1965, Kim Jong-il wrote about how the state was the "loving mother" of all the people. Military song lyrics in the North always reference defense of the motherland and how the "country I call my mother I now know is the General's [Kim] bosom."[27] Paintings of Kim Il-sung purposively accentuated softer, almost effeminate features of Kim's face and depicted workers with youthful, rosy-cheeked loving expressions all aimed at equating political loyalty with filial piety. The message was clear: you could not disagree or disrespect the state. You could not even contemplate it, just as one could not disrespect one's mother or father.

Juche ideology also fed the leadership's control because it constituted a mix of rigid doctrine and complete flexibility. For example, the doctrine would call for self-reliance, but at the same time, the North would rely heavily on Soviet and Chinese patron aid. How could one claim self-reliance and dependence at the same time? *Juche* would justify this apparent contradiction by stating that such dependence was still *juche* because it was doing what was good for Korea. So, xenophobic and self-serving nationalism was used to obfuscate any apparent contradictions in theory and practice. Similarly, the ideology called for total subservience to a leadership that effectively starved its people while it built nuclear weapons and palaces for the Kim family. Again, all contradictions were washed away with rationalizations of sacrifices that were good for the state and for the cause of the Revolution.

The primary arm of *juche* ideology and control in North Korean society during this time was the Korean Workers' Party. During the Cold War years, the party controlled the government and the military and was considered the vanguard organization of the masses. The highest body within the party was the Central Committee of the Politburo, which acted as an executive committee of advisers to Kim Il-sung. The party had about three million members, who were the privileged in North Korean society. The government was composed of the National Defense Commission, the State Administrative Council (cabinet), and the Supreme People's Assembly. The National Defense Commission (NDC) was responsible for military affairs and national defense. (This institution's role would increase after the death of Kim Il-sung in 1994 under the reign of Kim Jong-il.) The Supreme People's Assembly was the ceremonial rubber-stamp legislative body of party officials for the leadership's decisions. (This organ is famous for the televised pictures of six hundred people voting uniformly with "yes" cards to all decrees.) The cabinet was stocked largely with KWP members, including cabinet ministers, provincial governors, and mayors. So if you were a young and ambitious North Korean, your career path to success was through the party. Moreover, as evident in the charter of the party, the primary criteria for being anointed as a member was loyalty to *juche* thought and Kim Il-sung. In an amusing book called *The Complete Idiot's Guide to Understanding North Korea*, Ken Quinones lays out the ten simple criteria: (1) believe in *juche;* (2) uphold Kim Il-sung and Kim Jong-il's leadership with unswerving loyalty; (3) believe in Kim Il-sung and Kim Jong-il's absolute authority; (4) believe in Kim Il-sung and Kim Jong-il's revolutionary thought as the backbone of society; (5) demonstrate unconditional loyalty in carrying out instructions; (6) continue to strengthen ideological solidarity; (7) emulate Kim Il-sung and Kim Jong-il; (8) return political confidence given to you by the State with unswerving loyalty to Kim Il-sung and Kim Jong-il; (9) work with the party to uniformly support the monolithic leadership of Kim Il-sung and Kim Jong-il; and (10) accept that the revolutionary task of Kim Il-sung and the state must be perfected and inherited generation after generation.[28]

Juche was not an instrument of control merely through beliefs. It's not like being an American: you believe in freedom and democracy and therefore show allegiance to your country. *Juche* was seared into the minds of every North Korean every day through repetitive indoctrination sessions. There was almost a biological and anatomical rationalization for loyalty that went along with the spiritual. *Juche*'s writings taught that the Great Leader (*Suryŏng*) Kim Il-sung was the brain, the party was the nerves, and the people were the arms, legs, muscle, and bone of the state. Two messages of obedience emerged: (1) without the brain, the rest does not function; therefore, there must be complete loyalty; and (2) independent thinking was not needed, since this was handled by the brain. The only critical thinking that was allowed was self-criticism based on guilt for not serving the leader well. These sessions took place in the KWP, of course, and its three million members, but *juche* was also taught through the various social institutions created in North Korea as forms of mass control. The Kim Il-sung Socialist Youth League taught *juche* to its five million members. The General Federation of Trade Unions educated urban workers. The Union of Agricultural Workers educated farmers in *juche*. The Democratic Women's Union educated women. Similar institutions for journalists, literary writers, lawyers, and others all acted as vessels for *juche* indoctrination.

THESE DAYS IN Beijing, it is not hard to find merchandise that caters to Westerners with a penchant for "Communist chic." Old portraits of Mao on T-shirts, Mao suits, the ubiquitous Mao cap have all become fashion icons and are readily available in markets in China. But I was surprised to find at one of these markets small lapel pins with the portrait of Kim Il-sung. They were about the size and shape of a dime. I immediately scooped up six and showed them a few days later to a member of the North Korean Six-Party delegation, curious to see what kind of reaction it would elicit. This individual eyed the badge carefully, examining it as a numismatist would eye a mint coin, and then tossed it back at me with a dismissive wave of the hand. "Fake," the individual said. "You must have gotten this in China, didn't you? They counterfeit our Great Leader's pins all the time. They do not respect for [*sic*] intellectual property!"

For anyone who has been to North Korea, the Kim Il-sung badge is the most apparent physical manifestation of *juche* control. Worn on the lapel of a suit or a blouse, the badges came into being in the 1960s and were a daily reminder of where one's allegiances stood. You might forget to kiss your mother good-bye one morning on your way out the door but you could not forget your badge. The badges came in different sizes and shapes, presumably designating a certain status within the party. If the badge was not enough of a reminder of the Great Leader's benevolence, the portraits of him—and, later, his son—could be found in every office, school, workplace, and leisure place. And in public places, tens of thousands of monuments, statues, murals, and portraits adorned the city, leaving no psychic space to think outside of *juche* ideology.

Juche was not just metaphysical, it was also physical. Cold War *juche* ideology taught North Koreans not only to learn from the Great Leader's words but also to labor beyond one's physical limitations for him. The economic manifestation of this concept was the Ch'ŏllima movement. Named after the legend of a flying horse in Korean folklore, Ch'ŏllima espoused the idea that on the backs of the workers, the state would fly to a socialist paradise. The leadership would routinely declare 150-day work campaigns to quadruple manufacturing, industrial, or agricultural production. It was adopted formally at a session of the Supreme People's Assembly in 1958, in partial response to changing economic conditions. The Soviet Union reduced support to the North after the failure of Pyongyang's first Three-Year economic plan to achieve balanced growth. (Moscow felt the North Koreans were overemphasizing heavy-industry development.) The reduced outside assistance subsequently led Kim to create a doctrine that would make up the difference by squeezing more production out of the hands of the workers. This was not, of course, the publicly stated rationale. *Juche* ideology instead said that Ch'ŏllima represented the self-directed enthusiasm of workers and their unconditional love for Kim. "Revolutionary zeal" led the workers to labor tirelessly and without sleep to exceed production targets. A typical story follows along these lines: Kim Il-sung visited the Kangsŏn Steel Plant in 1956. He talked directly to the workers about the imperatives of industrialization in order to fend off aggression from the United States and its puppet regime in South Korea. The workers responded in exemplary Ch'ŏllima fashion. "Reportedly moved by the emotion of [Kim] sharing the burdens of the state personally with the Premier, the Kangsŏn workers were recounted as holding a rally immediately and resolving to boost production [to] 120,000 tons of rolled steel in 1957 at the mill, which had a rated capacity of only 60,000 tons. Predictably, the heroics at Kangsŏn spurred workers in other places to build blast furnaces of 300,000-ton capacity in a single year, to lay an 80-kilometer [50-mi] railway in 75 days, to fabricate 13,000 machines over and above the plan in a year . . ."[29] Squeezing as much as possible out of the workforce based on revolutionary zeal was both an economic policy and an effective form of political control.

In the 1960s, as part of its industrialization, North Korea designed an energy strategy based on thermal electricity plants that would be fueled by coal. This seemed like a prudent move, given the large deposits of coal in the country. A Ch'ŏllima movement was started to force workers to excavate more coal by working longer days and on twenty-four-hour shifts. This was destined to fail. Coal-mining technologies in the West could produce as much as eleven tons of coal per minute from a single machine operated by two people.[30] But forcing workers to labor longer hours for the Great Leader was an instrument of control.

People do not understand stories out of North Korea where the masses would build a bridge brick by brick, or where hundreds of laborers would manicure a lawn by cutting each single blade of grass, dutifully disposing of the sheared portion in a bag.[31] There are even stories of how workers who prepare rice for the Great Leader inspect each grain to make certain it is of top quality. You ask how can people do that? It is part of the Ch'ŏllima mentality and *juche* ideology.

IF YOU STAND at the demilitarized zone and stare in the direction of North Korea, you will see, carved into the side of the hill, a word in Korean script (*Han'gŭl*) that spells "*chaju.*" *Chaju* or *chajusŏng* means "self-reliance" and is synonymous with the term "*juche.*" In fact, it was the nameplate often used by the Park Chung-hee regime in the 1970s to justify his economic development plans. With *juche,* however, North Koreans saw themselves as the authentic Koreans. The emphasis on Korean uniqueness, homogeneity, and pure-bloodedness constituted a myth that all Koreans on both sides of the division believed. The theme of independence from predation by outside great powers was also a mandate that all Koreans believed in. The difference was that the North could claim that they were not a "foreign-occupied" power like the South. Nowhere was this more evident than in July 1972, when the two Koreas met amid the growing détente in the region among the great powers. Not to be outdone or overtaken by these events, the South Korean KCIA director and Kim Il-sung's brother met secretly and devised a joint statement. The joint statement talked about Korean independence and unity against external interference in Korean affairs. It called for unification without reliance on or support from outside sources. It praised the aspiration of a greater Korean national unity. The fact that the themes in the statement resonated with North Korean propaganda, not South Korean political principles, was revealing of how much Kim owned the nationalist narrative. And because Korean nationalism was synonymous with anti-colonialism and anti-Japanism, Kim could always claim that Park, because he served the Japanese military during the occupation period, was not a "true Korean." Moreover, allowing American troops to remain in the country as a front line of defense from Japan (the notion that they were there to deter a second North Korean attack is never part of the narrative) further denigrated Park. Carving Park's term *"chaju"* into their hillside was essentially a North Korean statement of confidence meant to convey that they were the true patriots, the authentic Koreans on the peninsula during the Cold War.

COLD WAR CONFIDENCE

The skeptic might ask, were things really this good for the North? Because of the country's decrepit state today and the South's position on the cutting edge of world affairs, how bad was it then? North Korea's advantages during the Cold War were certainly not comparable to the yawning gap in capabilities that the South enjoys today. However, the Cold War constituted an era of genuine competition between two social systems on the peninsula, and the North exuded a genuine confidence about its future that befit its bloated propaganda and statements.

For example, in April 1946, Kim Il-sung gave a speech about land reform, except that his audience was the *South* Korean people. He called for the promise of bringing to the people in the South "democratic reforms" enjoyed by the people in the North.[32] Kim was referring to a major land-reform law promulgated in the North the previous month, which distributed to rural families 720,000 new plots of land formerly owned by Japanese colonial authorities. This meant that two-thirds of Korean farmers, who previously had been tenant farmers to the Japanese, were now landowners. Though output and taxes had to be paid back to the state, this reform created tremendous loyalty and support of the government in Pyongyang. At this time in the South, however, there was no land reform to speak of. Instead there was political chaos as more than fifty political parties were fighting to gain power, the economy was in runaway inflation, and labor strikes were rampant. Even though Rhee in the South completed land reform in April 1949, Kim Il-sung went further on May 1950 in a radio address to the South Korean people, in which he claimed to have a better land reform program than in the South, which he promised to start immediately if the South Korean people sought unification. The date of this offer is important, because it came only one month before the North Korean invasion, and was clearly meant as a way to "soften up" the southern people to see a brighter future with the North. (Some argue that Kim's land-privatization was a political ploy designed solely to prepare for war. Its purpose was to seduce dissatisfied southerners as well as to increase agricultural productivity and stockpile food in advance of the war. After the war, the North collectivized everything and used land and food as instruments of control.)

Kim Il-sung was the provocateur on the peninsula, always seeking opportunities to exercise leverage. When Park Chung-hee came to power by military coup in the South in 1961, rumors flew that the unknown general might have communist leanings. The Kennedy administration, for example, was initially very concerned about Park's political colors, the concern stemming from U.S. military occupation reports that he was once arrested as the leader of a communist cell within the Korean military academy following the 1948 Yŏsu rebellion where the ROK government brutally put down a revolt among army troops. Park was sentenced to death by a military court, but then-president Rhee commuted the sentence on the advice of James Hausman, an American military adviser who had known the young Park personally and saw value in him. Park then provided the Americans and South Koreans a list of communists in the ROK army for counterintelligence purposes, and for his deeds was given a new start.[33] After Park instigated the coup, Kim Il-sung was so confident of his position on the peninsula that he sent a secret emissary to Seoul in hopes that he could get Park to join Kim's revolution. Though the plan did not work (Park said no in the strongest possible terms: he had the emissary executed), it was a sign of Kim's confidence of his position on the peninsula.

In the 1960s, Kim tried to actively propagate his place as the next leader of the Communist movement among Third World countries. China's self-absorption in its destructive Cultural Revolution opened a space for Kim, and he had no hesitation about claiming his new role. In November 1967, he published a proclamation in the government newspaper *Rodong Sinmun,* titled "Let's Turn the Spearhead of Fighting Against U.S. Imperialism," appealing to national liberation movements in Southeast Asia, Cuba, and Latin America. In July 1968, he led with a new slogan, "Cutting Off the Limbs of U.S. Imperialism Everywhere," in which he described how Vietnam and North Korea together were each breaking one leg of the "American bandit." He then called on Cuba and Latin American countries to tear off one of America's arms and called for African countries like Ghana, Guinea, and Mali to tear off the other arm, finishing with a flourish, "If the small countries jointly dismember him, the American bandit will be torn apart." He also published a major treatise later that year, timed to the anniversary of the death of Bolivian guerrilla Che Guevara, on Kim's leading the great revolution of the peoples of Asia, Africa, and Latin America.[34] These actions upset the Chinese, who saw the North Koreans as "revisionist" and "bourgeois." (It would not be until 1969, when China began to emerge from the Cultural Revolution, that Sino-DPRK relations improved.) But it especially upset the Vietnamese, who pointedly stated that they spilled blood expelling the American imperialists from Asia, not the North Koreans.[35] Vietnam saw that Kim, then only fifty-five years old, would surely outlive Mao and Ho Chi Minh, and cynically derided the North Koreans for seeking the mantle as the next leader. Kim may have been opportunistic in trying to capitalize on a period of Chinese domestic radicalization and Vietnamese distraction, but this opportunism was fueled by a confidence that the struggle with the South was then only a small part of a wider ambition.

While Nixon's 1972 visit to China elicited acute abandonment fears in Seoul, Pyongyang reacted with confidence. Kim told Hungarian president Pál Losonczi and Cambodian prince Sihanouk in the autumn of 1971 that Nixon's visit would eventually lead to U.S. expulsion from Vietnam:

The U.S. would stumble from defeat to defeat. The Americans attempted to isolate China, they occupied Taiwan and continuously threatened the

PRC. But China developed into a mighty anti-imperialist revolution-
ary power in Asia, and the American blockade came to a shameful end.
Nixon's visit to Beijing would now prove the bankruptcy of America's
anti-Chinese policy. Just as the United States came to Panmunjom with a
white flag after its defeat in the Korean War, Nixon will head to Beijing.
His visit will be that of a loser, not a victor. This will constitute a great
triumph for the Chinese people and all revolutionary people worldwide.
Now the USA will have to withdraw next from South Korea, Taiwan,
Indochina and Japan.[36]

Reading this passage, one is struck by the unusual level of confidence,
even bravado, expressed by Kim, when compared with the utter fears of
U.S. abandonment expressed by his South Korean counterpart.

In April 1975, as the final battle for Saigon was slipping away from
the United States, Kim Il-sung traveled to Beijing for an eight-day state
visit. Deng Xiaoping, who was then vice chairman of the Chinese Communist Party, greeted Kim at the airport amid great pomp and circumstance. Deng took Kim directly to Zhongnanhai to meet with Chairman
Mao and with Premier Zhou Enlai to discuss the strength of their bilateral relations and emerging geopolitical trends in the region. Kim then
visited Nanjing and took a cruise on the Yangtze River. At a banquet
with Premier Deng, Kim toasted the impending North Vietnamese victory and the end of U.S. imperialism in Asia.

Dear Comrades and Friends,

A great revolutionary transformation has taken place in the East and
the look of Asia has radically changed since the Second World War.

The colonial Asia, the underdeveloped East of yesterday, has disap-
peared once and for all and new Asia has been born that advances to-
ward independence, progress, and prosperity.

The U.S. imperialists started going downhill after their ignomini-
ous military defeat in the Korean war [sic] and have sustained repeated
setbacks in their aggressive wars in Indochina, and their hostile policy
towards China has gone bankrupt. All this proves that no desperate ma-
neuvering on the part of the imperialists can block the liberation struggle
of the peoples or stop the victorious advance of socialism.

Nowadays the U.S. imperialists are again being dealt fatal blows and are sliding into an inextricable quagmire of ruin in Indochina. Yesterday the National Liberation People's Armed Forces of Cambodia defeated the traitorous Lon Nol clique, the stooges of U.S. imperialism, and finally liberated Phnom Penh.

This is a great victory won by the patriotic Cambodian people in their five-year-long heroic struggle against U.S. aggression and for national salvation, and it is another shameful defeat sustained by the U.S. imperialists in Asia.

This glorious victory of the Cambodian people over U.S. imperialism and its stooges is an important contribution to the anti-imperialist national liberation struggle of the oppressed nations and a historic event that will exert a great influence upon the development of the situation of Southeast Asia as a whole.

Availing myself of this opportunity, I warmly congratulate the National Liberation People's Armed Forces of Cambodia on their shining victories in the operation to liberate Phnom Penh, and in the cause of liberation of the whole country under the leadership of the National United Front of Kampuchea with Head of State of Cambodia Samdech Norodom Sihanouk as its Chairman, and the Royal Government of National Union of Cambodia.

Now in South Viet Nam, too, the Saigon puppet clique is being dealt strong punitive attacks by the South Vietnamese people and the People's Liberation Armed Forces and is on the verge of collapse.

In Asia the imperialists have resorted to various methods and tricks one after the other, such as direct armed intervention, neocolonialist rule through their puppets, and the "New Asia Policy" to make Asians fight among themselves; however, they have been unable to save themselves from doom and reached such a dead end that they can no longer hold out in Asia.

We actively support the struggle of the Indochinese peoples against U.S. imperialism and its lackeys, and the anti-imperialist national liberation struggle of all the Asian peoples.[37]

GDR (German Democratic Republic, East Germany) archives record extraordinary conversations between Erich Honecker, East German general secretary of the Socialist Party, and Kim Il-sung in the 1970s and 1980s. Honecker was one of Kim's closest friends among Communist bloc leaders, and the two leaders exchanged visits on a regular basis and held extensive ruminations about the state of world affairs. In these discussions, the level of confidence expressed by Kim was striking. When Honecker visited Pyongyang in December 1977, Kim expressed supreme certainty of the North's ascendancy on the peninsula. He drew a picture of political chaos in the South and the likelihood that the Park regime would soon collapse. He concluded by saying, "The DPRK will patiently continue its work with respect to the South so that Park Chung-Hee becomes even more isolated and the struggle for democratization can be continued."[38] After Park was assassinated in 1979, Kim proclaimed that the South was in disarray, filled with landlords and capitalists, and under occupation by U.S. imperialists; by contrast, the North was a politically stable socialist paradise where everyone lived in peaceful bliss. Kim saw no need to do anything proactive to capitalize on Park's assassination. He preferred to sit back and watch the masses in the South rise up in revolt.

Kim Il-sung was hosted by Honecker in East Germany several years later, after an interim government in the South was overthrown by a second military coup at the hands of General Chun Doo-hwan. The North Korean leader mapped out his strategy for undermining the South, focusing on the growing anti-Americanism there. He noted that unification was soon within his grasp and even connoted that divine intervention was on his side—a strange reference to Catholics in the passage below even though the North was an atheist state:

> The struggle by the population of South Korea is currently intensifying. In the past the South Korean populace either feared the Americans or worshipped them. These two tendencies are in decline . . . The demand for sovereignty would mean extricating itself from U.S. domination. The young people and students of South Korea are currently waging an energetic battle for this. The Chun Doo-Hwan regime is even worse than the Park Chung-Hee regime. There are dogs that are somewhat belligerent and others that are downright vicious. This Chun Doo-Hwan regime is like a vicious dog . . . The entire population and even many Catholics in

*South Korea are unleashing a vigorous struggle against the Chun Doo-
Hwan regime.*[39]

North Korean confidence was also manifest in the various proposals
it made to the Americans for a peace treaty. Rather than a sign of weakness, the proposals, made in a written letter to Congress in 1974 and then
in secret messages to Secretary of State Cyrus Vance through Pakistani
intermediaries in 1977, demanded two preconditions for peace treaty
discussions: (1) the United States should withdraw all military forces
from South Korea; and (2) any peace treaty negotiation should take place
between Washington and Pyongyang and should exclude the South
Koreans. Far-fetched as these proposals may sound today, they exuded
a certainty on the part of Kim that once U.S. forces were withdrawn,
the South Korean masses, given the unpopularity of their leader, would
join with the North. Moreover, the proposals were aimed at enticing the
Americans into disengaging from Korea with the fake offer of a permanent peace ending the Korean War.

RECKLESS BELLIGERENCE

If you take a trip as a government official abroad, you usually have a clear
schedule laid out in advance of your arrival, complete with the timeline
of meetings, speaking events, and dinners. When you go to North Korea,
however, you are entering a black hole. You can request meetings with
key counterparts, but there is never any confirmation in advance, only
a vaguely positive or negative response, such as "I am sure he would like
to see you," or "I am not sure he will be available at that time but we will
check." Upon arrival, you are asked to hand over your passport. You are
then given an itinerary for the visit. Mine listed a series of meetings, dinners, orchestra performance, and then an entry that read "Visit to USS
Pueblo." I had never asked for this visit and so it was a bit surprising.
I told my two colleagues from the Defense Department, who were accompanying me, that we could do everything else on the schedule but
we would politely decline this visit. We told our civilian colleagues on
this trip, Governor Richardson of New Mexico and former secretary of
veteran affairs Anthony Principi, of our intentions, and they said that

they understood the sensitivities for standing U.S. officials to visit the ship, but that they would go in order not to offend our hosts. Our North Korean interlocutors politely asked us what we would like to do instead. They offered us a visit to the giant, seventy-foot-tall (21 m) bronze statue of Kim Il-sung, which we also declined. The sight of White House and Pentagon officials standing before this statue was a photo op we wanted to avoid. (We ended up visiting a department store, since I was curious of how the economy was doing.) When the rest of the party returned from the visit to the *Pueblo* in Wonsan Harbor, we asked how it went. Former secretary Principi, a consummate diplomat and about as good-natured as they come, was visibly upset at the propaganda and lies spewed about the ship and the spectacle of what had become a tourist attraction for North Koreans. The capture of the USS *Pueblo,* he said, was an act of war in which American servicemen were tortured. Long ago as this was, it is nothing to celebrate.

North Korea had no qualms about flexing its military might during the Cold War. By the late 1960s to early 1970s, it had built up the fourth largest standing army in the Communist bloc at 408,000 troops, with fourteen of its twenty-three divisions forward-deployed on the demilitarized zone. For every year between 1968 and 1979, the North outspent the South militarily,[40] in spite of having a population of less than half of South Korea's during this period.[41] In terms of military equipment, the RAND Corporation estimated that between 1970 and 1975, South Korea had only 13 percent of the North's total allotment, and this balance would only reach near parity in 1984.[42] And as for the "defense burden," which is simply the percentage of a country's economic spending that is devoted to the military, since the end of the Korean War in 1953, South Korea has not once had a greater burden than its northern counterpart.[43] While this figure certainly has less meaning today with a South Korean economy that is over thirty-seven times larger than that of the North,[44] during the years of relative equality up until the late 1960s, it was, indeed, significant. It is in these years, too, that North Korea's well-trained, well-fed, and highly motivated elite special forces units started to play a more significant role. By 1970 they are estimated to have numbered approximately 15,000, climbing to 41,000 by 1978 and approximately 81,000 in the early 1980s.[45] Through these years, they conducted high-profile assassination attempts such as the 1968 Blue House infiltration, trained Third World Communist militaries, and supported international revolutionary organizations and terrorist groups. Today, the South Korean Ministry of National Defense estimates that North Korean Special Forces may total as many as 200,000 personnel.[46] Based on North Korea's observations of the U.S. wars in Iraq and Afghanistan, these elite forces are believed to have recently stepped up their nonconventional and guerrilla tactics training, such as planting roadside bombs and the use of other improvised explosive devices (IEDs).[47]

Pyongyang undertook numerous military provocations in violation of the 1953 armistice truce, all aimed to destabilize the rival regime in the South. The fact that the North carried these out despite the risk of escalation was another manifestation of its confidence. One campaign ran from the 1960s through the early 1970s, claiming the lives of over forty Americans and hundreds of South Koreans. The capture of the USS *Pueblo* in February 1968 was about as provocative a violation of the truce as the North could manufacture, short of war. The North captured the U.S. intelligence ship while it was in international waters on a routine operation. One of the crew of eighty-three was killed in the ship's seizing, the rest, including Captain Lloyd Bucher, were held for eleven months and beaten until Bucher was forced to confess to spying. While Bucher remained resistant as long as he could, he was forced to buckle when the North Koreans threatened to execute his crew in front of him, one by one, beginning with the youngest man. In the negotiations for the crew's return, the U.S. side asked to see evidence of their well-being. North Korean captors prepared the crew for a picture, in which captives held up their middle fingers and told their captors it was a Hawaiian "good luck sign." One of the crew members, Stu Russel, recounts how "the finger became an integral part of our anti-propaganda campaign. Any time a camera appeared, so did the fingers."[48] The picture showed that the Americans were well and still defiant, but when the North understood through a *Time* magazine article that they had been had, many beatings ensued. The North's refusal to release the *Pueblo* crew even led the Soviets, in bilateral discussions with Kim Il-sung, to advise him to lower tensions by ending the ordeal, since he had made his point and milked all the propaganda value from it already.

The ten-month crisis finally ended in December 1968 with a written apology from the Johnson administration, which was later disavowed once the crew was returned.

In January 1968, the North dispatched a thirty-one-man commando team to assassinate South Korean president Park Chung-hee. Their mission, according to the sole captured member, Kim Sin-jo, was to cut off Park's head, photograph it, and return to the North by February 8 to celebrate the twentieth anniversary of the Korean People's Army.[49] The team, disguised in South Korean army uniforms, infiltrated deep into South Korean territory over the course of three days, and slept in cemeteries and sewers to avoid detection. Kim Shin-jo was an army lieutenant and led the squad whose mission was to take out the bodyguards at the Blue House. The team made it as far as the front gate of the presidential compound—about two hundred yards from Park's personal quarters—when they were questioned by a policeman who sensed something unusual about the group. When police confronted the commandos, a firefight broke out, killing thirty-five South Korean soldiers and wounding sixty-four soldiers, police, and civilians. All of the commandos were killed, except for Kim. According to a 2009 interview with Kim, he recalled how he underwent months of interrogation and confessed to all the details of the plan after befriending a South Korean general who convinced him that his only salvation would be to confess and to start a new life. While in prison, Kim received many letters from Christian families in South Korea, and eventually converted to Christianity, later becoming a Protestant clergyman in 1997. (The North Koreans executed his parents when this news became public.)[50] The trail that these commandos took has since been opened by the South Koreans as a tourist site.

The list of additional provocations during this period is long. In April 1969, on Kim Il-sung's birthday, the North shot down a U.S. EC-121 navy intelligence plane while it was conducting a routine reconnaissance mission, killing all thirty-one crew aboard. The very same route, a cautious fifty nautical miles (58 mi, 93 km) from the North Korean coast, had been taken by reconnaissance aircraft over two hundred times in the previous three months without incident. Yet, on this date, the North Koreans claimed the plane had penetrated far into their airspace, and that their air defenses had "scored the brilliant battle success" of downing the aircraft with a single shot.[51] In June 1970, three North Korean agents tried again to assassinate the South Korean president by an attempted terrorist bombing at the national cemetery in Seoul during a twentieth-anniversary ceremony remembering the Korean War. In August 1974, another assassination attempt against Park took place at the hands of a North Korean–trained assassin, Mun Se-gwang, who tried to shoot the president in the national auditorium while he was giving a speech on Korean Independence Day. The shots missed Park but they struck the first lady, the well-liked Yuk Yŏng-su, in the head, killing her instantly. Park's daughter is a prominent conservative politician and possible presidential contender in South Korea today.

The North Koreans also engaged in provocations along the main military border area separating the two Koreas. From 1972, the North started to dig a series of infiltration tunnels into South Korean territory. These tunnels were reinforced with concrete, electricity, lighting, weapons storage, and a railway system that could move as many as eight to ten thousand special forces and light infantry troops into the South each hour. ROK forces discovered the first tunnel in November 1974, about two-thirds of a mile (1 km) south of the military demarcation line, when patrols saw steam rising from the ground and thought they had lucked upon a natural hot spring. In February 1975, a second tunnel was found about three-quarters of a mile (1.2 km) into the South. Blast markings in the tunnel showed that it had started three miles (5 km) inside the North. A U.S. report in 1977 acknowledged that the North was actively seeking different covert invasion routes into the South and could probably infiltrate by land, sea, or air to almost anywhere in the South. Two more tunnels were discovered in 1978 and 1990,[52] each of which would have allowed approximately thirty thousand military personnel to pass through per hour. The third tunnel, discovered in 1978, was approximately a mile long (1.6 km), 240 feet underground (73 m), and had five separate exits into the South. The 1990 tunnel was an even greater feat of engineering, stretching nearly one and a half miles (2.1 km) long and 475 feet deep (145 m).[53] Like the Blue House commando raid trail, these tunnels are now tourist attractions.

In August 1976, North Korean soldiers bludgeoned to death with axes a team of American soldiers in a premeditated act of murder. A U.S. and South Korean detail was preparing to trim a row of poplar trees in the Joint Security Area near the Bridge of No Return (named as such because of its role as the last transit point for returning prisoners of war). The fifth of five trees blocked the line of sight between two checkpoints, and the detail was going to do some routine trimming as was the practice during the summer months. North Korean soldiers confronted the detail and demanded that they stop the operation. A fight broke out. Thirty North Korean reinforcements showed up, immediately outnumbering the detail. The head of the detail, Captain Arthur Bonifas, and First Lieutenant Mark Barrett were hacked to death in a senseless act of violence. The incident led to a mobilization on both sides and the Ford administration's order for an armed platoon, twenty-seven helicopters, and a squadron of B-52s flying overhead to return to the scene to finish the mission. "Operation Paul Bunyan" cut the tree down and placed a monument that remains there today.

The provocations continued into the 1980s. The North tried on at least two occasions to assassinate Park's successor, President Chun Doohwan (1980–1988). In 1982, they planned to kill Chun during a visit to Gabon but aborted the operation at the last minute. According to Koh Yŏng-hwan, a North Korean diplomat-turned-defector who was involved in the plot, it was called off at the last minute because it was decided that an assassination in an African country would have squandered the North's much-valued, much-needed African support in the U.N. General Assembly.[54] During a state visit to Burma in October 1983, Chun narrowly escaped death when a terrorist bomb was planted by the North in the ceiling of the mausoleum at the national cemetery in Rangoon. Chun's motorcade was delayed in traffic and arrived late for the wreath-laying ceremony. The ROK ambassador's car, however, arrived on time just as a bugler was practicing for Chun's arrival. North Korean agents mistook this car to be Chun's and remotely set off the bombs, obliterating the structure and burying half of Chun's cabinet ministers under piles of rubble and steel. Twenty-one people died, including the foreign minister, minister of economy, deputy prime minister, and presidential adviser.[55] Despite the carnage, only one of the three bombs planted in the roof detonated successfully. The three North Korean agents were eventually captured (one blew himself up with a grenade) and confessed to the plan. As recalled by a foreign ministry official who witnessed the horrible incident, the South was caught completely off-guard by this blatant attack on a third country's soil. The traveling party and presidential security detail was at a loss as to how to maintain security, as they were in a foreign country without any sense of whether there would be a follow-up attack. The official recalled that the United States stepped in quietly to provide support and military oversight to ensure that the delegation and the bodies arrived home safely. He recalled that this is what only a true ally like the United States was capable of doing, in ways that would never become public but would be remembered.

In each of these instances, the United States and the ROK considered responding militarily to these deliberate acts of aggression. After the 1968 Blue House raid, Park Chung-hee implored the Johnson administration to launch an offensive against the North. After the 1976 poplar tree ax murder, then–secretary of state Henry Kissinger wanted the Ford administration to bomb the North. Over the years, options ranged from laying mines and seizing North Korean ships to air strikes against military targets and nuclear bursts at sea. But in the end, Washington averred, seeking instead to increase military exercises with the ROK and reinforcing capabilities in the region, rather than risk a proportionate military retaliation that could escalate rapidly to an all-out war. This was probably the prudent decision, but it only fed North Korean confidence that they held all the escalation cards on the peninsula.

BACK TO THE FUTURE: "*NEOJUCHE* REVIVALISM"

In 1977, North Korea became the only country in the world to declare that it had reached the final stage of socialist utopia. In their own minds, they believed it. The Cold War years were the best days for North Korea. Cupboards were full, the military was strong, the rival South was troubled, and the North had many friends in the socialist world.

How can we be so certain of this? Because North Korea, today, is trying to return to these principles. It is building a new ideology for the next generation of leadership to succeed Kim Jong-il. This process started around 2008 but has been accelerated with Kim's death in 2011. I call it "*neojuche* revivalism." It is a return to the principles and propaganda of the 1960s and 1970s, when in North Korean minds they were strong, but with an even harder line and more dogmatic than before. This more conservative strand of *juche* continues to espouse complete loyalty and subservience to the leader, and in particular highlights the ascension to the throne of Kim Jong-il's twentysomething-year-old son Kim Jong-un. It continues to espouse the uniqueness of the Korean race, the need for independence from external predatory powers, and the weakness of the South as puppets of American and Japanese imperialism.

This new strain of *juche* is different in two respects. It is reactionary in its rejection of the opening and reform policies that were tried from the mid-1990s to the mid-2000s. These halfhearted attempts at reform coincided with the decade of Sunshine Policy in South Korea, when Seoul under progressive governments sought to shower the North with unconditional economic engagement. As will be discussed later in the book, this experimentation period failed miserably, in large part because the North Korean regime was unwilling to take real steps to liberalize their system, for fear of losing political control. In reality, the halfhearted nature of these reforms led to a massive failure of the food, energy, and economic infrastructure starting from the mid-1990s. Rather than tie this poor performance to the state, *neojuche* revivalism flips the script: it uses revivalism to rationalize that the problems of the 1990s were precisely because they experimented with "polluted ideas" and now they are returning to purity.

The new ideology calls for a return to the core principles that made North Korea great during the Cold War, and discards the attempted periods of experimentation and reform as deviant turns that dirtied the mind and spirits of Koreans. This new strain of *juche* is also different in that it stresses the concept of "*sŏn'gun*" ("military-first") politics. This is an artifact of Kim Jong-il's rule of North Korea, in which he privileged the military above all as the key decision-making body. *Neojuche* revivalism continues to stress *sŏn'gun* politics and, in particular, wholeheartedly associates the drive for nuclear weapons with the country's achievement of "*kangsŏng tae'guk*" ("rich nation, strong army").[56] The result of all this is that North Korea is going back to the future—the next generation will inherit a revivalist and reactionary ideology from the Cold War that is more conservative, unrepentant, and ever more dogmatic.

The reader might ask, what possibly could lead the North Korean *juche* gurus to believe this will work? After all, we all know North Korea is isolated, but are they that delusional?

Ideology is the core of the state. Without ideology, there is no godlike Kim family, and there is no North Korea state in its current form. As renowned *juche* scholar Park Han-shik notes, "[The] DPRK has used ideology as the primary basis of regime legitimacy."[57] Ideology becomes more important because the state cannot derive its legitimacy from its poor performance in providing food, energy, and sustenance to the people. The ideology for a new leadership, moreover, cannot be the same one associated with Kim Jong-il. His period of rule failed in every respect except one, in North Korean eyes, and that is the creation of nuclear weapons. A North Korean perestroika is impossible, because it would mean inevitably giving up some degree of control, which the leadership will never allow. My friends who are China scholars remain eternally optimistic about North Korea's reform prospects because they assume that if China could tolerate some decentralization to implement Deng's modernization reforms, then a small country like North Korea certainly could. But North Korea does not have a Deng Xiaoping. Moreover, it still sees political control as more important than economic development. North Korea became somewhat infatuated with what South Korea did in the later years of the Cold War, growing economically while holding political control. But then the burgeoning middle class that emerged from such development demanded democratization in the mid-1980s and authoritarian governments in the South wilted under the pressure. The North then saw the perils of that model.

The only ideology that North Koreans experienced with any degree of success in their own history was the one during the Cold War. In the collective memory, this was the best of times. They know nothing else. Moreover, there is little room for experimentation with any other ideology. With a super-successful South Korea directly on their border, Pyongyang probably feels as though there is little room for mistakes as they try to affect a shaky power transition from a sick, elderly father to his inexperienced son. Thus, they build an ideology that mixes the two elements—conservative *juche* ideals but laced with *sŏn'gun* politics—

with the one achievement that Kim Jong-il promised—status as a nuclear weapons state.

Evidence of this *neojuche* revivalism is abundant. In 2002, when North Korea was attempting halfhearted economic reforms, Kim Jong-il was quoted as saying that foreign trade is important and that trade must be conducted according to market principles. But now, the leadership is de-emphasizing this rhetoric and moving back to principles of Cold War–era Ch'ŏllima mass mobilization and labor-intensive production. One German scholar, Rüdiger Frank, who has tracked this very closely, pinpoints a significant trip by Kim Jong-il in December 2008 to Kangsŏn steel complex. Kangsŏn is the home of the Ch'ŏllima movement. Kim Il-sung declared in 1958, at the very same steel complex, that ideologically inspired workers could use their hands to overcome any impediments imposed by lack of technology or capital. The shift to *neojuche* conservatism is also evident in the propaganda statements. While public references to Ch'ŏllima numbered less than ten in the last four months of 2006, since 2009, there have been over forty references. As Frank concludes, "Ch'ŏllima is replacing the creative application of market principles."[58] Similarly, references to "*kangsŏng tae'guk*" ("rich nation, strong army" or "powerful and prosperous nation") have now been replaced by ubiquitous references to *socialist* rich nation, strong army, appearing over one hundred times in official Korean Central News Agency (KCNA) broadcasts in the first quarter of 2009. In January 2001, when the North was experimenting halfheartedly with reforms, Kim Jong-il justified the changes in the official newspaper, *Rodong Sinmun,* "Things are not what they used to be in the 1960s. So no one should follow the way people used to do things in the past." By contrast, in March 2009, Kim Jong-il was quoted as saying the country should return to core principles and that the state should "energetically lead the masses by displaying the same work style as the officials did in the 1950s and 1960s."[59]

This depiction of an idealized past can also be seen by simply flipping through a few of the North's "Joint New Year's Editorials." The Joint New Year's Editorial is an article that is annually published on January 1 in North Korea's three leading newspapers, the *Rodong Sinmun* ("Worker's Daily"), the *Chosŏn Inmin'gun* ("KPA Daily"), and the *Ch'ŏngnyŏn Chŏnwi* ("Youth Daily"), and basically lays out the overall direction of the regime for that year. In 2007, the editorial made no mention of Ch'ŏllima, but in 2008 this number increased to four, and in 2009 it was up to nine. The 2009 editorial describes how, at Kangsŏn Steel Complex, the "Dear Leader" Kim Jong-Il "kindled the torch of a new revolutionary upsurge," touting his visit as "a great event that has brought about a turning point in the development of our Party and revolution *as that in December 1956 when Kim Il Sung set the great Chollima Movement in motion.*" The article also calls for the North Koreans to display their "indomitable spiritual strength" that has been "cultivated and built in the flames of Songun" and to bring about this new revolutionary upsurge, "*like our forefathers who had ushered in a great Chollima era.*"[60] This harkening back to the past is not limited to references to Ch'ŏllima. As stated above, references to "*kangsŏng tae'guk*" ("a prosperous and powerful nation") follow a very similar pattern and are used to bring forth images of a great revolutionary past. In the 2006 Joint Editorial, "*kangsŏng tae'guk*" wasn't mentioned, and in 2007 it increased to only a single reference. Yet in 2008, there were thirteen references to "a prosperous and powerful nation," two in 2009, five in 2010, and twelve in 2011, including in the title of the article itself.[61] Many of these references also include the word "socialist," to emphasize the glory of the early Cold War days. For instance, the 2008 editorial announces that the "road we are taking is the road of *Juche,* the road of Songun, opened by Kim Il Sung; the objective of our advance is a great, prosperous, and powerful *socialist* country."[62] The following year, the editorial declares that the "whole country and all the people, *as in those years of bringing about a great Chollima upsurge after the war,* should launch a general offensive dynamically . . . opening the gate to a great, prosperous, and powerful nation"[63] (emphasis added to all quotes above). With these references, the Kim regime is creating a simple formula in the minds of average North Koreans: the purely socialist past was good; the ideologically impure influences of the present are bad; so if we do things as they did in the past, all will be good in the future.

THE COLD WAR era was North Korea's heyday. But if adherence to *juche* ideology during the Cold War was considered a successful practice, the rise of *neojuche* conservatism today is an act of desperation. It represents a last-gasp effort to define a new legitimacy for the state that has failed miserably in fulfilling its end of the social contract. For reasons discussed in the ensuing pages, North Korea has become a prisoner of its own ideology and its own Cold War successes. Its hope to return to the "good old days" is severely misplaced. *Juche* was possible then because of massive inputs from the Soviet Union and China. Even with continued Chinese assistance, it is not possible to sustain today. And yet, the regime knows of no other way to try to justify its continued hold on power. This is an unsustainable situation.

CHAPTER THREE

ALL IN THE FAMILY

A DISCO BALL SHIMMERS FROM THE CEILING. STROBE LIGHTS FLASH ACROSS THE translucent tiles of the dance floor, pulsating to the rhythmic beat of salsa music. No, this is not a scene from the Odyssey nightclub made famous by John Travolta's gyrating hips in the 1970s movie *Saturday Night Fever*. It is Banquet Hall Number 8 in Pyongyang, where Kim Jong-il partied. In this dance hall, it is said, Kim treated his guests to banquets and burlesque shows. Indeed, on one occasion, according to his former chef who escaped the North, Kim sometimes would indulge in excesses manifesting his total control:

> *During a banquet one night, a group of live dancers in the entertainment entourage were performing a disco dance. Suddenly, Kim Jong-il ordered, "Take off your clothes!" The girls took off their clothes, but then Kim told them to take it all off. They seemed surprised and could not hide their bewilderment, but they could not object to the Dear Leader's orders. In awkward embarrassment, they stripped down and continued their performance in the nude. . . . After a while, he turned to his cabinet staff members and instructed them, "You guys dance with them too." And soon enough I, too, was ordered to dance. However, he cautioned us, "You'll dance, but you won't touch. If you touch, you're thieves."[1]*

This story is just one of the many that have informed the folklore of the mysterious and eccentric North Korean leadership. There probably is no other leader of a nation-state today that is the butt of more ridicule than Kim Jong-il of North Korea. Students in my classes at Georgetown know Kim best from the hilarious puppet caricatures in the 2004 movie

Team America depicting an angry little Kim singing "I'm So Ronery" as he clutches his nuclear bombs. Indeed, Kim has become an integral part of political cartooning in newspapers around the world, imaged in his Mao suits, bouffant hairdo, and elevator shoes.

The silliness sometimes seeps into policy. During a round of Six-Party Talks in Beijing, as we waited for a meeting with the Chinese, we sat in our delegation room in the Diaoyutai complex, which was adjacent to the North Korean delegation room. I glanced over to see members of our delegation huddled around someone's iPod, giggling loudly. They were watching a scene of Kim Jong-il from the movie *Team America,* when one of our members, a jaded foreign service officer, thought it would be "funny" to take the iPod into the adjacent room and show it to the North Koreans. We decided against this impromptu introduction to American pop culture, and probably avoided a diplomatic incident. (We did, however, share it with our South Korean allies for a good laugh.)

The jokes about the North Korean leadership, however, fill a black void of reliable information about the successive generations of Kims that have run North Korea. The dearth of understanding would not be so troubling if this country were not a dictatorship with a million-man army, ballistic missiles, and nuclear weapons. Adjectives such as "opaque," "unpredictable," "irrational," "reclusive" are often used to describe what we basically know little about. Unlike our knowledge of other world leaders, we have little ground truth about the Kim family. Our intelligence community has less information about the North Korean leadership than that of any other country in the world today. Only one former U.S. president (Jimmy Carter) has met both the dad (Kim Il-sung) and the son (Kim Jong-il). And until this year, no American had ever laid eyes on the grandson (Kim Jong-un), the twentysomething-year-old heir to the throne. The fact that, until late September of 2010, the only picture we had of the grandson, the new leader of the world's renegade nuclear state, was of him as a grade-schooler is both historically unprecedented and downright frightening.

THE DAD: KIM IL-SUNG

The first leader of North Korea, Kim Il-sung, was born on April 15, 1912, in the village of Man'gyŏngdae near the capital city of Pyongyang. I have visited the site, now a tourist attraction nestled atop mountains over-looking the city. His beginnings were undeniably modest, and North Korean authorities have done nothing to lionize the site, perhaps desirous of accentuating his rise to greatness—the North Korean version of the American Dream.

The state's story of Kim Il-sung launches from these origins depicting him as a glorious revolutionary from the day he was brought into the world. He is credited with many accomplishments, including the founding of an anti-imperialist league at the age of nineteen, and then the founding of the Korean Communist movement. Kim Il-sung's destiny was to become the country's leading freedom fighter against the Japanese colonizers. According to the story line, he led guerrilla forces against the Japanese and ultimately defeated them at the end of World War II and expelled permanently the hated occupiers from the Korean Peninsula. Kim then became anointed as the leader of the country. In this official history, there is no mention of the United States and the atomic bombs in 1945 that led to Japan's unconditional surrender. There is no mention of the role of the Soviet Union in installing Kim as the North Korean leader in late 1945, and the rally of 300,000 held for his welcoming, in which he turned up wearing a Western suit with numerous Soviet military medals pinned to his chest.[2] Every North Korean child today believes that the Korean War was started by South Korea and the United States in a surprise attack on June 25, 1950. They believe that Kim Il-sung repelled the Americans and within three days drove U.S. forces south to the Pusan perimeter. There is no mention of the Chinese intervention in the war, nor that the instigator of the war was Kim himself. Kim Il-sung has since been recorded in North Korean history as the ultimate leader, the epitome of everything Korean, and everything good in the world. Though he passed away in July 1994, the government designates him as the Eternal President of the country, forever alive in the spirit of North Koreans, even as his body lies in state in the Kim Il-sung Mausoleum on the outskirts of Pyongyang.

Here is the real story. Kim Il-sung was born as Kim Sŏng-ju. He was a Christian, not a Communist. What is significant about his birth date (aside from being the same day that the *Titanic* sunk) is that this was only twenty years after the 1882 treaty of amity and commerce with the

United States, which paved the way for Western missionaries to come to the peninsula. These missionaries touched Kim's father, Kim Hyŏng-jik, born in 1894, who spent his school years at the first private American Christian School in Pyongyang (Sungsil Middle School). By all accounts, he was a young man of faith. He eventually became a Presbyterian elder who worked during the day as an herbal pharmacist and taught at a small rural Christian school southwest of Pyongyang. As Japanese occupation authorities carried out draconian policies to colonize Korea, Hyŏng-jik traveled in 1916 to China as a young man and met up with Chinese nationalist and anti-Japanese movements, for which he was arrested and imprisoned for one year when he returned to Korea. The experience seared him. He participated in the March 1, 1919, Independence Movement, a nationwide peaceful demonstration of Koreans against Japan's occupation. The Korean calls for independence went unheard by the world, and Japanese authorities ruthlessly suppressed the demonstrators. Seeing no future in a country ruled by the hated Japanese, Hyŏng-jik left his homeland the following year, taking his family to Manchuria. He died there a young man, at the age of only thirty-two. Kim Il-sung's mother, Kang Pan-sŏk, was the daughter of a local schoolteacher and Presbyterian elder and was herself a devout Christian, having served as a deaconess in a local church.[3]

Kim Il-sung, the eldest son of the family, was only seven or eight years old when his family moved to China. They lived in the Korean-populated Jilin Province, where he was educated in Chinese schools and ended his formal education in the eighth grade. The official state history records that Kim Il-sung founded the Korean People's Army in 1932, but this is incorrect. He joined anti-Japanese guerrilla movements that were looking for Chinese and Korean nationalist recruits after Japan colonized Manchuria. Kim was a twentysomething, ambitious man displaced from his homeland. He spent the next twenty years in the Communist movement in China, and like many young nationalist Koreans saw this as a career path and devotion to the Korean independence cause.

According to one of the best accounts of Kim—written by Suh Dae-sook, an emeritus professor at the University of Hawaii—Kim organized his first guerrilla unit in 1932 but started to make a name for himself the following year at the Battle of Dongning. Chinese guerrillas attempted to take this Japanese-held city but were outgunned and found their unit surrounded. Professor Suh writes that Kim's unit was able to distract the Japanese, thereby facilitating the escape of the Chinese commander of the unit. Thereafter, Kim became a known quantity among the Chinese and a marked man among Japanese colonial authorities. How great a fighter Kim really was is unclear, but he was clearly no slouch. According to some sympathetic accounts, he was commanding a division-size guerrilla unit by 1936 and had Chinese commanders reporting to him at the tender age of twenty-five. Professor Suh confirms that most of Kim's fighting was in 1938 and 1939, in southern and southeastern Manchuria. He became a target of Japanese colonial police, who tried to capture his unit. According to Japanese military records, the bounty on Kim's head went from 20,000 yen ($10,000) to 200,000 yen ($100,000). As the war in the Pacific against the United States heated up, Japan sought to fully assimilate its colonies in Manchuria and Korea to fuel the war machine. Koreans were forced to change their names to Japanese. All were forced to give up their faith and worship the Japanese state religion (Shinto) and pledge allegiance to the emperor. Resistance was not tolerated, and pacification campaigns to root out Korean and Chinese "extremists" grew more intense. Kim Il-sung and his band of fighters could not withstand the pressure. He was eventually forced to retreat to the Soviet border, and by the end of 1941 crossed it for refuge in the Soviet Union, where he stayed until 1945. Kim trained with the Soviets as an infantry officer. He learned Russian. He started a family with his wife, Kim Chŏng-suk, who had joined his guerrilla unit in 1935 as a sixteen-year-old orphan, a food worker. Chŏng-suk gave him two sons and a daughter, and the two young parents lived a fairly normal life during these years. She died in September of 1949 while delivering a stillborn baby at only thirty years of age. This was a truly tragic loss for Kim, and he is said to have carried fond memories of her and mourned this bereavement for all his years.[4]

What is interesting about these early years of Kim's life is that the first great Communist leader of North Korea, a revolutionary and a patriot, who owned the Korean nationalist narrative during the Cold War over the rival in the South, enjoyed about as bourgeois and non-Korean a middle-class upbringing as one could have imagined. He was a Christian before he ever became a Communist. He lived in Korea only nine years of his first thirty-three. And he became a Communist by accident, driven by a patriotic groundswell that inhered in every young and relatively educated Korean man who had been rendered country-less by Japan's unlawful takeover. The majority of Korean families stayed at home trying to make a new life under a new system. But the families who resisted by voting with their feet sought refuge in China, and their young adults, like Kim, found common patriotic cause with Chinese revolutionaries, but not necessarily ideological truth. North Korea's true first Communist was not Kim but a man by the name of Yi Tong-hwi. With other leftist Christians, Yi established a secret society known as the New People's Association (*Sinminhoe*). The group was accused in 1911 of an assassination attempt against the Japanese resident-general, and Yi fled to southern Manchuria. Yi was disappointed that the West, despite its principles of self-determination, did not come to Korea's aid, and he looked to the newly empowered Russian Bolsheviks for help to form the Korean People's Socialist Party (*Hanin Sahoedang*) in June 1918. He set up operations in Khabarovsk in Siberia and harbored ambitions to form an army outside of Korea to liberate the country from Japan. Yi later became a leader of the Koryŏ Communist Party (*Koryŏ Kongsandang*) in 1919 and eventually premier of the Korean government-in-exile in Shanghai. His extremist views—and willingness to take money directly from Moscow to fund his movement rather than the provisional government-in-exile—led to a breakup of the party. Yi died of an unknown illness in 1928.

KIM IL-SUNG SETTLED in to his new Russian surroundings. He enrolled in a Khabarovsk Infantry Officers School and rose to the rank of captain. Kim ended up leading a multiracial reconnaissance battalion of two hundred Russians, Koreans, Chinese, and other regional ethnicities. Under what was known as the Eighty-eighth Special Independent Sniper Brigade, Kim and his comrades were charged with collecting intelligence on Japanese troop movements in Korea and China. The training was said to be rigorous, running from six A.M. to ten P.M. daily, and as a result of his partisan lifestyle, Kim's health was not particularly good, despite his youth. He was said to have been thin and emaciated, and at certain times unable to participate in some of these exercises and to lead reconnaissance missions.[5] This was a far cry from the official history of Kim being the active liberator of his country and master tactician, charging after the Japanese on the front lines of battle. Kim first started to appear in photos with Soviet military officers in 1945, and clearly saw his future better assured by Moscow than by Beijing. After the Japanese surrender, the Chinese Communists confiscated the former colonizer's weapons and started a civil war against the Nationalists. Kim, however, stayed with his newfound Russian friends rather than return to China. In the end, this strategy paid off for him handsomely. The Allied Powers could not fulfill their promise, embodied in the 1943 Cairo Declaration, to give Korea independence "in due course" after Imperial Japan's surrender. Korea's status remained undetermined until at Potsdam, in July 1945, the United States and the Soviet Union agreed to divide the Korean Peninsula into temporary occupation zones along the thirty-eighth parallel. Though the issue of Korean independence would formally be taken to the U.N.-administered nationwide election, the emerging Cold War spheres made clear that the division was not temporary.

It was in this context that Soviet intelligence handpicked Kim as the indigenous figurehead to lead the Soviet occupation zone. Stalin approved this choice—not for some well-thought-out reason but as a last-minute decision, since he had no real plan for the occupation. According to Soviet archives, Kim arrived in Korea on August 22, 1945. He was only thirty-three years old, and had been out of the country for about twenty years. Kim's Korean was not very good, though he was fluent in Chinese and conversant in Russian. Soviet authorities fed him a speech to learn and practice reading aloud in Korean. Relative to other "freedom fighters" against the Japanese, Kim was an unknown quantity. He was not like his counterpart in the South, Syngman Rhee, a seventy-year-old political giant who spent years in the United States studying at Harvard and Princeton, and who led an international appeal for Korean independence—or Kim Ku, a well-known revolutionary leader and the last president of the Korean provisional government-in-exile. Soviet authorities probably preferred Kim because they could assure his loyalty. Moscow did away with potential competitors like Cho Man-sik, a popular sixty-two-year-old leftist Presbyterian deacon, by spreading rumors that he was a Japanese collaborator and then by placing him under house arrest. All of these signs point to Kim Il-sung, the first "Great Leader" of

North Korea, as little more than a puppet of an unpopular Soviet occupation of northern Korea. While Western history books record how the United States was wholly unprepared for their takeover of the southern half of the peninsula (General John Hodge was given only days to divert to Korea a force that was training for the occupation of Japan), they do little justice to the extreme unpopularity of the foreign occupation in the North. In a handwritten document recently unearthed and translated by the Woodrow Wilson Center, a young Soviet lieutenant colonel describes some of his occupying comrades' conduct. He claims that the "immoral behavior of our servicemen is horrible. Regardless of rank, they indulge in looting, violence, and misconduct every day here and there." He goes on to describe how the "sound of gunfire never stops at night in areas where our troops are stationed," and that "drunk and disorderly soldiers commit immoral behavior and rape is prevalent."[6] Despite this horribly deviant behavior by Soviet soldiers, Kim continued to praise his patrons in every public speech, contrary to the sentiments of his countrymen. Kim traveled in these early months with an entourage of Soviet soldiers who saved him in March 1946 from an assassination attempt when an alert soldier got his arm blown off while deflecting a live grenade tossed at the young North Korean leader during a public appearance. But this discontent did not bother Soviet authorities; they valued Kim as an instrument of absolute control over the North Korean people. Moscow opposed the U.N. plan for national elections in the two halves of Korea, which it perceived as favoring the more populous U.S.-backed South Korea. On September 8, 1948, three weeks after Syngman Rhee assumed the helm of the newly established Republic of Korea, Kim Il-sung completed his unlikely rise to power by becoming leader of the newly established DPRK.

Kim Il-sung worked assiduously to consolidate his power once he took the reigns of leadership in Pyongyang from the Soviets. By 1949, he had purged all potential opposition leaders either through public executions or by throwing them into newly created labor camps, the precursors to the infamous gulags that are today widely condemned by human rights advocates. Kim became totally dependent in these early years on assistance from the Soviets, which is perhaps another reason Moscow felt they could control him. Recently released archives from the Russian

Federation reveal the extent to which Kim was beholden to the Kremlin. In the spring of 1949, the young North Korean leader made one of several trips to Moscow with a laundry list of needs. Kim told Stalin that the DPRK's very existence relied on continued Soviet aid. Stalin asked what kind of aid. Kim responded with a long list: machines, equipment, spare parts for industry, communications, transport, technical specialists, irrigation structures, hydroelectricity plants, metallurgical plants, steam engines, electric locomotives, textile machinery spare parts, a fifty-eight-kilometer (36-mi) railroad track, transport planes, pilots, teachers, Russian language instructors, automobiles, oil, and $50 million in credits.[7] Stalin responded with a curt "Fine," and then their conversation turned to other topics, such as the South Korean military, the U.S. presence on the peninsula, and foreign trade. Throughout the conversation, Stalin repeatedly poked fun at the North Korean leader, asking him if he was "afraid" of the South Korean military and telling Kim he appeared to have "filled out" since his last visit, but the North Korean leader seemed to have misunderstood or disregarded Stalin's banter.

But even as Kim became materially dependent on the Soviet Union, the regime started to create an indigenous official narrative of "self-reliance" ideology and myths about the leadership, which were wholly independent of its patron. The state erected the first statue of Kim Il-sung in 1949, marking the beginning of the personality cult. A rewriting of Korean Communist history took place, in which the stories of critical figures such as Yi Tong-hwi were completely erased from the annals. On the one-year anniversary of the founding of the Korean People's Army, Kim Il-sung first referred to himself as the "Great Leader," or *"Suryŏng,"* drawing on a term used during the Koguryŏ dynasty to denote maximum—or supreme—leadership. As this cult of personality gained momentum, Kim gave orders that all references to Soviet support be erased from North Korean history. To this day, North Koreans believe that the Korean Workers' Party was founded by Kim Il-sung rather than the Soviet Union occupying forces.

In the previous chapter, I talked about *juche* as an ideology of control. *Juche* transformed from a political ideology into a cult of personality and semi-religion from 1949. The one statue of Kim Il-sung in 1949 grew to an omnipresent thirty thousand monuments and images by 1982 and to over forty thousand by 1992.[8] The state took draconian measures to erase any influences, political and religious, which might detract from fidelity to Kim. Over two thousand Buddhist temples and Christian churches were burned. As Jasper Becker notes, the persecution of Christians was especially intense given the relative success of the missionaries in Korea compared with other parts of Asia. Kim incarcerated over a hundred thousand Christians and spread rumors that missionaries were Western spies who branded Korean children with hot irons and sold their blood.[9] The irony of these measures was obvious to the few who knew Kim's background, growing up in a Christian household; and the objectives were clear: Kim was replacing God with himself in the minds of North Koreans. Through destroying others, he made himself the Creator of everything material and spiritual in the North Korean state. Nothing existed before him. State propaganda thereafter referred to Kim as superior to Christ in love, Buddha in benevolence, Confucius in virtue, and Mohammed in justice. Kim also was made out to be a great warrior and the steadfast protector of the Korean people, and was reputed to have fought a hundred thousand battles against the Japanese in ten years. Yet, as a North Korean defector would later write, if this were true, Kim would have had to engage in twenty-eight battles a day, without interruption, for each day from 1932 to 1941.[10] During the Korean War, known as the Fatherland Liberation War in North Korea, the Korean People's Army is described as being led by the indomitable fighting spirit of Kim Il-sung. Official accounts describe how despite "U.S. material and numerical superiority in its offensives, the KPA men firmly defended the heights of the Fatherland, not surrendering even an inch of land to the enemy."[11] One of Kim's official biographies further describes him returning home after liberating the country, and becoming so immediately busy building the party, the state, and the army that he didn't have time to change from the cotton flannel uniform he had worn on the battlefield for the past twenty years. The use of racialized propaganda was also not beyond the North Korean leadership. As North Korean propaganda expert B. R. Myers attests, over the course of the past sixty years, through state propaganda, the people of North Korea have been led to believe that they "are too pure-blooded, and so too virtuous, to survive in this evil world without a great parental leader."[12] Their racial purity and homogeneity, the story goes, renders them dangerously vulnerable unless they are under the care and protection of the Great Leader. Over the years and to this day, the United States has been depicted as "bloodthirsty Yankees" and South Korea as "warmongering puppets." In contrast to the "paradise" of North Korea, the South is depicted as hell on earth, where destitute students sell their blood to pay for textbooks and the American imperialists drive their tanks over children just for sport.[13] This twisting of history might seem crazy. But it was logical for Kim. The purpose of history was not truth; it was political control through legitimation of the leadership and through total loyalty.

I ARRIVED AT the foreign ministry building in Pyongyang for a meeting with the North Korean vice minister. This structure sits at the south end of Kim Il-sung Square, which you often see in CNN video footage of goose-stepping North Korean soldiers leading a military parade of missiles and tanks. There were no soldiers on this spring day in April; instead, the square was filled with North Korean women in traditional colorful Korean dress, rehearsing songs for an upcoming festival. The music piped through the public-address system echoed through the hallways of the barren lobby as I entered the building. As I waited for the vice minister's aide to retrieve me, I stared over the shoulder of my three North Korean minders at a wall mural depicting the Great Leader Kim smiling radiantly as he was giving instructions to young diplomats following him. The whole aura of the painting suggested a political rendition of the Pied Piper story (except for the propaganda music over the loudspeakers). But then I noticed something about the artist's portrayal of Kim's face: blushed cheeks, soft and round face, and thin, glossy lips. At the time, the artist's interpretation of Kim's face struck me as unusually feminine, which I found strange. I thought better not to ask, lest my minders decide I was having hallucinations from spending a day too many in Pyongyang.

In the end, of course, I was not imagining things. The personality cult built around Kim Il-sung was not just spiritual and political, it was also filial. The iconography portrayed Kim not as a stern, disciplined father figure to the people but as a loving mother. Photos and artwork depicted the soft-cheeked leader, holding farmers and children close to his bosom, appealing to the working proletariat to show sentimentality and piety to Kim as they would do to their own mother. Ri Myŏng-hun, the seven-foot-nine (236-cm) North Korean basketball player who flirted with a possible career in the National Basketball Association in the 1990s, once told foreign reporters that he was honored to play basketball "in the bosom" of Kim. The state therefore created a narrative in which the job of the citizens was to work for and care for the mother (Kim), who was constantly toiling to provide for the family (state). The Great Leader was also depicted as virtuous (whose Mom is not?), frugal, and austere—thus sowing seeds of guilt among those who felt the state was not providing enough. A typical news report from the official mouthpiece KCNA, broadcast nationwide, went as follows:

> *The Leader did an on-sight inspection at a local factory. He received reports about how the workers met their production quotas ahead of schedule in order to show their loyalty to the Leader. The Leader then offered to share his simple lunch of grains, vegetables, and soup with the workers. The workers were so impressed by the generosity of the Leader to share his small and simple meal with them, they sobbed with tears of joy and pledged to work even harder to please the Leader.*

Filial piety is not a Marxist concept, but it is an Asian one. Kim's grip on the people was therefore accentuated by the fusing of the Stalinist personality cult–like order with these neo-Confucian values. Bizarre as it sounds, it was very effective. People still felt great sentimentality for Kim and the revolutionary cause even as they suffered from relative deprivation. They were taught to believe that even under hardship, the Great Leader was more frugal and working even harder than the proletariat, so how could anyone complain? When Kim died in 1994, tens of thousands mourned in the streets as if they had collectively lost their mother. A recent study by the respected scholar Park Kyung-Ae found that interviews of North Korean defectors today find sentimentality expressed for the leadership even as they expressed great anger with the political system.[14]

I recount this history because it casts an ordinary pall on the official and extraordinary narrative of Great Leader Kim's accomplishments as the first ruler of the country. There is no denying he is immortal in the minds of North Koreans, but his story contains puzzles and imperfections that were very human. In this vein, Kim Il-sung's sustained rule after the DPRK's birth in 1948 is almost as puzzling as his rise to power. Here was this bourgeois young Christian man who became a competent but unheralded anti-Japanese independence fighter based in Manchuria, who then got handpicked by the Soviets to run a country at the age of thirty-three. The young and inexperienced leader then pressed his two benefactors, Stalin and Mao, to support his plan to invade South Korea, promising success. Kim attacked on June 25, 1950, starting a war of Koreans against Koreans, sooner than either Stalin or Mao had expected, and his adventurism in the end cost the Chinese an estimated 800,000 lives.[15] Moreover, the war effectively cost the Chinese the territory of Taiwan, which the United States committed to defend during and after the war. It cost the Soviets hundreds of millions of dollars in material and equipment. In spite of these huge mistakes, Kim remained in power in North Korea, accumulating total and absolute control. Why didn't the Chinese or Soviets kick him out after the Korean War and replace him with someone else? How did Kim turn the country from socialism to a bizarre cult of personality?

A number of factors contributed to this outcome. The imperatives of the Cold War made it so that the Soviets could not abandon North Korea even after its failed and costly attempt to unify the peninsula. Korea had become a critical proxy war in the global struggle with the United States. Neither Washington nor Moscow intrinsically valued the peninsula, but both assigned high strategic value to it—meaning they could not allow it to fall into the hands of the enemy. From Stalin's point of view, Kim may have had his flaws, but he had to stick with him. Internal splits within the Chinese leadership after the war were fortuitous for Kim Il-sung as well. Peng Dehuai, who was commander-in-chief of Chinese forces during the Korean War, wanted to oust Kim for his mistakes. Peng would have probably been successful had he not fallen into disfavor with Mao. Peng's criticism of Mao's Great Leap Forward eventually led to his demise, thereby allowing Kim to stay in place. Geopolitics also operated to Kim's advantage. The emerging split within the Communist bloc between the Chinese and the Soviets benefited the North Korean regime handsomely as both capitals vied for the allegiance of the North. Thus, rather than being rejected by Stalin or Mao for his failed war, Kim was courted by both in the years following the war, as Stalin and Mao wanted to legitimate their dominance in the movement by having smaller Communist countries, like the DPRK, on their side. In international relations theory, we call these "structural explanations," which basically means the confluence of forces in the strategic environment would have benefited Kim—or any other leader, for that matter—at the time. But there is another specific answer for Kim Il-sung's iron grip on the leadership mantle, which has less to do with structure and everything to do with the agency of a particular individual: the rise of his first son, Kim Jong-il.

THE SON: KIM JONG-IL

I want to introduce this mercurial figure to readers by explaining a less well-known but critical role the Son played in the state-building of North Korea. Kim Jong-il was known to be a cinephile. His favorite movie of all time was *Gone with the Wind,* and this affection apparently is widely shared by North Korean elite. In both official and sidebar meetings with North Korean counterparts, I would be thrown off by sudden North Korean references to the American classic. In one tense session of negotiations when we confronted our counterparts with the consequences of failure to denuclearize (i.e., U.N. sanctions, etc.), the North Korean negotiator tilted his head back and said, "Well, frankly, Scarlett, I don't give a damn." It brought levity to the moment, although the North Korean said it in all seriousness and with an artistic flair. Kim Jong-il apparently liked James Bond movies, too, and reportedly enjoyed *Die Another Day,*[16] which portrays an ambitious and ruthless son of a North Korean general who plans to take over the world with a laser-firing satellite. (The son eventually kills his father in the movie's climax.) He had a video library of over twenty thousand movies and has written books on filmmaking. In 1978, he orchestrated the kidnapping of the famous South Korean director Sin Sang-ok and actress Ch'oe Un-hŭi because he liked their movies. The Son spent his early years producing many of the propaganda films and revolutionary operas for the state. This was not just Kim's hobby horse, nor his ambition to become North Korea's next Martin Scorcese. Instead, it was part of a deliberate effort to elevate his father to demigod status. These films and the maternal-like depictions in art of the leadership created loyalty through appealing to the sentimentality of the revolution and through weaving together political loyalty and filial piety.

Indeed, Kim Jong-il played a major role in the deification of his father and the transformation of a Korean Communist system into the bizarre personality cult–based regime that it is today. This transformation was driven by the politics of family succession. The Son found himself in intense competition with his father's younger brother (Kim Yŏng-ju) and his stepbrother (Kim P'yŏng-il, from the father's second marriage) for the mantle of designated successor. Kim Yŏng-ju was his brother's trusted representative in the occasional secret talks that took place with the South Korean CIA in the 1970s. It is also said that he worked at a Japanese-owned store while the family was in exile in Manchuria, and that he spent the early half of the 1940s living in Hawaii, returning only after liberation in 1945.[17] Kim P'yŏng-il is said to be a debonair, English-speaking diplomat who served as DPRK ambassador to Hungary, Bulgaria, Finland, and is currently ambassador to Poland. In his younger years, he was a spitting image of his father, and his military service bestowed popularity upon him with this powerful faction, something Kim Jong-il couldn't have claimed to have.[18] Hwang Jang-yŏp, the highest-level defector ever from North Korea, who served as mentor and confidant to the Kim family, once told me that the rivalry among these individuals was intense and that it was entirely based on who could put Kim Il-sung on a higher pedestal. As I mentioned earlier, the frail, eighty-seven-year-old Hwang, who was the founder and a former teacher of *juche* ideology, came to Washington to deliver a speech at the Center for Strategic and International Studies (CSIS). Because of persistent North Korean assassination threats, he arrived with an FBI detail of eight officers, which turned out to be a necessary precaution, as only weeks later, South Korean officials arrested two North Koreans posing as defectors, who were sent to kill Hwang. Hwang talked about how the competition between Kim Jong-il and his relatives led to excesses of the personality cult prevalent today. In 1965, shortly after joining the party and heading up its Propaganda and Agitation department, Kim Jong-il ordered party officials to publish the first biography of his father for external consumption, which introduced the world to all the absolutisms of the Great Leader. In the early 1970s, Kim Jong-il headed a government agency known as the "4-15 Creation Group," named after his father's birthday, which was in charge of creating personal monuments to his father. Kim ordered the construction of over twelve thousand monuments and statues in his father's name, including the Man'gyŏngdae birthplace (1969), *Juche* Tower (1982), and the Arch of Triumph (1982) modeled after the French monument.

He constantly showered his father with gifts, including a bulletproof Mercedes-Benz, which now sits in the Kim Il-sung Mausoleum on display. In 1972, to commemorate his father's sixtieth birthday (a celebration known in Korean as *Hwan'gap*), the Son ordered the building of a massive, $800 million, seventy-foot (21-m) gilded statue in the center of the city, known as the Great Monument on Mansu Hill.

By 1992, there were a total of over forty thousand pieces of iconography.[19] The Grand Monument upset both the Soviets and the Chinese. Moscow believed that such grandeur in the context of the global socialist movement, of which North Korea was a part, should only be reserved for Stalin. Deng reportedly was very upset with the extravagance of the statue when he first saw it. This eventually led the North Koreans to strip the gold leaf off of the statue and redo it in the bronze gild that visitors see today. In the end, however, the monuments worked for Kim Jong-il's purposes: in April 1974, he was formally anointed as the successor to his father and took on the moniker of the "Dear Leader," a full twenty years before he would eventually take power. Kim Jong-il's image did not start to appear in portraits in government offices until around 1988, in large part because once he had become the designated successor against all other contenders, he had no need to usurp his father's position, instead waiting in the wings for his day. Ironically, the most significant piece of iconography in the Son's likeness stands outside the entrance of the nuclear facility at Yongbyon, where the North produced plutonium for nuclear bombs. It is a fifty-foot (15-m) monument of Kim Jong-il standing with scientists and soldiers, with a slogan encouraging the scientists to promote the nation's defense.

Kim Jong-il's efforts to create a virtuous, frugal, and austere aura around his father contrasts starkly with the reported excesses associated with the Son's lifestyle. He romped around eight different palaces, connected by underground train, each complete with a golf course, indoor wave pool, home movie theater, video game room, regulation basketball courts, horse stables, and shooting ranges. Each palace is detectable with overhead commercial satellite photography, all constantly illuminated against the surrounding darkness and fully staffed, in large part so that no one can determine which one he is visiting at any given time.

The late Kim was an avid consumer of things Western, including CNN and MTV, video games (Mario Kart was reportedly a favorite), and music ranging from the Rolling Stones to the Beach Boys. During former secretary of state Madeleine Albright's meeting with him in October 2000, Kim let on that he was a huge National Basketball Association fan, which prompted the secretary—now a Georgetown University professor—to give him an autographed basketball from NBA icon Michael Jordan. Robert Carlin, a former State Department official, who accompanied Albright on that trip, recalled:

> We were looking for something that was a little more meaningful than a bottle of scotch or a miniature Statue of Liberty or a Buffalo Bill book—something with more importance to him . . . [h]e may have been initially surprised by it, but you could tell he was pleased. I don't think he expected it. It was a very personal gesture, in a sense. . . . It showed him we went through some effort to get the signature. They realized it wasn't just an ordinary ball.[20]

The ball now sits in the Museum of International Understanding, which displays all the gifts given to the Dear Leader. It sits next to a hunting rifle given by Vladimir Putin and a crocodile bag proffered by Fidel Castro. Subsequent to Albright's gift, Jordan's management team was approached in 2001 with an official invitation to visit North Korea and play for the Dear Leader. South Korean conglomerate Samsung, which sought to improve inter-Korean relations under the South Korean government's Sunshine Policy of engagement, offered to underwrite the bizarre event. Jordan, who probably abhorred involvement in a diplomatic dance aimed at trading his signed basketballs for Kim's basketball-size nuclear bombs, graciously declined the invitation.

There are more lurid reports that Kim enjoyed the company of Norwegian models and that he retained constantly replenished "joy brigades" of women who entertained him. He stocked a spirits cellar of over ten thousand bottles of the world's finest wines and liquors, and until his death in 2011 was one of the single biggest foreign customers of Hennessy Paradis Cognac. The Son, as evident from his paunch, loved food, and stories told by his former chef, Fujimoto Kenji, are impressive. Fujimoto recounted how Kim ordered him to go on global buying sprees to bring the best items back to Pyongyang for Kim's consumption. The chef went to Tsukiji fish market in Japan to buy nearly three thousand pounds (1,360 kg) of the best sushi and squid, and to Mistukoshi department store in Ginza to buy red-bean rice cakes and Japanese cigarettes; he then went to Thailand for the best papayas and mangoes, to Czechoslovakia for Pilsner draft beer, to Denmark for bacon, to France for Perrier water, and to Iran and Uzbekistan for pistachio nuts and caviar.[21]

Moreover, the Son did not cut down on his excesses. They became even more egregious, particularly as his countrymen went through difficult economic times. Swiss trade statistics show that at the height of the famine in the 1990s, he imported $2.6 million worth of luxury Swiss watches. In 1995, he paid $15 million for U.S. professional wrestlers to do exhibition matches in North Korea—the most money at the time that professional wrestling ever made for a foreign event. A few years later (1998), he paid $20 million for two hundred new S-500 Class Mercedes limousines.[22] Kim was entirely willing to satisfy his taste buds during the famine. In 1997, Italian gourmet chef Ermanno Furlanis and a team of chefs went to North Korea for three weeks at the invitation of the government. They were put up in a seaside villa and were provided with three fully equipped kitchens to teach North Korean chefs how to cook Italian foods. In an interview in 2001, Furlanis recounted that he explained the need for a special type of oven in order to properly bake pizza dough, and it was brought to him a few days later. He also recounted how the North Koreans mistakenly provided French wines and cheeses to the chefs. When Furlanis pointed out the error, all the materials were taken away and replaced a few days later with a collection of the finest Italian cheeses and Bartolo wines from his home country.[23] Yi Yŏng-guk, a former bodyguard of Kim Jong-il who later defected to South Korea, assessed that his former boss's excesses made the extravagant Philippines dictators Ferdinand and Imelda Marcos look like paupers. In a 2005 interview, Yi explains that Kim "has at least ten palaces set in sprawling grounds . . . They contain golf courses, stables for his horses, garages full of motorbikes and luxury cars, shooting ranges, swimming pools, cinemas, fun-fair parks, water-jet bikes, and hunting grounds stocked with wild deer and duck."[24]

THE MIND BOGGLES at comprehending what sort of individual was capable of such decadence. According to the official history, the second leader of North Korea was born in a secret military camp on February 16, 1942, on Mount Paektu, which is the mythical birthplace of the Korean race. As the annals record, his birth was foretold by a swallow, and the heavens celebrated with a double rainbow and the appearance of a new star in the night sky. The real story, however, is less spectacular. Kim was born as Yuri Irsenovich Kim in the Russian town of Vyatskoye near Khabarovsk, when his father was a captain in the first battalion of the Soviet Eighty-eighth Brigade—a guerrilla unit composed of Chinese and Korean exiles. Details on these years are scarce, because it is not part of the official history, but according to interviews with North Koreans close to the family in Russia at the time, Kim attended a Russian school with other children of the Eighty-eighth Brigade, where they were taught Stalinism-for-preschoolers. The future leader of North Korea apparently did not like the sessions very much, according to one South Korean newspaper report, because he spent his time disobeying teachers and biting other classmates.[25] He had a younger brother, Kim P'yŏng-il, known as "Shura," born in 1944, who drowned when he was three years old, and a younger sister, Kim Kyŏng-hŭi, born in 1946. He also had two stepbrothers (Kim P'yŏng-il, named after the drowned boy, who is the abovementioned ambassador to Poland; and Kim Yŏng-il, who died in 2000 in Germany) and one or two stepsisters from later marriages of his father.

The sister, Kim Kyŏng-hŭi, appears to be the most important female in Kim's life. Kim was deeply affected by the death of his mother, Kim Chŏng-suk, who died in childbirth when Kim was only seven years old. He has invoked his mother's name when referring to Kyŏng-hŭi as "[M]y only blood family whom I was asked to take care of by my mother till the moment she died." There are stories that recount how Kim and his baby sister awaited from the hospital news of their mother's state and cried in each other's arms when she was gone. After the death of their father in 1994, Kim grew even closer to his sister. The Japanese national security adviser to then-premier Abe Shinzo (2006–2007), Koike Yuriko, wrote in 2010 that Kim Jong-il told the Central Committee after his father's death, "Kim Kyong-hui is myself, the words of Kim Kyong-hui are my words, and instructions issued by Kim Kyong-hui are my instructions."[26] North Korean defector Hwang Jang-yŏp described to me in 2010 that the sister was the only person Kim Jong-il could truly trust, which gave her enormous power behind the scenes. Her husband, Chang Sŏng-t'aek, who holds the number two position in the party, Hwang explained, is only powerful because of his marital ties to the Kim family. The sister graduated from Kim Il-sung University and held the relatively unassuming position as deputy director of the light industry department. She later served on the Party Central Committee in 1988 and Supreme People's Assembly in 1990. In September 2010, she was promoted to the rank of four-star general in the army and elected to the twelve-member Central Committee of the Party—which put her in a more prominent leadership role, alongside Kim Jong-il's youngest son

With the end of the Japanese occupation, Kim Jong-il returned to Korea when he was around three or four years old, in the fall of 1945. He attended primary and middle school in Pyongyang, where he was known to be a bit of a renegade and found himself in different types of trouble with teachers and with house help at home. Only a few months after his mother's death, Kim was sent to China (probably Jilin) while his father attacked the South in the Korean War. Undoubtedly, he saw this separation of the family not as his father's fault but that of the American imperialists, which certainly instilled in him a hatred of the United States. In 1964, he graduated (with top academic honors, of course) from Kim Il-sung University, where he majored in political economy. According to the official history, he wrote twelve hundred works during his illustrious college career, including "The Characteristics of Modern Imperialism and Its Aggressive Nature." His personal life reads like a script from *The Sopranos*: Kim's first wife, Kim Yŏng-suk, was the daughter of a party official and was picked by his father in a Korean-style arranged marriage. This marriage bore one daughter, Kim Sŏl-song, who has never been seen in public. Kim soon lost interest and fell for Sŏng Hye-rim, a then-famous North Korean film actress. A woman of *Yangban* roots (pre-twentieth-century Korean aristocracy), Sŏng was married, but when the Dear Leader falls for you, you don't have much of a choice. Her husband was sent away to France and she gave Kim his first son, Kim Chŏng-nam. Sŏng traveled frequently to Moscow and later died there in 2002. Sŏng's niece and nephew later defected to France, where the nephew gave interviews about life inside the Kim family. He was later found dead in South Korea. Kim's taste for women in the arts was again apparent in his next partner, Ko Yŏng-hŭi, a Japanese-born ethnic Korean who was a member of the Pyongyang dance troupe. She gave birth to Kim's other two sons, Kim Chŏng-ch'ŏl and Kim Jong-un. She died, reportedly during cancer treatment, in Paris in 2004. Kim's last-known mistress was Kim Ok, who served as his personal secretary since the 1980s. A pianist by training, she graduated from Pyongyang Musical College, and reportedly became a confidante and caregiver for Kim.[27] Much younger than Kim, she is in her forties and was part of the DPRK high-level delegation that visited Washington for consultations with Defense Secretary Bill Cohen during the Clinton administration. She is also reportedly involved in the activities of Bureau 39, which handles Kim Jong-il's personal funds.[28] Her relationship with Kim Jong-il's sister, Kim Kyŏng-hŭi, is not known.

Kim Jong-il was nothing like his father. While his father had bona fide, albeit inflated, revolutionary credentials as a freedom fighter against the Japanese, Kim Jong-il had none to speak of. If anything, he had a reputation as an antihero, a spoiled and pampered prince-in-waiting. His father was a handsome and physically big man for a Korean, while his son was short at five feet, one inch (155 cm, hence the height-compensating elevator shoes and the bouffant hairstyle), with an omnipresent paunch. (Madeleine Albright noted that when she met him in 2000, she was wearing high heels, and so was he.) Kim's behavior manifested insecurity about his deficiencies—there are reports that in addition to his four partners, Kim had several other mistresses and some nine additional illegitimate children. He also worked systematically at assuming positions of power in the North Korean government. After university, Kim joined the party and put himself in charge of the propaganda machine, instructing writers and artists to produce over eight thousand revolutionary films and operas in honor of his father. He ordered the construction of seven massive movie studios around the country. I drove past one of these on the outskirts of Pyongyang—a long, sprawling complex of low-rise white buildings and warehouses that make Fox Studios in Los Angeles look small. The story lines of all of these propaganda films and musicals were vehemently anti-American and about paying the ultimate sacrifice for Kim Il-sung. *Wŏlmido* is a story about a North Korean battalion of the Korean People's Army defending a small island (Wŏlmi) off the coast of Korea during MacArthur's landing at Incheon during the Korean War. The story ends with the battalion, fighting valiantly against all odds, ultimately dying in their defense of the small piece of North Korean Motherland. The musical score emphasizes the sentimentality of the Revolution: "In his bosom, I live and die. / I long for his bosom at all times. / The country I call my mother / I know now is the General's bosom."[29] Ordinary citizens were required to watch these movies and then discuss the virtues of serving Kim Il-sung. School competitions were not spelling bees but contests to see which students could recite the most passages from a revolutionary movie. The theory behind this propaganda was simple and also attributed to Kim. The Revolution always needed a Supreme Leader. Masses alone were not sufficient for the cause. They needed to be led by a single leader who was the "brain and spirit" of the Revolution, while the masses were the body. This became the essence of Kimilsungism. It is reported that Kim also instructed the Korean Central News Agency in 1964 about the ideological mission of the organization to be the mouthpiece of the Great Leader's ideology broadcast throughout the world. KCNA today is the primary organ of news coming out of North Korea to the outside world, and has become replete with colorful phraseology denouncing the United States as "imperialist warmongers,"[30] the Japanese as "reactionaries steeped in the idea of militarist aggression to the marrow of their bones,"[31] and South Korea as "a tundra of human rights where dictatorship and suppression prevail."[32] Individuals are also not spared the KCNA's wrath, having referred to former U.N. ambassador John Bolton as "human scum and [a] bloodsucker,"[33] former vice president Dick Cheney as "the most cruel monster and bloodthirsty beast,"[34] and former defense secretary Donald Rumsfeld as "a political dwarf," a "human butcher," a "fascist tyrant who puts an ogre to shame," and the "kingpin of evil" who puts "Hitler into the shade in man-killing and war hysteria."[35] We have Kim Jong-il to thank for this.

The Son never served a day in the military, and yet in a militaristic society where revolutionary credentials are a requirement of leadership, he had to have some. It is now believed, both through scholarly research and through interviews, that Kim compensated for this by his involvement in a number of terrorist acts during the 1970s and 1980s. Kim is believed to have ordered the 1976 poplar tree incident. The North Korean defector Hwang Jang-yŏp maintained that Kim was the mastermind of the 1983 terrorist attack on the South Korean presidential delegation during a state visit to Burma. The Son is also believed to have orchestrated the 1986 bombing of Gimpo International Airport, killing five and injuring over thirty. Hwang also maintained that Kim was responsible for orchestrating the 1987 terrorist bombing of a Korean Air civilian passenger plane over the Andaman Sea, killing all 115 passengers and crew on board, which was designed to sabotage Seoul's bid to host the upcoming 1988 Olympics. In September 2002, Kim admitted to Koizumi the abduction of thirteen Japanese citizens between 1977 and 1983. The North under Kim Jong-il has also been an active sponsor of terrorism, aiding the Japanese Red Army (JRA) in their 1970 Japan Airlines hijacking, their 1972 Israeli airport attack, and subsequently harboring a number of their members. As recently as 2000, the DPRK is also suspected of having sold tens of thousands of small arms to the Moro Islamic Liberation Front in the Philippines,[36] and between 2006 and 2009 potentially provided arms and training to the Tamil Tigers of Sri Lanka and Hezbollah in Lebanon.[37] It is through these types of activities that the Son tried to bolster his revolutionary credentials and strengthen the legitimacy of his rule.

Kim cemented his position as the eventual successor, and probably fashioned himself as the ideological father of North Korea's personality cult. At the young age of thirty, he was elected to the Party Central Committee in 1972, and thereafter became a member of the elite Politburo and party secretary for organization and guidance. From this powerful position, he targeted all elements potentially disloyal to his father, which, coincidentally, also paved the way for his eventual ascension to the throne absent any rivals. Nothing either got to or left Kim Il-sung without being filtered through Kim Jong-il. By the mid-1970s, Kim Jong-il's portrait started to appear in public places paired with his father's ubiquitous image. At the 1980 Party Congress, the Son's position as the successor was cemented when he became a member of the presidium of the party Politburo. By the age of thirty-eight, he became the fourth-highest ranking person in the Politburo, second in the Party Secretariat, and third in the Military Commission.

Despite his anointed position, the Son remained the recluse. Reports proliferated of his on-the-spot guidance alongside of his father in different parts of North Korea, but rarely was there ever footage of his activities. North Korean citizens have never heard his voice in public except on special occasions. He seldom traveled abroad, and mostly only to China. The hagiographers went to work building the official personality cult of the Son, ranging from his exploits as a young revolutionary to his eleven hole-in-ones on an eighteen-hole golf course. Some believe that the Son basically was running the daily operations of the country from 1985 onward, even though his father was still the leader. Should this be true, then the Son only knew the revolution as a losing race against its southern competitor. It was from the mid-1980s that the insurmountable economic gaps between the two Koreas became visible to the world. Electric power shortages became evident. According to defector accounts, food rations got smaller in the 1980s, and the days of bumper crop harvests became a memory of the 1970s. Consumer goods were in short supply. Productivity rates started to decline and infrastructure started to decay. Meanwhile, the South's economy was growing at a double-digit percentage clip. South Korea started to make inroads in diplomatic and trade ties with Eastern bloc countries, with Hungary being the first in 1987 and culminating with the Soviet Union three years later. In the ultimate statement that must have impressed upon the Son that the competitive legitimation battle with the South was a lost cause, Seoul hosted the world at the 1988 Olympic Games. Visitors to North Korea during this period, as well as defectors, recall how the pace of the country seemed frenetic: people working incredibly hard in mass mobilization campaigns for the Dear Leader in order to keep up with the South, but with lesser and lesser productivity due to dilapidated equipment. It should therefore come as no surprise that during these years of the Son's unofficial rule, the North pursued the ultimate equalizer: nuclear weapons. In 1985, the North signed the Nuclear Non-proliferation Treaty (NPT)—largely as a quid pro quo to gain access to more Soviet nuclear know-how—this, ironically, said more about Kim's nuclear ambitions than about his nonproliferation intentions. Kim Jong-il inspected the Yongbyon nuclear facility and gave scientists and workers there gifts, such as Japanese TV sets, as rewards for their great work in securing the nation's safety. During this period, the North also reportedly conducted underground nuclear tests, as it refused to fulfill the safeguards and inspection obligations of the NPT.[38] Two larger reactors—a fifty-megawatt (MW) and two-hundred-megawatt facility—were also under construction during this period. The North Korean leadership is fond of saying that a nuclear-free Korean Peninsula was the Great Leader Kim Il-sung's last wish. This may be true, but it certainly was not the wish of his son. On the contrary, the only contribution that Kim Jong-il arguably made to the Revolution was nuclear weapons.

It is during these years of Kim's rise that mysterious references to an all-knowing "Party Center" (*Tang Chungang*), which was upgraded to a "Glorious Party Center" (*Widaehan Tang Chungang*), began to emerge in local newspaper editorials. This was a propagandistic effort on the part of the Son to anchor his place as the exalted imparter of guidance and wisdom in the party and in the psyche of the North Korean people. Kim also resorted to cruder tactics, such as fairly large-scale purges of rival party members by exiling, imprisoning, or "arranging accidents" for them.[39] The Son also introduced a new term of reference for the state ideology— "Kimilsungism"—which placed the focus less squarely on *juche* ideology and more centrally on his father, and by extension, on the emerging Kim dynasty. Kim's period of unofficial rule peaked in the early 1990s. In December of 1991 he became supreme commander of the People's Army. In April 1992, he was promoted to the top military rank of marshal alongside top-ranking military official and Kim family loyalist O Chin-u. And in April 1993, Kim became chairman of the party's central military commission. (The parallels to the power transition to the youngest son, Kim Jong-un, discussed below, are uncanny.) Kim's coming-out party was his observance and speech at a major military parade through Kim Il-sung Square. The speech—the first public statement by the Son—was terribly uninspiring and poorly delivered, leading some to surmise that the reclusive leader was hiding a speech impediment. (Former secretary of state Madeleine Albright later confirmed, after her October 2000 meeting with Kim, that the man was lucid and decisive.) Over these years, the Son is said to have harbored a number of fairly idiosyncratic traits, such as being extremely secretive and suspicious, pathologically jealous, highly reclusive, and noticeably uncomfortable in public.[40] In Politburo meetings, he is said to have regularly shown up late and severely hungover, and other times to belligerently dominate the discussion.[41]

ON JULY 8, 1994, Radio Pyongyang broadcast a single statement of immense proportion for North Korea:

The Great Heart has stopped beating.[42]

The sudden death of the Father gave the Son his moment to take up formally the job for which he had been groomed his entire life. Rumors persist to this day, however, that Kim Jong-il's ascension to the throne was of his own making. In the spring and summer of 1994, the Father, Kim Il-sung, was fairly stressed out as foreign relations swung wildly within months between war and peace. In June, the nuclear crisis reached an apex with the United States when Pyongyang defied U.S. threats and unloaded a batch of fuel rods from the nuclear reactor in Yongbyon, which was the first step to amassing plutonium for nuclear weapons. The Clinton administration responded, as then–secretary of defense William Perry has described, by drawing up plans for a possible military strike against North Korea. While the two countries looked as though they were on the brink of war, former president Jimmy Carter met with Kim Il-sung in Pyongyang and through an extraordinary piece of personal diplomacy negotiated a solution that would eventually form the basis of the October 1994 U.S.-DPRK nuclear agreement. One of the conditions of U.S. diplomacy was that the North improves relations with the American ally in the South. Kim responded by agreeing to the first-ever leaders' summit with ROK president Kim Young-sam (1993–1998). It was during his preparations for this summit that the story becomes fuzzy. According to accounts by defector Hwang Jang-yŏp, the Father was apparently hidden away in one of his remote villas in the Myohyang Mountains. He was deep in argument with the Son about the details of the upcoming summit, including whether the Father should go to the airport to receive the leader, what honorifics should be used to address him, and, in particular, whether the North should turn out the requisite thousands of citizens to welcome the South Korean leader. The Son was vehemently opposed to giving the despised ROK leader any face while the Father believed it was the proper thing to do. (Later, when Kim Young-sam refused to send condolences to the funeral, Kim Jong-il referred in public to the ROK leader as a "filthy dirt-bag.") At the time, the Father was already upset at the Son for problems related to mismanagement of the economy. The Father had only recently become aware of how bad the economic situation was in his country outside of Pyongyang, and was genuinely upset that his son had not informed him accurately of the dire state in the provinces. Kim Il-sung saw his meeting with Carter and the upcoming summit with the South Korean president as an opportunity to rectify the situation, presumably expecting large amounts of assistance from these two countries. The two argued, and the Father apparently suffered a heart attack shortly thereafter; he was found a few hours later facedown on the floor of his bedroom. Kim's regular doctor was not present, replaced by a young, inexperienced physician. Doctors and emergency equipment were rushed to the mountain resort, but due to bad weather one of the helicopters crashed and the other was unable to reach him at the villa in time and he died on July 8, 1994. Further details remain unknown. It is hard to imagine that a medical team was not by Kim Il-sung's side wherever he traveled. And, mysteriously, all of the doctors, bodyguards, and aides who were present at the time have all since died or gone missing in the gulags of North Korea.

What was so interesting about the Father's death was that it was met with a genuine outpouring of grief in North Korea. The state required, of course, that the population come out in mourning, but the footage of the citizens displaying deep sorrow did not look faked. The people had been taught to love the Great Leader like their own mother and god, wrapped into one. The psychic and spiritual void created by his death was apparent in the tears of the people. The Son—the Dear Leader— took the reins of power amid massive speculation that he could not run the country. South Korean analysts in the summer of 1994 affirmed to me that the Son would not last through the end of the calendar year. He did not have the experience, the loyalty of the military, nor the charisma to replicate his father. The fact that the country would soon enter the worst period of food shortages approximating a famine only fueled these predictions of collapse. The Son did not declare himself the leader right away. Instead, he figuratively brought his father back to life. After a period of mourning, Kim Jong-il passed an amendment to the Constitution in 1998, declaring Kim Il-sung the "Eternal President" of North Korea. He built a massive mausoleum, in which Kim is entombed. He declared a new calendar, in which Year Zero is 1912, the birth year of Kim Il-sung (hence, 2012 is 100 after-the-birth-of-Kim), and April 15 is basically Christmas in North Korea (except kids don't get presents). On July 26, 1998, the Son was formally elected to the Supreme People's Assembly as the leader of the country.

KIM JONG-IL'S DEATH AND LEGACY

When Kim Jong-il formally took the reins of power in 1998, no one would have predicted that only a decade later, he would suffer a stroke, and then only three years after that, he would die of a massive heart attack. And yet, as this book went to press in late 2011, the North Korean news agency broadcast the announcement on December 19 that shocked the world: Kim had died of "an advanced acute myocardial infarction, complicated with a [sic] serious heart shock" due to "physical and mental over-work in caring for the North Korean people." Despite the relative brevity of Kim Jong-il's rule, he left some major legacies for the country.

From the start of his rule, the Dear Leader knew his weaknesses and tried to compensate for them. His time in office was based on a tight alignment with the military. Known as "military-first" politics (*sŏngun chongch'i*), this put Kim Jong-il as chairman of the National Defense Commission. Up until this point, the NDC was known as the highest military organ of the state in control of national defense, but it sat alongside other organs, including the Cabinet, Supreme People's Assembly, judiciary, and, most important, the party. As leader of the NDC, Kim Jong-il effectively made this the primary decision-making body in the government. Composed at this time of seven generals and three civilians, the NDC supplanted the party as the heart of the state. Today *sŏngun* politics is the fundamental defining feature of North Korean life. Far from solely being the protector of the North Korean people, the military is a provider of food, services, technical assistance, and revolutionary education. Members of the military are regularly tasked with tilling the fields, fixing the faucets, and unclogging the toilets of everyday North Koreans, ensuring the uninterrupted influence of the military in North Korean society. The conscription system of compulsory service for up to twelve years and mandatory part-time service until age sixty ensures that all are filially, if not directly, connected to the military. According to Professor Park Han-shik, when asked in recent years what type of man they would like to marry, single North Korean girls and women most often respond, "A soldier."[43] This may seem anecdotal, but it is representative of something much larger. Through the elevation of the NDC and the primacy of *sŏngun* politics, the Kim regime eliminated any separation between the military and civilian spheres, to the point that North Korean culture is essentially a military culture.

The Son's formal rule of North Korea was short, relative to his father's half-century at the helm. If Kim had lived to his father's ripe age of eighty-two, he would still only have ruled the country from 1994 to 2023, a mere twenty-nine years. Instead, at his death in 2011, he had run the country for only seventeen years. His rule was marked only by challenges and failures. The biggest challenge that became evident to the world in the 1990s was food. Upon taking power, Kim contended with the collapse of the North's food system and the onset of famine-like conditions. In the years leading up to the famine, the regime tried to deal with food shortages with a "Let's Eat Two Meals per Day" campaign to cut overall consumption, but these measures proved inadequate.[44] It was in the mid-1990s, though, that the "socialist paradise" truly began to look more like a living hell. In what the regime referred to as the "Arduous March" ("*Konan-ŭi haenggun*"), somewhere between 600,000 and a million North Koreans eventually perished as a result of a particularly deadly combination of ill-advised government policy and natural disaster.[45] This encompassed between 3 and 5 percent of the total North Korean population and brought unimaginable pain, suffering, and deprivation to the North. This constituted one of the worst famines suffered by an industrialized society in modern nation-state history, largely due to economic mismanagement. World Food Programme (WFP) appeals, which annually averaged over 920,000 metric tons (MT) from 1995 to 2001, helped to alleviate the situation, but the suffering was intense in North and South Hamgyŏng Provinces. There were reports of food riots and rumors of an assassination attempt against Kim, with one of his bodyguards allegedly attempting to shoot him in March 1998.[46]

Kim's biggest failure related to botched efforts at economic reform. The North Korean attempt at economic opening, which started in July 2002, was a flawed effort, motivated more by the absence of government supplies (and therefore control) to sustain the public distribution system than by any genuine attempt at ending price controls, rationing, and allowing markets to take over. In simple terms, Kim did not stop government rationing because he wanted to transform North Korea into a free-market economy. He stopped the rationing because the government had no supplies, food, clothing, or rice left to ration. Once the supplies did become available again, Kim reinstituted the ration system as a form of political control. Moreover, on more than one occasion, the state issued unilateral redenomination of the national currency. Why? By redenominating the currency and allowing citizens to exchange only a fixed amount, the measure effectively wiped out the savings and extra cash made by North Koreans from entrepreneurial activities, thereby making them once again dependent on state handouts. Kim believed that political control is more important than economic growth. Kim was once asked about a proposal to bring Club Med to North Korea. The vacation business, famous for building resorts in out-of-the-way exotic and secluded places, could find many such places in the mountains and beaches in the North. The business could be a source of employment and revenues for a starving economy. Kim rejected the proposal because of the risks of exposing people to outsiders, and the fear of losing control. Bureaucrats were only interested in repairing the North's economy as it was, rather than developing it through interaction with the outside world. In a conversation with the association of North Korean residents in Japan (*Chosen Soren*), Kim added, "We don't want hordes of tourists to come here and spread AIDS."[47]

Kim's only positive accomplishment (he had many negative ones), aside from building nuclear weapons, was a short-lived makeover in his public image. This coincided with the June 2000 summit with South Korean president Kim Dae-jung (1998–2003) and his hosting of Secretary of State Madeleine Albright in October 2000. The North Korean leader demonstrated confidence, knowledge of world affairs, and wit in these meetings, which was displayed to the world. Whether or not this was a deliberate attempt to shed the "recluse" image he had garnered over the years, Kim told his South Korean counterpart that he had traveled the world secretly and that he was far from the strange, alien-like creature portrayed in Western media. Images of Kim smiling and laughing during the summit captivated a South Korean audience and started to change the way he was viewed. Once a rogue and sinister character, he was now perceived by average South Koreans as everything from "normal" to "statesman-like" to even "cuddly." *Time* magazine was so taken by this new Kim that they named him "Asian of the Year" in 2000. Kim revealed to Albright that he surfed the Web and had an e-mail address. She described him as "an intelligent man who knew what he wanted. He was isolated, not uninformed . . . Despite his country's wretched condition, he didn't seem a desperate or even a worried man. He seemed confident."[48] Charles Kartman, who accompanied Secretary Albright on the trip and participated in talks with Kim, characterized him as:

> *A reasonable man, who was fully engaged with us for that very extensive period that Secretary Albright was with him . . . I never saw his attention wander. I never saw him lose the thread. I always found him to be completely on the point and with a lot of energy, and able to make decisions . . . our observation . . . was that this is a man you could do business with. He always seemed to be somebody who had a sense of humor, was personally attentive to the people that he was hosting . . . I hate to use the word, lest I be criticized later, but . . . I would say he was gracious.*[49]

The poor state of the country was never the threat to Kim Jong-il's longevity as leader; instead, it was his health. Kim reportedly suffered from a series of ailments. A number of these were connected with his heavy-drinking habits. Defectors who were Kim's former bodyguards reported that in the 1970s Kim was an alcoholic and chain-smoker, and had heart and liver problems. He was occasionally pictured in the press wearing rather trendy dark sunglasses, but this was less a fashion statement than cataract problems. In the 1990s, rumors surfaced that he had diabetes and kidney problems. True or not, his health condition was bad enough that Kim told former PRC president Jiang Zemin in 2000 that he had quit smoking and drinking hard alcohol. Questions about his health were confirmed in August 2008, when he suffered a stroke. The leader disappeared from the public eye for several months. He did not appear in September 2008 at the sixtieth-anniversary celebrations of the founding of the DPRK. He also missed the celebration of the founding of the Korean Workers' Party the following month. Rumors surfaced that Kim suffered a relapse in November 2008. (I once gave a speech to the annual convention of Korean-American spine and neurosurgeons in Washington, D.C. After the speech, one of the older neurosurgeons came up to me and told me that he was once asked by European colleagues to review an MRI scan of a brain that had suffered a cerebral hemorrhage. He was not told the identity of the patient, but only that the patient requested a second opinion from a Korean neurosurgeon. To this day, the doctor is convinced it was a scan of Kim's stroke-stricken brain.) As speculation mounted that Kim was seriously ill, DPRK authorities released pictures showing Kim performing his and his father's trademark "on-the-spot guidance," but experts believed the pictures were Photoshopped. When Kim finally appeared at a televised party meeting, the severity of his health problems was clear. He had lost a great deal of weight and was walking with a limp. Those who traveled with former president Bill Clinton to meet with Kim Jong-il in 2009, on a mission to retrieve two American journalists who had been detained in North Korea, noted that Kim seemed lively and fully composed, but at the same time he walked with a limp and showed weakness and trembling on the left side—all telltale signs of a stroke victim. Kim's subsequent public appearances in October 2010 made clear that at the age of sixty-eight, the leader was on the decline. In 2011, Chinese authorities ironically kept telling outsiders that Kim Jong-il's health had improved so much that he had reportedly started drinking and smoking again. Pictures of a heavier-set Kim appeared in 2011 to validate the Chinese argument. But clearly these arguments were wrong and offered testament to how little even the Chinese knew about the situation inside Pyongyang.

Some may wonder why Kim Jong-il was never blamed for his terrible rule of the country. Leadership security in a paranoid dictatorship like North Korea is generally kept within the family. Very few have access to the leader, and an elaborate system of monitoring—not unlike those described in George Orwell's *1984*—ensures that there is no mutiny within the ranks. There were two rumored assassination attempts on the life of the Dear Leader by bodyguards (about the only people who could get close enough to Kim). A widely reported incident occurred in April 2004, when two parked trains filled with ammonium nitrate and fuel exploded at Ryongch'ŏn rail station, near the Chinese border, killing 170 and wounding hundreds. Kim Jong-il's train passed through the same station nine hours earlier en route from China, which led many to believe this was an assassination attempt. Korean Central News Agency, which, as a security precaution, never reports on Kim's movements, announced that Kim had returned safely to Pyongyang, presumably to dispel immediately any rumors that he had been killed.

Dynastic leadership succession in North Korea was never in doubt. Kim's health problems from 2008 to 2011 made clear the need to prepare for the next power transition. Handing power over to a son, in North Korean minds, was the normal order of things. Madeleine Albright once asked Kim Jong-il over dinner what country's model he admired. Unsurprisingly, Kim chose Thailand, because of its strong tradition of royalty and its fierce independence. (Thailand is the only small Asian country that was never colonized.) Indeed, shortly after Kim's sixtieth birthday in 2002, *Rodong Sinmun* published a long editorial about how the final victory of the Revolution needed to be multigenerational—if it could not be accomplished by the Father, then it would be accomplished by the Son, and if not by the Son, then by the next generation. "The next generation" referred to one of the three Grandsons.

THE GRANDSONS

In April 2001, Japanese intelligence officials were tipped off that a "person of interest" would be entering their country from Singapore. A portly Asian man in his thirties arrived the next day at Narita Airport. He was sporting an expensive gold Rolex and was carrying a wad of U.S. currency. He was accompanied by two women, decked out in designer clothing and carrying Louis Vuitton handbags, and a young boy. Immigration officials knew something was strange, because the name in the man's passport was "Pan Xiong" but the passport was from the Dominican Republic. (Even in today's era of globalization, how many Chinese-Dominicans do you know?) They detained the party and took the man in for questioning. When asked the purpose of his visit, the man responded that he was taking his family to Disneyland. After about one hour of silence in response to a litany of questions by immigration officers, the man finally admitted to paying $2,000 for the fake passports. But the next utterance stunned the officers in the room. The detained man said, "I am Kim Jong-il's son." The eldest grandson of Great Leader Kim Il-sung then said he was hungry and asked if the officials could get him a hamburger.

In Confucian tradition, the eldest son usually inherits the family business. For quite some time, it was believed that Kim Chŏng-nam, the man who was eventually denied his visit to Tokyo Disneyland and deported from Narita International Airport, was groomed to be the eventual successor. The oldest of three sons by two women, he was the only child to be born out of Kim Jong-il's relationship with Sŏng Hye-rim, the actress with whom Kim became smitten even though they were never officially married. Kim Jong-il showered the eldest son with gifts when he was a child, even as the illegitimate son of an extramarital affair. In the 1990s, Kim Chŏng-nam held posts in the military and in the party. But the Disneyland incident, among other problems, apparently put him out of contention, and since then, the eldest Grandson, now about forty years old, has spent more time living outside of North Korea. He has his father's habits, enjoying gambling, fast cars, and alcohol, and for his efforts, he receives a reported $500,000 allowance that pays for his villa in Macau overlooking the South China Sea. Unlike his dad, he does not prefer Mao suits, instead sporting gold jewelry, stylish blue jeans, and designer shoes. He lives a bizarrely normal life, taking taxis to Korean restaurants or gambling in the Altira Hotel. Japanese reporters follow him like paparazzi and occasionally he will talk to them and to others who seek him out. In June

2010, when there was speculation about Kim Jong-il's heart problems, he told Korean reporters that his father was in good health. When asked in 2009 whether the eldest Grandson of Great Leader Kim Il-sung was the heir to the throne or whether he was in hiding in Macau because of the Disneyland thing, he responded, "If I were the successor, would you see me in Macau wearing these casual clothes and taking a holiday? I am a North Korea citizen who has the right to live in Macau and China. To call me a fugitive from North Korea is completely incorrect." In January 2012, Chŏng-nam became an outspoken critic of the power transfer from his dead father to his younger half-brother. Quoted in a book by a Japanese journalist, Chŏng-nam expressed skepticism that the regime could avoid collapse. Such signs of open discord were previously unheard of in the Kim clan.

That leaves the other two Grandsons of Kim Il-sung: Kim Chŏng-ch'ŏl (b. 1981) and Kim Jong-un (b. 1985 or 1987). It became clear in the fall of 2010 that the youngest of the boys, Kim Jong-un, is the heir apparent. Only twenty-seven or twenty-eight years old (we do not know his age for certain), the young man was given the rank of a four-star general in September 2010 though he has never served in the military. He was also made the number two in the Central Military Committee of the Party. These two appointments were nearly identical to those of Kim Jong-il some twenty-five years earlier, and effectively signaled that the youngest Grandson of Kim Il-sung would be prepared as the next leader of the country. In February 2011, just days before his father's seventieth birthday, he was given a senior position on the National Defense Commission, which is the top decision-making organ under Kim Jong-il's military-first doctrine. Kim Jong-il's sudden death in December 2011 forced an accelerated dynastic succession process that heaped additional titles on the junior Kim aimed at cementing his leadership position. Kim Jong-un was immediately anointed with the title of "Great Successor." The official news agency later reported in December that he was made "Supreme Commander" of the Korean People's Army. On December 31, Kim was referred to by a National Defense Commission statement as the "Great Leader" and new postage stamps were issued of him with his late father. The rush to build his leadership credentials have continued into 2012, including pictures of him meeting with military officials in the field (squeezing his rather rotund body into a tank cockpit) and new propaganda documentaries building the junior Kim's very own cult of personality.

We know remarkably little about the Grandson of Kim Il-sung. If his father, Kim Jong-il, was enigmatic, the Grandson, or the "Great Successor," is a black box. His coming-out party was an extraordinary session of the Korean Workers' Party, the first since 1966, in September 2010, in which the world caught its first glimpse of the five feet, nine inch, two-hundred-plus-pound young man (175 cm, 90 kg) standing next to his aging father. Internet chat rooms in South Korea immediately started to make fun of the Young General, ridiculing his weight (in a country of starving people) and calling him the "Great Eater." In North Korea, however, citizens knew even less about him, presumably because the government wants to control and mete out every piece of information and every image. A British friend of mine, who had taken his family to Pyongyang for a vacation (the family prides itself on choosing unusual vacation destinations) at the time of the party celebrations, struck up conversations with people leaving Kim Il-sung Square.

He asked them what they thought of the young leader, and they responded with superlatives about his intelligence and greatness, but they then asked my friend if he had seen pictures of Kim Jong-un. It was as if the next leader had been hidden from their view, like a god, up until his rushed unveiling after Kim Jong-il's death. Then the government could not do enough to get as many images of the young leader out to the public as possible to avoid the perception of any gap in the dynastic succession. Kim Jong-un's ubiquitous round face appeared in photos, films, posters, and paintings. For the outside world, the initial images were of a young man blubbering at his father's funeral, and then standing reluctantly before a massive audience in Kim Il-sung Square, speechless but being presented to the nation as the Great Successor. These pictures were later replaced by the Grandson's own trademark "on-the-site" inspections throughout the country, laughing with military soldiers and farmers just as his grandfather did. For the world, and for the North Korean people, Kim Jong-un's appearance was clearly calculated to look like the spitting image of his grandfather some sixty years prior, when the Soviets first unveiled Kim Il-sung to the North

Korean people. Some South Korean news reports claim that the new North Korean leader underwent cosmetic surgery to bring Kim Il-sung to life in the young man.

I believe that part of the reason for this has to do with the creation of a new ideology for Kim Jong-un that is like his grandfather's. But it is also because the North Korean people still hold general affection for Kim Il-sung while they appear to be less enamored with Kim Jong-il, despite the mandatory wailing and grieving at the latter's state funeral.

Promoted along with Kim Jong-un were his aunt Kim Kyŏng-hŭi and her husband Chang Sŏng-t'aek. Kim's sister was made a four-star general in the People's Army, and she holds a key position in the party's Politburo. Chang Sŏng-t'aek was promoted to number two in the National Defense Commission in June 2010 and heads the Ministry of Public Security and the State Security Department, two powerful agencies. Ri Yŏng-ho, a younger general, in his sixties, was also promoted to a four-star general and placed on the Standing Committee and the Central Military Committee of the Party. This series of moves made clear the desire to keep leadership succession within the family, carefully balanced among the key agencies. General Ri is the exception to this family rule, but he remains graced by his close relationship to Kim Jong-il and Chang Sŏng-t'aek. These four individuals make up the collective core of the leadership to follow Kim Jong-il. Their positions represent a balance between the party and the military, which means an elevation of the Korean Workers' Party's status relative to the "military-first" years of Kim Jong-il. But there is no doubt as to who will lead in the end. The Grandson is the next great leader and the entire apparatus is designed to ease him into the position, which many believe to have been set up to compensate for a rushed leadership transition, given Kim Jong-il's declining health.

WHO IS THIS not-yet-thirty-year-old "Great Successor"? The most interesting fact we know about him is that he spent part of his life being educated outside the cloistered North. He spent two years, from about 1998 to 2000, attending the Schule Liebefeld Steinhölzli, a German-language state school near Bern, Switzerland.[50] I met a classmate of his who attended the school while her father, a South Korean, was working in the country. Sŏng-mi (pseudonym)[51] recalled that there were not many Koreans or Asians in the city or at the school, so "everyone kind of knew each other, or knew when a new kid arrived." The school was fairly small, with class sizes of about thirteen to fifteen students. One day, dinner conversation at Sŏng-mi's table turned to news of the arrival of a new family from Korea. Her mom was surprised that she had not heard in advance about this, given the normally close-knit community of South Korean expatriate families, but then later heard from a Japanese parent at the school that the family was from North Korea. Sŏng-mi's parents, naturally curious about the new family, looked to catch a glimpse of them at the daily pickup of children at the end of the school day. But the young boy's folks never showed up. Instead, a black van arrived daily and whisked the boy off. Finally, parents' day arrived, and Sŏng-mi's family approached the boy at the reception and asked in Korean, "Are your parents here? We would like to meet them." The boy responded curtly, *"Uri ŏmma appa yŏgi ŏpsŏ"* ("My parents are not here")—with a heavy North Korean accent. The response surprised Sŏng-mi's parents, because the boy used non-honorific Korean, which is an unusual sign of disrespect to elders in Korean society. This made Sŏng-mi angry and she thought ill of the boy.

Sŏng-mi remembers Kim Jong-un as a soft-spoken child. He went by an alias name, Pak Ŭn, and said his family worked at the North Korean embassy in Switzerland. Pak Ŭn always had another Korean boy as a companion at the school. The two were never apart. He participated in many of the activities at school, including sports (basketball) and drama. Sŏng-mi's parents were curious as to whether Pak Ŭn's folks would show up for the school play, but instead a woman in a black mink coat arrived, toting a top-of-the-line video camera. She taped the whole performance, presumably to send back to Pyongyang for viewing. Sŏng-mi lost interest in figuring out Pak Ŭn's mysterious family. One day, she was on the school playground swings waiting for her parents to pick her up. Staring at her dangling feet above the ground, as kids tend to do on swings, she was startled when Pak Ŭn appeared behind her and said in Korean, without emotion, "Can I give you a push on the swing?" She turned away and said, "No." He responded, "It's okay, I can give you a push." She responded, *"Hajima!"* ("Don't do it!"). The Grandson of

Kim Il-sung then gave her a gentle push anyway. She turned and yelled at him, *"Hajimalago!"* ("I told you not to do it!"), and screamed at him to go away. The young boy then quietly moved away with his head down, defiant in anger.

In 2009, a journalist and I once discussed the vacuum of information available on the Grandson, and concluded that the only way to learn more about Pak Ŭn was to track down former classmates and teachers at the Schule.[52] Through interviews, he found that the Grandson arrived in Switzerland in August 1998 and lived in a flat on an unassuming suburban street conveniently located near a pizza parlor, bank, and market. A mother of one of Pak Ŭn's schoolmates said that Pak told her son (now a chef in Austria) that his father was the leader of North Korea. As Sŏng-mi's parents had discovered, no one could ever confirm this, because the parents never showed up at school events, substituted for by an array of embassy officials.

According to his friends, Pak Ŭn was not unlike your average teen-ager. He loved video games and action movies, and was a big NBA fan. He played pickup games regularly, and, by all accounts, was pretty good and very competitive. His idols, like his father's, were Michael Jordan and the Chicago Bulls, and his room was filled with posters of Jordan, Toni Kukoč, and Kobe Bryant of the Los Angeles Lakers. He apparently has attended some NBA exhibition games in Europe.

Pak Ŭn's German was not very good, so he took language courses to get up to speed. His German was decent by the time he left, and his schoolmates say that he also spoke some English. His curriculum was certainly different from what one might get in North Korea. He took classes on Swiss history from 1291; Swiss government and democracy; and a class on parties and elections, which included study of the U.S. 2000 presidential election campaign. He left as suddenly as he arrived: the schoolmates remembered that their basketball buddy disappeared in the middle of the school year without any notice. Teachers and administrators at the school were given no notice and have not heard from him since. As one classmate said, "He never came to school again. He totally disappeared . . . [w]e were just playing basketball—now he is going to be a dictator . . . I hope he is a good leader, but dictators are usually not that good."[53]

The Grandson of Kim Il-sung returned to Pyongyang, where he enrolled in the military academy, graduating in 2006. The hagiography being created for him initially described him as the Young General with "twenty-first-century high-tech skills." After Kim Jong-il's death, his moniker became the Great Successor. It was reported in early 2011 that all North Korean citizens were required to watch a program about Kim Jong-un's great leadership. He is described as a "genius" able to speak German, French, Italian, and English, and actively learning Chinese, Japanese, and Russian. The broadcast also explained that the Great Successor understands the need for the country to become a "self-sufficient nuclear power" after he learned of the aggression of American imperialism. Not to be outdone by the godlike acts of his father and grandfather, he was also reported to be encouraging farmers to grow more food and, on one of his on-the-spot inspections, the Great Successor miraculously created a new synthetic fertilizer that could grow fifteen thousand tons of wheat on a nine-thousand-square-meter (96,875-sq-ft) plot of land.[54] He has been associated with projects developing the infrastructure of the country, including a hundred-thousand-unit housing project. His birthday in 2010 was celebrated in North Korea like a national holiday, where official propaganda described the "morning star of Venus shining brightly on Mount Paektu," the mythical birthplace of the Korean race.

The Great Successor has spent much of his time building credentials with two key constituencies: the DPRK military and China. Just as his father needed military credibility to fulfill his role as a leader of the Revolution, the Grandson, according to press reports, built his around belligerent acts including the March 2010 sinking of the South Korean naval vessel *Cheonan,* killing forty-six sailors. South Korean intelligence leaked to newspapers that Kim and his son gave medals to the submarine unit responsible for the torpedo attack. In October 2010, South Korean press also attributed the unprovoked North Korean artillery shelling of a South Korean island Yeonpyeong to the building of Kim Jong-un's credentials. It was reported that the Grandson visited the artillery units that shelled the island, and that within North Korea propaganda spread that the Great Successor is an artillery expert and is well-versed in battle tactics of conventional military defense. The Great Successor also visited training exercises at the missile site where the North launched its larg-est barrage of ballistic missile tests in July 2006 in protest against the Bush administration's policies. On his birthday in January 2012, state-run media broadcast a new documentary in a frenzied effort to further build the junior Kim's military credentials. The program claimed that Kim Jong-un helped his father to coordinate the April 2009 ballistic mis-sile test (which slapped away the Obama administration's initial efforts at engagement). In the missile-test control room with Kim Jong-il, the Great Successor was reported to have proclaimed, "I had determined to enter a war if the enemies dared to intercept [our missile]." The broad-cast contained images of Kim Jong-un riding a white horse (something his father was depicted doing in propaganda paintings), driving a tank, playing pilot in the cockpit of an airplane, and participating in a firing exercise, "making the New Year's first sound of gunfire." Kim Jong-un has spent an inordinate amount of time kowtowing to Chinese officials as well, meeting with virtually every high- and low-level delegation that came to North Korea. These efforts have been reciprocated by the Chi-nese. In the immediate aftermath of Kim Jong-il's death, at a dinner in Georgetown, a senior ROK foreign ministry official related to me that the Chinese called in the ambassadors of several countries in Beijing, includ-ing the ROK and Japan. The Chinese message to these envoys was that the leadership transition to the junior Kim was under way, that all par-ties should exercise restraint, and that no one should disrespect the au-tonomy of the DPRK. This pissed off the ROK official to no end because China was essentially behaving as if the North were a new province of its own rather than as sovereign Korean territory.

AN ENLIGHTENED LEADER?

The unanswered question still remains as to whether the Grandson's education in Switzerland influenced his thinking about his own coun-try. Life in Liebefeld and Bern could not have been more antithetical to that in North Korea: an open and direct democracy in which citizens exercise national referendum to contest the government. A presidency that rotates every year. Constitutionally and in practice, the state guar-antees freedom of expression, religion, assembly, and association. It has a firmly entrenched rule of law, a wholly independent judiciary, and legally protects the rights of religious, ethnic, and linguistic minorities. It is a system in which, with enough signatures, even the voters can initiate legislation. At $56,370 per capita GDP, Switzerland boasts the world's third-highest level of individual wealth,[55] has the eighth-freest press in the world, and in 2009 was ranked by Transparency International as the fifth-least corrupt country on earth.[56] Does this experience make a difference in the mentality of Kim Il-sung's Grandson? The education director in Liebefeld believes so. "There is a big difference between attending a school in a free country and a school where everyone has to salute," said the director. "[Education] is a question of culture." He believes the next leader of North Korea "will take something away that will have an effect on his life." Do we have an enlightened leader?

Probably not. His youth is not the issue. After the Korean War, Stalin picked Kim Il-sung, the first leader of North Korea, at the tender age of thirty-three. Kim Jong-il began climbing the party ladder when he was thirty years old, and was anointed as the successor to his father at the age of thirty-eight. For the Kim family dynasty, picking them young is the natural requisite for forty to fifty years of continuous rule.

No, the real problem is the system itself. Even if the young Kim is enlightened, there are three obstacles. True reform in a post–Kim Jong-il era would require the courage to loosen the very political instruments of control that allow the regime its iron grip on the people. The dilemma the young Kim faces is something I wrote about long ago in *Foreign Affairs*, referring to Kim Jong-il—that he needs to reform to survive, but the process of opening up will undeniably lead to the end of his political control. For North Korea, this was perhaps the most important lesson of the end of the Cold War.[57]

Even if Kim Jong-un were an enlightened leader who has the courage to attempt such reform, he would be dealing with a generation of institutions and people that are the most isolated in North Korean history. The generals, party officials, and bureaucrats of the Cold War era were far more worldly than those of the post–Cold War era. Kim Il-sung's generation was able to travel freely to Eastern bloc countries. Kim used to spend time with Erich Honecker in East Germany and Nicolae Ceausescu in Romania. By contrast, Kim Jong-il's generation saw Ceausescu get executed in the streets, the Chinese Communist Party nearly lose power to student demonstrations in 1989 in Tiananmen Square, and dictators in the Middle East falling to the Arab Spring. The generation of leadership the young Grandson will inherit sees nothing comforting about the outside world. They are afraid of their own shadow. Nowhere was this more apparent than in the way the regime responded to the demonstrations in Egypt in 2011. North Korean authorities banned all news of the public revolt that toppled the Mubarak government. To the extent that it was reported, the North described the protests as being generated by anti-American demonstrators. The regime also banned all forms of public and private gatherings, including in restaurants and open-air markets. This paranoia clearly stemmed from the uncomfortable parallels to their own situation that they might have seen. Kim Jong-il and Hosni Mubarak both ran dictatorships. The two were friends, which was one of the reasons why Orascom, an Egyptian telecom firm, got the exclusive contract for North Korea's cell phone market. And just as Kim had plans to hand power over to his son, Mubarak planned to do so with his son, Gamal, albeit unsuccessfully.

Finally, despotic regimes like North Korea cannot survive without ideology to justify their iron grip. And as I discussed earlier in the book, the ideology that accompanies the Great Successor's rise appears to look backward rather than forward. "*Neojuche* revivalism" constitutes a return to a conservative and hard-line *juche* (self-reliance) ideology of the 1950s and 1960s—harkening back to a day when the North was doing well relative to the now richer and democratic South. *Neojuche* revivalism is laced with *sŏn'gun* (military-first) ideology that features the North's emergence as a nuclear weapons state (Kim Jong-il's one accomplishment during his rule). The revolution in North Korea died long ago but the Great Successor will be forced to cling to the core but outdated ideological principles that worked during the Cold War. It is no coincidence that Kim Jong-il frequented visits in his last two years of life to factory towns that used to be the center of North Korea's mass worker mobilization (Ch'ŏllima) movements of the 1950s. It is no coincidence that NKEconWatch's Web site, which has the best Google Earth imagery of the North, has reported the rebuilding of chemical and vinylon factories that were the heart of Cold War–era Pyongyang's now-decrepit economy.

The Great Successor has also been calling for an agricultural revolution similar to that pursued in both the South and the North in the 1960s and 1970s, stressing greater mass labor mobilization to meet production targets. There are reports of sweeping changes in economic laws designed to strengthen the government's central control. Legal statutes that had previously allowed for some innovativeness and entrepreneurship at the local levels have been completely erased and replaced with provisions calling for central government control over all decisions. All housing and food supplies are to be controlled by the state. All residents in Pyongyang are to carry, at all times, their government-issued residency cards. As one expert, Kim Yong-hyŏn of Dongguk University in South Korea, described, the regime is seeking tighter internal control rather than economic reform.[58] Public executions in North Korea more than tripled in the past year. The army reportedly has shoot-to-kill orders for unauthorized attempts to cross the Yalu or Tumen Rivers into China. Public bulletin boards carry government warnings banning the use of Chinese-made cell phones or foreign currency under the threat of death. The number of inmates in North Korean gulags has increased disproportionately.

As a general rule, brittle dictatorships do not implement reform of their systems during periods of leadership transition except if the dictator is a strong, dynamic, and charismatic individual: Deng Xiaoping in China. Gorbachev in the Soviet Union. The not-yet-thirty-year-old boy-leader, the Great Successor, does not yet meet this bar. He and his coterie of supporters will have their hands full transacting a rushed dynastic succession, let alone entertaining grand thoughts about fundamental transformation. Some believe that this leadership succession has been carefully planned out in excruciating detail after Kim Jong-il suffered a stroke in 2008. They point to the well-executed state funeral, and the rush of propaganda thereafter, building the new personality cult of the Great Successor. Undeniably some planning must have taken place, but Kim Jong-il had twenty years or more to prepare for his inheritance of the family business. Kim Jong-un had barely twenty months. The state funeral went off without a hitch because the North already had a playbook for this event when Kim Il-sung died in 1994 (even dusting off the same 1976 Lincoln Continental hearses). In North Korea, it is not possible for anyone, even members of the Kim family, to say "Hey guys, let's prepare a plan for when Kim Jong-il dies." This is a country where an undusted portrait of the leader can get you thrown into a gulag. Based on past precedent, it is safe to say that the powers-that-be in Pyongyang thought they would have at least five to ten years to ease the Grandson into position. Now they are making up the playbook as they go. When Kim Jong-il took over, it was literally years before he came out into the open as the leader. This was largely because he was already running the country on a daily basis for at least fifteen years prior. The frenzied propaganda campaign that put Kim Jong-un in front immediately after his father's passing reflects less certainty and more insecurity about a rushed transition process, and the need to show cosmetically that all is working inside Pyongyang. Yet even if a path for this third North Korean dynastic succession is laid out in the coming months and years, the road leads to a dead end because of the ideology. This revivalist ideology leaves little room for reform and opening, because it blames the past decade of poor performance on "ideological pollution" stemming from experiments with reform. The Grandson of Kim Il-sung faces a clear dilemma: the state he inherits is not sustainable under this new *neojuche* revivalist ideology; yet it is the only ideology that can legitimate the new leadership.

THE INFORMATION IN these pages only scratches the surface of the enigmatic Kim family's rule of North Korea. We know less about the inner workings of this family than we do about any other sought-after intelligence target, including the late Osama Bin Laden. While it is undeniable that the Father, Kim Il-sung, governed North Korea in dictatorial fashion, he also ruled during a period of North Korean greatness, at least in North Korean eyes, when the regime was strong and the steadfast Communist nation was buttressed by Soviet and Chinese patronage. The Son, Kim Jong-il, was responsible for creating the cult of personality of his father and of himself. He then oversaw two decades of North Korean decline, including famine and deprivation the likes of which the citizens of the country have never seen since the end of the Korean War. The Son's militarization of the political leadership and creation of nuclear weapons remains his only contribution to the state's history. The Grandson, Kim Jong-un, inherits a country in disrepair, and despite his cosmopolitan upbringing (relative to other North Koreans) is constrained by a state ideology that looks backward to his grandfather's days rather than forward. And it builds on the nuclear legacy of his father. Reform and opening in this *neojuche* ideology is equated with spiritual pollution. This new synthetic of an ideology ensures that the Grandson of the Great Leader Kim Il-sung shall be the true emperor with no clothes.

CHAPTER FOUR

FIVE BAD DECISIONS

GOATS.

This was once thought to be an antidote for North Korea's economic ills. The terrain in the northern portion of the peninsula is mountainous and not suitable for farming. There are no green plots of grass for grazing cows, and therefore no source of dairy products or meat. So, in 1996, the North Koreans started a campaign to breed goats. These mountain animals are a good source of milk and meat; moreover, they feed on the shrubs tucked away high in the rocky terrain. The goat-breeding campaign led to a doubling of the goat population almost overnight, and tripled it within two years. This solved a short-term problem, but it had long-term consequences that were more destructive. The goats completely denuded the areas they inhabited, chewing up every single shrub in sight. This then had the effect of removing the last line of the land's defense against the annual massive rains. The result? Annual monsoons led to deluges of biblical proportions, which wiped out the little remaining arable land and flooded the coal mines that were a source of energy. This only worsened the chronic food and energy shortages. The goat story is a microcosm of North Korea's economic trap. The undertaking of measures as a short-term expedient exacerbates a long-term problem, for which there is no long-term solution.

FIVE BAD DECISIONS

The North Korean economy is a puzzle. How does a country that in 1945 emerged as one of the most industrialized societies in Asia decline to the point of famine and near-collapse over five decades? The end of World

War II saw the emergence of a state that benefited greatly from Japanese colonial economic development. As a centrally planned socialist economy in the early Cold War years, the North did quite well, certainly better than the South. The Korean War destroyed all of these advantages. The United States did more bombing runs in the North and laid more ammunition on the country than it did in all of World War II. But China and the Soviet Union worked quickly to rebuild the country, and the North experienced an economic boom in the 1970s when per capita income outpaced the South and industrial production was growing at a staggering 15.9 percent. From the 1980s, however, things started to slow down. Production targets could not be met. Equipment and machinery broke down. By the 1990s, the economy was in free fall, registering negative growth rates for the first time in its history. The decade ended with a terrible food shortage. Since then, the economy has been on life support with help from the Chinese, but with no real chance of recovery. Today, the per capita GDP of the country is just under $1,000, while that in the South is nearly twenty-two times higher.[1]

This nightmarish odyssey is all the more amazing given that North Korea's 47,000 square miles (120,538 sq km) of territory is rich in resources. Lying beneath their feet are estimated to be over 100 billion metric tons of limestone, 14.7 billion tons of coal deposits, 6.5 billion tons of magnesite, 3 billion tons of iron ore, 12 million tons of zinc, 1.2 million tons of nickel, and substantial deposits of silver and gold. The U.S. Geological Survey assesses North Korea's reserve of coal, iron ore, and limestone as comparatively large, given the size of the country and potentially having impact on global markets.[2] It has significant untapped reserves of magnesite and is believed to be a source of rare earth materials. A Goldman Sachs report estimated the value of North Korea's mineral deposits at 140 times the country's GDP.[3] Some European drilling companies believe there may be oil deposits in the seas west of the country. How did economic failure happen? And why is it impossible for the regime as it is currently structured to implement true economic reform? I believe Pyongyang made five bad historic decisions that doomed its economy. North Korea's economic decline in many ways approximates the perfect storm. Poor choices by the leadership both exacerbated the economy's vulnerabilities and exhausted its assets. It did not seek to reform, instead relying on handouts from China and the Soviet Union to survive, and when this assistance dried up, the economy collapsed. Contributing to the free fall of the economy were major natural disasters that wiped out indigenous sources of food.

BAD CHOICES

The first of the five bad decisions came in the aftermath of the Korean War, when Kim Il-sung focused exclusively on heavy industrial development. Kim had at his disposal very willing patrons in Moscow and Beijing to help rebuild the country. During the early Cold War years, the Soviet Union and the People's Republic of China were virtually the North's only sources of aid and trade. According to declassified CIA documents, in September of 1953 the USSR granted North Korea $250 million in aid, half to be used for the military, a quarter for light industry, and the final quarter for heavy industry. In December of the same year, the Soviets remitted North Korea's war debt and eased the terms of repayment for pre–Korean War loans.[4] The Chinese also chipped in, supplying an estimated 45 percent of North Korea's total trade in the 1950s with an annual value of about $100 million.[5] And from the onset of the Korean War to the end of the decade, China is estimated to have granted the North over $500 million in aid and loan credits.[6] All in all, during the 1950s, the North received in excess of $1.65 billion in aid from its Soviet and Chinese benefactors.[7] Kim took advantage of this support and rebuilt the economy with a particular emphasis on heavy industry. The lack of attention to agriculture and light industry would not have been a problem if the regime engaged in more trade. What other countries, however, might have seen as trade-based interdependence, North Korea saw as trade-based vulnerability. In compliance with the *juche* ideology, the regime emphasized self-sufficiency in food, agriculture, and light manufacturing. What emerged therefore from the Korean War was a quintessential mercantilist strategy aimed at promoting the growth of state power through heavy industrialization. On August 5, 1953, only two weeks after the armistice signing, Kim Il-sung gave a speech titled "Everything for the Postwar Rehabilitation and Development for the People," the focus of which was on reconstruction and expansion of heavy industries. Iron and steel plants, heavy machinery, mining, chemical fertilizers, and oil refineries were all projects that were seen to constitute the basis of national power that would eventually overthrow the South. In the Three-Year Economic Plan of 1954–1956, 81 percent of resources went into heavy industry; by contrast, only 19 percent went into light industry. This produced a terribly distorted economy that focused entirely on producers and almost totally ignored consumers. Despite all of the help from the Soviets and from the Chinese, Moscow was uncomfortable with the lopsided nature of development. They saw clearly that the DPRK plan defied rational economics. For a centrally planned economy with heavy industrialization, the rural workforce needed to be mobilized into an industrial workforce. Yet this would then deplete the labor force necessary to sustain agricultural self-sufficiency. Even without the strain of heavy industry, the North Korean economy was not suited to be self-sufficient in agriculture under the best of circumstances. With only 20 percent arable land, North Korea was a rugged mountainous terrain with a cold northern climate that allowed for only short crop seasons. A normal country would have traded aggressively in order to meet its food needs, but the regime undertook other far-fetched ideas to maintain the semblance of self-sufficiency. In the 1980s, for example, as food stocks were depleting, the government tried land reclamation projects on the west coast of the peninsula in order to create more arable land, but this failed. From that point forward, the regime relied increasingly on patron aid from China to meet its food shortfalls.

THE CH'ŎLLIMA MOVEMENT

The second bad decision was to rationalize economics in terms of ideology rather than letting economics trump ideology. Rational economics for North Korea was something called the Ch'ŏllima movement. An economic manifestation of *juche* ideology, Ch'ŏllima espoused the idea that any shortfalls could be made up for by the "revolutionary zeal" of the people, which would result in superhuman productivity gains that could outpace that of any other economy. Started in the mid-1950s, Ch'ŏllima was, in part, a response to decreased Soviet support after the first Three-

Year Plan, which ended in 1956 and which Moscow thought overemphasized heavy industry and stressed the economy unnecessarily.

The Ch'ŏllima ideology drove massive inefficiencies in the economy because it always substituted longer work hours for technological innovation. In the 1960s, for example, North Korea decided to build electricity plants based on thermal power and coal. This seemed like a smart move given the country's large coal deposits. With help from the Soviets, they proceeded to build the Pyongyang Thermal Power Plant and the Pukch'ang Thermal Plant. The size and scale of these plants, however, presented the North with an unexpected problem—they could not excavate enough coal to feed the plants. Using antiquated blasting technology, the North could excavate only about five or six tons of coal per day. In the West, by comparison, continuous coal-mining technologies allowed one machine operated by two workers to produce exponentially more than this output in a day. The North's answer was simply to force the workers through the Ch'ŏllima mentality to work longer hours to increase productivity. Ideology also trumped economics when it came to considering alternative sources of power. By the 1970s, the North had set out targets for total energy production, which it hoped to meet with hydropower plants. In fact, they built one sprawling plant that had a total new projected capacity of 4.4 million kilowatts, but they were only able to produce 250,000 kilowatts. Naturally, this raised the question of whether the DPRK should consider oil-burning power plants, but Pyongyang rejected this idea out of hand for reasons of *juche*. Kim Il-sung affirmed the righteousness of this decision:

> *Certain scientists have in former days suggested that oil-burning stations should be built, saying that oil-power stations can be built in less time than hydroelectric plants. That is true. However, if we build oil-burning stations, we will have to import oil from other countries, for it is not available in our country. This is contrary to our party's policy of building an independent economy. Therefore, I did not accept the scientists' suggestion and decided to build power stations that rely on the resources of our own country.*[8]

Formally introduced at a session of the Supreme People's Assembly in June 1958, Ch'ŏllima broke the backs of the workers. It was a labor exploitation policy that only added further irrationality to economic policy by putting party hacks in positions of decision-making. Committees of ideologues were sent as supervisors over plant managers to enforce loyalty. Making laborers work harder under tough conditions is challenging enough with the offer of material incentives. But the only "incentives" under Ch'ŏllima were attainment of spiritual purity and the imperative to manifest ideological zeal. The dangers of seeming "impure" by not meeting production targets were obvious.

The next two decades saw the North increasingly diverting resources to the military at the expense of the regular economy. The Seven-Year Plan of 1961–1967 sought to contract heavy industry in its first three years, which one might think foretold efforts to rebalance the economy. As initially announced, the 1961–1967 Seven-Year Plan aimed at bettering living conditions, including promises of bigger, healthier diets from an improved agricultural sector and the availability of more consumer goods as the light industrial sector was strengthened. On the contrary, however, the resources were redirected to a massive military buildup, not to light industry and agriculture. As the Cold War heated up, North Korean leaders largely abandoned the rebalancing of the economy starting in the early 1960s and instead focused on building an "impenetrable fortress," pulling resources from other sectors and further straining already weak budgets and living conditions. In December 1962, the DPRK announced a four-point military modernization program to: (1) arm the people; (2) modernize weaponry; (3) fortify the country; and (4) train each solder.[9] Workers moved from plants to building vast underground tunnel networks to house artillery and military equipment. The entire society was militarized for men from the ages of fifteen to forty-five and for women from eighteen to thirty-five. (A Young Red Guard was created for those fifteen to seventeen years old.) Strains on the economy from this redirection of resources became apparent. All of the target goals of the Seven-Year Plan fell behind schedule so that authorities had to extend the plan another three years, to end in 1970. Once again, low priority was placed on the people, with no emphasis on light industry or agriculture. Pyongyang's economic policies constituted abuses of human rights.

DEBT

The third bad decision took place in the 1970s. It related to foreign debt. The DPRK continued the same trends of the previous decade as economic resources were diverted to the military. Despite having half the population, North Korean military spending exceeded that of the South every year from 1968 to 1979. The buildup of this decade included increasing the size of the armed forces from 485,000 to 680,000, which was twice that of the ROK. By 1980, troop numbers stood at 720,000 and continued to swell, with the majority deployed along the thirty-eighth parallel with their sights set on the South. Special forces grew from 15,000 (1970) to 41,000 (1978). The military began Scud missile development, boosted its submarine and surface fleet, and the air force grew to over 200 attack planes. The army added 2,500 armed personnel carriers, about 1,000 heavy tanks, and 6,000 or so artillery tubes and rocket launchers. Military doctrine was revamped to increase the speed, power, and lethality of attacks in combat, focusing on rapid advance and infiltration tactics. In spite of its relatively limited technological base, by 1992 the North had twice the number of tanks and artillery that the U.S.-ROK defenses had in the South.[10]

Academic Lee Hy-Sang, who has written one of the best scholarly treatments of the North Korean economy, has noted that this obsession with aggrandizing the military was driven by ideology as much as it was by external security threats. Self-reliance required the strongest military one could muster. The net effect, however, was an increasingly reckless and irresponsible approach to the economy.[11] In order to offset the strain of the military budget on the economy, the DPRK should have directed efforts at excavating coal and other mineral resources to trade for hard currency, which might then have been used to finance heavy industry development, light industry, and to address energy shortages. Instead, the government decided to engage in massive borrowing from foreign markets. At the time, it seemed like the right decision. Sino-American rapprochement and U.S.-Soviet détente transformed relations between the East and West, and in this wider political context Western European countries were willing to extend credit to countries like North Korea. More important, the North began looking over its shoulder as the 1970s saw the gradual acceleration of South Korean growth and development of major heavy industries like the P'ohang Steel Complex.

So, in 1972, Pyongyang borrowed $80 million from France to build a fertilizer plant. The following year, they borrowed another $160 million, from the United Kingdom, to build a cement factory. In 1974, they borrowed $400 million from countries including Japan for large-scale plant equipment. In fact, between 1970 and 1975, the North borrowed approximately $1.2 billion before foreign governments realized that Pyongyang could not service the debt. These numbers do not account for whatever else might have been provided to the North from Eastern bloc countries and China. Thus, in 1976, the debt market dried up for the North as precipitously as it had opened to them six years earlier. Trapped by its own self-reliance ideology, the North could not do things normal nations would, such as issue bonds to finance its debt. Today, North Korea's external debt is estimated at $12.5 billion and no one expects them to pay it off. An attempt was made to pay back some of this in 1990 and 1991, but the DPRK has long since defaulted on its long-term debt. Pyongyang has occasionally asked Russia and former Soviet satellites like the Czech Republic to forgive the majority of the debt. In response, these countries have asked for North Korea to repay part of the debt through barter. Pyongyang asked Russia in 2007 to make a "high-level political decision" to forgive $8.8 billion in unpaid debt. In August 2010, Prague asked for zinc ore as repayment for an outstanding $10 million in unpaid loans from the Cold War when it provided Kim Il-sung with machinery and equipment. Pyongyang responded that it would provide four hundred tons of "heavenly ginseng root" worth some $500,000. Since annual consumption of the root in the country was barely two tons, this would have kept Czechs well-stocked with ginseng—which, among its many reported benefits, boasts of enhancing sexual vitality—for two hundred years.[12] An unusual secondary market has emerged for North Korean debt that a few courageous investors have dared to enter. It sells DPRK debt paper at about 6 cents on the dollar, based on the bet not that Pyongyang would ever repay but that under a future unification scenario, South Korea would want to reestablish North Korean creditworthiness as it worked to gradually reintegrate the two systems. If Seoul were to take on this debt, it could repay it all, speculators hope, with only one week's addition to its foreign exchange reserves. Even if Seoul were to pay off only a portion of the debt, speculators could make six to seven times what they have paid for North Korean paper.

OLYMPIC ENVY

The fourth bad decision came in the 1980s, when the North invested in several economic mega-projects, all of which failed. If you had to name one person who unwittingly contributed to North Korea's bad economic decisions of the 1980s, it was the late Juan Antonio Samaranch. Why not Kim Il-sung? Because in 1981, Samaranch, as head of the International Olympic Committee (IOC), oversaw the awarding of the 1988 Olympics to Seoul. This outcome was in many ways North Korea's worst nightmare. It bestowed international accolades on the rival regime, which hit at the heart of the DPRK's legitimacy. Seoul would be only the second East Asian city in modern Olympic history—after Tokyo in 1964—to host the premier summer games. The South's economic takeoff alone was hard enough for the North to swallow, but at least they could hide that fact from their people. The Seoul games promised to be South Korea's "coming out" party on the world stage, showcasing its double-digit economic growth and industrial wares in the same way they did earlier for Tokyo. To have this celebration all happening on North Korea's border threatened core legitimacies the regime tried to uphold about itself. At first, the North set forth proposals to cohost the games, which the South begrudgingly listened to. But when negotiations with the IOC and Seoul failed due to inordinate North Korean demands, the leader-in-waiting, Kim Jong-il, resorted to terrorist attacks on South Korean airplanes and airports to scare away visitors, the most horrific of which was the bombing of a South Korean passenger airliner in 1987. Matters for the North only became worse when both China and the Soviet Union announced their plans to participate in the Seoul games after very successful lobbying efforts by the South Koreans.[13] With the summer games having been plagued by superpower boycotts in 1980 (Moscow) and in 1984 (Los Angeles), the Seoul games were shaping up to be the most widely attended and most important Olympics of the twentieth century.

All of this created, for lack of a better term, "Olympic envy" on the part of the North. The regime engaged in a series of wasteful large-scale projects throughout the 1980s. These were prohibitively expensive endeavors aimed to compete with the South as well as mobilize labor to work harder for the state. These projects, several of them left unfinished, had the effect of hollowing out the economy—which, in conjunction with the cutoff of Soviet and Chinese pation aid at the end of the decade, laid the groundwork for collapse in the 1990s. One project was for tideland reclamation. North Korea was short of arable land and therefore sought to create some 300,000 hectares (1,160 sq mi, 3,000 sq km) of land on the west coast of the peninsula. This was a massive project, which dredged tidal flats that were submerged under one to two meters of water (3 to 6 ft) and turned these into usable farmland. It became known in Korea as the "find new land" project. The North managed to complete about 20,000 hectares (77 sq mi, 200 sq km) over a decade until Kim Il-sung's death in 1994, after which the project was left uncompleted. The West Sea barrage was a $1.77 billion project to build the longest dam in the world, longer than the Panama and Suez Canals. The dam was to cut across the Taedong River, which would serve to irrigate the newly reclaimed tidelands on the west coast of the peninsula. Three divisions of North Korean military troops were put to work on this project, which ultimately was also left uncompleted.

Some of these mega projects even sought to defy earth's natural forces. One of these was a hydrothermal project at T'aech'ŏn power station. It aimed at building a forty-meter (130 ft) tunnel underneath a mountain that would serve to divert flowing streams into a nearby river. The purpose was to raise the water volume of the river, thereby increasing the hydrogeneration capacity of the river. Another massive failure was the Sunch'ŏn Vinylon Complex. This was a second-generation vinylon complex that was to annually produce 100,000 tons of vinylon, a synthetic fiber referred to, within the DPRK, as the "*juche* fiber." The project failed because the North could not perfect a new technology for production of ammonia, which was critical to less costly large-scale production of vinylon. However, rather than perfecting the new technology before building the plant, the North proceeded on both at the same time. Thus, when they could not perfect the ammonia production technology, and Soviet funding ran out, the entire project failed—all 250 plants and

52,000 tons of equipment were rendered pretty much useless at a cost of over $5 billion. In the end, it seems the whole vinylon industry was more important to the North politically than practically or economically. The material is supposed to be durable and highly heat-tolerant, but excessively stiff, uncomfortable, largely resistant to dye, and prohibitively expensive to produce for any countries other than the DPRK.[14] While the rest of the world produced and used the more practical nylon, North Korean schoolchildren were forced to sing the praises of the "*juche* fiber" in revolutionary songs, such as "Ode to Vinylon," "Three Thousand-ri of Vinylon," and "Vinylon, Pride of My Country."[15] Another massive failed project was the Sariwŏn potassic/potash fertilizer plant. The project started in 1988 with the goal of increasing production to 500,000 tons of potassium fertilizer each year. This was, again, a case of building a larger-scale plant at the same time that they were trying to perfect new technology that would make a larger capacity of production affordable. In this case, aside from the fertilizer, it was technology for producing aluminum using a local mineral, feldspar—rather than the traditional input, bauxite—that proved not to work. And so, the project, worth about $3.5 billion, failed after Soviet funding dried up again.

As if these failures were not enough of a cautionary tale to economic planners, in 1989 North Korea underwrote the World Festival of Youth and Students. This was their answer to the Seoul Olympics, and they invested in massive infrastructure-building as if they were hosting their own Olympics. Spending somewhere in the range of $4 to $9 billion, the North built, at breakneck pace, 260 major facilities in two years, among them 12 athletic facilities, including a 4,000-seat table-tennis stadium, 3,000-seat badminton stadium, and the 150,000-seat Rŭngrado May Day Stadium, which was the largest stadium ever built at the time in Asia. Four new hotels were erected for the occasion, the most famous of which was the 105-story Ryugyŏng Hotel. Built in the shape of a black obelisk, the structure towers over the Pyongyang skyline. Construction began in 1987 and was to be finished by the 1989 Youth Festival. The hotel was meant to have three thousand rooms, seven revolving restaurants, and to be complete with casino and nightclub on the banks of the Pot'ong River. At 330 meters tall (1,080 ft), it was at the time the tallest hotel project in the world. Like all the other wasteful projects of the 1980s, this, too, was left unfinished. In 1989, construction was halted because of design problems, one of which was reportedly that planners realized the elevators could not operate in the angular elevator shafts that were built to the shape of the overall hotel. The project was completely halted in 1992 for lack of money. Undoubtedly embarrassed by this massive failure, the DPRK initially tried to deny the existence of the hotel—despite its towering presence over the Pyongyang skyline—by airbrushing it out of pictures, but this charade did not last long. Looking like a palace that Darth Vader might inhabit, the structure was named by *Esquire* magazine in January 2008 "The Worst Building in the History of Mankind"—a "hideous" structure that has remained unfinished and unoccupied for two decades despite sapping 2 percent of the country's GDP to build it.[16] In 2008, Egypt's Orascom Group started to refurbish the Ryugyŏng tower, some believe, as Pyongyang's condition for awarding the Egyptian company with a $400 million exclusive cell phone contract. The estimated costs to finish the hotel range as high as $2 billion. The plan is to have the hotel open in 2012 to commemorate the one-hundredth birthday of Kim Il-sung, but this, too, is likely to set the North Koreans up for another high-profile failure, as there are numerous construction problems, including concrete rotting in the building's foundations after having sat exposed for two decades.[17] Tearing down the building would make the most sense. Driving past this structure, I was impressed by its size, as it dwarfs everything in the vicinity, even the monuments to Kim Il-sung. However, I could not help but view it less than the symbol of North Korean modernity and "strong state," and more as a tombstone to the economic mismanagement of the 1980s.

SOVIET ABANDONMENT

The massive outlays of capital, manpower, and energy for the Potemkin projects of the 1980s drained the economy, paving the way for utter collapse in the ensuing decade. The key variable for collapse was the end of Soviet and Chinese patron aid. The end of the Cold War in Europe had ripple effects in Asia. Through a very effective *Nordpolitik,* or Northern Policy, South Korea reached out to Eastern European countries and the Soviet Union for commercial and trade-based ties irrespective of competing ideologies. I will spell out the details of the policy in later chapters,

but the primary result of this policy was the breakthrough normalization of diplomatic relations with Moscow in September 1990. If the Seoul
Olympics were not enough of a blow to the DPRK's core legitimacy, the
official recognition of its archrival in the South by one of Pyongyang's
biggest supporters was worse. The political impact was clear, but the economic impact of Soviet–South Korean normalization was deadly. Suffering from their own economic problems, Moscow benefited from a
massive $3 billion loan from the ROK as part of the normalization deal,
and had no intention of seeing any of these assets offset by increased
liabilities of patron aid to the North. So, almost immediately upon normalization, Moscow informed Pyongyang that it was cutting off patron
aid to the North and instead demanded that the North now pay market
prices. Moscow also indicated that it was terminating military cooperation with the North. This had an additional economic impact, because
it terminated another form of revenue to the regime from the export of
Soviet-designed military equipment and arms sales.

The effect of Moscow's abandonment was both immediate and devastating. For decades, Pyongyang had enjoyed favorable trade terms with
the Soviet Union and with China in the form of subsidized barter trade,
patron aid, and debt-financed trade. The end of this assistance spelled
the breakdown of the economy. Russia accounted for 49.5 percent of total
DPRK trade in 1985. By 1993, this dropped an unimaginable sixfold. Total
trade with the Soviet Union plummeted to less than $100 million by 1994,
one-thirtieth of what it had been four years prior.[18] Soviet-made imports by
the DPRK sat at about $175 million in 1990, but by 1992 they were less than
$10 million, and by 1994, basically nonexistent.[19] In 1987, the Soviet Union
sent North Korea nearly 50 percent of its food imports, and in 1988, it was
still close to 25 percent, totaling nearly $100 million for the two years. Yet
over the course of the following six years, as the famine was fast approaching, the Soviets sent somewhere between just $20 and $25 million, many
years sending nothing at all.[20]

But the worst-hit sector was energy. North Korea, which used to import oil at the greatly discounted rate of 25 percent of market prices, was
now saddled with a hopelessly unaffordable oil bill. Pyongyang had been
importing about 3.5 million tons per year, but after the change in terms, oil
imports dropped by more than 50 percent in one year, down to 1.5 million

tons. In 1990, petroleum imports had fallen to 410,000 tons, and by 1991, to just 45,000. And while crude oil made up nearly 22 percent of the North's imports from the Soviets in 1987, by 1990 it was just under 7 percent.[21] This was one of many areas to be impacted by the decrease in Soviet support, but it was distinct in that it had ripple effects throughout the economy. The reduction in oil imports hurt domestic coal production, because the ammonium nitrate necessary for explosives in blast mining required petroleum products that were now in short supply. The lack of oil hurt annual crop production, because it led to a decline in the production of chemical fertilizers. Exacerbating the energy shortages was the perceived need to irrigate the remaining precious arable land that existed despite the fertilizer shortages. This, in turn, hurt the North's one semi-successful source of domestic power production—hydropower. Because the lack of oil led to a decline in chemical fertilizers, the regime was forced to store water in order to flood rice paddies during the spring-season planting of seedlings. But this diversion of water reduced the capacity to produce hydropower. Moreover, the lack of oil made it impossible to compensate for the electricity shortfall with other forms of power to pump water into the fields. The lack of crude oil basically rendered the economy unable to function. Electricity stopped flowing, transportation stopped, machinery stopped. Large-scale agriculture became impossible. Trucks, trains, and tractors ground to a halt. Vital economic sectors saw drastic declines. Steel production, for instance, went from 3.1 million tons in 1991 to 1.7 million by 1994. Cement production atrophied by 55 percent, going from 8.9 million tons in 1989 to 3.9 million in 1993. And chemical fertilizer went from nearly 1.7 million tons in 1989 to just over 1.3 million by 1994, a near–24 percent reduction. In 1993, it was reported that many factories were running at a mere 20 to 30 percent of their full capacities.[22]

China initially boosted aid to their Communist brethren in the aftermath of Soviet abandonment. By 1993, Beijing provided 77 percent of North Korea's fuel imports and 68 percent of their food, but this was only temporary. Beijing normalized diplomatic relations with Seoul shortly after the Soviets did, and subsequently also declared an end to patron aid and demanded that all transactions for fuel and food now be paid in cash or barter. In spite of the fact that China replaced the Soviet Union as the North's number-one patron in these years, the early 1990s saw a fairly steep decline in aid and trade from Beijing. Sino-DPRK trade was never more than half of what the Soviets' had been, and showed great fluctuation, receding by 31 percent in 1994, 3 percent in 1996, and nearly 40 percent in 1998. In 1989, the Chinese exported over 1.1 million tons of crude oil to the North. But by 1994, this figure had dropped to 830,000, and by 1999, to just over 300,000.[23] Though China tried to reverse course in the later-1990s, as the North's famine set in, the trend continued. By 1999, due to these political developments and the atrophy of the North Korean economy, the total trade volume between China and North Korea was about a quarter of that of 1990.[24] Aid followed a similar trajectory. While official aid in 1991 is estimated to have floated around $230 million, by 1994 it was a lot closer to $100 million.[25]

It was in response to this crisis that Pyongyang made its fifth and most dire decision. As economist Lee Hy-Sang notes, the North could have adapted to the crisis in a couple of ways. They could have tried to boost exports in order to pay for needed imports, but there was not much that the economy could produce that it could sell on international markets, except for goods made with gulag labor (discussed in chapter 5), or some illicit items (discussed below). Moreover, the regime remained under a phalanx of trade sanctions because of its deviant behavior on the nuclear front. The United States maintained trade sanctions dating back to the Korean War, which restricted the export of all goods except humanitarian aid–related ones. North Korea was under additional sanctions due to its place on the State Department's list of states that support terrorism, which prohibited trade and denied the country access to international financial institutions and Export-Import Bank funding. The North was placed on this list by the Reagan administration in 1987, after the bombing of a South Korean passenger airliner over the Andaman Sea. Another set of sanctions levies the highest import duties possible on any North Korean–origin item imported by the United States, and another set of sanctions—for North Korean proliferation activities and nuclear test of 2006—overlap with the previously described ones. Even after many of these sanctions were lifted by the Clinton administration in 1995 and 1999, as part of the 1994 nuclear agreement, North Korea could not rely on trade to address its needs.

Another way to deal with the crisis might have been commercial

borrowing to help the regime through the tough times. But Pyongyang's credit reputation among both Western and Eastern bloc lenders
was shot after the defaults of the 1970s and an outstanding debt of $12
billion owed to banks and governments. This left one other alternative, which was to seek foreign assistance from the United Nations, foreign governments, and NGOs. But as two preeminent scholars of the
North Korean economy, Noland and Haggard, have argued, the North
completely mismanaged the situation. First, allowing their pride and
ideology to impede need, Pyongyang refused to acknowledge the seriousness of their situation to the outside world. They had brief interac-
tions with the World Food Programme and the ROK in the early 1990s,
but these did not result in substantial assistance. Instead, the North
waited almost two years before seeking some assistance from Japan in
1994 (Japan provided the North with 378,000 metric tons of food the
following year),[26] and then, not until 1995, did they decide to make an
international appeal for help. Second, despite the fact that food constituted some 70 percent of all the outside assistance the North was
receiving in the 1990s through 2000, the regime created unacceptable
terms for the assistance they were to receive. The government was completely inflexible with regard to access and monitoring requirements
for food donations from the United Nations and from NGOs. For example, despite the fact that the WFP 1998 appeal for 680,000 tons of
food for the DPRK was the largest in history, the regime only allowed
twenty-four monitors for a country the size of Pennsylvania the year
prior. They denied entry to the U.N. Special Rapporteur on the Right
to Food, Jean Ziegler, even though the United Nations was responsible
for feeding easily one-third of the North Korean population. And for
nearly ten years from the program's inception, the regime denied entry
to any Korean-speaking WFP staff, in order to minimize contact with
the population. Moreover, they reacted violently to any attempts to tie
international assistance with a government commitment to correct
some of the structural problems in the economy. Indeed, during one
1998 U.N. meeting on agricultural assistance, the North Korean delegation participated in an earnest fashion with positive disposition. But
when one of the non–North Korean participants mentioned the need
for "reform," the North Korean delegation closed their binders and

walked out of the room, despite the fact that they desperately needed the assistance being offered to them.[27]

North Korea's obstinate refusal to consider any serious reform as a condition of receiving assistance led to its fifth bad economic decision. Pyongyang effectively turned North Korea into an economy dependent wholly on external aid to survive. Rather than augmenting the economy with this foreign aid as a way to divert national resources to needed reforms, the government simply consumed the aid as a form of revenue. In the decade following the flood, the DPRK received over $2.3 billion in assistance from the world. A good part of this was in the first three years (1995–1998), when it received $1 billion in international assistance, including $349 million from U.N. agencies, $352 million from South Korea, and $299 million from NGOs and other governments. The WFP provided over 4 million tons of food. It is estimated that the United States, ROK, Japan, and China accounted for over 80 percent of total food aid to North Korea from the 1995 flood through 2007.[28] All the while this aid was being consumed, the regime continued to divert precious scarce national resources to the military buildup and its military-first politics. By the end of the 1990s, the economy was wholly one-third dependent on foreign aid.

Moreover, because the regime was doing nothing really to increase the supply of any economic resources, they simply chose to suppress demand by calling on workers to "eat two meals a day" and "tighten their belt two more notches" for the sake of the Revolution. This was an untenable situation. While the world community continued to put up with North Korean intransigence, and the WFP annual appeals for North Korea continued to get answered by well-meaning countries, sooner or later, countries and NGOs would become fed up with the North's inflexibility that violated every norm of humanitarian giving. By 2002, donor fatigue among Western countries started to set in with declining contributions to the WFP annual appeals. WFP staff hated working in North Korea with government counterparts who would lie on a daily basis to restrict access, yet at the same time make outrageous demands that the WFP provide gas to fuel the military's vehicles that would pick up rice donations from ports, and subsequently divert some 30 percent of it to its own coffers. Other NGOs, such as Médecins Sans Frontières (Doctors Without Borders), left the country earlier than that, in 1998, when the regime demanded that they stop providing patient care and instead only give out medicine. Oxfam and UNICEF followed. By 2005, the only countries that were giving to the North were South Korea and China.

Corruption also became endemic to the North in these years. As the famine began to envelop the country, dire need forced vast numbers of North Koreans to fend for themselves for the first time. This created new vulnerabilities among everyday North Koreans, and new opportunities for party apparatchiks to prey upon them. The mass movement of people roaming the countryside in search of food, unofficial trade and transit across the Chinese border, and a massive influx of food aid created opportunities for North Korean officials to profit every step along the way. Officials could be paid to forge travel documents, bought off to look the other way during cross-border transit, and bribed to distribute more aid to certain areas or certain families. These KWP officials were often as hungry as average North Koreans, so these bribe offers were not exactly a hard sell. During the Sunshine Policy years in the South, the fact that so much of the aid was donated without even a modicum of monitoring requirements exacerbated this problem. The breakdown of central control of the public distribution system and the hundreds of millions of metric tons of food that flooded into the country meant that local officials had unprecedented power and leverage over those around them. And as Lord Acton famously stated, "Power tends to corrupt, and absolute power corrupts absolutely." This was particularly true in the North Korean case, as there was no rule of law and no real legislative infrastructure to deal with corruption on an official level. Today, corruption seems to have become the grease for the wheels of North Korea's crippled economy. Yi Tong-hun, a defector from the North who fled in 2006, describes how "corruption in North Korean authorities has exceeded all conceivable limits. Bribes are required for everything, from getting a travel permit to obtaining the references needed to enter a good college."[29] In the words of North Korea expert Andrei Lankov, the "abuses are so systematic that corruption has become an incurable disease."[30] As an aid-dependent economy, North Korea truly became a black hole for foreign assistance, because no positive reform was coming of it and no one could confirm whether the donations were going to the neediest or being diverted to the military. The policy of "suppressed demand" made the population even more vulnerable to starvation and disease. It was in this context that monsoons of biblical proportions hit North Korea in 1995.

MONSOON SEASON IS a regular occurrence on the Korean Peninsula. Usually arriving in July or August, the rains are welcomed as a respite from the heat of the summer, and are usually followed by a dry and hot remainder of August. In 1995, the effect of torrential rains was exacerbated by the subsistence crisis the regime was already facing. The energy crisis, created by the drop-off in trade with the Soviet Union, caused many North Koreans to deforest the countryside in search of lumber for firewood the previous winter. Denuded lands then became vulnerable to flooding. The August 1995 floods basically broke the back of the North Korean economy and led to the great famine. It destroyed the four western provinces in the North, and wiped out about 70 percent of the annual rice harvest and over 50 percent of the maize harvest. The International Federation of the Red Cross reported that over 100,000 families were rendered homeless and over 400,000 hectares (988,422 acres) of arable land was destroyed. Vital economic infrastructure was laid waste to, energy supplies were ravaged, and because they were stored underground, between 1.2 and 3 million tons of emergency grain reserves were lost.[31] Roads, bridges, and rail systems were torn apart, hospitals and health clinics destroyed, and water supply and irrigation systems rendered useless. It was noted at the time by the U.N. Department of Human Affairs that flooding of this magnitude had not taken place in the DPRK in at least seventy years.[32] In September 1995, Pyongyang finally acknowledged the gravity of the situation and made an unusual international appeal for help. Pyongyang submitted humanitarian aid requests to the U.N. Department of Humanitarian Affairs, WFP, World Health Organization (WHO), UNICEF, and Red Cross, estimating that the floods caused $15 billion in damages (an inflated figure that was more than the DPRK annual GNP). The international community aimed to feed 8 million people who went starving because of a 2-million–ton shortfall of food. WFP efforts peaked in 2001, when they raised 1.5 million tons exclusively for North Korea. The WFP initially started an appeal for aid to help an estimated 500,000 needy, but it soon realized that it was trying to feed 8 million, and subsequently engaged in one of the largest emergency food operations in its history. It is noteworthy, however, that the regime continued to deny any economic mismanagement on its part, instead explaining the need to stem solely from the summer monsoon that flooded their lands. The pain and suffering of the great famine of the 1990s is chronicled in chapter 5. Ultimately, the famine was the result of five very bad decisions outlined above, which informed a half century of horrific economic mismanagement. The statistics are staggering: it is rare for an industrialized economy such as North Korea's to contract in size, but starting in the 1990s, the country experienced negative growth up until 1998, shrinking by nearly 46 percent in the process.[33] By the 1990s, machinery no longer worked, fuel and electricity were absent, and factories had ground to a halt (although employees still had to go to "work" for daily indoctrination sessions). The country could not meet 50 percent of its food needs. The ration system broke down. Food riots at distribution centers and warehouses were reported. The famine killed as many as a million people, who did nothing to deserve such a fate.

ILLICIT ACTIVITIES

THE "TONY SOPRANO OF NORTH KOREA"

The North Korean economy by the 1990s was one-third dependent on foreign aid and one-third based on commercial (minerals, metals, agriculture, and fishery products) and arms exports. It is widely believed that an equal third of the economy is based on illicit activities. As a result of these activities, over the years North Korea has been granted a number of rather ignominious titles, such as "Gangster Regime,"[34] "Wiseguy Regime,"[35] "Narco Korea,"[36] and its leader Kim Jong-il has been called the "Tony Soprano of North Korea."[37] Since the late 1960s and early 1970s, the North has been involved, to varying degrees, in the production and trafficking of narcotics, fake currency, money laundering, the production and distribution of counterfeit products, insurance fraud, and the smuggling of humans, precious metals and stones, and endangered species parts. These criminal activities have financed North Korea's ballooning national debt, kept its military machine churning on, helped keep Kim and his cronies in the lap of luxury, and even potentially advanced the North's nuclear and missile programs. While, like all other aspects of

North Korea, the facts here are murky at best, there is no doubt that the regime in Pyongyang has and continues to direct a variety of criminal activities to advance the interests of the state. What is occurring in the North is a novel form of state criminality. Generally, corrupt leaders will have gangster connections (such as Slobodan Milosevic of Serbia), will turn a blind eye to criminal activity within their state (allegedly, such as Hamid Karzai in Afghanistan), or will lack the capacity to effectively deal with powerful criminal organizations (such as Felipe Calderón in Mexico). Yet in North Korea, while the regime certainly does not have a monopoly on the criminal activity that takes place within and around its borders, a great deal of it has been and continues to be directed from up on high, by the offices of the leadership itself. It practices a special form of "criminal sovereignty,"[38] in that its status as a nation-state in the international system protects it from the risks and consequences that individuals and non-state organizations would normally face for partaking in such activities. It uses the protection of its territory and the organs of its government to enable or to carry out crimes for profit. In sum, it is a criminal state par excellence.

For the past four or five decades, the North Korean leadership has sanctioned or participated in the commission of a variety of criminal activities involving multiple actors and organizations, spanning nearly every continent on the globe. Since the mid-1970s, when North Korea began defaulting on its international debts, the regime began to look to transnational criminal activity as a means of supporting its faltering economy. Because the central government was unable to pay for many of its embassies abroad, the regime initiated a policy of "self-financing" for its overseas diplomatic missions.[39] This policy encouraged North Korean diplomats to find high-profit, time-efficient means to finance the embassies in which they worked, and narcotics trafficking and other illicit activities fit this bill perfectly. Diplomats began smuggling drugs and gems in their diplomatic pouches and used their diplomatic immunity to protect them from prosecution. Over time, the North's illicit network branched out, involving military personnel, intelligence officials, foreign criminal syndicates, and terrorist organizations. These activities rose steadily since the early 1970s, but saw a marked increase during the famine years as the North Korean economy began to implode.[40] Today, while estimates vary greatly, most open-source material regarding North Korean criminal behavior put the profits from these activities somewhere between $500 million and $1 billion per annum,[41] and showing no signs of slowing.

A key question though is whether North Korea's criminal activity is merely state-sanctioned or is actually state-directed. Are the Kim family and the Politburo in Pyongyang simply allowing local officials and criminal organizations to commit transnational crimes, or are they, in fact, ordering these activities to be carried out to profit the regime? In the early years, North Korean criminal activity was largely state-centered, with narcotics and counterfeit materials being produced within the DPRK and trafficked abroad by North Korean diplomats. During this time, North Korean criminal activity was directed from the infamous "Bureau 39" of the Korean Workers' Party. This institution has been headquartered in downtown Pyongyang, just blocks away from the foreign tourist–frequented Koryŏ Hotel, since its inception in the 1970s to fund Kim Jong-il's rise to power.[42] This office is thought to have as much as $5 billion stashed away in offshore bank accounts from Macao to Switzerland to Luxemburg, and uses these funds to direct its criminal enterprises, fund military and WMD-related (weapons of mass destruction) activities, and buy loyalty from North Korean Party elites.[43] Its representative offices are stationed at every major port and rail junction across the DPRK, and it has liaison offices in every province, city, and county in the North, allowing North Korean officials from all over the country to operate with ease.[44] North Korean counterfeit products are known for their extremely high quality, and North Korean drugs such as methamphetamines, for their high purity. This is due to the safety that the state provides in the production of these products, with the use of resources that only a state can afford. Counterfeit currency, pharmaceuticals, and cigarettes are manufactured in state-run factories, and narcotics grown or produced on state-run farms and in state-run labs.[45] The North Korean regime uses merchant ships and naval vessels, foreign diplomatic posts, and state-run companies to run its criminal enterprises. It employs middlemen, uses front companies and foreign entities, and constructs complex financial arrangements to cover up its complicity. There is simply no question that a great deal of North Korean transnational criminal activity is state-directed rather than state-sanctioned. But its criminal empire is certainly not confined to the North Korean state.

Through its smuggling networks, the DPRK government has employed, partnered with, and even been employed by a variety of organized-crime groups and terrorist organizations. Historically, the North Koreans tended to operate with non-state organizations with which they shared ideological affinity, such as the socialist terrorist organization, the Japanese Red Army. Yet as the years have progressed, these ideological ties have become less and less important, and profit, more and more. Over the years, the North has been suspected of dealing with the Japanese Yakuza, Chinese triads, South Korean criminal organizations, Irish mobsters, Russian mafia dons, and Southeast Asian crime groups. The North Koreans use these groups to buy, sell, and transport illegal drugs, counterfeit products, and precious stones on the international black market. It is even reported that the North Korean government provides safe haven to members of foreign criminal organizations within the DPRK territory, to employ in currency counterfeiting and drug production facilities.[46] Kim Yŏng-il, a defector who was formerly an official in North Korea's National Security Agency, attests that in the 1990s, opium produced on state-run farms was "processed and refined into heroin under the supervision of several drug experts who were brought from Thailand to assist the North Korean government in its drug production program."[47] There have also been reports of members of the Burmese underworld helping the North establish its drug labs, Taiwanese criminal delegations being hosted by North Korean officials, and Chinese and Taiwanese counterfeiters running factories within the DPRK territory.[48] What seems to have developed, and what the North Korean authorities have recognized, is a mutually beneficial, symbiotic relationship between themselves and these transnational criminal organizations. The North Korean state provides these crime groups with high-quality, high-purity products such as narcotics and counterfeit goods, the safety of sovereign territory or territorial waters, and vast economic and logistical resources. The criminal organizations, in turn, provide the North with greatly reduced levels of risk, the security of plausible deniability, and allow the state to stay out of "turf wars" over illicit economic markets.[49] But the North is not simply an employer of these non-state actors. The *"Pong-su* incident" of April 2003—when a North Korean crew was caught on a North Korean state enterprise–owned ship (the *Pong-su*), attempting to smuggle 125 kilos (275.6 pounds) of Burmese-origin heroin to Australia—shows that the North is also willing to be a transporter for organized crime groups.[50] By partnering with these types of organizations, the North has been able to garner considerable sums of money to keep the regime afloat.

One of the most important sources of illicit revenue for the regime in Pyongyang comes from the growth, harvesting, manufacturing, processing, storage, sale, and transport of illegal drugs. A 2008 report by the Congressional Research Service on the subject points out that "since 1976, North Korea has been linked to more than 50 verifiable incidents involving drug seizures in more than 20 countries,"[51] including Bulgaria, Ethiopia, Germany, Singapore, Turkey, Venezuela, and Zambia, among many others. While the North has produced and trafficked a variety of drugs, including cocaine, hashish, and illegal hallucinogenic tablets, it has historically focused most centrally on the production and distribution of opium and opiate derivatives, such as heroin, and methamphetamines, more commonly known as "crystal meth." Initially, the North Korean government dabbled in the trade, buying and selling foreign-produced drugs on the international market. In the mid-1970s, however, the regime began to cultivate and harvest opium plants as a matter of state policy, and to refine and export heroin across the globe. All collective farms were ordered to devote 25 acres to poppy fields and opium production.[52] The regime continued to invest in these activities to compensate for lost arms sales revenues after the conclusion of the Iran-Iraq War in 1988. A major shift in North Korean drug production took place in the famine years of the mid-1990s, when torrential rains and persistent droughts forced the regime to shift its focus to the non-weather-dependent manufacture of methamphetamines.[53] Skyrocketing demand in China, Japan, Russia, and Southeast Asia (along with higher profit margins than heroin) is also said to have influenced this decision.[54] The regime currently maintains the capacity to produce fifty tons of opium and ten to fifteen tons of methamphetamines per year,[55] and while the estimates here also vary widely, the North is thought to procure between $70 and $200 million in profit through these activities.[56] Defectors describe the North as a "narco-state in which all aspects of the drugs operation—from schoolchildren toiling in poppy fields to government-owned processing plants to state-owned cargo ships and trading companies—are controlled by Kim [Jong-Il]."[57]

Recent years have seen a marked decline in DPRK drug activity, with its name not even showing up in the annual *UN World Drug Report* since 2007.[58] A 2011 State Department report also affirms that for eight consecutive years there have been "no known instances of large-scale methamphetamine or heroin trafficking to either Japan or Taiwan with direct DPRK state institution involvement."[59] The reasons for this decline could be many, but chances are that the North hasn't had a sudden change of heart. It is more likely that the regime is focusing on other important illicit activities, such as producing its world-renowned high-quality "supernotes."

In 1994, two North Korean trading company executives carrying diplomatic passports were arrested in Macao for attempting to deposit US$250,000 in high-quality counterfeit $100 notes to a local bank. In 1996, a North Korean trade counselor to Romania was expelled from the country for exchanging $50,000 in fake U.S. currency; in Ulan Bator, another DPRK official that same year was arrested for dumping $100,000 in U.S. currency on the black market. And in 1998, a DPRK party official was caught trying to exchange $30,000 in U.S. notes for rubles. These seem to have been among the first public appearances of North Korea's "supernotes," but they certainly weren't the last. Since the mid-1990s, North Korean–origin counterfeit U.S. currency has shown up in places ranging from Manila and Belgrade to Las Vegas and San Francisco. The supernotes, known to North Koreans as *kattalio*, are estimated to generate between $15 and $100 million in profit for the North Korean regime.[60] These notes are of such high quality that most analysts trace their origin to North Korea's state mint, the Trademark Pyongyang Printing House, otherwise known as "Number 62 Factory."[61] They are believed to be printed on a $10 million Intaglio-type printing press (the same type used by the U.S. Bureau of Currency and Engraving) purchased from Japan, using Hong Kong–bought paper and ink from France.[62] In August of 2005, the FBI completed two ongoing undercover operations focusing on China's triad crime syndicates, code-named "Royal Charm" and "Smoking Dragon." The string of arrests across Atlantic City, Los Angeles, Las Vegas, Chicago, Philadelphia, and San Francisco led to the seizure of large quantities of ecstasy and methamphetamines, counterfeit cigarettes and pharmaceuticals, and a reported $4.5 million in North Korean–origin counterfeit U.S. currency of "exceptional quality."[63] In October of the same year, former head of the Official Irish Republican Army (OIRA), Sean Garland (known as "The Man with the Hat"), was arrested in Belfast, on an extradition application, by the U.S. government, on charges of running a ring that distributed supernotes in Belarus, the Czech Republic, Denmark, Great Britain, Ireland, Poland, and Russia.[64] Currently, the notes are said to have a global circulation of approximately $45 million,[65] but in reality it is nearly impossible to make such estimates, for as one U.S. government official put it, "We have no idea how much they're counterfeiting, because it's so good."[66]

But the North's counterfeiting activities don't end with high-quality currency. Over the past few years, North Korea has gained notoriety for its high chemical purity and high-quality packaging in counterfeit cigarettes and pharmaceuticals.[67] There are thought to be around a dozen factories within the DPRK territory devoted to producing multiple brands of American and Japanese cigarettes. Most estimates of the regime's profit from black-market cigarettes range from $80 to $160 million annually, carrying a street value of as much as $720 million.[68] Intelligence gathered by satellite imagery and the Japanese coast guard is reported to show North Korean ships regularly transferring containers of counterfeit cigarettes onto ships registered in Taiwan, Cambodia, and Mongolia.[69] Cities in Belize, Greece, Japan, the Philippines, Singapore, and the United States are among the thirteen hundred locations worldwide in which North Korean counterfeit cigarettes have surfaced.[70] In 2006, federal indictments alleged that organized crime groups arranged for one forty-foot (12 m) container of North Korean–origin counterfeit cigarettes to enter the United States each month, each individual container costing as little as $70,000 but fetching a street value of $3 to $4 million.[71] Along with fake Marlboros, the North Koreans are also adept producers of counterfeit pharmaceuticals. Most notable among these are sildenafil and tadalafil, known more commonly by their brand names, Viagra and Cialis. Like the knock-off cigarettes, these erectile dysfunction meds are also said to be expertly packaged and of extremely high chemical purity.[72]

On top of their narcotics trade, their supernotes operation, and their counterfeiting of cigarettes and Viagra, the North Koreans are believed to engage in a variety of other illicit activities to keep the leadership's coffers full. One such example is the trafficking of endangered species and animal parts, with DPRK diplomats having been caught in the past trying to transport hundreds of pounds of elephant tusk and rhino horn.[73] Precious metals such as gold are also thought to be traded on the black market by members of the North Korean regime.[74] Nor is insurance fraud beneath the DPRK government. It is believed that by falsely reporting accidents, such as a 2005 helicopter accident and an early 2006 ferry accident, the North may have profited in the excess of $150 million in 2006 alone.[75] And finally—and perhaps most sadly—human beings are another one of North Korea's important "commodities" in their illicit network. In the U.S. State Department's June 2010 Trafficking in Persons (TIP) Report, North Korea is designated, along with just 11 other countries (out of 177) as a "Tier Three human trafficker."[76] This designation is reserved for countries that do not even meet the minimum standards for prevention of human trafficking within their territory and are making no effort to do so, and the North has carried this label since 2003. Through its prison camp slave-labor network, foreign work operations such as Russian logging and Mongolian mining camps, and the sale of North Korean brides across the border to rural Chinese buyers, the North Korean regime has proven itself to be among the worst of the worst in one of the most abhorrent of human rights violations.

A key question going forward is to what extent the North Korean government would potentially be able to curtail its transnational criminal activities. There is some concern over the degree to which the North's elicit economy has become "institutionalized," with its smuggling networks and drug production operations having possibly taken on a life of their own.[77] A second and equally important question is whether Pyongyang would be willing to modify its criminal conduct. This makes one wonder, with the North Korean economy in shambles, its inexperienced leadership, and the country receding further and further into global isolation, whether the leadership will up the ante with regards to transnational criminal activities. Of course there is no way of knowing what the regime has planned, but they obviously have to do something. And at this point, the light of reform doesn't appear to be at the end of North Korea's long, dark economic tunnel.

WHITHER REFORM?

Because the United States does not have diplomatic relations with, or an embassy in the DPRK, our protecting power is Sweden. It was therefore with great appreciation that I accepted an impromptu invitation from the Swedish ambassador Mats Foyer in Pyongyang to attend a reception at his residence after my long day of official meetings with our North Korean interlocutors. I thought it would be interesting to interact with the NGO and diplomatic community that would be in attendance, and the promise of a glass of Merlot after three days of North Korean liquor added to the allure. Upon arrival, I was locked into a conversation with the Chinese ambassador in Pyongyang, who berated me for the Bush administration's neoconservative policy toward North Korea and scolded me for the administration's belief that it could collapse the deceivingly sturdy regime. He carried a brief better than any hard-line North Korean I had met. After disengaging myself from this unpleasant exchange, I met a young couple from New Zealand, who were doing microfinance in North Korea. Admiring their adventurist spirit (who does microfinance in North Korea?) and their stories of the equivalent of Costco runs to the Chinese border, I asked what exactly they did in Pyongyang. They admitted that microfinance in North Korea amounted to teaching basic accounting, inventory, and business administration skills. The lack of such basic training is apparent in the country. Some of the academic exchanges that have taken place with schools such as Syracuse University (U.S.), the University of Warwick (UK), University of Essex (UK), the University of Sydney (Australia), and Australian National University have aimed to teach woefully undertrained North Koreans these basic skills.[78] Indeed, North Korean bureaucrats have shared company with and received sage advice from some of the greatest financial minds in the Western world. I recall a session in New York City in 2008, in which luminaries such as the former vice chairman of Goldman Sachs Bob Hormats (who, appropriately, was also former senior economic adviser to Henry Kissinger and managed U.S. diplomatic and economic relations with China during its late-1970s reforms), and former chairman of the Federal Reserve Paul Volcker sat with a visiting delegation of North Korean economic and financial experts and offered them five hours of counsel on economic reform. To this day, I do not know whether these North Koreans had any understanding of who these senior American figures were, or how much it would have cost had Volcker or Hormats billed them for the consultation. But the failures of the North Korean economy are not caused by these undertrained bureaucrats, or the absence of any Nobel Prize laureates in economics in their own universities. Technocrats know very well the extent of the problems. Nor is the problem that North Koreans are somehow genetically incapable of economic reform and growth. One need only look at the South Korean experience to see the preposterousness of such a proposition.

The primary cause for the bad economic choices of the last fifty years sits at the very top of the political structures in Pyongyang. And the only obstacle to genuine economic reform relates to the leadership's prizing, at any cost, its iron grip on the regime. The North Korean leadership faces in its own minds a fundamental reform dilemma. They need to open up to survive, but in the process of opening up, they unleash the forces that lead to the regime's demise. Resisting the system in North Korea today is virtually impossible, because the society is so closed. The masses are preoccupied with basic subsistence. And the elite seek only to ensure their relative share of the sparse gains that could be had from the system rather than contemplating a change of it. Any openness begins to generate a spiral of expectations and inexorable forces for change— the overturning of systems like North Korea occur not when things are at their absolute worst, but when they begin to get better. The North Koreans have seen this happen in South Korea, where economic growth and a burgeoning middle class eventually precipitated the downfall of military dictatorships. They have also witnessed this throughout Eastern Europe and with the fall of the Soviet Union. The Kim family and its cronies know that true economic reform will ultimately improve the lives of the North Korean people, but this will also set off a spiral of expectations. Once the people taste the sweetness of change, they become impatient for more rapid change, if not revolution. China, when it undertook modernization reforms under Deng Xiaoping some forty years ago, was willing to risk a degree of political decentralization for economic growth, because, as Deng famously said, "To get rich is glorious." For the North Korean leadership, however, political control is still the most valued currency.

HALFHEARTED REFORMS

For these reasons, pundits misjudge signs of economic reform in North Korea. The moment Pyongyang appears to undertake measures that could vaguely be associated with marketization or entrepreneurship, there are clarion calls that reform is finally afoot in the country. But these so-called reforms end up disappointing all, because they are, at best, tactical actions done out of temporary need (for reasons described below). Even when the North tries measures to open the economy a crack to invite trade and investment, these efforts are halfhearted because of the political masters' fears that they might lose control. One area of attempted economic reform and opening, for example, centered on special economic zones (SEZs) set up by the DPRK on the border with China (Sinŭiju Special Administrative Region) and Russia (Rajin-Sŏnbong Free Economic and Trade Zone). North Korean authorities had grand visions that these zones would attract foreign investment, but the way they mishandled all aspects of these enterprises demonstrated a fundamental lack of business knowledge, an inflated sense of self-importance, and a fear of losing control. These zones were created in the 1990s as North Korea's response to the end of the Cold War and to rival South Korea's very successful *Nordpolitik* outreach to communist nations. Pyongyang thought it could also capitalize on the thaw in inter-Korean relations occasioned by a 1992 agreement on political reconciliation signed between the two governments, and the conclusion of the 1994 nuclear agreement with the United States. These SEZs, it was hoped, would constitute a solution to the North's growing economic malaise. Rajin-Sŏnbong (now known as Rasŏn) is a 465-square-mile (1,200-sq-km) special economic zone in the northeast corner of North Hamgyŏng Province, butting up against the 12-mile (19-km) border with Russia along the Tumen River. Sitting 800 kilometers (500 mi) from the capital, the zone was established to promote growth by attracting foreign investment, and to serve as a hub for regional transportation.

Sinŭiju was a special administrative region that sits in the northwest corner of the country, in Pyongan Province, just across the border from the Chinese city Dandong. The Chinese-Dutch orchid and property tycoon Yang Bin (listed in *Forbes* in 2001 as the second-richest man in China) was appointed by the North Koreans to be the first governor of the region, but Yang was shortly thereafter arrested by Chinese authorities on charges of forgery, bribery, fraud, and tax evasion, and is currently serving out an eighteen-year jail sentence in Shenyang. They enacted a Joint Venture Law and some laws to protect foreign investments, but really little else in terms of a juridical infrastructure governing taxes, operating regulations, liability, and a host of other requisite issues. This would require a level of transparency that the political masters would not be comfortable with. They naively assumed that simply announcing that they were open for business would draw hordes of hungry investors.

The projects garnered some initial Western investment, but this was largely in building infrastructure and refurbishing ports in the SEZs. Manufacturing investment, which was what the North had hoped for, did not come—in large part because of dilapidated infrastructure, official corruption, and only partial adherence to agreed-upon economic reforms in the areas. According to a British journalist who traveled to Rasŏn in late 2010, the city still seemed stuck in a "Stalinist time warp," with traffic consisting mostly of oxen-driven carts and Chinese-style lorries, and infrastructural construction carried out by men with picks, shovels, and wheelbarrows. There are no streetlights in the area, and because of poor drainage, the city's main square becomes "a sea of mud" on days when it rains.[79] Sinŭiju has never really resurfaced since Yang was arrested in the summer of 2003, though there was some talk of its being relocated to Wihwa Island on the Yalu River as recently as 2009.[80] These projects are basically in a perpetual state of "talk" with very little "action," with the North Koreans simultaneously trying to attract investment (more like aid) while fighting off the need for reform, and having very little success in the process.

The other area of attempted reform in this period regarded inter-Korean trade. The first recorded trade between the two Koreas was in

November 1988, in the form of a forty-kilogram (90-lb) box of clams that arrived in Pusan. The next was a shipment of 612 pieces of Korean artwork that arrived in Pusan on January 1989. But here again, the North set conditions that aimed to circumvent the fundamental reform dilemma—i.e., conditions that maximized their cash inflow but minimized any interaction that could have deleterious effects on the population. Thus, almost all of the initial trade with the South was conducted through intermediaries, so that the North could claim none of it was of South Korean origin. Direct trade started in 1991, on a barter basis, but even here the North set out conditions. The delivery of South Korean rice, for example, in exchange for North Korean anthracite could not be delivered in bags that had anything written on them indicating South Korean origin.

Many believed that a sweeping set of reforms enacted by the North in July 2002 was the real deal, after a decade of halfhearted and failed efforts. As these reforms emerged at the end of the 1990s out of a collapsed economy, famine, energy shortages, and negative growth, many believed the North had finally learned to put aside ideology and obsession with political control as the only way to survive. I was asked to testify before the U.S. Congress on the meaning of these reforms after they were enacted. I made a prediction then that the reforms, which looked great at the time, were temporary and tactical. I would have been happy to be proved wrong, but regrettably, I wasn't.

JULY 2002 REFORMS

The July 2002 market liberalization reforms undertaken by North Korea were generally associated with four measures. The first was a basic monetization of the economy. The government abolished the coupon system for food rations, relaxed price controls, thereby allowing supply and demand to determine prices. In order to meet the rise in prices, the government also hiked wage levels—for some sectors by as much as twentyfold (from 110 won/month to 2,000 won/month), and for other "special"-wage sectors (government officials, soldiers, miners, farmers) by as much as sixtyfold. Small-scale markets sprouted up all over North Korea, and the public distribution system broke down. Second, the government abandoned the artificially high value of the North Korean won, depreciating their currency from 2.2 won to $1 to 150 won to $1. This measure was aimed at encouraging foreign investment and providing export incentives for domestic firms. Third, the government decentralized economic decisions. Measures entailed cutting government subsidies, allowing farmers' markets to operate, and transplanting managerial decisions for industry and agriculture from the central government into the hands of local production units. Enterprises have to cover their own costs. Managers have to meet hard budget constraints. Fourth, the government pressed forward with special administrative and industrial zones to promote foreign investment in the Sinŭiju Special Administrative District, Kaesŏng industrial project, and the Kumgang (Diamond) Mountain tourism project.

At the time, these reforms were hailed by the outside world as historic. They represented the first attempt in the regime's history at widescale economic change. People focused on the fact that the regime was recognizing flaws in the socialist-style economy as the source of the problem rather than blaming its economic woes on outside actors.

> ... the socialist economic management method is still immature and not perfect. ... If we stick to this hackneyed and outdated method, which is not applicable to the realities of today, then we will be unable to develop our economy.[81]

By decentralizing decisions, and separating the local economy from the central economy, these pundits lauded, local governments and counties could set their own production levels and prices, which encourages competition. State-owned enterprises were now given incentives to meet government production targets and then sell surplus on the open market for profit.[82] Visitors to North Korea noted a new, albeit limited, spirit of entrepreneurship. Caritas and other international relief organizations reported makeshift small-scale markets with kiosks selling drinks, cigarettes, and cookies, as the public distribution system broke down.[83] The government's sanctioning of these open-air markets—where consumers could purchase goods at (lower) prices not determined by the government—was widely seen as a harbinger of major change. A description by the *Guardian* in 2003 gave a sense of the optimism: "Compared with the dusty, quiet, almost empty state department stores, Pyongyang's Tongil Market is a hive of activity and noise. Shoppers haggle noisily with the 150 or so stall holders for a staggering range of goods; second-hand Japanese TVs, Burmese whiskey, and Korean dog meat. Most of the goods are from China. Some—including Western diarrhea pills, which sell for 3 [pounds sterling] apiece—are kept under the table. Prices are determined by the market, not—as is the case everywhere else—by the state . . . The openness and activity suggest that Tongil market is the best hope for North Korea's future—one that would bring it closer in line with the successful economic reforms that have transformed neighboring China."[84] Policy pundits jumped on this bandwagon, claiming that Kim Jong-il should be encouraged in his efforts to reform "by stealth" without confronting his domestic opponents to change. ROK president Kim Dae-jung proclaimed that these reforms represented the North Korean leader's acute "intellectual ability and discernment [as] a reform-minded and the type of man we can talk with in a common-sense fashion." Peter Maas wrote in the *New York Times* that Kim was reform-minded like a Korean Jimmy Carter but with a "harmless feudalism." And Don Gregg, former U.S. ambassador to the ROK and close friend of Kim Dae-jung, proclaimed that the reforms showed the DPRK wanted to emulate the Park Chung-hee model of state-led capitalism.[85]

The significance of these reforms, however, did not guarantee their success. The measures proved not to constitute the equivalent of North Korea's religious "conversion" to capitalism. Neither the language nor the nature of the reforms carried the same conviction of those seen in China or Vietnam. More important, many of the reforms were motivated situationally rather than dispositionally—i.e., they constituted coping mechanisms to deal with immediate problems rather than a wholesale, prescient shift in economic ideology. Pyongyang authorized monetization of the economy and authorization of farmers' markets to buy and sell goods, for example, largely because the public distribution system had broken down. The government simply had no goods to ration to the public. It could no longer provide the measly 600–700 grams of daily food allotment to it citizens (800 grams for the elite), so it had to allow markets for subsistence. They knew this meant giving up some control, but there was no choice in the matter. In the decade after the 1995 flood, for example, the PDS for food was about 80 percent supplied by international assistance. So, when there was no food, the government suspended the PDS and allowed markets to operate. But when food arrived, they reinstituted the PDS. The PDS, in this sense, was not a system to ration things equitably: it was an entitlement distribution system that formed the basis of social and political control.

Similarly, local managers were given more leeway not because the central government "trusted" their entrepreneurial capabilities but because state-owned enterprises were experiencing plunging outputs and high absentee rates for workers, which required some drastic measures to incentivize them. Monetization of the economy looked like another significant departure from the North's socialist ways, but it had the effect of asserting political control over the elements of the economy that constituted the biggest threat—black market entrepreneurs. The activities of these individuals were the collective answer to market failure. They operated underground and traded in goods that the government could not supply (or could supply at inflated government prices). Farmers would sell their produce in these markets after meeting state production quotas. International aid recipients would keep some of the rice, but then take a portion of their allotment to the black market to fetch a high price. Consumers would spend money sent to them by relatives in China or South Korea to acquire secondhand VCRs and watch forbidden South Korean soap operas. These constituted threats, in the minds of the political masters, precisely because they operated outside the control and eye of the Orwellian state. In this regard, the lifting of price controls and devaluation of the currency undercut these entrepreneurs (and the general population) by rendering their cash holdings a fraction of their value while also causing massive inflation.

These reforms ultimately failed as they created more problems than they solved. The lifting of price controls led to runaway inflation: low supply and low output brought significant increases in prices and further devaluation of the won. By comparison, China's initial price reforms in 1979 drove up the price of rice by 25 percent. In North Korea, the price after the reforms went up by at least 600 percent, and the value of won dropped from 150 for $1 to 700 for $1.[86] Fixed-income workers were devastated by these dynamics, as were the military and laborers. (Farmers were hurt marginally less, because they benefited from the inflated prices of their produce.) The North only managed to squeak by because of the aid from China and South Korea. North Korea needed to meet the upward pressure on prices created by the reforms with either increased production (not feasible yet) or increased imports. The growth in North Korean imports in years following the 2002 reforms was largely financed by aid inflows from Seoul and Beijing. As Nicholas Eberstadt argues, Chinese aid went well beyond what was publicly reported, with the best indicator probably being the trade deficit between the two countries: "The DPRK's seemingly permanent merchandise trade deficit with China actually constitutes a broader and perhaps more accurate measure of Beijing's true aid levels for Pyongyang (insofar as neither party seems to think the sums accumulated in that imbalance will ever be corrected or repaid)."[87] During this period, it was reported that Beijing provided some $470 million in aid annually to North Korea, amounting to 70 to 90 percent of fuel imports and 30 percent of grain imports.[88] China increased shipments of corn and wheat in early 2003; and during a visit by chief PRC legislator Wu Bangguo in October of 2003, in a meeting with North Korean Politburo member Kim Yŏng-nam, the Chinese reportedly offered $50 million in aid.[89] Japanese media reported that the aid was nominally for a glassworks plant, but Pyongyang could spend the aid at their discretion.[90] Food was an important component of Chinese aid during these years, officially averaging over 287,000 metric tons from 2000 to 2007, and peaking at just over 450,000 metric tons in 2005.[91] The Chinese also built numerous factories and other production facilities for little or no cost, provided the North with between 600,000 and 700,000 metric tons of oil annually at "friendship prices" (highly subsidized by the PRC government), and allowed the North to run up massive trade deficits, with an implicit understanding that they likely wouldn't be repaid.[92]

Chinese trade with the North also absolutely exploded over these years. While trade with China made up a substantial 20 percent of all North Korean commerce in 1999 and 2000, by 2004 this figure had just about doubled, totaling 39 percent.[93] The increases in value of this trade were equally impressive. At the turn of the millennium, it sat at $488 million, but would more than triple in value to nearly $1.6 billion by 2005.[94] In 2003, China also increased overall trade with North Korea by nearly 40 percent, according to the Korean International Trade Association. North Korean fuel imports from China rose 53.2 percent to $187 million, backfilling the end of U.S. shipments of fuel oil after the breakdown of the nuclear agreement at the beginning of 2003. In addition to Chinese trade and aid, the North received easily over $1 billion in aid from a South Korean government and public then enraptured by the Sunshine Policy. During President Kim's first full year in office, South Korea provided the North with just $29 million in food, fertilizer, and humanitarian aid. But this number climbed rapidly during his and President Roh's tenure, reaching a whopping $635 million in 2007.[95] Food aid exhibited a similar pattern. Starting at just 12,000 metric tons in 1999, it would average just under 370,000 metric tons over the following eight years, topping out at 542,000 in 2003.[96] Inter-Korean trade was another important source of support for the ailing DPRK economy. Total trade between North and South was equivalent to about $78 million in 1998. But this figure, too, increased rapidly, doubling by the following year ($144.4 million), doubling again by 2002 ($298.8 million), and reaching a high of nearly $800 million by 2006.[97]

As one longtime international aid worker very familiar with North Korea put it figuratively during these years, "North Korea has its own 911 number—access to state-of-the-art health care, agricultural support, and aid . . . and that number rings in Seoul."[98] The ROK Unification Ministry estimates that since 1995, $2.4 billion in aid has been provided to North Korea by Japan, the United States, South Korea, the European Union, and the United Nations (food, fertilizer, medicine, and fuel oil). From 1995 to 2007, China, South Korea, the United States, and Japan provided over 80 percent of North Korea's food aid, and from 2000 onward, it was generally over 90 percent. But from the years 2002 to 2005, the North got the majority of its food from just China and the South, and in 2006 and 2007, they provided it all.[99] Indeed, these aid "revenues" constituted the most successful part of Pyongyang's so-called reforms. As noted above, the economy became perpetually dependent on foreign aid for one-third of its needs. This inflow of cash and goods without any adequate supervision by NGOs or the state created ripe opportunities for corruption to take hold.

Thus, the one major national effort at economic reform in 2002 never amounted to what it was made out to be. Many argued that the unprecedented and far-reaching nature of the July 2002 measures demonstrated North Korean intentions to seek integration into the international community, to receive engagement by the United States and allies, and to trade their nuclear programs for help from the outside world. The danger of fixating on the economic reforms was that these optimists were giving much more credit to North Korean security preferences than they deserved. Even if we gave the North the benefit of the doubt on their economic reforms, there is no logical link between DPRK desires to reform on the economic front and a change in their security intentions. To seek economic reforms *and* pursue a ramping up of national power through nuclear weapons and ballistic missiles proved not only plausible but also fully consistent with Kim Jong-il's concept of *kangsŏng tae'guk* or "rich nation, strong army." But the point is that the DPRK could divorce its economic intentions from its security preferences. Economic reform does not necessarily mean they are equally interested in trading away their nuclear weapons—a common and mistaken assumption made by many analysts of the economic reforms. Pyongyang could, in fact, want to have its cake and eat it, too.

DPRK'S "MOONSHINE" POLICY

It was no coincidence that the DPRK's most vigorous economic reforms overlapped with South Korea's Sunshine Policy. Two liberal administrations in Seoul, those of Kim Dae-jung and Roh Moo-hyun (2003–2008), pursued unconditional economic engagement on a large scale for one decade. The two presidents believed that they had to convince the regime that its external environment was benign and that no one was out to collapse Kim Jong-il's house. The Kim and Roh administrations pursued economic engagement both to pacify the belligerent North and to spur slow reform. These objectives, in turn, would avoid a DPRK collapse and the dreaded "hard-landing" scenario for unification, which would be prohibitively costly to the South Koreans. Every time the Kim Jong-il regime responded to Seoul's unilateral offers of assistance, these South Korean governments felt validated in their hopes that their policies were working.

But Pyongyang had its own Moonshine Policy. Accepting such assistance in hard times was a no-brainer. While it led the gullible South Koreans to believe in their Sunshine Policy, it played ROK aid at home as "gifts" to its Great Leaders from the weaker South, all the while keeping both hands in their southern brethren's deep pockets. Pyongyang agreed to two major inter-Korean economic projects that became the hallmark of the Sunshine Policy. It also agreed to two summit meetings in which South Korean presidents traveled to Pyongyang to pay their respects to Kim Jong-il. Seoul hailed all of this as a transformative change in the DPRK. The Kaesŏng Industrial Complex and the Kumgang Mountain tourism enterprise constituted new steps in inter-Korean economic cooperation. The Kaesŏng Industrial Complex is a joint North-South industrial park located just across the DMZ in North Hwanghae Province, forty-three miles (70 km) from Seoul. Housing over 120 South Korean companies, the eight-hundred-acre complex employs over 47,000 North Korean workers earning approximately $45 a month. (Sadly, this is a far better opportunity than most in the North.)[100] Workers produce a wide variety of goods, such as pajamas, motorcycle helmets, socks, printer cartridges, and fish nets, for export to South Korea and around the world.[101] The start-up costs for the complex were $374 million, 40 percent of which was provided by the South Korean conglomerate Hyundai-Asan and the remainder was left up to the South Korean government.[102] The Kumgang Mountain tourism project, for its part, was in operation starting in 1998, and hosted over 1.9 million South Korean tourists since its inauguration.[103] Two-night, three-day packages ranged from $230 (250,000 Korean won) to $1,140 (1,250,000 Korean won) per person, depending on the time of year and quality of accommodation.[104] Here visitors took in the breathtaking scenery of the T'aebaek mountain range area, soaked in natural hot springs (called *onchŏn* in Korean), and sampled North Korean cuisine, art, and culture; all, of course, under the watchful eye of North Korean minders. (I discuss this in greater detail in chapter 9.)

The more successful Seoul believed its Sunshine Policy was, the more effective was Pyongyang's Moonshine. Kaesŏng and Kumgang were acceptable to the North Korean leadership because they met two core conditions. First, the projects funneled large sums of cash to the leadership.

The agreements for these projects mandated a sum of $942 million to be transferred from Hyundai-Asan to the North Korean government; much of it in cash and heavily front-loaded over a seventy-five-month period (approximately $150 million per year).[105] While the exact profit figures are a matter of dispute, the Kaesŏng Industrial Complex is additionally thought to generate between $20 and $34 million annually in hard currency for the North Korean regime.[106] Given that the complex has been in operation since 2005, but only really in full swing since 2007, a conservative estimate of the DPRK's total revenue is upward of $80 to $135 million in cash profit alone. Kumgang Mountain tours, too, have been an important source of support for the regime. While the amount of hard currency Kumgang generated for the regime is unknown, from 2001 up to the program's cancellation in 2008, the South Korean government provided the North with over $76 million in aid through the program.[107] These may sound like trivial amounts to the average American—used to a national debt in the tens of trillions—but its impact on North Korea's $28 billion GDP is certainly significant.[108] In this regard, the epic June 2000 summit between Kim Dae-jung and Kim Jong-il, which won the former a Nobel Peace Prize, was also a cash cow for the latter. It was later revealed that Seoul paid $500 million for the meeting.

Second, neither project had the potential for enlightening the people and empowering forces for change. In the case of the Kaesŏng Complex—a joint venture that married South Korean capital and technology with North Korean labor to produce watches, flatware sets, and other light manufactured items for export—Pyongyang carefully managed the terms of this endeavor. South Korean managers were not allowed to pay North Korean workers directly. Instead, they paid a DPRK government intermediary, who did not pay the workers. This became apparent in 2005–2006, when the South Korean government invited foreign journalists to Kaesŏng as part of a publicity campaign for the Sunshine Policy. Journalists quickly figured out that even as the DPRK intermediary negotiated higher wages each year from the South Korean companies, it was, at best, paying a small fraction of those wages to the workers. In lieu of wages, workers were receiving three meals per day and a clean work environment. The North also screens all workers for their "loyalty" to the regime before they are eligible to work at Kaesŏng. A nearly-all-female workforce was selected (a factory full of young men posed too many risks), and contact between South Korean managers and the workforce is restricted by the North. South Korean managers are sequestered off into their own cafeteria during lunch hour, and, if need be, are treated in segregated medical facilities. In the instances when the South Koreans do communicate with their Northern counterparts, they reportedly have trouble understanding each other, as a result of how much their languages have parted ways since the early fifties.[109] Party music, militantly singing praises to Kim Il-sung and Kim Jong-il, blares out of loudspeakers on the factory walls. In 2005, the South Korean press reported rumors that a Romeo and Juliet–style romance between a South Korean man and a North Korean woman had blossomed in the complex. But Kaesŏng's South Korean workers wrote these off as dubious, for the simple reason that the North Korean women in the complex are never alone. According to one such worker, "There are big social differences between us. There is no sense of the individual in North Korea . . . they even go to the toilet in pairs."[110]

In the case of the Kumgang Mountain complex, all foreigners were separated from the regular population not only by the site's secluded location on the mountainous east coast of the peninsula, but also by fences, barbed wire, and a phalanx of guards. Military personnel were stationed at regular intervals throughout the tour area, raising bright-red flags when tourists committed infractions such as taking unauthorized pictures or straying away from the pack. "Environment rangers" stood tense, with watchful eyes, on the lookout for breaches of tour regulations, and ready to spout official party line at the drop of a hat. Fines were handed out, too, for carrying contraband items such as cellular phones or cameras with telephoto lenses, or for taking pictures while riding on the bus.[111] Large granite rock-faces throughout the tour are engraved with North Korean slogans, such as "Long live *Suryŏng* (Great Leader) Kim Il-sung, who has sacrificed his lifetime to bring happiness to us," and "Let's devote our lives to *Suryŏng* Kim Il-sung!" These propaganda messages are said to be absolutely immense, with each individual character standing as tall as thirty feet (9 m) and as wide as twenty-six feet (8 m), carved over two feet deep (60 cm) into the rock.[112] Serious missteps, moreover, were not tolerated. One group of tourists found this out the hard way in July 2008, when North Korean guards shot a fifty-three-year-old South Korean woman in the back for inadvertently trespassing into a restricted area on the beach. (The tours were suspended after this incident.) Meanwhile, the regime annually made between $80 and $85 million off the project with no real impact on the population.[113] It is these sorts of projects that qualify as "economic reform" in the minds of Sunshine Policy advocates. When the obvious problems regarding North Korean restricted access and stifled reform are pointed out, Sunshine proponents respond with lectures about the need for patience and magnanimity on the order of decades before true change will be visible in the North. This probably coincides very well with the North's Moonshine Policy.

North Korea practiced Moonshine with China as well. Every time Kim Jong-il made a visit to China, his Chinese interlocutors urged him to visit factories and cities to see the benefits of capitalism with Communist characteristics. Over the past decade, Kim willingly visited a wide variety of facilities in China, including fiber optics, computers, telephones, laser technology, computer software, and a human genome complex. The table below lays out the number of times Kim did this in the last decade.

VISITS BY KIM JONG-IL TO CHINA, 2000–2011			
DATE		FACTORIES	LOCATION TOURED
2000	5/1/00	Zhongguancun IT complex	Beijing
		Lenovo computer	
2001 (1/15-20)	1/17/01	Shanghai Hua Hong NEC Electronics Company Ltd	Shanghai
	1/18/01	Shanghai GM Motors factory (w/ Premier Zhu Rongji)	
		Paosan steel mill	
	1/17/01	Shanghai Bell Telephone Equipment Co. Ltd	
	1/19/01	Zhangjiang high-tech complex	
		Shanghai Pudung software complex	
		Human genome research center	
		Shanghai Sunqiao Modern Agriculture Development Zone	

VISITS BY KIM JONG-IL TO CHINA, 2000-2011		
DATE	FACTORIES	LOCATION TOURED
2006 (1/10-18)	1/11/06 Chang Fei Optical Fiber & Cable	Wuhan, Hubei Province
	1/11/06 Fiber Home (communication technology)	
	1/13/06 VTRON Technologies Ltd (display, information visualization)	Guangzhou, Guangdong Province
	1/14/06 Industrial and Commercial Bank of China software development center	Zhuhai, Guangdong Province
	1/14/06 Gree Electric Appliances Inc. (air-conditioning)	
	Eastcompeace Smart Card Co. Ltd	
2006 (1/10-18)	1/15/06 Huawei Technologies Co. Ltd (telecommunication equipment)	Shenzhen, Guangdong Province
	Han's Laser Technology	
2010 (5)	5/3/10 Dalian Port, Shipyard	Dalian, Liaoning Province
	5/4/10 Dalian Development Area	
	Intel factory	
2010 (8)	8/26/10 Jilin Chemical Fiber Group Co. Ltd.	Jilin, Jilin Province
	8/28/10 Agricultural exhibition	Changchun, Jilin Province
	Jilin Agricultural University	
	Changchun Li Chi Motors (FAW Group)	
	8/29/10 Harbin Engineering University	Harbin, Heilongjiang Province
	Steam turbine factory	
2011 (5/20-26)	5/20/11 Hailin Farm	Mudanjiang, Heilongjiang Province
	5/21/11 First Automotive Works Group	Changchun, Jilin Province
	Northeast Changchun Core Area Planning Construction Hall	
	5/23/11 China Resources Suguo (supermarket)	Yangzhou, Jiangsu Province
	Jeifang Automotive Company	
	Yangzhou Smart Valley (tech)	
	5/24/11 Panda Group Co. (electronics)	Nanjing, Jiangsu Province
	Supermarket	
	5/25/11 Digital China R&D Center	Beijing

With each visit to a Chinese plant, journalists and scholars proclaim a new chapter in North Korea's economic transformation. And each time they are proven wrong. Kim invariably made these trips to appease his Chinese hosts (and to receive the requisite aid packages), but had no intention of reforming. Many times, on the sidelines of Six-Party Talks, I would ask Chinese counterparts about the need to push the North to reform economically. The Chinese would look at me like I was some sort of idiot, responding, "Do you think we have not told them this before? We have told them many, many times!" I asked if they referred the North to China's own experiences as a template to be emulated. Again, I was looked at like some sort of Martian, with the response that the Chinese have always lectured the North about the comparison. The North Korean response was: (1) "Don't lecture us"; and (2) "North Korea is not China." I then asked, what about a comparison to Vietnam? But the North Korean answer, the Chinese said, was the same (but with a twist): (1) "Don't lecture us"; (2) "North Korea is not Vietnam"; and (3) "We still face a threat from the American imperialists, which Vietnam does not, because it defeated the United States in a war." (!) Arguably, North Korea's Moonshine Policy has been more successful than South Korea or China's Sunshine Policy.

In the end, the source of North Korea's five bad economic decisions and the impediments to reform are the same. These are flaws of the political leadership, not of economic expertise. Only when the regime prizes wealth and growth more than its vice-like grip on power will true economic reform come to the North.

NEOJUCHE REVIVALISM

North Korea is in the midst of making a sixth bad decision. Like its past, the economic future of North Korea will be dictated by political ideology rather than rational economics. As I have argued throughout this book, the post–Kim Jong-il ideology is taking a harder-line conservative turn, a hybrid of 1950s–1960s *juche* self-reliance messages and 1990s *sŏn'gun* (military first) capabilities as a nuclear weapons state. This *neojuche* revivalism characterizes the economic reforms of the mid-1990s to mid-2000s as a temporary straying from the core ideology. The reforms failed not because of government incompetence but because they represented spiritual pollution rather than innovation; a recipe for disaster rather than an antidote for recovery. Economically, this means that Pyongyang is returning to the megaprojects of the 1980s and a rejuvenation of the Ch'ŏllima spirit. We have seen large projects like the February 8 Vinylon Complex in South Hamgyŏng Province (not to be confused with the Sunch'ŏn Vinylon Complex mentioned earlier), the Ryongsong Machine Complex, and the Hŭngnam Fertilizer Complex being refurbished in the past two years. These large endeavors require large amounts of resources and will last as long as the Chinese continue to fund them. But, in the end, they are about political control more than they are about economics. They try to sap every bit of labor and individualism out of the population as they prepare for a new leader to command undisputed loyalty.

CHOCO PIES

One cannot help but wonder whether the small but stifled steps already taken toward reform have left an indelible mark on North Korean society. The political leadership uncorked the bottle cap of reform only slightly, for fear of losing control, but even this small release can ignite forces beyond the Kim family's iron grip.

The best example of this? Choco Pies.

Choco Pies are the popular South Korean equivalent of the American Oreo cookie or Hostess Twinkies. It is a confectionary treat manufactured since 1974 in South Korea by the Orion Company. It consists of two chocolate-covered cookies sandwiched together by a bed of marshmallow (so it's actually more like an American s'more or MoonPie). These individually wrapped, 120-calorie treats have been a non-nutritious staple of every South Korean child's diet for years, and lately Choco Pies have garnered a significant part of the local cookie markets in China, Vietnam, Uzbekistan, Japan, and Indonesia. At the Kaesŏng Industrial Complex, I noted earlier that the DPRK government did not allow the workers to be paid fully in wages directly by South Korean companies. The management, however, did compensate the workers with hot meals in the factory cafeteria and a small monthly stipend. In 2005, one of the ROK businesses operating at Kaesŏng started to reward their workers with one or two Choco Pies per day. The female laborers tasted the treat and knew they had something of value. Popularity of the Choco Pie spread and other South Korean businesses at Kaesŏng put in orders with Orion to have ten thousand boxes shipped immediately. DPRK workers, however, stopped eating them and started to hoard them for sale outside of Kaesŏng. ROK unification officials said that soon after distribution of the Choco Pies started, the factory trash-handlers could hardly find a spent wrapper. Rather than being consumed daily at Kaesŏng, many of these Choco Pies were selling on the black market for as much as $9.50 per pie. (They cost about 45 cents at your local 7-Eleven in South Korea.)[114] According to a Japanese newspaper report, nearly 2.5 million Choco Pies are traded in North Korea today. Kaesŏng workers quickly figured out that selling one of these confectionary delights could fetch one-sixth of their monthly wage.

Choco Pies tell a larger story of how even the smallest opening can encourage an entrepreneurial spirit. As stifled as the North Korean population was from experiencing the real fruits of opening and reform, the small steps taken by the regime during the period of Sunshine Policy opened their eyes to an economic life outside of the state's PDS. The thriving black markets have created entrepreneurs who are working for themselves rather than for the Dear Leader. These underground markets started to sprout up after the famine years as the people could no longer rely on the government to provide food or products. You can find them everywhere. A recent newspaper report estimated that a majority of people in North Korea admit that they rely on the black market to obtain goods because they cannot obtain them from the government distribution system. The wealthier in North Korea might sell stored food in the markets at prices higher than the government-set price. International assistance in the form of grains and rice would find its way to the black market. Farmers gained a sense of individual ownership by tending small, thirty-*p'yŏng* (about the size of a football field) private plots of land to sell their produce in the market, while they pay token attention to weed-filled collective-farm plots. Traders sell anything they can in these markets, ranging from scrap metal scavenged from an idle factory to banned South Korean DVDs smuggled in from China. Factory workers pay their foreman a bribe to be signed in as working on the state payroll (which has not paid them in months), but then they spend the day fishing squid to sell in the markets. Consumers in these markets got a sense of individual purchasing power. They had savings to buy a widget in the market. This was not a widget rationed to them, so they had to choose which one they wanted in the market and bargain for the best price. People were making economic choices that previously had not been given to them by the state.

Because of Kaesŏng, tens of thousands of North Korean women today, though not paid market wages, still have the experience of working in a modern South Korean–made factory and receiving three meals a day in a clean cafeteria. These women will not revolt against the government, but they will tell others of their experiences. Nearly 2 million ROK tourists have passed through the Kumgang tourism project, and thousands have taken tours of the Kaesŏng facility. The North Korean government collected a boatload of cash through this, but at the same time, they exposed their own workers and guides to the sight of affluent South Koreans. A German writer on Korea, Rüdiger Frank, captured best the anger that such exposure can create among North Koreans. Recalling his own experience in Germany, Frank recalled how a cash-starved East German government opened its highways to visitors from West Germany. East Germans had heard about the affluence on the other side of the Wall, but seeing it was a completely different thing. The sight of shiny new BMWs, Mercedes-Benzes, and Audis angered many East German men, who worked hard their entire lives only to drive an old Trabant. As Frank notes, the anger was not taken out on West Germans but on their own government for being so inadequate. This accumulated frustration was ultimately let out in the autumn of 1989.[115]

This anger was clearly on display in North Korea in 2009 and 2010. In November 2009, the regime proclaimed a surprise redenomination of the national currency. The public was given no forewarning. They were told that they had one week to exchange old currency notes for new ones at a ratio of 100 to 1. Moreover, citizens could exchange no more than 100,000 won. Exchanges beyond this amount would be at a rate of 1,000 to 1. Citizens were told to deposit any excess currency in the state-run banks. This measure, the first of its kind in seventeen years, was designed to crack down on private markets and to reassert state control over the economy. It wiped out in one stroke lifetime savings of households by rendering any amount beyond 100,000 won virtually valueless. For one family, what was once a lifetime of savings of $1,560 tucked under the mattress was now worth $30 amid a soon-to-be-worthless pile of bills. Entrepreneurs were effectively being sought out for punishment as well, because any excess currency or working capital they deposited in banks targeted them by state authorities as involved in nonsocialist activities.

The redenomination measure created panic and anger throughout the population. The ceiling of 100,000 won meant that families could convert only enough money to buy the equivalent of a fifty-kilogram (110-lb) bag of rice. The one-week time frame created outright panic as North Koreans looked to buy foreign currency on the black market, or buy goods that might retain value with the old currency. This led to massive price increases and shortages in the markets. An interview with one family captured the desperation and despair of the moment:

> He emptied the living-room cabinet drawer that held their savings and split it with his wife and daughter, telling them, "Buy whatever you can, as fast as you can." The three bicycled furiously to Chongjin's market. "It was like a battlefield," he said. Thousands of people frantically tried to outbid one another to convert soon-to-be worthless money into something tangible. Some prices rose 10,000 percent, he said, before traders shut down, realizing that their profits soon would be worthless, too. The three said they returned home with 66 pounds [30 kg] of rice, a pig's head, and 220 pounds [100 kg] of bean curd. The construction worker's daughter had managed to purchase a small cutting board and a used pair of khaki pants. Together, he said, they spent the equivalent of $860 for items that would have cost less than $20 the day before.[116]

The government tried then to shut down the markets, set state prices on goods, and ban the use of foreign currency. But unlike other times, when the citizens responded with passiveness, this time there were widespread reports of social discontent. Some families committed suicide out of hopelessness once their savings had been wiped out by the government. Others substituted anger for despair. Graffiti criticizing Kim Jong-il appeared on the sides of buildings. People were heard loudly denigrating the government—an action that could easily get one thrown into a gulag. There were reports of attacks by people against local police who were patrolling the markets and trying to restrict hours of operation. And in Hamhŭng City, citizens were displaying unusual signs of civil disobedience by burning their old currency in the public square.

The unprecedented nature of this openly expressed anger was manifest in the government's response. Pyongyang tried increasing the ceiling on exchangeable currency per household to 150,000 won, but citizens remained angry. None would deposit excess currency in the banks as the government had directed. Popular anger was so strong that the government took the unusual step of issuing a public apology for the sacrifices the people were making for the Dear Leader. Government backtracking was evident in the offer of compensatory wages at old wage rates, which effectively resulted in a hundredfold increase in income with the new currency.[117] This then caused market chaos, as confidence in the new currency's value also collapsed and the value of North Korean bills, old and new, was unknown. Public anger was spontaneous and unorganized, but still the government had never expected it, nor knew how to deal with it. In the end, the state resorted to tried-and-true tactics—it executed two government officials, including the Korean Workers' Party director of finance, Pak Nam-gi, in a stadium in Pyongyang to assuage discontent. They also executed an inordinately large number of citizens, reportedly as many as fifty-two in the immediate aftermath of the redenomination, while they had only sixteen public executions in all of 2010 prior to the currency redenomination measure. These presumably were intended as a deterrent from further civil unrest.[118]

The state of the North Korean economy since the 2009 currency redenomination has not gotten any better. Shortages of food and other goods are still reported. The government has no capital. Three out of four factories today are mothballed. Inflation is rampant, and a poor harvest in 2011 ensures more hardship. And no one seems to be exempt from the dire economic times, with even the military reportedly being forced to subsist on animal feed.[119] A colder-than-average winter in 2010–2011 and an outbreak of foot-and-mouth disease among North Korean livestock have significantly raised the risk of starvation among the North's people. Life expectancy (67.2) remains below figures from the late 1980s (70.2) and well short of that of the South (79.8).[120] The regime has even apparently halved the official size of Pyongyang, to reduce the number of loyal residents it needs to support.[121] Pockets of protest are said to have broken out, with average North Koreans gathering in small groups, shouting, "We can't live! Give us fire! Give us rice!"[122] The government has responded to this crisis in the very same four steps they have taken in the past. First, when the government had nothing left to ration through the public distribution system, they removed restrictions on markets to allow people to fend for their subsistence through this mechanism. Second, to meet food shortages, they do not contemplate long-term reform or sustained means to purchase food, but seek handouts from the international community to tide them over until the next harvest. This year, Pyongyang already made requests of E.U. countries and the WFP to resume food shipments. The DPRK representative at the United Nations also asked the United States to resume food shipments that Pyongyang unilaterally suspended in March 2009. Third, they seek out the lowest-hanging fruit among international benefactors. Thus, Pyongyang has also recently demonstrated interest in restarting the inter-Korean projects that have the potential to once again funnel large amounts of cash to the regime. Finally, they rely on their trusty ally in Beijing. They continue to ask the Chinese for help, and in return for this help, Kim Jong-il and his son continued to pay token visits to high-tech factories.

The eternal optimists will confirm with these measures their proclamations that the North is cycling out of its belligerent phase of 2010 with the *Cheonan* sinking and Yeonpyeong Island artillery attacks, and is returning to engagement in 2011 and 2012. These foolhardy people will once again point to the government's tolerance of market mechanisms as a sign it is contemplating fundamental reform. They will make the leap from the regime's expedient actions to full-throated declarations that the heir, Kim Jong-un, is rejecting a harder-line ideological direction in favor of an enlightened reform path.

In truth, however, the economic policies of the post–Kim Jong-il era will be held prisoner to ideology and to the regime's obsession with not losing control. The government's leniency on market restrictions will last as long as the government cannot support the PDS. But once it can, it will reimpose control and stifle as much free enterprise as possible. After a period of international food assistance helps to replenish stocks, Pyong-yang will once again reinstate onerous restrictions on access and moni-toring and will eventually eject humanitarian aid workers on charges of "spying." And the North will continue to pursue Moonshine projects with the ROK as a way to secure large sums of cash, and will react with threats if Seoul tries to propose any conditions regarding transparency or reciprocity. Dr. Pak Hyŏng-jung of South Korea's Korea Institute of Na-tional Unification (KINU) is one of the most astute observers of North Korea's internal machinations. He argues that the leadership, ironically, felt very comfortable with its position in the year between North Ko-rea's first nuclear test (October 2006) and the summit with ROK presi-dent Roh Moo-hyun in October 2007. Why? Because their nuclear test succeeded in pressing the Roh government to engage with Pyongyang as a means of pacifying the threat, ultimately leading to the summit in 2007, which promised many benefits to the North. Moreover, Pak argues, once they received these Moonshine benefits, the government had the sustenance that enabled it to reimpose market restrictions: "With having acquired the prospect of receiving increased economic assistance from the South at the second summit in October 2007, [the] North Korean regime felt safe to intensify anti-reformist policy, which would be sure to deteriorate the sterility of the economy. The regime significantly raised the level of market crackdown from October 2007 . . ."[123]

The only variable that changes in this sad economic algorithm is the North Korean people. With each expedient nod to the market by the cash-strapped economy, the regime is unwittingly exposing mothers, fa-thers, sons, daughters, aunts, and uncles to capitalism, to the generosity of outsiders, and to the flaws of its own economic policies. The change is microscopic but it is real, so that the next time the government tries its old ways of reasserting control over the economy and wiping out the people's savings, there will be a different response. In 2011, North Ko-reans banned all news of the public demonstrations in Egypt and Libya that toppled dictatorships in these countries. They banned all public gatherings, and put tanks in the main square as a warning for a reason: they sense popular dissatisfaction as a result of the last two decades of economic mismanagement. And the regime's ideology of *neojuche* con-servatism, which accompanies Kim Jong-un's rise to power, offers no economic solution. It promises only more bad economic decisions. North Korean people are too oppressed to revolt the way we saw in the Middle East. They have no weapons and have no capacity to organize against the state. They have been taught to praise Kim Jong-il and Kim Jong-un, to hate the Americans, Japanese, and South Koreans, and to be distrustful of the Chinese. But if there is one issue that animates their hatred and anger against the omnipotent state, it is economics. It is not human rights abuses, or their international isolation because of nuclear weapons, or the corrupt bureaucracy that cause average citizens to set fires in the streets or yell at local police. Anger mounts when the government allows the people to fend for themselves, they succeed in some small fashion, and then the state tries to reassert control by taking this away.

THE FATHER OF Sunshine Policy, the late Nobel laureate and ROK president Kim Dae-jung, was right that the world's economic engagement could plant seeds of change in the North. But Sunshine Policy advocates were wrong in their belief that this change would be gradual. Their hope was for market reform to be led by an enlightened DPRK government that over decades would take advantage of the world's proffered hands to prevail over entrenched domestic hard-liners. The North would then, through reform, close the economic gap between the North and South, thereby paving the way for a gradual integration and unification—the so-called soft landing. Sunshine Policy was not about fomenting revolution. Yet the agent of change that we all point to rising from the ashes of the North Korean economy is the people. Precisely because of the economic failures of the past decades, they have been forced, out of the need for survival, to view the world differently, to think for themselves rather than for the state. It is hard to imagine enlightenment out of utter poverty, but that is what is happening slowly in North Korea. And when this anger erupts, it will be violent and bloody.

CHAPTER FIVE

THE WORST PLACE ON EARTH

MEANDERING THROUGH THE STREETS OF PYONGYANG, ONE CANNOT HELP BUT BE IMpressed by its wide thoroughfares and massive structures. The capital city of North Korea is a carefully manicured and organized piece of urban planning. Like most Communist cities, it is built to impress with large plazas, iconic architecture, and scenic vistas. There is no litter on the streets and no graffiti. There are no homeless as you might find in any major city in the West. The air is clean. There are no traffic jams. One afternoon, as I was being driven back to my guesthouse from the foreign ministry, I watched children walking home from school, like kids everywhere. Their uniforms were a little disheveled after a day's use, and they were laughing and joking happily as they chased each other down the sidewalk. Office workers were smoking cigarettes as they waited for the bus. Women, not dressed extravagantly but also not dressed poorly, were strolling home with shopping bags full of purchases made at the local store. Passing the main entrance to Kim Il-sung University, I was reminded of the university where I teach. Not in the sense that Kim Il-sung University is surrounded by multimillion-dollar Georgetown townhouses, but in the sense that one saw college-age students who looked carefree, full of enthusiasm, and welcoming of life's opportunities. Every student had a clean-cut and well-kept appearance (no grunge look in Pyongyang!).

SOCIALIST PARADISE

Looking at life in Pyongyang, one hardly gets the impression often given in the Western press that this is a country on the verge of mass starvation and collapse. There is no sign of conspicuous wealth, but also no sign of poverty. On the contrary, it looks like a modest but well-functioning population that seems quite content living its everyday lives. I thought to myself, "I guess this is their Socialist paradise." Some who have traveled to North Korea point to this scene that I have described to discount all of the claims of human rights abuses in North Korea. They argue that people are well taken care of. They argue that those who want to try the North Korean leader in the International Criminal Court (ICC) for his treatment of his people are ideological neocons looking to undermine the regime. They argue that the government is fulfilling its end of the social contract, and while there is no democracy, there is "good governance." Some further argue that a Western definition of human rights is not everyone's. The U.S. version of human rights, defined as individual liberty, is not what North Koreans value. Instead, it is freedom from external predation and foreign intervention that is a paramount "human right." On this score, the regime has done well by its people.

This type of cultural-relativist argument may work for high-minded scholars, but not for most others. The average commonsense person does not demand that every country share the U.S.'s democratic values, but does expect society to allow those who excel to do well, those who need help to receive it, and all to be treated with human dignity. North Korea meets none of these criteria. It is a system that denies its citizens every political, civil, and religious liberty. It severely punishes with physical and mental abuse any perceived violation of laws, without any juridical fairness. And it allows its citizens to starve while the governing elite lives in relative splendor. One would never get this impression in Pyongyang, because Pyongyang city-dwellers are by far the most privileged. Indeed, one cannot live in the capital city without some connection to the party, military, or bureaucracy. Part of this status is determined by family lineage, which means that if your family has party ties, you could do well. It also means that on any day, someone could knock on your door and take you to jail because a distant relative two generations prior was discovered to be a Japanese collaborator. Life looks normal at first glance, but if one stares only a few seconds longer, the cracks become evident. North Korea would like you to believe that their people enjoy all of the creature comforts of modern society. For example, in October 2010, CNN broadcast from Pyongyang a story about how cell phones were prevalent in the North. Second-unit shots showed young, smiling citizens chatting happily away on their cell phones on a street corner. Sure, these phones may be prevalent among the elite and party loyal, but these are not available for purchase by any North Korean citizen (unlike in the South, where smart phones are ubiquitously seen in the hands of grade-schoolers to grandmas); moreover, the service area is limited to local calls only. Instead, most "elite" citizens in Pyongyang use public telephone booths, which became clear to me one afternoon when I saw on several streets scores of people lined up behind orange bubble-like structures. I soon realized that these were city-dwellers lining up to make their one phone call of the day. Visitors to North Korea are sometimes invited to attend Sunday services at a Christian church, which leads them to believe that there is a degree of freedom of religion in the country, while their guides dutifully explain that it is promised in the North Korean constitution. But the reality is that there are three government-controlled churches (two Protestant, one Catholic) in the country for foreigners. The government bans any other form of organized worship as counterrevolutionary and grounds for charges of treason against the state. Buddhism, widespread in Asia, is accepted in the North, within limits, as a philosophy, but not as a religion. The existence of deep underground Christian movements in the North is a telling sign of the absence whatsoever of any freedom to worship anything but Kim Il-sung.

The neat, orderly streets seen by visitors to Pyongyang are that way because there is no traffic. A car is another indicator of privilege and status. Tourists who return from Pyongyang claim that they saw BMWs, Lexuses, and Mercedes-Benzes in the streets, so they conclude the country is doing fine. These cars, of course, don't belong to average citizens but serve to chauffeur VIPs and dignitaries. As I was driven around in a sedan, I did not see anything but an occasional VIP car or military vehicles. I finally noticed one old beat-up four-door compact. It was orange, rusted, and with no windows. I was told the car was a "taxi." Official sedans whiz by, which may carry dignitaries or Chinese businessmen, but you don't see average North Korean moms driving their kids to soccer practice or salarymen commuting to work. On the contrary, everyone walks or rides ancient and dangerously overcrowded 1960s vintage

Check Out Receipt

Saline District Library
734-429-5450
http://salinelibrary.org

Monday, August 7, 2017 7:17:46 PM

Title: The impossible state : North Korea, past
and future
Call no.: 951.93   Cha
Due: 09/05/2017

Total items: 1

****

You can now pay your library fines
online at http://salinelibrary.org

buses. There is also a subway system, which doubles as an underground network of tunnels and bomb shelters. The only times that my car had to stop due to traffic was in the late afternoons, when hundreds of students, still dressed in school uniforms, were marching down the main thoroughfare. Kids who had been playfully walking home from school the previous hour were now expressionless, walking in unison behind a lead sign board that designated their work unit. In school, 33 percent of the curriculum is devoted to the personality cult of Kim. (Typical course titles are the "History of Revolutionary Activities," "Poetry of Kim Jong-il.") Children are taught that Kim gave them their clothes, toys, and books, and to love Kim more than they love their parents. They are taught that they can live without their parents but they cannot live without love for and undying loyalty to Kim Il-sung.

Outside of the capital city, the situation deteriorates rapidly. Kaesŏng, the second-largest city, is most well known in the West for the gleaming new joint industrial complex built by the South Koreans. But outside of this structure, the city is in dire straits. Apartment dwellings not only have no heat, they have no windows. Outside the city, farmers use old and diseased oxen to till the land; there is no mechanization visible. The paved roads, despite their infrequent use, are cracked and potholed to the point that they would even make riding a bicycle difficult. The mountains surrounding the area are brown and gray, having long been stripped of all of their trees. Children in grubby clothes can be seen running barefoot among herds of skinny goats. Large, military-green Korean War–era ambulances lumber along, over the bumpy roads. The area hosted bus tours from South Korea from late 2007 to late 2008, and tourists reportedly found it reminiscent of the South in the 1960s.[1] Most interesting to me was that no one seemed to be in a hurry. Observed by one Italian chef, who once was asked to make pizzas for the Kim family: "[Y]ou caught sight of people squatting on their heels, their legs folded under them as if doing knee bends. They appeared to be waiting around for something— though it was impossible to tell what this might be, or how long they have been waiting for it, or how long they intended to go on waiting."[2] Asian cities are known for being fast-paced: people rushing to meetings; friends late for a date; car horns honking. None of that exists in North Korea. There is far less to life in this dark kingdom than meets the eye.

Absolute poverty rates in North Korea are over 30 percent of the population. The health-care system, which is said to provide universal coverage, is broken beyond repair. The system services the elite, military, and party members, but no one else. In 2006, the World Health Organization estimated the North Korea government has one of the lowest expenditures on health care in the world, at approximately $1 per person. Medical facilities have power shortages and lack basic supplies. There is no clean water supply and no sterile environments. Hospitals are forced to reuse hypodermic needles. Surgeries are performed without anesthesia. Doctors have long been cut off from payments by the state and therefore barter cigarettes, food, and alcohol from patients for medical treatment. No medicines are available and only the well-heeled can afford to buy medicine on the black market and bring it to the hospital for administering. Tuberculosis, cholera, malaria, typhoid fever, and dengue fever are among the diseases still prevalent in the North.[3] This is not a model of "good governance" that absolves the state from charges of human rights abuse.

THE WORST PLACE ON EARTH

The only reason that we cannot claim that North Korea is the worst human rights disaster in the world today is because we are not allowed to see the extent of it. The victims are faceless and nameless, whether they are forced to study Kim Il-sungisms, banished to live in gulags, or tortured and executed for trying to escape the country. No one has a claim to be treated fairly and equally with rights that inhere in one's dignity as a human being. On the contrary, individualism in North Korea is taught by the state to be a normatively bad trait, because the rights and duties of the citizen are based on the collective. The country maintains the tightest grip on its internal workings, so that the world can never find an individual around whom to organize a cause. Human rights groups, for example, do not have an Aung San Suu Kyi, as in Burma, or a Kim Dae-jung, as in South Korea, that could act as a nameplate for human rights abuses. Without names or faces, the North Korean human rights abuses become an abstract policy problem.

President Bush tried to humanize the issue. On April 28, 2006, he hosted a six-year-old girl named Kim Han-mi in the Oval Office. She is the daughter of a young family that tried to escape from North Korea when the mother was five months pregnant with Han-mi. The family hid in China, where Han-mi was born, and then tried to defect by entering the Japanese consulate in the northeastern Chinese city of Shenyang. Their attempted defection was captured for the world to see as two Chinese guards tackled the mother as she tried to make it through the consulate gates onto foreign diplomatic territory. Pigtailed Han-mi, then four years old, stood at the entrance to the consulate, crying as she watched her mother beaten by the guards. In the pre-brief before the Oval Office meeting, the president stared at the picture that captured this horrific but heroic moment. We explained to him that the girl was now six years old and that she did not speak any English, and that the family may be a little bit in awe of the moment, coming only a few years from the life as defectors to a visit to the White House. (Thanks to the help of human rights advocate Suzanne Scholte, the family made the trip to Washington on very short notice.) President Bush stared pensively at the picture, said nothing, and walked over to the door through which guests enter the Oval Office. The door flung open and Han-mi, sporting a pink dress and pigtails, was the first to enter the room. President Bush flashed a big smile and then swooped up Han-mi in his arms as though she were his own granddaughter. Any nervousness in the room melted away at that moment. With the girl in one arm, he motioned with the other, inviting the parents to sit down and tell the story of how they left the North and made a new life in the South. Han-mi, clearly excited and giggly, sat next to the president in the chair normally reserved for visiting heads of state, and swung her legs as she showed the president a card she made in anticipation of her meeting with him. Like a grandfather, the president stopped his conversation in midstream, pulled out his reading glasses, and then studied the pictures together with Han-mi, complimenting her artistry. When the father finished telling his story of escape from the North, the president asked him what he was doing now. Han-mi's father responded that he was living in Korea. The president stated that he knew that, but wanted to know what he was doing for a living now. The father apologized for misunderstanding the question and responded, "Oh, I sell cars for Kia Motors," which the president found wonderful. He then looked at Han-mi's mother and expressed genuine admiration for her strength and courage to find a better life for their child.

The entire meeting was extraordinary, and one could not help but wonder what was going through the family's minds. When the press came into the room, President Bush made clear what was on his mind:

> *I have just had one of the most moving meetings since I've been the president here in the Oval Office. . . . I talked to a family, a young North Korean family that escaped the clutches of tyranny in order to live in freedom. This young couple was about to have a child, and the mom was five months pregnant when they crossed the river to get into China. They wandered in China, wondering whether or not their child could grow up and have a decent life. They were deeply concerned about the future of their child. Any mother and father would be concerned about their child. . . . The world requires courage to confront people who do not respect human rights, and it has been my honor to welcome into the Oval Office people of enormous courage. . . . We're proud you're here. I assure you that the United States of America strongly respects human rights. We strongly will work for freedom, so that the people of North Korea can raise their children in a world that's free and hopeful . . .*[4]

On a separate occasion, in June 2005, the president hosted North Korean defector Kang Ch'ŏl-hwan. Kang and his family lived a fairly normal and comfortable life in Pyongyang. During the Japanese occupation, Kang's family was among the thousands that colonial authorities forced into labor conscription programs in Japan. Kang's grandfather occupied an important position as a community leader of the ethnic Korean minority living in Japan and, after the end of the war, returned to Pyongyang to settle. One night, guards burst into his house and took him and his family to a political concentration camp on alleged charges against his grandfather pertaining to treasonous activities as a collaborator with the colonial Japanese. In the blink of an eye, the life of this ten-year-old boy was turned upside down. The only belonging he managed to take with him was his fishbowl. He would spend the next ten years of his life in the camp. He was released in 1987 and then defected in 1992 to China, and then South Korea. He wrote of his experiences in a book titled *Aquariums of Pyongyang: Ten Years in a North Korean Gulag* (2001). Though I had used the book to teach my classes at Georgetown, it was a relatively obscure work, and I never anticipated that the president would read it, until it was recommended to him by Henry Kissinger. (Bush was a voracious reader, contrary to what many may think; studious staff could not keep up with his reading list.) The president became deeply interested in Kang's story. He knew it so well that he corrected a fact I had flubbed about Kang's family in a briefing paper. He asked to meet the author. This was the first meeting between a sitting American president and a North Korean defector. It was a private gathering (i.e., not on the official schedule), and we only released a picture to the press, but several accounts of the event have since become available. During the forty-minute visit, the president asked Kang to describe his life imprisoned in a North Korean gulag.[5] Kang, who now lives in South Korea and works as a journalist for the major daily newspaper *Chosun Ilbo,* recounted how even at the age of ten, he was forced to do hard labor. Bush said that the world did not pay enough attention to human rights abuses in the North and that it broke his heart to hear stories of pregnant women and children starving in the country while the military lived in relative splendor. He asked Kang what he thought would be said in North Korea if they knew that he was meeting with the U.S. president, to which Kang responded, "The people in the concentration camps would applaud." The president then asked Kang to autograph his copy of *Aquariums,* which he still considers to be one of the most important books he read during his presidency.[6]

Han-mi's family, Kang Ch'ŏl-hwan, and other victims of North Korean human rights abuses said afterward that never in their wildest dreams did they ever imagine a journey from the worst place on earth to the White House. They said that only a country like the United States would care about what was happening to the people of North Korea. As I escorted Kang to his meeting, we entered the White House compound through the front entrance to the West Wing. It was an overcast and rainy day, and he paused at the front as the Marine guard opened the door. He glanced at the entrance and naively asked if this was really the White House. I explained that this was the West Wing, where the president worked, and that there was the larger main residence of the White

House. He took all of this in with some awe, and said under his breath, "There truly is a God."

President Bush's meetings with North Korean defectors were part of a larger effort to reach out to human rights advocates around the world. But in the case of North Korea, these meetings had the effect of attaching names, faces, and inspirational stories to the North Korean human rights issue. The president was never under the impression that a couple of meetings with defectors would somehow magically solve the problems in North Korea. But he used the tallest soapbox in the world to draw global attention to the issue, as well as to humanize it. This was especially important to do with a country like the North, which through opacity tried to dehumanize the issue and make it abstract, distant, and a lower priority than their nuclear weapons programs. The North tried to create a dynamic in which the United States and other members of the Six-Party Talks would be deterred from pressing Pyongyang on human rights because Washington would not want these issues to stand in the way of ongoing nuclear negotiations. But President Bush, to his credit, would not accept such arguments. He was moved by the defector accounts, and in meetings with other world leaders would talk about them, raising the world's consciousness about the problem.

GULAGS

Life in the political prison camp is worse than death . . . You cannot imagine how harsh the living conditions are. They eat rats, grasses. Their living conditions are indescribable.

—MR. YI K, FORMER PRISON GUARD[7]

When North Korea collapses, the gulags will be revealed as one of the worst human rights disasters in modern history. Hundreds of thousands of nameless and faceless men, women, and children waste away in the camps. Many have been thrown into the gulags with very little forewarning and without a trial. "Crimes" amounted to no worse than sitting on a picture of Kim Jong-il. Another crime punishable by hard labor was allowing a portrait of the Great Leader to collect dust. Other punishable crimes were humming a South Korean pop song and com-plaining about the lack of merchandise in the state-run department store. And yet another, punishable by six months in a gulag, was watch-ing a Hong Kong action film on VHS.[8] These hardly constitute crimes severe enough to warrant banishment anywhere else in the world. As in any society, there is socially deviant behavior in North Korea that requires law enforcement. But many of these illegal acts are "survival crimes"—a mother pilfering rice from a rations warehouse to feed her starving children, a farmer underreporting production quotas, or a fa-ther stealing medicine from a hospital for his sick family.

There are today about five main gulags in North Korea. (There used to be as many as fourteen, but they were consolidated to five in the late 1990s.) Each encampment holds between five thousand and fifty thou-sand prisoners, depending on its size and scale, the largest of which is estimated to be thirty-one miles long (50 km) and twenty-five miles wide (40 km).[9] All but one of these camps are administered by North Korea's National Security Agency (NSA), the intelligence organization tasked with monitoring of domestic activity, border control and im-migration, and international intelligence gathering. Individuals who find themselves in the camps are subject to arbitrary arrest and impris-onment, without trail or any sort of judicial process. They are simply picked up by authorities and brought to the camps, facing torture until they confess to whatever "crime" their captors have accused them of, often regardless of whether or not they even committed it. The camps themselves are surrounded by four-meter-high walls (13 feet), which are topped with barbed and razor wire, or electrical fencing. Intermittent guard towers are staffed by heavily armed guards with orders to shoot-to-kill if anyone tries to escape. Some of the camps are divided into a number of zones, depending on one's sentence. There are "revolutioniz-ing zones," where individuals are all serving shorter-than-life sentences and therefore are subject to intensive reeducation in revolutionary doc-trine and the thought and scholarship of Kim Il-sung. Then there are the "total control zones," in which individuals are sentenced to life im-prisonment, and are simply kept well-controlled rather than being "re-educated." These individuals will never breathe the air of freedom (to the extent that that is possible in North Korea), until perhaps they are on the very verge of death, and then the authorities will release them to go off and die elsewhere.

The camps originated after World War II as prisons to hold enemies of the state who were landholders, collaborators, religious leaders, and family members of disloyal Koreans (i.e., those with family members in the South). With the outbreak of the Korean War, the camps were expanded to include those who were seen as collaborators with U.S. and U.N. forces. Anyone seen as a potential political threat to the Kim family was thrown into the camps, whether they were from the party, military, or bureaucracy. Koreans returning from Japan (like Kang Ch'ŏl-hwan's family) ended up here as well. Students who studied abroad or diplomats who were seen as "polluted" by outside ideas were also fair game. While the camps have existed as long as the current regime in Pyongyang, they took on a new significance in the regime's repression strategy during the early post–Cold War and famine years. With the loss of its Soviet patron, the decomposition of its economy, and the rapid decline of its food distribution, the North Korean leadership found itself facing theretofore unseen infractions of its systematic, dictatorial control. Unauthorized migration, black market activity, quiet murmurings of discontent, and defection into China all became far more prevalent during these years, and with them, arrests skyrocketed. Today, the prison camp system is a fundamental pillar of North Korea's repression and political control strategy; an indispensable aspect of the Kims' totalitarian rule. In total, there are about 200,000 to 300,000 individuals imprisoned today. An estimated 1 million people have died in these North Korean gulags.

The conditions in the gulags are subhuman. Perhaps the best way to convey this is to describe the average day in a North Korean gulag. Generally, inmates are woken up between four and six A.M. to begin their slave-labor. The types of work the prisoners are tasked with vary greatly, but are often hard, physical labor for men and young female prisoners, such as mining, logging, brick-making, and general construction. The work conditions on these sites are incredibly dangerous, with large numbers of work-related deaths and defectors reporting the shockingly high counts of amputees, cripples, hunchbacks, and other generally deformed prisoners as a result of their toil. The older or weaker men and women are forced to carry out light manufacturing jobs, such as sewing clothes and making belts and shoes, and they are driven no less hard than their younger, stronger counterparts. The work is ceaseless and subject to highly strict quotas, which are enforced brutally. Punishments for working too slow or not making a quota range from reductions in already-measly food rations to prolonged solitary confinement to physical abuse to torture. The work is often not interrupted by lunch (because there usually is none), but prisoners, if they are lucky, are allowed to feed on local weeds and grasses as they slave away. Usually, the only justifiable reason to provide prisoners with a break is to gather them to witness a public execution, most often for prisoners who have tried to escape. Execution methods run the gamut, but are similar to those practiced outside prison walls in North Korean society (see below), including hanging, shooting, stoning (which requires prisoner participation), and, in one particularly grotesque case, being dragged behind a moving car.[10]

Work ends at around six P.M., and the prisoners are sent back to their living quarters to prepare for the meager portions they will receive for dinner. In the North Korean state, prisoners are allocated whatever is left over after the elite, military, loyal class, and Pyongyang and other urban residents are fed, which is essentially nothing. For this reason, on top of their paltry portions of corn, spoonfuls of grain, or a few leaves of cabbage, prisoners are forced to subsist on bugs, beetles, snakes, and, on good days, rats, along with the grasses, barks, and wild foods they collect while working. Kim, a young man who spent four years in a North Korean gulag, describes the food condition:

Malnourishment made life . . . very difficult . . . We were always hungry; and resorted to eating grass in spring. Three or four people died of malnutrition. When someone died, fellow prisoners delayed reporting his death to the authorities so that they could eat his allocated breakfast.[11]

This combination of strenuous, unrelenting labor and the meager portions of food prisoners subsist on results in what North Korean human rights expert David Hawk calls "permanent situations of deliberately contrived semi-starvation."[12] Defectors attest to losing huge amounts of weight during their stays in the gulags, with one man in his twenties getting down to sixty-six pounds (30 kg) upon release.[13] New prisoners, when they first arrive, are reportedly awestruck by the emaciation, disfiguration, and discoloration of the camps' inhabitants,[14] experiencing something reminiscent of what United States and other Allied forces must have felt when they first stumbled upon Nazi concentration camps in Germany and Poland.

After dinner, prisoners are required to carry out a somewhat perverse and Orwellian ritual referred to as "self-criticism." In these sessions, the prisoners gather around and spend two or so hours confessing the wrongs they committed that day. Even if prisoners don't feel as though they committed any, they basically have to make them up to avoid being harshly punished for what would be viewed as defiance or dissent. Owning up to these transgressions, real or contrived, results in even more draconian work quotas and longer hours, often for whole work-units under a system of "collective responsibility." After self-criticism, prisoners are sent off to bed, where they sleep on the hard floor without blankets. In some cases, they are crammed into rooms with eighty or ninety other prisoners, in rooms that are just sixteen by twenty feet (5x6 m, that's three and a half square feet per prisoner!).[15] In the camps, men and women work, sleep, and generally live strictly separately, coming together only for public executions and other "important" collective activities. This is part of an effort to maintain control and prohibit sexual contact, to avoid a new generation of "counterrevolutionaries." If prisoners survive the night and manage to get some sleep, despite the frostbite they suffer for much of the year, they only get up the next morning to begin the routine once again.

The most well known of the camps is Yodŏk concentration camp. Located in South Hamgyŏng Province about seventy miles (115 km) northeast of Pyongyang, the camp sits in a valley surrounded by four mountains. It is a massive facility and is estimated to be about twenty miles (32 km) long and twenty miles wide. The perimeter is confined by a large brick wall, covered in barbed and electrical wire and surrounded by live minefields to deter escape. Watchtowers, set at one-kilometer intervals (0.6-mi), are equipped with machine guns to prevent any riots (although one was rumored to have occurred in 1974). Anti-aircraft guns ensure against external attacks. The one thousand or so guards that patrol these walls are personally equipped with grenades and fully automatic assault weapons, and are often accompanied by viciously trained guard dogs. Yodŏk alone holds over fifty thousand prisoners, who are zoned into categories as political prisoners, criminals, or descendants of either category. Because the state can imprison you for acts that were committed by your ancestors three generations earlier, no North Korean is safe. There is no judicial process that supports these imprisonments. You could be sent here without warning, and for indefinite time periods.

The camps focus on two tasks: reeducation and forced labor. Prisoners perform slave labor such as working in coal mines (often without tools or safety equipment), building roads and bridges, and producing textiles and other light manufacturing. Some items, including clothing and artificial flowers, are made in these camps for export. The factories in these camps have become a source of hard currency for the regime, so prisoners were often forced to work long hours to make production quotas. In one case, the factory was to meet an order from Japan for handknit sweaters. But once the sweaters were made, complaints ensued that the yarn had become tainted by the unsanitary conditions in the camps. Prisoners were beaten for being dirty, which, of course, was not their choice. In another case, prisoners were required to make doilies for export to Poland. Stitching intricate patterns into the white material was difficult, and prisoners were beaten for making poor-quality products and punished with reduced food rations. Those who did well would be forced to work longer hours in order to meet production quotas. In yet another case, prisoners were forced to make paper flowers for export to France. Each prisoner had a production quota of a thousand flowers per day, which averaged to about sixty flowers per hour or one per minute. If they did not meet this quota, or if they made inferior products, they would be punished.

The guards in the camps are taught to treat the prisoners as subhuman. There are incentives to prevent rioting and to kill any escapees, which sometimes leads the nastiest guards to randomly shoot prisoners in order to win the awards. Mr. An, a former prison guard, claims that "[a]s a prison guard, you couldn't treat the inmates as human beings. If you did, you'd get punished. If anyone resisted, or tried to run away, we could shoot to kill . . . It was a horrible place, where women and men are killed very cruelly. Some of the methods are too horrible to repeat."[16] Mr. An also confirmed reports that some prison guards force inmates to attempt to climb the fences, just so they can shoot them down for recreation or target practice. Mr. Lee K, another former prison guard, describes the treatment of prisoners in a gulag he worked in:

> *People in the facility were beaten every day with sticks or with fists. In the evening, they had to make time for an "ideological struggle" . . . This was an official time for the inmates to fight with each other, and the guards indirectly provoke violence. The prisoners had to endure physical punishments . . . There were many different ways of beating. Those who attempted to escape . . . [had] their hands tied behind their back and they were hung on the wall for three to seven days. They were handcuffed and guards would stomp on the handcuffs . . . I witnessed these types of atrocities quite often.*[17]

Aside from the physical abuse many prisoners suffer, female inmates in particular are subject to the pain and humiliation of sexual abuse. Chi, a fifty-four-year-old who was detained after being repatriated from China, describes her experience:

> *During pretrial detention, I was humiliated, abused. The guards—who were all men—touched my sexual organs, breasts with brooms. All the guards during the pretrial detention period were male. I was alone when I was interrogated. I was beaten for speaking up, as were others.*[18]

Some of the most horrific accounts are of North Korea's infanticidal policies in the gulags. If a woman is pregnant when she is detained, or becomes pregnant during her internment in the camps, she will be subject to forced abortion or, upon birth, her child will be summarily killed. As a result of severe malnutrition, these women often have highly irregular menstrual cycles, and it is quite common for women in North Korea's gulag system to not know of their pregnancy until quite late in their term. A female defector who was in a gulag in Ch'ŏngjin City attests to these harsh realities:

> *[I]f it is found that a woman is pregnant, they administered a medicine to abort. If the woman gave birth to a baby, they covered it with vinyl and placed it facedown and killed it. Seven women gave birth to children*

in that prison and they killed all of them. The women were in labor in the prison cell and all the female inmates assisted with the birth. On April 1, 2000, I was arrested and I witnessed seven children born during the period of May to June and they were killed.[19]

When the women are defectors who have been repatriated from China, these policies are often ethnically motivated: to prevent half-Chinese, half-Koreans from "polluting" the North Korean race. When they aren't, these women are simply told that they are carrying "the children of betrayers" in their wombs, and that this is unacceptable.[20] Ch'oe Yong-hwa, a "shy and soft-spoken" twenty-five-year-old woman from North Hamgyŏng Province, ended up in a North Korean prison camp after crossing the border in search of food during the famine. One of her duties during her incarceration was to assist a late-term pregnant female inmate. On one fateful day, she witnessed the prison staff administer a labor-inducing injection, and, upon birth, the infant was suffocated with a wet towel right in front of the mother, who fainted in horror.[21] Another defector, a sixty-six-year-old grandmother, had a similar yet even more horrific experience. Being unable to perform hard, physical labor, she was also tasked with taking care of pregnant women in the detention center in Sinŭiju in eastern North Korea. The grandmother witnessed the birth of a child to a twenty-eight-year-old mother, known as Lim. Right after the child was born, a guard grabbed it by its leg and tossed it into a plastic box nearby. Here the child, among others, was simply left to die, as was the standard practice in this particular facility. When the box filled up, it would be taken outside to be buried. A North Korean human rights report describes what the grandmother witnessed next:

Two days later, the premature babies had died but the two full-term baby boys were still alive. Even though their skin had turned yellow and their mouths blue, they still blinked their eyes. The agent came by, and seeing that two of the babies in the box were not dead yet, stabbed them with forceps at a soft spot in their skulls.[22]

As terrible as the place may be, some who go to Yodŏk can eventually gain release. Located outside of Pyongyang, Sŭnghori is another major concentration camp that has been seen in satellite photos, but because no one is known to have survived it, little information is available about it except that those considered "incorrigibles" are banished there. (Kang Ch'ŏl-hwan's grandfather was sent here.) Defectors' accounts suggest it is the most feared concentration camp in North Korea. There are other camps, less severe than Yodŏk. These qualify as prisons or labor camps, but they are distinguished by the existence of a judicial process and fixed-term sentences. But still, the conditions here are so bad that many, even if not banished for life, die from of disease or starvation.

REFOULEMENT

Refoulement is coercive expulsion of political refugees. China has been actively engaged in efforts to sweep up and forcibly repatriate North Korea refugees who enter its territory. As a signatory to the 1951 U.N. Refugee Convention and the 1967 Protocol to that convention, China is obligated to recognize a political refugee who flees his country because of fear of political persecution. The United Nations High Commissioner for Refugees (UNHCR) is the agency that ensures that once an individual is considered a refugee, they are accorded certain rights, resources, and protection. Parties to the convention, including China, have an obligation to the principle of non-*refoulement,* meaning that "No contracting State shall expel or return (*"refouler"*) a refugee in any manner whatsoever to the frontiers of territories where his life or freedom would be threatened on account of his race, religion, nationality, membership of a particular social group or political opinion."[23] China has consistently refused to recognize North Koreans as refugees, and has been forcibly repatriating them, pursuant to a 1986 bilateral agreement with Pyongyang.

The overwhelming majority of North Korean refugees exit through China. Numbers are very hard to come by, since no organization is allowed to conduct a systematic survey. The Chinese official estimate is about 10,000. But activists, press, and other governments put the number as high as 100,000 to 300,000. The DPRK, of course, does not report any migration statistics, and in a 1993 census only stated that "migrant numbers going into and coming out of our country are neglected."[24] A 2008 census made no mention of migration out of the country. The

United Nations puts the number at between 30,000 and 50,000. (The population of North Korea is about 22 million.)[25] The majority of these migrants are women—as high as 75 to 80 percent. (Male numbers may be underestimated because they are in hiding to avoid deportation from Chinese sweeps.) The majority is also classified as "distress migration"—movements across borders without official documentation out of economic deprivation and chronic food insecurity.[26] The movements of people into China started in the mid-1990s and grew steadily, peaking at the end of the decade. There were other routes through Southeast Asia (Vietnam and Thailand) and Mongolia, but only a trickle have succeeded. One famous case involved the Vietnam government turning over 480 North Korean defectors to the South, but this was a onetime event. About 20,000 North Koreans have managed to exit through China, finding permanent settlement in third countries. The overwhelming majority end up in South Korea, where the government provides resettlement assistance that is generous compared with other countries.[27] Refugees are accorded South Korean citizenship, and live at a transition facility known as *Hanawŏn* for three months of education and job training to deal with the challenges of integrating into fast-paced South Korean society.[28] According to a 2010 U.S. government report, 1,211 North Koreans have sought asylum in England, Germany, and Canada. The United States, under a new resettlement program, has taken in 96 refugees.[29] Only about 14 percent seek to settle in China, because of the fear of *refoulement*.

Most North Korean defectors come from North Hamgyŏng Province, which is one of the poorest parts of the country. They cross the porous Sino–North Korean border into Jilin Province's Yangbian autonomous prefecture, populated by 2 million ethnic Koreans.[30] Some escapees find work in Jilin, usually menial labor jobs under poor conditions, but still better than what was available in North Korea. Others, mostly women, marry Chinese farmers or laborers as a way to start a new life. There are stories of North Korean families who sell their daughters for cattle on the Chinese side in order to feed themselves as well as give their child a chance at a better life.[31] It is estimated that over ten thousand children have been born to Chinese men with North Korean women (who are not given naturalization rights). As one can imagine, this dynamic creates opportunities for human trafficking, which has become a major problem.

Women are victims of rape, forced prostitution, and bride-selling, and activists report that as high as 80 to 90 percent of North Korean escapees may be victims of some form of trafficking. (North Korea is rated as a Tier 3 country in the U.S. State Department's Trafficking in Persons Report—the lowest possible rating.) One such example is of Ms. Ryo, who was in her early twenties when she left North Korea for China in 2001. After she and her uncle crossed the Tumen River, they were abducted and separated by a group of local Korean-Chinese traffickers. Ms. Ryo eventually managed to escape her captors and made her way to a Korean church in Yanji, which was also hiding some sixty North Korean defector children. The church deacon recommended a job for Ms. Ryo, as a housekeeper and Korean teacher for the grandchildren of a local family. But when she showed up for her first day of work, she was subject to a rude awakening. The reality was that she had just been sold by the church deacon for 5,000 renminbi (approximately $600) to the family for their thirty-year-old son. Ms. Ryo describes her experience:

> *The son had a mental problem . . . He always stayed beside me and the only thing he wanted was for us to always have sex. When I became depressed, he beat me. If I was beaten, I could not walk for a week. He beat me on my face and my body and all my body was bruised black-and-blue.*[32]

After four months of such treatment, Ms. Ryo made her escape in desperation. The son was determined to keep her there, so when he went to work or to sleep, he would hide all of her clothes. But one day, after being "beaten very seriously," Ms. Ryo snuck out of the house at five A.M., "wearing only [her] underwear and house slippers." She made her way to another Korean church, this time, thankfully, to be helped on her eventual journey to South Korea.[33]

Despite international criticism, the Chinese government refuses to consider these escapees as political refugees and instead classifies them as illegal economic migrants that require deportation. Beijing is supposed to allow the UNHCR access to these migrants to determine whether they qualify for refugee status. The UNHCR established an office in China in 1995 in order to handle refugee flows from Vietnam, but the office has been denied access to evaluate North Korean cases. In practice, Beijing does not return every escapee. It is difficult to enforce the 1986 agreement with North Korea religiously. But whenever high-profile cases emerge, or the international community puts pressure on Beijing, the government argues that such acts constitute a violation of its sovereign borders and therefore they are obliged to address illegal immigration decisively. China's worst nightmare is a flood of millions of North Korean refugees that would add to unemployment problems and potentially destabilize the North. Granting them widescale refugee status could trigger this flood.

From about 2001, China started to crack down on these cases more severely. The police increased the tempo of border patrols, repatriations, and security around foreign diplomatic compounds. The latter was in response to some high-profile attempts by North Koreans to rush through gates of foreign embassies and consulates. The motive was to storm onto a third country's embassy compound, which constituted sovereign territory, in the hopes that that country would allow the UNHCR access to determine their refugee status. Chinese authorities built green chain-link fences around the perimeter of the U.S. embassy compound in Beijing to prevent defections. Barbed wire was strewn across the tops of the fences and the fences were set a few yards outside the main walls in order to ensure that North Koreans would fall between the newly built fence and the old wall if they tried to jump it. Chinese living in Yanbian are offered rewards of $500 for turning in any North Korean migrants and are fined large sums ($3,600) if they are caught aiding any refugees.[34] Periodic sweeps are conducted by police agencies to round up North Koreans (particularly young men) for deportation. As the numbers of defectors increased, China stepped up the sweeps in Jilin Province, and arrested thousands of Korean-Chinese residents of Yanbian who were involved in the refugee business, all in order to create a deterrent against increased flows. According to most studies, these efforts have been effective. The numbers of North Koreans illegally in China have declined, according to one estimate, from 75,000 in 1998 to about 10,000 in 2009.[35]

The average North Korean is not allowed to travel within the country. Leaving your village requires a special travel pass. Attempting to defect, in this regard, is a major crime that, according to the North Korean penal code, is punishable by a sentence ranging from a minimum of seven years to death, depending on the offense. Once *refouled*, these individuals are thrown into labor/interrogation prisons along the Sino–North Korean border. Generally, *refoulees* are asked three questions: (1) "Why did you leave?" (2) "Did you contact any South Koreans?" (3) "Did you go to a church?" Those who answer that they left the country only in search of food are treated marginally more leniently. (*Refoulees* also can bribe DPRK officials with their earnings in China.) But those who are found to have met South Koreans or missionaries are harshly tortured, as part of "reeducation." All women discovered to be pregnant are forced to have abortions. Pak Chŏng-il was a twenty-four-year-old male who was forcibly repatriated by the Chinese. He was sent to an underground prison in Ch'ŏngjin, where he was placed in a row of cells holding ten prisoners each. He was not allowed to talk, nor move. He was interrogated while being beaten with chains, belts, and sticks over the course of weeks. The only food he received were kernels of corn and a salty broth. He was forced to clean latrines without any implements.[36] As the numbers of forcibly repatriated North Korean men grew since the 1990s, Pyongyang started to hold them separately from the general prison population, for fear of information dissemination of what they might have seen while in China.

Another such example is of a former military radio operator from North Hamgyŏng Province. After his discharge from the military, he became a courier, transporting goods between North Korea and China. But on one unauthorized trip, he was arrested in Yanji and repatriated back to the North to face detention. He was tortured and interrogated for a number of weeks until he was sent to a hard-labor prison camp. During his interrogation he was accused of listening to South Korean radio while in military service, and of wanting to go to South Korea, neither of which was true. At the camp, he toiled away, making bricks and being deprived of the most basic levels of nutrition. He became so emaciated—or so "skin and bones," as he puts it—that before he was discharged, he was unable to climb a flight of stairs or to carry a few bricks. Because he wasn't allowed to bathe or change his clothes, he became covered in lice and sores. In the end, the authorities released him just so he wouldn't die while in their custody.[37]

These are just a fraction of the horrific human stories. The world's utter ignorance of the courage and fortitude of these individuals who attempt to escape is tragic. When the Chinese forcibly repatriate, they send the North Koreans back on buses with curtained windows, to ensure anonymity. Of the hundreds of thousands who have tried to escape, similar numbers have been tortured and killed, yet there is not a single identifiable name or face associated with the practice of *refoulement* that would be known around the world. There are more defector accounts now that reveal the extent of the horror, but their stories circulate among a small expert community and NGO advocates. These groups have organized to put pressure on the Chinese government to allow the U.N. High Commissioner for Refugees to have access to escapees to determine whether they can be classified as political asylum–seekers. Yet there is no Nelson Mandela–type figure or a story that captures the public's imagination and sense of justice.

President Bush tried to draw attention to this problem by issuing a White House statement on *refoulement* on March 30, 2006. It read as follows:

> *The United States is gravely concerned about China's treatment of Kim Chun-Hee [Ch'ŏn-hŭi]. Despite U.S., South Korean, and UNHCR attempts to raise this case with the Chinese, Ms. Kim, an asylum seeker in her thirties, was deported to North Korea after being arrested in December for seeking refuge at two Korean schools in China. We are deeply concerned about Ms. Kim's well-being. The United States notes China's obligations as a party to the U.N. Convention relating to the Status of Refugees and its 1967 Protocol, and believes that China must take those obligations seriously. We also call upon the government of China not to return North Korean asylum seekers without allowing UNHCR access to these vulnerable individuals.*

Thirty-one years old, Kim Ch'ŏn-hŭi had family members who successfully defected to South Korea. Kim was imprisoned in the North for eight months because of the "disloyalty" of her family. Her five-year-old son died during this time. After her release, she snuck into China in September 2005 and hid for two months. She then tried to enter a Korean school in Dalian, hoping to reunite with her family and win consideration as an asylum-seeker. The school would not accept her, however, and Kim was forced into hiding again, fearing her actions would almost certainly be reported to Chinese authorities, who would seek to forcibly repatriate her. She traveled in secret back to Beijing and the following month tried to defect through another Korean school. This time, Chinese authorities were ready and immediately arrested her. Kim's family in South Korea contacted politicians and NGOs, making her case known. They feared her *refoulement* would mean torture and death. U.S. embassy officials in Beijing, ROK officials in Seoul, and U.N. officials all issued démarches asking Beijing not to deport Kim to North Korea and consider her as a potential political asylum-seeker under China's obligations as a signatory to the U.N. Convention on Refugees. Chinese officials responded only that Kim's case was under review. A visit to Beijing by the U.N. High Commissioner for Refugees António Guterres March 19–23, 2006, provided an opportunity for the Chinese to release Kim, but nothing was forthcoming from Beijing. Then, on March 24, the day after Guterres left, the Chinese informed the U.S. embassy in Beijing that Kim had been deported to North Korea. Chinese handling of this high-profile case enraged South Koreans and American officials, who stated privately that Beijing basically lied to avoid any further pressure. Kim Ch'ŏn-hŭi's fate after being deported remains unknown. She has been almost certainly imprisoned and tortured for having the courage to seek a better life outside the North.

The White House statement on Kim Ch'ŏn-hŭi was the first of its kind, and yet Kim's case is typical of thousands who try to escape the North. No other country has singled out one North Korean refugee by name and sought their rescue at the highest levels of government. The statement was released only weeks before a visit by Chinese president Hu Jintao to the White House, and in his meetings with Hu, President Bush specifically raised Kim Ch'ŏn-hŭi's case. Critics argue that Bush pursued the human rights issues with North Korea as part of a regime-collapse strategy because he despised Kim Jong-il. Or that he was uninterested in negotiations with the North and therefore castigated the regime's human rights abuses as a way to submarine any potential talks. Nothing could be further from the truth. As his former adviser on Asia Mike Green described, Bush certainly had no love for the North Korean leader, but he was motivated by the sheer horror that such human rights abuses could still take place in the twenty-first century, and that no one stood up for an oppressed population that could not stand up for itself.[38] The statement on Kim Ch'ŏn-hŭi was meant to draw the world's attention to a problem by humanizing and by giving voice to one individual as a representative of the masses of unknown others.

While the people of North Korea have certainly borne the brunt of the regime's human rights abuses, these atrocities have not necessarily stopped at "water's edge." Aside from the acts of terrorism, transnational crime, and arms trafficking outlined in the previous chapters, the DPRK regime is suspected of having abducted over 180,000 citizens of foreign countries since its inception in 1948.[39] In the early years, they were mainly well-educated and trained ethnic Koreans from South Korea and Japan, who could help build the North Korean state. But as years progressed—and the North's intelligence needs for expertise in foreign language and culture increased—the scope of abductions broadened. Foreigners disappeared from places as far-flung as France, Italy, Guinea, Japan, Lebanon, Macau, Malaysia, the Netherlands, Romania, Singapore, and Thailand, only to later turn up in North Korea. Some abductees were quite literally carried off through the use of brute force. Others were lured to the North through promises of employment and a better life. And yet what they all share in common is that once they were in the "Hermit Kingdom," the *vast* majority would never set foot outside its borders again, requisitioned to a life of servitude in the name of the Dear Leader and the North Korean state.

You might wonder what sort of society would tolerate the level of inhumane treatment that is seen in North Korea. Certainly, one explanation has to do with the omnipotence of the government that makes social resistance difficult. Yet another has to do with *juche* ideology, which does not tolerate questioning of the state. But another permissive condition rests in society itself. Korea emerged out of World War II as one of the most class-stratified societies in Asia. Prior to the Japanese occupation, Chosŏn-dynasty Korea was organized around a three-tiered class system with *yangban* (scholars, government officials, landowners) at the top of the social hierarchy, followed by commoners, and finally, outcasts. This society bestowed rights upon aristocrats and outcasts in completely different ways. Outcasts were treated as subhuman and not accorded the fundamental right to human dignity. Not only was slavery an accepted practice, but hereditary slavery was common in the Korean society. Despite its classless Communist society, North Korea adopted very similar elements of this class stratification. This is known as the *"sŏngbun"* system. Started around 1946 and becoming fully established by the 1960s, *sŏngbun* has three dominant categories for society: the loyal, the wavering, and the hostile classes (with fifty-one subcategories). The loyal, or core, class consists of Korea Workers' Party members, politicians, and military elites. This class enjoys "rights" defined as preference in education, employment, housing, food, and marriage. The wavering class consists of peasant workers. The impure or hostile class consists of pro-Japanese colonial collaborators, criminals, former landowners, businessmen, and families of defectors. Every North Korean has a place in this system that is only nominally determined by one's own actions. One's place is also determined by one's ancestors. Thus, if you were a young North Korean man, who truly believes in the system and works hard, it would not really matter, because your *sŏngbun* record may show your grandfather to have been a Japanese collaborator, in which case you would be eternally banished to the hostile class. In the Chosŏn dynasty, or in North Korean society today, this three-tiered system essentially means that it was perfectly legitimate to endow those in the lower class with fewer rights than those in the privileged class. Moreover, the subhuman treatment of outcasts is not anathema but expected as just a part of the way things are. The point of this is not to say that North Korean society condones human rights abuses, but that the society created by the government promotes the idea of an underclass that legitimately can be abused. This is part of the "socialist paradise."

THE GREAT FAMINE

Small children in tattered rags, with wizened, old faces and blotchy skin pick through the mud in search of kernels of corn or seeds of grain, dropped or discarded by those who are buying and selling on the black market. Their bare feet are ashen-gray and caked in dirt from months and even years of having no shoes to wear. Their clothes are filthy, worn, and gray from years of wear-and-tear without having been washed. The contours of their skulls can be seen through their thinning, patchy, discolored hair, a result of chronic protein deficiency and malnutrition. As they stumble about, their infected eyes appear sunken, deep in their sockets, and their cheekbones jut out from their wasted faces in a shocking, almost violent manner. Many have protruding bellies—which, disturbingly, resemble their Dear Leader's, though theirs are not from an overfeeding of cognac and fine European cheeses but from the edema they suffer, a result of organ failure. These are the *kkot chebi* ("flower swallows") of North Korea, the orphaned or abandoned, wandering, homeless children that began to appear in the thousands as the famine emerged in the early nineties.[40] To them, Kim Il-sung's modest, 1960s promise that all North Koreans would "wear silk clothes, eat white rice with meat soup every day, and live in well-heated tile-roofed homes" is, indeed, distant.

A U.S. NGO team went to North Korea in February 2011 to assess food needs in provinces outside of the main city of Pyongyang. They found seven-year-old boys who weighed only seven kilograms (15 lb). They found that 60 percent of the population in these provinces rely on "alternative food"—the grinding up of tree bark and grass in cornmeal to supplement a fifteen-hundred calories daily intake, which is lower than the U.N.-recommended minimal intake. Many suffered from digestive problems because of these alternative foodstuffs. The NGO team interviewed individuals and asked them when was the last time that they had a piece of protein in their diet, defined as a piece of meat, fish, beans, or such. It was telling that many of these individuals knew to the day when they did. One said he had a piece of meat six months earlier—on his birthday. Another said he had one egg a month earlier to celebrate the New Year.[41]

If you had to choose one key driver for the outflow of North Koreans, it would have to be the food situation. North Koreans started to cross into China from the mid-1990s when the government ration system for distributing food to citizens started to experience shortages. Defector interviews show that only 9 percent of North Korean refugees cite political reasons for leaving the country, while 55 percent say they left for lack of sustenance.[42] The great famine that swept across North Korea from 1995 to about 1998 wrought upon the country a degree of havoc and destruction never before seen by its people. Though the numbers are a matter of dispute, the most rigorous estimates put excess mortality as a direct result of the food crisis at between 600,000 and 1,000,000; 3 to 5 percent of the total North Korean population.[43] Shortages of food are among the most tragic of humanitarian crises, forcing the most devastating of situations upon its sufferers. Having to decide how to allocate food within a family, abandoning one's own children, selling one's body for a meal or two, taking one's own life, and watching loved ones slowly waste away to the ravages of hunger and disease are all experiences that were widely felt by the North Korean population during the famine. It unleashed the type of hunger and deprivation that turns brother against brother, even mother against child.

For as long as human rights have existed, the "right to food" has been an inseparable part of the concept. Article 25 of the 1948 United Nations Universal Declaration of Human Rights states that all have the "right to a standard of living adequate for the health and well-being of himself and of his family, including food, clothing, housing and medical care."[44] Article 11 of the International Covenant on Economic, Social, and Cultural Rights (ICESR), to which North Korea acceded in 1981, states that "States Parties to the present Covenant recognize the right of everyone to an adequate standard of living for himself and his family, including adequate food, clothing, and housing," and recognizes "the fundamental right of everyone to be free from hunger."[45] At the 1996 World Food Summit in the midst of the famine, representatives from 185 countries, including the DPRK, reaffirmed the "right of everyone to have access to safe and nutritious food, consistent with the right to adequate food and the fundamental right of everyone to be free of hunger."[46] And so, when a state proves unwilling, or even unable to guarantee basic nutritional sustenance for the entirety of its population, it commits a grave violation of human rights, as North Korea has done for so many years. The right to food is not merely a tangential humanitarian concern, but is itself a fundamental human right.

It must be stated that a centrally controlled, socialist, totalitarian state suffering a food crisis of this magnitude is certainly no anomaly. Political economist Nick Eberstadt even goes as far as to say that "episodic but severe food shortages are, in fact, a characteristic and arguably predictable consequence of the twentieth-century Marxist-Leninist state's approach to economic management and economic development."[47] The Soviet Union suffered tremendous mortality as a result of famine in 1921–1922 (9 million dead) and in 1946–1947 (2 million). The then-Soviet-controlled Ukraine suffered a famine of its own in 1932–1934, leading to the deaths of over 7 million Ukrainians. The Great Leap Forward in the People's Republic of China from 1958 to 1961 resulted in an astounding 33 million dead. Cambodia under the Khmer Rouge suffered a famine from 1977 to 1979, leading to the deaths of as many as 2 million Cambodian men, women, and children. During the leadership of the Communist military junta known as the Derg, in Ethiopia, the population suffered famine from 1983 to 1985, leading to as many as 1 million deaths.[48] And Communist-controlled Mongolia and North Vietnam also experienced serious food shortages during the first ten years of their rule.[49] These horrific events add credence to Nobel Prize–winning economist Amartya Sen's famous claim that "no famine has ever taken place in the history of the world in a functioning democracy."[50]

It is also important to recognize the qualitative difference between the famine in North Korea and past famines in places such as Somalia. Somalia suffered famine for a period from 1991 to 1993, leading to the deaths of as many as half a million of its people. This famine was a result of a combination of drought, conflict, and a central government in the capital Mogadishu, which literally controlled only a few city blocks. One can certainly hold the Somali government liable for its lack of capacity, yet in North Korea, the leadership had much higher levels of state capacity and managed to strictly control the bulk of its population. And the regime was certainly aware of the crisis early on, as indicated by Kim Jong-il's 1996 statement that "the most urgent issue to be solved at present is the grain problem . . . the food problem is creating a state of anarchy."[51] Beyond that, rather than simply having its hands tied by its incompetence, the regime in Pyongyang continued to spend vast sums of money on luxury goods, sophisticated defense technology, and allocated food rations away from North Korean civilians to its military personnel.

Throughout the early 1990s, as the famine was heating up, North Korea is estimated to have spent 25 percent of its GDP on its military budget.[52] And in 1999, as the country was receiving massive amounts of food aid at the tail end of the famine's devastation, the government purchased forty MiG-21 fighter aircraft and eight military helicopters from Kazakhstan.[53] Further, once food aid started flowing in, in 1996, the regime began to simultaneously reduce its commercial food imports, essentially using the aid as a substitute rather than a supplement, and perpetuating the famine in the process.[54]

THE CAUSES

The causes of the North Korean famine are many, but they centrally revolve around misguided government policy in Pyongyang. Although North Korea had periodic food shortages in the mid-1940s, 1950s, and early 1970s, the real problems began with the collapse of the Soviet Union at the end of the Cold War. Beginning in 1987, with their own economy in disarray, the Soviets began to cut all forms of aid, trade, and investment in the DPRK, causing a tectonic shift in the North's international economic position. By 1993, imports from Russia were a mere 10 percent of the levels from 1987 to 1990,[55] and would eventually peter out to insignificance. The steep decline in the fuel, fertilizer, and pesticide/herbicide imports upon which North Korea so critically depended had immediate and adverse impacts on the state's ability to maintain sufficient levels of agricultural production. What followed was the gradual decomposition of the state-run public distribution system, and with it, disaster.

The public distribution system was the sole means of obtaining food for 60 to 70 percent of the North Korean population since the early 1950s.[56] The PDS aggregated harvested crops from collective farms, distributed food among the urban population, and allocated volumes based on a complex and multilayered system of entitlements. North Korean economics experts Stephan Haggard and Marcus Noland point out that the most recent forms of classification in the DPRK consist of fifty-one distinct categories of person, each with its own certain right to entitlements based on age, occupation, family background, regime loyalty, and the like.[57] Nutritional experts generally believe that an adult needs, at the very least, about five hundred grams (1.1 pounds) of food per day to maintain a normal level of health. In theory, North Korean Special Forces and heavy laborers are entitled to eight hundred grams (1.76 pounds) of food per day, but the members of Special Forces get a 7:3 rice-to-corn ratio, whereas the laborers only get 6:4. On the other end of the scale are preschool students and the aged and disabled, who are entitled to three hundred grams (0.66 pounds) of food daily.[58] The South Korean Ministry of Unification estimates that the prisoners in North Korea's gulags receive, on average, the ration of a child between two and four years old, a mere two hundred grams (0.44 pounds).[59] All of these entitlements are subject to modification, depending on whether one is considered a member of the "core," "wavering," or "hostile" class, which itself is determined by one's family background and perceived allegiance to the regime. The North Korean leadership has and continues to use the allocation of food and access to health care and educational opportunities to confer benefits for loyalty or to punish dissent, making it a decisive tool of political control for the political elites in Pyongyang.

The PDS started to show mild signs of breakdown fairly early on. In the 1960s, for instance, white-collar workers were supposedly entitled to and received 700 grams (1.54 pounds) of food per day through the system. But this number had, in actuality, gradually decreased to 608 grams (1.34 pounds) by 1973 and to 547 grams (1.2 pounds) by 1987.[60] In 1992, the government initiated a "Let's Eat Two Meals per Day" campaign to help deal with the food shortages that were crippling the PDS. Private markets sprang up all over the country. Hordes of the *kkot chebi* described above began to swarm these markets and urban centers in search of food. The numbers of defectors swimming across the Yalu and Tumen Rivers into China began to skyrocket, and with them, the number of executions and political prisoners. Food riots are even said to have broken out in North and South Hamgyŏng Provinces,[61] an unheard-of level of disorder in the ultra-orderly totalitarian state. Villages were abandoned wholesale, as residents emigrated en masse after food stocks and sources were completely exhausted, leaving only the dead behind. At least some of these migrants flooded into Pyongyang in search of any form of nutrition, eventually leading the regime to forcibly deport them from the capital, as it was dealing with its own shortages.[62]

In May of 1994, as the world was concerned with the first nuclear crisis with the North, Chinese sources were referring to what was occurring as the "worst food crisis in history"[63] in the DPRK. By 1997, the regime's heralded control tool, the PDS, was estimated to be supplying just 6 percent of the population, and by 1998 it wasn't supplying anyone for large portions of the year.[64]

The steady decline of the PDS was compounded by a series of catastrophic natural disasters that befell the North. In 1995 and 1996, there was flooding on a biblical scale. On a particular day in North Hwanghae Province, 877 mm (34.5 inches) of precipitation was recorded in just seven hours,[65] more than the state of Vermont's annual average (855.7 mm [33.7 inches]). This flooding was followed by periods of severe drought in 1996 and 1997, and a typhoon in August 1997. The flooding, drought, and typhoon not only wiped out existing crops but also destroyed an estimated 85 percent of the country's hydroelectric capacity and ravaged its coal-power capabilities.[66] This severely hampered the state's ability to generate electricity, and therefore the few collective farms that survived the natural disasters had little ability to carry on large-scale agriculture. None of this would have been disastrous had the regime in Pyongyang maintained adequate emergency stocks of food, but the inefficient nature of the PDS and its multiyear decline rendered these reserves grossly inadequate.

Finally, there were simple issues of geography. North Korea is relatively far north, running from the thirty-eighth parallel up to the forty-third, which accounts for its harsh winters and a relatively short growing season. It is also not abundant in highly arable land, with only approximately 20 percent of the territory being cultivatable.[67] As a result, historically the northern part of the Korean Peninsula was the industrial rust-belt, and the south, the agrarian heartland. Yet wholly contradictory to these geographic realities, soon after its foundation, the DPRK implemented its *juche* ideology, which emphasized self-sufficiency in all areas of life, including in agriculture and food production. Given the North's high population-density ratio to its allotment of arable land and its relatively short growing season, for much of its history the regime feverishly tried to keep up with demand by overusing fertilizers and chemicals, and by continuous cropping, a practice that leads to soil erosion over time.

The North is also highly mountainous compared to its southern counterpart, with this type of topography covering approximately 80 percent of the territory.[68] Because of its desire for self-sufficiency and the need to keep up with demand, the regime's solution was to deforest and cultivate hillsides, exacerbating the soil's erosion.[69] Their overreliance on fertilizers and other chemicals also proved disastrous, for when they lost their Soviet patron in the late 1980s, they lost the vast majority of these crucial inputs. Again, these geographic realities wouldn't be a problem if the North simply had had an open economy, traded in the international market, and imported the bulk of its food. But its stubborn faith in a system of central economic control and complete self-reliance essentially doomed it from the start.

LIFE WITHOUT FOOD

And so, a combination of misguided government policy, massive geopolitical shifts, natural disasters, and unfavorable geography led to the eventual loss of as many as 1 million North Korean lives. The extent and the scale of the deaths was truly harrowing, as defector Ms. Kim attests to:

> I personally know about fifteen people who died of hunger. In the case of an acquaintance of mine, her entire family died. There were so many deaths; we got used to seeing dead bodies everywhere—at train stations, on the streets.[70]

Because of the aforementioned social stratification and harsh central control, certain areas of the country and particular classes and occupations experienced more death than others. In a 1998 survey of almost seventeen hundred refugees, 85 percent of respondents said that North and South Hamgyŏng Provinces were the hardest hit, and 88.7 percent believed urban areas to be more severely affected than rural ones.[71] The most likely to suffer under the famine were those who were jobless, or those in marginal jobs such as construction. But by far the most vulnerable were infants, children, and the elderly. In five short years, between 1993 and 1997, the infant mortality rate of North Korea increased by over 25 percent, from forty-five per thousand to fifty-eight per thousand.[72] A 1998 World Food Programme survey covering eighteen hundred children aged six months to seven years found the prevalence of stunted growth as a result of malnutrition to be over 60 percent.[73]

But while these certain groups and areas were hardest hit, no one except the Kims and their inner circle seemed to be fully protected from the ravages of the famine. For instance, Mr. Lim, a soldier from Hwanghae Province, describes how many men in his unit died as a result of malnutrition:

> *You know they were hungry. And then you don't see them for a while. Eventually, someone finds them dead in their own home. That was quite typical. And then there were those who died on the street, after wandering around to find food. There were so many dead people that the authorities often couldn't find surviving families, so they would bury them in fives or tens in hills, without even coffins.*[74]

When the worst of the famine set in, the tyranny of hunger refused to discriminate, despite the regime's complex classification schemes. Kim Yŏng, a defector who was in a North Korean prison camp from 1996 to 1998, summed up the general misery, lamenting, "There are so many miserable stories. People pick undigested beans out of the dung of oxen to eat. They compete to take the clothes off of dead bodies to wear. It is not a human world."[75]

It must be made clear though that it is not hunger per se that leads to the majority of the death in famine situations. Rather it is the plethora of diseases, some infectious, that emerge among populations with malnutrition-induced, weakened immune systems, and in this regard North Korea was no exception. Tuberculosis, an acute respiratory illness, was rife among the North Korean population, and anemia, a common blood-oxygen-level disorder, was also widespread. Cholera, an intestinal infection often carried by dirty water, was brought on and exacerbated by the repeated flooding in the country, causing the deaths of many malnourished soldiers and civilians.[76] And malaria, a parasitic disease, was said to have increased dramatically over the course of the famine.[77] Added to this list are the simple health issues that often end up proving deadly, like prolonged diarrhea among children and eye infections leading to blindness. Further, there are the longer-term health implications of chronic malnutrition, such as major digestive dysfunction, heart failure, declines in brain function, and trauma-induced long-term psychological damage. There are also increased miscarriages and premature births, elevated levels of stillbirths, and reduced conception due to malnutrition, which carry significant demographic implications.

All of these health crises would be manageable in any country with a functioning health system, but over the course of the famine, the North Korean medical system all but completely crumbled. Kim, a twenty-six-year-old defector from North Hamgyŏng Province, claimed that "it's no use going to hospitals because they don't have any medicines. It's better to buy medication at markets or directly from Chinese merchants."[78] Sŏng, a fifty-six-year-old woman, also from North Hamgyŏng Province, describes having her appendix removed without any form of anesthetic, because of the lack of medical supplies in the country:

The operation took about an hour and ten minutes. I was screaming so much from the pain, I thought I was going to die. They had tied my hands and legs to prevent me from moving. I was hospitalized for one week and then I recovered for about a month at home.[79]

Unfortunately, it gets even worse. A twenty-four-year-old man, Hwang, suffered a similar fate: a train accident necessitated him having his lower leg amputated without so much as an Advil.

Five medical assistants held my arms and legs down to keep me from moving. I was in so much pain that I screamed and eventually fainted from the pain. I woke up one week later in a hospital bed.[80]

And so the people of North Korea trudged along on their "Arduous March" ("*Konan-ŭi haenggun*") as the regime called it. What the widespread lack of food resulted in was a number of heartbreaking coping mechanisms to which many North Koreans resorted. Hwang, the young man mentioned above, for instance, was one of the thousands of *kkot chebi* in the North, and he describes how he coped:

I normally ate one meal a day. I was always hungry. If I had something to eat, I would eat it all—even if I was full, I would still continue eating because I didn't know when I would have the chance to eat again. Also because I was homeless, I couldn't take the food with me, so I just finished it in one go.[81]

Others had different methods of coping with the relentless gnawing hunger they were afflicted with. One common method was making food "go further" by supplementing it with wild food. Roots, grasses, tree barks, and different types of stalks and bulbs were added to the measly portions that the PDS allocated, not for their nutritional value (of which they mostly had none), but to mimic the sensation of fullness. These near-indigestible foods would wreak havoc on the digestive systems of those who ingested them, and by 1996 the U.N. estimated that they made up some 30 percent of the North Korean diet.[82] Hwang describes his experience with these "alternative foods," as the regime referred to them:

I ate several different kinds of wild foods, such as neung-jae, *which is a wild grass found in the fields. It's toxic—your face swells up the next day. Other grass and some mushrooms are poisonous, so you could die if you picked the wrong one. Sometimes I mixed corn powder with pine tree bark, which gave me digestive and bowel problems but I needed to add something to my food to satiate my hunger . . . I knew all these foods had little nutritional value, but I still ate them to fill my stomach.*[83]

A twenty-seven-year-old man from North Hamgyŏng Province, Park, explains that "[s]ome wild greens or roots can be dangerous or difficult to digest." He goes on to tell of how he often "suffered from stomach ache or diarrhea," and that "during a particularly rough patch . . . [he] also ate food you normally feed to pigs."[84] During the worst of the food shortages, in its desperation, the regime in Pyongyang even added wild food to its stocks and distributed it, mixing 30 percent corn or maize residue with grasses, bulbs, and seaweeds to make non-nutritious "food bars."[85]

Forms of criminal activity, previously unheard of in the North, also became far more common during the famine. There were even instances of parents selling their own children, with one case in which a parent parted with their eight-year-old daughter for a mere 4,000 yuan. (Today that is approximately $600.)[86] There were also reports of people being executed for mixing human flesh with pork and selling it in the markets. These reports were taken seriously enough for the U.N. World Food Programme (WFP) to request access to certain markets where "special meat" was supposedly being sold, yet they were turned down by the regime.[87]

When all hope was lost, many turned to suicide rather than continue to suffer the agony of living. When they had families suffering with them, they often felt it better to commit suicide collectively rather than allowing their loved ones to go on alone, as a male defector attests to:

> *Many people died of hunger, each day . . . I saw a whole family dead, under a bridge. The father thought it would be better to die than to live on. So they went outside and . . . froze to death.*[88]

The existential terror of repatriation is not surprising, for during the years of the famine, public executions became an integral part of North Korean life. As the famine worsened, public executions are said to have increased in lockstep, peaking between 1996 and 1998.[89] Typical crimes resulting in execution were theft, the slaughtering of livestock for food, and, often, defection. Local villagers, including children, were regularly forced to witness these executions, and there are even reports of elementary-school teachers being made to bring whole classes.[90] Shops were ordered to be closed while these grotesque ceremonies were carried out, and defectors report seeing execution by hanging, shooting, garroting (seated strangulation by chain, wire, or rope), and, in one particularly disturbing case, being burned alive with relatives being forced to light the pyre.[91] In North Korea's gulags, there were other ways in which individuals and even children were forced to partake. Kang Ch'ŏl-hwan describes how he and other children were forced to stone other prisoners to death:

> *You were ideologically unsound if you didn't join in throwing stones. There was no other option . . . Stones would pile up under their feet and*

their skin peeled away, bleeding. Their bodies shook for about three min-
utes, until they took their last breath . . . You saw it so often, you got used
to it.[92]

LASTING EFFECTS

While the very worst of the famine was over by 1999, what has transpired
since is that the country has basically settled into a chronic and prolonged
state of food crisis. In spite of brief periods here and there, the World Food
Programme has never *really* left, and the North Korean regime, appropriately, has never *really* returned to importing large quantities of food.
But where the consequences of the famine are present most disturbingly
is among the next generation of North Koreans, the "stunted generation"
as they are often called. In 2003, a WFP/Food and Agricultural Organization (FAO) joint report found malnutrition among youth in the country
to be "alarmingly high," found chronically in 39 percent of children.[93] In
2004, the stunting rate in South Hamgyŏng (47 percent) and Ryanggang
(46 percent) Provinces was considerably worse than that of Pyongyang (26
percent).[94] A UNICEF report covering 2003–2008 found that 45 percent
of children under five were stunted; 9 percent were suffering from wasting
diseases; and 25 percent were underweight, 7 percent severely so.[95] Most
recently, in 2009, the World Food Programme estimated that 37 percent
of North Korean children under five continue to be malnourished, and
that one in three women were malnourished and suffered anemia due to
poor diet.[96] A telling and, sadly, very well-known sign is the simple comparison between young boys from South and North Korea. A 2004 assessment found that in the South, the average seven-year-old boy is 125
centimeters tall (4 ft 1 in), and weighs 26 kilograms (57 lb). His northern
brother is 105 centimeters tall (3 ft 5 in), and weighs a mere 16 kilograms
(35 lb).[97] Even after North Korea is long gone, this generation of children
will bear the scars of the regime's lasting legacy of abuses.

POLICY

What has the world done to address these abuses? The gulags of North
Korea started to come to the attention of NGOs and the international

community since 1974. The context was an Amnesty International campaign for the release of two Westerners, Ali Lamada of Venezuela and Jacques-Emmanuel Sédillot of France. Both individuals were recruited by the North Korean foreign ministry to translate the works of Kim Il-sung into Spanish and French. Lamada was a well-known poet and member of the Communist Party in Venezuela. Sédillot was a linguist and a former colonel in the French Republican Army who had served in Spain during the Spanish Civil War and in Algeria during its war for independence. What these two people saw as a temporary job turned into a nightmarish ordeal. Even as Communists, they found the Kim Il-sung propaganda way over the top and made critical remarks about the regime. Lamada was first placed under house arrest for his insubordination, but when he refused to submit, he was sentenced to twenty years of hard labor on charges of espionage. Lamada was banished to a prison cell with no bed or blanket despite freezing temperatures. Sédillot suffered a similar fate. The governments of Venezuela and France intervened with help from the Romanian president—a close friend of Kim Il-sung—to get the two released in 1974. Sédillot died in Pyongyang before he could return to France, but Lamada lived to write about his experiences. He wrote about how life in the North was worse than anything he could have imagined. He literally almost froze to death in prison, succumbing to frostbite.

Stories about the gulags started to emerge in the late 1980s and 1990s, largely based on defectors' testimony. The first major NGO report was published in December 1988 by the Minnesota Lawyers International Human Rights Committee and Human Rights Watch Asia, which outlined the camp system. Prisoner accounts emerged with Kang Ch'ŏl-hwan's work, but some also came from An Hyŏk, who escaped to China in 1992, and from An Myŏng-ch'ŏl, a former prison guard, in 1994. As the famine pushed more defectors out of North Korea, accounts of these and others started to get published in South Korean newspapers, attracting international attention. In December 2002, the *Far Eastern Economic Review* published the first satellite photos of a gulag in North Hamgyŏng Province. An important vehicle for raising awareness has also been the series of annual conferences held by Freedom House. Supported by congressional funding, starting in 2005, these meetings have been held in Seoul, Brussels, Rome, and Washington, D.C., and have provided a platform for sharing stories about the conditions within North Korea.

When it became clear to the international community that North Korea was in the midst of a food crisis of catastrophic proportions, food aid donors moved quickly to try and bring some relief to the country's people. In 1995 and 1996, the World Food Programme delivered over half a million metric tons of food aid each year. The years 1997 and 1998 saw over 900,000 metric tons and almost 800,000 metric tons, respectively. From 1999 to 2002, WFP annually donated over 1 million metric tons of food aid to the North, peaking at 1.5 million in 2001. In total, since the program started working in the country in 1995, it has delivered over 12.2 million metric tons of food to the people (and, by extension, the military) of North Korea. To put this in context, North Korea is the third-greatest recipient of food aid in WFP history, behind only Ethiopia (19.2 million metric tons) and Bangladesh (14.3 million metric tons), and appeals began in these countries some seven years before those in the North.[98] The regime in Pyongyang worked hard to hamper the international community's efforts. WFP requires certain amounts of monitoring and access in order to ensure that the food gets to those in the greatest need. Initially, the regime aggressively curtailed access, allowing WFP staff into just seven of North Korea's eleven provinces. By 2000, access had improved somewhat, but there were still huge swaths of territory in North and South Hamgyŏng, Chagang, Ryanggang, and Kangwŏn Provinces that were totally off limits.[99] Pyongyang limited WFP staff to a maximum of fifty workers. It did not want any staff to be Korean-speakers, for fear of information dissemination. It is estimated that as much as 30 percent of donated food was diverted toward the military.[100] The regime violated all four basic norms of humanitarian aid—access, transparency, nondiscrimination, and a focus on the most vulnerable.

These attempts to procure as much food aid as possible with as little transparency as possible posed humanitarian dilemmas for countries like the United States and Japan, which contributed to the WFP annual appeal for North Korea. The United States has been one of the largest donors to the annual appeal for North Korea, providing over 2 million metric tons since 1996, and it stated that it would provide as much as

50 percent of the annual appeal if the North allowed access and monitoring.[101] When the North did not meet this standard, the United States stopped providing food aid in the summer of 2006. In May 2008, USAID restarted a food donor program for North Korea. Under this program, 500,000 metric tons of food aid was to be delivered to the North, 400,000 of it through the WFP and the remaining 100,000 through a consortium of NGOs such as Global Vision, Mercy Corps, and Christian Friends of Korea. This breakthrough came after Pyongyang agreed to allow greater access to previously prohibited regions (every province except Chagang and Ryanggang), increased monitoring of the delivery of the aid, and larger numbers of Korean speakers as part of the aid team. But by March 2009, the North had begun to renege on its agreement pertaining to access, monitoring, and general transparency, and by September, the U.S. component of the WFP appeals had ground to a halt.[102]

Japan was also a major donor until 2001, when revelations regarding North Korea's abduction of Japanese citizens in the 1970s outraged the nation. While China does not reveal the full amount of support it gives, around 500,000 to 1 million tons has made its way across the border every year since 1995. Both China and South Korea did not help resolve the dilemma, as they provided food on a bilateral basis to the North, with few strings attached, thereby undercutting any attempts by the WFP to demand greater access and monitoring with the promise of more food. Under the "Sunshine Policy" of Kim Dae-jung and the "Peace and Prosperity Policy" of Roh Moo-hyun, South Korea was annually the largest or second-largest donor of food aid to the North. The majority of their aid was donated bilaterally, with few monitoring mechanisms in place. Donations averaged over 400,000 metric tons between 2001 and 2007, peaking at just under 550,000 metric tons in 2004.[103] For China's part, according to the World Food Programme, it has donated a total of over 3 million metric tons to the North Koreans since 1996, averaging at about 230,000 metric tons per year.[104] But these official statistics don't tell the whole story. The deliberately opaque way China reports aid figures to the WFP makes it nearly impossible to distinguish between food aid and commercial food exports, and makes the true volume of Chinese aid to North Korea basically unknowable. But as an indication of where the true figure may lie, from 1997 to

2008, the exports of cereals alone to North Korea (which have yet to be paid for, hence, "aid") have only dipped below the 100,000 metric ton mark on two occasions, in 2004 and 2006.[105] This also doesn't include accompanying regular shipments of corn, rice, and the other forms of food aid that the Chinese regularly send, indicating a total figure substantially larger than the WFP and the rest of us are privy to.

WFP Food Aid to the DPRK

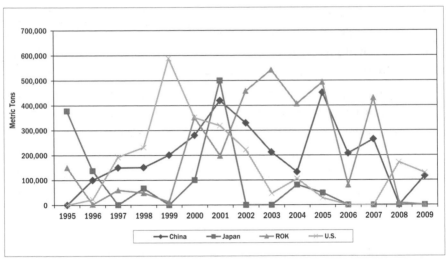

Source: The World Food Programme (2011).

Total WFP Food Aid to the DPRK, 1995–2009

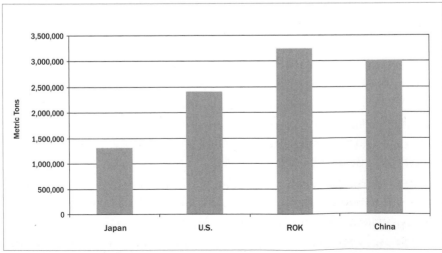

Source: The World Food Programme (2011).

U.S. POLICY

U.S. policy over the years has generally prioritized security issues with North Korea over human rights. When human rights atrocities first became known to the world in the mid-1990s, U.S. policy was preoccupied with a more proximate threat in the clandestine nuclear weapons program being pursued by Pyongyang. The Clinton administration focused their efforts on an agreement to freeze the program in 1994, followed by years of challenging implementation. From 2001, both the Congress and the George W. Bush administration became more active on the issue. President Bush had a proactive mind-set on the problem that went deeper than his oft-cited statement recorded in Bob Woodward's book *Bush at War:* "I loathe Kim Jong Il! I've got a visceral reaction to this guy, because he is starving his people."[106] The president said on many occasions privately that the United States needed to bring attention to the plight of the people in the North because no one else in the world would. He understood the limitations of what could be done given the opacity of the regime, but he always said that he wanted his presidency to be remembered as one that tried to make measureable improvements in the lives of the North Korean people.

Congress helped greatly in this regard by passing, in 2004, a landmark piece of legislation on North Korean human rights. The North Korean Human Rights Act established that human rights should be an integral element of U.S. policy toward North Korea. It called on China to stop *refoulement* and to allow the UNHCR access to North Korean migrants. The act maintained that U.S. food aid to North Korea must only be given on the condition of adequate access and monitoring to ensure that the needy are being helped. It also called for enhanced radio broadcasting and information dissemination into the North, to break the regime's grip on information and to empower the people. Toward these ends, the act authorized $20 million every year for assistance to North Korean refugees, $2 million for promoting human rights in North Korea, and $2 million to promote the freedom of information within the country. The act allowed for the eligibility of refugee status for legitimately qualified North Korean cases, and called for the establishment of a refugee resettlement program. Finally, the act called for the creation of a special envoy for the promotion of human rights in North Korea.

President Bush worked with this legislation to put together the first-ever comprehensive policy to promote human rights in North Korea. In August 2005, he appointed a special envoy, Jay Lefkowitz, who had been a domestic policy adviser in the first term and was a close confidant of the president. Lefkowitz worked with the White House to draw the world's attention to the issue with the visits to the Oval Office by the North Korean defectors Kang Ch'ŏl-hwan and the family of six-year-old Han-mi. President Bush instructed the State Department and Department of Homeland Security to establish a North Korean refugee resettlement program, which led to the first resettlement of six refugees in the United States in May 2006. As of June 2010, this program has resettled a total of ninety-six North Korean refugees in the United States, with a further fifteen cases pending.[107] While most defectors choose to resettle in South Korea, this program led by example—it was the first of its kind outside of Korea; moreover, it set no limit or quota on the number that can come to the United States. On the president's instructions, we also saw to it that the September 2005 joint statement of the Six-Party denuclearization talks included some mention of human rights, albeit obliquely. Section 2 of the agreement stated: "The DPRK and the United States undertook to respect each other's sovereignty, exist peacefully together, and take steps to normalize their relations subject to their respective bilateral policies."[108] The reference to "respective bilateral policies" was diplomatic talk for a variety of outstanding issues that would need to be resolved before the United States would grant political normalization. These included North Korea's aggressive conventional force posture, missiles, and human rights.

In 2008, the Bush administration allocated $4 million in assistance to U.S. NGOs to help several North Korean rural and provincial hospitals by improving their electrical supplies and by providing medical equipment and training. These items were carefully chosen to meet the president's desire to see measureable improvements in the lives of North Koreans, but to avoid any aid diverted to military use. In 2006 and 2007, Lefkowitz also pushed for increasing radio broadcasting into the country through new programming for Voice of America and Radio Free Asia.

In May of 2008, the U.S. Agency for International Development started a major food aid program of 500,000 metric tons for the North but only after adequate access and monitoring was allowed for the NGO consortium and WFP participants. Seventy-five inspectors in nine field offices were offered unprecedented access, especially with the permitted use of Korean-speakers. As noted earlier, the North abruptly ended this in March 2009, with only a little more than 130,000 tons received, as tensions grew worse on the nuclear front. There were other elements of the U.S. government that had North Korean human rights as part of their portfolio, particularly in the State Department's Population, Refugees, and Migration Bureau and in the Bureau for Democracy, Human Rights, and Labor, but nothing captured the world's attention like the sustained focus of an American president. To ensure continued attention to the issue in the next administration, President Bush reauthorized the North Korea Human Rights Act in October 2008.

One can say without prejudice that the Bush administration did more to take on the human rights problems in North Korea than any other administration. There were delays in implementation of the NKHRA, which upset some advocates. As I mentioned earlier, critics saw these actions as veiled efforts either to collapse the regime or to vent Bush's personal loathing of Kim Jong-il. There was also a widespread perception among many Bush naysayers and former Clinton-era negotiators that one could not criticize Pyongyang on human rights abuses and hope to have a credible negotiation on the "real" issue—nuclear weapons. Therefore, they argued, Bush raised human rights as a way to submarine concurrent diplomatic negotiations on the nuclear program, which Bush hawks believed would lead nowhere. While no one person can speak for the intentions of all, I do not believe any of these explanations motivated Bush on human rights. His concern for the plight of the people was about as genuine as any human being could have had. His conviction on this issue was deep, as he told Woodward, "Either you believe in freedom, and want to—and worry about the human condition, or you don't."[109] These views were not restricted to North Korea, as the president hosted political dissidents from other repressive states, such as Burma, China, Cuba, Russia, Syria, and Venezuela as part of his Freedom Agenda. But on North Korea, he was emotionally moved by the stories of the defectors. He remembered every detail, and would then relay these stories to other world leaders he met in bilateral summits or at events like the G8. This had the effect of internationalizing the issue at the highest levels of government in a way that no NGO could have been capable of doing. It would only be a mild exaggeration to say he was on a one-man crusade to bring the world's attention to the issue.

The Obama administration picked up the mantle by appointing a new special envoy and ambassador, Robert King, in April 2010. King's appointment was in a full-time capacity (unlike that of Lefkowitz, who held a part-time position in addition to his full-time legal practice), and he was a known quantity to many on Capitol Hill, which was seen as important, considering the Congress's role in legislating the creation of the position. Given the closed regime in Pyongyang, much of the battle for human rights is fought on the outside, by increasing awareness (as President Bush did); offering refugee resettlements; and supporting international conventions like the International Convention on Civil and Political Rights and the International Convention on Economic, Social, and Cultural Rights (both of which North Korea is a party to), which single out the abuses of the Pyongyang regime. But sooner or later, if there is to be any improvement in human rights, advocates will have to negotiate directly with the regime. In this regard, King is arguably the only American who could conceivably have a credible dialogue with the North Koreans on human rights. A longtime senior aide to the late Congressman Tom Lantos (D-CA), King accompanied the congressman and his wife on trips to North Korea. I was asked to meet with the congressman and King after one of their trips. Lantos, seventy-seven at the time, said he had been treated very well upon his arrival in Pyongyang and had been extended every courtesy. However, in the first substantive meeting with the North Koreans, his interlocutor sat rigidly at the table and opened a briefing book from which he started reading a long and detailed diatribe about American imperialism and aggression against the Korean race. Lantos listened patiently for a few minutes and then politely raised his hand, gesturing for a pause in the one-way conversation. The congressman, a Holocaust survivor, then said politely in a tone that resonated with years of life experiences, "Young man, I am very appreciative to be hosted so well by your government and people. Thank you. But as for this discussion, I am an old man and frankly do not have time for this. If you would like to put away the talking points and have a genuine discussion, I am happy to do that with you." The congressman and King relayed how the North Korean was initially startled and did not know how to respond. However, after a moment, he closed his book and proceeded with the meeting. While Lantos reached no major breakthroughs with the North, he and King were able to have a real conversation about human rights like no other American could have. Appropriately, in May 2011, Ambassador King became the first human-rights envoy to travel to Pyongyang. Although much of his discussions focused on humanitarian aid (i.e., food aid assessment) rather than on human rights abuses, the fact that he was in the country was a small victory. In this issue area, there are so few of them.

South Korea's policy on human rights in North Korea is complex and highly politicized. There is no denying that South Korea has done the most of any other country to resettle refugees and to help them reintegrate in society. Seoul has also provided annual tranches of food aid and fertilizer as humanitarian assistance intended to help women and children. But while the U.S. approach has sought to trumpet the abuses in the North as a way to draw the world's attention to the problem, the South has preferred a quieter approach. This was especially true during the decade of politically progressive governments in South Korea (1998–2008), which sought explicitly to avoid voicing any public criticism of the North Korean regime. During these years, Seoul shied away from associating itself with the new U.S. envoy Lefkowitz and abstained from voting on U.N. human rights resolutions on North Korea. These governments believed that full-throated criticism only unnecessarily aggravated inter-Korean relations. Thus, when summits took place between the two Koreas in 2000 and in 2007, human rights were not on the agenda, displaced by a focus on enhanced economic cooperation and political reconciliation. Political conservatives in South Korea, on the other hand, frame human rights issues—such as the return of prisoners of war, reunion of 11 million families divided by the Korean War, and the return of abducted South Korean citizens—to be frontline issues in dealing with the North. They do not see political reconciliation as possible with the currently constituted regime and view human rights as a key barometer of real reform in the regime's intentions (versus tactical and temporary bouts of cooperation on the nuclear issue). Conservatives have called for bringing Kim Jong-il before the International Criminal Court. They are less concerned about "offending" Pyongyang with the call for respecting human rights. Governments such as Lee Myung-bak's (2008–2013) have not disavowed humanitarian food and fertilizer assistance, but they have explicitly tied substantive economic cooperation with improvements in the human rights issues (and denuclearization).

The ultimate unanswered question on human rights abuses is why do the North Korean people take it? Regardless of how isolated they may be from the world, surely they must understand the illegitimacy of a government depriving its citizens of basic food and subsistence? When will the revolution take place?

Not yet. One can hazard several guesses as to why. The first relates to the strong arm of the government. There is no freedom of assembly in North Korea, and the only organized and armed social institutions with tools of enforcement belong to the state. The police, internal security forces, and military ruthlessly extinguish any sign of social disorder. With such an infrastructure in place, to put it mildly, peasants in the North don't even have pitchforks to rise up against the regime.

A second potential explanation for the population's docility relates to the closed nature of the system. The government works very hard to deprive the people of any information about living standards outside of the country. North Koreans are taught, for example, to believe that South Korea is a poor country, much worse off than theirs. They are taught that southerners eat rats and live in a crime-filled and underdeveloped society. Thus, the people may not be revolting because they may think that times are tough everywhere.

The regime's capacity to maintain such an iron grip on information, however, is rapidly dissolving. In the 1980s, North Korean propaganda used to show films of student demonstrations in the South to prove that the country was in chaos and the masses were revolting. Then people started to notice that the buildings and streets in the newsreels of Seoul were modern and advanced, which undercut the lies that had been propagated. The government responded by subsequently blurring the footage of urban scenes in the South to get only its own message across. North Koreans are increasingly smuggling in VCRs from China, on which they watch South Korean soap operas and movies that are the rage across Asia, and see the incredible prosperity of that country. More North Koreans who return from China spread information about life on the outside, and more people have access to shortwave radios as alternate sources of information to the government's propaganda. The increased flow of information will ultimately spell the end of the regime in the future, but right now, it is not enough to incite a widespread revolt.

I think these explanations make sense, but a third one impresses me the most: revolution, at least right now, is simply too grand a dream for the people. When one is as poor as a North Korean, one's immediate concern is not to overthrow the system, it is merely to survive. Fathers and mothers are not concerned with how to act on their disenchantment with the government; instead, they are preoccupied with questions like where to find the next meal for their children or how to stay warm in subzero temperatures. Revolt is not on the radar screen. Ironically, the time at which the North Korean people are more likely to throw down their chains is when they see an improvement in the standard of living. Downtrodden populations, as Montesquieu said, do not seek revolt when they are at their absolute worst but when their circumstances start to get better. This sets off a "spiral of expectations," when society becomes impatient and wants change for the better to come faster. This spiral of expectations is only likely to inspire North Koreans to action after a period in which there is real economic reform that puts food on the table and money in their pockets. But it is precisely the fear of this spiral of expectations that motivates the regime to keep its people downtrodden and weak, and to reject real reform.

It is interesting that there does not appear to be an organized and politically active dissident exile community. In Eastern Europe, vibrant dissident groups played a major role in forcing changes at home. But experts observe that this is nonexistent in the case of North Korea.[110] Small groups have formed, such as the Democracy Network against North Korean Gulags, which was founded in 2003 by former political prisoners (http://www.nkgulag.org/); or Committee for Democratization of North Korea, which was created in 2000 by DPRK defector Hwang Jang-yŏp. Despite the existence of such groups, the level of anti–North Korea regime sentiment among refugees is not as high as one might expect. This ambivalence stems, in part, from the fact that many of the defector community are preoccupied with reintegration challenges in South Korean society. Defectors, though ethnically Korean, are still treated with prejudice for their accents, undereducation, and physical diminutiveness caused by their poor nutrition. They end up in low-paying menial jobs, have trouble marrying into society, and generally lack opportunities. The dropout rate from school for North Koreans, for example, is over 13 percent, which is ten times higher than that for South Koreans. The unemployment rate is 14 percent, versus the national average of 4 percent. In 2011, the ROK National Policy Agency released the results of a study showing that over 50 percent of defectors who had resettled in Seoul make a monthly income of less than 1 million won ($893), which puts them below the lowest average wage (housemaid) recorded in the South Korean census. By contrast, the average South Korean makes well over 2.5 million won ($2,232) a month.[111] Many defectors, moreover, still identify themselves as North Korean (33 percent) rather than as Korean or South Korean, and still have affection for the notional idea of North Korea though they may have animosity toward the government. Indeed, many defectors still express fondness for Kim Il-sung, which says something about the residual strength of the *juche* ideology even as they deplore the conditions that forced their escape and express anger at corrupt lower-level bureaucrats.

All of this means that the international community must continue to carry the burden of improving the human rights situation in North Korea. While there are many issues that need to be addressed, five items top the agenda: first, the PRC must stop *refoulement* of North Korea migrants and must allow the UNHCR access to determine who would be qualified as political refugees. Second, future South Korean governments, progressive or conservative, must adhere to an inter-Korean agenda that includes respect for human rights. In particular, while humanitarian assistance such as food for children should endure, any large-scale economic assistance should be linked with family reunions and return of detained South Korean citizens. Third, future U.S. administrations should continue to set the example of permitting qualified DPRK refugees to settle in the United States. Fourth, the DPRK must be encouraged to demonstrate rectification of its human rights problems as a key condition for acceptance into the international community. This includes not only allowing adequate monitoring and access for assistance from humanitarian groups, but also beginning a dialogue with international organizations about how to depart from current practices, which meet internationally recognized standards for forced labor and slavery. Ultimately, this dialogue should lead to a path where Pyongyang opens the camps to international inspection and decriminalizes the movement of people within the country. The agenda is clear, but achieving this will be extremely difficult.

Finally, what policymakers fail to understand is that an emphasis on human rights abuses does not necessarily detract from addressing U.S. and Asian concerns about North Korea's nuclear and military threats. Aside from President Bush, U.S. officials have treaded lightly because they fear that criticism of the regime's gulags will somehow make Pyongyang less willing to negotiate denuclearization. On the contrary, the North must be encouraged to believe that any improvement in their treatment of citizens will register positively in the world as a regime that is on the mend and seeking better relations. Negotiators focus on denuclearization agreements that have verification protocols for each step either side makes. This is required between counterparts like the United States and North Korea, who have decades of mistrust between them. Even when Pyongyang takes steps in fulfillment of existing nuclear agreements, people are skeptical of whether their cooperation is genuine or merely tactical. However, if Pyongyang were making small steps in fulfilling nuclear agreements *and* also showing improvements in their human rights record, the latter would lend enormously more credibility to the former. People would then believe the regime is serious about changing its old ways. At the moment, I admit that these thoughts amount to aspirations more than actionable policy, given the harder-line direction in which the DPRK is leaning. Yet human rights must remain on the U.S. agenda with North Korea. If they do not, then, as one defector said to me, "If America does not stand up for the abused people in North Korea, then what other country in the world would even care?"

CHAPTER SIX

THE LOGIC OF DETERRENCE

SPECIAL OPERATIONS FORCES WOULD PENETRATE SOUTH KOREAN DEFENSES WITH predawn airdrops and shore landings. These forces would sabotage power stations, telephone lines, cell and Internet networks, and bridges, to paralyze the population. Artillery at the rate of hundreds of thousands of rounds per hour would rain on the city of Seoul and its unwitting population of 24 million. Panic would ensue as millions would try to escape the city, clogging all highway arteries out of Seoul while troops would use those very same roads to move north to defend against the aggression. A missile arsenal of 600 chemically armed Scuds would be fired on all South Korean airports, train stations, and marine ports, making it impossible for civilians to escape. One hundred Nodong missiles targeted toward Japan with chemical weapons would complicate the battlefield environment and delay the inflow of some 500,000 U.S. reinforcements to supplement the 28,500 already stationed in Korea. DPRK submarines and semisubmersibles south of the Tsushima Strait would serve the same purpose, torpedoing U.S. ships carrying troops and supplies from Japan. This would set the stage for the mass invasion. Over 700,000 troops, 2,000 tanks, and mechanized forces would advance southward rapidly, trying to penetrate ROK defensive positions and cover the fifty miles (80 km) or so to overtake Seoul, roughly the short distance from Washington, D.C., to Baltimore, before the United States and ROK could mount a response. Once in Seoul, at minimum, the DPRK would seek to hold the capital city hostage, or, at a maximum, exploit it as a base of resupply and operations for advancing on the rest of the peninsula.

As wars go, this would be the most unforgiving battle conditions that could be imagined. An extremely high density of enemy and allied forces—1 million DPRK troops, 660,000 ROK troops, and 500,000 American forces—over 2 million mechanized forces all converging on a total battle space spanning the equivalent of the distance between Washington, D.C., and Boston. The United States would flow in 4 to 6 ground combat divisions, including Marines and Army, 10 wings of Air Force aircraft, and 4 to 5 Navy carrier battle groups.[1] Soldiers would be fighting with little defense against DPRK artillery, aerial bombardments, and in an urban warfare environment polluted by 5,000 metric tons of DPRK chemical agents. There is no uncertainty about the outcome of this war. The United States and ROK would win, but not without four to six months of high-intensity combat and many dead. U.S. commander in Korea, Gary Luck, famously told President Clinton that a second Korean War would kill 1 million, would cost the United States $100 billion, and would cause $1 trillion worth of industrial damage. Such a renewal of hostilities would indeed be an ugly sequel to the 1950–1953 war, which never officially ended. In a small shack on the northern side of the DMZ, empty of any adornment except for a small wooden table and four chairs, the two sides signed a cease-fire agreement that stopped the bloodshed. Up to 2.7 million Koreans, 33,692 Americans, and as many as an estimated 800,000 Chinese were killed.[2] The two Koreas, even today, remain technically at war, with the most heavily fortified border in the world. An estimated 70 percent of North Korea's army (approximately 510,000 troops) and half of its naval and air forces (approximately 85,000) are deployed within a hundred kilometers (62 mi) of the border.[3] Many of these forces are well-protected by a vast network of more than 800 underground facilities and hardened artillery sites sitting on or near the DMZ. Each of these bunkers are said to contain enough military equipment to arm up to 2,000 men, including mortar shells, arms and ammunition, and even South Korean military uniforms and name tags so the KPA troops can disguise themselves in the event of an invasion.[4]

Despite this precarious situation, the Korean Peninsula has remained remarkably stable. There have been occasional firefights between the two patrols, skirmishes along water boundaries, and even more bloody altercations (e.g., 1976 poplar tree ax murders), but on the whole, the standoff has remained just that, a standoff. The DMZ spans 150 miles (240 km) across the waist of the peninsula at the thirty-eighth parallel and is one mile wide on each side. Cordoned by barbed-wire fences, heavily mined, and with over a thousand guard posts and bunkers, this slice of earth was a product of the 1953 armistice that banned all activity except for one farm village on each side. Residents in these villages live under a strict curfew and eerily at peace in the heart of a war that never ended. When I was convoyed from Pyongyang to the DMZ in 2007 to bring back the remains of American servicemen who had been killed in the war, I recall entering the DMZ on a narrow single-lane bridge from the north. The road from Pyongyang to the DMZ is a long, straight two-and-a-half-hour ride with little that qualifies as scenery. Barren farmlands, hills denuded of trees, an occasional machine-gun nest is about all there is.

You arrive at the checkpoint for the DMZ, which is right out of a movie script. Armed soldiers stand on a dusty road in front of a phalanx of concrete barriers, machine-gun nests, and a massive metal reinforced gate with barbed wire strewn across it. Beyond the rusted metal and wire gate is a single-lane bridge that leads over a ravine into the DMZ. Once you enter this area, it is like an oasis. The vista turns beautifully green as you enter land that has literally been untouched and undisturbed by human hands for over sixty years. Nature has thrived in this space out of the destruction of war beyond anyone's imagination. The area has become a natural wildlife habitat, with over 150 species of rare birds and wildflowers, 2,900 species of plants, 16 rare species of mammals, and 67 other endangered species of mammals. It is literally a piece of Eden in the middle of a military standoff. The area is adorned by natural waterfalls, and tourists today can hike areas adjacent to the DMZ leading to Daeam Mountain and see rare breeds of flowers, rare grasshoppers, wild deer, and red-bellied frogs. A typical and unforgettable sight was empty shell casings and a rotted-out army helmet sitting amid a field of bright yellow wildflowers, literally untouched for over half a century because the area remains a live minefield. How has the DMZ remained so peaceful for over fifty years despite the absence of a peace treaty and despite the heavily armed standoff?

THE LONG PEACE

Though the public discussion of North Korean threats always focuses on the nuclear question, the conventional military balance has been at the crux of the long period of peace since 1953. Peace exists because deterrence works. South Korean forces, supported by anywhere between 225,000 and 28,500 U.S. troops stationed on the peninsula,[5] undergirded by a robust alliance, have deterred any North Korean contemplation of launching a second war. Conversely, North Korean capacity to inflict high casualties on the South has deterred aggression from Seoul. The bottom line is that this array of forces has made the Korean Peninsula a good place to wage a defensive war, but not a good place to start an offensive one.

North Korea has been deterred from war because it knows that it could not get very far with an offensive thrust southward despite its forward-deployed posture. It knows that the United States would rapidly reinforce its presence by flowing in tens of thousands of troops at the first sign of conflict. Pyongyang also understands that South Korean forces today are a far cry from their debilitated state in the 1950s, and have evolved into one of the world's top militaries. The ROK military is half the size of that of the DPRK in numbers, but it is by far better equipped and better trained. In absolute terms, ROK defense expenditures ($27.6 billion per annum) are nearly four times that of the DPRK ($7–$8.6 billion) and based on an exponentially larger GDP, which means Seoul can spend these amounts and more on its military with comparatively less strain on the economy. (Military spending amounts to between 25 and 31 percent of the DPRK's $28 billion GDP.)

THE CONVENTIONAL MILITARY BALANCE ON THE KOREAN PENINSULA		
	ROK	DPRK
Personnel (active)	655,000	1,190,000
Personnel (reserve)	4,500,000	6,489,000
ARMY		
Tanks	2,414	4,060
Armed Personnel Carriers	2,880	2,500

THE CONVENTIONAL MILITARY BALANCE ON THE KOREAN PENINSULA		
	ROK	DPRK
Artillery	11,038	21,000
Anti-aircraft Guns	330	11,000
Surface-to-Air Missiles	838	3,400
Army Helicopters	424	0
NAVY		
Submarines	23	70
Surface Combatants	47	3
Coastal Patrol Combatants	111	383
Amphibious Landing	71	290
Naval Combat Aircraft	8	0
Naval Helicopters	29	0
AIR FORCE		
Combat Aircraft	490	620
Helicopters	56	441
Unmanned Arial Vehicles	103	0

Source: *The Military Balance, 2011* (London, UK: IISS, 2011).

Despite the well-worn CNN footage of goose-stepping soldiers and parades of tanks, North Korean equipment is poor. About half of its weapons are 1960s vintage; and the other half is older than that. North Korean pilots get very little flight training time (just twenty hours per year) because of rampant fuel shortages and would be no match for ROK pilots flying in Boeing F-15K Slam Eagle fighter jets. Most of North Korea's fighter aircraft are J-5s, J-6s, and J-7s, all introduced between the mid-1950s and the mid-1960s. The majority of North Korea's main and light tanks, too, such as the T-34, T-55, T-62, and PT-76, entered into production between the early 1940s and early 1960s. Similarly, most of their armed personnel carriers, like the Type-531 and the BTR series, entered somewhere between the 1950s and late 1960s. In the South, on the other hand, well over half of the tanks are of modern design and currently in production, as are their armed personnel carriers. The differentials in speed, accuracy, agility, and power of these units would likely overwhelm the North with relative ease. And while, at first glance, the North seems to outweigh the South in amphibious landing vehicles, North Korea's ten largest landing ships (Hantae-type) have a capacity of just 3 tanks and 350 troops. The South, on the other hand, has a Tokto-type amphibious ship, with a capacity of 10 tanks and 700 troops, three Un Bong–types holding 16 tanks and 200 troops apiece, and two Alligator-types, carrying as many as 20 tanks and 300 troops each.[6]

The DPRK armed forces exhibit characteristics of a very politicized military in the sense that it is top-heavy. There are many generals, but there is not a strong cohort of mid-level officers who constitute the heart of a fighting force. In addition, the lack of any real combined-forces training makes unclear how interoperable the different branches of the DPRK military really are. In his 2010 *Annual Threat Assessment,* former director of national intelligence (DNI) Dennis Blair sums it up well, saying North Korean conventional capabilities "are limited by an aging weapons inventory, low production of military combat systems, deteriorating physical condition of soldiers, reduced training, and increasing diversion of the military to infrastructure support. Inflexible leadership, corruption, low morale, obsolescent weapons, a weak logistical system, and problems with command and control also constrain the KPA capabilities and readiness."[7] While the obsolescence of DPRK equipment and training does not mean they are rendered harmless—no matter how old the gun or artillery system is, it can still fire on Seoul and do damage—it does mean they ultimately will be defeated by U.S.-ROK combined forces. And the North Koreans know that.

The unforgiving terrain of the peninsula also makes attack difficult. There are only a handful of potential invasion corridors through which DPRK forces must flow, and their advance could be slowed long enough for U.S. tactical aircraft to inflict major damage. All roads northward from Seoul to the DMZ are adorned with large concrete barriers that would be blown up to block an enemy tank's advance southward. Rivers, marshes, and rice paddies also make it very challenging for an army to advance. (Also, up until the early 1990s, the United States had positioned 280-mm nuclear cannons, Honest John nuclear-tipped missiles, in South Korea, and atomic demolition mines to contaminate areas against DPRK advance.)[8] However, more than the terrain, the density of U.S.-ROK deployed forces conveys to the adversary the difficulty of advancing. U.S.-

ROK force density is about one division per ten kilometers (6 mi) in this area, which is about three times higher than the norm. At the start of the conflict, the United States would only have two brigades of the army's Second Infantry Division on the ground, but it could triple the force size within ten days from pre-positioned forces in Japan, Guam, and Hawaii. The United States could, in short order, bring to Korea modern heavy ground divisions that would exceed those of the DPRK. It could bring airpower three times that of the combined North and South airpower. At the height of the conflict, these forces would number between 500,000 and 600,000 troops deployed with over three hundred fixed-wing aircraft, F-117 Stealth bombers, F-15e strike fighters, and B-1 and B-52 bombers deployed from Guam. And, unlike the DPRK, the United States and ROK maintain a constant tempo of joint and combined exercises to ensure readiness and interoperability.

North Korea has a stock of five thousand metric tons of chemical weapons, one of the largest in the world. War scenarios postulate that the North would deploy these weapons at transportation hubs (railways, ports, airports) and U.S. bases in Korea and Japan to try to slow the U.S. capacity to respond. But experts believe that the United States has the capability to operate in a chemical environment and would be able to adjust.[9] The one exception would be if the North persistently disbursed a very high volume of potent chemical weapons across a wider area, in which case their own military, not well-equipped for chemical warfare, would be impeded.

Pyongyang also understands that if it were to attack again, the likely U.S.-ROK response would not merely be to defend and block a southward advance, but to roll back the regime for good. Since the early 1990s, Operational Plan (OPLAN) 5027—the joint U.S.-ROK war plans for war on the Korean Peninsula—has seen its emphasis shift from limited to defending the South in response to an attack to offensive maneuvers north of the border, reportedly involving some 400,000 personnel and effectively ending the Kim regime.[10] Bill Clinton could not have made this point any clearer when he said a nuclear war started by the North would mean the end of the country as they knew it.[11] Those who believe the United States, bogged down in wars in Iraq and Afghanistan and the nuclear and tsunami disasters in Japan, would be unable to respond to an attack are dead-wrong. United States Forces Korea (USFK) officers state that U.S. airpower would be fully capable of responding according to the battle plan, and enough ground forces would be available for this military contingency, even if the reinforcement pace might be slightly delayed.[12]

THE DPRK UNDERSTANDS, therefore, that it faces a formidable, well-trained, well-equipped, and well-organized U.S. and ROK military—should it ever consider a second invasion. They are deterred from a massive invasion because they know they would lose, and this rational calculation has been at the core of the peace on the DMZ for the past fifty-plus years. But what about the U.S. and ROK? Given their demonstrated capabilities, can Washington and Seoul contemplate moving northward in a preemptive fashion? The simple answer is yes. However, the more realistic and complex one is that the estimated price of such a campaign in terms of bloodshed has been so prohibitive that no U.S. administration since the Korean War has been willing to undertake the risk.

The most significant conventional deterrent is the North's artillery arrayed along the DMZ. The largest artillery force in the world, of 13,000 systems and 2,300 multiple rocket launchers, some of them armed with chemical weapons, are targeted southward. Short of dropping tactical nuclear weapons in the battlefield, it would be impossible for the United States and ROK to neutralize all of this without the North first inflicting major damage on Seoul. Here is a very simple example: North Korean artillery travels at about one-half kilometer (0.3 mi) per second. Even if ROK counterartillery radar ten kilometers (6 mi) away could pick up the incoming round, track it back to the source, and counterfire, this would take, at best, one to two minutes. In the interim, each artillery tube would have gotten off between five and twelve rounds before being neutralized. North Korea military expert Narushige Michishita estimates that since 2001 the North has been capable of firing approximately 500,000 artillery rounds per hour (nearly 140 rounds per second!) into Seoul, laying waste to one-third of the metropolis in that time.[13] This would obviously mean the death of tens, if not hundreds of thousands of people. The United States and ROK could neutralize this force, but it would take several days. There is also little that a civilian population could do to prepare for such an attack. The warning time for Seoul residents of an incoming North Korean artillery shell is measured in seconds (about forty-five), not even minutes, and certainly not hours. If the North fires chemically armed weapons, the death toll would be even higher. Pyongyang effectively holds Seoul's population hostage, which is their best deterrent against attack. In most imaginable circumstances in international politics, the physics of this alone poses a credible deterrent to a preemptive strike.

Beyond the artillery, 70 percent of the DPRK's military manpower is concentrated within 100 kilometers (62 mi) of the DMZ. All ground units are fully mechanized. The KPA even has 80 or so U.S.-made Hughes MD-500 helicopters, which they mysteriously acquired through a third party in the mid-1980s. The DPRK air force is about 110,000 in manpower, but it's not a potent force. Most bombers are over fifty years old, and an air battle on the peninsula would constitute the equivalent of a Ford Model-T (J-series) against a Porsche (F-15s). The navy's most dangerous element is their submarine force. Believed to have about 50 submarines and approximately 20 midget submarines, the dangers posed by this became apparent in March 2010 when a DPRK submarine force ambushed and torpedoed a ROK naval vessel.

The North's Special Forces are the most rigorously trained, well equipped, and dedicated personnel in the Korean People's Army. Their harshly regimented training is said to include all aspects of infiltrations and covert operations, even the use of kitchen utensils, such as forks and spoons, as weapons.[14] These Special Forces squads, through their rigorous training, can reportedly march fifty kilometers (31 mi) with a forty-kilogram pack (88 lb) over mountainous terrain in just twenty-four hours.[15] According to North Korean military expert Joe Bermudez, the results of all this training are "tough, intensely trained fighters who [are] . . . ready to obey orders and to suffer privations that could cause mutinies in other armies."[16]

Just as battle terrain does not favor a North Korean advance southward, it is no less forgiving to a northward advance. There is no easy axis of approach to Pyongyang similar to, for example, the broad expanse of desert that U.S. forces exploited in getting to Baghdad. It is about 165 kilometers from Seoul to Pyongyang (102 mi), with about six potential invasion corridors, but only one main paved one that runs north of the DMZ. U.S.-ROK supply lines along this route could be easily targeted by even a decrepit air force. Off the main roads, the terrain is hilly, mountainous, and heavily mined, with the only large flat spaces being soft marshes and rice paddies that would not be conducive to the advance of a large mechanized attack. North Koreans reportedly have also invested heavily in IEDs after watching carefully U.S. difficulties in Iraq. Moreover, this entire peninsula, the equivalent of a distance between Washington, D.C., and Boston—600 miles (965 km) long by 130 miles (210 km) wide—would have a higher density of enemy and allied mechanized forces in battle, over 2 million, than was concentrated in Central Europe during the Cold War. While North Korean forces are not well equipped, most experts believe they would put up a fight. In numbers, this is a 1.1-million-man army, compared with the last U.S. military-on-military war in Iraq, where the enemy numbered only between 250,000 and 400,000. The DPRK army is the fourth-largest standing army in the world behind China, the United States, and India (with only a fraction of the population). It can be bolstered with 7.5 million reservists. Most estimates believe the DPRK military would fight harder than the Iraqi army, because of their severe indoctrination. Even in the most favorable war scenario, the Pentagon predicts that hundreds of thousands would die.[17]

What about a decapitation strike? How feasible is this for U.S. and ROK forces either as a discrete military action or as part of a larger preemptive attack? The Kim leadership's whereabouts constitute a very difficult intelligence target, given the lack of much on-the-ground assets or operatives who have penetrated their elite. The world's primary insights into the North are from overhead satellite photos, which is the less-than-ideal method of targeting individuals. The fact that we did not have a picture of Kim Jong-un, the designated next leader, until 2010 gives one a sense of the gaps in requisite intelligence to carry out a decapitation strike. The task is even more challenging given the numerous precautions the North has taken for decades. All of Kim Jong-il's known official residences remain fully alit (in a land without electricity) and occupied by personnel so that one cannot pinpoint his location. It is also reported that the Dear Leader had a number of look-alikes: body doubles that he used for fear of terrorist attack or assassination.[18] In Pyongyang, there are over eleven thousand underground facilities. All key buildings and palaces are linked with a deep underground network to allow for quick escape if attacked. Nuclear bunkers reportedly exist underneath the main subway system in the city that is already three hundred feet (90 m) underground. After the experience of American bombing and napalm during the Korean War, the North sought refuge by burrowing deeper underground than anyone else in the world, making the country like a block of Swiss cheese, with caverns and tunnels everywhere.[19] Entire command centers, factories, and logistics nodes are housed deep underground. Airfields and runways are built inside mountain ridges. Food and fuel supply depots are buried deep inside the earth to provide enough sustenance for six months. Beneath Kim Il-sung Square reportedly lies a bunker command post large enough to accommodate a hundred thousand men with a fresh-water and ventilation system, and a thirty-kilometer-long (19-mi) tunnel that leads out of the cities into nearby mountains.[20] Kim Jong-il was said to have a security detail, the "2-16 Unit" (named after his birthday), of about a thousand men, many of whom are culled from the best of the elite Special Forces unit. They have no contact with the outside, and no two members of the unit share family ties, in order to ensure strict loyalty to Kim. Based on the account of one former bodyguard, who escaped after being sentenced to a prison camp, the guards formed an impenetrable ring around the Dear Leader.[21] Kim also allegedly had his own underground network of "undisclosed locations." He was rumored to have disappeared for about six weeks into these hideaways near the border with China and Russia after the U.S. invasion of Iraq, presumably because he feared he might be next. The killing of Osama Bin Laden and the capture of Saddam Hussein certainly demonstrate that the U.S. has the wherewithal to carry out a decapitation operation, but it would not be easy and would require exquisite intelligence.

WHAT, ME WORRY?

If adversaries on both sides of the DMZ are rationally deterred from starting a war, then what is there to worry about? This is often the calculation of money managers who invest in Korea. Every time Kim

Jong-il or his son do something provocative, private capital reacts with surprisingly little anguish, largely because they believe deterrence will hold. Pyongyang may do ornery things for tactical advantage, but in the end, it knows that large-scale military attack would be tantamount to suicide and that dictators value their survival more than anything. The bullish markets, therefore, shrug off any DPRK provocations as temporary blips.

There is no denying that conventional deterrence has held on the peninsula since 1953, and it is likely to hold another half-century in terms of deterring a second DPRK invasion of the South. However, there are other dynamics, short of an all-out war on the Korean Peninsula, that are equally dangerous. Some of these relate to developing weapons systems; others relate to dangerous and misinformed strategic thinking on both sides of the peninsula. The danger today is that one of these variables can lead us to war in Korea in a manner very different from that in June 1950.

REACH OUT AND TOUCH . . .

With the North Koreans' continuing development of nuclear weapons, and their development of intercontinental ballistic missiles, North Korea is becoming a direct threat to the United States . . . I don't think it's an immediate threat . . . But on the other hand, I don't think it's a five-year threat.

—SECRETARY OF DEFENSE ROBERT GATES, JANUARY 11, 2011[22]

North Korean missiles are good; indeed, they are the best available on the world market for countries not allied to the United States.

—PROFESSOR BRUCE CUMINGS, UNIVERSITY OF CHICAGO[23]

The United States has failed for over twenty years to deter DPRK development and testing of its ballistic missiles. This failure stands in stark contrast to the record of success in deterring a second armed invasion. DPRK missiles are a strategically critical complement to the country's nuclear weapons program. A large, unwieldy nuclear bomb that is dropped from an airplane, like in World War II, is not nearly as strategically impactful as a miniaturized warhead that can be placed on the top of a long-range missile to be fired at the United States or Japan. The North has been developing for decades precisely this strategic capability to reach out and touch others.

Today, North Korea still faces three obstacles to delivering a ballistic missile on the United States. It has not yet perfected a three-stage missile launch despite three attempts in 1998, 2006, and 2009. It has not yet demonstrated a capacity to put a nuclear warhead on a missile. And it has not yet shown it can manufacture a reentry heat shield for a long-range ballistic missile. (Ballistic missiles exit the atmosphere on launch and then descend through the atmosphere and therefore must withstand intense heat without blowing up before meeting its target.)[24] Having said this, however, they have come a remarkably long way in the development of their program. Moreover, as the quote by Defense Secretary Robert Gates above clearly acknowledges, the DPRK is well on a trajectory to overcome these obstacles in the near future. The table below documents how woefully incapable we have been in deterring North Korean missile tests.

NORTH KOREAN BALLISTIC MISSILE TESTS, 1984-2011		
DATE	TYPE	DESCRIPTION
April/Sept. 1984	Hwasŏng-5 (Scud-B)	Scud-B missile.
June 1990	Hwasŏng-6 (Scud-C)	Upgrade to Scud-C.
July 1991	Hwasŏng-6	Successful Scud-C test.
June 1992	Nodong (ND)-I	Failed test.
May 29~30, 1993	Hwasŏng-5 Hwasŏng-6 Nodong-1	Launched without pre-notification to international community. Nodong fired in direction of Japan.
August 31, 1998	Taep'odong (TD)-I	First test of three-stage missile. First and second stages separated approximately 300 km and 1,380 km respectively from the launch site. Overflew Japanese archipelago.

NORTH KOREAN BALLISTIC MISSILE TESTS, 1984–2011		
DATE	TYPE	DESCRIPTION
July 4~5, 2006	Taep'odong-II	Launches a series of short- and medium-range missiles, including one long-range Taep'odong-II ballistic missile. The TD-II failed 40 seconds after the launch but has an estimated range of 3,600 to 4,300 km.
April 5, 2009	Taep'odong-II	Largest launch vehicle tested by DPRK to date. A three-stage missile with successful separation of first and second stages but failed to put a satellite into orbit. If perfected, would be able to reach continental U.S.
July 2~4, 2009	KN-01 Short-range missiles; Scud-C, Scud-ER; Nodong	Four short-range missiles and an additional seven missiles fired on July 2 and July 4, respectively. July 2 tests were KN-01 missiles that traveled approximately 60 miles before dropping into the sea. July 4 tests involved two Scud-C missiles, two new Scud-ER missiles, and three medium-range Nodong missiles, reportedly traveling 240–310 miles
Early June, 2011	KN-06 Short-range missile	A single short-range (approx. 150 km) surface-to-air missile is tested off North Korea's west coast.

The DPRK possessed an early and intense interest in getting into the missile business, both for security and for sales. The origins of the program date from the 1960s, when the DPRK acquired engine guidance and design technology from the Soviets. While the Soviet Union stopped short of providing the North with ballistic missile technology, they introduced them to free-rockets-over-ground (FROGs), surface-to-air missiles (SAMs), and coastal defense antiship missiles.[25] But it was not until the 1970s that the program got a big boost from China. A 1971 agreement had Beijing help Pyongyang develop ballistic missiles, cruise missiles, and antiship missiles, transferring technology on missile engines and airframe designs. Of particular significance was a joint development program for the DF-61, liquid-fueled medium-range ballistic missile system, though it would eventually be canceled with Deng Xiaoping's rise to power in China.[26] Experts believe a good part of the North's missile technology appears to be of Soviet origin, but this does not necessarily mean it all came from Moscow. A significant volume came to North Korea through the Middle East. Egypt and Syria provided Soviet-based missile technology for the North's Scud missile between 1976 and 1981, long after the Soviets stopped transferring it to Pyongyang. The North Koreans then learned how to build the Scud by taking it apart piece by piece and putting it back together again (known as reverse-engineering). The first reverse-engineered Scud-B missile, known as the Hwasŏng-5, was tested successfully in April and September of 1984. Production of these missiles started shortly thereafter. Iran immediately became a customer, as they wanted the Hwasŏng for use against Iraq and agreed to finance part of the DPRK's production in return for scores of the finished product. In 1990, the North successfully tested an upgraded version, the Hwasŏng-6, which was a reverse-engineered Scud-C missile with an increased range of five hundred to six hundred kilometers (310–373 mi). The North began full-scale production of this missile after the 1990 test.

The North continued with development of the longer-range Nodong missile. They did this by bundling together four Hwasŏng engines, with the first prototypes being completed in 1991. The Nodong had a range of a thousand to fifteen hundred kilometers (620–930 mi), depending on the size of the warhead, and was first tested in 1993, reportedly in the presence of Iranian and Pakistani customers, reaching a distance of five hundred kilometers (310 mi).[27] These missiles were reportedly launched from the Musudan-ri test site without any requisite notification to the international community, and were targeted on a maritime buoy in the direction of Japan, creating, for the first time, real public concerns about the emerging missile threat from the DPRK. While the Nodong did not fly its full distance, some experts believe it was a successful test, and only limited in distance with a purposeful under-fueling of the missile to avoid landing it too close to Japan. This conjecture appears plausible, as the North began production of the Nodong shortly thereafter, amassing an arsenal of about a hundred by the end of the decade. Today there are estimated to be about two hundred deployed and operational, which allows the North to target anywhere in Japan.[28]

Having perfected the Nodong, North Korea proceeded to develop a 1,500 to 2,000 kilometer (930–1,240 mi) long-range ballistic missile known as the Taep'odong-I (TD-I). This was the regime's first attempt at a three-stage missile, using a Nodong missile as the first stage and the Hwasŏng (Scud) missile as the second stage. The dramatic first test of this missile was in August 1998, which the North justified as a satellite launch. The missile overflew the Japanese archipelago and constituted an equivalent of the Sputnik launch for the Japanese public, awakening the population to the existential missile threat to their national security. (Japan invested heavily in ballistic missile defense thereafter.) The missile failed to put a satellite into orbit, but it demonstrated a surprisingly early technical capability to develop multi-stage missiles: the first stage separated approximately 300 kilometers (185 mi) and the second stage about 1,380 kilometers (860 mi) from the launch site. In spite of a declared missile-testing moratorium from 1998 to 2006, which Pyongyang hoped would gain it massive assistance from the ROK, Japan, and the United States, its rocket scientists continued development of the missile programs even without overt testing. The objective was to perfect a longer-range—3,600 to 4,300 kilometer (2,240–2,670 mi)—Taep'odong-II (TD-II) missile, which would be able to reach the continental United States. The DPRK tested the TD-II for the first time unsuccessfully, as part of its largest barrage of short- and medium-range ballistic missile tests in July 2006. The TD-II failed forty seconds after the launch, but still worried governments about unimpeded improvements in the North's programs. The same missile was tested again in April 2009, with much more success. Justified as the launch of a satellite (but using the same elements of a ballistic missile test), the "Ŭnha-2" constituted the largest launch vehicle ever tested by the DPRK, three times the size of the TD-I (four Nodongs strapped together as the first stage and a Nodong as the second stage).[29] The launch took place in an eastward direction toward Hawaii, overflying Japan's Honshu Island. Despite Pyongyang's claims that it successfully placed its Kwangmyŏngsŏng-2 satellite into orbit in nine minutes,[30] the U.S.

Northern Command (USNORTHCOM) reported that the first stage landed in the East Sea/Sea of Japan while the remaining stages fell into the Pacific Ocean along with their payload.[31] Nevertheless, experts saw the missile as a significant advancement over previous prototypes and estimated it to have the potential capacity to reach Hawaii, Alaska, and possibly the West Coast of the continental United States when perfected.

Make no mistake: this is a very successful missile program and a very real threat. The Taep'odong missile arsenal will make the DPRK the first country besides China and Russia to be able to target U.S. cities with nuclear weapons, possibly within four years. In addition, North Korea today is one of the world's biggest exporters of missiles, and therefore one of the biggest sources of horizontal (selling to others) ballistic missile proliferation. Missile sales constitute a major source of hard currency (or crude oil from the Middle East) for the regime. The North can produce well over a hundred Scud-type missiles annually with ranges of three hundred to five hundred kilometers (186–310 mi). These are not of poor quality. The Hwasŏng-6 can be fitted with a 680-kilogram (1,500-lb) conventional bomb and is a fairly accurate missile out to 480 kilometers (300 mi), which meets the needs of most customers, many of whom have beefs with the United States or its allies. Pakistan has had a long relationship with North Korea, originating in the late 1980s. The Ghauri missile arsenal is basically modeled on the Nodong. The two states forged close ties through the 1990s, trading largely in conventional arms. But the relationship took on more alarming implications, when in 2002 it came to light that the "father of the Pakistani bomb," nuclear scientist Abdul Qadeer (A. Q.) Kahn may have aided the North Koreans in getting their uranium enrichment program off the ground.[32] Iran has been another big client. In 1987, it bought a hundred Hwasŏng Scuds for $500 million and used these in the Iran-Iraq War in 1988. Iran's Shehab-3 missile, too, is a knockoff of the Nodong. Iranian engineers are believed to have been present at a number of North Korea's groundbreaking missile tests, and over the years have paid in crude oil for some of their purchases of missiles, artillery systems, midget subs, and other arms. The North has also used its tunneling expertise to help Iran build tens of thousands of meters of underground bunkers and tunnels, designed to withstand bunker-busting munitions. In 2003, Saddam Hussein gave the North $10 million as a down payment on a missile production facility in Iraq, before he was ousted from the country. Syria, too, bought $500 million in Scud-C missiles in 1990, and has continued to collaborate with North Korea in more advanced Scud designs over the years. Other customers include the United Arab Emirates, Libya, Yemen, and Egypt.[33]

While we have deterred a second DPRK invasion of the South, we have not been able to deter the development, testing, or proliferation of these missiles. Since 2006, U.N. Security Council sanctions, financial sanctions, and counterproliferation measures like the Proliferation Security Initiative (PSI), aimed at intercepting shipments of missiles and missile parts, have constituted the world's efforts at stopping these programs, albeit with limited success. Ballistic missile defense, a $500 to $800 billion investment meant to defend the continental United States against an incoming rogue missile, has succeeded in tests, but has yet to be tested against a North Korean missile launch, and therefore has not acted as a deterrent against further testing or development. Indeed, one of the first policy statements attributed to Kim Jong-un after his father's death was his determination to wage war if the United States tried to intercept one of its missile tests.

Much as hawks might hate to admit it, the most effective means of stopping the North's missile threat, thus far, has been through negotiation. The Israelis were the first to try in 1993. When Iran was set to buy 150 Nodong missiles, Israeli foreign minister Shimon Peres was ready to offer Pyongyang $1 billion in investments and technical assistance with the North's gold mines if they would cancel the deal. But after the North announced its intention to pull out of the Nuclear Non-proliferation Treaty in March 1993, the United States intervened to try to stop the deal, and by August these talks screeched to a halt.[34] The last time such negotiations with the United States showed promise was during the Clinton administration. The United States held several rounds of bilateral negotiations between 1996 and 2000, with the objective of stopping the North's long-range ballistic missile program. President Clinton was ready to provide $1 billion annually as compensation for lost revenues if the North gave up their missile development and sales. In return, the DPRK would have had to adhere to Missile Technology Control Regime (MTCR) guidelines, which would limit the range of their arsenal to 300 kilometers (185 mi) and the payload to 500 kilograms (1,100 lb). The deal eventually fell apart over several issues, including the North's unwillingness to eliminate existing stocks, the lack of a satisfactory verification protocol to ensure the North would meet its obligations, and the administration's cautiousness in committing to a Clinton–Kim Jong-il summit before a finalized deal was struck. The Bush administration did not pick up where Clinton left off, focusing the majority of its effort on stopping the nuclear program. The Obama administration, in its first three years in office, has not engaged the DPRK on missiles, either. This essentially means that the program has continued unabated for the past decade. No one expects that the North will start firing missiles at random on the United States once it achieves the capability to do so. But such a capability will certainly affect perceptions of the strategic balance, and will increase North Korea's propensity to coerce others (given its proven capacity to reach out and touch others with retaliation).

Should the current or a future administration engage in negotiations over these missiles, the to-do list would be long: it would start with the imposition of a testing ban to prevent further advances in technology. It would then include agreements to stop further development of launchers, the rollback of existing missile deployments, and the elimination of existing missile stocks. Another target would be to impede continued cooperation with Russian experts. The North has an unusually high rate of success for the tests it has conducted, which has led many experts to believe they are benefiting from technical assistance from Russian scientists who are operating outside of their government's control. In terms of compensation, the North would undeniably demand large sums of money in return for restricting its missile program as it did with the Israelis and with the United States. A novel idea has been for an international consortium to help the North launch a geosynchronous communications satellite, which would enable telephone and television broadcasting coverage. There is an international precedent for this in Kazakhstan (2006), Vietnam (2008), and South Korea (1998). Pyongyang has justified its past long-range missile tests as attempted satellite launches. Such an arrangement would give the North what they presumably want (they claimed the last two TD-II tests were satellite launches) without giving them the launch technology. In the unlikely event that the DPRK accepted such an arrangement, a verifiable agreement would still need to be struck on eliminating existing stocks and future production—hardly an easy feat.

TERROR

The two agents posed as an elderly Japanese father and his pretty daughter as they boarded Korean Air Lines Flight 858 in Baghdad, Iraq, on November 29, 1987. They had trained together for four years to carry out this mission. In order to make the KAL 858 flight, the two had flown a circuitous route to avoid detection, from Pyongyang via Moscow, Budapest, Vienna, and Belgrade, to board the Bangkok-bound plane. The woman, Kim Hyŏn-hŭi, was a twenty-six-year-old daughter of a DPRK foreign ministry official, who was recruited as a covert operative in 1980. The man was Kim Sŭng-il, a seventy-year-old father of seven from Pyongyang. Once on the plane, they planted the bomb, a package of C-4 explosive in a radio encasement with a timer set to explode after the plane stopped over in Abu Dhabi. The two deplaned in Abu Dhabi, and nine hours into the flight, KAL 858 blew up over the Andaman Sea, killing everyone aboard. Once authorities realized KAL 858's demise was no accident, they immediately sought out the fifteen passengers who had deplaned in Abu Dhabi. The two DPRK agents were caught two weeks later at the airport in Bahrain, trying to make their way out of the region. Trained for such situations, the man immediately ingested a cyanide tablet and killed himself. Kim Hyŏn-hŭi, however, failed to act quickly enough and was captured alive. She confessed to the plot after one month of interrogation by the South Koreans. She revealed that the DPRK government directed the mission, and that she had been trained in Japanese by a woman who was later identified by the Japanese government as one of the scores of citizens that had been abducted by North Koreans. Kim later became something of a celebrity in South Korea. While in captivity, she received many letters from young South Korean bachelors offering to marry her. She wrote a best-selling autobiography titled *Tears of My Soul* and donated the proceeds to the victims of KAL 858. Kim ended up marrying one of her bodyguards, a former South Korean intelligence agent, and currently lives under constant security protection in an undisclosed location in South Korea.

The primary use of force against the ROK has been asymmetric, through terrorist acts that eventually are found to be of North Korean origin. Conventional deterrence is not well-suited to deal with this threat. As noted in chapter 2, the DPRK has propagated numerous deadly terrorist attacks. In 1982, Canadian police stopped an assassination attempt against ROK president Chun during an official visit to Canada. Chun narrowly escaped a terrorist bombing the following year during a visit to Rangoon, Burma. In 1986, a terrorist bombing at Seoul's main international airport killed five and wounded thirty. And throughout the 1970s, the government engaged in the practice of abducting South Koreans and foreigners (including Japanese and Europeans) to use them to train spies.

The DPRK has no known terrorist links today, and in a deal related to the 2005 Six-Party agreements, the Bush administration removed North Korea from the state sponsor of terrorism list in 2008. (States can be listed for providing planning, training, logistics, and material support to terrorist organizations, or for providing financial or other forms of assistance.) However, there is no denying the history of links to various non-state guerrilla groups and other nefarious characters. During the 1970s, the North provided weapons and training to guerrilla groups in Latin America, including Argentina, Bolivia, Brazil, Chile, Guatemala, Mexico, Nicaragua, Paraguay, Peru, and Venezuela. Kim Il-sung had good relations with Zimbabwe's dictator Robert Mugabe and equipped his army with tanks, APCs, artillery, and small arms. In the 1970s, the DPRK worked with the Japanese Red Army faction, providing refuge to their agents, most notably when they hijacked civilian airliners from Japan. Some authors claim the DPRK ran terrorist camps that trained Third World revolutionaries and others, including the African National Congress, PLO, Popular Front for the Liberation of Palestine, Hezbollah, and the Tamil Tigers.[35] In 1971, Sri Lanka kicked out DPRK diplomats for allegedly funneling support to the People's Liberation Front, which was bent on overthrowing the government.

Much of this activity at the time was driven by Kim Il-sung's desire to establish himself as the Socialist leader of the Third World. For most of the 1980s, Pyongyang funded the Iran side of the Iran-Iraq War, providing munitions, artillery, Scud missiles, and navy craft. It also sought missile deals with Saddam Hussein in Iraq after the war. In 1988, the

United States designated North Korea as a terrorist state, making it ineligible to receive assistance from international financial institutions like the World Bank and International Monetary Fund. Public knowledge of these sorts of nefarious activities appeared to die down in the 1990s and early 2000s, but with some notable exceptions, including nuclear cooperation with Syria and, more recently, reportedly with Burma. In recent years, the North Koreans have been suspected of helping the Burmese develop a nascent nuclear weapons program in the north of the country. This relationship came to the fore of international attention in the summer of 2009, when the North Korean ship *Kangnam-1* was tracked for days as it reportedly headed for Burma carrying arms, only to eventually turn back to the North under international pressure. North Korea has also been tied, in more recent years, to an Islamic terror organization in the Philippines, having reportedly sold them tens of thousands of small arms.[36] It has even been reported that the DPRK sold weapons to Al Qaeda affiliates in 2005, according to a *Washington Post* report.[37]

BIOCHEMICAL WEAPONS

Among the more menacing threats the DPRK poses to the millions living in the Seoul metropolitan area is its vast chemical weapons stocks and its biological weapons potential. North Koreans' initial knowledge of biochemical weapons originates in the Japanese occupation prior to and during World War II. The Imperial Japanese Army maintained a biochemical and nuclear weapons research center in Hŭngnam, South Hamgyŏng Province, which they notoriously used to experiment on POWs and stockpiled biochemicals along the North Korea–China border. According to most estimates, the DPRK initiated a chemical weapons program in the early 1950s and its biological program in the 1960s. In 1987, North Korea acceded to the Bio and Toxin Weapons Convention (BTWC), and in 1989, to the Geneva Protocol banning biochemical weapons use, but remains one of just five countries that hasn't signed the Chemical Weapons Convention (CWC).[38] While estimates vary widely, most open-source literature places North Korean chemical weapons stocks at between 2,500 and 5,000 metric tons, with the capacity to produce an additional 4,500 tons per annum.[39] The North is thought to possess nerve agents such as sarin and VX gas, blister agents like mustard gas, blood agents, choking agents such as phosgene, and a number of vomiting agents. And in spite of its prohibitions, the DPRK is suspected of pursuing biowarfare capabilities, including plague, cholera, anthrax, and smallpox, which could potentially be weaponized. It is even suspected that the North Koreans have passed on some of their biochemical capabilities to other states, such as Syria, who is now thought to have the largest chemical stockpile in the Middle East.[40] But, perhaps most important for the South Koreans, many assume that a number of the North's long-range artillery systems along the DMZ are equipped with chemical munitions, ready to launch at a moment's notice.[41]

THE SPIRAL OF MISCALCULATION

If the DPRK is deterred from invading South Korea again, their missiles are not yet capable of reaching the United States, and they no longer appear to be in the terrorism business, then why should we be worried? Are the money managers right that we need not worry?

The dangers stem from the overall desperate nature of the regime, given their isolation, opaque dictatorship, and tendency to communicate with the world through violence rather than through diplomacy. When one combines this with their burgeoning weapons capability, including missiles, nuclear, and other WMD, the chances of North Korea's lashing out are still, unfortunately, very real.

DOUBLE OR NOTHING

In particular, there are two things that worry me. The first is North Korean rationality. I don't mean this in the sense that they are crazy. On the contrary, though the caricatures of Kim Jong-il as the "plutonium madman" color the public commentary of North Korea, I believe the leadership, whether it was Kim Jong-il or today, centered around Kim Jong-un, is eminently rational. They may be misinformed about the outside world, but they are rational. The fact that conventional deterrence has held indeed offers evidence of a degree of rationality in Pyongyang. But what is concerning is that sometimes even rational actors, when they become especially stressed, can do dangerous things. That is, countries, when pushed into a corner, have a tendency to lash out rather than whither away. This does not mean they experience a bout of insanity; rather, it becomes perfectly rational to contemplate a desperate action.

In social science jargon, this is sometimes explained through prospect theory.[42] The simple idea is that humans tend to become more risk-acceptant as their situation worsens, and tend to be risk-averse when they are doing well. Think about gambling: if you are at the blackjack table in Atlantic City and having a good night, generally you are risk-averse and desirous of protecting your winnings—i.e., you are not likely to view a "double or nothing" bet as rational. However, if you are having a bad night and losing profusely, then you become more risk-acceptant—i.e., the "double or nothing" bet begins to look appealing as you try to recoup losses. This very simple idea applies to North Korean belligerence. If Pyongyang is in the domain of losses, it is likely to see "double or nothing" bets—such as disrupting the peaceful status quo—as a useful way to try to recoup losses and threaten others into assisting it. Because Pyongyang benefits less from the prosperous peace in Asia than others, it has less vested in the status quo. Moreover, if this status quo is a losing one for Pyongyang, the leadership will start to look for any measures to stop the losses from occurring. This "anything to stop the bleeding" mentality is not craziness. On the contrary, it is quite rational the more desperate one becomes. So the danger from North Korea is that this type of risk-acceptant rationality will lead it to undertake provocative actions short of all-out war.

In 2010, the DPRK fired 180 artillery shells on the South Korean island of Yeonpyeong. After a routine live-fire exercise (aimed away from the North) in the area on the morning of November 23, the North Koreans fired bursts of artillery shells on and around the island in the early afternoon. Two South Korean Marines and two local construction workers were killed in the shelling, with an additional nineteen injured and dozens of properties destroyed. The shelling forced an evacuation of the island and temporary closure of Incheon International Airport, a major hub of air travel in Asia, only seventy-five kilometers (45 mi) away. By any metric, this was an act of war and a violation of the 1953 Korean War armistice. It constituted the most serious conventional military attack since the 1968 attempted commando raid on the South Korean presidential palace, and the first artillery attack on South Korean territory and civilians since the war. Unlike the torpedo attack on the South Korean naval vessel, *Cheonan,* only a few months earlier, there was no perceivable rationale for the attack (i.e., DPRK apologists claimed the *Cheonan* sinking was in retaliation for a prior inter-Korean naval altercation in disputed waters).

Why did the DPRK carry out such a potentially destabilizing attack? Were they not concerned about starting a war? Cable news media chalked it up to another bout of DPRK unpredictability, perhaps aimed at establishing the credentials of the young son, Kim Jong-un, who at the time was being groomed to take over for his ailing father. But this violent act could be entirely rational viewed from the perspective of a country that sees itself increasingly in a losing situation. Absent food assistance from the conservative Lee government in Seoul or other such benefits that North Korea had grown used to during a decade of free-flowing engagement from earlier, progressive South Korean governments, Pyongyang grew increasingly desperate to reverse the trend. Japan, which had previously been the world's biggest donator of food, was no longer giving. The United States had stopped giving assistance in 2009. A poor harvest, tighter U.N. sanctions, and the onset of a cold winter all may have led Pyongyang to view it as perfectly rational to undertake a limited conventional provocation in order to shatter the status quo, and try to force others to compensate it for maintaining the peace. Moreover, this is not a crazy calculation. It is eminently rational as a response to what is perceived as a losing situation. All-out war as an option would have been irrational, because it would have been met with a swift and devastating response from the United States and ROK, probably resulting in the end of the regime. However, a limited but significant conventional provocation, short of all-out war, would be enough to get everyone's attention, threaten stability and prosperity of the South and the region, and require others to seek a solution that did not escalate the situation but brought it back to a stable peace. The fact that this strategy appears not to have worked for Pyongyang (the ROK government did not respond by offering the DPRK goodies to play nice) does not negate the fact that the rationale I describe is an entirely plausible one. This calculated act of belligerence is, in effect, a double-or-nothing bet by the North, which has worked for them time and time again.

A study I directed at the Center for Strategic and International Studies in Washington, D.C., tracked all DPRK provocations on a weekly basis from March 1984 to the present. It charted these provocations against all periods of negotiation involving the United States. The finding was that every DPRK provocation for the past thirty years has been followed within months (on average: 5.9 with the United States, 6.3 with South Korea) by a period of dialogue and negotiations in which the North got something they needed. In October 2006, the North's nuclear test was a brazen act that led to international condemnation, U.N. Security Council sanctions, but also a period of intense negotiations with the United States. Similarly, during the Clinton administration, the North launched its three-stage Taep'odong-I over Japan at the end of August 1998, and by October the two were holding missile talks in New York. That's playing a pretty good hand with a bad set of cards. The point here is not to argue that this was the primary cause for the Yeonpyeong Island shelling. Instead, it is to demonstrate that there is a logic to North Korean belligerence that cannot be deterred in the same way a second DPRK invasion has been successfully discouraged.

This same logic could lead to limited acts of belligerence in the future, not only with artillery but could extend to terrorism, ballistic missiles, or even the limited use of its chemical and biological weapons stockpiles. What if the North fired a ballistic missile in the direction of Hawaii, U.S. missile defense systems were able to track it but unable to shoot it out of the sky, and the missile purposefully landed nine hundred miles (1,450 km) off the coast in the Pacific Ocean, demonstrating a successful launch and guidance system? Or what if the DPRK fired more artillery, this time slightly to the east of Yeonpyeong Island, so that it fell within thirty miles (50 km) of Incheon International Airport, forcing the closing of a major hub of air travel in Asia? Would the United States and the ROK go to war over this act? Given other commitments around the world and a dwindling defense budget, it is highly unlikely that Washington would. Might it retaliate with a missile strike on the DPRK missile launch pad or artillery positions? Possibly, but the chance of escalation with North Korean artillery raining on a hundred thousand U.S. expats in Seoul would make any American president think twice. Yet, at the same time, we could not leave the problem completely unaddressed. We would need to do something that punished the North for such a brazen act, but also would want to reduce the tension and take things off of an escalatory track so that the president could move on to address other pressing issues of the day. History has shown consistently that the response has been some initial sanctions (which the DPRK can tolerate), but then some diplomacy, which gives the North what they want to make them stop, in this hypothetical, firing more missiles in the direction of Hawaii. Undeniably a risky act by the DPRK, if it were to occur, but one that would be entirely rational from a "double or nothing" mind-set, and one that is hard to deter.

MISUNDERSTANDING NUCLEAR DETERRENCE

Another threat posed by the DPRK that cannot be managed by conventional deterrence is Pyongyang's possible misunderstanding of the strategic implications of their possession of nuclear weapons. Recently, DPRK behavior has become increasingly provocative. In 2009 alone, for example, Pyongyang conducted a long-range ballistic missile test in April, a second nuclear test in May, sentenced two U.S. journalists to over a decade of hard labor in June, conducted more missile tests in July, and had a naval skirmish with the ROK Navy in November. In 2010, the North sent submarines to torpedo an ROK naval vessel (March); it then fired artillery on Yeonpyeong Island in November; and it also revealed defiantly to the world that it was pursuing a uranium-based nuclear program in violation of all standing agreements with South Korea and its obligations to the NPT regime. The concentrated frequency of these acts, even more so than their magnitude, is especially worrying. Why do these provocations happen despite the fact that deterrence against DPRK aggression has held since 1953? What worries me in this instance is not the failure of conventional deterrence but that the North, once again, may have made the rational calculation that violence pays. Except that the difference from the "double or nothing" calculation is that this aggression is motivated by Pyongyang's view that its nuclear weapons render it invulnerable to retaliation by others.

What is disturbing about Pyongyang's belligerence over the past three years is not only that the acts are coming in rapid succession faster than ever before, but that they also are accompanied by a plethora of assertions by the North of their nuclear weapons status. Just days after its first test in 2006, the DPRK officials announced that the North had "acquired the status as a full-fledged nuclear weapons state."[43] After their second test, in 2009, they nonchalantly quipped that it is "nothing strange and quite natural for a nuclear weapons state to conduct a nuclear test."[44] Since this latter test, these types of assertions have increased, with an editorial in late 2009 citing how North Korea had demonstrated its "dignity and honor, prestige and might, as a . . . full-fledged nuclear weapons state."[45] Among these various assertions, the DPRK even claimed to be a "responsible nuclear weapons state."[46] The North has also adopted a number of pet names for its arsenal, calling it its "all-powerful treasured sword," or its "invincible might."[47] At the October 2010 Workers' Party assembly, Vice Marshal Ri Yŏng-ho, one of the key military figures in the emerging coterie of advisers around the next leader, Kim Jong-un, proclaimed to the foreign press, "If the U.S. imperialists and their followers infringe on our sovereignty and dignity even slightly, we will blow up the stronghold of their aggression with a merciless and righteous retaliatory strike by mobilizing all physical means, including self-defensive nuclear deterrent force [sic], and achieve the historic task of unification."[48] And in late 2010, KCNA announced that the North Korean military machine was "getting fully prepared to launch a sacred war of justice of Korean style based on the nuclear deterrent at anytime."[49]

These statements may reflect the leadership's belief that they have truly attained the status as a nuclear weapons state and therefore they are invulnerable to retaliation by others. On the sidelines of Six-Party Talks, when negotiations were going nowhere, we would engage in heated exchanges with the DPRK, in which my North Korean counterpart would state unequivocally that the United States should stop dreaming about denuclearization and should simply accept the DPRK as a nuclear weapons state. Nuclear weapons were the only way to ensure against U.S. aggression. He put this in terms I will never forget: "You attacked Afghanistan because they do not have nukes. You attacked Iraq because it did not have nukes. You will not attack us. And you will not attack Iran." The U.S.- and NATO-led airstrikes on Libya in 2011 to prevent mass killings of antigovernment rebels probably only reaffirmed this logic. Qaddafi's mistake, in North Korean minds, was that he gave up his WMD capabilities to the Bush administration in 2003. A KCNA broadcast could not have been more clear:

> The present Libyan crisis teaches the international community a serious lesson. It was fully exposed before the world that "Libya's nuclear dismantlement," much touted by the United States in the past, turned out to be a mode of aggression whereby the latter coaxed the former with such sweet words as "guarantee of security" and "improvement of relations" to disarm itself, and then swallowed it up by force. It proved once again the truth of history that peace can be preserved only when one builds up one's own strength as long as high-handed and arbitrary practices go on in the world. The DPRK was quite just when it took the path of Songun and the military capacity for self-defence built up in this course serves as a very valuable deterrent for averting a war and defending peace and stability on the Korean Peninsula.[50]

The threat posed in this instance is the mirror-opposite of the "double or nothing" provocation out of desperation. Pyongyang's belief instead is that it has attained a position of strategic superiority on the peninsula. That is, the regime now feels it is invulnerable to retaliation, so it has no qualms about carrying out limited but significant provocations that leverage the peaceful status quo in ways that rattle Americans and South Koreans. With their newfound nuclear deterrent, Pyongyang can provoke at liberty until it bullies the South into submission. After all, every time the DPRK carries out these attacks, Seoul's first concern is to avoid panic in the South and capital outflows by jittery investors. The purpose of these provocations would be to force Seoul to give the North cash, food, and energy to get it to stop provoking. This is otherwise known as extortion, and in North Korean minds, it becomes even more effective if their nuclear weapons render them invulnerable to retaliation.

The North Koreans are, of course, wrong in this view. They have no demonstrated second-strike capability (the capacity to withstand a first strike by the enemy and respond with a nuclear strike). Indeed, there is no evidence that they have even weaponized a nuclear warhead. The United States and ROK, therefore, are not deterred from retaliating against a North Korean provocation. Yet what we understand is not nearly as important as what they may believe. The continued references to their nuclear deterrent reflect a degree of confidence that we have not witnessed before. Perhaps they are further advanced in their capabilities than is readily apparent. Or, more likely, they may believe incorrectly that their nuclear tests and long-range ballistic missile tests have demonstrated enough of an existential nuclear capability to make any country think twice about striking it. Again, the point is that if they think this way, conventional deterrence that stopped a second Korean war will not stop further limited provocations like the *Cheonan* sinking or Yeonpyeong Island shelling. And their continued provocations under these circumstances would not be crazy but perfectly rational.

One might question whether Pyongyang already possessed such a deterrent based on its artillery, which it could rain on Seoul at a moment's notice. Yes, this is true. But the fact that the regime has been lately focusing so much on its nuclear deterrent raises another worrisome issue. The constant references to their nuclear weapons may manifest an increasing lack of confidence in their artillery systems, which have been deployed along the DMZ for over half a century. For the most part, these artillery pieces have been poorly maintained, and may increasingly be in a state of disrepair. Hence, the regime focuses on its nuclear deterrent as the answer. Why is this doubly dangerous? Because if a crisis arises in the future, the DPRK will have less confidence in its conventional deterrent and more in its nuclear shield. If deterrence fails, this will logically lead to a spiraling "use it or lose it" dynamic. That is, once the regime realizes they are not invulnerable to attack, they will become very worried that not just their artillery but their nuclear weapons would be at risk of being neutralized by an attack. This would cause them to move up the escalation ladder more quickly, contemplating not just conventional retaliation but also, potentially, nuclear retaliation: use them before you lose them.

This shift in strategic thinking in the North is taking place at a time when things are also changing in the South. After the shelling of

Yeonpyeong Island, in 2010, a new mood of anger and defiance took hold in the ROK. Previously, when the North provoked, South Koreans would take it in stride, almost embarrassed before an international audience about the actions of a crazy uncle in the attic, and try to get on with their lives. There was an attempt to be magnanimous and to avoid unnecessary escalation. But the Yeonpyeong shelling made Koreans acutely aware of the deteriorating strategic spiral they were locked in. Unlike the *Cheonan* sinking, which took place at sea in the dead of night and without witnesses, the artillery shelling of the island happened in broad daylight and was captured on cell phone cameras, the images immediately going viral all over the world. The uniform reaction was one of a demand for the government to strike back next time and to no longer permit the North to carry out its belligerence at will. President Lee Myung-bak stated very clearly in a national address that Seoul's patience had run out, and that the next provocation would be met by force. As he addressed the nation less than a week after the incident, President Lee vowed with particular emphasis: "If the North commits any additional provocations against the South, we will make sure that it pays a dear price without fail."[51] Starting in May 2010, the South Korean government undertook a bottom-up review of their strategy led by scholar and national security expert Yi Sang-u. Military officials subsequently rewrote their military rules of engagement in March 2011, shifting from "passive deterrence" to "proactive deterrence." The details of this are not known, but essentially, the old rules of engagement were weighted heavily toward preserving stability and de-escalation (i.e., "report first, do not respond militarily"). The new rules are reportedly "to act first, and then report," and to not rule out preemption as a form of defense against imminent DPRK attacks. What this means is that at the next bit of DPRK mischief, the ROK will let the planes and the missiles fly in response, rather than sit idly. This new, forward-leaning military position by Seoul was somewhat worrying to U.S. officials. On the one hand, Washington saw the need to deter further provocations; on the other, it did not want its ally to overreact. South Korean military officials' assurances that they could "control the escalation ladder" created more concern than calm that both countries could miscalculate, entrapping the United States in a war.[52]

WAR?

The confluence of these strategic logics presents an unstable situation on the peninsula, which I outlined in my testimony before the Congress in March 2011.[53] Seoul has basically reoriented its military to respond to the next action by the North. Meanwhile, the North believes its nuclear capabilities deter states from retaliating against it. Pyongyang, therefore, feels uninhibited in pursuing its coercive strategy aimed at leveraging the peaceful status quo against Seoul to reap benefits. The North acts with another attack, the South responds with military force. Both sides escalate in response to each other.

This spiral of miscalculation can lead to war.

As recently as December 2010, many officials were worried about just this spiral. The ROK decided that it would respond to the Yeonpyeong shelling by conducting its own live-fire artillery exercises on the island. The North warned that such an act would be akin to a declaration of war and that it would respond by turning Seoul into a "sea of fire," with confidence that the ROK would not dare fight back. Like a sucker-punched boxer itching for a chance at redemption, the Lee government was prepared to respond with force to any DPRK provocation during the drills. The Chinese grew concerned about the deteriorating situation and approached the United States to see whether Washington could stop the ROK from carrying out the exercise, but to no avail. The Russians called for an emergency meeting of the U.N. Security Council only hours before the exercises were scheduled for the same purpose. An eight-hour, closed-door emergency session was held at the Security Council, but to no avail, with China blocking any statement including even the mention of the DPRK shelling of Yeonpyeong Island. During the session, the North Korean ambassador to the United Nations, Sin Son-ho, reportedly threatened that war on the peninsula could easily spread worldwide, and referred to the South Korean drills as "gangster-like." Nevertheless, the South prepared by equipping a fleet of fighter jets with air-to-surface missiles, capable of striking the North Korean coast in case of retaliation. The North Koreans readied their own defenses, deploying more surface-to-air and surface-to-ship missiles along their coast. The island was nearly fully evacuated on the eve of the drills, with fearful residents scooping up their children and belongings in preparation for the worst. Some residents stopped by a local church for a final prayer before heading to the South Korean mainland. Others defiantly refused to budge, preferring to stay on the island where they had spent their entire lives. Seoul delayed by a day but eventually did carry out the exercises, and Pyongyang did not take action. After the ninety-minute drill, a North Korean official dismissed the exercise as being "not worth reacting to," but behind the scenes there was a flurry of activity. A crisis in this instance was averted only because Beijing messaged urgently to its North Korean ally that it would not support an escalation of the crisis by Pyongyang. The United States reportedly also appealed to Seoul to minimize direction of the artillery fire northward, and to focus firing westward to avoid any miscalculation on the part of the North.[54] Though a potential war was forestalled, this hardly gives one confidence that the deterrence dynamic on the peninsula is stable.

IN INTERNATIONAL RELATIONS, we often talk about the three ways that nation-states employ the use of force: defense, deterrence, and compellence (punishment). Defense is the act of repelling an attack. Deterrence is the threat of unacceptable retaliation against the adversary to prevent an attack. And compellence is the application of force (sanction) as punishment until the adversary changes behavior. The bottom line is that the United States and ROK have been good at deterring a second North Korean invasion for over sixty years. The two allies are also good at defense. If deterrence failed, Washington and Seoul would not just repel an attack, but through execution of a battle plan—cited in the media as OPLAN 5027[55]—would also roll back the regime.[56] The United States and ROK have also, over the decades, arrayed a plethora of compellent tools in the form of U.N. Security Council resolutions (UNSCR), bilateral trade sanctions, counterproliferation activities, and financial sanctions to try to influence and shape DPRK behavior. But what continues to vex policymakers is our inability to deter missile and nuclear testing and development. Moreover, the deterrence that has kept the peace on the peninsula is not well-suited to these limited but deadly military provocations short of an all-out war. Whether the North pursues these out of desperation or out of a belief in its nuclear deterrent, the threat to the peninsula is that a logic may be emerging in the North that violence is rational and beneficial, which creates an inherently unstable situation.

How can we address this problem? The first step is to try to deter through continuous military exercises. Readiness by both the ROK and U.S. militaries is obviously an important component of deterrence. But in the North Korean case, it may be useful particularly because the DPRK military is less likely to provoke directly into the teeth of strong U.S. and ROK readiness. Provocations tend to be carried out in areas where the DPRK sees vulnerabilities, which only became apparent to the general public after the fact. Thus, for example, the sinking of *Cheonan* made clear the weaknesses in ROK anti–submarine warfare capabilities, which Seoul and Washington subsequently fixed through exercises. The Yeonpyeong attack revealed weakness in ROK counterbattery radar, and was followed by improvements. This increased tempo of exercising helps to neutralize the North's "hit-and-run" strategy of provocations. It requires much effort and is not foolproof, but it is necessary. After all, the North needs only find one weakness to exploit next, while the South needs to train and exercise across the entire spectrum of capabilities and potential contingencies. In this regard, the ROK has instituted some seventy-one to seventy-three recommendations for reform of their defense capabilities, ranging from changes in doctrine to new weapons capabilities. Known as "Defense Reform 307," these plans aim to create the ROK wherewithal to respond promptly with force to any future provocations. While Seoul sees it as imperative to reestablish conventional deterrence, this heightens the potential for escalation of hostilities with the next North Korean provocation.

In addition to military exercising and defense reform, there are policy alternatives to address these threats, both of which would seem terribly unappealing to most. First, if DPRK provocations are being pursued out of desperation, then the world needs to do things that move the regime away from seeing the "double or nothing" bet as a rational option. This means enacting policies that give North Korea a larger stake in the peaceful status quo than it now has. This might mean food assistance and economic engagement, or other items it might value enough so that bad behavior could mean their forfeiture. Such a policy by the United States and ROK would come under severe criticism, and would be seen as rewarding bad behavior, succumbing to DPRK extortion tactics, and offering only a temporary reprieve. The North, moreover, could exploit such outreach by simply raising the price whenever it wanted to in order to remain peaceful. It would be hard for any administration to accept this.

If the DPRK pursues violence out of the mistaken belief that they hold a superior position because of the nuclear weapons, then the appropriate policy would be to undertake measures to disabuse them of this misperception. It is entirely plausible that strategists in Pyongyang do not adequately understand the literature on nuclear deterrence, in which case, one policy might be to engage with the DPRK military on the ABCs of stable deterrence, what constitutes a second-strike capability, and how the survivability of weapons systems can be achieved. The United States conducted such exchanges with the Soviet Union to minimize the chances of miscalculation during the Cold War. It also conducted such exchanges with China, once the latter became a nuclear weapons state. Understanding the vulnerabilities of their own capabilities might reduce DPRK bravado and overzealousness.

This policy option, too, would be met with widespread disdain. Allies like Japan, Australia, and the ROK might understand the logical need for such a strategic nuclear dialogue, but at a political level would see it as outright abandonment by the United States. Such a dialogue would effectively convey a clear political message that the United States has resigned itself to accepting the DPRK as a nuclear weapons state, and had given up on denuclearization. Furthermore, many would see such a dialogue as signaling the effective end of the NPT regime, since the worst violator would essentially be recognized for its nuclear capabilities. Any administration would be vilified on these counts.

It is no wonder that North Korea is known in the policy world as the "land of lousy options."

CHAPTER SEVEN

COMPLETE, VERIFIABLE, AND IRREVERSIBLE DISMANTLEMENT (CVID)

THE FACILITY WAS NESTLED DEEP IN A CANYON, WITH THE EUPHRATES RIVER TO THE north and the broad expanse of lifeless desert to the east. After many years of careful and quiet work since 2001, it was nearing operation. Without the help of outside partners, the project could never have been completed, and once loaded with fuel, it would provide a means of producing the weapons-grade plutonium necessary for making nuclear bombs.

But this facility at Al-Kibar would never see its inauguration. Ten F-15s left Ramat David Air Base around eleven P.M. on September 5, 2007, for what appeared to be routine exercises. The evening made it unusual but not exceptional for the pilots from the Israeli Air Force's Sixty-ninth squadron to take to the sky. The planes took off south of the port city of Haifa toward the Mediterranean Sea, but once the evening flight exercise was ostensibly completed, the true task began.

Known to only a few as Operation Orchard, seven of the ten F-15s dropped to altitudes below radar range as they cruised toward the eastern desert sands of Syria. Once the jets entered Syrian airspace, they evaded fire from Syrian AA missiles. The first target was a radar station near Tall al-Buad, which was destroyed with laser-guided precision munitions. Next, the planes reached the provincial town of Deir ez-Zor area and set their sights to the east on the Al-Kibar facility, only eighty miles (130 km) from the Iraqi border. This was at least the second covert operation against the facility authorized by Israeli prime minister Olmert in two months, the first one having been an aborted attempt to take soil samples and survey the reactor. The Israelis, however, needed little confirmation in their own minds about the existential threat posed by Al-Kibar.

Just after midnight, the residents of Deir ez-Zor were awakened by the sound of distant explosions lighting up the black skies. The F-15s destroyed the central hull of the reactor facility "lit up" by Shaldag special forces commandos on the ground, who had infiltrated the day prior.[1] AGM-65 Maverick missiles and five-hundred-kilogram (1,100-lb) bombs left the facility in an ashen heap. The F-15s thundered home, reporting "mission accomplished." Prime Minister Olmert called Turkish prime minister Recep Tayyip Erdogan to explain what he had just ordered, and to apologize if the pilots "inadvertently" crossed into Turkish airspace. (Discharged fuel tanks from the jets were found in Turkey.) Olmert's message to Syrian leader Assad was more direct: this was a limited action. Israel had no other targets beyond Al-Kibar. Olmert would be happy to leave the issue alone if Syria would do the same. On October 10, 2007, a Syrian team finished a cleanup operation of the burned remains of the reactor facility, destroying any traces of construction and burying everything—figuratively and literally—underground.

The destroyed secret nuclear facility at Al-Kibar was a gas-cooled, graphite-moderated reactor. Only one country in the world has built this type of reactor in the past thirty-five years—North Korea. According to a video that was released after the bombing and sourced by authoritative intelligence officials, Syria's reactor was nearing operational capacity by August 2007, and therefore the Israelis sought to destroy it before it could be fueled. The video goes on to say: "We are convinced, based on a variety of information, that North Korea assisted Syria's covert nuclear activities, both before and after the reactor was destroyed . . . We have information spanning more than a decade that indicates sustained nuclear cooperation between Syria and North Korea."[2]

Both the U.S. and Israeli governments remained conspicuously silent about this veritable act of war. There were no proclamations or statements, and officials ducked all questions about the incident. But the act spoke for itself. The Al-Kibar reactor was in many ways America's worst nightmare—North Korea's three-decade drive for nuclear weapons had now crossed a new threshold. The Kim regime not only posed a "vertical proliferation threat," which refers to the augmentation of its own weapons capabilities, it was now a "horizontal proliferation threat"—transferring nuclear materials and know-how to aid other regimes with nuclear ambitions that wish to do harm to the United States or its allies. Efforts by the United States and the world to obtain "complete, verifiable, and irreversible" removal of nuclear weapons from North Korea had failed. How did this happen?

ORIGINS OF THE NUCLEAR AFFLICTION

The first party with an interest in nuclear technology on the Korean Peninsula was the Japanese. During the occupation period, colonial authorities discovered deposits of uranium ore and graphite in northern Korea, which they used in their experimentation with nuclear technology. After the end of World War II, North Korea enjoyed a mutually beneficial relationship on nuclear issues with Soviet Union, without whom they could not have had a nuclear program. (After China conducted its first nuclear test in 1964, Kim Il-sung was rebuffed by Mao when he asked for nuclear cooperation.) Moscow needed large amounts of uranium ore in their efforts to develop nuclear weapons, and found a ready supplier in the North. The North was interested in learning all it could about the nuclear fuel cycle. Kim Il-sung sent hundreds of scientists to study at the Institute for Nuclear Research at Dubna, near Moscow. The North brought home this knowledge and created its first nuclear physics laboratory at the National Academy of Science. Kim Il-sung ordered a nationwide survey of all natural minerals, including uranium ore, and in the mid-1960s created a nuclear research complex at Yongbyon, which he staffed with scientists trained in Moscow. The first research reactor was built with Soviet help and went into operation around 1967, a Soviet IRT-2 megawatt research reactor at Yongbyon fueled by enriched uranium. North Korea worked feverishly to develop indigenous expertise. In 1973, the Department of Nuclear Physics and the Department of Radiochemistry were opened at Kim Il-sung University; and at Kimch'aek University, departments specializing in nuclear materials, nuclear reactors, and nuclear engineering were also created.

It was in the late 1970s and 1980s that DPRK interest in nuclear weapons development, as distinct from nuclear energy, became more apparent. In addition to its reactor cooperation with the Soviets, in the mid-1970s, the North initiated on its own a secret nuclear program based on a five-megawatt reactor at Yongbyon. As a condition of continuing nuclear cooperation, Moscow required that North Korea allow international inspections of the reactor, to ensure that it was not being utilized to produce material that could be used for nuclear weapons. Subsequently, in 1977, Pyongyang concluded an agreement with the international watchdog agency, the International Atomic Energy Agency (IAEA), and allowed inspections of the research reactor it had cooperated on with the Soviets, but not access to the "second reactor." In 1985, the Soviets pressured Kim Il-sung to become a signatory to the Nuclear Non-proliferation Treaty, but the DPRK refused to sign a safeguards agreement, which is an obligation of NPT members. Meanwhile, it was becoming clear to U.S. officials from the early 1980s that the North was building a clandestine nuclear weapons—not nuclear energy—program. In 1985, the U.S. intelligence community revealed for the first time that it detected high explosives testing by the North and had evidence the North was building secret nuclear facilities in pursuit of a weapons program.[3] These facilities included not just the five-megawatt reactor but a six-hundred-foot-long (180-m), six-stories-tall radiochemical laboratory that could be used to reprocess weapons-grade plutonium from the spent fuel rods. The five-megawatt reactor facility started to operate in 1986 or 1987, and was estimated to be capable of producing six kilograms (13 lb) of plutonium annually, enough to make one bomb. The North claimed the facility was for civilian energy research purposes, but satellite photos revealed the absence of any of the requisite power lines or infrastructure for generating electricity. These photos also indicated the construction of larger, fifty-megawatt and two-hundred-megawatt reactors in the same vicinity from about 1984. Should these facilities have been completed, they would have been capable of producing two hundred kilograms (440 lb) of plutonium, enough for thirty bombs per year. By the start of the 1990s, the North had demonstrated a capability to maintain a complete nuclear fuel cycle using domestically produced materials.[4]

It had also demonstrated a troubling tendency to make agreements about their nuclear program but implement none of them. The North signed the NPT in 1985, for example, but did not sign a safeguards agreement until January 1992, some seven years after it had promised to. Pyongyang signed a joint denuclearization declaration with the ROK in early 1992, which instituted a comprehensive ban on the peninsula of all nuclear-related activities, but they could not reach any subsequent agreements on a bilateral North-South inspection regime or on other verification issues. The issue started to creep onto the U.S. foreign policy radar screen. In July 1990, the *Washington Post* reported on new satellite photos confirming the existence of plutonium reprocessing facilities. An influential column written by Leslie Gelb of the *New York Times* in April 1991 warned that the next major security threat in the aftermath of Iraq's rebuffed invasion of Kuwait was the nascent nuclear program in North Korea.[5] Acceding to the safeguards agreement meant that the North would have to allow inspections, which it finally pledged to do in the summer of 1992. Prior to his visit to the Yongbyon facility, IAEA official Hans Blix was provided briefings by U.S. intelligence officials, including a virtual tour of Yongbyon and designated areas of concern. IAEA officials had visited only once before, in 1977, and therefore had little on-the-ground experience with the facility.

During Blix's visit, the DPRK showed him a small vial of powdered plutonium and said that they had indeed reprocessed about three ounces of plutonium in 1989, from eighty-nine damaged fuel rods, but that this was experimental. A series of inspections that summer showed, however, that the DPRK was not telling the truth. In what would be the first of several occasions where the DPRK underestimated the capacity of nuclear forensics, Yongbyon officials allowed IAEA inspectors to take swipe samples of the equipment used to produce plutonium and of the waste storage tank pipe. With help from technicians in the U.S. Air Force, the IAEA discovered different rates of decay of the particle samples. They also found disparate isotopic signatures between the swipe samples and the waste samples. All of this indicated that the North has reprocessed plutonium on at least three occasions in 1989, 1990, and 1991—contrary to what the North initially reported to Blix. Concerns about North Korean diversion of nuclear materials for military use mounted, and in February 1993, the IAEA exercised an obscure measure calling for "special inspections" of two nuclear waste sites in the North, access to which would provide a much better picture of plutonium production. Pyongyang scoffed at this demand, claiming that the IAEA was a puppet of U.S. aggression and that no other NPT member had ever been subjected to such "special inspections." From this point on, a dynamic began that has become familiar to all who have given even cursory attention to the nuclear problem as it has been covered in the newspapers.

GROUNDHOG DAY

The casual news consumers, upon hearing about the latest antics of Kim Jong-il, might roll their eyes complaining about yet another rerun of the same nuclear crisis. They would not be terribly wrong. Recounting the nuclear crises with North Korea is a bit like the movie *Groundhog Day*. The script looks something like this: the IAEA declares the North is in violation of the NPT; Pyongyang threatens withdrawal from the NPT; the United States and United Nations condemn and sanction North Korean intransigence; and North Korea retaliates by undertaking production of more plutonium and/or a nuclear test. Throughout these ordeals, the North Koreans have accumulated approximately thirty to fifty kilograms (66 to 110 lb) of plutonium, enough to make five to eight nuclear bombs,[6] and have contributed to the destruction of two international denuclearization agreements.

CRISIS NO. 1: THE AGREED FRAMEWORK

The first nuclear crisis occurred in 1994. In January, the director of the CIA went public with the estimate that Pyongyang had accumulated enough plutonium for one to two nuclear weapons. North Korea remained defiant in its rejection of special inspections, and the IAEA inspectors, though in the country, were prevented by the North from carrying out their inspection duties. IAEA head Hans Blix reported to the United Nations that the DPRK was not in compliance, and the United States sought sanctions. The IAEA confirmed in May–June 1994 that the North was removing spent fuel rods from the Yongbyon reactor without international inspectors to observe the process. At the time, this was about the most provocative and defiant act the regime could take. Not only did it constitute the first step to refueling the reactor and potentially producing more weapons-grade plutonium, it also constituted a clear breach of a red line drawn by the United States and the world community. Pyongyang then announced it was cutting off all ties with the international watchdog IAEA, basically conveying that it was going to pursue nuclear weapons in full defiance of the nonproliferation treaty.

In response, the United States considered military options to take out the facility. This ran the risk of escalating to an all-out war on the peninsula (discussed in detail below). The gravity of the situation was evident in the hoarding shoppers emptying out grocery stores in South Korea in case of conflict, and the State Department advising American citizens to leave the country. In June 1994, North Koreans invited former U.S. President Jimmy Carter to Pyongyang to meet with Kim Il-sung. Carter discussed with Kim the outlines of a potential agreement based on elements of the then-suspended negotiations. Acting as a private citizen, but with the authority of a former president, Carter called the White House from Pyongyang and told the administration that the North was willing to step down from the crisis and reintroduce IAEA inspectors. For the United States, the presence of inspectors was not the issue, since they had been in the country before but had been prevented from doing the work they needed to do. The United States agreed to reenter the negotiations if Carter could seal a commitment by Kim not to reprocess spent fuel and not to refuel the reactor.

Carter's trip and the subsequent U.S.–DPRK Agreed Framework averted an escalation of the first crisis in October 1994. The result of four months of intense negotiations led by my friend and former dean at Georgetown, Bob Gallucci, in his capacity as assistant secretary of state for political-military affairs, and his DPRK counterpart, the then-senior vice minister of foreign affairs Kang Sŏk-ju, the agreement essentially offered energy assistance, political normalization, and economic benefits in exchange for a freeze within one month and eventual dismantlement of the North's nuclear program. The freeze referred to operations at the plutonium production facilities at Yongbyon and the construction of the two larger, fifty- and two-hundred-megawatt reactors at T'aech'ŏn. North Korea also committed to eventually allowing the IAEA to verify compliance through special inspections, and agreed to allow the eight thousand spent fuel rods to be canned and stored, with plans to eventually remove them from the country. In return, the United States agreed to provide the DPRK with two state-of-the-art light-water reactors (LWRs) with a combined capacity of two thousand megawatts to compensate for their professed loss of energy by giving up the Yongbyon reactor. Until these reactors were operational, the United States promised to provide annual shipments of 500,000 tons of heavy fuel oil (HFO), amounting to roughly $50 million per year and commencing within three months of the agreement.[7] The LWRs would be financed through a multilateral consortium known as Korea Energy Development Organization (KEDO), which included the ROK, Japan, and the United States, along with a collection of other international partners.[8] The lion's share of the cost of the LWRs, however, was footed by the ROK, totaling $3.2 billion, and by Japan, picking up the remaining $1 billion.[9] The Agreed Framework also called for the eventual normalization of political relations, beginning with a reduction in trade and investment barriers by the United States within three months, and the eventual establishment of liaison offices, followed by ambassadorial relations. The United States also committed to provide formal assurances against the threat or use of nuclear weapons against the DPRK. The concept behind the agreement was reciprocal moves where fulfilled commitments by one side would be met with fulfilled commitments from the other. Ultimately, the agreement envisioned this path of reciprocity to lead to the full dismantlement of the three reactors. A confidential minute delineated the timetable of 2004–2005 for the two LWRs, as well as the terms of the nuclear freeze, which included all facilities at Yongbyon and a DPRK pledge not to build new ones.

The Agreed Framework averted a potential war on the peninsula, but still came under heavy scrutiny. The implementation of the agreement was tortuous from the start with both sides claiming the other was not living up to its terms. There were concerns about DPRK nuclear cheating at a suspected underground facility at Kumchangri in 1999. Pyongyang complained about U.S. failure to lift sanctions, deliver oil, and complete the LWRs on schedule. (HFO deliveries fell behind schedule, but they were eventually all made.) Republicans won the midterm elections only weeks after the agreement was signed, and they raised many doubts about its effectiveness. Critics disputed the Clinton administration's claim that LWRs were more proliferation-resistant than the graphite reactors they would replace, particularly in the hands of North Koreans who could not be trusted with any nuclear capabilities. A freeze of the North's programs was viewed as suboptimal, because Pyongyang could always reverse their promises, critics argued.

The latter points were unfair. Any negotiator is always trying to get the maximum and irreversible concessions first, but if the other side is uncooperative, then one must work with what they can achieve or walk away. The freeze did not eventually stop the North from restarting activities at Yongbyon, but it did succeed in stopping the construction of the fifty-megawatt and the two-hundred-megawatt reactors, which, if operational, would have produced thirty bombs annually. This was perhaps the most lasting accomplishment of the Agreed Framework.

CRISIS NO. 2: THE SIX-PARTY TALKS

The second crisis occurred in October 2002. In the aftermath of the June 2000 summit meeting between the North and South Korean leaders, as well as a breakthrough summit meeting in September 2002 between the Japanese prime minister Koizumi Junichiro (2001–2006) and Kim Jong-il, experts widely proclaimed the end of Cold War antagonisms in East Asia and the dawn of a new era.[10] The Korea summit appeared to validate Seoul's full embrace engagement policies and significantly reduce perceptions of threat. The Pyongyang Declaration with Japan opened the potential for large-scale assistance and normalized relations between longtime adversaries. There were growing concerns amid this happiness, however, that North Korea was covertly developing the capacity for a second nuclear program, this time based on uranium rather than plutonium. Such a program would have been in violation of all standing agreements the North had made with South Korea and the United States, and a clear violation of the NPT regime. The George W. Bush administration, still reeling from the attacks of September 11, designated North Korea as part of an "axis of evil"—a renegade regime that, along with Iraq and Iran, might fuel WMD terrorist threats to the homeland. In October 2002, a U.S. delegation led by Assistant Secretary of State James Kelly arrived in Pyongyang and called upon the North to address concerns that it was making purchases of high-strength aluminum and other items consistent with the pursuit of a uranium enrichment program in violation of standing agreements. His North Korean counterpart responded defiantly that the DPRK was entitled to such weapons, but then later denied that they had such a program.

This diplomatic confrontation sparked the second crisis. The United States ended HFO supplies to the North on the grounds that it could not certify to Congress that the DPRK was in compliance with the terms of the Agreed Framework. The IAEA adopted a resolution calling on the DPRK to come clean on its secret uranium program. Pyongyang denied that it had such a program despite what it conveyed to Assistant Secretary Kelly, and proceeded to reverse every element of the 1994 agreement. It restarted its nuclear reactor, kicked out international monitors, removed seals on the facilities, and disabled the monitoring cameras. It refueled the Yongbyon reactor in January 2003 with rods that could potentially produce enough plutonium for six to seven more weapons, and declared its withdrawal from the NPT regime effective immediately. In February 2005, just as the DPRK foreign ministry made its most definitive statement to date that they possessed nuclear weapons, the threat of North Korea proliferating nuclear materials to others came into stark relief when the White House officials Michael Green and William Tobey undertook a mission to Beijing, Seoul, and Tokyo to convey U.S. concerns that, sometime in 2004, Libya received nearly two tons of uranium hexafluoride suspected to be of North Korean origin. The material was not fissile in itself (not immediately usable in a nuclear device), but if fed into nuclear centrifuges could have been enriched to make it weapons-grade.[11] The following month, Pyongyang asserted its sovereign right to test its long-range missiles, and in April, it did not deny that it would sell its wares to terrorists if pushed into a corner by the United States. Between 2003 and 2005, it also undertook a massive reprocessing campaign, fueling and then defueling the Yongbyon reactor with batches of eight thousand fuel rods, which were then culled for their plutonium. According to experts, the North now had amassed an additional five to eight bombs worth of plutonium.[12] The Bush administration's mantra henceforth was that it would not negotiate anything with North Korea except the "complete, verifiable, and irreversible dismantlement" (CVID) of its nuclear programs.

SIX PARTIES, NOT TWO

Contrary to popular opinion, President Bush never had, nor asked for, a plan to collapse the North Korean regime that he despised so bitterly. He knew peaceful diplomacy was the best option for denuclearizing North Korea, but he wanted a different format for doing so. This gave rise to the logic behind the Six-Party Talks. After the breakdown of the 1994 agreement, President Bush had no qualms about seeking sanctions to punish North Korea, but he also knew that some form of diplomacy was eventually needed. The previous bilateral agreement broke down because of DPRK cheating, but it also constituted a negotiating algorithm that was not entirely favorable to the United States. Because the United States was negotiating on behalf of not only itself but also the region, to get rid of Pyongyang's nuclear threat, the U.S. negotiators were, in effect, doing all of the heavy lifting. After every negotiating round with the North Koreans, U.S. lead negotiator Gallucci would have debriefing sessions with his South Korean and Japanese counterparts, and would be confronted by a then-hard-line government in Seoul cynically asking, "So, what did you give away to the North Koreans today?" Regional actors would urge the Americans to negotiate a good agreement with the DPRK to end the nuclear program, but would also urge Washington not to threaten the use of force that might destabilize the region. Moreover, any leverage that Washington might exercise was undercut by Pyongyang's primary ally, China, which was both backstopping the regime with food and energy assistance, and securing their own interests against DPRK instability.

This was not the negotiating dynamic that Bush wanted to reengage in. It made no sense to allow countries in the region that were most directly threatened by their North Korean neighbor to free-ride off the negotiating efforts of the United States but at the same time demand that the United States solve the problem while others sat on the sidelines. The advantage of negotiating bilaterally with the North was that the United States was in control, but its freedom of movement was inevitably curtailed by allied complaints, or neutralized by Chinese backdoor support to Pyongyang. Thus, President Bush called for a new negotiating forum, with guidelines that were clear: the new forum should include those regional players whose interests were directly affected by the problem so that they would have a real stake in the outcome. These countries should also have some political influence and material leverage on Pyongyang in order to be effective. They should also have influence in the wider international community should the negotiations fail and the issue be referred to the U.N. Security Council. And there were to be no free-riders.

South Korea was an obvious choice. Kim Dae-jung's and Roh Moo-hyun's Sunshine Policies toward North Korea constituted both a potential source of incentives in the negotiations and sanctions (through the withholding of benefits). Moreover, it was better to have any ROK handouts to the North regulated in some manner by the pace of the larger nuclear negotiations rather than on a wholly separate and unregulated track. Japan was another obvious choice. It was a global power whose security was directly threatened by the North's nuclear program, and it was a potential source of massive economic assistance to the North on the back end of any future agreement. These two allies, moreover, would give the United States a strong foundation in any multilateral negotiating forum.

China was considered a critical country. As North Korea's only great power patron after the end of the Cold War, Beijing exercised an inordinate amount of influence on the North through its economic assistance, and party and military ties. A burgeoning nuclear program would render China's immediate region unstable, and so it had direct stakes in the outcome. The previous bilateral U.S.-DPRK negotiation allowed China to coast with minimal cost or commitment. Beijing could piggyback on the stability provided by any U.S. denuclearization agreement, but at the same time, it could keep the regime in Pyongyang afloat to maintain a friendly buffer. The idea arose, therefore, not only to include China but also to place it as the chair of the negotiations. Beijing's face and reputation would now be associated with the success or failure of the denuclearization effort. The international attention Beijing would garner in this multilateral negotiation, it was hoped, would widen the aperture of its traditionally parochial views on North Korea.

Finally, Russia was considered a useful player. It had the history of nuclear cooperation with the North and was a potential player in any alternative energy arrangements for the Northeast Asian region. It was not initially in the concept (in part because Putin called for the United States to work directly with the DPRK), but once the talks started to take shape, Moscow changed its tune. Equally important, Russia along with China were permanent members of the U.N. Security Council, which was a body inevitably drawn into play when Pyongyang did provocations.

There was no belief that simply changing the format of the negotiations would magically achieve denuclearization of the North. However, variations of the new "five-to-one" logic in the Six-Party Talks offered potential advantages over the old format. Five countries—the United States, Japan, South Korea, China, and Russia—telling Kim to trade his weapons for benefits and entry to the world community—was a lot more credible than one country doing so. Having the North Koreans make commitments to five countries at once also reduced the opportunities for Pyongyang to say different things to different parties (as they had done, for example, when they acknowledged the existence of the uranium program to Assistant Secretary Kelly in 2002 and then denied it to other parties afterward). Finally, negotiations for the United States always started with a minimum coalition of three (United States, Japan, ROK) and aimed to achieve five (plus China, Russia) against one.

The Six-Party Talks, which formally started in August 2003, undeniably had their challenges. The United States had never participated in a formal multilateral negotiation in which China held the permanent chair. This meant that in the negotiation of any agreements, the Chinese team held the pen, which gave it great influence over the outcome. Trying to coordinate policy positions among three, five, or six parties was no easy feat. Assistant Secretary Kelly once famously described the process as akin to "herding cats." And, at times, not everything went according to the blueprint. The engagement-oriented South Koreans under Roh Moo-hyun sometimes strayed from a tougher U.S.-Japan line in the talks, instead advocating more American flexibility alongside the Chinese. On more than one occasion, the United States and China butted heads over fashioning a way forward. But in the end, the Six-Party Talks represented the first multilateral institution since 1945 that dealt with security issues and involved all of the key powers in Northeast Asia. This in itself was not a trivial accomplishment.

The metric for success, however, was not the mere establishment of the institution but the results it achieved. Here, the Six-Party Talks did manage to get further, in terms of denuclearizing North Korea, than the previous agreement. It resulted in not just a freeze of the Yongbyon program, but also the disablement of critical parts and, ultimately, the dismantlement of portions of the program. The key agreement in this regard was the September 2005 Six-Party Joint Statement. The first multilateral denuclearization document of its kind in Northeast Asia, the agreement had four major components: nuclear weapons/security; political relations; economic and energy assistance; and regional security.

All parties agreed that the goal of the Six-Party Talks was the verifiable denuclearization of the Korean Peninsula. In this regard, the United States reaffirmed that it did not have any nuclear weapons on the peninsula, and South Korea reaffirmed its commitments to a 1992 denuclearization agreement with the North that Seoul would not possess, develop, or transfer nuclear weapons (an agreement that Pyongyang had already obviously violated). While these two commitments were essentially a restatement of the status quo, they were necessary in order to get the most important statement in the document, which was North Korea's commitment "to abandon all nuclear weapons and existing nuclear programs, and to return at an early date to the Treaty on the Non-Proliferation of Nuclear Weapons and to IAEA safeguards."[13] This constituted the first-ever DPRK acknowledgment in writing, to all members of the region, that it had nuclear weapons, that it would give them up, and that it would end all associated nuclear programs. The reference to "existing nuclear programs" was important, because every party understood this to mean North Korea's commitment to end its efforts to build a uranium enrichment capacity outside of its plutonium program at Yongbyon.

The North claimed that it had the right to peaceful uses of nuclear energy, but given that no one believed the reactor at Yongbyon was for civilian energy purposes (U.S. lead negotiator, Assistant Secretary of State for East Asian and Pacific Affairs Christopher Hill, used to tell the North in formal negotiations that the Yongbyon facility could produce plutonium for bombs, but that it could not produce enough electricity to power a lightbulb), this North Korean claim was included as a sop to their negotiators. Pyongyang was insistent on receiving the light-water reactors that they were promised in the previous, 1994 agreement. This was strongly resisted by the United States, in part because such a concession would smack of a Clinton-era agreement, but more important, because of the view that the North could not be trusted with any nuclear capacity, particularly one that included any form of uranium enrichment. In the end, the State Department lawyers accepted a terribly verbose phrase that connoted a vague willingness to discuss at an appropriate time, in the distant future, "the subject of the provision of a light-water reactor." This wording was not to be construed by any party to be equated with a commitment to provide a light-water reactor (let alone the two proffered in the 1994 agreement). It was only a vague commitment to discuss the topic, and there were no secret minutes or confidential clauses that delineated specifics such as the capacity of the reactor, how it would be provided, and who would finance it. Moreover, the key understanding among all parties was that the so-called appropriate time to discuss the topic of an LWR was after the DPRK had abandoned all nuclear weapons and returned to full compliance with NPT and IAEA safeguards.

The political portion of the agreement laid out all parties' commitment to principles of the U.N. Charter, which outwardly appears like a vague reference but was the result of intense efforts to force the DPRK to admit to the need to improve the human rights conditions in its country in accordance with the charter. The United States committed to exist peacefully together with the DPRK and agreed to the eventual establishment of a bilateral working group to normalize diplomatic relations; Japan committed to do the same with North Korea; and in both cases, the understanding was that issues outside of the nuclear context—such as abduction cases for Japan and DPRK human rights abuses and missile programs for the United States—would be dealt with in these channels.

The third portion of the agreement dealt with energy issues in which the United States and other parties committed to provide energy assistance to North Korea as compensation for the freezing of their nuclear program. And the last portion of the agreement committed to discussing a broader peace mechanism for the peninsula and for regional security.

The agreement was weak on specifics deliberately, because the logic was that trying to nail down specifics in a big and new multilateral negotiation would tie everyone down in a morass of detail. The objective, as lead U.S. negotiator Hill termed it, was to reap an "early harvest," through a broader vision agreement that laid out the ideal end states that all parties sought in the negotiation. Given the levels of distrust between the United States and DPRK and China, this was an efficient way to start the negotiations.

The Six-Party Joint Statement was widely heralded at the time as an important breakthrough in addressing the second nuclear crisis. Few imagined the Bush administration would ever enter into an agreement with the North, but such a view misunderstood the president's and Secretary of State Condoleezza Rice's commitment to address the problem through peaceful diplomacy. From early on in her tenure as the nation's chief diplomat, Rice called "deep dive" sessions on Friday afternoons on North Korea and Iran—an unusual commitment to think through the problem despite her busy schedule and travel. Held in her suite on the seventh floor at the State Department, she conducted these like the Stanford professor she was, asking many questions and soliciting arguments and counterarguments about the road forward. In Asia, the agreement was heralded as a major breakthrough for the security and prosperity of the region. Asians saw the Six-Party Joint Statement not just as a denuclearization agreement on North Korea but also as a sign of the United States and China working together in a consultative fashion to undergird the security of the region. Scholars who had long opined about the need for a security institution like NATO in Asia scribbled furiously about the significance of the Six-Party Talks. As we stood next to our North Korean counterparts in the Diaoyutai grand hall, with cameras flashing, their lead negotiator said to me in Korean, *"Kkŭtkkaji kapsida,"* meaning "let us take this agreement to its successful end." The South Korean lead negotiator oversold the agreement to the press as the final solution to the nuclear threat (in part to get himself promoted to national security adviser). The Chinese were so excited by the buzz that they created Six-Party pencils, folders, and fans (but no T-shirts).

But the meaning of the agreement to the average person hit home for me at Narita Airport. After finishing the round of talks in Beijing, it was customary for then-national security adviser Steve Hadley to send me to Japan for consultations. Japan, of course, had its own negotiators at the talks, but I would routinely go to debrief at the Prime Minister's Office as a sign of alliance solidarity. The Prime Minister's Office appreciated an American view on the talks outside their internally dominant foreign ministry. At Narita Airport, I was met by airport personnel with a wheelchair. (I had broken an ankle running in Chevy Chase the week prior to the Six-Party Talks.) Tired after several consecutive days of sixteen-hour negotiations and a sleepless night of doing press background briefings on the agreement, I could barely stay awake as the attendant wheeled me through the terminal to an awaiting embassy car. As I arose from the chair, I realized that the attendant's constant chattering was not to her colleagues but to me, thanking the United States for saving her country from North Korean aggression. Pouring myself into the backseat of the car, I awkwardly thanked them, all the while knowing that we were still very far from accomplishing what the young lady had given us credit for.

CRISIS NO. 3: THE 2006 NUCLEAR TEST

"I can't believe I have to read this fucking statement," U.S. chief negotiator Chris Hill mumbled under his breath at the plenary session of the Six-Party Talks. The third nuclear crisis with North Korea started to brew almost immediately after the conclusion of the September 2005 Joint Statement. The context of Hill's remark was the delivery of each country's closing statements in the final plenary Six-Party session celebrating the Joint Statement. Washington had sent a pretty strongly worded statement for Hill to read, which downplayed any of the media's euphoria over the agreement and soberly delineated all of the problems with the DPRK regime and the need this time for complete, verifiable, and irreversible dismantlement. In between all of the niceties that an occasion such as this required, the U.S. closing statement read: "[The United States will] take concrete actions necessary to protect ourselves and our allies against any illicit proliferation activities on the part of the DPRK," and included a stated desire to address North Korean "human rights abuses, biological and chemical weapons programs, ballistic missiles, terrorism, and illicit activities."[14] Sitting next to Hill, I had a clear view of the head of the DPRK delegation, Kim Kye-gwan, listening to the U.S. closing statement. In his hands, he had a prepared text to deliver, but as he listened to the toughly worded U.S. statement, he slipped his prepared remarks back into his briefcase. Instead, when it was Kim's turn, he extemporized a brief closing statement, which essentially said that while the six parties had "climbed a mountain" to achieve the Joint Statement, he could see on the horizon that there were even larger mountains to climb. He was right.

Despite the landmark agreement in September 2005, it would take over seventeen months before even the first steps of implementation were agreed upon. The problems started immediately. The day after the agreement, the North Korean foreign ministry denied the international press reports on the ambiguity and noncommittal aspect of the Joint Statement's references to LWRs, and announced its demand that the United States provide light-water reactors to Pyongyang and "should not even dream" that the DPRK will give up their nuclear weapons before then.[15] More important, North Korea proceeded to boycott the negotiations for over one year in response to financial measures undertaken by the United States in September 2005.

"We want our $25 million back." This was about the only thing the DPRK negotiators said for over one year after the September 2005 Joint Statement. This was because the Treasury Department and law enforcement agencies had been investigating DPRK financial activities related to money laundering, counterfeiting U.S. currency, and other illicit activities. On September 15, 2005, only four days before the Six-Party agreement, the Treasury Department issued an advisory under Section 311 of the Patriot Act to U.S. financial institutions to beware of doing business with a Macau bank, Banco Delta Asia (BDA), on the grounds that it was engaged in money-laundering activities related to North Korean accounts at the bank. Treasury also cited evidence that BDA circulated North Korean "supernotes"—extremely good counterfeit of the U.S. $100 bill. At the time, the Section 311 on BDA seemed like an innocuous law enforcement action. We provided the North Korean delegation at the Six-Party Talks with a copy of the Treasury announcement, and they read it without any recognition of what it might mean. But soon thereafter, the acronym "BDA" was etched forever in their minds.

Upon learning that one of their banks was designated by the U.S. Treasury Department as a money launderer, Macau regulatory authorities immediately took control of the bank and froze for investigation all North Korean accounts, amounting to about $25 million. Moreover, once other bank presidents and bank regulators around the world learned of the Section 311, they, too, sought to freeze or expel all North Korean assets in their banks. While this action had little effect on the average North Korean (who does not have overseas bank accounts or hard currency), it had a dramatic impact on the elite, who suddenly found that they could not access their stashes of cash around the world. The North Korean leadership quickly learned that there was only one thing potentially worse than losing their nuclear weapons, and that was losing their financial reputation. Accounts were frozen. If a bank asked the North to remove their accounts, they could not deposit their cash elsewhere. Front companies for the North Korean government could not wire money. For most banks, there was little thought given to their draconian actions: maintaining the bank's financial reputation as free from dirty accounts was much more important than keeping North Korean assets, which constituted a miniscule portion of the bank's total deposits.

North Korea returned for a round of Six-Party Talks in November 2005, two months after the Joint Statement. The South Koreans and Japanese came to the talks ready with plans for implementing the September 2005 agreement, but the DPRK had only one talking point: "We want our $25 million unfrozen in BDA." The talks lasted no longer than two days, and it became clear that this sum of money came to represent for Pyongyang the financial problems they now faced around the world. Our Treasury officials explained that the mere return of this paltry sum of money would not solve their problems. Now that North Korean bank accounts were reputed to be potential facilitators of drug trafficking, counterfeiting, and laundering, no bank would want their money even if they got their $25 million back. The only way to rectify the situation was for the North to prove to the financial world that they would no longer engage in such illicit activities, which was, of course, hard for them to do given that these activities constituted some 33 percent of the entire economy. The North Korean delegation was both defiant and stunned. They claimed a U.S.-led conspiracy to stain Pyongyang's good reputation. But they knew that this was a sanction that they had never seen before and that their leadership was vulnerable. The Chinese hosts were both panicked and upset that the Six-Party agreement was collapsing only weeks after it was signed. The liberal South Korean government refused to accept U.S. claims and questioned whether the U.S. counterfeiting charges were credible (which made President Bush very angry). At a banquet dinner during the talks hosted by the Chinese foreign minister, however, the North revealed the significance of the action. After much ceremonial toasting with Chinese *baijiu,* an inebriated member of the North Korean delegation leaned over to us and mumbled, "You . . . you Americans finally have found a way to hurt us." As we drove through the Beijing streets in our embassy convoy back to the St. Regis hotel that evening, I overheard one of our delegation members on the phone to his wife, "Honey, we should be home soon . . . looks like we are done here for a while . . ."

Many critics have described the BDA action as a deliberate attempt by hard-liners in the Bush administration to sabotage the September 2005 Joint Statement. They point to the uncanny coincidence of timing, with the Treasury action taking place only four days (September 15, 2005) before the Joint Statement (September 19, 2005). Neoconservatives in the administration, it was charged, basically ginned up BDA as a way to undercut our negotiators. This popularly held view is wrong on several counts. First, the negotiators were as much a part of the BDA action as the so-called neocons were a part of the negotiations in Beijing. Second, the BDA investigation and the Six-Party negotiations operated on separate tracks. The former had been an ongoing law enforcement and intelligence operation for years, the conclusion of which came to fruition before any agreement on Six-Party Talks was within sight. In fact, rather than submarine the negotiations, the BDA action was delayed in the summer of 2005 in respect of the start of the July 2005 round of Six-Party Talks. It was only when we were unable to reach agreements in this round after two weeks of negotiation (July 26 to August 7), and returned to Washington for a recess in August 2005, that the decision was made that BDA could no longer be delayed. Moreover, at the time the interagency decided to move forward on BDA, we knew we were returning to Six-Party Talks in the near future, but no one had any idea that we would be able to achieve agreement on the Joint Statement; hence, the decision could not have been reached with the explicit purpose of submarining an agreement that had not yet happened. Third, and most important,

President Bush could not tolerate DPRK illicit activities, especially the counterfeiting of U.S. currency, which the president rightly considered an act of war. He wanted the BDA action to move forward in order to stop future actions. At the same time, however, he wanted the Six-Party Talks to produce an agreement on denuclearization. These two were not incompatible, in his mind.

North Korea's response to BDA triggered the third nuclear crisis. Their frustration with the effectiveness of these so-called new financial sanctions was evident in a prophetic statement made to South Korean colleagues in April 2005.[16] At a "track two" meeting (an unofficial meeting of policy experts at which government officials are also present) in Tokyo of the Northeast Asian Cooperative Security Dialogue (NEACD), an academic version of the Six-Party Talks, North Korean officials, once again under the influence of alcohol, told their South Korean counterpart, Ch'ŏn Yŏng-u, that they would now "light a fire under the American monkey's ass," since the talks were now stalled.

The North followed through with these threats first in July 2006, with its largest-ever display of missile tests, firing seven ballistic missiles, including its longest-range Taep'odong-II and an array of Scud-C and Nodong missiles. The Taep'odong-II, which the DNI assessed as having the potential to deliver a nuclear payload to the continental United States, failed.[17] The other six tests included short- and medium-range Scud-C and Nodong ballistic missiles launched from the Kit'taeryŏng base, all were successful. Then, on October 9, 2006, the regime conducted an underground nuclear test near P'unggye. Seismic data indicated a yield of less than one kiloton, but the DNI confirmed that air samples collected a day after the explosion detected radioactive debris consistent with an underground plutonium-based nuclear explosion.[18] The North told China it expected a yield of four kilotons, which suggests that the test was less than successful, and experts estimate the North used six kilograms of plutonium (13 lb) for the test.[19] In response to these unprecedented acts, the U.N. Security Council passed two resolutions (UNSCR 1695 and UNSCR 1718) condemning Pyongyang, and implementing a range of sanctions against it. These resolutions also marked the first time that China and Russia, two traditionally close allies of the North, signed on to Security Council resolutions against the regime.

GAME CHANGER?

The October 2006 nuclear test was commonly referred to as a "game changer" both inside and outside governments. It constituted the ultimate nuclear provocation short of attack and crossed yet a new red line in DPRK brazenness. Though the test was not entirely successful, it took us to a place we had never been before. The liberal South Korean government feared that the nuclear test would cause the United States to take off the diplomatic gloves and address the issue now with military force. Indeed, in President Bush's first phone call after the nuclear test with South Korean president Roh Moo-hyun, Roh was so concerned that he was barely even listening to Bush's calm, methodical call for taking the issue to the U.N. Security Council for a strong resolution, and instead the ROK president rapidly read talking points about how the United States should not provoke a war in Korea. (This was obviously not a good phone conversation.) Others believed that the nuclear test was such an affront to China that Beijing would finally clamp down on the regime and use its vast material leverage to choke the regime into giving up its nuclear weapons.

In the end, neither of these was true. Beijing did take tougher measures, most of which took place out of the public eye. In addition to taking the unprecedented step of signing on to two UNSC resolutions against North Korea, it also curtailed economic and political cooperation through unseen but all-important party-to-party channels and PLA-to-KPA (People's Liberation Army–to–Korean People's Army) channels. But it hardly abandoned the regime. As for the United States, the Bush administration did not respond with thoughts of attack, but instead tried to turn lemons into lemonade. The immediate diplomatic reaction when things go awry, as they did in October 2006, is to find a manner of leveraging the bad outcome in ways that can achieve positive longer-term objectives. What this meant for Rice was that the nuclear test would lead to a period of sanctions to punish Pyongyang, but it would eventually pave a path back to diplomacy where the United States would be in a stronger position to implement the Joint Statement. The aftermath of the third nuclear crisis was, therefore, a cycling back to a period of diplomacy between 2007 and 2008, which resulted in unprecedented progress in denuclearizing North Korea. After the BDA case had sent shivers through the North Korea elite and its money-laundering activities for over a year, the United States committed to returning the $25 million.[20] More important, the February 2007 initial actions agreement laid out the first steps in denuclearization. North Korea agreed to halt operations at the Yongbyon reactor within sixty days in return for an initial shipment of 50,000 tons of heavy fuel oil. Pyongyang would then provide a complete and verifiable declaration of all of its nuclear weapons and nuclear programs, and disable all of its existing facilities in return for an additional 950,000 tons of heavy fuel oil or its equivalent. The action plan also established five working groups to implement the Joint Statement: a denuclearization working group; an economic and energy working group; a DPRK-Japan working group on bilateral relations; a U.S.-DPRK working group; and a working group on the creation of a Northeast Asian Peace and Security regime. The DPRK put particular emphasis on the U.S.-DPRK group's efforts at removing Pyongyang from the U.S. state sponsor of terrorism list. The U.S. emphasis was on completing disablement within a specified time frame (by the end of 2007), in order to avoid a protracted process as the DPRK was wont to do. In negotiations, we pressed so hard on a 2007-end time frame, that our DPRK counterparts' uneasiness became manifestly evident as the pressure of their elbows literally broke through the glass coffee table upon which we were negotiating. Despite delays, from September 2007, Chinese, Russian, South Korean, Japanese, and American experts were making trips to Yongbyon, drawing up plans for disabling the reactor.

By November 2007, an eleven-step program for disablement of Yongbyon was started. The North also provided the U.S. State Department envoy, Sung Kim, with samples of high-strength aluminum tubes that were the source of U.S. concerns about uranium enrichment, as well as with eighteen thousand pages of operating records from the Yongbyon reactor and the reprocessing facility dating back to 1986. In June 2008, the DPRK took its first step in dismantling the reactor when it invited CNN and the international press to Yongbyon to witness the destruction of the cooling tower at the facility. Pyongyang also provided a declaration of its nuclear programs to China as chair of the Six-Party Talks. The declaration stated that the DPRK had thirty kilograms (66 lb) of plutonium (which was less than the U.S. intelligence estimate),[21] but did not declare a uranium-based program, only acknowledging U.S. concerns that such a program might exist in the DPRK. The North also agreed to a timetable for full dismantlement of the facility, and would allow further site visits, review of documents, and interviews with its nuclear technicians as part of the verification process.

These steps did not happen for free, of course. The North continued to receive heavy fuel oil and the Bush administration agreed to delist Pyongyang from the terrorism list, since it no longer met the legal requirements (i.e., perpetrating an act or aid to a terrorist organization in the preceding six months). The latter was a very controversial step for allied Japan, which considered the unresolved cases of DPRK abductions of its citizens in the 1970s as grounds for keeping DPRK listed. Nevertheless, the judgment was to accept the nuclear declaration and move forward, because any flaws in the declaration would be found in the verification process. Taken as a whole, however, this period resulted in unprecedented steps in the denuclearization of the Yongbyon facility, which we had never achieved with the North before. Even the *New York Times,* harshly critical of every aspect of Bush's North Korea policy, acknowledged that the process started by the February 2007 agreement contained DPRK denuclearization "commitments [that] go well beyond the requirements of the 1994 deal negotiated by the Clinton administration."[22]

CRISIS NO. 4: OBAMA AND THE 2009 NUCLEAR TEST

We have some problems with this.

This comment by the DPRK Six-Party negotiator on a U.S. draft of a verification protocol of the North's nuclear declaration started the cycle back to crisis mode from late 2008. The Six-Party Talks almost faltered on North Korea's refusal to provide a clear and comprehensive declaration of their nuclear holdings. Chris Hill averted a breakdown with a last-ditch effort in the autumn of 2008 to come up with a compromise solution on the declaration, including an unusual format where Pyongyang would have a written declaration for certain parts of the program and an unwritten understanding for other parts that would be sanctioned by the other members of the Six-Party Talks. There was much controversy over this unorthodox format; moreover, concerns about the uranium program mounted when U.S. forensics on the aluminum tubes and operating records brought back from Yongbyon showed traces of enriched uranium. Yet the declaration appeared to focus only on plutonium while vaguely acknowledging U.S. concerns about uranium. The leniency on the declaration was only accepted because all discrepancies would be addressed in the verification process. The North reportedly agreed verbally to allow a standard IAEA-based verification protocol that would allow international inspectors to do site visits and "scientific sampling" to verify any concerns the United States might have. North Korean authorities, however, were not willing to put these commitments in writing, and the White House would not accept Hill's less-than-specific formulation. North Korea's reluctance to accept a standard IAEA-based verification procedure for their nuclear declaration made obvious to many that Pyongyang may have been willing to give up its now-decrepit Yongbyon reactor to dismantlement, but that it was not willing to give up its weapons or other nuclear secrets. Many speculate that another key variable for the breakdown of negotiations was Kim Jong-il's stroke in August 2008, after which negotiation responsiveness on the DPRK side precipitously declined. The December 2008 round of Six-Party Talks ended without agreement, and the stage was set for a deterioration of relations once again. There would not be another round of negotiations for well over three years.

> To those who cling to power through corruption and deceit and the silencing of dissent, know that you are on the wrong side of history, but that we will extend a hand if you are willing to unclench your fist.
>
> —PRESIDENT BARACK OBAMA,
> INAUGURAL ADDRESS, JANUARY 20, 2009[23]

The Obama administration came into office prepared to advance the ball on North Korea. During the campaign, candidate Obama promised to promote a more forward-leaning diplomacy with isolated regimes than his predecessor did. To his credit, he held no partisan bias on North Korea in accepting the results of Bush's Six-Party Talks, and wanted to press ahead by engaging in the high-level bilateral and multilateral consultations necessary to accelerate implementation of the Joint Statement. Soon after taking office, in February 2009, the administration appointed an experienced diplomat, dean of Tufts University Fletcher School and former U.S. ambassador to South Korea, Stephen Bosworth, as the U.S. special envoy for North Korea policy, who found out about the offer just as he returned from an academic visit to Pyongyang. Sung Kim, a U.S. Foreign Service officer who succeeded me as deputy head of delegation for the Six-Party Talks, was promoted to ambassador for his good work, and was retained as the special envoy for the Six-Party Talks. Kurt Campbell, the new assistant secretary of state for East Asian and Pacific affairs, with top cover from his close friend Undersecretary of State Jim Steinberg, would manage the policy along with the NSC's senior director for asian affairs Jeff Bader and director for Asian Affairs Danny Russel. Thus, the administration had assembled a strong team ready to undertake serious engagement with the North.

They spent most of their time, however, dealing with North Korean provocations. Political winds had shifted considerably on the peninsula with the December 2007 election of the first conservative government in South Korea in a decade. Lee Myung-bak, a pragmatic businessman-turned-politician, declared the end of the Sunshine Policy and called for a hardheaded engagement policy with Pyongyang in which Seoul would no longer dole out unconditional gifts but instead would invest in engagement only if it provided a return in terms of human rights or denuclearization. Rather than living up to the multibillion-dollar commitments that the previous Seoul government had made to Pyongyang only two months before Lee's election, the new government dispatched its deputy Six-Party negotiator Hwang Joon-kook to Pyongyang in January 2009 as a sign of the type of engagement Seoul was interested in. Hwang's mission was very specific: to negotiate Seoul's purchase of the remaining batch of eight thousand fresh fuel rods from the North so that they could no longer fuel the Yongbyon reactor. When the North asked for an exorbitant sum of money, President Lee rejected the price as unreasonable and Hwang returned home.

Very comfortable with the ten years of Sunshine Policy that benefited the North immeasurably, Pyongyang was offended by Lee's perceived high-handed and hard-line approach, so, when Obama took office one year later, the North was already on a path to provocations. In February 2009, KCNA announced that the regime was preparing to do a satellite launch based on its long-range ballistic-missile technology. The escalating crisis followed an almost predictable pattern thereafter. The Obama administration warned that such a test would be a violation of UNSCR 1718 and said it would move to the U.N. Security Council for further action if the launch took place. The Lee government in Seoul supported the U.S. position, and in March 2009 announced that it would consider joining the PSI to curb DPRK weapons trade, which the previous ROK government refused to do. Completely unmoved by these warnings, Pyongyang conducted its test of the Taep'odong-II on April 5, 2009. The missile went farther than any previously tested, with the first stage landing in the Sea of Japan and the payload landing in the Pacific Ocean. The U.N. Security Council condemned the test, and North Korea responded by saying it was formally withdrawing from the Six-Party Talks, would no longer be bound by its agreements, and "would never ever participate in the talks again."[24]

On a trip to New York City afterward, the DPRK's deputy Six-Party negotiator Ri Gŭn could barely contain his anger, saying that all of the Six-Party members had "betrayed their trust" in calling for a U.N. statement condemning the North's rocket launch. On April 16, it subsequently kicked out all international and U.S. monitors from Yongbyon and announced its intention to reprocess eight thousand fuel rods, thereby unwinding all that had been done as part of the Six-Party agreements.

On U.S. Memorial Day (May 25) in 2009, North Korea conducted its second underground nuclear test. More powerful than the first test, the U.S. Geological Survey registered an underground explosion with a seismic magnitude of 4.7 on the Richter scale. The DNI released a statement that the yield was a few kilotons (experts believe somewhere between two and eight kilotons).[25] The DPRK announced that the test was successful and "helped to settle scientific and technological problems arising in further increasing the power of nuclear weapons."[26] The U.N. Security Council passed a third resolution (UNSCR 1874), tightening sanctions against the DPRK, and the ROK announced its accession to the PSI, a multilateral coalition aimed at interdicting WMD transfers. North Korea accused the ROK and the United States of declaring war and claimed that it was no longer bound by the 1953 armistice. The North carried out two conventional military provocations against South Korea, torpedoing a ROK naval vessel in March 2010 and then firing 180 rounds of artillery on a small South Korean island.

In September of 2009, the DPRK provided a written statement to the U.N. Security Council, which essentially announced its possession of a uranium enrichment program despite years of denying it to the Bush administration. The key phrase read: "Experimental uranium enrichment has successfully been conducted to enter into the completion phase."[27] Then, in November 2010, the regime revealed to a visiting American scientist a completed and fully operational uranium enrichment facility at the Yongbyon nuclear site, in contravention to all standing agreements and despite its denials of such a program to the Bush administration eight years earlier. This brazen act confirmed what the Bush administration had claimed since 2002 and had been ridiculed for by critics such as the *New York Times,* which doubted Bush's uranium enrichment charges as "sensational" and a deliberate and fabricated attempt to submarine the diplomacy.[28] Another outspoken critic, Leon Sigal, referred to the uranium charges as Bush's "propagating inexactitudes" because he loathed the DPRK regime.[29]

Few believed these critics anymore. The international community condemned Pyongyang for its actions, and concerned parties called for tighter sanctions and counterproliferation activities in the United Nations. Obama's policy, known as "strategic patience," thereafter called on the North to adhere to "complete and verifiable" denuclearization, and to return to the Bush-era Six-Party agreements. Obama promised no serious diplomacy until the North showed evidence of better behavior, ceasing provocations against the South and refraining from more missile and nuclear tests. Despite threats of further provocations from the North including a third nuclear test, Obama remained firm in his position until Pyongyang signaled a true change in behavior. Until that point came in the future, Obama's policy was not discernibly different from the very hardheaded position of the Bush administration, which Obama supporters criticized so vociferously a few years earlier.

Your first sight upon arrival in North Korea: the ubiquitous portrait of Kim Il-sung at Suwon airport. *Paul Haenle*

After-school activities are all in service of the Dear Leader. Here, a student work-unit marches through the city. *Paul Haenle*

The central square in Pyongyang, aptly named Kim Il-sung Square. The unfinished triangular tower of Ryugyŏng Hotel towers in the background. *Paul Haenle*

DPRK women's brigade leaving the September 2010 celebrations in a truck near Pyongyang square.

TOP: Built to stand taller than the original in Paris, this Arch of Triumph was erected to commemorate Kim Il-sung's battles against the Japanese and was unveiled in 1982 on Kim's seventieth birthday. *Paul Haenle*

BOTTOM: The fount of knowledge: Juche tower. *Paul Haenle*

The author politely declined a North Korean invitation in 2007 to visit this larger-than-life monument—in no small part because the picture of a White House official bowing to the statue would probably have ended his career in government. *John Pavelka, Creative Commons*

All in the family.
The Father of the nation, Kim Il-sung.
Three Lions/Hulton Archive/Getty Images

The Son and late
Dear Leader,
Kim Jong-il.
*Dmitry Astakhov/
AFP/Getty Images*

The Great Successor, the Grandson,
Kim Jong-un. Notice the striking
resemblance. *Associated Press/Kyodo*

Dubbed by *Esquire* magazine "Worst Building in the History of Mankind," the exterior of the hotel has since been refurbished with glass panels courtesy of China. *Paul Haenle*

Recent reports are that traffic in Pyongyang has increased, but with their robotic movements these tall, slender traffic ladies tend to direct air currents more than cars. It's been said that if you stare long enough, you can get one of them to smile. *Paul Haenle*

Doing things the old-fashioned way. A tractor is a rare sight on farms in North Korea. *Paul Haenle*

The most vivid international image of denuclearization was the June 2008 collapse of the cooling tower at the Yongbyon nuclear facility. Note the tower's absence in the second photo and a close-up of the remains of the tower after it was demolished. There was much more, however, to their nuclear activities than this program. *Paul Haenle*

Pre-brief for President George W. Bush in advance of his meeting with North Korean defectors in the Oval Office. (*Behind the president, from left to right:*) Deputy National Security Adviser J. D. Crouch, Special Envoy for North Korean Human Rights Jay Lefkowitz, the author, and National Security Adviser Stephen Hadley. *Paul Morse*

The author and his family meeting with President Bush to say good-bye. The president is giving the author's oldest son a presidential lapel pin. *Eric Draper*

The author pre-briefing the president at dawn in the Oval Office before a phone call to Japanese prime minister Junichiro Koizumi. *Paul Morse*

THE PROBLEM IS NOT THE UNITED STATES, STUPID

A sampling of *New York Times* editorials on North Korea from 2003 to 2008 consistently shows criticism of the Bush administration's North Korea policy. These influential scribes blamed Bush for failing to engage in direct talks with Pyongyang (viz Six Party Talks). They considered sanctions as largely "gratuitous obstacles" and a "sideshow." They faulted as an "avoidable error" the administration's raising the issue of the North's clandestine uranium nuclear program; and denigrated as "quibbling" the administration's precondition that any negotiations be about the permanent and irreversible denuclearization. Most clearly, every editorial during this period blamed North Korea's nuclear breakout on the U.S. refusal to negotiate. "For six years, President Bush rejected any serious diplomacy with North Korea. That obstinacy made the world a more dangerous place," said one editorial.[30] The paper even claimed as truth the unfalsifiable proposition that if only Dick Cheney and the neocons had not withheld diplomacy, the Six-Party agreements of 2005 and 2007 could have been reached four, five, or six years earlier.[31]

Fast-forward to August 2009. After the North welcomed the Obama administration into office with a missile test, nuclear test, and then the arrest of two American journalists, Euna Lee and Laura Ling, on the Sino–North Korean border, the *New York Times* editorial pages supported Obama for exactly the same policy elements for which they had criticized Bush: refusing bilateral talks with North Korea; demanding as a precondition verifiable and irreversible denuclearization; and enforcing U.N. Security Council resolutions and other sanctions against the DPRK. In the end, the newspaper credits Obama's administration, now in its third year of non-dialogue with North Korea, with a "firm and patient" policy—exactly the same policy moniker that the editors characterized as empty posturing by the Bush administration.[32] This is less a commentary on the inconsistency of the op-ed pages of American newspapers than it is a statement on how two presidents, arguably at opposite ends of the foreign policy spectrum, ended up in similar hardheaded policies on North Korea. To me, at least, this shows that the primary cause for the cycle of diplomatic crises over North Korea's nukes for the past twenty-plus years is the behavior of the North

Korean regime itself rather than some flaw in U.S. policy or past presidents. This may seem obvious to the casual observer, but it is not at all the case with elite newspaper journalists, academics, or the news media.

BLAME AMERICA

What I find astounding about the story of nuclear diplomacy with North Korea is that, on balance, as much blame is placed on the United States for its failure as is placed on the policy mandarins in Pyongyang. Several individuals have led this charge—many of whom are scarred by the Vietnam War–era of never-trust-thy-government—and placed the responsibility for a nuclear North Korea squarely at Washington's doorstep. Because they are regarded as scholars and policy "experts," they are sought out by the cable news media and newspaper opinion pages for comments on the North Korea *crise du jour,* which then creates a prevailing narrative that the public and political partisans cling to. The story goes something like this: North Korea's latest nuclear provocation stems from United States' unwillingness to heed the North's "cry" for help as a weak, isolated country that is desirous of relations with the world. Washington does not address the North's insecurity because it needs to justify U.S. post–Cold War defense needs to have an enemy against which to target its military programs and ballistic missile defense budgets. Moreover, "hawks," whether Republican or Democrat, want to collapse North Korea, not negotiate with it. Why, then, should we be surprised that Pyongyang continues on its nuclear path?

Former *New York Times* correspondent Leon Sigal, for example, placed blame for North Korea's nuclear misdeeds squarely in the hands of the Clinton administration. Impeded by a Republican-controlled Congress after the November 1994 midterm elections, President Clinton "backpedaled" on implementing the terms of the October 1994 nuclear agreement, Sigal argues, rather than expend political capital to stand by the deal. This delay in implementation gave North Korea the pretext for breaking out of the agreement with a secret second nuclear weapons program. Because bad behavior was a response to America's prior sin, he characterizes the North's actions not as agreement-breaking but as a perverse diplomatic "olive branch" by an insecure regime wanting to work with the United States rather than fight it.[33]

With regard to the October 2002 meeting, when the United States confronted North Korea with information that Pyongyang was cheating on the 1994 U.S.-DPRK nuclear agreement by undertaking a second covert nuclear weapons program, Georgy Toloraya, a Russian foreign ministry official in charge of Asian affairs, wrote openly that U.S. accusations were a "lie" and that North Koreans were the innocents.[34] A New York Times editorial in April 2008, titled "Now He's Ready to Deal," applauded the restart of on-again, off-again nuclear negotiations, but the "he" in the title was a critical reference not to Kim Jong-il but to the U.S. president. The editorial staff basically blamed North Korea's nuclear breakout on the United States in non-nuanced terms: "For six years, Mr. Bush rejected any meaningful negotiations. The result? Pyongyang kept adding to its plutonium stockpile—it now has enough for eight or more bombs—and tested a nuclear device."[35]

Selig Harrison is a nonpartisan expert who has contributed much ink to the blame game for North Korea's nuclear ambitions. I consider him nonpartisan because he has consistently castigated every past American administration—Republican or Democrat—for failing to live up to agreements with Pyongyang. When North Korea did a ballistic missile test in April 2009 and a second nuclear test in May 2009, he blamed these outcomes on the "[Obama] Administration's naive attempts to pressure North Korea into abandonment of its nuclear and missile programs." When Pyongyang followed these acts with the March 2009 abduction of Laura Ling and Euna Lee of Current TV, and sentenced them three months later to twelve years of hard labor, Harrison blamed President Obama's refusal to negotiate their release as showing "callous disregard" for American lives. Urging Washington to negotiate under such duress was apparently not an issue for Harrison, who, like the other scholars, viewed the North as engagement-ready and its nasty behavior as largely an outgrowth of American neglect.[36]

These arguments often dominate the public policy debate. They are terribly wrong for two reasons. First, they presume that Americans can fix any problem if they just put their mind to it. In the North Korean case, this means that merely sitting down with the rambunctious North

Koreans and dealing with them in a respectful negotiation should result in agreements to dismantle their nuclear weapons. On the contrary, the issue is far more complex than this. Moreover, some problems may be too hard to solve. Vice President Cheney, who had a reputation in the media as one of the "neocons" in favor of collapsing the North Korean regime as the solution to the nuclear problem, was, in actuality, one of the most thoughtful voices behind the scenes. In all of his years of encountering different foreign policy challenges, he saw few as difficult as North Korea. The problem could not be solved by military force because of the inordinate costs of war and the sheer unpredictability of the regime's leadership. And from whatever diplomatic angle one viewed the problem, every potential solution traversed at least one party's core interests, whether these were Chinese, American, or South Korean.

Second, these "blame USA" arguments simply do not do justice to the decades of hard-fought diplomatic efforts of past administrations. Undeniably, there have been periods in U.S. foreign policy, such as in the aftermath of September 11, when there was much less tolerance for reaching out to Pyongyang in the face of its belligerence. But these periodic lapses only underscore a diplomatic record, taken as a whole, which demonstrates over twenty years of sustained efforts by Washington to seek a peaceful diplomatic solution to the denuclearization of North Korea.

I feel it is important to lay out this record for readers to judge for themselves whether or not the North's nuclear weapons threat can be blamed on the U.S. unwillingness to negotiate with a rogue regime. One could certainly criticize past U.S. presidents for being unsuccessful at wresting these weapons away from Kim's little hands, but a careful analysis shows that one cannot accuse Washington of not trying.

REAGAN'S MODEST INITIATIVE

Diplomatic outreach by the United States began under Ronald Reagan. In what became known as the "Modest Initiative," Reagan put forth a basic engagement template for negotiations, in which the United States would provide inducements for North Korean behavior that was compliant with international norms. From 1983, a series of small initiatives were taken by the State Department, aimed at establishing an open channel of dialogue. These measures supported similar efforts being made by the South Koreans and were based on concerns about nuclear threats, as well as a growing recognition that the North's emerging economic problems and its international isolation posed an inherently destabilizing threat in Northeast Asia. The purpose of the contacts, therefore, was to encourage Pyongyang to adopt policies that would bring it more fully into the world community. Each time, however, these initiatives were undercut by North Korean belligerence.

On February 26, 1983, the State Department announced that it would allow U.S. diplomats to "converse naturally" with "DPRK" counterparts. What might otherwise have been seen as an innocuous measure was quite significant. The State Department referred publicly to Pyongyang by its official name rather than "North Korea," which connoted a sign of diplomatic respect. Moreover, until this point, American diplomats were not permitted to interact or converse with North Korean counterparts in official settings (e.g., a multilateral gathering like the U.N.) or social settings (e.g., a cocktail party at a third country's embassy), reflecting the state of affairs between two countries still technically at war. The initiative had been under discussion with the South Koreans for six months and was coordinated so that the United States would notify its allies in Seoul if any contacts were made. But after North Korean agents attempted to assassinate ROK president Chun in Rangoon, Burma, in October 1983, killing half of Chun's cabinet, contacts were forbidden.

After about five months, the Reagan administration again told its diplomats to "start chatting" with North Korean counterparts through informal contacts. As an additional measure, Washington relaxed some travel visa restrictions. But in November 1987, North Korean terrorists blew up a South Korean civilian airliner, Korean Air 858. Reagan again cut off contacts and grew concerned about more potential terrorist attacks by the North Koreans to disrupt the Seoul Olympics scheduled in September 1988, particularly after the International Olympic Committee rejected Pyongyang's high-handed demands to cohost, and after Eastern bloc countries, including the Soviet Union, agreed to participate, making this the most widely attended Olympiad since the successive boycotts of the 1980 Moscow Games and the 1984 Los Angeles Games. Thus, Secretary of State George Shultz stated publicly that Reagan's commitment to the "Modest Initiative" continued in principle but that Washington would not resume contacts until after the Seoul Olympics were successfully concluded.

Reagan kept his word. Relaunched in October 1988, Modest Initiative eased the comprehensive embargo on trade by allowing for the review of trade in humanitarian goods. It also allowed U.S. citizens to travel to North Korea on a case-by-case basis. The State Department offered to promote unofficial cultural, athletic, and academic exchanges. To promote political exchanges, State Department officials were permitted to discuss "substantive matters" with North Korean counterparts in "neutral" settings in New York (where the only official North Korean representation existed in the United States at the United Nations), or in other capitals. Moreover, a semi-official line of communication was set up at the American and North Korean embassies in Beijing, through which messages could be passed directly between the two countries. This might seem a bit underwhelming, but at the time this "Beijing Channel" was a major step forward between two countries that did not recognize each other, and had never had routine diplomatic communications. The Modest Initiative led to working-level meetings between the two sides at Beijing's International Club, in which messages drafted in Washington would be transmitted to the U.S. embassy in Beijing, which would then request a meeting with the political minister from the DPRK embassy. Reagan also permitted North Koreans to receive travel visas to visit the United States on a case-by-case basis for nongovernmental and unofficial athletic, cultural, and academic exchanges. The first Beijing Channel meeting took place on December 6, 1988, during which the North Koreans delivered a letter from then-foreign minister Kim Yŏng-nam to Shultz. In August 1991, the State Department issued a visa to the first North Korean civilian since the Korean War, Kang Dae-yŏng, to attend the burial of his mother, a Korean-American. The first export license for humanitarian goods was given in 1991 to a private company in New Jersey for the export of foodstuffs to the North. Eventually, nearly $100 million worth of grain was sent before the initiative was stopped in 1993 because the North was not remitting payments.[37]

BUSH 41: BEGINS HIGH-LEVEL BILATERALS

Reagan's successor took even bolder engagement steps with the North. In the first fifteen months of the George H. W. Bush administration, the United States held fifteen bilateral meetings with the North. This factoid is only remarkable in that it undercuts the conventional wisdom today that Republican administrations oppose engagement and abhor sitting at the table with rogue regimes like North Korea. The first meeting was held only four days after Bush took office. In that meeting, the United States conveyed a response to Foreign Minister Kim Yŏng-nam's letter. The North was so pleased with the meeting that they did a rare press conference afterward. China's foreign minister Qian Qichen also expressed satisfaction that the so-called Beijing Channel was now operating. The pace of these bilateral meetings proceeded at about one per month and they largely centered on the conditions that each side considered necessary to normalizing political relations. For the United States, the main issues were prevention of North Korean terrorism, recovery of the remains of American soldiers killed in the Korean War, resumption of North-South Korean dialogue, and improvement of North Korea's human rights record. A key demand by the time Bush took office was also North Korean compliance with IAEA safeguards. By 1988, U.S. satellite intelligence had revealed alarming evidence of North Korean facilities designed for reprocessing of plutonium for making nuclear bombs and evidence of construction of two larger plants (fifty-megawatt and two-hundred-megawatt reactors) beyond the experimental five-megawatt reactor at Yongbyon.

For North Korea, the issues were the removal of U.S. forces from the peninsula, negotiating of a formal peace treaty ending the war, the termination of U.S.-ROK military exercises, and an upgrading of U.S.-DPRK bilateral dialogue. Pyongyang used this channel to routinely castigate the Americans—at the fifth meeting, on November 1, 1989, the DPRK blasted the United States for holding the annual Team Spirit exercises with the ROK, and at the seventh meeting, on January 19, 1990, the North Korean delegation showed up but refused to talk to the U.S. side in protest over Team Spirit. It never agreed to discuss the nuclear issues, maintaining that this was a discussion between the IAEA and

North Korea (which, by the way, contradicts their current stance in the Six-Party Talks, of wanting to discuss this only with the United States). Pyongyang also refused to address American entreaties for the North to resume dialogue with South Korea. Under the Roh Tae-woo government (1988–1993), Seoul was embarking on a very successful *Nordpolitik* engagement effort with Eastern European countries and with the Soviet Union, which eventually led to fully normalized relations with all of the North's Communist patrons. The Modest Initiative by the United States was a corollary effort to break down Cold War barriers on the peninsula. But Roh's diplomatic successes in Europe were threatening to Kim rather than comforting. Occasionally, Pyongyang would respond with bizarre proposals, as they did in the fifth meeting (November 1989) when the delegation tabled a personal proposal from the Great Leader himself, called the "New Epochal Save-the-Nation" plan.[38] Presumably modeled on Reagan's famous "Mr. Gorbachev, tear down this wall" remarks, Kim called for the removal of the nonexistent 150-mile-long (240-km) "concrete wall" separating the two Koreas and for negotiations leading to the full opening of the inter-Korean border. When puzzled recipients of this proposal noted that there was no "wall" separating the two Koreas as there was in Germany, the best that North Korean counterparts could come up with was the dismantlement of local antitank barriers set up in the South to defend against future North Korean invasion.

These talks did result in some positive measures beyond the diplomatic wrestling over agenda items. As a goodwill gesture, North Korea repatriated the remains of five soldiers killed during the Korean War, and at the ninth meeting, on May 15, 1990, the United States expressed appreciation and called for the repatriation of more remains in the future. This eventually became a regular operation involving the U.S. Defense Prisoner of War–Missing Personnel Office (DPMO). Between 1991 and 1994, the North repatriated what it claimed were the remains of 203 additional Korean War servicemen, but based on scientific testing and comingled personal effects, the DPMO estimated that as many as 400 servicemen could have been represented in these remains. During former president Carter's 1994 surprise visit to Pyongyang, Kim Il-sung accepted his proposal to hold regular U.S.–North Korean joint field activities (JFAs) to recover U.S. remains within North Korea. And from

1996 up until its suspension in 2005, thirty-seven joint field activities were held, leading to the repatriation of 233 sets of remains.[39] From its inception up to its suspension in 2005, the United States provided the DPRK with nearly $28 million to cover the costs of the joint field activities. A seven-member delegation from the North was also flown to and housed in Bangkok for the annual negotiations with DPMO, at a sum of about $25,000 per year.[40] Payments are supposed to have been literally made in cash—containers full of U.S. paper currency.[41]

But then the Bush administration took three unprecedented steps to advance the dialogue. In September 1991, Washington announced its support of admission of North Korea to the United Nations as part of a dual-entry formula in which both Koreas would finally become formal members of the United Nations. On the twenty-seventh of the same month, President Bush announced that the United States would unilaterally withdraw all land- and sea-based tactical nuclear weapons from around the world, including in Korea. And then, in January 1992, Washington announced that it would discontinue the annual U.S.-ROK Team Spirit military training exercises that the North had complained so bitterly about.

These were major steps. The U.N. measure, though it also benefited the ally South Korea, was a de facto expression of respect for the DPRK as a sovereign and independent nation-state—something that Pyongyang craved from the United States. Though official U.S. policy never acknowledged the presence of nuclear weapons in Korea, the September 1991 nuclear proclamation addressed a major North Korean concern about U.S. nuclear threats. Moreover, the United States indicated its willingness to allow for North Korean inspections of U.S. military bases in South Korea as part of two major inter-Korean accords on political relations and on denuclearization, signed in late 1991 and early 1992.

The culmination of this momentum was then the highest-level U.S.-DPRK meeting, on January 22, 1992, between Undersecretary of State for Political Affairs Arnold Kanter and Korean Workers' Party Secretary for International Affairs Kim Yong-sun. Kanter, the third-highest official in the State Department, greeted Kim on the East Side of Manhattan, where the U.S. mission to the United Nations was located. This being Kim's first trip to the United States, he arrived in style, in his best suit (Kanter recalled that the North Korean official was clearly the best-dressed individual in *both* delegations) and in a black limousine.[42] Kanter recalled how the unprecedented senior level of this meeting caused heartburn among conservative elements within the administration and precipitated a fierce interagency battle over what he was allowed to say to the North Koreans. With Kanter were Richard Solomon, assistant secretary for East Asian and Pacific affairs; Douglas Paal, NSC senior director for Asian affairs; and James Lilley, assistant secretary of defense for international security. In a meeting that lasted over six hours, he conveyed to Kim the primary U.S. concern, which was for the North to join the IAEA and allow for international inspections of its nuclear facilities. The undersecretary also enumerated the "obstacles" to "improved U.S.-DPRK relations," which was essentially the list of agenda items discussed through the Beijing Channel that would be part of a normalization dialogue.[43] (Hard-liners in the administration, Kanter recalled, would not allow him to use the words "diplomatic normalization" in his presentation—stating the "obstacles" to "improved relations" was the clever circumlocution.) Kim Yong-sun ran through his list of normalization preconditions, which included the end to U.S. hostile policy, and the removal of nuclear weapons and troops from the South. Then, in a quintessentially out-of-left-field moment, Kim also raised a strange proposal for greater U.S.-DPRK cooperation to contain the remilitarization of Japan, perhaps hoping to exploit contentious U.S.-Japan trade relations at the time.

The Kanter-Kim meeting would be the last high-level meeting during the Bush White House, with relations gradually getting worse through the remainder of 1992 and 1993, eventually leading to the first nuclear crisis. Again, many characterize the Kanter-Kim meeting as a pivotal moment in which the U.S. interagency, divided in its views on engaging a rogue regime, managed to handcuff American diplomats and snatch defeat from the jaws of victory. Scholars and journalists cite U.S. rejection of Kim's desires for a joint communiqué from the meeting as a sign of North Korean readiness for progress and U.S. recalcitrance.[44] The State Department issued a terse five-line statement, saying only that the meetings were "useful and constructive." They blame U.S. internalization of a diplomatic modus operandi, in which a mere meeting with the DPRK was the "carrot" and the message was the "stick," for creating the subsequent lack of progress. But the reality is that despite curtailed talking points given to U.S. diplomats, both the formal meetings and the long private conversations between Kim and Kanter allowed for a full explanation of U.S. intentions. Furthermore, Kanter's meetings, even if they did not result in a joint communiqué, did result in North Korean cooperation. Eight days after the meeting in New York, North Korea signed the safeguards agreement with the IAEA in Vienna and then ratified the agreement in a special session of the Supreme People's Assembly the following April. On May 4, 1992, North Korea submitted its nuclear material declarations to the IAEA, declaring seven sites that were then subject to IAEA inspection. A bad meeting or lack of U.S. engagement could hardly have produced this result. It was only after Pyongyang started to reject the terms of IAEA inspections, prevaricated on discrepancies in nuclear declaration, and refused to implement the inter-Korean accords, that things started to get worse, leaving Bush's successor to take up the mantle of engagement once again.

CLINTON: "NON-HOSTILE INTENT"

"A million, a hundred billion, and a trillion."

When then–American commander of U.S. Forces Korea, General Gary Luck, was asked to clarify what he meant, the general explained that a second Korean War would result in 1 million casualties, would cost the U.S. $100 billion, and would cause $1 trillion in industrial damage. President Clinton recoiled at this estimate. It was June 15, 1994, and he sat in the Oval Office about to make a decision that could take the United States to war in Korea. Defense Secretary Bill Perry and Joint Chiefs of Staff chairman John Shalikashvili gave the president three options to respond to North Korea's defiant actions. Despite being warned expressly by the United States not to unload nuclear fuel rods from the reactor at Yongbyon—the first step to making plutonium for nuclear weapons—North Korea crossed this red line on May 8, 1994. They blocked international inspectors' access to their nuclear facility and then, on June 13, defiantly announced Pyongyang's withdrawal from the IAEA.

While the Clinton administration was not ready to go to war over lies told by North Koreans to IAEA inspectors regarding the history of their nuclear program, it made clear to Pyongyang that Washington would consider all options to prevent the future growth of a nuclear weapons arsenal. Perry instructed the military to draw up contingency plans for a surgical strike on the nuclear reactor at Yongbyon to prevent the North from recovering the raw material from the eight thousand, yard-long, two-inch wide (90 x 5-cm) fuel rods to make nuclear bombs. Cruise missiles deployed by F-117 stealth fighters would do the job. Perry explained that the discreet mission could be accomplished successfully with little risk of radiation fallout. But, he added soberly, he also believed the preemptive attack could result in an all-out war.

Another option was to seek a tough sanctions resolution in the U.N. Security Council. But this diplomatic course also risked war. Robert Gallucci, the U.S. chief negotiator, recounted to the Oval Office attendees that he had been told personally by his North Korean counterpart in their last encounter that a U.S. move to sanctions through the United Nations would be taken by Pyongyang as an act of war. North Korea reiterated in a June 5 statement, "Sanctions mean war, and there is no mercy in war."

Clinton deliberated over a third option, which was a significant force-augmentation package for Korea. This would entail the addition of ten thousand combat-ready troops, F-117 stealth fighters, long-range bombers, and an additional aircraft-carrier battle group. North Korea would almost certainly read such a buildup of U.S. forces as a precursor to war, and would react with either a mobilization of their own, or worse, with a preemptive attack before the United States could amass their forces (an important lesson Pyongyang learned from observing the 1991 Persian Gulf War). Secretary Perry assessed all options as bad. But to do nothing as the most opaque and unpredictable regime was driving to acquire nuclear weapons was disastrous. Clinton started leaning in the direction of the force-augmentation package. After all, if the United States moved to sanctions or a preemptive strike, it would need the forces ready to respond.

But this could not be done quietly, given the risks. Already, in South Korea, the Kim Young-sam government did its largest civil defense exercises in years. Stock markets dropped 25 percent in two days and shelves in grocery stores were being emptied by shoppers preparing for a potential crisis. A *Washington Post* op-ed by Brent Scowcroft and Arnold Kanter, urgently titled "The Time for Temporizing Is Over," called for a U.S. military strike on the reprocessing plant in Yongbyon if the DPRK did not allow inspectors back in.[45] The U.S. ambassador, James Laney, instructed families of his embassy employees to consider taking home leave early, as an "early summer vacation." Back in Washington, Perry knew that a force-augmentation package of the kind being considered would also require an order for American civilian evacuation. Once that became public, chaos would ensue.

It was amid this crisis that former president Jimmy Carter called in from Pyongyang. Carter had received an invitation from Kim Il-sung to visit in 1991, 1992, and 1993, but he obliged State Department requests to decline the invite in order to avoid complicating the diplomacy. But as the situation worsened, Carter took matters into his own hands. Gallucci briefed the former president in Plains, Georgia, the week prior to his Pyongyang trip. (When Gallucci was leaving after finishing his briefing, the former president called him back, for what Gallucci presumed to be additional questions. Carter then asked his wife, Rose, to bring in two shopping bags of peanuts for Gallucci to take home.) During the briefing, Carter grew concerned that there was no plan for direct high-level contact with North Korea and told Clinton that he was going to visit Pyongyang, given the developments at hand. Clinton opposed this, but on the counsel of Vice President Al Gore, he agreed on the condition that Carter went as a private citizen and not as an official envoy. Carter arrived in Seoul on June 13, and went into North Korea on June 15, 1994.

When the White House aide entered the Oval Office to notify the meeting participants that Carter was calling in from North Korea, President Clinton reached toward the phone but was told that Carter asked to speak to Gallucci. Clinton glared as Gallucci went to the outer office to take the call. When he returned to the Oval Office to explain what Carter had proposed, there was, at first, disbelief, followed by seething anger; with at least one participant suggesting Carter's actions approached treason.[46] Cognizant that they had just been subjected to a fait accompli by the former president, Vice President Gore reasoned that there would be ways to make lemonade out of this lemon.

Going to the precipice of war led to the most sustained period of U.S. engagement with North Korea since Bush 41's efforts with the Kanter-Kim dialogue. Rightly or wrongly, the Clinton administration went to extraordinary diplomatic lengths with the DPRK to advance political relations and reduce levels of distrust. The key piece of U.S. diplomacy in this regard was the 1994 Agreed Framework, discussed above. However, it was not the only piece. In June 1993, in order to suspend North Korea's withdrawal from the NPT, the United States provided nonaggression assurances to the DPRK, stating that the United States agreed to principles of not using force or threatening to use force (June 11, 1993). Moreover, as part of the Agreed Framework, Clinton included an extraordinary personal letter of assurance to Kim Jong-il, dated October 20, 1994, stating that Clinton would use the full powers of his office to facilitate arrangements for the financing and construction of the $4.2 billion light-water reactors and funding for the HFO deliveries. In the pedantry of diplomacy, one of the most symbolic aspects of such a letter is how the DPRK leader should be addressed by an American president when the two countries do not have diplomatic relations. President Bush, for example, had some trouble addressing the North Korean leader by his desired obsequious title. For President Clinton, however, this was barely an afterthought, as the letter was addressed to "His Excellency Kim Jong Il, Supreme Leader of the DPRK."

Clinton not only conducted nuclear diplomacy with the DPRK, he also held the most serious negotiations to date on their missile program. These began in April 1996 in Berlin, where the U.S. agenda was to obtain DPRK adherence to the Missile Technology Control Regime, which would limit the payload and range of their ballistic missile program (a missile capable of carrying no greater than a five-hundred-kilogram [1,100-lb] payload within a range of three hundred kilometers [185 mi]) and control the sales of missiles, components, and technology. The United States pressed forward with several rounds of these talks despite DPRK provocations, including the August 1998 test of the long-range Taep'odong-I missile, which provocatively overflew Japan. When concerns arose that the regime was flouting the Agreed Framework by keeping a secret underground facility at Kumchangri in 1998–99, the United States agreed to provide compensation in the form of food assistance in order to inspect this facility.

From 1999, the Clinton administration undertook high-level bilateral engagement in order to move the diplomatic ball forward. Former Secretary of Defense William Perry was appointed by the White House in 1998 as policy coordinator for North Korea, and Perry traveled to Pyongyang in May 1999 as a presidential envoy, delivering a letter from Clinton to Kim Jong-il that promised normalized relations, sanctions-lifting, assistance, and security assurances in return for denuclearization. Perry's diplomacy paved the way for the unprecedented visit of Kim Jong-il's special envoy, Vice Marshal Jo Myŏng-rok, to the White House in October 2000. Jo was given the red-carpet treatment and met with Clinton in the Oval Office, the first DPRK official ever to do so. The October 12, 2000, Joint Communiqué emerging from this visit was hailed at the time as a true breakthrough in U.S.-DPRK relations. It talked about how U.S.-DPRK relations could be fundamentally transformed on the heels of the June 2000 inter-Korean summit, and that a peace agreement ending the Korean War was the vehicle for doing this. The United States offered a statement of nonhostile intent and promised to work with Pyongyang to "make every effort in the future to build a new relationship free from past enmity."[47] Secretary of State Madeleine Albright reciprocated Jo's visit one week later by becoming the first chief American diplomat to visit North Korea and meet with Kim Jong-il. News of Albright's trip blanketed the airwaves. (The DPRK allowed almost all international media in to cover it.) She visited a North Korean elementary school and danced with the schoolchildren as well as attended a show at a stadium where hundreds of thousands in attendance performed with synchronized placards displaying a Taep'odong missile launch. Albright spent six hours with Kim Jong-il, in a meeting the primary purpose of which, from the DPRK side at least, was to secure a visit by President Clinton. In press statements, Albright talked about the beauty of the city of Pyongyang with its "heroic monuments." She described Kim as "a very good listener and a good interlocutor. He strikes me as very decisive and practical and serious."[48] Although Albright qualified all of her remarks by noting that she carries no "rose-colored" glasses when it comes to Communist regimes, her positive characterization of Kim lives on. Albright's visit per se was unprecedented, but it was also so because she explicitly stated that the purpose was to prepare for a potential summit with President Clinton in Pyongyang. In the end, this did not materialize, because of the United States' inability to get a deal on North Korean missiles (the North was willing to curtail development of their longer-range ballistic missiles for billions of dollars in compensation, but they were unwilling to part with the shorter-range and fully deployed Nodong missiles, which posed direct threats to Japan and the ROK), and also because the disputed U.S. presidential election became the White House's primary focus of attention. Over eight years, the Clinton administration amassed three agreements (1993 Joint Statement, 1994 Agreed Framework, and 2000 Joint Communiqué) and almost a fourth, on missiles, before it left office. This was more than any previous administration. It used some of its best diplomats and Korea experts to achieve this. Again, whether one agrees or not with Clinton's approach to North Korea, few can deny that the United States went the extra mile to engage in diplomacy despite DPRK provocations and concerns about their cheating on existing agreements, and despite very strong criticism at home from politicians both in and outside of the Democratic Party.

BUSH 43: ENGAGEMENT BEYOND EXPECTATIONS

Taken together, Clinton's agreements of 1993, 1994, and 2000 set out a model of quid pro quo for denuclearization: energy assistance, economic assistance, food, security assurances, political normalization, and a peace treaty in return for North Korean denuclearization. While these offerings had existed implicitly in the initiatives of previous administrations, they were made explicit under Clinton. George W. Bush basically ended up offering similar incentives in return for denuclearization.

Given the administration's well-known distaste for Clinton-era agreements—what many referred to as the "ABC" syndrome ("anything but Clinton")—many might find this assessment incredible. The common view is that Bush was not at all interested in diplomacy with the DPRK regime. This was most certainly the verdict of major opinion leaders such as the *New York Times* editorial page. As evidence, people pointed to then-secretary of state Colin Powell's retraction of statements he made early in March 2001 about the administration's plan to "engage with North Korea to pick up where President Clinton and his administration left off."[49]

This judgment is not accurate. There were undeniably individuals who strongly believed that denuclearization could not be achieved without regime change, but "regime change" as a policy was never the subject of any internal North Korea policy meeting or any external meeting with allies. Thus, it is fair to say that some held this attitude, but the attitude never translated into a strategy. The strategy, as stated many times by President Bush, was threefold: (1) to seek verifiable and irreversible denuclearization; (2) to resolve this problem peacefully; and (3) to do so through diplomacy of the Six-Party Talks. Bush never took off the table the use of military force, and indeed postulated it to Chinese president Jiang Zemin in 2003,[50] but there were no real military options that did not carry high risk of escalation to all-out war in Korea; moreover, taking out the Yongbyon nuclear complex (which a military strike could do) would not guarantee an end to the program, given speculation about other hidden sites.

Early evidence of the commitment to diplomacy was the result of an internal U.S. government policy review. As tortuous and protracted as this was, according to those who participated in it, the final judgment of this review was, in principle, to support the 1994 Agreed Framework and proceed with its implementation. The precondition, however, was that the North needed to address U.S. concerns about its pursuit of acquisitions consistent with an alternative uranium enrichment program in violation of the agreement.[51] When the North broke out of the agreement in 2002, Bush's focus then moved to a multilateral diplomatic approach in which the dynamic was to get five regional countries in unison to persuade the North of a better path. Particular focus was put on alignment with China. As North Korea's biggest patron, China had the most material leverage on Pyongyang. This relationship existed not only in the reported trade figures but also in the vast and unseen relationships between the Communist parties of the two countries and between the militaries. Members of the Chinese leadership, such as State Councilor Dai Bingguo, also had close personal ties with the DPRK leader. Bush framed diplomatic cooperation on denuclearizing North Korea as a key test of China's emergence as a responsible great power in the international system, and as a key test of the U.S.-China partnership. There were many things that Beijing and Washington might have different views on, including Taiwan arms sales, human rights, and Tibet, but the absence of nuclear weapons on the Korean Peninsula was one issue on which the two leaders had little disagreement. In addition to challenging the Chinese to do better on North Korea, Bush's diplomacy also aimed to delicately handle South Korea. Under a progressive government that was ideologically tied to the Sunshine Policy and unconditional engagement, the challenge was to channel and modulate Seoul's assistance to Pyongyang in a coordinated fashion with the overall pace of Six-Party Talks. Otherwise, an unregulated stream of South Korean assistance to the North would undercut any leverage exercised by others in the Six-Party Talks. Again, the purpose of these diplomatic machinations was not to collapse the regime by starving it; instead, it was to create a dynamic where five countries were in unison sending the same message to North Korea: give up your nukes for a better path and better life with your neighbors.

What about Bush's human rights agenda? In his memoir, *Decision Points,* President Bush wrote that while an estimated one million North Koreans died of starvation, "Kim Jong-il cultivated his appetite for fine cognac, luxury Mercedes, and foreign films."[52] So, there is no denying that he wanted to do things to raise world consciousness about the problem and to improve the lives of North Korean citizens. But pursuing this objective was not at odds with seeking denuclearization. The president believed one could pursue both of these, and indeed, if the United States was to ever normalize political relations with this country, there would have to be substantial improvements in both areas—human rights and denuclearization. He rejected the concept put forward by some of his diplomats that the United States could not criticize the regime on human rights because this would undercut the nuclear diplomacy. That argument, the president believed, was North Korea's game, which he would not play.

Bush's diplomacy was therefore more principled in its emphasis on human rights. Many have argued that it was ultimately more destructive because the North initially recoiled at the tougher language out of Washington compared with the Clinton administration, and undertook a reprocessing campaign that created more plutonium for nuclear weapons. But again, this blanket statement presumes two judgments, one of which is unfalsifiable and the other has been proven wrong. First, it presumes that the North would not have made more plutonium or done a nuclear test if the United States simply abided by the 1994 agreement. This is impossible to prove. Moreover, even when the United States was abiding by the 1994 agreement, the North was constantly threatening breaches of the agreement. Second, it presumes that the U.S. accusations of a secret uranium program by the North were based on fabricated intelligence. The events since October 2002, when the United States first confronted the North with this evidence, have proven this wrong. In 2010, Pyongyang not only admitted to such a program but also showed it to an American scientist.

In the end, the Six-Party agreements constituted the fruits of the administration's diplomatic efforts. The 2005 and 2007 agreements were packaged differently, but they offered many of the same elements that twenty-plus years of U.S. diplomacy with North Korea has put on the table: economic and energy assistance, security assurances, and the promise of political normalization. Working groups were set up for each of these issue-areas. The U.S.-DPRK working group on normalization eventually led to North Korea's removal from the state sponsor of terrorism list and the lifting of some economic sanctions. The added new dimension, given the multilateral nature of the diplomacy, was the offer to North Korea of a Northeast Asian peace and security mechanism. The idea behind this working group was to demonstrate to North Korea, through dialogue and through specific measures, the vision of what sort of East Asian region Pyongyang would live in once it gave up its nuclear weapons. The objective was for the six parties to reach agreement on a set of norms, rules, and procedures that would proffer mutual security and cooperation in North Korea's neighborhood. In 2008, the Bush administration also agreed to one of the largest food aid packages ever for North Korea. This provided 500,000 tons of food to the regime through the WFP and a consortium of U.S. NGOs. The agreement came with a protocol on monitoring and access that ensured the food was reaching the neediest rather than being diverted to the military.

The final element I would mention in Bush's diplomacy with North

Korea is flexibility. Again, this is not a trait that one would normally associate with the Bush administration. But on more than one occasion, when flexibility was necessary to move the diplomatic process forward, the administration did so rather than fall on its sword. At the beginning of 2007, the administration was faced with two important decisions—whether it should return the frozen $25 million in North Korean accounts at BDA, and whether it should meet North Korea on a bilateral basis outside the venue of Six-Party Talks. Until this point, the administration adhered firmly to the principle that it would not do either as a way to maximize leverage. But when it became clear that Pyongyang would be willing to begin serious implementation of the denuclearization agreement, including starting the critical disabling of their nuclear facilities, if the administration showed some flexibility on these elements, a decision had to be made, and it could only be made by the president. In the end, he authorized the return of the funds as well as authorized us to begin bilateral discussions in Berlin, Germany, in January 2007. The result of this flexibility was deeper inspections, insights, and dismantling of the program than the United States had ever got in two decades of dealing with the problem. Similarly, at the end of 2007, when North Korea was hesitant to provide a full declaration of the nuclear holdings by the December 31 deadline, aides believed that at this late stage, a letter from the president that conveyed his personal commitment to see the process through to the normalized political relations was critical to pushing North Korea across the goal line. Bush provided such a letter. As one commentator put it, "Kim Jong-il is someone whom Bush famously loathed. He's quoted as saying he loathes Kim Jong-il and called him a pygmy, and the attitude was that you don't talk to evil, you end it . . . that Bush would, at this point, directly contact—send a personal letter to Kim Jong-il—is a remarkable turnaround from that."[53]

OBAMA: STRATEGIC PATIENCE

Question: Would you be willing to meet separately, without precondition, during the first year of your administration, in

Washington or anywhere else, with the leaders of Iran, Syria,
Venezuela, Cuba, and North Korea, in order to bridge the gap
that divides our countries?

Senator Obama: I would. And the reason is this, that the notion
that somehow not talking to countries is punishment . . . is
ridiculous. —BARACK OBAMA, JULY 24, 2007 [54]

This notion [that] by not talking to people we are punishing them
has not worked. It has not worked in Iran, it has not worked
in North Korea. In each instance, our efforts of isolation have
actually accelerated their efforts to get nuclear weapons. That
will change when I'm president of the United States . . .
—BARACK OBAMA, SEPTEMBER 26, 2008 [55]

Talking to advisers to the campaign in 2008 and then White House and State Department officials who were in charge of the policy in early 2009, I got the clear sense that the administration wanted to pick up where the Bush administration had left off, and wanted to accelerate the process of negotiations, shedding what they perceived to be Bush's reluctance to engage in high-level bilateral negotiations. Obama stated clearly that the United States harbored no hostile intent toward Pyongyang, which had been a main condition of North Korea engagement with the United States. Moreover, he made clear that he did not consider talking or face-to-face negotiations with the North Koreans as revolting or distasteful. He made his commitment to the multilateral negotiating forum and to moving forward with the September 2005 Joint Statement clear to the other members of the Six-Party Talks—Japan, China, Russia, and South Korea.[56]

After the DPRK conducted the missile and nuclear tests in the spring of 2009, and then revealed its secret uranium enrichment program in 2010, the Obama administration did not default to a hostile policy but continued to demonstrate a commitment to engagement. Obama offered to send former vice president Al Gore to North Korea to achieve the release of the two kidnapped American journalists, Laura Ling and Euna

Lee. When the North Koreans rejected Gore as too "low-level," Obama agreed to send former president Bill Clinton. Clinton spent two days in Pyongyang, much of it with DPRK leader Kim Jong-il. While Clinton's sole mission was the return of the two Americans, he conveyed to Kim his personal view that the Obama administration was ready for serious negotiation despite the DPRK missile and nuclear tests. In December of 2009, the White House dispatched senior envoy Steve Bosworth to Pyongyang, and in an extraordinary sign of U.S. diplomatic intentions, Bosworth carried a personal letter from President Obama to Kim Jong-il. While both Bush and Clinton sent letters to Kim, it was after long periods of negotiations and was meant to help push the implementation of agreements past the finish line. In this case, the letter came very early in the administration, and was concealed by the White House until press inquiries mounted. While they would not disclose the contents of the letter (again, in contrast to past practice where the letters were all released to the public), reports stated that the letter assured Kim of U.S. commitment to negotiations and the benefits that could accrue to Kim should he recommit to the Six-Party Talks.[57]

When North Korea responded to these overtures with the sinking of the South Korea naval vessel *Cheonan* in March 2010, followed by the artillery shelling of Yeonpyeong Island in November 2010, the administration initiated a policy that came to be known as "strategic patience." This policy essentially stated that the United States remains committed to diplomacy—that is, the United States seeks a peaceful diplomatic solution to the denuclearization of the Korean Peninsula, and that it remains committed to the Six-Party Talks and to fulfilling its commitments in the denuclearization agreements of 2005 and 2007. However, in the face of the string of DPRK provocations in 2009 and 2010, Washington was willing to wait for a period of time in which Pyongyang could demonstrate some positive and constructive behavior and a willingness to negotiate in earnest. In the interim, a premium was placed on coordinating policies closely with Japan and South Korea, and on the tools of coercive diplomacy, including counterproliferation measures, U.N. Security Council sanctions, and financial sanctions. Strategic patience would not reward the regime and thereby devalued Pyongyang's attempts to use provocations as a means to attract attention. More important, it highlighted positive behavior by the North (i.e., denuclearization or human rights steps) rather than a mere cessation of provocations, as the path back to high-level diplomacy.[58] Concerns about a third nuclear test and escalatory provocations eventually inclined the Obama administration in 2011–2012 to seek a path back to the Six-Party talks in the aftermath of Kim Jong-il's death, although this has proceeded at a halting and slow pace.

The record of diplomacy is pretty clear. The United States has tried for over twenty years to denuclearize North Korea through diplomacy. Administrations, with very different foreign policy agendas and ideologies, have all negotiated with the North, however unappetizing that may have been. Each had its own flavor, but the overall direction of engagement has been far more carrot than stick. Though packaged differently, each administration, including the current one, has offered benefits that would help the DPRK reenergize its economy, feed its people, and reenter the prosperous region in which it lives. Two former U.S. presidents have met with the North Korean leader to convey this vision. The last three U.S. presidents have each sent personal letters to Kim Jong-il to signal at the highest levels the president's personal commitment to negotiations. All have failed miserably, but not for lack of trying.

To blame the DPRK's nuclear program on the United States is terribly misinformed. Harsh critics may argue that the North undertook provocations like missiles, nuclear tests, or plutonium reprocessing in response to U.S. failure to meet the requirements of their agreements. However, there is a clear distinction that needs to be made between falling behind on implementation of an agreement versus breaking core elements of it in bad faith. American administrations are certainly guilty of the former, falling behind in fuel shipments, for example; but, in the end, every shipment was made, even if it was terribly late. This flaw is qualitatively different from cheating on core elements of the agreement such as building new nuclear facilities in secret. To equate these two is wholly inaccurate.

So, what do the North Koreans really want? If twenty-plus years of offers by the United States, including personal appeals from three U.S. presidents—in addition to a chorus of encouragement from regional neighbors—is not enough to convince Pyongyang to partake in the benefits of the most prosperous region of the globe, then what else could they possibly desire? The answers are discouraging.

SO, WHAT DO THEY REALLY WANT?

We remained deadlocked over a particular clause in the document. Our counterparts across the table demanded language that we thought to be unacceptable. Yet in an effort to move the already faltering negotiations forward, we agreed to send the language back to Washington overnight for approval. This was the fourth round of the Six-Party Talks in September 2005. The talks had been suspended previously for well over a year, and the Bush administration, in its second term, was reengaging in a way it was not in its first term. At issue was North Korea's demand that we put in writing a statement of American nonhostile intent. The clause in question stipulated the United States "would not attack North Korea with nuclear or conventional weapons."[59] To my surprise, the language came back the next morning, having been approved in Washington. When we came back to the negotiation session at the Diaoyutai State Guesthouse with the accepted language, we could see the looks of surprise on the faces of the other negotiators, including the North Koreans. At that point, the Russians suddenly asked the Chinese chair for a recess from the drafting session for the agreement led by each country's deputy head of delegation. They held a bilateral meeting with the North Koreans. In this meeting, they told the North, according to my Russian counterpart on their delegation, "The Americans are serious. You see this [clause the United States has accepted]? This is called a negative security assurance. We tried to get this from them throughout the Cold War and were unsuccessful."

It seemed to me at the time that the DPRK finally received the security guarantee and the end to "hostile" U.S. policy that they had long sought. Yet after holding this out as a precondition for progress, in subsequent rounds of negotiations they proceeded to brush this off as a meaningless commitment, a piece of paper that guaranteed nothing in terms of North Korean security. Today, the clause remains buried in the 2005 Joint Statement, bereft of any significance, despite all of the intent to make it the definitive statement of U.S. nonhostile intent.

Negotiating with North Korea is all about contradictions. What can be important one day can become unimportant the next. A position they hold stubbornly for weeks and months can suddenly disappear. But these contradictions tell us a lot about core goals that may lie beneath Pyongyang's rhetoric and the provocative actions over the years. Understanding these core goals, moreover, offers insights into how spectacularly unsuccessful North Korean leader Kim Jong-il has been as he prepares to step down.

In the paragraphs below, I offer an assessment of what the North Koreans ultimately want with their recent spate of provocative behavior. It is not based solely on formal statements or evidence per se of their stated policy objectives. What is often stated through the mouths of their foreign ministry officials is only a part of the Pyongyang leadership's broader goals. Instead these judgments are also informed by the experiences and "gut instincts" of those who have negotiated with the regime over the past sixteen years.

At the June 11, 2009, hearing on North Korea before the Senate Foreign Relations Committee, the normally taciturn and eminently reasonable Richard Lugar (R-IN) responded in stern tone to one of the panelists who trotted out the same tired arguments blaming U.S. inaction and lack of negotiations for the North's May 2009 nuclear test. The experienced senator responded: "I will say respectfully, professor, of course we want negotiations. The whole point we're trying to make is the North Koreans have deliberately walked away from it, have shot missiles across Japan, have done a nuclear test. Of course [the United States government] want[s] negotiation, but until we really do something as an international community, I don't see much movement in that respect."[60] Lugar is right that negotiations have been proffered to Kim Jong-il and Kim Jong-un, yet the North continues to threaten and refuses to come to the table.

So what do they really want?[61]

THEY WANT NUCLEAR WEAPONS . . . FOR KEEPS

In social science, graduate students learn about a term called "Ockham's razor." Proposed by William of Ockham, a Franciscan monk living at the turn of the fourteenth century, the principle is *"Pluralitas non est ponenda sine necessitate,"* which translates as "entities should not be multiplied unnecessarily." This has been adopted in social science theorizing to mean that the best theories or explanations are often the simplest ones. Hence, applying Ockham's razor, the simplest explanation for North Korean nuclear tests and provocations is the desire to improve their nuclear weapons and ballistic missiles. Countries do not pursue ICBMs (inter-continental ballistic missiles) or nuclear weapons simply to accumulate negotiating chips. Pyongyang's devotion of massive amounts of very scarce resources to such projects suggests it actually wants to acquire these capabilities and be accepted by the world as a nuclear weapons state. It is unlikely to be willing to trade them away in return for international acceptance and a peace treaty with the United States. Missile and nuclear tests conducted from 2006 until today—whether they succeed or fail—are opportunities to demonstrate, learn from, and improve upon their nuclear weapons and short- and long-range delivery capabilities. The April 2009 missile test, for example, believed to be a test of the long-range Taep'odong-II ICBM was more successful than the July 4, 2006, ballistic missile test that failed in its ascent stage. The July 4, 2006, tests of seven ballistic missiles about three hundred miles (480 km) into the Sea of Japan appeared aimed at improving the accuracy of their short- and medium-range arsenal. Similarly, the May 2009 nuclear test registered seismic magnitude wave activity of 4.7, indicative of a three- to eight-kiloton weapon, which is larger than the "fizzle" test of October 2006 of less than one kiloton (0.5–0.8 kilotons), according to scientific analysis in the public domain.[62] Rather than "upping the ante" with the United States or seeking attention, as many of the post-test analyses argue,[63] Pyongyang seeks to build a better nuclear weapon and ballistic missile, and there is no substitute for learning by doing.[64]

The North Korean leadership may want nuclear weapons, but is that all that they want? After all, you can't eat plutonium. This logic leads many to argue that Pyongyang seeks nuclear weapons only for lack of a better deal out there offering North Korea food, energy, and a new relationship with the international community. The problem with this logic is that the Kim family has been offered such a deal, twice. The 1994 Agreed Framework negotiated by the Clinton administration initially froze North Korea's plutonium production facilities at Yongbyon in return for U.S.-supplied heavy fuel oil, but the agreement also laid out the vision of a peace regime, normalized relations with the United States, and economic and energy assistance for denuclearization.[65] The 2005 Six-

Party Joint Statement, as noted above, offered all of these benefits and more in return for the same denuclearization. It is no wonder, then, that members of subsequent U.S. administrations have stated their disinterest in buying the same horse again.

THEY WANT AN INDIA DEAL

I believe that North Korea wants a deal ultimately, but not one that requires full denuclearization on their part. In later rounds of Six-Party Talks, North Korean negotiators used to demand that the Bush administration deliver the light-water reactors for civilian nuclear energy promised by the 1994 agreement negotiated by Clinton. They asserted in formal sessions that this was the quid pro quo for giving up the small experimental reactor at Yongbyon, ostensibly for nuclear energy, but from which they produced plutonium for nuclear weapons. Yet in the course of sometimes heated talks, the North Koreans would assert to Ambassador Chris Hill that the United States should simply accept North Korea as a nuclear weapons state, much as they had done for India and Pakistan. When they were told that this was not likely (nor should they want to be treated like Islamabad), their negotiators countered that the Six-Party Talks should not be about the one-sided denuclearization of North Korea. This was tantamount to "stripping them naked" without any corresponding actions. Instead, the talks, they argued, should be about mutual nuclear arms reductions between two established nuclear powers, they would say, "You know, like you used to have with the Soviet Union during the Cold War."

Engagement-oriented doves have always maintained that North Korea is willing to trade their nuclear weapons for security. Hawks say that the North equates nuclear weapons with ultimate security. But the record of negotiations implies that the Kim family's true goal may be a deal with the West, but not the deal believed by the doves. Pyongyang has told countless visiting American scholars and experts in recent months that the U.S. government should simply accept North Korea as a nuclear weapons state.[66] As their candid comments, alluded to above, demonstrate, moreover, their model may be to turn the Six-Party Talks into a bilateral U.S.-DPRK nuclear-arms reduction negotiation, in which the North is accorded a status as a nuclear weapons state. The ideal outcome of this negotiation, in the North's view, is a situation similar to the arrangement that the United States negotiated with India. That is, an agreement in which North Korea is willing to come back under International Atomic Energy Agency safeguards and monitoring, but it is also assured of a civilian nuclear energy element (i.e., Pyongyang's long-held desire for light-water reactor technology and a national energy grid capable of supporting these reactors). Most important, they would want to control a portion of their nuclear programs outside of international inspection, which, in their eyes, could then serve as their nuclear deterrent. This was, of course, the most controversial element of the U.S.-India civil nuclear energy agreement. Pyongyang would certainly want a great deal in return for these "concessions," including energy assistance, economic development assistance, normalized relations with the United States, and a peace treaty ending the Korean War. But on the nuclear side of the equation, they want the rules of the nonproliferation treaty regime essentially rewritten for them as such rules were done for India.

The North Koreans have never tabled an India-type agreement as a formal negotiating position at Six-Party Talks or in bilateral dialogue with the United States. Despite their relative isolation from the world, perhaps they understand that such a position is a bridge too far. And, frankly, they would have been laughed out of the room for proposing this formally, even by the Chinese. But the North Koreans are acutely aware that the ground constantly shifts in a protracted negotiation, and what seemed implausible at one point could become plausible later. After all, they witnessed the Bush administration move from a position of non-dialogue during the first term to President Bush's writing a personal letter to Kim Jong-il at the end of its second term.

But that is not all that North Korea wants. North Korean leader Kim Jong-il's death in 2011 has led many experts to see Pyongyang's recent nuclear and missile tests as a way to kill two birds with one stone. The tests established the North's nuclear status and security from external threats so that the power transition to the son could be carried out without worries. The tests also served to secure the Dear Leader's place in Korean history as having bequeathed to the nation the ultimate weapon against all future enemies in fulfillment of *kangsŏng tae'guk* ("rich nation, strong army"). After all, even dictators need to polish their legacies.

Yet on closer analysis, the recent provocations don't appear to represent the final jewels in the crown for Kim Jong-un. Indeed, the nuclear tests and ballistic missile barrages in 2009 may have represented desperate attempts to achieve the bare minimum of more ambitious goals, like an India-type deal, rather than the mere demonstration of nuclear capabilities. If an India deal was the Dear Leader's ultimate goal, he fell far short of that. What the world saw as Kim Jong-il's successful second nuclear test (and our failure to stop him) may actually have been the last gasps of a dying regime, bankrupt materially and ideologically, trying to secure the first step in a longer-term and distant goal of becoming the next India. Like the poor student who rushes to finish the exam before time runs out, Kim raced against the geriatric table to achieve the minimum for his son rather than the maximum for his legacy.

THEY WANT THE HOUSE OF KIM . . . FOREVER

Apologists for North Korea often argue that the regime's nuclear programs derive from insecurity. The small, isolated state had few friends during the Cold War and even fewer ones after East Germany and the Soviet Union collapsed. When China normalized relations with South Korea in 1992, the relationship between Pyongyang and Beijing, which had been "sealed in blood" through the Korean War, was never the same thereafter. Pyongyang validated the apologists' theories by saying that they desired an end to the hostile policy of the United States, and they pointed to comments like Bush's "axis of evil" or Obama's U.N. sanctions as evidence of this hostile policy. While virtually no one in the United States (or the world, for that matter) believes that any U.S. president is itching to attack North Korea, it is natural for a small, paranoid state to have such concerns, apologists argue.

There is some truth to this claim, and for this reason the United States has stated on countless occasions that it does not have a hostile policy toward North Korea. U.S. negotiator Chris Hill was fond of saying that the United States did not have a hostile policy toward North Korea but that it did have a hostile policy toward its nuclear weapons.

The North's response, once it received such assurances, even at the presidential level? Words were not enough, they said. The United States must document its nonhostile policy. So, in September 2005, the North Koreans won the aforementioned negative security assurance that they had long sought. This assurance went further in text than the statement of nonhostile intent provided by the Clinton administration in October 2000, which read, "As a crucial first step, the two sides stated that neither government would have hostile intent toward the other and confirmed the commitment of both governments to make every effort in the future to build a new relationship free from past enmity."[67] As I noted at the outset of this section, all of the other parties were impressed by this statement, including the Russians and Chinese. Yet the North dismissed this as a piece of paper with no meaning. It ended up on the scrap heap of other security assurance statements for North Korea given by the president, secretary of state, or national security adviser of past administrations dating back to George H. W. Bush. The table at the end of this chapter provides a list of all of these statements. A glance at this list makes it hard to argue Washington has not been sensitive to DPRK insecurities.

So what do they really want? I believe that the North wants a special type of "regime security assurance" from the United States. This is different from a negative security assurance. The North seeks a deeper, more fundamental form of protection for the Kim family and its cronies, which is more problematic for the United States to give. The desire for this very personal type of security assurance stems from the fundamental reform dilemma that the DPRK faces: it needs to open up to survive, but the process of opening up could lead to cracks in the hermetically sealed country precipitating the regime's demise.[68] Thus, what Pyongyang wants is an assurance from the United States, not against nuclear attack, but that it will not allow the House of Kim (that is, Kim Jong-un, his aunt and uncles, and other relatives) to collapse as Pyongyang (partially) denuclearizes and goes through a modest reform process and opening to the outside world.

This type of regime assurance must be an even more prescient concern for the North Korean leadership, given Kim Jong-il's sudden death. The leadership transition to Kim Jong-un, the youngest of his three sons, who lacks any experience or revolutionary credentials like that of his grandfather Kim Il-sung, would be an inherently unstable process in the best of times. The fluidity created by Kim Jong-il's sudden death in combination with the imperative for reform probably makes regime assurance a top-line preoccupation.

So, if escaping the horns of the reform dilemma had been one of the leadership's goals, here, too, they have failed miserably. Kim Jong-un has inherited a regime that has neither reformed economically nor gained an ounce of international goodwill to help it out of its current state.

AMERICA'S CONUNDRUM?

Where does this leave the Obama administration and future U.S. governments? If the goals for North Korea enumerated above are correct, then the negotiations, if they ever resume, will invariably reach a dead end. The United States is unlikely to offer the post–Kim Jong-il leadership a civil-nuclear deal like that of India, and absent any real improvement in the human rights situation, no American president could possibly offer regime assurances to the butchers of Pyongyang. This pessimistic prognosis should not, however, mean abandoning the opportunity to negotiate. If the choice is between dealing with a dictator with a runaway nuclear weapons program or one with a program capped and under international monitoring, the latter surely serves U.S. and Asian interests better. The Six-Party Talks or any future derivative can still serve the purpose of freezing, disabling, and degrading North Korea's nuclear capabilities, even as the stated goal remains total denuclearization.

By signaling a willingness to negotiate with the North during his administration through envoys Steve Bosworth and Sung Kim, Obama positioned the United States well for a negotiation track and the sanctions track. The emphasis has been on implementing the sanctions in U.N. Security Council Resolution 1874, passed in the aftermath of the May 2009 nuclear test, and institutionalizing a multilateral counterproliferation regime against North Korean WMD. Many initially criticized the resolution as lacking teeth, because it did not authorize the use of force in its provisions for inspection of suspect North Korean cargo. But after the DPRK ship *Kangnam* reversed course because the government of Burma (Myanmar) stated publicly its intention to comply with the provisions of 1874 and inspect the cargo, critics began to appreciate the potential for building an effective counterproliferation mechanism. Ironically, the resolution institutionalized, in a U.N. context, the Proliferation Security Initiative of the Bush administration, making it both more effective and more inclusive. One of the challenges the administration will continue to face is to keep the Chinese honest in terms of complying with the sanctions in UNSCR 1874 even after the North Koreans show interest in returning to the table for negotiations. Removing sanctions against DPRK proliferation should not be a quid pro quo for the resumption of multilateral or bilateral negotiations, tempting as this might be for Beijing to advocate.

The other negotiation trap that Obama and future U.S. administrations must avoid is the dilemma of "relative reasonableness." What this means is that every agreement in the Six-Party process is negotiated with painstaking care in which parties hammer out specific quid pro quos, the synchronization of steps, timelines, with concomitant rewards and penalties. Yet sooner or later, Pyongyang commits brinksmanship and demands more than it was promised or does less than it should. While everyone accepts that the DPRK is being completely unreasonable, they also realize that a failure of the agreement could mean the failure of the Six-Party Talks and the precipitation of another crisis. To avoid this, the parties end up pressing the U.S., certain that the only chance of progress can be had from American reasonableness rather than DPRK unreasonableness. The result is that any additional American flexibility is widely perceived in the region as evidence of American leadership, but is viewed in Washington as some combination of desperation and weakness.

So that's the playbook. The talks, if ever resumed, will never achieve what either Washington or Pyongyang wants, but they serve as a way to manage the problem, contain the proliferation threat, and run out the clock on the regime. Indeed, in early 2012, the Obama administration said as much when it evinced a willingness to seek a path back to negotiations with the North Koreans after three years of "strategic patience." Administration officials, concerned about the new leadership in Pyongyang conducting a third nuclear test and other escalatory provocations against the ROK, rationalized the return to Six-Party talks as a form of "crisis containment" or "preemptive crisis management" as they watched to see whether the young and inexperienced Kim Jong-un could hold things together after the death of his father. There will definitely be a mess on the back end when the Kim family falls from grace. But planning today for that eventuality with Seoul, Beijing, and Tokyo could help tidy things up. Obama and future U.S. administrations would do well to consider a set of separate dialogues, either bilaterally or plurilaterally among the United States, South Korea, and China. Kim Jong-un's future is uncertain, and, if internal leadership struggles ensue, there is no telling what could emerge (or fall apart) in Pyongyang. While the United States and South Korea have restarted planning how to respond to a sudden collapse scenario north of the thirty-eighth parallel, they need to also begin a quiet discussion with China. The purpose of such a discussion would be to create some transparency about the relative priorities and likely first-actions by the three parties in response to signs of political instability in the North. Presumably, the United States would be interested in securing WMD weapons and materials, and South Korea would be interested in restoring domestic stability. China would be interested in securing its border against a mass influx of refugees. Koreans are suspicious of China's intentions in a North Korean collapse scenario, given Beijing's investment in the North's mineral resources, but such a three-way discussion is important to ensuring China's support in any United Nations Security Council resolutions that might accompany sudden change in the North. Coordination in advance helps to minimize misperception and miscalculation in a crisis.

RECORD OF U.S. SECURITY ASSURANCES TO THE DPRK, 1989–2011			
DATE	ADMINIS-TRATION	STATEMENT	CONTEXT
February 27, 1989	George H.W. Bush	"I will work closely with President Roh to coordinate our efforts to draw the North toward practical, peaceful and productive dialogue, to insure that our policies are complementary and mutually reinforcing."	Presidential Address to ROK National Assembly
January 6, 1992	George H.W. Bush	"If North Korea fulfills its obligation and takes steps to implement the inspection agreements, then President Roh and I are prepared to forgo the Team Spirit exercise for this year."	President Bush News Conference with ROK President Roh Tae-Woo

RECORD OF U.S. SECURITY ASSURANCES TO THE DPRK, 1989-2011			
DATE	ADMINIS-TRATION	STATEMENT	CONTEXT
June 11, 1993	George H.W. Bush	"The Democratic People's Republic of Korea and the United States have agreed to principles of: - Assurances against the threat and use of force, including nuclear weapons; - Peace and security in a nuclear-free Korean Peninsula, including impartial application of fullscope safeguards, mutual respect for each other's sovereignty, and non-interference in each other's internal affairs; and - Support for the peaceful reunification of Korea. In this context, the two Governments have agreed to continue dialogue on an equal and unprejudiced basis."	1993 U.S.-DPRK Joint Statement
July 10, 1993	William J. Clinton	"We are seeking to prevent aggression, not to initiate it. And so long as North Korea abides by the U.N. charter and international non-proliferation commitments, it has nothing to fear from America."	Presidential Address to the ROK National Assembly
June 5, 1994	William J. Clinton	"I approached them in the spirit of peace… I would like to have a relationship with North Korea… But we are not trying to provoke North Korea. We are only asking them to do what they have already promised to do."	President Clinton, CBS Interview
June 22, 1994	William J. Clinton	"We also always kept the door open. We always said—I always said I did not seek a confrontation; I sought to give North Korea a way to become a part of the international community. I have sought other means of personally communicating to Kim Il Sung that the desires of the United States and the interests of the United States and the policy of the United States was to pursue a nonnuclear Korean Peninsula and to give North Korea a way of moving with dignity into the international community and away from an isolated path…"	Presidential Press Conference on North Korea

RECORD OF U.S. SECURITY ASSURANCES TO THE DPRK, 1989-2011			
DATE	ADMINIS-TRATION	STATEMENT	CONTEXT
October 21, 1994	William J. Clinton	"The U.S. will provide formal assurances to the DPRK, against the threat or use of nuclear weapons by the U.S."	1994 U.S.-DPRK Agreed Framework
April 17, 1996	William J. Clinton	"The four-party talks are simply a way of providing a framework within which the South and the North can ultimately agree on the terms of peace in the same way that the armistice talks provided that framework 43 years ago. And if the United States can play a positive role in that, we want to."	President Clinton, News Conference with ROK President Kim Young-Sam
September 17, 1999	William J. Clinton	"Our policy of seeking to ease tensions, prevent destabilizing developments, and explore the possibilities of a different and better relationship with North Korea, are fully in accord with the positions of our allies. So is our staunch support for the Agreed Framework, which is the linchpin of our effort to end North Korea's nuclear weapons program."	Secretary of State Albright, North Korea Briefing
October 12, 2000	William J. Clinton	"Hostility between our two nations is not inevitable, nor desired by our citizens, nor in the interests of our countries… This is why we must seize the opportunity to take the concrete steps required to open a new and more hopeful chapter in our relations."	Secretary of State Albright, Speech at Dinner with North Korean official, Gen. Cho Myŏng-rok
October 12, 2000	William J. Clinton	"[T]he United States and the Democratic People's Republic of Korea have decided to take steps to fundamentally improve their bilateral relations in the interests of enhancing peace and security in the Asia-Pacific region … As a crucial first step, the two sides stated that neither government would have hostile intent toward the other and confirmed the commitment of both governments to make every effort in the future to build a new relationship free from past enmity. . . . In this regard, the two sides reaffirmed that their relations should be based on the principles of respect for each other's sovereignty and non-interference in each other's internal affairs, and noted the value of regular diplomatic contacts, bilaterally and in broader fora."	2000 US-DPRK Joint Communiqué

DATE	ADMINIS-TRATION	STATEMENT	CONTEXT
		RECORD OF U.S. SECURITY ASSURANCES TO THE DPRK, 1989–2011	
February 20, 2002	George W. Bush	"We're a peaceful people. We have no intention of invading North Korea. South Korea has no intention of attacking North Korea. Nor does America. We're purely defensive, and the reason we have to be defensive is because there is a threatening position of the DMZ, so we long for peace. It's in our nation's interest that we achieve peace on the peninsula."	President Bush, Joint News Conference with ROK President Kim Dae-Jung
May 1, 2002	George W. Bush	"[The] president made it clear that we were willing to talk to them any time, any place, and without any preset agenda."	Secretary of State Powell, Senate Hearing
October 22, 2002	George W. Bush	"The United States hopes for a different future with North Korea. As I made clear during my visit to South Korea in February, the United States has no intention of invading North Korea. This remains the case today."	Presidential Remarks in Meeting with NATO Secretary General Lord Robertson
October 27, 2002	George W. Bush	"We have no intention of invading North Korea or taking hostile action against North Korea."	Secretary of State Powell, News Conference at APEC in Los Cabos
February 7, 2003	George W. Bush	"[We] have no intention of attacking North Korea as a nation… We're prepared to talk to them."	Secretary of State Powell, Senate Foreign Relations Committee Testimony
October 20, 2003	George W. Bush	"[What] [the President] himself has said, which is that there is no intention to invade North Korea. But the President is very committed to the six-party talks, believes that it is the forum in which we are most likely to get a satisfactory resolution of the nuclear problem on the Korean Peninsula. And so he reiterated the importance of moving those talks forward. . . . We are not going to go in, all guns blazing, say take it or leave it, this is it."	National Security Adviser C. Rice, Press Briefing

RECORD OF U.S. SECURITY ASSURANCES TO THE DPRK, 1989–2011			
DATE	ADMINIS-TRATION	STATEMENT	CONTEXT
October 27, 2003	George W. Bush	"The president has made it clear that he has no intention of invading North Korea or attacking North Korea."	Secretary of State Powell, "Meet the Press"
February 11, 2005	George W. Bush	"The North Koreans have been told by the president of the United States that the United States has no intention of attacking or invading North Korea."	Secretary of State C. Rice, News Conference in Luxembourg
July 12, 2005	George W. Bush	"Now that they've decided to return to the talks, let's just remember that we have stated that this is a sovereign state, that we have no intention to attack it…"	Secretary of State C. Rice, SBS Interview in Seoul
September 15, 2005	George W. Bush	"The United States affirmed that it has no nuclear weapons on the Korean Peninsula and has no intention to attack or invade the DPRK with nuclear or conventional weapons…"	2005 Six-Party Talks Joint Statement
October 10, 2006	George W. Bush	"The United States of America doesn't have any intention to attack North Korea or to invade North Korea… But the United States somehow, in a provocative way, trying to invade North Korea—it's just not the case."	Secretary of State C. Rice, CNN Interview with Wolf Blitzer
October 11, 2006	George W. Bush	"The United States affirmed that we have no nuclear weapons on the Korean Peninsula. We affirmed that we have no intention of attacking North Korea. The United States remains committed to diplomacy…. But the United States' message to North Korea and Iran and the people in both countries is that we have—we want to solve the issues peacefully."	Presidential News Conference
November 18, 2006	George W. Bush	"Our desire is to solve the North Korean issue peacefully. And as I've made clear in a speech as recently as two days ago in Singapore, that we want the North Korean leaders to hear that if it gives up its weapons—nuclear weapons ambitions, that we would be willing to enter into security arrangements with the North Koreans, as well as move forward new economic incentives for the North Korean people."	President Bush, Meeting with ROK President Roh Moo-Hyun

RECORD OF U.S. SECURITY ASSURANCES TO THE DPRK, 1989–2011			
DATE	ADMINIS-TRATION	STATEMENT	CONTEXT
June 26, 2008	George W. Bush	"First, I'm issuing a proclamation that lifts the provisions of the Trading with the Enemy Act with respect to North Korea. And secondly, I am notifying Congress of my intent to rescind North Korea's designation as a state sponsor of terror in 45 days. The next 45 days will be an important period for North Korea to show its seriousness of its cooperation. We will work through the six-party talks to develop a comprehensive and rigorous verification protocol. And during this period, the United States will carefully observe North Korea's actions—and act accordingly... Multilateral diplomacy is the best way to peacefully solve the nuclear issue with North Korea. Today's developments show that tough multilateral diplomacy can yield promising results."	Presidential Press Conference on North Korea
July 31, 2008	George W. Bush	"I will do nothing to undermine the six-party structure, the credibility of the six-party structure, and our partners."	President Bush, Roundtable Interview By Foreign Print Media
February 15, 2009	Barack H. Obama	"Our position is when they move forward in presenting a verifiable and complete dismantling and denuclearization, we have a great openness to working with them... It's not only on the diplomatic front... the United States [has] a willingness to help the people of North Korea, not just in narrow ways with food and fuel but with energy assistance."	Secretary of State H. Clinton, En Route to Asia
April 5, 2009	Barack H. Obama	"The United States is fully committed to maintaining security and stability in northeast Asia and we will continue working for the verifiable denuclearization of the Korean Peninsula through the Six-Party Talks. The Six-Party Talks provide the forum for achieving denuclearization, reducing tensions, and for resolving other issues of concern between North Korea, its four neighbors, and the United States."	Presidential Statement on North Korea Launch

RECORD OF U.S. SECURITY ASSURANCES TO THE DPRK, 1989–2011			
DATE	ADMINIS-TRATION	STATEMENT	CONTEXT
April 5, 2009	Barack H. Obama	"The United States and the European Union stand ready to work with others in welcoming into the international community a North Korea that abandons its pursuit of weapons of mass destruction and policy of threats aimed at its neighbors and that protects the rights of its people. Such a North Korea could share in the prosperity and development that the remainder of northeast Asia has achieved in recent years."	U.S.-European Council Joint Statement
June 16, 2009	Barack H. Obama	"So I want to be clear that there is another path available to North Korea—a path that leads to peace and economic opportunity for the people of North Korea, including full integration into the community of nations. That destination can only be reached through peaceful negotiations that achieve the full and verifiable denuclearization of the Korean peninsula. That is the opportunity that exists for North Korea, and President Lee and I join with the international community in urging the North Koreans to take it… We are more than willing to engage in negotiations to get North Korea on a path of peaceful coexistence with its neighbors, and we want to encourage their prosperity."	President Obama, Joint Press Availability with ROK President Lee Myung-Bak
November 14, 2009	Barack H. Obama	"Yet there is another path that can be taken. Working in tandem with our partners—supported by direct diplomacy—the United States is prepared to offer North Korea a different future. Instead of an isolation that has compounded the horrific repression of its own people, North Korea could have a future of international integration. Instead of gripping poverty, it could have a future of economic opportunity—where trade and investment and tourism can offer the North Korean people the chance at a better life. And instead of increasing insecurity, it could have a future of greater security and respect."	President Obama, Tokyo, Japan

RECORD OF U.S. SECURITY ASSURANCES TO THE DPRK, 1989–2011			
DATE	ADMINIS-TRATION	STATEMENT	CONTEXT
November 19, 2009	Barack H. Obama	"Our message is clear: If North Korea is prepared to take concrete and irreversible steps to fulfill its obligations and eliminate its nuclear weapons program, the United States will support economic assistance and help promote its full integration into the community of nations. That opportunity and respect will not come with threats— North Korea must live up to its obligations."	President Obama, Joint Press Conference with ROK President Lee, Seoul
November 11, 2010	Barack H. Obama	"I want to reiterate that along with our South Korean and international partners, the United States is prepared to provide economic assistance to North Korea and help it integrate into the international community, provided that North Korea meets its obligations."	President Obama, Joint Press Conference with ROK President Lee, Seoul

CHAPTER EIGHT

NEIGHBORS

NORTH KOREA'S NEIGHBORS ARE BOTH THE BANE OF ITS EXISTENCE AND THE SOURCE of the regime's uncanny resilience. Japan was once the largest provider of food assistance to the DPRK until 2002, but now it remains locked in a death struggle with Pyongyang over the fate of Japanese citizens abducted and taken to North Korea in the 1970s. China is the sole source of external support for the regime today; but at the same time it pursues a predatory economic policy, exploiting the North's resources to feed its own growth. North Korea needs Chinese support but resents being treated by Beijing as one of China's poor provinces. The Soviet Union, which supported the regime throughout the Cold War, dropped it like a hot potato in 1990, when Moscow normalized relations with the South. It has since done as little as necessary to maintain its interests on the peninsula. Kim Il-sung once had a profitable way of dealing with its two big patron neighbors—playing off the rivalries between the two competing Communist powers to maximize benefits from each. And it simply used the others in the region as the justification for its siege mentality and draconian control at home. But today, the DPRK is flailing about in the region—unhappy with its dependence on China but having no other real alternatives.

CHINA: MUTUAL HOSTAGES

For the late DPRK leader Kim Jong-il's seventieth birthday in February 2011, the Chinese sent a special delegation to Pyongyang. It was led not by the foreign ministry but by state councilor and head of public security Meng Jainzhu. Meng wished Kim Jong-il a successful succession process from him to his son in the future, and offered Kim a *Shou Tao*—a large, maroon-colored porcelain peach—as a birthday gift. Traditionally given by Chinese as gifts to elderly folks, the *Shou Tao* symbolizes longevity, and with this gift, the Chinese people's desires for a long and healthy life for Kim Jong-il.

From this episode, we can learn five basic facts about the relationship between the DPRK and its only real patron in the international system today. The first basic fact is that while other nations speculated how long the stroke-stricken North Korean leader could have lived, China was unabashedly pronounced in its desires to see Kim Jong-il remain in power for as long as possible, even as it fully supported the succession process. Second, China's policy toward North Korea is unlike that toward any other country in Beijing's orbit. The Chinese refer to it as a special relationship, often described by the adage "as close as lips and teeth." Policy toward North Korea is not made in, nor led by, the foreign ministry, which shepherds China's diplomacy with an eye to its national interest and international reputation. Instead, this relationship is made, managed, and protected by the International Liaison Office of the Chinese Communist Party, the People's Liberation Army, and the Ministry of Commerce. For China, the relationship is treated almost as a domestic issue, given the commercial ties between the North and China's poor northeastern provinces, Jilin and Liaoning. The third basic fact about China-DPRK relations is that despite the professed unique relationship, there is no love between the two. In public, the two speak only platitudes of one another. I sat through many a dinner in Beijing during the Six-Party Talks where the DPRK and Chinese delegates would share protracted and obsequious toasts about the rich history and everlasting friendship between the two. Whenever the press took photos, the DPRK would be shuffled into position next to the Chinese ahead of the other Six-Party members. It was all smiles and hugs.

This public image, however, stands in stark contrast with the private relationship. On the one hand, DPRK's distrust of the Chinese is palpable. On the other hand, Beijing views the North as a huge albatross around its neck from the Cold War. Its bad behavior, which China is forced to acquiesce to, drags China's name through the mud and tarnishes its international reputation. The Chinese would often express their frustration to us about dealing with its stubborn neighbor. And behind closed doors at Six-Party Talks, one could occasionally hear the two sides shouting at one another, at which point the staff at the Diaoyutai would usher intrigued parties away from the embarrassing scene.

The fourth basic fact is perhaps the most significant and disappointing: despite China's frustration with its poor and pathetic neighbor, it will never abandon it. There were three periods, arguably, when Beijing contemplated changes in their support of the DPRK. At the end of the Korean War, authorities were indignant at what Kim's invasion had cost China. At the end of the Cold War, when Beijing normalized relations with South Korea in 1992, it had to balance relations with Pyongyang against a new and economically vibrant partner in the South, creating tensions. And after the first nuclear test in 2006, Beijing was so upset with the North's actions that it undertook some punitive measures. But these were brief episodes in an otherwise consistent policy of support for North Korea. This underwriting of the regime has only become more apparent after Kim Jong-il's death in 2011 and the accelerating of the process to hand over power to his youngest son, Kim Jong-un. In the end, China's support derives less from some anachronistic Communist allegiance than from the fact that the two are mutual hostages: North Korea needs China to survive. It hates this fact of life and resists all Chinese advice to change its ways. China needs North Korea not to collapse. It hates this fact. And as the only patron supporting the decrepit regime today, it is, ironically, more powerless than it is omnipotent, because the regime's livelihood is entirely in Chinese hands. It must, therefore, countenance bad DPRK behavior, because any punishment could destabilize the regime. Pyongyang knows this, and deftly leverages its own vulnerability and risk-taking behavior to get sustenance, diplomatic support, and protection from its ambivalent big brother against the South Korean and American "aggressors."

DON'T PULL MY CHAIN

For how long has the DPRK been pulling China's chain like this? And how did China end up in this far-from-ideal position with its neighbor?

The formative event for the relationship was the Korean War. This war seared in Chinese minds the strategic importance of the northern portion of the Korean Peninsula as a strategic buffer on China's northeast border, which must be preserved. North Korea was never intrinsically valuable to China as a trading partner, as a model of Communism, or as a military ally. Instead, its paramount value to the Chinese was as an asset to keep out of the hands of other adversaries. When Mao won the revolution in China, he showed allegiance with the North by transferring all ethnic Korean troops who had fought with the Chinese against Japanese colonizers to the North Korean army, and by promptly recognizing the country in October 1949. After Kim Il-sung's brash decision to invade the South, Mao grew very concerned at what appeared to be Kim's fatal mistake once U.S. forces repelled the initial invasion and launched a counteroffensive that pushed north of the thirty-eighth parallel with the objective of reaching the Yalu River. The newly established Communist nation could not afford to have the United States military, an ally of the Nationalists in Taiwan, in a united Korean Peninsula directly on its border.

Mao's predicament in 1950 would become a recurring one in relations with the North. Regardless of how flawed the North's behavior was, Beijing was forced to support it for its own strategic interests. Mao told Kim and Stalin in July 1950 that he would intervene in the war if U.S. troops pushed farther north, threatening China's fourteen-hundred-kilometer (870-mi) border with Korea, and in October 1950 he kept that promise, committing 200,000 ground troops. Thus, while Stalin only provided some air support, Mao saw up to 800,000 of his soldiers die in the war to keep the Americans away from his border. The war was costly for China. It devoted over 1.45 million troops to the war and incurred a debt of $1.3 billion.[1] Among the hundreds of thousands of young Chinese men who lost their lives was Mao's son, Anying. The cost was not only in terms of men and matériel, but it ended any hope of Sino-American reconciliation, which was still the hope of many in the United States despite the revolution in 1949. Moreover, China paid the ultimate price in that the war led to U.S. support of Taiwan. The United States interposed the Seventh Fleet in the Taiwan straits and inked an alliance with Taipei. Beijing also underwent what would become two decades of U.S. trade embargoes and sanctions, and adversarial relations with the West, all because of North Korea's choices.

After the war, rather than abandon Kim Il-sung, Beijing stayed close. It kept 300,000 troops in the DPRK for some five years after the war, and signed its first bilateral economic agreement in November 1953, providing the North with $320 million in restoration costs over the following four years, supplying them with coal, cloth, cotton, grain, building materials, communication equipment, machinery, and agricultural equipment. The Chinese also agreed to send skilled workers and engineers to aid in reconstruction and to train local North Koreans.[2] In 1961, Beijing cemented its relationship with Pyongyang by signing the Treaty of Friendship, Cooperation, and Mutual Assistance. This treaty codified a de facto security guarantee already provided to the North by binding the two parties to extend military assistance if either suffered an attack, to not enter into any alliance relationship directed against the other, to not interfere in the internal affairs of the other, and to consult together on important international issues of mutual interest.

Kim Il-sung deftly secured a steady diet of Chinese support through the Cold War years despite Beijing's own economic difficulties.

NORTH KOREA–CHINA ECONOMIC RELATIONS, SELECTED YEARS (MILLIONS OF US$)		
YEAR(S)	TRADE VOLUME	PRC TO DPRK AID
1950–1954	---	508.5
1955	9.5	
1956	14.5	
1957	58.6	
1958–1960	---	
1961–1964	---	105.0
1965	180.3	
1966–1967	---	
1968	100.0	
1969	110.0	
1970	115.1	
1971	116.7	
1972	283.0	
1973	336.0	
1974	390.0	

NORTH KOREA–CHINA ECONOMIC RELATIONS, SELECTED YEARS (MILLIONS OF US$)		
1975	481.9	
1976	395.0	1.6
1977	374.4	
1978	454.3	
1979	647.2	
1980	687.3	258.7
1981	540.4	
1982	586.1	
1983	531.8	
1984	528.0	
1985	473.0	
1986	514.3	
1987	513.3	
1988	579.1	
1989	562.8	
1990	506.1	

Trade data 1955–1957 from Joseph S. Chung, The North Korean Economy: Structure and Development *(Stanford, Calif.: Hoover Institution Press, 1974), p. 110; Aid data 1950–1969, 1976, and trade data 1965 from Eui-Gak Hwang,* The Korean Economies: A Comparison of North and South *(Oxford, UK: Oxford University Press, 1993), pp. 200–201, 204; Trade 1968–1969 from Youn-Soo Kim,* The Economy of the Korean Democratic People's Republic, 1945–1977 *(Kiel, Germany: Kiel German-Korean Studies Group, 1979), p. 120; Trade 1970 from Chae-jin Lee,* China and Korea: Dynamic Relations *(Stanford, Calif.: Hoover Press, 1996), p. 140; Trade data 1971–1990 from Pong S. Lee, "The North Korean Economy: Challenges and Prospects," in Sung Yeung Kwack, ed.,* The Korean Economy at a Crossroad *(Westport, Conn.: Praeger, 1994), p. 173.*

The driver of this cooperation was the perceived need to shore up the Communist bloc in the face of the U.S.-led "iron triangle" of Japan, South Korea, and Taiwan. But Kim was especially skillful at exploiting intra-Communist bloc competition between the Soviet Union and China to win benefits for himself. (See chapter 2 for more on the Sino-Soviet split.) Because of the Sino-Soviet split, Beijing could not afford to lose North Korea's allegiance if it was to fulfill its aspiration of leading the Asian and African continents in a peasant-based revolutionary movement that competed with the Soviet model of gradual socialist evolution. Thus, Beijing was compelled to support Pyongyang regardless of how it might have disapproved of Kim's policies. In the context of the Sino-Soviet split, the DPRK was arguably China's most critical partner, much more so than it was to the Soviet Union—after all, if Beijing could not even secure the allegiance of its closest Asian Communist brethren, how could it possibly make the claim that it would lead the rest of Asian and African Communists (the Soviets, by contrast, already led the Eastern bloc)? Once again, the DPRK's value to Beijing was strategic more than intrinsic (i.e., keeping it away from the Soviets), but this was all that Kim Il-sung needed to yank on China's chain. He gravitated between the two Communist patrons, leaning in one direction and then the other to achieve his needs. China courted the DPRK after Khrushchev's 1956 "de-Stalinization" speech, knowing that Moscow's denunciation of Stalin's personality cult threatened Kim's own rule. It lost Pyongyang's support during the Cultural Revolution as Kim tilted slightly back toward the Soviets.[3] During the 1970s, when Chinese politics stabilized, Sino-DPRK relations warmed once again, and those with the Soviets cooled, evinced by the fact that not a single Soviet Politburo member visited the North between 1971 and 1978.[4] Meanwhile, the Chinese treated Kim in grand fashion with state dinners and cruises with Mao and Zhou Enlai on the Yangtze River. And after Deng Xiaoping's rise to power in 1978 and the initiation of the reform era in China, Beijing continued to court the North, offering a model of reform for the DPRK to follow.

While estimates vary widely, it is believed that China provided about 20 percent of the $4.75 billion worth of aid that was delivered to the North between the end of World War II and 1984. China helped the North Koreans to build capacity in industry and energy, at one point placing over ten thousand workers in the country working on the construction of a number of hydroelectric power plants and providing a steady diet of oil and fertilizer at low cost.[5] While, officially, the majority of this aid was given in the form of "loans," as the years went by the Chinese understood well that they would not be seeing their money again. Though the relationship was "sealed in blood" on the field of battle during the Korean War, there was hardly any love shared. China was both embarrassed by and detested Kim Il-sung's over-the-top personality cult. Kim Il-sung bit his tongue when receiving goodies from Beijing, but would occasionally let loose, criticizing Beijing to others in uncouth terms. For instance, China's 1958 withdrawal of troops is believed to have been spurred, at least in part, by a personal dispute between Kim and Mao. At a 1957 Communist World summit in Moscow, Kim asked Mao to hand over a number of North Korean defectors who had just escaped massive purges of "reactionaries" within the KWP. Mao refused, and reportedly lectured Kim on his need to be more accepting of alternate views and learn from divergent perspectives within the party. This irritated Kim, and, apparently grasping at straws, he began to complain about the Chinese military presence in the North, claiming it was a violation of DPRK sovereignty. Without a hint of hesitation, an equally perturbed Mao brusquely assured Kim that all troops would be withdrawn, and within one year, they were.[6] This was also seen during the Cultural Revolution, as the North Korean leadership sanctioned the continuous blasting of anti-Chinese propaganda through loudspeakers across the Sino–North Korean border, and both sides even recalled their respective ambassadors at certain points.[7] In his report to the Korean Workers' Party Conference of October 1966, Kim overtly hinted at China deriding "Left opportunism" and the perversion of "Marxism-Leninism in a dogmatic manner [which] leads people to the extremist action under superrevolutionary slogans."[8] In Vladivostok, in December 1966, Kim described the Cultural Revolution to the Soviet general secretary Leonid Brezhnev as "massive idiocy" and declared that the DPRK would follow a self-reliant path independent from China. Similarly, North Koreans talked disparagingly to the Cubans about how Mao's senility was sending China down the wrong path, and joked that perhaps Korean ginseng root would bring him back to his senses.[9]

The feeling, as they say, was mutual on the Chinese side. The Chinese could not stand having to clean up North Korea's mess and at the same time throw at it money that was wasted on ridiculous personality-cult projects. After the Korean War, China chafed at how Kim Il-sung had dragged Beijing into a horrific war with the United States. During the Cultural Revolution, posters in Beijing referred to Kim as a "fat revisionist" and a "disciple of Khrushchev," and widely circulated Red

Guard articles charged him with being a "counterrevolutionary," a "millionaire," an "aristocrat," and a "capitalist."[10] And just as Kim had criticized the excesses of the Cultural Revolution, Deng Xiaoping deplored Kim's personality cult. On a visit to Pyongyang in September 1978, on the occasion of the DPRK's thirtieth anniversary, Deng was taken to pay respects to the giant gold statue of Kim Il-sung. Deng, who was trying to rid China of Mao's personality cult, was appalled at the statue and, reportedly, "eyed the figure with fury." He complained to the North Koreans in private that the statue was one of the most wasteful things he had ever seen and was deeply offended that Kim was spending the aid he received from China on projects like this.[11] The Chinese were reportedly also disdainful of Pyongyang's terrorist attacks against the South. Deng was furious, for example, at North Korea for staging the October 1983 assassination attempt against South Korean president Chun Doo-hwan during a state visit to Burma, which killed half of Chun's cabinet. This was not out of any newfound love for the South, but because the Chinese had just days earlier conveyed to the Americans, on behalf of the DPRK, a proposal to do three-party talks involving the Reagan administration and the two Koreas. These deadly antics by the North made Beijing look foolish in the world's eyes.

A CHANGE OF HEART?

There were three times when Beijing contemplated a change of heart in its support of the DPRK. The first of these was in the aftermath of the Korean War. China was indignant at how Kim Il-sung's folly had cost it nearly 800,000 lives, a fratricidal war with the United States, and the loss of Taiwan. Peng Dehuai, who was commander-in-chief of Chinese forces during the Korean War, argued forcefully for Kim's expulsion and might have succeeded had he not also criticized Mao's Great Leap Forward, which put him in disfavor among the Chinese leadership, ultimately leading to his demise. The second moment came with Beijing's normalization of diplomatic relations with South Korea in August 1992. Until normalization, China maintained a strict "one-Korea" policy, only recognizing and interacting with the North. It did not consider the regime in Seoul legitimate, seeing it merely as a proxy for the

U.S. security threat. However, beginning in the 1980s, growing trade ties with the ROK started to change Beijing's perspective. This trade was initially indirect, through third parties like Hong Kong and Japan, but steadily grew from $40 million in 1979 to $222 million in 1984 and to $518 million by 1985. A key turning point in the relationship occurred in May 1983, when a hijacked Chinese civilian airliner was forced to land in South Korea. Seoul and Beijing were put in the position of having to engage in direct negotiations on the safe return of the aircraft and crew, which went unexpectedly smoothly for both sides. Resolution of this incident produced goodwill that led to increased cultural and sports contacts. The 1986 Asian Games, held in Seoul, were deftly used by South Korea as a tool of engagement with Beijing. These games were a slimmed-down regional version of the Olympics, which Seoul used as a dress rehearsal for the Seoul Olympics two years later. Early on, Seoul lobbied China to participate in the 1986 event. It wanted to secure China's commitment to attend the Seoul Games after two successive boycotts of the previous two Olympics, by the Americans in 1980 and by the Soviets in 1984. The plan was to treat Chinese teams and officials very well, hope that they would perform in the games and win a lot of medals (they indeed won the most gold medals), and create goodwill on both sides. All of this not only ensured Beijing's participation in Seoul's Olympics two years later, it also precipitated a boost in trade volume in 1985–1986 to over $1.5 billion, which then constituted 80 percent of South Korea's total trade with socialist countries. By 1989, China-ROK trade was over ten times that of China and North Korea, and small- and medium-size South Korean companies made China their second-largest investment destination.

Then, in 1990, China succumbed to another bit of South Korean sports diplomacy. The next major event in Asia after the 1988 Olympics was Beijing's hosting of the 1990 Asian Games. China saw the successful staging of this event as a prelude to an eventual bid for the Olympics, but the problem it encountered was that it had no practical experience at hosting a major international sporting event, even on a regional scale. Moreover, little help was forthcoming from the world community because of international outrage after the draconian government suppression of demonstrations in Tiananmen Square in 1989.

Seoul, however, made the conscious decision to go against the grain and help the Chinese.

ROK president Roh Tae-woo personally lobbied Asian leaders not to boycott the Asian Games. He encouraged over 22,000 South Korean tourists to attend the games (a large number, given the absence then of diplomatic relations between the two countries). South Korea's Hyundai and other carmakers donated some four hundred vehicles to be used to transport athletes around the games. While others were cutting off economic ties with China, South Korea provided over $15 million in advertising revenue. One estimate put ROK public and private sector support for the Beijing Asiad at $100 million.[12] Beijing pulled off a successful event, and four months later informed the International Olympic Committee of its intention to bid for the 2000 Olympics.[13]

The Chinese were eternally grateful for ROK support. At the conclusion of the Asian Games, in 1990, the two countries established trade liaison offices. The following year, China dropped its long-held opposition to South Korea's bid to become a member of the United Nations, which allowed Seoul finally to gain a seat in the international organization after decades of trying. These trends made Sino–South Korean normalization two years later a foregone conclusion. On August 24, 1992, ROK foreign minister Yi Sang-ŏk and PRC foreign minister Qian Qichen signed a joint normalization communiqué in which the two sides agreed to establish "enduring relations of good neighborhood, friendship, and cooperation on the basis of . . . the principles of mutual respect for sovereignty and territorial integrity, mutual nonaggression, noninterference in each other's internal affairs, equality and mutual benefit, and peaceful coexistence."[14] In the wake of the signing, the two sides were ecstatic. President Roh called the normalization "a significant turning point in world history" and "the beginning of the end of the Cold War in East Asia."[15] And although Beijing had to be more subdued so as to not antagonize their North Korean allies, even the then-hard-line premier Li Peng called the move "a very important event in relations between China and the ROK and has great significance for peace and development in Asia and the world."[16]

China's shift from a one-Korea to "two-Korea" policy in 1992 constituted a watershed policy change second only to its 1950 decision to enter the Korean War. It is attributable to a confluence of factors. First and foremost, the outreach to the ROK would not have been possible absent Deng's push for modernization reforms in the 1980s. This reform mandate made South Korea intrinsically valuable as a trade and investment asset to Beijing, much more so than North Korea, which was only an economic liability to China. Second, South Korea's *Nordpolitik,* or Northern Diplomacy, which emphasized Seoul's interest in building mutually beneficial economic relations with Communist countries, also provided a welcoming environment for Deng's economic modernization plans. The combination of these two initiatives gave both sides the confidence that their political leadership was supportive of a rapprochement. Third, and perhaps most important, Gorbachev's willingness to seek his own détente with China ended the Sino-Soviet split in 1989. In May of 1989, the culmination of years of effort and gradually improving Sino-Soviet relations was realized in Mikhail Gorbachev's historic summit with Deng Xiaoping in Beijing, the first by a Soviet leader since a fractious visit by Nikita Khrushchev in 1959. These developments had the effect of drastically reducing the strategic value of the DPRK to China as it no longer had to worry about the ramifications of "losing" the North to the Soviet orbit. The embrace of South Korea did not mean total abandonment of the North. Beijing moved much more cautiously than the Soviet Union, which rushed to normalization with Seoul two years earlier than China and then drastically cut its assistance to Pyongyang. But it did mean Beijing was no longer playing favorites on the peninsula, and would reorient its policies to obtaining benefits (i.e., trade and investment with the ROK) rather than merely preventing losses (i.e., sustaining the DPRK). Thus, when Pyongyang protested about South Korean trade and investment in China, Beijing ignored it and proceeded with little hesitation. When Kim Il-sung personally complained to his Chinese interlocutors that Beijing should limit the size of the ROK delegation to the 1990 Asian Games and should ban the ROK flag from the opening ceremonies (because Beijing had not yet formally established diplomatic relations with the ROK), China politely declined both requests. And when Pyongyang demanded that China not allow South Korean companies' billboard advertising (for which tens of millions of dollars were paid to Chinese sponsors of the games), Beijing authorities simply ignored the request.

China saw a two-Korea policy as best serving its own interests. It managed its new relationship with South Korea fairly successfully—the subsequent fifteen years in ROK-China relations were a virtual honeymoon, with popular feelings of economic opportunity, Confucian kinship, and reconciliation after thirty years of non-dialogue pervasive on both sides. There were even some short-lived concerns in the West that the ROK was falling back into China's gravitational orbit and away from the U.S.-based alliance system.[17]

While China did not abandon North Korea during this period, it changed the terms of the relationship to ones that were more economically rational for Beijing. After normalization with Seoul, China stopped supplying crude oil, coal, and fertilizer to the DPRK at so-called friendship prices, and stopped providing interest-free loans. Because the North could not pay these prices, bilateral trade dropped from $900 million in 1993 to $550 million in 1995.[18] Food exports to the DPRK fell by more than half between 1993 and 1994. Though the North was even more dependent on China than ever after the collapse of the Soviet Union, it was deeply offended by China's decision to normalize relations with the ROK. Pyongyang denounced Beijing for betraying the relationship and abandoning it. What ensued was essentially a period of non-dialogue for almost ten years. No senior Chinese official went to the DPRK between 1992 and 2000, even as China quietly continued a minimal amount of assistance to the North to maintain a basic level of stability. And Kim Jong-il did not visit China for almost the entire decade after Beijing's normalization with South Korea. Between 1992 and 2001, while Chinese investment in North Korea was a paltry $5.1 million, ROK investment in China was more than $13 billion. Sino-ROK trade topped $35.9 billion by 2001 while that between China and the DPRK was only $325 million.

To this day, some Chinese observers believe the shift in policy was a mistake. While it was inevitable that Seoul and Beijing would normalize relations, China's shift in policy toward the DPRK was, according to some, too abrupt and too focused on China's economic gains with the ROK, while neglecting the larger strategic benefit in maintaining the DPRK. Thus, after China's decision to reduce subsidized trade, critics argue, the North fell into its worst period in the mid-1990s—a nuclear weapons crisis with the United States in 1994, and then the famine from 1995, which precipitated real fears in China of possible instability on the peninsula. Famine-induced migration of starving North Koreans across the Sino-Korean border raised the nightmare scenario for Beijing that a collapsing DPRK would send hordes of refugees into its northeast provinces. The response between 1995 and 2001 was to track back to the traditional policy of keeping the DPRK afloat. By the beginning of 1995, the Chinese resumed subsidized trade, providing over 1.2 million metric tons of crude oil and 1.5 million metric tons of coal. It also upped food contributions, providing about 550,000 tons annually in this period, about 10 percent of the North's annual grain requirements. These donations supplemented what the World Food Programme's emergency appeals for DPRK were already bringing into the country. (China largely keeps secret its figures for food and fuel supplies to North Korea. It does not release full food aid information to the WFP International Food Assistance System Database. It also does not impose any monitoring requirements on the food to ensure it is going to the neediest.)[19] China also tried to reestablish political ties with Kim Jong-il after Kim Il-sung's death in 1994, but the Son was so upset, it was not until 1999 that the two governments reconciled. Two visits by Kim Jong-il to China in June 1999 and May 2000, big celebrations in July 2001 commemorating the fortieth anniversary of the 1961 Friendship Treaty, and a September 2001 visit by President Jiang Zemin to North Korea all had the effect of consolidating relations and returning to normalcy China's embrace of its little communist brother.

IT WAS SUNDAY EVENING, October 8, 2006, and I was in the kitchen doing the dishes after dinner. My wife put the boys to bed and I was looking forward to a light run to wind the evening down before another week of the frenzied pace at the NSC. Just then, the phone rang. It was the White House situation room and they alerted me to await a call on my STU (Secure Telephone Unit) phone. When you work at the NSC and you are asked on a Sunday evening to take a secure call, it is never good news. The STU rang and I picked up the receiver. The duty officer said that the sit room had word from the U.S. embassy in Beijing, via the Chinese, that a North Korean nuclear test was imminent. I asked how much time. The sit room officer said that the DPRK informed the Chinese embassy in Pyongyang, which relayed the information to Beijing. Beijing then relayed it to our embassy and then to the situation room. I said, "Okay, so how much time?" The response, "Well, sir, probably about forty-five minutes." I threw on a suit (the Bush White House did not approve of staff wandering around the West Wing in jeans, even after hours, as a sign of respect for the office) and brought an extra shirt, knowing it would be at least forty-eight hours before I would come home again. Soon after my NSC colleague Dennis Wilder and I arrived at the situation room ready to brief senior officials on the current status and implement instructions from National Security Adviser Stephen Hadley, the test took place. Seismic monitors detected an explosion at the P'unggye nuclear test site that we had been watching for months. The site was about 380 kilometers (236 mi) northeast of Pyongyang and only 130 kilometers (80 mi) from the Russian border. The explosion produced a tremor of about 4.2 magnitude. While this was a small test, about the equivalent of five hundred tons of TNT, which raised some speculation that it might just have been a high-explosives test, WC-135 "sniffers"—aircraft that collect atmospheric samples—later confirmed the presence of Krypton 85, indicating a nuclear test, albeit only a partially successful one.[20] As we worked throughout the night in the situation room, coordinating statements on the test with allies, preparing the president's statement, and preparing policy alternatives for Hadley, Secretary Rice, and the president to deliberate on, I wondered to myself what impact this test would have on China's support for its poor Korean province.

There was no country more outraged by the nuclear test than China. Beijing, in unison with other countries in the prior weeks, had been warning the DPRK through all of its communication channels in the foreign ministry, party, and military not to conduct a test. From China's perspective, a nuclear test would be an unprecedented act that defied the nonproliferation agreements and would remove any ambiguity about whether the North had the bomb. Prior to the test, Chinese negotiators would sometimes deflect statements of alarm about the DPRK by asking "how do you know they even have a bomb and not just some plutonium?" They could do this no longer. The nuclear test did not threaten China per se, but it did violate the primary maxim: to avoid a crisis and instability on the peninsula. Pyongyang understood this, and thus, in Beijing's eyes, the nuclear test amounted to the ultimate sign of disrespect and irresponsible behavior that Kim Jong-il could have levied against China, short of starting a second Korean War. It was almost as if Pyongyang dared China to abandon it, leveraging its own vulnerability with a sense of confidence in the end that once again, China would support the regime and clean up its mess. The test was also meant as a clear signal to the world that no one, not even China, could tell Pyongyang what it could and could not do.

China's initial response reflected anger and serious reconsideration of the terms of the relationship. Soon after the test, the foreign ministry released a statement strongly condemning the test, calling it a "brazen" act, which was the language the Chinese usually reserved only for their adversaries. PRC president Hu Jintao told President Bush over the phone that he was outraged at the test and dispatched Foreign Minister Li Zhaoxing to Pyongyang. Li, who was fond of reciting poetry with a radiant smile to foreign visitors, engaged in an uncharacteristic dressing down of the North. He essentially called Kim Jong-il a liar for having told Chinese officials many times in the past that he was committed to denuclearization in accordance with the last dying wish of his father. But they went ahead and did a test anyway. Li apparently told the North Koreans bluntly, "You've gone over the line. This is totally unacceptable. You have to promise this won't happen again."[21] The PLA—who was a key actor in the "real" and unseen bilateral relationship—were as upset about the lack of consultation prior to the test as they were about the act itself. They felt that Pyongyang would never do something as brash as this without first letting Beijing know. In fact, a PLA delegation led by a general very close to Hu Jintao was in Washington for a previously scheduled trip after the nuclear test. The general and his delegation were invited to meet privately with National Security Adviser Steve Hadley in the West Wing to discuss the nuclear test. The meeting was never made public and was, admittedly, a rarity, but given the circumstances, it was deemed necessary to hear PLA reactions. The general relayed that the military was very upset with North Korea. He said the PLA refrained from warning the DPRK not to test. He said it was not the military's place to do that, but that they did request information about what the DPRK was up to, and were deeply offended when these requests were summarily ignored. Then, after the test, the military demanded a briefing on what had happened, which the North also ignored. The PLA general waved his hand in disgust, saying the DPRK does not listen to anyone, not even China. Just then, President Bush entered Hadley's office for a rare "drop-by"—a seemingly impromptu visit by the president to convey a brief message, which is choreographed internally by the NSC in advance. The generals all jumped to attention with big smiles on their faces at this unexpected but welcome treat—a sign of respect to the PLA given by President Bush, which the general could duly report back to his superiors. The president was relaxed and thanked the general for coming over. The general said, according to one account, "[The DPRK is] out of control, they're just totally out of control," and that for China, "it's not the same sort of relationship."[22] The president then got serious. He told the general what he told Hu Jintao on the phone. In October of 2002, he and Jiang Zemin sat at his ranch in Crawford, Texas, and agreed that North Korea should not be allowed to have nuclear weapons. Now, North Korea has done a nuclear test in China's backyard. What were the Chinese going to do about it? It was both a question and a challenge to China's manhood.

The nuclear test prompted very serious debates within China about a fundamental shift in policy. On the one hand, some Chinese leaders, mostly of a younger generation, were sick and tired of North Korea's antics. By almost any metric, China's future on the Korean Peninsula was with the richer and more vibrant South, where total annual bilateral trade and investment were literally one hundred times greater than that with the North. Moreover, the status quo was no longer stable, as proven by the North's nuclear test. The test could prompt countries like Japan to consider, at a minimum, more active missile defense cooperation with the United States, and at a maximum, greater militarization on their own. It was time to cut China's losses and abandon this decrepit and dying regime. On the other hand, there were others, who believed that China's longer-term interests were still best served by the North Korean buffer, regardless of how angry China was in the aftermath of the test. Any change in the status quo on the peninsula that gave South Korea (as a proxy of U.S. influence and military presence) a position directly on China's border, next to its northeast provinces, was a fundamental threat to Chinese interests. The best path forward, therefore, was to calm the situation, draw the United States and DPRK back from crisis, and return to the negotiating table.

The initial manifestations of this internal debate were some tough Chinese actions. On October 15, 2006, Beijing signed on to U.N. Security Council Resolution 1718 (as did Russia), which denounced the test as a clear threat to international peace and security, and called for member states to block the sale or transfer of items related to the North's WMD programs, missiles, and weapons. It banned the North from exporting such materials, banned the export of luxury goods into the North, and authorized the inspection of cargo originating from and destined for North Korea. Moreover, this was a Chapter Seven resolution (article 41), which China signed on to, meaning the sanctions were mandatory and thus enlisted China in the sternest U.N. Security Council measures against the North since the Korean War.[23] Beijing also took some quiet but significant measures in its bilateral relations that were never made public. According to one account, this included the cutoff of military spare parts, suspension of some oil shipments, and curbing of money transfers from Chinese banks.[24] When we pushed the Chinese to explain what else they were doing, our interlocutors admitted that if China cut off all sustenance, the regime could last only months, but that this was not a feasible course of action. Instead, China had stopped cooperation on several projects—including work on the Dandong Bridge connecting the North to Liaoning Province, through which the majority of economic interaction took place. Ambassador Chris Hill pressed further, asking what evidence there was that the North understood China's intention to inflict punishment for the nuclear test. Without going into details, the Chinese essentially explained that Pyongyang had been calling since the test, but that the Chinese were not answering the phone.

But as in the past, this tough behavior did not last long. China soon fell back into its pattern of preserving minimum stability on the peninsula. Its initial tough actions against the North were largely designed to stop further nuclear tests, as opposed to definitive arm-twisting to achieve denuclearization. This became apparent in meetings only a week after passage of UNSCR 1718 between Secretary Rice and State Councilor Tang Jiaxuan. Rice's trip to Korea, Japan, China, and Russia was for the purpose of reassuring allies and mapping out the diplomatic path forward. In Seoul and Tokyo, she reaffirmed the U.S. nuclear umbrella and U.S. defense commitments, which were welcomed in the region, but a testy exchange with the progressive ROK president Roh took place in Seoul, where Roh essentially blamed the United States for the nuclear test because of the Treasury Department's sanctions on Banco Delta Asia, which resulted in Macao's freezing of DPRK assets. Roh said the United States must engage with North Korea to avoid more tests. I stared at my foreign ministry counterparts across the room with a "you cannot be serious?" look. They were visibly uncomfortable with Roh's remarks. Rice's eyes sharpened. She was angry, but in a calm and measured tone responded that the United States would not succumb to this brinksmanship and that the proper response now was to cut off Seoul's economic cooperation as punishment for the test. In Beijing, the meetings with the Chinese leadership were only more disappointing. After meeting with Hu and Premier Wen, Rice's key meeting was with State Councilor Tang. Tang had just returned from North Korea, where he had met with Kim Jong-il to deliver a stern message from President Hu. So we expected to hear what that message was, what was Kim's response, and how the United States and China could work together to press Pyongyang to denuclearize. Instead, we got an uninspiring performance in classic Chinese "muddling through." Tang made requisite statements about China's outrage at the test, but soon receded into a diplomatic defensive crouch, deflecting U.S. demands for China to put more pressure on the DPRK. It was clear from Tang's remarks that the Chinese, after much internal debate, once again chose the low-risk and low-commitment path, which was to call for the United States to be more flexible and more active in engaging with the North. When asked what China would do, Rice's various interlocutors said that Beijing stood ready to host the resumption of the Six-Party Talks (an empty statement), and that it would continue to ensure that the North would not perform another nuclear test. (This obviously failed in May 2009.)[25] An unprecedented DPRK misdeed constituted the ultimate test of Beijing's patience, but it did not change the policy. Total Chinese trade with the DPRK increased in the two years following the late-2006 nuclear test by as much as 41 percent between 2007 and 2008. And economist Marcus Noland found that after UNSCR 1718, Chinese exports of luxury goods (a banned item under the resolution) increased 140 percent between 2007 and 2008.[26] These numbers don't lie.

CHINA'S PREDATION

In the morning darkness of March 26, 2010, an ROK naval vessel, *Cheonan*, was on patrol in waters off the west coast of the peninsula. The ship's hull was suddenly impacted by an underwater explosion, which broke the ship cleanly in half. There was little that the doomed crew could do. Of the 104 young Korean seamen on board, 46 died in the worst loss of life suffered from a military attack since the Korean War. A joint investigation, involving the ROK, United States, Great Britain, Australia, and Sweden, lasted six months. On September 13, the investigation concluded, based on forensics of the recovered pieces of the ship and a study of eighteen possible scenarios for the sinking, that the *Cheonan* was attacked by an underwater torpedo of DPRK origin. It was later reported in the press by leaked intelligence sources that DPRK submarines were in the waters around the *Cheonan* at the time of the attack, and that an award ceremony was held for a submarine crew after the attack.[27]

While countries around the world condemned North Korea for this heinous act, China remained conspicuously silent. It did not accept the results of the investigation, and would not acknowledge that the attack was a violation of the 1953 armistice of which China is a signatory. Nor would it accept high-level intelligence briefings on the incident offered by the United States. When ROK president Lee Myung-bak met with Chinese president Hu Jintao on April 30, just weeks after the *Cheonan* sinking, Hu reportedly greeted him by offering condolences on the recent "accident." Lee looked puzzled. Hu went on to say that China had suffered, too, recently victimized by the Sichuan earthquake (May 12, 2008). According to Blue House officials, this attempted act of commiseration infuriated Lee. Hu was equating the premeditated attack on the *Cheonan* with a natural disaster in order to protect the DPRK from blame.[28] China also blocked any U.N. Security Council resolution that blamed the *Cheonan* sinking on North Korea. This disturbing pattern of behavior by Beijing continued throughout the rest of the year. Following the *Cheonan* sinking, in November 2010, North Korea carried out artillery attacks on Yeonpyeong Island, a small South Korean island off the west coast of the peninsula. Unlike the *Cheonan* sinking, which happened in the dead of night, the Yeonpyeong Island shelling took place in broad daylight, captured on television around the world. Yet Beijing again remained mum, only making token calls for calm and stability as it sought to protect its North Korean province. The cost of these actions for China was quite high in South Korea. Across the board, South Korean views of China turned wholly negative after over almost two decades of positive feelings and profitable economic relations since normalization in 1992. In the wake of the shelling of Yeonpyeong Island, 91 percent of South Koreans were dissatisfied with China's reaction to the attack, and nearly 60 percent favored a strong protest, even if doing so damaged economic relations with the Chinese.[29] As one Blue House official confided to me, "The Chinese have shown their true face."

MINING THE MINERALS

China's response to the DPRK provocations of 2010 seemed very much out of sync with that of the rest of the world. Why? I believe it is because Beijing has been following a deliberate strategy of economic predation with the North. This started from about 2007 and has been largely engineered on the Chinese side by the Chinese Communist Party and the People's Liberation Army, not the foreign ministry. In October 2009—only four months after North Korea's May 2009 nuclear test, which took place only seventy kilometers (43 mi) from the Chinese border—Premier Wen Jiabao visited North Korea to celebrate the sixtieth anniversary of the establishment of diplomatic relations. Kim Jong-il and Wen signed a host of education, tourism, and economic development agreements that represented a deepening of relations between the international department of the Korean Workers' Party and international liaison office of the CCP. This effectively ended the debate within China about North Korea policy in the wake of the October 2006 (and May 2009) nuclear test. This was followed in March 2010 by Kim Jong-il's visit to Beijing. This prescheduled visit took place only weeks after the *Cheonan* sinking, and despite personal entreaties from ROK president Lee to postpone the meeting, Hu hosted Kim with the equivalent of a White House state visit, with pomp and circumstance not seen since the Cold War days. The DPRK delegation was huge in scale, and the scope of the party-to-party meetings was unprecedented. Kim was generously lauded in meetings with Hu, Wen, Vice President Xi Jinping, Vice Premier Li Keqiang, and all nine members of the Politburo standing committee. The fact that the rest of the world was outraged over the *Cheonan* sinking did not deter the Chinese from carrying out their systematic strategy to consolidate relations with North Korea.

The formal principles of this approach were laid out during a second visit by Kim Jong-il to China, in the northeastern city of Changchun, in August 2010, where the two countries committed to: (1) maintain high-level contacts; (2) reinforce strategic cooperation; (3) exchange views on domestic and diplomatic issues; (4) increase people-to-people exchanges; and (5) strengthen coordination in international and regional affairs. During these meetings, Premier Wen Jiabao told Kim that China would never abandon its traditional relationship with the DPRK and would always seek to improve the country's economic livelihood. PRC foreign ministry sources considered this meeting to be a "disaster" given that the CCP- and PLA-led initiatives with the DPRK not only cut out the foreign ministry but ran contrary to the world's reaction to DPRK's 2009 nuclear test and 2010 provocations.

The latter statements by Wen about economic livelihood point to an extractive economic strategy designed to exploit the DPRK's natural resources. According to separate studies by John Park at the U.S. Institute of Peace and Drew Thompson, formerly at the Nixon Center and now in the Defense Department, this strategy has been in place since about 2007, when China made two significant investments in the Musan Iron Mine and the Hyesan Copper Mine.[30] China's growth-driven demand for mineral resources has doubled over the past decade and now makes up over 20 percent of world consumption. In 2009, China consumed almost 50 percent of the world's steel output. It needs access to coal, iron, copper, gold, zinc, and nickel, among other mineral resources to ensure continued growth. North Korea is a natural nearby source for China.

As I noted earlier, the U.S. Geological Survey estimates that North Korea's reserves of coal, iron ore, limestone, and magnesite are substantial by world standards, given the small size of the country, and if mined, would have an impact on global markets.[31] A Goldman Sachs study by Goohoon Kwon estimated the value of the North's mineral deposits to be worth 140 times the country's GDP.[32]

This is a match made in heaven, from China's perspective. Prior to 2004, the Chinese had no mining investment in the North. Today, an overwhelming 41 percent of Chinese joint ventures in North Korea are in extractive industries.[33] While the majority of Chinese joint ventures in the North are run by small- and medium-size enterprises, the sole two of China's top one hundred industries that are in the DPRK are in extractive industries of iron and steel: Wuhan Iron and Steel and Tangshan Iron and Steel. While North Korean mineral exports to China were a mere $15 million in 2003, they were in excess of $213 million in 2008.[34] The top export items from the DPRK to China in 2010 were iron ore, coal, and copper. North Korea is also known to be a potential source of rare earth minerals. Molybdenum, for example, has been found in large quantities in the DPRK. Akin to a rare earth, molybdenum is used as a critical ingredient in steel that allows pipelines and water wells to retain high strength against extreme temperatures and against corrosion.[35] The Chinese could mine this resource in their own country, but they can do it cheaper, setting their own price, and without cumbersome health regulations, in North Korea. Eight of China's fifty-six joint ventures in the DPRK are in molybdenum. It is believed that China has additional informal and, in some cases, illegal operations in rare earths in the North.[36] The DPRK accepts all of these contracts, even though they know Chinese intentions are predatory, seeking to suck all the resources off the peninsula. But it gains badly needed hard currency and also the benefits of some of these minerals, since the North Koreans cannot extract them on their own.

The recent resource push into North Korea tracks with a larger trend of increasing joint ventures. Starting with one fertilizer factory in 1997, Beijing started joint ventures that exploit North Korean labor and environment free from regulation. While 2003 saw just 4 new projects form, this jumped to 20 in 2005, 40 in 2006, 24 in 2007, and 14 in 2009, totaling just under 140 today.[37] These partners on the Chinese side tend to be smaller companies, not the big state-owned enterprises (except for Wuhan and Tangshan Iron and Steel). This neomercantile strategy by China plays a big role in explaining its decision to support the ongoing leadership transition in North Korea. Beijing is thought to have hosted the young son, Kim Jong-un, on at least two occasions: once on a "secret visit" in June 2009, and a second time when he visited as part of his father's delegation to Beijing in August the following year.[38] While others see the death of Kim Jong-il as a wholly unstable transition, the Chinese have chosen to support it by essentially owning a piece of North Korea, which provides resources to the regime and ensures that the new leadership will remain compliant with China's policies.

In keeping with the overall mutual hostage nature of this relationship, this is not an allegiance built on brotherly Communist love. Private Chinese companies constantly complain about the uncertainties of doing business in North Korea, the lack of business practices, and the absence of a juridical base. Anti-Chinese sentiment among North Koreans, in turn, has become more pronounced, according to some scholars.[39] China demands economic reforms in North Korea, not because it is concerned about the North's future, but because such reforms would benefit Chinese businesses operating there. North Koreans increasingly chafe at the growing dependence on the haughty Chinese, who treat them like dirt and dictate the terms of the relationship. This is hardly Communist brotherly love, but it is cooperation. It is an illusion to believe that China will work with the United States and the ROK on denuclearizing North Korea as its top priority. China has a host of other priorities that rank higher than that of the United States and ROK, and it will follow its own path in achieving them vis-à-vis the North.

"IT'S DOMESTIC POLICY, STUPID"

One of these priorities is not, as is commonly believed, China's obsession with avoiding a flood of millions of North Korean refugees across its borders if the North were to collapse. Sure, Beijing does not want to see the North collapse. But the main benefit of stability is not stemming refugee flows. The main benefit is development of China's northeast provinces, Jilin and Liaoning, which maintain a fourteen-hundred-kilometer (870-mi) border with the DPRK. Traditionally, Jilin and Liaoning were, during the planned-economy period in China, fairly well-off provinces, because they hosted much of the state-owned heavy industries. But with Deng-era reforms and restructuring of the economy, these provinces saw massive layoffs and shuttering of companies deemed uncompetitive. Beijing's leaders thusly saw its northeastern provinces grow increasingly poorer while the coastal provinces grew richer. To rectify this imbalance, Beijing has pushed forward with a "revitalize the Northeast" campaign to enhance economic development, raise employment levels, and raise income levels. North Korea is a big part of this domestic campaign. In addition to the business in extractive industries, which helps the two provinces, Liaoning Province has benefited greatly as the primary entry and departure point of DPRK-China trade. (75 to 80 percent of all trade passes through Dandong.) Jilin is a landlocked province, and there are opportunities to be had in accessing the Rajin port in the DPRK to increase trade and exports. Rajin is the northernmost ice-free port in the area, and Chinese ambitions are to raise Jilin's share of GDP from trade (now at a meager 10 percent) to approximate those of other provinces (average of 70 percent). Business between Jilin and North Korea is further facilitated by the fact that Jilin hosts the largest number of overseas ethnic Koreans in the world (about 2 million), many of whom reside in Yangbian Prefecture. China's long-term plan has always been to link the cities of Changchun, Jilin, and Tumen with the Rajin port only fifty kilometers (31 mi) away.[40] With Jilin and Liaoning Provinces accounting for a combined 62 percent of all Chinese joint ventures with North Korea, Beijing's policy toward the North is motivated more by domestic development priorities than it is by twisting North Korea's arm to denuclearize. That, unfortunately, is the sad truth.

These domestic economic priorities also drive China's aid policy to North Korea. The primary purpose of such aid is not to cement "brotherly love," nor is it to stop refugees from crossing the border. Instead, the aid serves to sustain a minimal level of stability and subsistence so that China can continue its economic extraction policies. Beijing does not make public any data on its bilateral food (non-WFP) aid or fuel assistance to the North, unlike the rest of the world. Some of this aid is in the form of outright grants, and some of it is disguised as "trade" but at greatly subsidized "friendship" prices, which essentially constitutes aid. Economists often point to the high bilateral trade deficits as evidence of subsidies from China. China's aid, and North Korea's reliance on it, has increased dramatically since 2002. The end of the Sunshine Policy in South Korea that came with the election of Lee Myung-bak terminated one major channel of assistance to the DPRK, leaving China as the sole handout-provider. Unlike South Korea, moreover, where aid decisions are made at the highest levels of government, Chinese aid flows through established party, military, and other channels. It is thus more institutionalized and more decentralized, and therefore relatively unaffected by political winds. Chinese aid is also completely unmonitored, so much of it is believed to go to the elite rather than to those in need. According to the WFP, for example, China is believed to be one of the largest providers of corn and rice to the DPRK since 1995, even though this aid went bilaterally to the North and not through the U.N. world food appeals for North Korea. WFP monitoring and interviews of households during their food distribution never found one case of Chinese food donations reaching villages, which leads one to believe it goes entirely to noncivilian populations in the North.

North Korea–China Trade, 1995–2008

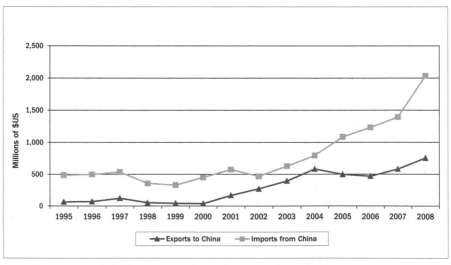

Sources: Global Trade Atlas, Using Chinese Data (data); Manyin in Kyung-Ae Park, ed., p. 81 (graph).

Chinese Energy Shipments to North Korea, 1995-2008

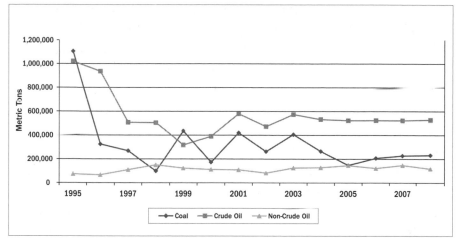

Sources: Global Trade Atlas, Using Chinese Data (data); Manyin in Kyung-Ae Park, ed., p. 81 (graph).

China's Export of Cereals to North Korea

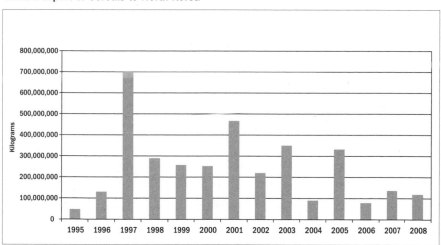

Sources: Global Trade Atlas, Using Chinese Data (data); Manyin in Kyung-Ae Park, ed., p. 83 (graph).

Chinese aid not only comes in the form of food and fuel. China has helped build infrastructure and factories in the North, usually around the port areas of Dandong and Rajin, that benefit Chinese businesses. Accurate numbers of just how much the Chinese provide are hard to come by, but Mark Manyin of the Congressional Research Service believes that since 2000, Beijing has provided almost 800,000 metric tons of crude and non-crude oil annually, and 200,000 metric tons of coal.[41] Stephan Haggard and Marcus Noland estimate, based on China's subsidized trade deficit with North Korea, that since the mid-1980s Beijing has provided in excess of $7 billion in handouts to the North. China still provides 80 percent of North Korea's imported consumer goods and at least 45 percent of its food.[42] And so, yes, Beijing certainly wants to prevent a deluge of refugees flooding across its border. And yes, the Chinese are more comfortable with a friendly yet weak and sometimes embarrassing North Korea on their southern flank than they would be with a rich, powerful, democratic, U.S.-aligned, unified Korea. And these factors undoubtedly play a role in Chinese aid policy to the North. But in the end, as former U.S. Speaker of the House Tip O'Neill would remind us, "all politics is local," and Beijing's priorities in its assistance to its belligerent little brother, North Korea, will likely continue to reflect this reality.

FOREVER STABLE

Finally, China's preference for sustaining a minimal level of stability in North Korea today is not only economically motivated, it is also deeply rooted in history and in China's perceptions of its Korean border that is completely at odds with views in the United States. We view the North Korean situation as fluid—a dead dictator, a failing economy, an inexperienced successor. All of these factors lend to an assessment of instability that must be prepared for. But in China's mind, North Korea is not a factor for instability, it is not a fluid situation; instead, North Korea is part of a stable status quo on China's northeast border that has been in existence since the tenth century. In China's mind, the Yalu and Tumen Rivers have, for centuries, been not only the established border but a zone of peace and stability. In 1962, China signed a treaty that delineated the border with Korea. As David Kang has argued, China ceded 60 percent of disputed territory with North Korea in this 1962 treaty, for the explicit purpose of cementing a permanent zone of peace on this northeast border.[43] China, a country with centuries of border disputes with others surrounding it, values this border as permanent and unchanging.

Thus China neither sees fluidity on its North Korean border, nor desires it. On the contrary, it equates stability and the absence of change with China's long-term interests. We, as Americans, underestimate the importance of this historical fact in China's mind. We think it should not be difficult for the Chinese to abandon North Korea, a wretched and lost cause that only creates problems for China. But our utilitarian calculations are different from those of China. For Beijing, every time the northern portion of Korea has undergone flux, the outcome for China has been bad. In the nineteenth century, instability in the form of Japanese advances into northern Korea led to China's defeat to Japan in the First Sino-Japanese War (1894–95). In World War II, the invasion of Manchuria by Japan came through a destabilized northern Korea. And in the Korean War, the U.S. advancement into North Korea after repelling the June 1950 invasion cost China almost 800,000 deaths. Where we see instability and potential opportunity in North Korea, the Chinese see historic dangers that can only be averted by continuing the status quo.

Critics might argue that China surely sees the gravity of North Korean misbehavior, and even if it wants long-term stability, it must see some advantage to using its enormous economic leverage to occasionally slap the North back into compliance. As commonsensical as this may sound, it has been empirically unproven. There were occasional reports of Chinese punishment in the spring of 2003 (when they supposedly cut off oil for a few days), and then after the 2006 nuclear test, but these were exceptions that proved the rule. Moreover, despite revisionist accounts of the first nuclear crisis in 1994, when, some argue, China played hardball with the DPRK, a careful reading of the data shows otherwise. In March 1993, when North Korea announced it was withdrawing from the NPT (the first country ever to do so), the IAEA Board of Governors passed a resolution condemning Pyongyang's noncompliance and calling for referral of the issue to the U.N. Security Council. China was one of only two countries that voted against the resolution (28–2, the other was Libya). Two months later, when North Korea announced to the IAEA that it was defueling the reactor at Yongbyon, giving it fuel rods from which to extract weapons-grade plutonium, the U.N. Security Council sought to stop the North. China abstained from the resolution. At the height of the crisis in June 1994, China again abstained from IAEA resolutions to cut off all assistance to the DPRK, and continued to tell

U.N. Security Council members that it opposed sanctions. In each case, Beijing's stance was unique and in juxtaposition to the general outrage expressed by the international community at DPRK truculence. This stance, however, is not at all surprising if one appreciates China's unique position and its desire to maintain a minimal level of stability. It is a low-cost, low-risk strategy that has little regard for who is right or wrong, instead prioritizing what is necessary from Beijing's viewpoint to keep the situation at hand from going off the rails.

The problem today is that China is both omnipotent and impotent in North Korea. It has great material influence as the North's only patron. Yet, as the sole patron, if Beijing shut down its assistance to punish Pyongyang for its bad behavior even temporarily, it could precipitate an unraveling of the regime, which would be even more threatening to China. Beijing has no metric by which to gauge how much pressure is enough to punish versus too much pressure that could lead to collapse. In the end, this dilemma typifies the mutual-hostage relationship: Beijing needs to keep the regime afloat, even though it hates the rigid ideology and costs to China's international reputation of being seen as a patron. Yet it cannot use its leverage, for fear of collapsing the regime like a house of cards. North Korea knows this, and therefore uses its vulnerability and unpredictability to get what it wants from China. It hates China's predator economic policies, but has little choice in the matter because it needs the hard currency.

The death of Kim Jong-il has not appeared to change China's course. On the contrary, in the aftermath of the Dear Leader's massive heart attack in 2011, Beijing behaved as if it had effectively adopted North Korea as a third northeastern province. Rather than see Kim's passing as an opportunity to abandon a sinking ship or at least adjust its course, Beijing tried its best to keep it afloat. After the December 19, 2011, shocking announcement, Beijing reportedly called the senior envoys for South Korea, Japan, Russia, and other countries into the foreign ministry for an emergency meeting. In this meeting, senior Chinese officials called for all parties to show respect for the dearly departed Kim Jong-il and the leadership succession to his young son, to exercise restraint and not seek to exploit the situation, and to do nothing to undermine the autonomy of the DPRK. China was the first country to express condolences for the death of the DPRK leader, the first to recognize Kim Jong-un by name as the rightful successor, and the first to extend an invitation to the new leader to visit its capital. Senior South Korean officials were deeply offended by China's behavior, one of whom confided to me, "This isn't their [China's] fucking peninsula . . . it's ours." While some observers hope that Kim Jong-il's death will unleash democratic regime change, China will work strongly against that possibility, especially if such efforts receive support from South Korea or the United States. Given that Beijing has the only eyes inside the North, Washington and Seoul could do little in response.

If there was ever a day when the world could look to China to help moderate North Korean behavior and solve problems, those days are long gone. Does China not worry about how a nuclear North Korea could create a "nuclear domino effect" in Asia, where other countries like Japan, in particular, might seek its own nuclear deterrent? Any concern about such a scenario coming to fruition for the Chinese is mitigated by two factors. First, the concern would be much greater in Beijing if the domestic politics of Japan were dominated by conservatives, which was not the case when the second nuclear test and ballistic missile tests occurred. Conservatives like Abe Shinzo (2006–2007) or Aso Taro (2008–2009) in earlier years capitalized on the DPRK threat in order to push forward a more proactive Japanese defense posture that did worry Beijing. But as long as the LDP and conservatives like Abe and Aso are out of power, China is less concerned about this scenario. Second, and ironically, China has confidence that the U.S. nuclear umbrella will be enough to keep the so-called cork in the bottle of renewed Japanese militarism. Instead, China, for its own unique and parochial reasons, has chosen to support the DPRK regime to the bitter end and countenance its bad behavior and growing nuclear capabilities. For the party and military leadership, North Korea is more an issue of domestic development of the Northeast provinces than it is a source of far-flung concerns about denuclearization and the sanctity of the NPT regime. And even for a Communist system, all politics is local.

RUSSIA: THE FORGOTTEN PLAYER

The Six-Party Talks have a certain aura of importance around them. Journalists from six nations, including major papers like the *Washington Post,* the *Wall Street Journal*, and *Financial Times*, descend on Beijing and stake out the hotels where the delegations stay, trying to pick up a quote or two as the officials set out for, or return from, the day's negotiations. Particularly ambitious reporters (usually Japanese) follow officials around like Hollywood paparazzi, catching them at the Starbucks or in the St. Regis hotel gym for a morning workout. (One actually followed me into the swimming pool.) At the Diaoyutai State Guesthouse, motorcades from each country enter the gates where a bank of television cameras await, filming B-roll. Security stands at attention at the main entrance, waiting for the delegations to arrive. We are ushered into the main plenary hall, where the five lead members of each country's delegation sit at a hexagonal, green-felted table with their support staff seated in rows behind them. Interpreters check to make sure their equipment is working. Once everyone is seated, the Chinese head delegate motions to open the doors and a rush of cameras roll in to set up for shots of the opening statements. It is controlled chaos as cameras are clicking everywhere and flashbulbs blind you in every direction. Sitting amid this scene, one is reminded that this forum is truly the first multilateral security negotiation in Northeast Asia since the end of World War II. It is the biggest news story in Asia.

EXCEPT FOR THE RUSSIANS

While throngs of cameras would crowd the other delegations, especially those from North Korea and the United States, the Russians would sit patiently at their end of the table, looking on with boredom as one camera might peel off from the pack to snap a quick photo of their delegation. After the plenary session finishes with the opening statements, delegations would leave the cameras and move into separate conference rooms for a series of bilateral meetings between the countries. The most important of these tended to be between the United States and DPRK, and the United States and China, which in themselves would produce multiple bilateral meetings as the United States would debrief Japan, ROK, and others on the contents of the meetings. The pace at times is furious, moving from one conference room to another. During the lunch hour, teams would huddle together, munching on the buffet food as they tried to figure out the next diplomatic moves. Occasionally, the United States and an ally would leave the Diaoyutai for an off-site lunch, trailed by a rush of paparazzi. Except for the poor Russians. Sitting in their delegation holding room, awaiting a call from the other nations for bilaterals, they would often be the last party to be informed of what was going on, and, to their credit, tended to be pretty mellow about it. At lunch, the delegation sat at its own table, liberally enjoying the buffet. I recall one member of the delegation planting himself in front of the big-screen television in the lounge area on the first floor, watching Chinese programming all day.

Russia is the forgotten player on the Korean Peninsula. When U.S. negotiators go to the region for consultations with Six-Party partners, Russia often gets left out. Obama's chief envoy, Ambassador Stephen Bosworth, had nine trips to the region and skipped Russia on all but one occasion.[44] At best, we would often ask Russian representatives to meet us in Beijing to avoid the extra stop. In the August 2005 round of Six-Party Talks, when the United States and DPRK were engaged in bilateral talks, some members of the U.S. delegation from the State Department felt little need to follow the common diplomatic practice of debriefing Japan, a key ally, on the proceedings. This upset the Japanese lead negotiator terribly, and when my NSC colleague Will Tobey and I went to their delegation room to mend fences, one member of their team blurted out, "Don't you treat us like the Russians! If you treat us like Russians, we will behave like Russians. We are not to be excluded like Russia!"

While Russia may appear of peripheral importance, no deal can be done without it. Any negotiation with North Korea requires Russian consent, because of Russia's critical role in any future multilateral energy deals for the DPRK. It is also a key player, given its vote as a permanent member of the U.N. Security Council, where DPRK actions often end up. Yet Russia is constantly underestimated and neglected when it comes to dealing with North Korea. Unlike China, Russia shares a small border of nineteen kilometers (12 mi) with the North and, therefore, does not associate Pyongyang's fate with its own border security or economic development of local provinces. Yet things that happen in North Korea impact Russia dramatically, and Moscow has no desire to see instability brewing on the peninsula. In this regard, Moscow seeks to play a role in addressing the problems of North Korea, but it faces twin dilemmas. First, relative to the other players, Russia has the least influence over the situation, yet it knows that, given its geographic proximity, misbehavior by the North Koreans can disproportionately affect it. When North Korean ballistic missile tests create greater impetus for cooperation between Japan and the United States on ballistic missile defense, this impacts Russia in ways over which it has no control. Second, Russian influence is greatest when things with North Korea are at their absolute worst. In other words, when parties are deadlocked and dialogue is nonexistent, that is when Russia plays an occasionally useful role in trying to jump-start negotiations and pull everyone out of the abyss. The dilemma for Russia is that if it is successful in getting the parties to reengage in dialogue, these parties quickly seek to reengage in direct negotiations with one another. The result is that Russia is marginalized once again. Thus, for example, Moscow supports economic reform in the North as a solution to the nuclear crisis, but it knows that if this support actually led to reform, it would be quickly marginalized as Pyongyang would look to Seoul and Beijing as its main partners. Moscow's role is best explained as a bit player; occasionally helpful, always critical, but never appreciated.

This was not always the case, of course. Historically, imperial Russia saw itself as a critical player on the peninsula, and coveted Korea as a window to the Pacific Ocean. In 1884, tsarist Russia established diplomatic relations with Korea and the following year opened a diplomatic mission in Seoul. Moscow's primary interest on the peninsula was for access to a year-round, ice-free Pacific port, something they didn't have with the port of Vladivostok just seventy miles (115 km) northeast of the Korean border.[45] At the end of the nineteenth century, Russia even went to war over Korea when, in 1896, the Russian legation in Seoul provided refuge to the fleeing King Kojong, who sought to escape Japan's domination on the peninsula. Japan responded by attacking Port Arthur at the tip of the Liaotung Peninsula, leading to the Russo-Japanese war in 1904. Japan's victory in this war—the first by an Asian country over a Western power, pushed Russia off the peninsula.

Aside from sporadic Soviet support of Korean anti-Japanese guerrillas in Manchuria during World War II (largely to draw Japanese forces away from Siberia), the Russians were marginalized on the peninsula for the next half-century until Japan's defeat in 1945. The Soviets moved quickly to occupy the northern half of the peninsula and had designs on all of it if it were not for the U.S. and U.N. decision to divide the peninsula into occupation zones. As the Cold War made these temporary zones permanent, the Soviets put their man, Kim Il-sung, in charge, formally recognized the North in October 1948, and signed its first economic agreement supporting the North in March 1949. It kept 120,000 troops in northern Korea until seven months before Kim's invasion of the South in June 1950, and then participated in the war by proxy, helping plan the invasion, aiding the Chinese, and providing some air support, but never contributing ground forces.[46] In July 1961, the Soviets inked a Treaty of Friendship, Cooperation, and Mutual Assistance, which had as its key clause: "Should either of the Contracting Parties suffer armed attack by any State or coalition of States and thus find itself in a state of war, the other Contracting Party shall immediately extend military and other assistance with all the means at its disposal." Like China, the Soviet Union extended through this treaty a security guarantee to the North and provided decades of material assistance and subsidized trade that enabled Kim Il-sung to thrive during the Cold War.

NORTH KOREA–SOVIET UNION ECONOMIC RELATIONS, SELECTED YEARS (MILLIONS OF US$)		
YEAR(S)	TRADE VOLUME	USSR TO DPRK AID
1950–1954	--	
713.25		
1955	84.9	
1956	105.0	713.25
1957	122.5	
1958	105.1	
1959	125.7	
1960	114.1	
1961	156.1	
1962	168.9	
1963	170.2	196.68
1964	163.6	
1965	178.1	
1967	218.3	

NORTH KOREA–SOVIET UNION ECONOMIC RELATIONS, SELECTED YEARS (MILLIONS OF US$)		
YEAR(S)	TRADE VOLUME	USSR TO DPRK AID
1968	293.1	196.68
1969	328.2	
1970	373.2	87.0
1971	502.4	250.0
1972	458.3	150.0
1973	485.2	109.0
1974	453.2	120.0
1975	496.1	186.0
1976	375.8	4.0
1977	446.0	--
1978	552.5	35.0
1979	749.8	75.0
1980	880.4	250.0
1981	601.7	145.0
1982	774.3	130.0
1983	667.8	40.0
1984	915.8	55.0
1985	1,349.2	93.0
1986	1,828.5	6.0
1987	2,074.1	-33.0
1988	2,634.3	-41.0
1989	2,531.8	-16.0
1990	2,715.3	0

Trade in 1955–1969 in J.S. Chung, (1974), p. 112; Trade 1970–1975 in C.O. Chung (1978), p. 157; Trade 1976–1983 in Pong S. Lee in Kwack, ed. (1994); Trade in 1984, 1986 in Joseph S. Chung, "The Economy," in Andrea Matles Savada, ed., North Korea: A Country Study *(Washington, D.C.: Library of Congress, 1993), Appendix; Trade 1987, 1989 in* Country Profile: North Korea, South Korea, 1994/94 *(London, UK: Economist Intelligence Unit, 1993), p. 74; Trade 1985, 1988, 1990 and aid data 1950–1976 from E.G. Hwang (1993), pp. 200–201, 204; aid 1978–1979 in* Handbook of Economic Statistics, 1984 *(Langley, Va.: Central Intelligence Agency), p. 117; aid 1980–1990 in Marcus Noland, "The North Korean Economy,"* Peterson Institute for International Economics Working Paper, *95-5 (1995), p. 73.*

Kim deftly used the rivalry between North Korea's two Communist patrons to maximize aid from each. Moscow was aware of this, but continued to shower the North with aid in the form of commodities, weapons systems, and natural resources to try to keep the North Koreans as far as possible from the Chinese and to maintain pressure on the Americans, as crises were erupting in the Middle East, Southeast Asia, and Latin America.[47] Once the Sino-Soviet split ended in 1989, however, the strategic value of Pyongyang to Moscow, much like to Beijing, declined while the potential for economic cooperation with the more prosperous South grew exponentially.

PERESTROIKA AND THE ABANDONMENT OF NORTH KOREA

The big shift in Soviet-DPRK relations took place in 1988–90, when Moscow and Seoul moved to end decades of non-dialogue and normalize diplomatic relations. The Soviets chose to view relations with North Korea in a wider context than through their two traditional lenses, the Cold War and the Sino-Soviet split. Soviet leader Mikhail Gorbachev saw a fundamental problem with the fact that his country was not benefiting from the economic vitality in Northeast Asia, and was instead only seen as a security threat. Through his perestroika in foreign policy, the Soviet leader sought reengagement with the region as a way to reduce wasteful military spending as well as to develop the Russian Far East.[48] He made this clear through three steps: first, in a speech in Vladivostok in July 1986, Gorbachev called for a new, more active, and engaging role for the USSR in East Asia, and offered a comprehensive set of proposals for reducing tensions in the region, ranging from nuclear no-first-use assurances to a ban on space militarization to expanded trade ties.[49] He offered partial solutions to two of Beijing's "three obstacles" to normalization—the Soviet occupation of Afghanistan, the 500,000 Red Army troops on the Sino-Soviet border, and Soviet support for Vietnam's occupation of Cambodia—announcing the withdrawal of 6,000 Soviet troops from Afghanistan, and possibly a "substantial part of Soviet troops in Mongolia."[50] The Chinese initially reacted coolly to Moscow's overtures, but in the end, this turned out to be the beginning of the end of the Sino-Soviet split that had existed for most of the previous forty years.[51] In September 1988, Gorbachev followed with a speech at Krasnoyarsk, where he explicitly called for an improvement in Soviet–South Korean relations, irrespective of the two countries' ideologies. In addition to these declarations, the Soviet Union demonstrated more leniency in handling South Korean fishing boats that were caught in Soviet territorial waters. Moscow also liberalized policies regarding repatriation of ethnic Koreans living on Sakhalin Island. In the past, very strict rules applied to allowing this minority population, sent to Sakhalin during Stalin's era, to visit Korea, but from the late 1980s, visa policies were noticeably relaxed. Following the Krasnoyarsk speech, Moscow increased academic and cultural exchanges with Seoul. Third, Gorbachev sought to reduce tension in Sino-Soviet relations by offering a further unilateral drawdown of troops on the border, which had been put there since the armed clashes in 1969. The dramatic announcement was made by Foreign Minister Eduard Shevardnadze in February 1989, during a visit to Beijing, and the 250,000 man draw-down was the final obstacle to be overcome before Gorbachev's historic summit with Deng just three months later.[52]

This new Soviet diplomacy coincided with the onset of Northern Diplomacy, or *Nordpolitik,* in South Korea. Modeled on West Germany's *Ostpolitik,* the Korean version, formed under the Roh Tae Woo government in 1988, stated that the ROK would seek normal relations with Communist nations on the basis of pragmatism and economic benefits, not of ideology. Seoul would do this while maintaining three core policy principles. First, the new foreign policy outreach would be grounded in a stable domestic-political situation at home; second, the outreach would be grounded in strong relations with traditional allies (i.e., the United States); and third, it would be grounded in a strong economy. *Nordpolitik* was a clear expression of South Korean confidence at the time.[53] Politically, the country had just gone through a peaceful transition to democracy in 1987. The economy was running at an extraordinary 12 percent annual growth rate, giving rise to an insurmountable economic gap with the rival North Korean regime. One of the unwritten goals of *Nordpolitik* was also to enable South Korea's admission to the United Nations. The Communist bloc opposed dual entry of the two Koreas to the United Nations, as this would symbolize a solidifying of the division on the peninsula. The two Koreas had observer status but were not permanent members. For South Korea, a country emerging by the late 1980s as an economic powerhouse and an international player, this was the ultimate humiliation.

The policy was enormously successful. South Korea normalized relations with a number of Eastern bloc countries, starting with Hungary (January 29, 1989), Poland (November 1, 1989), Czechoslovakia (March 1, 1990), Bulgaria (March 23, 1990), and Romania (March 30, 1990). They then moved on to the rest, with Estonia (September 6, 1991), Belarus and the Ukraine (February 10, 1992), and, finally, Croatia (November 18, 1992). Moreover, as *Nordpolitik* led to the normalization of relations with Eastern bloc nations, each dropped its opposition to U.N. entry for Seoul, with the result in September 1991 that South Korea gained long-sought admittance to the international body. With great pride, ROK president Roh Tae-woo became the first Korean president to address the General Assembly in October of 1991. *Nordpolitik* also succeeded in obtaining Soviet participation in the 1988 Seoul Olympics. Being a frontline Cold War state, South Korea was especially concerned that its moment in the sun as only the second Asian host of the Summer Games would be marred by superpower tensions. The South Koreans thus lobbied Moscow very hard to participate in their games, making it the first Olympics in eight years with the full participation of the world. The Olympics created tremendous goodwill between the two countries, and were followed by a series of economic contacts and semi-official political meetings between the two sides from 1988 to 1990. These contacts led to the establishment of trade offices by the South Korean government-backed KOTRA (Korea Trade Promotion Association) and the Soviet chamber of commerce in the summer of 1989. Consular functions were added to these trade offices in February 1990. These burgeoning contacts were finally consummated at the highest political level in June 1990 in San Francisco. Presidents Roh and Gorbachev held the first ROK-USSR summit in postwar history in a hotel room and agreed in principle to establish formal diplomatic relations. Relations were established in September 1990, followed by two additional summits—in Moscow (December 1990) and Cheju Island (April 1991)—in which the two leaders reaffirmed their new relationship: the Soviets provided a formal apology for the first time for the KAL 007 shootdown in 1983, and the two countries inked a major economic agreement, including a $3 billion loan.

Eduard Shevardnadze was assigned the task of giving the North Koreans the bad news. The Soviet foreign minister traveled to Pyongyang in September 1990 to explain to the longtime ally that Moscow was going to normalize relations with South Korea. Before leaving, he told reporters he was "counting on a frank discussion" with his counterparts in Pyongyang, but he likely had little idea of just how frank it would be.[54] The North Koreans knew the purpose of Shevardnadze's trip, and had no inclination to take the news well. Normally handled with great respect, the Soviet foreign minister was given the lowly treatment of a director-general. He waited patiently for his call on DPRK leader Kim Il-sung, and was finally told that Kim would not see him. Instead, he was met by the Son, Kim Jong-il, who reportedly spoke to him in a dismissive and insulting manner. Shevardnadze eventually met Foreign Minister Kim Yŏng-nam to deliver the news. Kim Yŏng-nam expressed anger at Soviet abandonment and called for Moscow to reinstate patron aid. When Shevardnadze told them that this was impossible, the North responded that without Soviet assistance it could no longer trust nor rely on Moscow in lieu of other international partners. Kim Yŏng-nam stated further, "henceforth we will have to take steps to supply ourselves with the few weapons that till now we have relied on the alliance for."[55] Like a good and cool-headed diplomat, Shevardnadze asked for time to consider his counterpart's comments, promising a response by the following morning. But in private, his blood boiled. The next morning he reiterated his country's position from the previous day, and was met by the same belligerence from Foreign Minister Kim. By now fed up with the situation, Shevardnadze told his interlocutors that North Korea must do as it sees fit, but he warned that the threat to develop nuclear weapons was not a good idea. He and his delegation ended up making a brusque exit, departing several hours earlier than was planned. Upon his return to Moscow, he was so disgusted that he reportedly saw no reason to soft-pedal the timeline for normalization in deference to Pyongyang and authorized the process to move forward as quickly as possible. Shevardnadze would later call his discussion with Foreign Minister Kim "the most unpleasant, most difficult talk of my life."[56]

Unlike the Chinese, who would fret endlessly over the decision to normalize relations with Seoul in 1992 and would try to assuage Pyongyang's fears of abandonment, the Soviet Union dropped the DPRK like a bad habit. Normalization with the South brought the Soviets $3 billion in loans, which Moscow was not about to spend on continuing to support the North. They had no qualms shedding the economic burden of sustaining the DPRK, and reaping benefits in the richer ROK. Moscow informed Pyongyang that it was immediately stopping patron aid to the North and indicated that it was terminating military cooperation. The impact of Moscow's abandonment was both immediate and devastating. Russia accounted for 53.1 percent of total DPRK trade in 1990; by 1993, this dropped to an astounding 8 percent, as the DPRK was now forced to pay market prices for Soviet goods, which it could not afford.[57] Total trade with the Soviet Union went from approximately $3.25 billion in 1990 to less than $100 million by 1994.[58] Soviet-bound exports to the DPRK in machinery, transportation, and manufacturing equipment dropped by more than tenfold by 1992.[59] Moreover, with the end of Soviet-subsidized pricing of energy that afforded the DPRK a 75 percent discount of market prices, DPRK oil imports dropped over 50 percent in one year, and petroleum imports dropped almost tenfold.[60] Without USSR necessarily being able to say it outright, it made obvious that Gorbachev's forward-leaning "new thinking" in foreign policy simply fit much better with the globally integrated, fast-growing, and economically modern South Korea than the belligerent, backward North. Just hours before his first meeting with President Roh in San Francisco, Gorbachev told Stanford students and faculty that "new winds are now blowing in Asia" and that he fully intended to adjust the Soviet sails accordingly.[61] In the aftermath of that meeting—one Roh would call "epochal"—Gorbachev told reporters he met Roh because of their two nations' burgeoning economic ties and, referring to Northeast Asia, added that "we must improve relations with everyone who lives there. We can't do it selectively."[62] And after the 1991 meeting between these two leaders on Cheju Island, Gorbachev sang the praises of the ROK, stating with great pride: "We have established good and durable relations with a country that has not just taken up a respected and promising position in the world economy, but is playing a more and more noticeably active and constructive role in world politics."[63] The juxtaposition with the North could not have been starker.

After the collapse of the Soviet Union, Russia-DPRK relations only grew more distant. Russian president Boris Yeltsin went further than Gorbachev, and demonstrated almost total indifference toward relations with Pyongyang while privileging those with Seoul. Yeltsin had an emotional reaction to the Kim regime, not unlike that of George W. Bush a decade later. Yeltsin was simply repulsed by the DPRK, and saw its leadership as weak, backward, and dictatorial.[64] For Yeltsin and pro-West factions in his government, led by Foreign Minister Andrei Kozyrev, the DPRK relationship was an anachronism of the Cold War, the Stalinist era. For them, the choice between the DPRK and ROK represented the choice between the old and new Russia, and therefore was not a hard one to make. There were some who still advocated for a more balanced relationship between the two Koreas, represented by Deputy Foreign Minister Georgy Kunadze and Deputy Director for Asian Affairs Georgy Toloraya. They and Kozyrev's eventual successor, Yevgeny Primakov, saw balanced relations on the peninsula as a means to reduce opportunities for American unilateralism. However, Yeltsin's desire to rewrite the terms of relations with Pyongyang was readily apparent in the renegotiation of the 1961 Treaty of Friendship, Cooperation, and Mutual Assistance. The key document of the Cold War alliance, the treaty committed Russia to automatically intervene in case of an attack on the DPRK. The treaty was good for thirty years and was, therefore, due to expire in 1991, but the collapse of the Soviet Union prompted Yeltsin to say the treaty was no longer valid. He wanted to do away with the automatic intervention, and told the DPRK as much in January 1992. Later that year, during a trip to Seoul, the Russian leader assured ROK president Roh Tae-woo that the 1961 treaty was no longer valid and existed in "name only." Pyongyang was deeply offended at this abandonment and refused to renegotiate the terms of the treaty. But Moscow did not care and eventually replaced Article One with a clause that called for mutual consultation only (not automatic intervention) in case of unprovoked attack.

The Yeltsin years represented the nadir in bilateral relations. Trade dropped to a paltry $50 million annually, and Moscow continued to require that all purchases be made on a cash basis only, not on credit or with barter. At the same time, economic relations with the ROK took off. While in 1992 the total trade volume between these two countries amounted to just $193 million, by 1996 it had increased nearly twenty-fold, to just shy of $3.8 billion. For the rest of the 1990s, trade between the two countries would remain well over $2 billion annually right up until the Putin era, when it absolutely exploded, averaging over $4.4 billion annually and peaking at $18 billion in 2008.[65] Politically, too, Yeltsin moved to warm relations with the South, clearly exemplified by his returning of the black box of downed Korean Air Lines Flight 007. In 1983, a Korean Air Lines flight bound for Seoul from New York was shot down after straying into Soviet airspace, killing all 269 passengers and crew on board. In a speech following the event, President Reagan called the action a "crime against humanity," and an Indian newspaper threatened it could be "the end of civil aviation as we know it."[66] In September of 1992, Yeltsin acknowledged for the first time the existence of black boxes from the flight, something that had theretofore been denied by Soviet and Russian Federation authorities. And just two months later, during a visit to Seoul, Yeltsin dramatically handed ROK president Roh Tae-woo the battered black boxes.[67] To add insult to injury, Pyongyang watched Moscow emasculate the terms of its military alliance while at the same time growing its military relations with the ROK—the ultimate abandonment. While the Soviets would not sell military arms to Pyongyang, they sold fighter aircraft, T-80 tanks, armored fighting vehicles, and antiaircraft missiles to Seoul as a way for Moscow to service its $3 billion loan from the 1990 normalization agreement (which the United States, as the traditional military supplier to its ally, did not appreciate). In November 1997, the two countries signed an agreement to increase bilateral defense cooperation.

These defense ties continued through the Putin era, starting in 2002, when the two governments signed an accord on prevention of dangerous military activity. The following year, Sergei Ivanov became the first Russian defense minister to visit Seoul and pay a courtesy call on ROK president Roh Moo-hyun. The ROK navy and air force engaged in combined maritime search-and-rescue operations with the Russian Pacific Fleet in 2003. In 2005, ROK defense minister Yun Kwang-ung visited Moscow and signed a joint agreement on arms transfers, joint technological development, and the establishment of an aviation hotline. The following year, the commander of the Russian air force reciprocated, visiting Seoul and meeting his counterparts there. Between 2003 and 2006, South Korea received six different weapons systems from the Russians, including helicopters and hovercraft, totaling over $500 million.[68] In 2007, the South sent its chief of staff of the navy to Russia for a visit, and in 2008, its air force chief. In 2009, South Korean defense minister Yi Sang-hŭi paid an official visit to Moscow in the wake of the North's second nuclear test, cementing a unified position with Russia. And in 2010, the Russian chief of general staff Nikolai Makarov held talks in Seoul with ROK chairman of the joint chiefs of staff General Han Min-ku and Defense Minister Kim Tae-yŏng.

RUSSIA'S NORTH KOREA policy under Yeltsin was essentially its South Korea policy. Yeltsin cared little about the DPRK as an ally or as a strategic asset. This raises the question: what does Russia want today in the DPRK that is not derivative of its relations with the ROK?

At the broadest level, Russian interests converge with those of the United States and others in that Moscow desires a denuclearized North Korea and seeks a peaceful diplomatic resolution of the problem. Russia seeks an end to the DPRK's missile threat as a way to counter U.S. ballistic missile defense in the region, which is seen as a threat to Russian interests. Following a July 2000 summit trip to Pyongyang, for example, Vladimir Putin announced speciously at the G8 Summit in Okinawa, Japan, later in the month that Moscow, as the only G8 member with regular dialogue with the DPRK, reached agreement with Kim Jong-il in which he consented to a testing moratorium on his long-range ballistic missiles programs if the United States and Russia would agree to launch two to three satellites annually for the DPRK. Putin then said that the end of the DPRK missile threat would remove the rationale for a BMD system in Asia and remove the need for the United States to renounce the ABM treaty. Russia does not want to see one power—particularly one hostile to Russia—dominating the peninsula, and threatening its Far Eastern border. It sees instability or a sudden collapse of the DPRK as not in its interests, and like China, it is concerned about potential refugee flows of hundreds of thousands into its vulnerable maritime region, where the Moscow central government does not exercise a great deal of control.[69] Russia has interests in the development of Rajin-Sŏnbong (Rasŏn), a special economic zone in northeastern North Korea. In addition to being the only year-round ice-free port on the Russian Pacific coast, the Rajin port is a potential gateway to economic interaction with the northeast provinces of China, which could help build the Russian Far East. Russia's ultimate dream is to run gas pipelines through northern Korea to the energy-hungry economies in the ROK, Japan, and other parts of East Asia, and to reconnect the Trans-Siberian Railway to enable cargo transport from Europe to Asia. The latter two objectives are advocated by Russian interlocutors in almost blind fashion. During Six-Party Talks, whenever we ran into a deadlock with the North Koreans over the nuclear issue, the Russian answer to breaking any deadlock was "gas pipelines and the Trans-Siberian Railway."

Despite being the first major Northeast Asian power to have relations with both Koreas from 1990, Russia's influence on the peninsula, particularly with regard to the North, has been impeded by the debt problem. Russia could have used debt resettlement as negotiating leverage to gain DPRK cooperation on other issues, but talks over this issue have been suspended since 2002, after the DPRK demanded Russia forgive the debt as a political gesture. Rightly, Moscow has insisted on repayment of the $8.8 billion rather that write it off.

PUTIN'S PERSONAL TOUCH

Russian president Vladimir Putin marked a shift in relations with the two Koreas after the one-sided policies of President Yeltsin. Putin wanted to reassert Russia as a great power in Asia and connect the region to development of Siberia and the Russian Far East. The Korean Peninsula became an area of interest because relations with Japan remained impeded by the sovereignty dispute over the Northern Territories, and relations with China were impeded by concerns about Chinese migration into the Russian Far East. Given Russia's growing energy wealth, Putin also wanted to counterbalance U.S. influence in the region and, in particular, to curtail U.S. plans for missile defense in the region, which Russia viewed as a capability that could undermine deterrence against a U.S. attack.

Using "personal diplomacy," Putin sought to expand relations with the DPRK in pursuit of the objectives outlined above. In the summer of 1999, he sent a delegation to the DPRK to resolve long-standing differences over the revision of the 1961 security treaty. Pyongyang never accepted Yeltsin's desire to free Moscow of any responsibility to defend the DPRK, as stated in the treaty, and months of difficult negotiations resulted in a revised treaty on February 9, 2000. The new treaty promised "gigantic plans" for cooperation in various industries, including metals, power, transport, forestry, and oil and gas.[70] It also contained a statement on the two countries' joint opposition to U.S. ballistic missile defense plans in Asia.

Subsequent to the treaty revision, Putin traveled to Pyongyang for a summit meeting. His July 2000 trip to the DPRK was not only the first by a Russian leader since the founding of North Korea in 1948, but also the first trip to an Asian capital by President Putin. And with Yeltsin's first Asia trip having been Seoul in 1992, in Kim's eyes, the sea change couldn't have been greater or more gratifying.[71] Putin tried to develop a personal friendship with Kim, referring to him as a "totally modern man" and as a "well-informed" leader. Following on the heels of the historic June 2000 summit between the two Koreas and agreements reached in that forum for reconnection of the railways between the two on the peninsula, the Russian leader proposed a $3 billion project to reconnect the Trans-Siberian Railway to the Korean Peninsula, a project that captured the imagination of ROK president and Sunshine Policy champion Kim Dae-jung. Kim Dae-jung raved about how such a railway would cut transit time for goods from Europe from thirty to forty days by sea to thirteen to eighteen days by direct rail. Russia and North Korea would both benefit from greater commerce and from transit fees. At the time, it sounded like a great plan (even though refurbishment of DPRK railways would promise to be an enormous project, given their antiquated nature and the disparate gauges of Korean and Russian tracks), to which Kim Jong-il responded positively. After the trip, Putin went to the G8 summit in Okinawa and conveyed the proposal for the United States and Russia to cooperate in satellite launches for the DPRK. (Kim Jong-il later denied that he had agreed to such a proposal, claiming it was meant "in humor".)[72]

Putin's visit was followed by a reengagement in military relations. Defense ministers from the two countries met in April 2001, followed by meetings of the two air forces and commanders of the adjoining border areas. These constituted the first substantive military exchanges since the collapse of the Soviet Union in December 1991, and resulted in two new military cooperation accords. The first was an intergovernmental cooperation agreement on the sharing of military technology and training, and the second, on military cooperation between the two defense ministries. The North, evidently keenly interested in Moscow's sophisticated military technology, reportedly requested that Russia sell it over $500 million in modern weaponry, but this deal never came to fruition.[73]

Kim Jong-il reciprocated Putin's visit in July–August 2001 by taking a twenty-four-day, 9,299-kilometer (5,780-mi) journey in his "leadership train" to Moscow. (Kim did not like to fly.) Agreements were reached on technical support for modernization of DPRK electricity power stations and railways and on use of DPRK labor forces in the Russian Far East as a way to service Pyongyang's $8.8 billion outstanding debt. But Putin would not agree to writing off the debt as a political gesture.[74] Despite this, Putin's personal diplomacy was fast at work. During the 2001 summit, Putin dispensed with the formal meal and instead invited Kim to his Kremlin apartment for a casual engagement. Kim was delighted by the invitation, and the impromptu meal made a strong impression on him. A Russian official who was present at the time said that the event had a noticeable effect on his personality, going from being "a little reserved" to "more open, trusting, [and] gentle." And Kim would reportedly admit as much, quoted as saying: "If I am treated diplomatically, I become a diplomat myself . . . Putin was sincere with me, and I opened my heart to him."[75] Kim described the Russian leader as an "honest man" to whom "one could bare one's soul." And Putin, in turn, described Kim as an educated and intelligent man with a crafty sense of humor. What came out of this trip was an eight-point DPRK-Russia "Moscow Declaration," signed by the two leaders. But far more important—for Kim Jong-il, at least—were the personal bonds forged. During his long journey back to Pyongyang, Kim is reported to have said:

Today everybody is using diplomatic terms like "partnership" and "strategic partnership." I told President Putin that we do not need to look for such a term to apply to our relationship. Putin agreed. It's all diplomacy, and what we need is sincerity. I don't want to be a "partner." You don't say "partner" with friends.[76]

Relations between the two were restored enough that Kim looked to Putin for support in the then-materializing Six-Party Talks. Initially, when the Bush administration put forward the idea in 2003, Russia was not included, in part because Putin insisted that the United States negotiate bilaterally with the DPRK. But Kim Jong-il, reportedly, personally telephoned Putin and asked that Russia not only participate but also host the talks, because he did not trust the Americans or the Chinese. Putin politely declined.[77]

The inauguration of President Dmitry Medvedev in May of 2008 brought with it the hope of significant change in Russian politics. As Putin's former chief of staff, he was an insider but had many of the characteristics of an outsider. For one, he rose to power at the tender age of forty-three, thirteen years Putin's junior. He also was trained as a lawyer and taught law at St. Petersburg State University, lacking Yeltsin's *nomenklatura* ties and Putin's KGB background. Many hailed the rise of Medvedev as a sign of the emergence of a modern, moderate, pragmatic, and perhaps even reform-oriented Russia on the world stage. And yet the reality hasn't been quite so rosy. Medvedev has operated in his presidency under the watchful eye of his former boss, with Putin sitting as prime minister, casting a great shadow over the Russian president. Just three months after Medvedev's inauguration, Russia invaded the disputed territory of South Ossetia, sitting between it and neighboring state Georgia, gave the Georgians a bloody nose, and withdrew. On North Korea, Russia under Medvedev was helpful in supporting a U.N. Security Council Resolution (1874) after North Korea's 2009 nuke test, but dragged its feet along with China in forming the U.N. Security Council Presidential Statement (in lieu of a resolution) in the wake of the *Cheonan* incident. In the end, due to their objections, the statement condemned the act but didn't single out North Korea (or anyone, for that matter) as the culprit. After the Yeonpyeong Island shelling, and the North's unveiling of a clandestine uranium enrichment facility in November of 2010, the Medvedev government was quick to condemn the North Koreans, but basically put forth talking points–type calls to a hasty return to the Six-Party Talks and for calm and restraint all around. And so, in spite of the rise of the young, post-Communist technocrat,[78] it seems that Russia still can't quite fully leave the Cold War behind it.

COLLATERAL DAMAGE

Given Russia's traditional exclusion from the affairs of East Asia, its inclusion in the Six-Party Talks was an accomplishment. Kim Jong-il's view of Russia as more of an honest broker than China constituted an important step in overcoming one of Russia's fundamental dilemmas when it comes to dealing with North Korea: its relative inability to influence DPRK behavior, despite the fact that Pyongyang's actions create real and diplomatic collateral damage in Russia. Russians, though they were the original supporters of North Korea's first research reactor at Yongbyon, feel they have little control over the crises resulting from North Korea's greatly expanded nuclear ambitions, and yet these crises lead to decisions that directly affect Russian core interests. Every time North Korea tests a ballistic missile, it potentially threatens Russia. As noted earlier, these tests provide justifications, in Russian eyes, for a U.S.-Japan missile defense system inimical to Moscow's long-term security interests. Moreover, these tests, though aimed to affect Japan, the ROK, and the United States, pose an existential threat to Russian territory, more so than any other country's, even though Russia is, arguably, an innocent bystander. The July 4, 2006, ballistic missile tests, for example, featured the TD-2 multistage missile among the seven missiles fired. The TD-2 failed forty seconds after launch, as it was headed eastward on a trajectory toward the United States, but what many don't know is that missile parts landed only 250 kilometers (155 mi) from Vladivostok. In addition, three of the other missiles splashed down in Russia's Exclusive Economic Zone (EEZ) and close to Nakhodka. In the aftermath of the test, the former head of Russia's Strategic Rocket Forces, Viktor Yeslin, vehemently criticized North Korea for firing missiles that do not have automatic self-destruct mechanisms when they veer off course. The 2006 nuclear test by the DPRK was conducted with little advance notice to Moscow, despite the fact that the test site is only 150 kilometers (90 mi) from the Russian border. Russians carried a deep fear, particularly during the Bush administration, that they would be the victims of nuclear fallout if the United States carried out a surgical strike on the Yongbyon nuclear facility.

Moscow has tried to avoid being the victim of DPRK collateral damage. Prior to being asked by Kim Jong-il to join the Six-Party Talks in 2003, for example, the Russians had made several proposals for a multilateral effort to rid North Korea of its nuclear weapons and to address outstanding security issues in the region. During the first nuclear crisis, in 1994, Russia proposed an eight-party conference on North Korea, involving the United States, Russia, Japan, China, the two Koreas, plus the head of the IAEA and the U.N. secretary-general. Moscow laid out a comprehensive road map, including denuclearization, noninterference in internal affairs, confidence-building measures, a peace treaty, and normalization of relations between the United States, DPRK, and Japan. In 1997, it proposed a ten-party conference on security in the region. This arrangement would include the same participants as the eight-party proposal, but added the two other permanent members of the U.N. Security Council (along with the United States, Russia, and China): Britain and France.[79] In January 2003, just as revelations about North Korea's violations of the standing nuclear agreement came to the surface, Russia was the first to propose the idea of a multilateral conference to deal with the issue. This was not empty political posturing, but, according to former Russian foreign ministry official Georgy Toloraya, offered a detailed plan that included about a dozen synchronized steps, starting with simultaneous declarations of a DPRK nuclear freeze and provision of U.S. heavy fuel oil. This would be followed by bilateral consultations on how to repair the 1994 Agreed Framework, which would include lists made by Washington and Pyongyang of demands made of the other. According to the Russian plan, the other parties would act as referees and honest brokers and would facilitate movement of the negotiations to the stated goals of a DPRK return to the NPT, guarantees of U.S. noninterference in DPRK domestic affairs, and mutual respect for sovereignty.[80] And at the June 2004 Six-Party Talks, it proposed turning the Korean Peninsula into a nuclear weapons–free zone (NWFZ). These are internationally legally binding, mutually agreed upon geographical expanses that ban the use, development, and deployment of nuclear weapons and include verification and control mechanisms. (These currently exist in outer space, on the sea bed, in Antarctica, in the ASEAN countries, the South Pacific, Mongolia, Latin America and the Caribbean, and the African continent.)

These were each serious proposals. Russia's interests in preparing these stemmed from a genuine desire to help the situation. Moscow sees itself as something of an honest broker in the group, situated between the U.S.-Japan-ROK camp on the one hand and the China-DPRK alliance on the other. The proposals were also motivated by a tactical calculation to avoid Russian exclusion from any discussions. According to Russian foreign ministry officials, Moscow complained bitterly that it was excluded almost entirely from the U.S.-DPRK negotiations that led to the 1994 Agreed Framework.[81] The 1997 proposal for a ten-party peace conference similarly was motivated by a desire to avoid being left out of the emerging U.S.-ROK-DPRK-China "Four Party" talks on a peace treaty for the peninsula, which the Russians were never formally briefed on and learned about only inadvertently through the South Koreans.[82] This is also why Moscow was prepared with an elaborate proposal when the Agreed Framework broke down in late 2002 and early 2003. In the current Six-Party Talks, Russia is not only a member but also chairs the Working Group on Northeast Asian regional security. And having been the U.S. representative to this Working Group, I can attest to Russia's professional preparations and management of this group. In total, these and other proposals today represent Russian desires to gain some control over a proximate security problem in which they have high stakes.

In spite of Russia's best efforts, however, Moscow's proposals are more often ignored by the other parties than welcomed. Even if recognized agreements and negotiating forums over the past twenty-plus years look eerily like some of these earlier Russian proposals, they are never realized until another party, like the United States or China, champions the idea. As frustrating as this must be, it reflects a fundamental Catch-22 with regard to Russian efforts to help: Moscow is most helpful when relations among the other parties in the region are at the absolutely worst, but once things start to improve, Russia is quickly sidelined. In other words, Moscow's desired role as an honest broker is realized when nuclear negotiations are hopelessly deadlocked or North Korean misbehavior has closed off all avenues of diplomacy. All parties have dug themselves diplomatically into tough positions with a plethora of preconditions before they reengage in dialogue. It is at these moments when Russia can play a helpful role—in large part because they have less invested in the deadlock. So, Moscow comes up with some ideas to move the process forward. These ideas help to break the ice. But then, once parties start to quietly reengage after an appropriate period of "being tough," Moscow gets shortchanged again, because each of the parties have greater interest in reengaging with the others than with Russia. Thus, for example, Russian proposals for a multilateral peace conference, by definition, would only be successful if it led to Moscow's sidelining, because momentum would lead the key parties to the Korean armistice—the United States, China, and the two Koreas—to engage with each other rather than with Russia. After the normalization of relations between the USSR and ROK in 1990, Moscow saw an opportunity to play a central role as the first major power to have full relations with the two Koreas. But it quickly found itself marginalized: Moscow could no longer influence Pyongyang, since it was not willing to give large amounts of help to the regime. This, in turn, reduced any expectations in Seoul that the Soviets still had juice in Pyongyang. After the October 2006 nuclear test took the diplomatic situation to its nadir, the United States, Japan, ROK, and even China were in no mood for dialogue with Pyongyang and saw its primary arena of action to be the U.N. Security Council. It was at that point that Russian deputy foreign minister Alexandr Alekseyev immediately went to Pyongyang days after the test to confirm that Pyongyang's intentions remained peaceful. Upon his return from the one-day visit, Alekseyev said the trip was "positive" and that he remained "cautiously optimistic" about North Korea's eventual return to the Six-Party Talks.[83] Alekseyev's trip helped in maintaining open dialogue channels during the crisis and eventually helped to facilitate a return to talks in February 2007. But once we engaged in intensive negotiations, the majority of these took place between the United States and DPRK, with support from the ROK and China, not with Russia. The upshot is that when Russia is most helpful, it is usually a manifestation of how bad the situation has become.

A BIT PLAYER

In the end, I think Russia's part in the North Korean problem is best described as a bit player. Its role is often peripheral, but at times it can be incredibly unhelpful at the most inopportune moments. I recall when North Korea conducted its first nuclear test in October 2006, and U.N. Security Council members were mobilizing for a resolution condemning the brazen act and implementing sanctions, Putin took some of the wind out of the UNSC sails when, on a Russian TV show called *Hotline with the President,* he blamed the DPRK test on U.S. "heavy-handed diplomacy" that, supposedly, pushed North Korea into a corner. Russian ambassador to Seoul Gleb Ivashentsov also said during the 2005 Banco Delta Asia action that Russia had neither been presented with nor possessed evidence of the charges of DPRK money-laundering, counterfeiting, and proliferation financing, calling it all "rumor-level talk."

Sometimes Russia follows its own parochial interests without an ear to the pace of negotiations. In part, this is not entirely Moscow's fault, as the other parties need to do a better job of including Russia, but it can result in some bizarre behavior. In the course of negotiations on the Six-Party agreement, for example, the United States understood that energy assistance to the DPRK would be part of a package to obtain denuclearization. For Bush counter-proliferation people, energy was defined as oil and conventional electricity, but not civilian nuclear energy in the form of light-water reactors. LWRs still had proliferation potential. The United States stood firm on this point, and won others to its side on the grounds that such long-term energy assistance questions should not be part of an initial agreement over the DPRK's freezing its nuclear programs and reintroducing international inspectors. Heavy fuel oil and electricity should be enough compensation, the United States argued. But then, completely out of the blue, the Russians were quoted in the press as saying the DPRK had a right to civilian nuclear energy and that Russia, if asked, would be happy to help supply the contracts for these reactors. This caused our delegation to hit the roof, as it deflated the U.S. negotiation position considerably.

But at other times, Russia can be important and helpful, often by surprise. I am not trying to demean a government, but when Moscow is helpful, there is a Forrest Gump–like quality to it that is both uncanny and mildly amusing. One such moment occurred during the fourth round of the Six-Party Talks. Allow me to recount in detail a story I noted at the outset of this chapter. The DPRK demanded a security guarantee from the United States as a pretext for their committing to denuclearization. It was a crucial stage of the talks, and momentum—that long-sought-after dynamic that every negotiator seeks to create—appeared to be building among the parties. China, as the host of the talks and the drafter of the agreement, pressed us hard to come up with a satisfactory statement that would push the DPRK to commit to giving up their nuclear ambitions.

We tried to craft language that did not depart from past precedent, conscious of the fact that unconditional statements of nonaggression could undercut the terms of our defense commitments to treaty allies—Japan and the ROK. However, to simply repeat past statements was not going to be enough. The Chinese, probably in consultation with the North Koreans, came back with revised language for the U.S. security guarantee. The proposed language went far beyond anything the United States had said before, and our initial reaction was that it would not be accepted in Washington, but we agreed to send it back overnight and await instructions. Though we explained to our superiors at home the negotiating context, I had serious doubts that it would be accepted. To my surprise, the following morning the proposed language was approved. We returned to the multilateral drafting session at the Diaoyutai, and told the Chinese that the proposed language had been accepted and that we had instructions from Washington to proceed. The Chinese delegate, who had doubts similar to my own, blurted out, "Really? Your side accepts this language?" The South Koreans and Japanese, also with looks of surprise, asked, "Really?" Even the North Korean delegation, after arriving habitually late for the negotiating session, was surprised by the demonstration of U.S. pliability. The key phrase of the statement read, "The United States affirmed that it has no nuclear weapons on the Korean Peninsula and has no intention to attack or invade the DPRK with nuclear or conventional weapons."[84]

At this point, the Russian delegation, which had remained fairly quiet throughout the several days of negotiations, abruptly asked the chair for a recess. The Chinese lead drafter, Cui Tankei, looked puzzled and questioned why, given that we had not yet even sat down to start the negotiation session that morning. Cui was also probably concerned that any delay might cause the U.S. or DPRK delegation to change their minds, and he did not want to lose momentum. The Russians insisted, however, and asked for a bilateral meeting with the DPRK delegation. The Chinese, being consummate hosts, granted the request. I joked to my Russian counterpart, "Well hurry up then before we change our mind." After about twenty minutes, the two delegations emerged from their bilateral meeting and rushed back into the drafting session. I chased after my Russian counterpart for a quick hallway debriefing. What he explained epitomized the sometimes surprising and helpful role Russia could play. He told me that the Russians, too, were surprised that the United States accepted the proposed language. In the bilateral with the DPRK, the Russians explained that the phrasing accepted by the United States amounted to a negative security assurance—i.e., an assurance that the United States would never be the first to attack. This was something, the Russians explained, that the Soviet Union tried unsuccessfully to get from the United States throughout the Cold War. Therefore, it was their estimation, they told the North Koreans, that the United States was quite seriously committed to reaching a denuclearization deal and that the DPRK should reciprocate. My Russian interlocutor said this with an earnest look on his face and then turned on his heels and headed for the coffee bar. I would have expected no less.

Of course, despite these Russian entreaties, the North Koreans never did reciprocate. They pocketed the negative security assurance after having demanded it for years and offered nothing in return. They had many other complaints that they wanted addressed, not least of which was Japan.

JAPAN: ETERNALLY UNRECONCILED

"Sorry folks. Can't pass. Gotta let the motorcade through." At first, the burly officer in NYPD blue would not allow us to disembark from the cab and walk down East 49th Street, where the Chinese restaurant was located. We tried to explain several times that the VIP delegation in the black GMC vans were the North Koreans, who were riding with State

Department diplomatic security escorts, and that we, the counterpart U.S. government delegation, were following them in plain taxicabs. One younger officer in our delegation told him that we were hosting the lunch, so we needed to get to the restaurant first to greet them, and blurted out in frustration, "Hey, we're the good guys, not them!" The officer retorted, in New York-ese, "Oh yeah? Den why are dey in the frickin' motorcade and youse on da street?" The VIP motorcade for the DPRK was courtesy of Ambassador Chris Hill, who wanted to treat the North Koreans well in our first meeting of the Six-Party bilateral working group between the United States and DPRK. The result was that Vice Minister Kim Kye-gwan and his delegation sped by with NYPD sirens blaring, while we stood on the street behind a police barricade, indistinguishable from other pedestrians who seemed uninterested in the temporary inconvenience. Once the delegation disembarked into the restaurant, the police removed the barrier and we ran down the street to catch up with them. The whole incident was mildly amusing, even more so to the North Koreans when we explained what had happened.

The conversation that followed over lunch was much more serious, however. We had just spent the entire morning in the Waldorf-Astoria residence of the U.S. ambassador to the U.N., discussing the various obstacles to U.S.-DPRK normalization of political relations. (John Bolton had left his post by then, allowing us to use the spacious private apartment out of range of the press, but the irony that the two delegations were discussing U.S.-DPRK political reconciliation in Bolton's former residence was not lost on the North Koreans.) The lunch discussion, however, was almost entirely about Japan. Chris Hill confronted the North Koreans, saying that it was completely unfathomable to him how the DPRK could ignore Japan. You need economic help, Hill lectured, and yet here was the world's second-largest economy directly on your doorstep, and you won't improve relations with them. He went on to say that it made no sense for the DPRK to allow a few unresolved abduction cases from over thirty years ago to impede relations.

The DPRK vice minister Kim Kye-gwan put down his chopsticks and responded angrily, "You want us to put the abductions issue behind us? We have. We tried to put it behind us in 2002. It's the Japanese that keep raising it. Why don't you tell them to stop raising it? We accounted for all the cases, living and dead. Abe knows that. He was there standing next to Prime Minister Koizumi in 2002 when we agreed. He was nodding his head in agreement, too. And now he is raising the issue for his political gain. We can never work with him."

Kim's outburst referred to then–prime minister Abe Shinzo, who, as deputy chief cabinet secretary, had accompanied Prime Minister Junichiro Koizumi for his breakthrough summit with Kim Jong-il in September 2002. It was during this trip that the DPRK leader made the bombshell admission that the North had, in fact, kidnapped citizens from Japan in the 1970s and used them to train North Korean spies to operate undercover as Japanese citizens. The DPRK leader's apology was meant to achieve closure on the issue and pave the way for reconciliation, normalization, and a fat aid package. Instead, it created a groundswell of anger among the Japanese public. Some of the anger was guilt-inspired, because Japanese society had, for decades, dismissed the stories of these kidnappings as the equivalent of *National Enquirer* stories about alien abductions. But much of it was directed against North Korea, which compelled conservative politicians like Abe to make a full resolution of this issue a precondition for improved bilateral relations.

EMOTION OVER REASON

This anecdote tells us a lot about a basic dilemma in relations between Japan and the DPRK. By almost any rational metric, both countries have an interest in reconciling relations. It would be an understatement to say Pyongyang needs economic help, and as Hill aptly noted, the DPRK could not have been blessed with a more proximate potential economic partner than Japan, one of the largest providers of official development assistance (ODA) in the world. Moreover, Japan has had experience with development on the Korean Peninsula, not just during the colonial period in the first half of the twentieth century, but more recently in contributing to the foundation of South Korea's economic boom in the 1970s. A normalization settlement like that reached between Seoul and Tokyo could provide Pyongyang with over $10 billion in grants and low-interest loans. (This number is based on the 1965 Japan-ROK normalization package of grants and loans of $800 million, adjusted for today's prices.)[85] North Korea's GNP is about $28 billion. So, the math is clearly favorable for Pyongyang.

For Japan, reconciliation would remove the most proximate threat to its national security. While the challenge of a rising China is a longer-term concern for Tokyo, North Korea's deployed force of a hundred Nodong ballistic missiles and two hundred or so Scud missiles are the greatest immediate threat to Japan's security today.[86] Unlike the longer-range Taep'odong missiles, which have failed several high-profile tests, the Nodong is a fully operational ballistic missile. These missiles, more-over, if armed with biological or chemical weapons, could do untold damage in Japan. Normalized relations would help to reduce this threat, and would fit with Japan's policy, since the end of World War II, to rec-oncile relations with all former adversaries. The DPRK is also the only country to have been formally occupied by Japan with which it has not normalized relations. The North Korea issue and a territorial dispute with Russia over the Kurile Islands in the north are basically the only major pieces of unfinished business left over from World War II, and the Japanese would welcome the opportunity to turn the page on these as well.[87] Normalization would also sit well with the sizable Korean resi-dent population in Japan (approximately 900,000), a portion of which is affiliated with the Chosen Soren, a pro–North Korean citizens' orga-nization.[88] Japan could import manufactured goods and metallurgical products, such as iron ore and copper, from the DPRK economy. And normalization would give the Japanese the opportunity to compete with China to tap into the North's supposed multitrillion-dollar mineral re-source deposits—that is, if the investment environment were to improve. Furthermore, ODA infrastructure projects are big business for the Japa-nese construction industry, which has had trouble keeping afloat during Japan's multidecade economic stagnation. Any normalization package would likely include a great deal of infrastructural development and would give a much-needed boost to Japan's ailing construction sector.[89]

Yet deep historical animosities prevent this outcome from being real-ized. Emotion has become a major driver of dynamics between the two sides. For the DPRK, there is a deep-seated hatred of Japan. North Ko-rean nationalism was born out of the Japanese occupation, and Kim Il-sung's qualifications, when he was chosen by Stalin as the first leader of the country, were more for his record as an anti-Japan guerrilla fighter than for his loyalty to Communism. Since then, anti-Japanism has been central to the regime's ideology. One of the poles around which the DPRK has wrapped its propaganda and the justification for its weapons has been the threat of renewed Japanese aggression against the Korean people. For North Koreans, Japan is "bad" in more ways than one: as a former colonizer, as an ally of the dreaded imperialist United States, and as a supporter of rival South Korea's economic development.

North Korea does not elicit the same sort of visceral reaction in Japan. It remains one of the few countries with which Japan does not have relations. (Tokyo even has relations with Burma, but not with North Korea.) For decades, North Korea registered as a distant threat that created, at best, a sense of indifference in Japan. North Korea was the enemy during the Cold War, but no more so than China, where Tokyo always had an inclination to improve relations whenever U.S.-China relations thawed. Likewise, during the détente years of the 1970s, Japan made minor overtures to Pyongyang to improve relations, much to the consternation of the South Koreans. But nothing much came of this. By the 1990s, the security threat posed by the DPRK's Nodong ballistic missile force became real, as it could target any of the Japanese home islands. The long-range ballistic missile tests in 1998, which overflew Japan, caused politicians and the general public to really acknowledge the gravity of the threat. The Japanese, however, approached all of these problems, unlike the North Koreans, in a rational and cool-headed manner. That was, until the 2002 abduction revelations. After Kim Jong-il's admission of guilt, the public's angry reaction heightened beyond anyone's imagination, and made the North "Public Enemy #1" in the minds of many.

KANEMARU, THE COWBOY

This is not to say that the two countries were too stupid to recognize the mutual benefits. From the 1980s, North Korea entered a phase where they tried to extract money and food from Japan. Joint venture laws enacted in the 1980s were meant to draw in Japanese investment. Then–foreign minister Ho Tam also entertained special envoys from the Nakasone government. A breakthrough came in 1990, when Liberal Democratic Party

(LDP) elder Kanemaru Shin led a parliamentary delegation to Pyongyang for a five-day visit. Kanemaru was a powerful political figure within the conservative LDP and held great influence behind the scenes as a king-maker in Japanese politics. Seeking his "Nixon goes to China" moment, the seventy-five-year-old Kanemaru brought Socialist Party (JSP) Diet-men with him and met with Kim Il-sung. Kanemaru wanted to bring the Socialists closer to the mainstream by including them in the visit, and to appease business interests in Japan associated with the Chosen Soren, who foresaw economic opportunities in the DPRK with normalization. There was also the thorny issue of two Japanese fishermen, who had been detained in the North for "espionage" after straying into North Korean territorial waters in 1983, which needed to be worked out. Kim Il-sung saw an opportunity to counter Roh Tae-woo's immensely successful *Nordpolitik* by making diplomatic inroads with Japan, and a way to gain massive amounts of economic assistance.

The meetings between the two went well and Kanemaru was report-edly completely taken by Kim's charisma. The DPRK leader proposed that Kanemaru's mission be a springboard to the opening of formal nor-malization talks, to which Kanemaru, without official instruction, agreed and promised that a settlement would include Japanese compensation for the colonial period and from 1945 to the present. At their press confer-ence in Pyongyang, Kanemaru grew emotional and shed tears over the need to reconcile relations between the two peoples. During their meet-ings, Kanemaru did raise U.S. concerns about the North's clandestine nuclear program, which Kim glossed over. The DPRK leader responded that the North had only an experimental reactor at Yongbyon and that Japan should not worry. "Trust me," Kim told Kanemaru. Seemingly as a goodwill gesture, the Japanese fishermen were released just weeks after the Kanemaru visit.

Kanemaru's mission was the definition of cowboy diplomacy. Though a very powerful elder in the ruling party, he traveled without any foreign ministry bureaucrats, and, probably to the latters' horror, allowed party politicians from the LDP and JSP to negotiate a joint declaration. The government of Japan immediately characterized the visit as an unofficial one, which did not commit Tokyo in any way. A few years later, Kane-maru himself would fall from grace when $51 million in gold bars, cash, and other assets were found in his home, leading to his jailing on charges of tax evasion.[90] Thickening the plot, it was widely reported at the time that the gold bars found in Kanemaru's home were stamped "North Korea."[91] However, in spite of all the uproar and controversy surrounding the trip, five weeks later Japan and the DPRK engaged in normalization talks in November 1990. The two governments held eight rounds of dialogue that lasted until 1992. As a result of the 1994 Agreed Framework and these talks, Japan started to provide humanitarian assistance to the DPRK, starting in the summer of 1995, and soon became the largest contributor of food assistance to the annual WFP appeal for North Korea. Two parliamentary delegations from Japan visited the DPRK in 1997 in an effort to spur the normalization talks on and to make progress on a normalization package of aid, apologies, and colonial reparations. The DPRK reciprocated in 1998 by allowing Japanese spouses of North Koreans, who had previously lived in Japan and since returned to the DPRK, to have contact and, in some cases, visit their families in Japan.[92]

After this high point, Japan-DPRK relations went through cycles of tension followed by thaw, typical of all countries that deal with the North. The August 1998 Taep'odong-I ballistic missile test marked the end of the period of Japanese infatuation with Pyongyang started by Kanemaru. The launch, though it failed, was still seen as a brazen act. (Pieces of the missile fell into the sea uncomfortably close to Japanese shores.) Also, at this time, there were new revelations about North Korean kidnappings of Japanese citizens in the 1970s. The government stopped food assistance in the aftermath of the test, expanded defense cooperation with South Korea, and began serious cooperation with the United States on ballistic missile defense. Six months later, in the most significant military action by Self-Defense Forces (SDF) since the Pacific War, Japanese navy vessels chased and fired upon two North Korean espionage vessels near the Japanese coast. In the fall of 1999, former secretary of defense William Perry conducted a congressionally mandated review of North Korea policy for the Clinton administration, one of the recommendations of which was that a Japan-DPRK normalization settlement would be one of the key financial incentives for the DPRK to denuclearize. The combination of Perry Review and Kim Dae-jung's Sunshine Policy led Japan to restart food assistance in the spring of 2000, a controversial decision for conservative lawmakers in Japan. This was followed by the start of ninth, tenth, and eleventh rounds of normalization talks from April to October of 2000. Talks faltered though, over several issues, the most important of which was North Korea's demand not only that they receive an economic assistance package comparable to what the ROK got when it normalized in 1965 (about $5–10 billion) but also an apology and compensation for damages experienced during the thirty-five-year colonial period. In 2001, Japan provided a massive food aid package, which helped to set an all-time high for food assistance to the DPRK, at over 1.5 million metric tons. In keeping with the topsy-turvy nature of relations, Pyongyang became deeply offended at a Japanese police raid of the Chosen Soren headquarters in November 2001 over charges that one of its executives was embezzling money, and unceremoniously stopped an ongoing investigation into the fate of Japanese abductees taken to North Korea. In December 2001, Japan coast guard vessels fired on and sank an intruding DPRK naval vessel, taking relations to a low point.

KOIZUMI'S GAMBIT

"What about a trip to Graceland?"

NSC staff are tasked with managing the overall contours and minute details of summit meetings between the president and foreign leaders. NSC senior director Michael Green and I tossed around the unconventional idea of a trip by President Bush and Prime Minister Koizumi to this hallowed piece of Americana. After all, it was an unconventional friendship. Bush and Koizumi were about as odd a couple as you could imagine in international relations. They had little in common, and could communicate only through interpreters (Koizumi spoke little English, and Bush no Japanese), yet the two leaders had one of the closest friendships in global affairs. Bush liked Koizumi's decisiveness, his unorthodox style, his domestic agenda of deregulation, and, of course, his love of baseball. Koizumi, who was not much of a grand strategist, loved American westerns and saw Japan's foreign policy as grounded in one key element—his good friend and cowboy George W. Bush. Among his many eccentricities, Koizumi was a big fan of Elvis Presley. He even created a CD with his favorite selections from the King with a Photoshopped cover of himself and Elvis. (The proceeds from sales went to charity.) The Graceland visit was intended as a symbol of this close and unique partnership—and it was initially denounced by every senior member of the White House as about the stupidest idea any staff member could think of (particularly coming from two ivory-towered professors). "Graceland? You mean, you want the president to go to Graceland with a foreign leader when we are in the middle of two wars??"

We shelved the idea on the trash heap of staff-originated proposals to make summits more interesting.[93] Until the president met with Koizumi on the sidelines of the U.N. General Assembly in New York in 2005. As they ended the meeting, Bush mentioned in parting that the two should do something interesting when Koizumi next came to the United States the following year, perhaps a trip to Graceland. Needless to say, after that conversation, everyone now thought it was not only a great idea but that it was *their* great idea. The trip was a huge success in the end, with the most memorable moments recorded in the press being Lisa Marie Presley's surprising command of Japanese (apparently, there are a lot of Elvis fans in the Land of the Rising Sun), and Koizumi's donning of a pair of the King's oversize, jewel-studded sunglasses, and air-guitaring an Elvis song.

Koizumi never did things in a conventional way, which was part of his appeal to a Japanese public that had long countenanced a bland train of cautious and ineffective prime ministers. He had an aggressive domestic agenda of deregulation that he was willing to stake his prime ministership on (by dissolving the cabinet and using his reelection as a popular mandate to push through reform). He dispatched—for the first time in postwar history—Japanese naval vessels to the Indian Ocean in support of the war in Afghanistan. And, in another first, he authorized putting Japanese troops on the ground in Iraq.

Koizumi was no less bold when it came to North Korea. From 2001, he authorized the Japanese foreign ministry to engage in secret negotiations, led by Director-General of Asian Affairs Hitoshi Tanaka. Tanaka, who reported directly to Koizumi, Chief Cabinet Secretary Fukuda Takeo, and Foreign Minister Tanaka Makiko, met secretly with DPRK officials in Beijing and had direct contacts with a high-level DPRK official known as "Mr. X." These talks paved the way for the September 17,

2002, visit by Koizumi to Pyongyang for a one-day unprecedented sum-mit with Kim Jong-il. The two-and-a-half-hour meeting produced a joint declaration known as the Pyongyang Declaration, which today still re-mains the primary reference document for relations. The declaration ad-dressed a range of issues, the most significant of which was an exchange of apologies: Japan made a statement of regret regarding the colonial past, while the DPRK offered a similar statement on the abductions issue. Tokyo acknowledged that economic assistance in the form of grants, long-term low-interest loans, and humanitarian assistance disburse-ments through international organizations would be offered to Pyong-yang after a normalization settlement is reached. In a nod to Japanese concerns that nonproliferation issues be addressed in the summit, the joint declaration contained a general statement regarding mutual agree-ment with regard to fulfilling "all related international agreements" per-taining to nuclear issues on the peninsula. Kim Jong-il also committed to maintaining a self-imposed moratorium on missile tests over Japan, which he had declared in September 1999. Koizumi's surprise summit, a major break from the difficult relations preceding it, was designed to jump-start bilateral Japan-DPRK relations. It was an unusual departure for Japan from its traditional proximity to U.S. policy, and from the cau-tious approach of the Bush administration. Arguably, it was one of the few bold moves by Koizumi that did not succeed. Normalization talks were not significantly aided by the summit, and any positive atmosphere was dramatically undercut the following month, during a U.S. bilateral visit with the DPRK, by the revelations of the North's pursuit of a second uranium-based nuclear program in violation of standing agreements. In the end, Japan-DPRK relations were stuck in the same place and on the same issues since Kanemaru's visit a decade earlier, despite good reasons for both sides to reconcile.

MEGUMI'S ABDUCTION

On a chilly November evening in 1977, thirteen-year-old Yokota Megumi meandered her way home from badminton practice with a friend in Nii-gata in central Japan. The young Megumi, described by her mother as "confident," "wise," and "full of life,"[94] parted ways with her friend at a traffic light, just 250 meters (820 ft) or so from her house. Carrying her book bag and her badminton racket, she headed home to finish up her homework in time for dinner. But she would never make it, and this was the last time Megumi was ever seen, as if she had vanished into thin air.

But Megumi wasn't the only one to go missing in these years. Just two months earlier, fifty-two-year-old Kume Yutaka, a reclusive, lonely divorcée, a security guard, disappeared one night from the coastal city of Ushitsu, in Ishikawa prefecture, 300 kilometers (185 mi) northwest of Tokyo.[95] In September of the same year, twenty-nine-year-old seamstress Matsumoto Kyoko disappeared after leaving home at around eight P.M. to head to her knitting class in Yonago, a city in southern Japan.[96] Tanaka Minoru, a twenty-eight-year-old employee of a local diner in Kobe, vanished after heading to Europe in June of 1978. That same month, Taguchi Yakeo, a twenty-two-year-old bar hostess and single mother of two from Saitama, dropped her children off at a day care in Tokyo and was never seen again.[97] The following month, twenty-three-year-old Chimura Yasushi (known lovingly as "Ya-chan" by his father)[98] and his girlfriend of the same age, Hamamoto Fukie, went missing while they were on a romantic date in their hometown of Obama, a city just north of Kyoto. Their car was later found, still running, on an observation deck close to the beach.[99] On July 31, 1978, twenty-two-year-old beautician Okudo Yukiko and her twenty-year-old university student boyfriend Hasuike Kaoru went missing after meeting for a date on Kashiwazaki Central Beach to watch the summer festival fireworks.[100] The following month, a third couple, twenty-three-year-old Ichikawa Shuichi and his girlfriend, twenty-four-year-old Matsumoto Rumiko, disappeared after telling relatives they, too, were going to a beach in Fukushima, on the very southern tip of Japan, to watch the sunset.[101] That same month, a "quiet, patient, [and] sensitive" fifty-two-year-old mother Soga Miyoshi and her nineteen-year-old daughter Hitomi, an assistant nurse at a local hospital, left their home in the town of Mano in Niigata to go shopping and never returned, leaving behind her husband, Shigeru, and second daughter, Tomiko.[102] In May of 1980, two young Japanese men—Matsuki Kaoru, a twenty-six-year-old graduate student of the prestigious Kyoto University, and Ishioka Toru, a twenty-two-year-old recent veterinary medicine graduate—disappeared shortly after meeting during their stay in Spain.[103] The following month, a single, forty-three-year-old cook from Osaka, named Hara Tadaaki, was sent to Kagoshima for a "job interview" by his employer and never came back.[104] And in July of 1983, twenty-three-year-old Arimoto Keiko, described by her mother as "fragile," "very quiet," and as "a follower . . . never [taking] the initiative," disappeared during a working holiday in London. Her father recounts how he couldn't help but imagine that she had been abducted into the sex trade, or was "beaten up, blinded, and forced to do terrible things." "I didn't dare mention it," he adds, but "there were times when I had such thoughts."[105] These seventeen individuals—from the young, chipper Megumi to the reserved and impressionable Keiko—have since been identified by the government of Japan as having been abducted by the North Korean government.[106]

Koizumi got more than he bargained for with Kim Jong-il's 2002 apology and admission that the North had kidnapped thirteen Japanese nationals in the 1970s and 1980s. (The North continues to deny responsibility for the others Japan suspects it of having abducted.) The Japanese wanted a definitive statement from Kim Jong-il at the summit rather than the vague promises, like in the past, to "investigate" the cases. Kim subsequently not only admitted North Korean responsibility for these abductions but also revealed that a substantial number of them were dead, including Megumi. The parents of Megumi and the abductions movement groups, like the Association of Families of Victims Abducted by North Korea (Kazoku-Kai) and the National Association for the Rescue of Japanese Kidnapped by North Korea (Sukuu-Kai), refused to accept these findings. Conservatives in the National Legislative Diet led by Abe joined forces with this right-wing populist movement. The DPRK subsequently provided Megumi's remains, though the Japanese later claimed DNA testing showed this was a falsification. Nevertheless, the strategic calculus at the government-elite level was that a major hurdle had been cleared in normalization dialogue. The view on the street, however, was quite different. The domestic-political reaction was one of anger and despair at the deaths—rather than express satisfaction at Kim's confession, the public expressed disbelief that a country could admit to kidnapping and possibly killing Japanese nationals and then be potentially showered with billions of dollars in economic assistance (pursuant to normalization). In fairness to the Japanese government, news about the actual fate of the abductees, reportedly, was not released by the North Koreans until the immediate run-up to the Koizumi-Kim summit meetings, but the net assessment is that the domestic anger was significant. The numbers don't lie. Gaimusho (Ministry of Foreign Affairs) reported that polling found that nearly 74 percent of Japanese remained dissatisfied with Kim Jong-il's "apology," and only 7 percent believed that the summit reflected a genuine change in the character and intentions of the DPRK regime.

In addition to Kim's apology, Koizumi achieved the return of the remaining five living abductees to Japan in October 2002. Negotiators probably calculated that any public anger would be undercut by a wave of euphoria at the prime minister's success in bringing back the five individuals for visits with their long-lost families. While the scenes of reunions captured the attention of the entire nation, they only created more anger. The terms of their return were that the visits to Japan would be temporary, only for one week, and that all five were expected to return to their families in North Korea. As an assurance against mass defection, Tokyo and Pyongyang agreed to disallow the spouses and children of the five abductees from accompanying them. What seemed like a practical measure (because the abductions happened at such an early age, most grew up in the North and married North Korean spouses; their offspring had grown up in North Korea and knew no Japanese), led to a national outcry in Japan that the hated North Koreans were holding the family members as hostages in the DPRK in order to force all of the abductees to return. The government of Japan had no choice. They could not enrage the public by sending these five back as planned, and were compelled to keep them in Japan in violation of agreements with the North. This outcome was about the worst of both worlds. It left the DPRK angry at Japanese untrustworthiness. It further fueled the Japanese public's raw anger. And it left the five abductees worse off than before, now separated from their family members.

Undeterred, Koizumi engineered another summit with Kim, in May 2004, in which he won the release of the family members of the abductees. Among those granted exit from the DPRK was Charles Robert Jenkins, a U.S. army soldier who abandoned his unit during night patrols on the DMZ and defected to North Korea in 1965. Jenkins, apparently, did not want to be sent to Vietnam and defected to the North, hoping to seek asylum at a foreign embassy and eventually be returned to the United States. Instead, he spent some forty years in North Korea, teaching English and appearing in DPRK propaganda films. While in North Korea, he married Soga Hitomi, the young Japanese assistant nurse who was abducted in 1978 and who was allowed to return to Japan in 2002. Jenkins and his two daughters initially did not seek to be reunited with Soga in Japan in 2004, for fear that Jenkins, seventy-one years old, would be court-martialed for desertion. The Bush administration would not grant Soga's plea for a pardon for Jenkins. He initially left the DPRK with his daughters for Indonesia, which does not have an extradition treaty with the United States. The family was reunited there, after which he eventually went to Japan with his daughters and served a one-month sentence for desertion before being released. The family now lives in Soga's hometown in Niigata.

In the May 2004 summit with Kim Jong-il, Koizumi also pressed the DPRK leader to relinquish his nuclear programs, and offered $100 million in assistance and 250,000 tons of rice as a goodwill gesture. The Japanese prime minister believed he had achieved a breakthrough with the North's commitment to negotiate in earnest on its nuclear programs, and, perhaps hoping to play the role that Great Britain had played in back-channel negotiations with Libya,[107] he told Bush at the G8 summit in Sea Island, Georgia, the following month that the North Koreans were ready to deal. Koizumi's entreaties for diplomacy carried weight with Bush, more so than those by Kim Dae-jung, which led the president to approve an initial proposal at the June 2004 round of the Six-Party Talks, offering energy assistance and other benefits in return for DPRK steps on denuclearization. But relations again took a nosedive in December 2004, when DNA testing revealed that the DPRK had falsified the remains of the deceased abductees that had been returned to the Japanese. This, once again, enraged the Japanese public, after which Japan stopped all assistance to the North. Koizumi's successors Abe Shinzo and Aso Taro, both conservative Japanese politicians, made resolution of the abductions issue a precondition for reengaging with the DPRK. The DPRK retaliated by maintaining that the issue was resolved in 2002 and that it wanted Japan expelled from the Six-Party Talks. When no one agreed to this, the North Korean delegation refused to acknowledge the presence of the Japanese delegation at the talks. Pyongyang stated that Japan has no right to demand anything from it and that Tokyo must show sincere redress of the historical past, including colonial reparations. It continues to maintain that Japan is the sworn enemy of the North Korean people. It condemns Japanese remilitarization. And it attacks ROK president Lee Myung-bak for his Japanese affinities. (He was born in Japan.) Japan became one of the strongest advocates of Security Council sanctions against North Korea for its ballistic missile and nuclear tests in 2006 and 2009. When an agreement was reached in 2007 to start denuclearization in return for shipments of heavy fuel oil, Japan stipulated that it would not participate in the energy shipments without satisfactory resolution of the abductions issue, leaving four countries (United States, China, Russia, and the ROK), rather than five, in the deal. While trade by each country with others in the region has increased by leaps and bounds, trade between Japan and the North has dropped to all-time lows.

Meanwhile, in April 2006, President Bush's Oval Office meeting with the mother and brother of abducted Japanese teenager Yokota Megumi turned the abduction issue into an international human rights issue. Yokota Sakie, silver-haired and dressed in a pale pink suit, had become a nationally recognized figure in Japan in her quest to find out the truth about her daughter. Unlike other members of the abductions movement, who had fallen into untoward rivalry, Mrs. Yokota remained above the fray, and was aptly described as "saintly" in her disposition.

She quietly showed the president a framed picture of Megumi in her school uniform, and a photo album of Megumi and her family. The president leafed through the album, respectfully asking questions, and then lightened the mood by telling Mrs. Yokota that she and her husband were quite a dashing young couple in the 1970s, which spurred Mrs. Yokota to a rare smile. Just before the press was brought into the Oval Office for the president's statement, Mrs. Yokota started to put the framed picture and album back into her bag. The president stopped her, and asked her to leave the picture on the side table between them. He said that way, when the cameras take pictures, Megumi's image would be between the two of them, and she might somehow see that. It was a moving moment that had everyone in the room misty-eyed. The president did a press availability (when the White House press corp comes into the Oval Office for photos and questions) where he told the world that he had just had one of the most emotional meetings of his presidency. He explained, without notes, in detail, the circumstances of Megumi's kidnapping, and said that he wanted deeply for this mother to be able to hug her daughter again. The soapbox of the Oval Office is about the most powerful platform there is for making news. Instantly, the story of Megumi and the kidnappings by the DPRK, which, until then, were known mostly to Japanese and Asia experts, became household knowledge around the world. President Bush recounted the meeting countless times to world leaders at the G8 and U.N. General Assembly sessions. The G8 did a statement on abductions, offering its support for ongoing efforts toward "a comprehensive solution" to "unresolved humanitarian problems such as the abduction issue."[108] The abductions became one of the stated conditions for U.S. designation of the DPRK as a terrorist state.[109]

Some experts lament how the abductions issue took Japan-DPRK relations completely astray from the two nations' interests. Some blamed the ultraconservatives in Japan, who were able to ride a wave of public anger and exploit the abductions issue to promote conservative politicians and a more muscular Japanese defense policy. Yet even when watershed changes in Japanese domestic politics in 2009 unseated the LDP and put progressive governments in power under the DPJ's (Democratic Party of Japan) Hatoyama Yukio (2009–2010) and Kan Naoto (2010–2011), these did not precipitate any substantive changes in Japan-DPRK relations. Thus, summit diplomacy engineered by one of Japan's most dynamic prime ministers, the promise of billions in aid, constant coaxing by the United States, and politically progressive governments in Japan have been unsuccessful in inching toward reconciliation in this difficult relationship. Dialogue has been reduced to an elementary-school level, as conveyed by a State Department officer who recounted what her Japanese counterpart debriefed regarding a rare Japan-DPRK bilateral meeting at the Six-Party Talks:

The Japanese opened the meeting by asking for an explanation of the fate of the abductees who were not returned in 2002, including the fate of Yokota Megumi.

The North Koreans responded, "We told you already, she is dead."

The Japanese responded, "No, you claim she is dead but we think she is still alive."

North Koreans, "No, she is dead."

Japanese, "No, she is alive."

North Koreans, "No, she is dead. They are all dead."

The meeting ends.

This, unfortunately, will remain the state of Japan-DPRK dialogue until a resolution of the abductions issue can be found.

CHAPTER NINE

APPROACHING UNIFICATION

IT ALL STARTED WITH COWS.

In June 1998, Hyundai conglomerate founder Chŏng Chu-yŏng led a convoy of trucks across the Demilitarized Zone into North Korea. He was going home. The eighty-two-year-old Chŏng, a native of T'ongch'ŏn in northern Korea, brought with him five hundred head of cattle. He was repaying a long-held debt. The eldest of eight children, Chŏng left grade school to support his family. After working on a railroad and at construction sites as a young man, Chŏng was ready to leave home and seek his fortune elsewhere. He decided to walk to the capital city of Seoul a hundred miles (160 km) away. In order to make his way, Chŏng stole one cow from his father to support his needs. Soon after he reached his destination, the peninsula was divided and he could never return home. In Seoul, Chŏng worked at a rice mill, and in 1940 he opened an auto repair shop. When U.S. occupation forces came into Korea after World War II, Chŏng won construction contracts from the United States and from the Korean government, including the building of a 250-mile (400-km) highway between Seoul and Pusan, under budget and ahead of schedule, which the World Bank had previously declared an unfeasible project. Chŏng went on to build the world's largest shipyard at Ulsan, benefited from U.S. contracts in Vietnam and the Middle East, and grew Hyundai to seventy-nine companies totaling $80 billion in revenues. Now, as one of the richest men in Asia, the Hyundai magnate sought to settle his debt with his homeland. As the first civilian to traverse the DMZ, Chŏng opened a new era in inter-Korean relations.

These cows marked the start of an era of so-called Sunshine Policy on the Korean Peninsula. The brainchild of former political dissident and Nobel laureate Kim Dae-jung, the policy, in its purest form, lasted about one decade, from about 1998 to 2008, during the governments of Kim and Roh Moo-hyun. It earned its moniker, "Sunshine Policy," from Aesop's fable of the North Wind and the Sun. The Wind and the Sun debated which was more powerful and agreed to test their capabilities by stripping a wayfaring man of his clothes. The North Wind went first and blew as hard and as cold as it could on the old man, but this only caused the man to pull his coat tighter around his collar. The Sun went next and shone light and warmth on the old man. After a moment, the man relaxed and removed his clothes to bathe in a stream. The fable's message of persuasion over force was a metaphor for introducing to the South Korean public and the world a new way of dealing with the DPRK. It focused on engagement and cooperation, rather than containment, as the way to reduce Pyongyang's insecurity, to create moderation in its behavior, and, ultimately, to facilitate reform in the DPRK and the conditions for inter-Korean reconciliation. "The challenge," as then–foreign minister Hong Sun-yŏng put it at the time, "is to construct policies that protect the national security of the South against the North's belligerence while simultaneously coaxing the North to expand engagement with the outside world. This would expose the closed North Korean society to international 'sunshine' and promote internal reform."[1]

A great deal of controversy surrounds the Sunshine Policy. At one point, it captured the world's imagination and garnered praise as a way to end the Cold War on the peninsula. However, after North Korea's provocations and nuclear tests, it was harshly criticized by some as a terribly misdirected policy.[2] In retrospect, the policy had three traits. First, it was supposed to be transformational, not transactional. What this meant was that the Sunshine Policy sought to rewrite the entire terms of inter-Korean relations. It would be implemented not through a tit-for-tat negotiation (i.e., "you give me this, and I will give you that"), but through a wholesale change in South Korean policies toward the North that would create the conditions over time to change North Korean behavior permanently. In the interim, informed by this long-term objective and not by short-term expedience, Seoul would countenance a lack of reciprocity by the North, since decades of mistrust and animosity do not melt away immediately.

Second, the Sunshine Policy was informed by a spirit of magnanimity, not maliciousness. It was based in a deeply held view that North Korea was not an inherently "evil" country (after all, its people were still Korean), but that its errant path was an accident of history. Great power politics led to Korea's unfortunate division in 1945, even though Korea was not a combatant in the Pacific War, and this division ultimately created the North Korea we see today. North Korea's flaws, in this sense, represented the ultimate manifestation of Korea's victimization as the "shrimp caught between whales."

Finally, the Sunshine Policy was about generosity, not pedantry. It reflected a confidence that South Korea had won the postwar and Cold War competition that had started between the two regimes since 1948. Favoring Seoul, the economic gaps were now insurmountable, the quality of life was hardly comparable, and the futures so widely disparate between the brightness of the South and the grim future of the North. The well-known satellite photo of the Korean Peninsula at night, where the southern half is awash in lights, compared with the utter darkness in the north, constituted the ultimate illustration of this outcome. And for Sunshine Policy advocates, this picture meant that it was time for the winner to give rather than withhold.

And give they did. By one ROK government estimate, the DPRK benefited from a total of $3 billion from the South during the decade of the Sunshine Policy.[3] This far surpassed what the North is estimated to have received from China during the same period ($1.9 billion). The highlight of the Sunshine Policy was the June 2000 summit between Kim Dae-jung and Kim Jong-il in Pyongyang. But this event did not come without a price. The ROK put up about $500 million in order to secure the meeting. While this, ostensibly, was for the purchase of "business licenses" to start economic cooperation projects in the North, this fig leaf of a justification fell away when the DPRK—at the time, inexplicably—at the last minute delayed the scheduled summit meeting by one day, because the money had not yet been transferred to their bank accounts. This revelation, first broken as a news story by American journalist Don Kirk in January 2003, caused an uproar in South Korea and prompted claims that Kim "bought" a Nobel Prize.[4] A subsequent investigation by state prosecutors fingered, as the fall guy, Hyundai's Chŏng Mong-hŏn, the fifth son of

Chŏng Chu-yŏng. Chŏng was indicted in June 2003 for passing nearly $200 million of a state bank loan directly to the North. In August 2003, he committed suicide by jumping off the twelfth floor of the Hyundai building in downtown Seoul.

SUNSHINE TROPHIES

The majority of the Sunshine Policy money went to two endeavors that became the signature projects, the Kaesŏng Industrial Complex and the Hyundai Kumgang (Korean for "Diamond") Mountain tourism project. The Kaesŏng Industrial Complex is a joint North-South industrial park located on the outskirts of Kaesŏng, a city of about 300,000 near the border between the two Koreas (just a ten-minute drive from the DMZ). Over one hundred South Korean firms operate there, employing 47,000 North Korean workers in a marriage of ROK capital and technology and inexpensive North Korean labor. The complex produces mostly light-manufactured consumer goods, such as running shoes, watches, chopstick sets, and the like. The South Korean government and businesses from the South have invested about $26.9 million, but about $26 million of this has gone to the government directly rather than in form of wages to workers. North Korea selects all of the workers, about three-quarters of which are young women from the city of Kaesŏng, and their interaction with South Korean managers and foremen is kept to a bare minimum. After the steep "social insurance" and "cultural" fees, the workers take home about $45 a month to work forty-eight hours per week, and get three square meals a day, which, in the North, is a reward in itself. Since Kaesŏng is so well quarantined off from the rest of the North Korean economy, the leaders in Pyongyang are in favor of the project, because it allows them to think like capitalists at their convenience. The latest demand from Pyongyang (after detaining an ROK executive for over four months at Kaesŏng) is for a new fee structure in which they will charge land-use fees as well as hike monthly wages from the current $75 to about $300, effectively undermining the cost advantage of being in Kaesŏng.[5] In a *Wall Street Journal* op-ed, President Bush's envoy for North Korean human rights, Jay Lefkowitz, also raised questions about human rights issues associated with the complex, citing as highly problematic the fact that workers make a mere $2 per day.[6] Others have followed his lead, highlighting the fact that North Korean labor laws don't protect workers at Kaesŏng from exploitation, discrimination, sexual harassment, and child labor, and don't allow them to strike or bargain collectively.[7]

In fostering his Sunshine Policy, Kim Dae-jung relied primarily on two groups: the big Korean *chaebŏls* (conglomerates, such as Hyundai, Samsung, and LG), who would provide the money, and South Korean NGOs, who would provide the people to transform relations. The Kumgang Mountain tourism project is as clear a representation of this as any. The Kumgang Mountain tourism project is a special administrative region in North Korea that allowed visitors to take in the sights and scenery of Kumgang Mountain; perhaps the most famous peak on the Korean Peninsula and the subject of Korean art and poetry dating back thousands of years. Visits, it was thought at the time, would allow South Korean people to feel romantic about North Korea and about the Sunshine Policy without having to deal with political realities of the regime in the North. It would also give the leaders in Pyongyang a stake in inter-Korean reconciliation while ameliorating their fears of threats from the South.

Hyundai's Chŏng Chu-yŏng was instrumental in the establishment of Kumgang. In early 1989, Chŏng made a trip to the North and requested that Kim Il-sung allow South Korea to develop the area. As Chŏng saw it, the tourist venture would help heal the wounds of scores of South Koreans who, like himself, had been separated from their homes in the North, and would also earn the North Koreans a great deal of foreign currency. In 1991, Kim Il-sung met with Reverend Mun Sŏn-myŏng, the founder of the Unification Church, the worldwide religious movement best known for holding "mass weddings" in which he and his wife simultaneously marry thousands of couples. Also a native of the North, Mun made his own proposal to Kim: to turn Kumgang into a vacation resort. It just so happened, though, that Mun's request was at a time when remissions from Japan to North Korea were falling, and, feeling somewhat strapped for cash, Kim Il-sung said yes. From here, a feasibility study was undertaken and plans drawn up. But not all were in favor of the endeavor. The South Korean government was initially reluctant to let tourists go up north, just as the North Korean military were not necessarily happy about having South Korean tourists in their country. Furthermore, the Unification Church wasn't able to bankroll the project. And so, when Kim Dae-jung, with his Sunshine Policy, came to power, the moment was ripe for Hyundai to seize. And as an initial gesture of good faith, Chŏng delivered the five hundred cows to North Korea through the DMZ.

In November of 1998, the first group of 900 South Korean tourists made their way up to Kumgang. By the end of 2001, 400,000 South Koreans had made the trip. Initially, it was very popular, with many elderly southerners venturing to the complex to walk, once again, on their native soil from which they had so long been separated. It also became a popular honeymoon destination, with couples claiming that rather than Saipan or Guam, Kumgang was "a more meaningful way" to start their marriage.[8] And yet, it was still not financially viable. Hyundai was contractually obligated to field a minimum number of tourists, and many months it had to fork over substantial amounts of money. To try and attract more tourists and cut expenses, a road was built in 2002 so that tourists could take a bus across rather than the ferry boats they had taken thus far. The two sides also agreed to set up a rail link to the west, connecting with Seoul and easing travel to the resort. (In the end, the two sides never managed to link their railways.) The number of tourists peaked at 250,000 in the year 2000, and until its suspension in July 2008, 1.9 million South Koreans made the trip.[9] In 2002, the resort hosted the first-ever inter-Korean reunion of families separated by the war: tearful events that reunited long-lost brothers, sisters, cousins, and even lovers after fifty long years. But the project as a whole remained a financial black hole for Hyundai, which, in the end, invested $600 million in Kumgang Mountain and ran it at an operating loss of about $300 million. The resort was constantly underfunded and in need of government subsidies to keep its doors open.

In total, Hyundai's eight projects in North Korea, including Kaesŏng and Kumgang, have amounted to $1.5 billion in investment. And while the South Korean government and business have swallowed these losses, the North has ended up profiting handsomely. Kaesŏng is thought to annually generate up to $34 million in hard currency for the regime, and Kumgang has cost the South Korean government $76 million in aid alone since its inception.[10] Add these to the $150 million or so that Hyundai-Asan transferred to the North Korean government on a yearly basis, and the numbers begin to take on some significance.[11] In the end, though, it was politics rather than economics that brought the Kumgang tourism project screeching to a halt. In July of 2008, Pak Wang-ja, the fifty-three-year-old South Korean wife of a retired police officer and mother of one, had gotten up early during her stay in Kumgang to watch the sunrise from the beach. As she made her way to her chosen vantage point, she reportedly stumbled into a restricted area of the site. Witnesses claim that they then heard two shots ring out within a ten-second interval, one of which struck Park in the torso and the other in the buttocks, killing her in short order. According to an eyewitness, three soldiers then ran out of the woods nearby and kicked her body to check if she was dead.[12] This led to a political crisis, and the Lee Myung-bak government ordered the tours suspended until further notice. And not a South Korean soul has set their foot in the tourism complex since.

Kim Dae-jung's successor, Roh Moo-hyun, continued the Sunshine Policy under a different name (the Peace and Prosperity Policy). Roh maintained Kim's policy of engagement even in the face of unprecedented North Korean provocations, like the 2006 nuclear test, because he believed that the belligerence was driven by core insecurities and paranoia on the part of the DPRK regime. The hallmark of the Roh policy was the October 2–4, 2007, summit, also in Pyongyang. The DPRK received several major infrastructure projects in the North, including ROK financial commitments to enlarge the Kaesŏng Industrial Complex beyond the pilot phase, to build a railway connecting Kaesŏng to Sinŭiju up the length of the northern portion of the peninsula, to build a highway connecting Kaesŏng and Pyongyang, and to build a port complex at Namp'o. These financial commitments were made literally weeks before the end of Roh's presidency, and while some critics saw it as an attempt by the progressive government (and the DPRK, for that matter) to lock in the next ROK president, I believe Roh's intentions were genuine, not political. He believed in the Sunshine Policy as the best way to deal with North Korea, and believed the policy was in South Korean national interests. During his presidential campaign, he insisted that "for the existence and prosperity of the nation, the Sunshine Policy is absolutely necessary, and thus must be carried on."[13] The projects he committed to, therefore, would have invested far beyond the $3 billion already given to the North.

AVOIDING UNIFICATION

The Sunshine Policy gained the support of many Koreans and the world community. The June 2000 summit featured an embrace by the two leaders, which was, undeniably, a cathartic event for all Koreans. The summit produced a joint declaration that, among other things, said the two sides agreed "to resolve the question of reunification independently and through the joint efforts of the Korean people, who are the masters of the country."[14] The words in this document were not nearly as important as the transformative effect the summit had. Young South Koreans described Kim Jong-il as "cute" and "cuddly," rather than as an evil dictator. The day after the summit, the numbers of those who feared a North Korean invasion dropped from 40 percent to 10 percent. South Korean soldiers asked their superiors if the summit meant that North Korea was no longer their enemy. According to South Korean polling data from the time, the summit brought Kim Jong-il's popularity ratings from 15.1 percent up to 50.2 percent, and positive images of North Korea went from 11.4 percent to 46.5 percent.[15] The event captured the front page of international newspapers, and Kim Dae-jung was widely praised for a transformative policy that reduced tensions in the region and raised the prospects of a new era of peace and cooperation in East Asia.[16]

But there was a practical yet silent motivator for the Sunshine Policy. That was the fear of unification. By the time Kim Dae-jung came into office in 1998, the economic gaps between the DPRK and the ROK were inordinately wide, exponentially more so than the gaps between the two Germanies at unification. In 1989, when the unification of East and West Germany took place, the West's economy was about ten times the size of the East's—a substantial gap to be filled to bring the two economies together. In Korea, the comparable gap was by a factor of thirty-two.[17] The DPRK had just emerged from the worst food crisis in the history of the country, which left as many as one million dead. Refugees were trickling into China by the thousands in search of food, and Beijing grew worried this would turn into a flood. There was widespread concern that the regime might finally be at the end of its rope, eight years after economic abandonment by its Cold War patrons. Adding to the problem, the ROK was in the midst of the worst financial crisis in its postwar history. The country suffered a severe liquidity crisis as credit dried up after a string of debt defaults nearly bankrupted South Korea. In the first few days of the crisis, the Seoul Stock Exchange tanked, the value of the Korean won plummeted, and within months, Moody's dropped the ROK's long-term credit rating six whole positions (on a twenty-one-position scale).[18] The last thing that the government in Seoul could contemplate was the enormous financial task of unification. The dreaded outcome was what was known as a "hard landing," a sudden collapse of the DPRK, which would be thrust upon the South Koreans to clean up and which would cost on the order of hundreds of billions, even trillions, of dollars.[19]

The unwritten purpose of the Sunshine Policy was, therefore, to avoid a hard landing. It was to push off unification for as long as needed, possibly for generations. The policy assumed the DPRK recognized that the key to survival was reform, and that the Sunshine Policy would nurture and encourage positive change in this direction. Eventually, engagement would facilitate a "soft landing," a slow and controlled process of integrating the two Koreas, but on a timeline that extended decades or even a half-century, which rendered unification irrelevant for any near-term government. In this sense, the DPRK and the ROK agreed on one clear aspect of the Sunshine Policy: to avoid unification. Kim Dae-jung clearly stated so in his inaugural address in 1998, when he said his goal was peaceful coexistence with the North and explicitly pronounced that "the longer-term goal of unification can wait." In his Nobel Peace Prize acceptance speech, Kim reiterated this point, saying, "Unification, I believe, can wait until such a time when both sides feel comfortable enough in becoming one again, no matter how long it takes."[20] Thus, while the Sunshine Policy was lauded by the Nobel committee in Norway, it was creating a decade-long narrative for a generation of younger Koreans that unification was normatively a bad thing—too expensive, too dangerous, and too difficult. Therefore, avoid it.

UNIFICATION DISCOURSES

This was not always the case, of course. For decades, the dominant narrative on both sides of the Korean Peninsula was about achieving unification as the overarching goal of the Korean people. During the Cold War, this could only be achieved through the victory of one side over the other. For North Koreans, the discourse centered on liberating the Korean people from U.S. military occupation and from exploitation by a South Korean government that was a "puppet" of American imperialism. The phrase that came to epitomize the view in the South was *"pukch'in t'ongil,"* or *"songgong t'ongil,"* which meant "march north" or unification by force. This discourse privileged unification as the immediate goal, but with obvious differences in terms of who should predominate. Compromise was alien to the relationship. On the contrary, *"pukch'in t'ongil"* was the ultimate zero-sum game between the two Koreas. One side's gain, no matter how minor, was the other side's loss. The relationship was one of mutual hostility, with shootings and firefights a nearly daily occurrence along the DMZ in the 1960s and 1970s, killing in aggregate over nine hundred soldiers and civilians. The only channel of official dialogue was through the military armistice commission (MAC). The purpose of the MAC was purely armistice maintenance and armistice violations, and there was no channel for peace talks or inter-Korean engagement or reconciliation. Any other channel, if it existed, was deemed not only illegitimate but illegal.

The two Koreas were locked into what scholar Samuel S. Kim once famously referred to as the "politics of competitive delegitimation."[21] This mentality was evident in things like the Syngman Rhee government-initiated version of the "Hallstein Doctrine" (this policy lasted from about 1953 to 1973), which stipulated that the ROK refused to have diplomatic relations with any country that recognized the rival North Korean regime. So, when countries like Republic of Congo sought in 1963 to recognize both Koreas as legitimate, Seoul ejected the Congolese embassy and declared its diplomatic personnel persona non grata. This zero-sum mentality was also manifest in South Korea's infamous national security law. It was illegal to have contact with North Koreans, to listen to any North Korean radio or television broadcasts, or to possess any materials or information about the North. Indeed, any mention of engagement with the North was deemed treasonous, and grounds for torture and imprisonment. Likewise, it was evident in the two countries' competition within the Non-Aligned Movement. In 1975, the DPRK applied and became a member of the fairly peripheral and loosely organized movement. Not to be outdone, however, South Korea felt compelled to apply, even though there was a better-than-even chance it would be rejected from membership because of the stationing of U.S. troops on its soil. (It was, in fact, denied membership.) Even when it came to U.N. membership, the DPRK would not accept a dual-membership formula that would bring both countries into the international organization, because it could not stand that the ROK would be accorded legitimacy in the United Nations, even if it meant the DPRK would be accorded the same legitimacy as an independent nation-state. For Pyongyang, the only formula that was acceptable was a "one-Korea" formula, which meant only a unified Korea under its rule. For this reason, the two Koreas never achieved permanent membership from 1948 until September 17, 1990.

Even the periods of brief thaw in inter-Korean relations were not the result of an early belief in the Sunshine Policy but derived from cold balance of power calculations. The DPRK, for example, made numerous proposals for improved relations with the South. These included a 1950 peace conference proposal (ironically, on the eve of the Korean War), a 1957 five-point peace treaty proposal, a 1960 unification proposal, and a 1974 letter to the U.S. Congress proposing bilateral negotiations with the United States to replace the armistice with a peace treaty. All of these proposed the establishment of a Democratic Confederal Republic of Koryŏ, identified as one nation (presumably, with the DPRK in charge) but operating with two systems. Each of these proposals, however, was designed to achieve one objective, which was the removal of U.S. forces from the ROK, and indeed this troop withdrawal constituted the precondition for every proposal.

The most significant interaction between the two Koreas during the Cold War period were a series of secret negotiations between Kim Il-sung's brother Kim Yŏng-ju and the chief of South Korean intelligence, Yi Hu-rak, which led to the July 1972 North-South Joint Communiqué. Both Koreas were somewhat paranoid about the emerging détente among their great power patrons, commencing with Nixon's trip to China in February 1972. The North hinted at an interest in starting talks, and the South responded by proposing Red Cross talks, which were essentially covert official talks, because both Red Cross delegations were stocked with as many intelligence officials as there were Good Samaritans. Three months of Red Cross talks started in August 1971 and went nowhere until the decision was made to bump the dialogue to a higher and more secret level. Chŏng Hong-jin, a Red Cross delegate from the South who was also deputy director of international affairs at the KCIA, went as scheduled to a Red Cross meeting on neutral territory at Panmunjom in March 1972, and then exited the back door of the building on the North Korean side and was whisked undercover to Pyongyang for direct talks. This paved the way for the visit of KCIA director Yi Hu-rak to make a series of covert return trips.

Staying secretly in North Korea, alone, at the height of the Cold War was not a comforting experience for South Korea's chief spy. According to a wonderful account of the events by Donald Oberdorfer, Yi was awakened late on his second night in Pyongyang and rushed into a sedan. Not told where he was being taken by the two burly officials in the front seat, Yi sat helplessly as the car roared down dark and empty rainswept streets. Yi was certain he was being taken someplace to be tortured. Instead, he was taken to a villa to meet the Great Leader himself, Kim Il-sung.[22] The July 4 communiqué, signed by Yi Hu-rak and by Kim Il-sung's brother Kim Yŏng-ju enunciated three principles of agreement between the two Koreas. One, unification must be achieved through the independent efforts of the Koreans and without external interference. Two, unification must be achieved peacefully and not by force. Three, the two governments committed to seeking national unity as a homogeneous people that transcends politics and ideology. While the surprise agreement was widely heralded as an important breakthrough for peace on the peninsula, the motivations for Seoul and Pyongyang were less benign. Each suffered intense fears of abandonment as their superpower patrons—the United States, China, and the USSR—entered into a period of détente with one another, and therefore the two Koreas sought a temporary reprieve in their otherwise contentious bilateral relations.

Moreover, the zero-sum nature of inter-Korean relations became evident shortly thereafter. Kim Il-sung saw the 1972 communiqué as a victory in luring the South Koreans away from the United States with the first clause that committed both countries to disavowing external interference in peninsular matters. North Korean ambassador to East Germany, Yi Chang-su, reported to his interlocutors in Berlin that the Park regime had "capitulated to this peace offensive," and that this tactical move by the North was undercutting the alliance between Seoul and Washington.[23] Pyongyang also saw the communiqué as a coup because the appearance of a thaw in Korea caused several countries in the Western bloc to establish relations with the North, thereby undermining the South's Hallstein Doctrine. Of course, this was not the way Park Chung-hee spun the agreement. The ROK president saw it as a clever way to "tether" the DPRK threat.[24] He said that putting a hand on the enemy's back is the best way to feel when he will attack you.

It was no surprise, therefore, that the two sides could barely agree in subsequent working-level meetings on an agenda for discussion, let alone reach any agreements. And only two years after the North-South Joint Communiqué, the North tried to assassinate the South Korean president, killing the country's beloved first lady Yuk Yŏng-su with a bullet through her head.

About one decade later, another set of exchanges were prompted by heavy rains and landslides in South Korea, which left 190 people dead and over 200,000 homeless. Seeing even a natural calamity in the South as a zero-sum win for itself, Pyongyang offered ostentatiously to send relief supplies as a propaganda ploy. President Chun Doo-hwan unexpectedly accepted the assistance. The Red Cross used this as an opportunity to restart North-South talks, which spanned from September 1984 to September 1985, and these led to some small-scale family reunions. While this period is also seen as a thaw in relations, it, too, was deeply embedded in competition. Chun initiated secret talks with the North alongside the Red Cross negotiations. These were facilitated by a Korean-American professor, Channing Liem. Liem was formerly the South Korean delegate (observer) to the United Nations, who left his position after Park Chung-hee's 1961 military coup to become a professor at State University of New York at New Paltz, where he was quite critical publicly of Park's martial law. (Chun came to power in a military coup in the aftermath of Park's assassination in 1979.) Employed as Chun's unofficial emissary, Professor Liem met with Kim Il-sung. During this meeting, Kim raised the idea of a summit. Talks then moved into the KCIA channel, where some forty-two secret meetings took place between the two sides since May 1985, including a secret trip to Seoul by former North Korean foreign minister Ho Tam, but these meetings fell apart when the DPRK demanded the end to the annual U.S.-ROK "Team Spirit" military exercises. Moreover, when the DPRK's flood-relief contributions arrived, the ROK ridiculed the poor quality of the clothing, rice, and building supplies sent by the North. It afforded South Koreans unique insight at the time into how much better off they were doing than their counterparts, and thus proved embarrassing to Pyongyang.

With the end of the Cold War, the discourse on unification then evolved to one dominated by a fixation on absorption—that is, for the North, avoiding it, and for the South, achieving it. Beginning from the late 1980s, the success of South Korea's *Nordpolitik* created a new, unwelcome geostrategic situation for the North. While the Roh Tae-woo government talked about northern diplomacy as a way to break down Cold War barriers and economically engage with Communist bloc neighbors on the peninsula, regardless of conflicting political ideologies, it was still informed by a healthy dose of zero-sum thinking. By normalizing relations with Pyongyang's two key allies, China and the USSR, Seoul achieved the ultimate humiliation and isolation of its rival, especially since neither the United States nor Japan recognized the North. Seoul's northern diplomacy created real fears of encirclement in Pyongyang, which facilitated two of the most substantive agreements in North-South relations to date: the Basic Agreement on Reconciliation (1992) and the Joint Denuclearization Declaration (1992). The first document put forward a comprehensive framework for ending the state of hostilities and fostering political reconciliation. It established the North-South liaison office at Panmunjom to deal with reconciliation issues and the North-South Joint Military Commission to implement and ensure non-aggression. The agreement contained clauses for mutual recognition, cooperation, consultation, and dialogue, and against internal interference, defamation, sabotage, and aggression.[25] The second document committed the two countries to refraining from manufacturing, producing, receiving, possessing, storing, deploying, testing, or using nuclear weapons. It also committed the two to refraining from harboring facilities that reprocessed plutonium or enriched uranium.[26]

While idealists on both sides may have wanted these major agreements on political reconciliation and denuclearization to catapult Korea into the post–Cold War era, as in Europe, neither government had the will to follow through. For Pyongyang, the fears of encirclement as a result of Seoul's northern diplomacy were real, after the USSR's normalization with the ROK in 1990 and Moscow's unceremonious end to patron aid and trade with the DPRK. In this regard, it saw the Basic Agreement as a way to reestablish itself on an equal footing with Seoul and cement peaceful coexistence as the status quo. Moreover, the agreement provided for a necessary semblance of a reduction in tensions while Pyongyang covertly accelerated its efforts to build a clandestine nuclear weapons program. For the South, the agreement was the beginning of a strategy to absorb the North. The ROK was experiencing a decade of double-digit economic growth, while the North's economy was shrinking and its people were starving. It had just won world acclaim for hosting the largest summer Olympics in recent history. The Cold War competition between the two systems on the peninsula was over. Seoul emerged victorious and it was brimming with confidence. Kim Young-sam, the next president of South Korea, spoke openly about unification by absorption as the next logical step after the Basic Agreement. With German unification happening before their eyes, South Koreans sensed that their time was inevitable and soon.

South Koreans' euphoria over unification was short-lived. It was replaced by what one could call the "German trickle-down" effect. We hosted an event in 1997 at Georgetown University, bringing together officials from South Korea's unification ministry and German officials who had worked on unification. During the two days, the German officials explained many of the problems they encountered, ranging from currency union to unemployment. The South Korean officials were furiously scribbling down everything that was said, much more so than what would be necessary for a reporting cable. When we asked during the coffee break what they found so important, they excitedly said that the discussion was extremely interesting to them. My first thought was, "You mean, you have not studied all of these problems already?" We left with an uncomfortable feeling that the ROK government had not yet fully absorbed the lessons of German unification. Koreans subsequently became acutely aware of the difficulties and complexities of uniting the two countries economically, politically, and socially. They learned quickly that these difficulties would be exponentially more acute given the even wider socioeconomic gaps between the two Koreas compared with that of the two Germanies.

What's critically important when considering the integration of two economies is the size of the population of the integrating economy and its per capita GDP. Certainly there are a great many other important factors, such as its technological base, natural resource endowment, and economic infrastructure. But when dealing with an economy as underdeveloped as that of the North, when it comes down to it, what policymakers will want to know immediately is how many new mouths there will be to feed, and how much they will need to be fed. In the case of Germany, when the reunification of East and West took place in 1989, the West had a population about four times that of the East, the former sitting at 61.7 million and the latter at 16.4 million. Its gap in average individual wealth, while great, wasn't drastic, with the average Westerner making just under $21,000 per year and the average Easterner, just over $7,000.[27] Also, from the early 1970s, the two Germanies engaged in fairly extensive trade, with West Germany being the East's second-greatest trade partner (8 percent of total), behind the Soviet Union.[28] And through the 1970s and 1980s, virtually millions of East and West German individuals would travel back and forth across the border, with tens of thousands even being allowed to resettle from East to West.[29] Among those who weren't able to travel, a significant number were at least able to watch West German television programs, establishing a familiarity and comfort with daily life across the border.[30] Thus, with a quarter of the population, a third of its average wealth, and extensive trade, travel, and social ties, the impact of unification, while significant, was not immediately detrimental to the prosperous West. Yet the view from the Blue House in the early Sunshine years was entirely different. In the year 2000, North Korea's 22.9 million people were nearly half of the South's 47 million, with South Koreans, on average, being fifteen times more prosperous than their northern counterparts.[31] Further, since 1953, North Korea had been wholly isolated from the South, with no travel, trade, or social contact. Studies emerged that estimated the cost of unification to be extremely expensive. While the estimated figures ran the gamut, none of them looked particularly welcoming to the South Korean leaders. For instance, in 1992, a special report of the *Economist* magazine (the Economist Intelligence Unit) estimated it would cost $1.09 trillion to bring North Korea's per capita GDP to within 70 percent of that of the South. The following year, the Korean Development Institute (KDI) estimated a figure of $658.2 billion. In 1997, Marcus Noland cited a figure of up to $3.17 trillion to get the North Koreans to within 60 percent of their southern counterparts.[32] In spite of the great variation in estimates, there is no doubt that these types of figures were enough to keep the South Korean leadership up at night. More recent studies are similarly varied. A 2005 RAND Corporation study cites a range of $50 billion to $667 billion over five years.[33] In 2009, Credit Suisse estimated unification costs to amount to $1.5 trillion. And a 2010 expert survey by the Federation of Korean Industries came up with a cost of at least $3 trillion.[34]

Just as these lessons started to sink in, Korea was hit by the liquidity crisis of 1997–1998. These resource constraints bounded the view of unification. What had once been seen as possible was now seen as impossible. This did not mean that Koreans disavowed unification. But it did mean that they would like to push unification as far into the future as possible. By the end of Kim Young-sam's term in office, he talked more about promoting a "soft landing" in North Korea than his earlier calls for absorption. Kim Dae-jung, his successor, was able to frame his ideological inclinations on North Korea as a practical necessity when he advocated the Sunshine Policy as the right solution for dealing with the North in the midst of a financial crisis. Arguably, the Sunshine Policy would have engendered much more opposition if there had not been a financial meltdown, but opponents were cowed into submission given the country's crisis mentality at the time. Precisely because unification was considered too expensive and difficult, the best course of action was to seek engagement with the North, try to help reform their system, reduce the South's security burden, and eventually affect a "soft landing."

As discussed in the economics chapter, North Korea countered the Sunshine Policy with its own Moonshine Policy, exploiting the South's generosity while offering little in return. Pyongyang engaged in economic cooperation projects, like the Kumgang tourism complex and Kaesŏng industrial site, but only because these self-contained projects offered the regime hard currency without requiring a significant opening up of the system to outside influence. Moonshine particularly exploited the Sunshine Policy's implicit assumption that the nuclear programs of the North were not the main problem. The Sunshine Policy generally downplayed the nuclear threat, seeing it largely as symptomatic of a deeper problem the regime had with insecurity and lack of reform. The Sunshine Policy assumed that once this insecurity was rendered moot and reform took hold, the nuclear problem would take care of itself. The Moonshine Policy's solution to this was to have its cake and eat it, too: Pyongyang would accept all that the Sunshine Policy provided to encourage reform, and would shape it in a way that would be minimally invasive to the regime. At the same time, it would continue to pursue nuclear weapons. Who benefited more from this period? At the end of the Moonshine period, the North had more nuclear weapons than before, avoided a near-collapse of the regime, and received $3 billion in cash from the South. At the end of the Sunshine period, the South had given political legitimacy to a progressive view on North Korea (in the past, such views were considered not only illegitmate but treasonous by law), had created two economic cooperation projects with the North, and had earned one South Korean president a Nobel Peace Prize. You can do the math.

TODAY'S UNIFICATION?

The Blue House, the South Korean presidential mansion, sits on a beautiful, lush, green compound at the base of a mountain. It was walled off from sight during the authoritarian days, but the streets leading to the facility were opened to the public with democratization in 1987. Unlike the White House, which actually feels quite small when you enter it, the Blue House entrance foyer opens to a high-ceilinged, grand staircase that leads up to sitting rooms, where the ROK president entertains delegations. In April 2011, our party walked through the spacious entrance and took an immediate right down a long red-carpeted corridor to a receiving room. Obama's former national security adviser and former Marine Corps commandant General James Jones, Clinton's former deputy secretary of defense and CSIS president John Hamre, Bush's former deputy secretary of state Richard Armitage, Georgetown professor Mike Green, and myself chitchatted with the Blue House staff around a circular tea table until President Lee arrived. He invited us to join him and led us halfway down the same corridor to a European-style dining room, plushly appointed in white and gold, to sit for a more detailed discussion.

Over the course of more than one hour, we listened to the ROK president talk about his view of inter-Korean relations. He explained that his team had a different view than the Sunshine Policy. For the Lee government, engagement was right only if it was reciprocated by the North. This was a notable departure from the previous decade's policies of unconditional engagement. The ROK president pointed to the two main proposals his administration had put forward for inter-Korean cooperation. The first was the "Denuclearization and Opening 3,000 (DNO 3,000)" proposal, in which Lee promised to raise North Korean income per capita to $3,000 per year within ten years if the North agreed to abandon nuclear weapons and open to the world. The other was the "Grand Bargain" proposal announced at the U.N. General Assembly in New York in September 2009. Lee promised to make massive investments in North Korean infrastructure, to construct a peace regime on the peninsula, and to end the era of North-South strife if the DPRK committed to denuclearization and addressed human rights concerns. Prior to entering politics, Lee was a legend at Hyundai, starting out as office staff and eventually becoming head of Hyundai construction around the world. Trained as a businessman, Lee believed that if he was to invest South Korean taxpayer money into engagement, then there should be a measurable return on that investment. He said inter-Korean engagement would not be measured simply by the creation of a dialogue process. The only thing that Lee promised to give unconditionally to the North was humanitarian assistance for children and pregnant women. All other assistance would be pegged to human rights (the return of ROK prisoners of war, abductees, and captured fishermen) and to denuclearization. Lee rightly believed that the South should not be a supplicant in this relationship, as it appeared to have been during the previous decade of the Sunshine Policy, when the ROK was always looking to please the North.

I thought to myself that Lee's remark about changing the overall tone of relations was evident early on in the administration. In March 2008, in one of his first statements about inter-Korean relations, the ROK first unification minister, Kim Ha-jung, delineated the principle that the speed and scope of inter-Korean economic cooperation would be decided by progress on the denuclearization issue. The new policy essentially said that inter-Korean meetings for meetings' sake were not enough; there had to be results. This constituted the mirror image of the Sunshine Policy's proclamation that "The [Sunshine] policy's value, however, lies not only in the end result, but also in the process."[35] Similarly, when the Lee government was faced with the North's perennial annual food and fertilizer shortfall, and was asked what his government would do, he responded with a very simple principle that spoke a great deal to how much change was apparent. Lee agreed to make some assistance available (fifty thousand tons of corn) on the condition that the DPRK request the assistance. If Pyongyang did not request it, then Seoul would not give. This might seem like pedantry, but it sent a clear message to the North that the days of Seoul knocking on the door, offering, unsolicited, to give the North food and fertilizer, were now gone. On the occasion of Kim Dae-jung's funeral in August 2009, the DPRK requested to send a high-level delegation to pay respects to the architect of the Sunshine Policy. After some internal debate, Seoul agreed to invite the delegation, composed of six officials, led by Workers' Party Central Committee secretary Kim Ki-nam and intelligence chief Kim Yang-gŏn.[36] But after this delegation arrived in Seoul, it presumed that it would be met by the ROK president and by the unification minister, and treated with VIP status, as had been the case during the Sunshine Policy. The DPRK group was shown every diplomatic courtesy, but they were also told that the ROK president had many visiting former heads of state attending the funeral and that, protocol-wise, the DPRK delegation (which did not have a former head of state) would not be first on the list. This came as a bit of a shock to North

Koreans, who had grown accustomed to being treated as South Korea's most important guest, but was a harbinger of the new policy.

Because of these changes in tone and atmospherics, many painted Lee's administration as packed with ideological hard-liners who are dead-set against any dialogue with the North. This is incorrect. Although there were undeniably hard-liners in the government, Lee and his national security team's stinginess on aid and his overall tough position today had less to do with ideology and more to do with the series of provocative actions taken by the North in 2009 and 2010. Ballistic missiles tests, nuclear tests, a ship-sinking, and artillery shelling of Yeonpyeong Island would have made even the most liberal government in Seoul take a tough stance. On the contrary, Lee was a pragmatist who sought to change the terms of the relationship and remove South Korea from the position of supplicant. Ultimately, the key determinant of Seoul's policy toward Pyongyang during Lee's administration was the degree of reciprocity that the North demonstrated. If the DPRK showed even a little interest in cooperating on denuclearization or on human rights, the Lee government reciprocated with a more conciliatory tone.

Regarding a summit, President Lee said that he was not averse to having one with the North Korean leader, but that he operated on the principle that he was not going to pay the North for a meeting. In this sense, he borrowed from the Koizumi template when the Japanese premier refused to pay anything up front for a meeting with Kim, on the principle that a summit would be in both countries' interests, not just one. Lee's government held such a view, and indeed, two weeks after our meeting at the Blue House, President Lee met with German chancellor Angela Merkel in Germany and said he would invite the DPRK leader to the 2012 Nuclear Summit in Seoul, but only if he undertook denuclearization. (The North Koreans subsequently rejected the invitation.) The irony of this is that while Lee's standoffish attitude created considerable tension with the North and caused Pyongyang to eviscerate the South Korean leader in its propaganda, Lee Myung-bak arguably was the ROK president that Kim most wanted to establish contact with. Those who traveled with former president Roh Moo-hyun to North Korea in 2007 recalled that when they first met Kim Jong-il, the North Korean leader politely greeted the ROK president but spent most of his time chatting with and trying to charm the delegation of business leaders that Roh brought with him. In this sense, Pyongyang has little use for South Korean politicians, and really wants to utilize them as a conduit to South Korean CEOs, because they are the ones who would know how to make money for the regime. Hyundai executives, moreover, garner special treatment in the North, compared with other South Korean *chaebŏls*, or conglomerates. In a country where your hometown, or *"kohyang"* is all-important, Hyundai's founder Chŏng Chu-yŏng was originally from the North Korean town of T'ongch'ŏn. Hyundai also built both of the trophy enterprises of the Sunshine Policy–era, the Kaesŏng and Kumgang Mountain projects. At Kumgang, Hyundai built the port facility for the tourism complex in an astonishing six months, which won Kim Jong-il's trust. Rumor has it that Hyundai executives were one of the few people who have ever changed Kim Jong-il's mind on anything. The North Korean leader met extensively with the company to try to convince them to invest in Sinŭiju in the northwest of North Korea. Hyundai subsequently did a feasibility study that did not offer a positive assessment. After reading the study, Kim Jong-il was persuaded that the project was not commercially viable and recommended instead the idea of developing Kaesŏng. He reportedly complained that his own economic officials did not have as acute an understanding of business and economics. One would imagine that a summit with South Korea's first "CEO president," and former head of Hyundai construction, was something the North truly desired despite its rhetoric to the contrary.

At the end of our meeting with President Lee in the Blue House, he went on to say that until that point, the DPRK had rebuffed all of his proposals for cooperation. He cited the shooting of a South Korean tourist in the back at Kumgang Mountain, the torpedoing of the *Cheonan*, and the firing of artillery on a South Korean island. He believed these attacks were out of desperation, given the regime's terrible state. He believed the DPRK was on its last legs, and was losing legitimacy among its people. He talked about widespread discontent stemming from the increasing trickle of information that is seeping into the country. The more the North Korean people learned, the more the regime's leadership had no future. Time was on our side, he said, and little should be done to divert the regime from its ultimate fate. Though he did not say it openly, it was clear to all of us that the ROK president had an elegant but simple algorithm in his mind for solving the problem of North Korean nuclear weapons, human rights abuses, and conventional military provocations against the South: unification.

"THE END OF History" is a phrase made famous by Francis Fukuyama at the end of the Cold War. Then at Office of Policy Planning at the State Department, Fukuyama used this to describe the historical progression of mankind throughout history between the forces of tyranny and freedom.[37] This battle between Communism and democracy culminated in the twentieth century, with the collapse of the Soviet Union signaling the end of history's progression as mankind would evolve to liberal democracy as the final form of government.

On the Korean Peninsula, I think we are gradually approaching the end of history.[38] What is interesting today is that not only in the Blue House, but across the conference circuit in five-star hotels in Asia as well as in the corridors of power in government capitals, the once-taboo topic of unification is now discussed more openly than ever in the past decade of the Sunshine Policy.

Why the change? It is certainly not because the United States has a newfound lust for collapsing the regime in North Korea. The Obama administration spurned the perceived hard-line motives of neoconservatives in the George W. Bush administration. Even though Obama's policies—demanding irreversible denuclearization; applying financial sanctions; carrying out military exercises; and demanding a North Korean return to, and reaffirmation of, the denuclearization commitments of the Six-Party Talks—looked hardly different from those of the Bush administration, Obama's inclinations were clearly toward dialogue and extending an open hand to Pyongyang, when the time was right.

No, the primary reason for the increased talk about unification has to do with three developments, all related to North Korea more than to South Korea or the United States. The first is the death of Kim Jong-il. In spite of periodic reports from the Chinese that Kim's health was a non-issue and that he was fully recovered from his 2008 stroke, the massive heart attack that killed him in December 2011 came as a shock to the world. Everyone inside and outside of Pyongyang knew the Dear Leader was ailing, but most gave him at least another five years. The attempted succession to Kim's youngest son amounts to a dynastic power transition that is questionable even in the best of times, and certainly far more shaky than the one that put Kim in power in 1994. While Kim Jong-il had over twenty years to prepare to take over for Kim Il-sung, Kim Jong-un has had barely twenty months. Junior Kim has had virtually no previous experience running the country. He has no preestablished relationships with the generals in the military as his father had cultivated just after Kim Il-sung's death. The regents who surround the young Kim include his aunt (Kim Jong-il's younger sister). She is the only remaining blood relative directly linked to Kim Jong-il. Rumors have it that she, too, is quite ill. Her death would leave Kim Jong-un's uncle as the only other key elder, who has developed his own loyalties and power base within the North Korean system. We have seen such an arrangement at other times in Korean dynastic history. The outcome: the uncle tried to murder the son.

Second, there is more talk about Korean unification now than in the past because of a growing realization that some twenty-five years of U.S. negotiation with North Korea has not led to successful denuclearization. In the past, many would have contested this proposition, blaming Washington for the negotiation impasses as much as Pyongyang. But after Obama's outstretched hand was slapped away by the North's ballistic missile test in April 2009, and its second nuclear test the following month, very few blame the United States anymore. In short, there is a growing realization that true, verifiable denuclearization of the Korean Peninsula can only come with unification. This is not an argument against continuing diplomacy, as U.S. governments have done; it is merely a realization that diplomacy's aims, while remaining maximalist (full denuclearization), will really amount to a crisis-containment exercise that temporarily impedes their bomb-producing capabilities until the regime collapses of its own weight and the real denuclearization process begins.

The third reason there is more talk about unification today is because the new and future leadership in North Korea does not appear capable of regime-saving reform. The massive Workers' Party rallies in North Korea in 2009 provided the world's first real glimpse of Kim Jong-il's youngest son, the not-yet-thirty-year-old Kim Jong-un, who was first anointed the named successor to his father through his early promotions to the rank of a four-star general in the army and second-in-command of the party. As I noted earlier, in a country of hyper-isolation and xenophobia, the so-called Great Successor does have a relatively cosmopolitan upbringing. He was educated for a period of his life in Western Europe, and speaks some German and some English. DPRK propaganda praises him as a "brilliant genius," wise beyond his years, with "high-tech twenty-first-century knowledge."

But even if Kim Jong-un is enlightened, the likelihood of real reform is small, because of the ideology that accompanies his rise. Despotic regimes like North Korea cannot survive without ideology to justify their iron grip. And the new ideology, *neojuche* revivalism, constitutes a return to a conservative and hard-line *juche* (self-reliance) ideology of the 1950s and 1960s—harkening back to a day when the North was doing well relative to the now-richer and democratic South. *Neojuche* revivalism is laced with *sŏngun* (military-first) ideology, which features the North's emergence as a nuclear weapons state (Kim Jong-il's one accomplishment during his rule). This revivalist ideology leaves very little room for opening, because it blames the past decade of poor performance on "ideological pollution" stemming from experiments with reform. True reform in a post–Kim Jong-il era is impossible, because it would require the courage to loosen the very political instruments of control that allow the regime its iron grip on the people. This was perhaps the most important lesson of the end of the Cold War and the Arab Spring for North Korea. Even if Kim Jong-un were an enlightened leader who has the courage to attempt such reform, he would be dealing with a generation of institutions and people that are the most isolated in North Korean history. The generals, party officials, and bureaucrats of the Cold War era were far more worldly than those of the post–Cold War era. Kim Il-sung's generation was able to travel freely to Eastern bloc countries. Kim used to vacation with Erich Honecker and Nicolae Ceausescu. By contrast, Kim Jong-il's generation saw the Chinese Communist Party almost lose power in Tiananmen Square, and more recently watched Middle East dictators get removed, one by one, from office during the Arab Spring. Moreover, an incredibly successful South Korea sits right on the border, giving the North little room to make further mistakes. The generation of leadership the young son inherits sees nothing comforting about the outside world. *Neojuche* revivalism is untenable in the long term. Mass mobilization of workers without reform can only work with massive inputs of food, fuel, and equipment, which the Chinese will be increasingly relied upon to provide. Beijing seems content to backstop its Communist brethren for the time being, especially after Kim Jong-il's death. But donor fatigue will eventually set in. Beijing officials confide that the regime would last only through one calendar year without the Chinese lifeline.

This is why people are talking about unification today. If this sounds too pessimistic, just imagine the following scenario:

> Korea is free of nuclear weapons, ballistic missiles, and chemical stockpiles as its development-oriented leadership realizes that this is the price for integration into the Asian and world economic network.

> $6 billion light-water reactors jointly provided by the United States, Japan, Russia, ROK, and China are operating in northern Korea.

> Washington and Tokyo have official representation in Pyongyang with foreign service officers busily at work granting travel visas and escorting visiting congressional and Diet delegations.

> Seoul is providing conventional electricity across the DMZ to northern power grids.

> Russia is running gas lines to Japan and South Korea through northern Korea.

> The Four Powers have signed a peace treaty ending the Korean War.

> Japan is providing $10 billion in assistance for major public works projects in northern Korea, supported by international financial institutions.

Today, does anyone think that this scenario is possible without significant regime-change and/or unification?

A NEW PARADIGM?

What does this new and final phase of unification discourse amount to? I am not certain. It is evolving, and has not yet been fully enunciated by any politician or scholar. Kathy Stephens, the very popular former U.S. ambassador in Korea, once described it as a "mood" at a roundtable with CSIS experts. A former political officer at the embassy in Seoul in the 1980s, and before that a Peace Corps volunteer in Korea, Stephens said that the one thing that felt different during her ambassadorship was a newfound willingness to talk about unification when, for the past decade, people just could not be bothered with it. Some critics opine that the discussion of unification is simply a manifestation of conservative government's rule in South Korea after a decade of Sunshine Policy. But I believe it is more than that, and embraces several elements.

First, this new discourse is based in *pragmatism* more than ideology. As stated above, the embracing of unification does not stem from a desire to collapse the DPRK regime, but stems from a rational realization that after decades of unsuccessful negotiations, the only true solution to tangible problems like nuclear weapons, human rights abuses, and the conventional military threat is through unification. Moreover, there are pragmatic concerns about the potential instability of the leadership situation in Pyongyang. South Koreans have no control over developments inside the North; and yet they know Kim Jong-il's death in 2011 makes the future uncertain. So there is a sense of urgency that had not existed before Kim's death. The Sunshine Policy's challenge was to prevent regime collapse stemming from starvation and economic decay. Money and food can help in that regard. But the challenge today is that money and food could not keep Kim Jong-il from suffering a second fatal stroke. Thus, there emerges a pragmatic understanding that Koreans must be prepared. ROK president Lee crossed this threshold in 2010, when he declared in a Korean Independence Day speech (August 15) that Koreans must start thinking about a unification tax in order to be financially prepared for the inevitable day.

Second, this new discourse is not a return to the Cold War–era *pukch'in t'ongil* policies of zero-sum competition, but is more *internationalist,* transparent, and open in its nature. In the past, Korean views of unification were very parochial. Koreans never wanted to discuss unification with any other parties for fear of external intervention by other powers in determining Korea's fate. Koreans may have been locked in a death struggle with one another, but it was *their* death struggle, and no one else's. When I left the White House, I participated, in early 2008, in several closed roundtable discussions with current and former government officials and academics from the ROK, the United States, and Japan. The topic was potential instability in the North and how the three democratic allies should respond. Japanese foreign ministry officials, in particular, were concerned that there was not enough discussion and planning among the allies, let alone with China. I was astounded at how South Korean interlocutors, many of them old friends and American-trained Ph.D.s with very cosmopolitan worldviews, completely shut down when they sensed that others wanted to talk about Korean unification. They were visibly uncomfortable with the discussion. It was a Korean issue, after all, and others should not be treading on this sacred ground. But after Kim's stroke in August 2008, a dramatic change took place. The new view understood that while unification is for Korea, there is a pragmatic acknowledgment that Koreans will indeed need help from the outside world to effect a successful transition. Moreover, it was to Korea's benefit to begin dialogue as early as possible in order to "socialize" the globe into thinking about unification the way South Koreans thought about unification. Discussions on unification thus became much more open and transparent, without the insecurities and "mind your own business" attitudes of the past.

What do we mean by "socialize" the globe about Korean unification? ROK leaders want to discuss unification with the world, because they want the U.N. Security Council, the European Union, and other members of the international community to support Seoul's actions and vision when the fateful day comes. In this regard, reaching out to the world now to talk about unification constitutes an effort to explain South Korean preferences as the lead player in any multinational effort. This is a far cry from previous Korean attitudes about unification. This socialization process also extends to Korea's twentysomethings and younger. These young, smart, and affluent Koreans grew up under a decade of Sunshine Policy and therefore hold negative (if any) views on unification, which they have been taught for years to believe was too dangerous, dirty, and difficult. Now these youths are being encouraged to think, prepare, and talk about unification in a way that was discouraged during the Sunshine Policy years.

One of the more interesting ways in which this socialization process is taking place is through a series of international conferences hosted in Korea since 2010. International conferences in Seoul, a global city, are about a dime a dozen, but the recent ones have a clear albeit subtle agenda. Using money from the unification ministry that used to be spent on economic handouts to the North under the Sunshine Policy, these conferences have unification as their primary theme. Prominent individuals from around the world are invited to opine on the topic, including luminaries like Colin Powell and Condoleezza Rice. These individuals invariably talk about how the division of Korea is a historical aberration and that a free and unified Korea is inevitable and is something that the world will support. Sitting in the audience of these Davos-style meetings are the requisite press and corporate leaders, but a special effort is made by the organizers to reach out to hundreds of Korean university students and high school students, who apply online to be selected to attend. These become some of the hottest tickets in town (what student would not want to hear Colin Powell?), and the students listen to how the world supports Korean unification and sees it as a normative good. Moreover, they hear this positive message from foreigners who are not encumbered by the domestic baggage associated with the liberal-conservative divide in Korea whenever a Korean politician or scholar calls for unification. At one recent conference I participated in at the Shilla Hotel in downtown Seoul, the organizers created a large white board, called "Unification Board." On this board, participating students were invited to write their thoughts about unification in multicolored sticky notes. I skipped an afternoon session of the conference to read the hundreds of scribblings on the colorful board. Many stated that they had never really thought about unification, or that they had only viewed unification as a "bad" thing that their generation should not be encumbered with. But with this conference, they felt as though their eyes were opened to the possibility that unification would benefit Korea, not hinder it, and that it was their generation's responsibility to think about how to prepare for it. This was fascinating to me. A process of socialization was taking place, in which old views were being uprooted and replaced by new ones.

Third, the new unification discourse is about *ideas* more than it is about power. In other words, the Cold War–era's *pukch'in t'ongil* policies were about relative power and the achievement of unification through only one path: the victory of one side over the other by force. But the new view says that what will eventually bring unification is not the use of force but the power and prevalence of ideas. These ideas relate to freedom, democracy, individual opportunity, and entitlement to human dignity. Once these notions start to seep into North Korean society, the game is basically over. This was the view that resonated greatly with President Lee in our discussions. Never once did he mention military force or sanctions as a way to collapse the regime; instead, the most potent challenge to the regime's legitimacy came from the trickle of information getting into the North from the outside. There were many transmission belts for this information. Economic migrants who work in China illegally and return to the North bring news about the outside. Radio broadcastings by Voice of America and Radio Free Asia get picked up near the Chinese border. South Korean movies, videos, and music seep into the country on thumbdrives and through a proliferation of smuggled DVDs, CDs, and videocassette tapes. NGOs float balloons into the North with packages of Chinese *renminbi,* food, and newspaper stories about the Arab Spring. President Lee espoused a confidence that slowly North Koreans were learning about the outside world, which would awaken them to the illegitimacy of their leadership.

Finally, the new unification discourse is about *opportunity* more than it is about threats. The previous view saw unification as too expensive and dangerous. Unification was, therefore, a threat of several orders. Closest to home, it posed a threat to the lifestyles of affluent Koreans. In Japan and China, it posed the threat of tens of thousands of refugees flooding their borders. In the United States, it posed the threat of loose nuclear weapons and potential conflict with China. This all added up to instability that the region did not need. Most of all, the process of unification had too many uncertainties that made no one comfortable. The adage that the "devil you know is better than the devil you don't know" was persuasive to many. The predominant way of thinking was that the late Kim Jong-il and his nukes may have been bad, but a collapsing regime with no clear leadership and loose nuclear weapons would be worse. But the new view expounds unification as perhaps the greatest opportunity in the postwar era—for the world and for Koreans. It argues counter to the narrative that the status quo is satisfactory by drawing attention to the costs that Koreans have had to endure for half a century living under the threat of war on the peninsula, all of which would be recouped.

One aspect of these recouped losses is the famous "Korea discount." This refers to the amount by which investors, both foreign and domestic, undervalue Korean investments relative to other places to put their money. For example, Moody's credit rating for Korea is A2, which is below that of the United States and the United Kingdom. The forward price earnings ratio for Korea is 10.8, compared with Japan at 21.6 and the United States at 15.7. These ratings all manifest concerns about both long- and short-term risk associated not just with the economic situation in the South, but the overall political situation.[39] Most other investment destinations do not have on their border a technical state of war (i.e., no peace treaty and only a cease-fire armistice), and an unpredictable dictator with nuclear weapons. Attacks like the sinking of the *Cheonan* and the artillery shelling of Yeonpyeong Island only reaffirm to investors that political risk exists in Korea that does not exist elsewhere. Foreigners own about 40 percent of the shares on the Korean stock exchange, which can create untoward capital flight at the first sign of belligerence. When North Korea tested a nuclear weapon and ballistic missile in May 2009, the KOSPI dropped 6.3 percent. Similarly, but to a lesser extent, after the sinking of the *Cheonan*, the won depreciated against the dollar and the KOSPI dropped nearly 6 points, declining by nearly 0.4 percent.[40] And the morning after the Yeonpyeong shelling, the Korean stock exchange opened 2.33 percent lower than the previous day's close (though it quickly bounced back).[41] And when the DPRK does provoke, the first reaction by the South Korean government is to project messages of calmness and tension-reduction in order to keep investors from running scared.

The point is that all these costs, borne by the Korean economy for over fifty years, would no longer be relevant, and would become part of the benefits associated with unification. Moreover, the end of the North Korean nuclear and missile threat in the region would signal the end of the Cold War and create confidence in peace dividends for all. Properly prepared for, unification could become the biggest positive-sum game in Asia for all parties. It would reap positive dividends for the entire region. Properly prepared for, unification will also result in net productivity gains higher than the costs associated with knitting the two countries back together. As Nick Eberstadt points out, in the short term, unification could help relieve the South's labor shortage, reduce pressure on wages and production costs, and enhance Korea's international competitiveness. In the longer term, the rebuilding of North Korea's industrial base and infrastructure could bring a sustained construction and technological boom, lower production costs, increase productivity, and allow architects of the new, unified economy the opportunity to lay the foundations for sustained economic growth.[42] As he puts it, "[T]he modernization of the North Korean economy could offer enormous spillover benefits for southern Korea. Nor would the benefits be limited to Korean nationals. Success in that venture would strengthen the framework for prosperity throughout Northeast Asia and the Pacific."[43] This is a positive and proactive view of unification, not a defensive and negative view. The result is that unification is now an "in my lifetime" concept. It is no longer something that Koreans should push off for generations and deny Korea its destiny.

"IN MY LIFETIME"

The final discourse on unification that I describe above is not naive. It harbors no false expectations that unification somehow has become an easier task. I believe all Koreans understand how difficult the task will be. It is not likely to come gradually, as Sunshine Policy advocates wish. It is probably more likely to come suddenly. Koreans will meet this challenge. They will have substantial support and help from Korea's allies, including the United States.

But they will also need a little bit of luck. If one looks at Korean history, luck is not a trait that has been in abundance. Korea has been invaded over nine hundred times in its two-thousand-year history. It was colonized for half a century, and upon liberation from the Japanese occupation was abruptly sliced in half even though it was not an enemy combatant in the war. And yet Korea has done so well. But as Seoul National University professor Paek Chin-hyŏn once said, luck does not come to those who are unprepared. It only comes to those who are ready.

In this sense, I believe that the unification ministry's efforts to reach out to the world and to the younger generation of Koreans through a series of international conferences and other outreach tactics is an excellent way to prepare. Money that once went fully to the North as part of "engagement" is now being put to use educating younger Koreans and socializing the world to how South Koreans see unification. President Lee's upholding of a unification tax was a watershed moment, essentially telling his country to be prepared. At CSIS, we have engaged in a project focused on the longer-term task associated with unification—how to reenergize North Korea's power sector; how to reconstruct its health system; how to manage the social security burden; how to reform education in the North; how to handle transitional justice. These are just a small sampling of the tasks ahead for this Herculean effort.

Finally, I believe that the new discourse on unification extends beyond the peninsula. Increasingly, countries are reaching the conclusion that the only real solution to the Korean question is unification. Japan, for example, long thought to be opposed to unification, views the costs of the status quo, with nuclear tests and ballistic missiles pointed at them from the North, as unacceptably high. Japanese officials, in fact, have been magnanimous in urging their U.S. and South Korean colleagues to have more serious discussions about unification contingencies, not even asking to participate in this, due to ROK sensitivities. While Russia supports North Korea, it also grows increasingly concerned that the nuclear program they once helped to create is now out of control. The United States has already stated in its June 2009 communiqué with the ROK that America aspires to see a Korea free and at peace.[44]

The one party that may not share this view is China. While, after the first and second nuclear tests, China has seen vigorous internal debate about where its interests lie on the peninsula, Beijing does not appear to be in favor of active discussions with any party about how to prepare for sudden change on the peninsula. Beijing's actions after the sinking of the *Cheonan* by a DPRK torpedo fell far short of their aspirations to be a responsible stakeholder and leader in East Asia. Deterring North Korea from undertaking other actions threatening to freedom of navigation in East Asian waters is a public good that China was uniquely positioned to provide. Such actions would have won it great praise and respect in the region. Yet, unfortunately, as outlined in chapter 8, China has clung thus far to an anachronistic view of the peninsula. While others saw Kim's death in 2011 as a moment for potential change, China saw it as a calling to promote continuity and a secure dynastic succession. One hopes that with greater dialogue among the United States, the ROK, and China, Beijing's party stalwarts will not view a united Korea as a geostrategic risk.

ROLLING UP THE SLEEVES

When the day comes, the actual tasks of unification will be daunting. Two scenarios are generally put forth for Korean unification: "gradual" and "sudden"—or otherwise referred to as a "soft landing" or "hard landing." It is difficult to assess which of these two possibilities is more likely. The dire condition of the North Korean economy and its people tends to point to the latter, but this is something that has been predicted, debated, and discussed since at least 1991, so there seems to be no reason to hold our breaths any longer. The preference of South Korea, the United States, and all other regional states would certainly be the former, but this is in no way a foregone conclusion, either. In reality, it will likely fall somewhere in between: not so hard as to cause mass calamity on the peninsula and in the region, but not so soft as to make reunifying Korea and rebuilding the North a simple, straightforward task. But whichever scenario plays out in the end, there are a number of policy priorities, which the government in Seoul will have to tackle, and potential problems, which it and its regional partners will have to face. This is something my USC colleague David Kang and I have recently been looking at with our Korea Project.[45] Although much work has been done both in the academic and policy worlds on military contingency planning for a North Korean collapse, far less work has focused on the longer-term but inevitable tasks of knitting the two nations together into one. And so, over the course of three years, we are gathering together North Korea experts and specialists of other regions and other functional areas to try and draw out lessons from other cases that may be applicable to unifying the Korean Peninsula. And thus far, even at this early stage in the project, we have come to some interesting conclusions.

The first and foremost challenge will be taking care of the shorter-term, immediate needs of the North Korean people. The closer to a hard landing the unification scenario is, the more important this particular challenge will prove to be. It has been estimated that the initial emergency relief costs—of food, medical care, daily necessities, and, in some cases, shelter—will at the very least total some $250 million per month and could reach as much as $1.25 billion.[46] The effectiveness with which this initial relief effort is carried out is crucial in winning the hearts and minds of what will likely be a shaken and bewildered northern Korean populace. This initial, large-scale humanitarian relief effort, targeted at the neediest—children, pregnant and lactating mothers, the elderly, and orphans—will be an important first step in gaining legitimacy in the eyes of the North Korean people and potentially quelling any large-scale rebellion, unrest, and mass migration. But there are limits to how much attention should be focused on immediate, short-term needs, for every day devoted to, and dollar spent on, providing immediate humanitarian relief is one that is unavailable for longer-term rebuilding of the northern economy and society. The key lesson for the Korean case, therefore, is to try to determine as early as possible in the process how and when to make the transition from handouts to the North Korean people to deeper investment in long-term restructuring. And the challenges there will be no less great than those of the immediate needs on the ground.

One crucial prerequisite for the successful unification of the Korean Peninsula will be the reconstitution of North Korea's infrastructure. And here, transportation will be a priority. Despite being 20 percent larger,[47] North Korea has less than a quarter of the total roadways of South Korea, and when paved roads alone are compared, North Korea actually has less than 1 percent (724 km/450 mi) of the South's total length (80,642 km/50,100 mi).[48] Furthermore, North Korea has just 37 airports with paved runways, as compared to the South's 72, and has 158 merchant marine vessels whereas South Korea has 819.[49] North Korea's seven major ports—Ch'ŏngjin, Haeju, Hŭngnam, Namp'o, Songrim, Sŏnbong, and Wŏnsan—too, will need refurbishment as they have greatly fallen into disrepair in recent years. One area where the North does have somewhat of a comparative advantage is in rail, with 5,242 kilometers (3,257 mi) of total length compared to 3,381 kilometers (2,100 mi) in the South.[50] But the North's system is highly inefficient, and, for the most part, has not been modernized since the Japanese occupation, and therefore its reconstruction will be another priority. An extensive road and rail network connecting North and South, and the necessary shipping and air infrastructure needed for northern Korea to connect to the global economy, will be critical in the longer-term strength of a unified Korean economy. Another infrastructural priority will be building up North Korea's pitiful communications network. Its sixty-year, self-imposed isolation has made it truly unmatched in this regard. For instance, in South Korea, when landlines and mobile phones are taken together, there are about 1.4 phones for each of the country's 48.8 million people. In North Korea, by contrast, there are a mere 1.6 million phones for its population of 24.5 million—that's just one phone for every fifteen people.[51] Furthermore, North Korea's near-complete absence of the Internet will need to be addressed. As a whole, South Korea currently has nearly 300,000 Internet hosts within its territory. In the North, this number is only 3, and only a handful of people have experience or exposure to the Internet, with the majority being only allowed to access a North Korean "Intranet." Enabling the northern half of the peninsula to connect to the South and to our increasingly interconnected world will be a key concern in the reconstruction of the country.

A third crucial infrastructural priority will be addressing power and energy. Currently, South Korea's electricity output capacity (417 billion kilowatt hours [kWh]) is nearly 19 times greater than that of the North (22.5 billion kWh), and this will greatly constrain northern growth. South Korea also consumes 137 times more oil on a daily basis (2.185 million barrels per day [bbl/day]) than does its northern neighbor (16,000 bbl/day), and has 20 times more length in oil and gas pipelines in its territory.[52] Substantial resources will, therefore, be needed in building up the North's infrastructure in the areas of transportation, communication, and energy.

A second area of concern will be population control. With the collapse of the North Korean state and the erosion of strict border control will come tremendous migration pressures. Years ago, it was estimated that the numbers of northerners heading south could number as many as 7 million—nearly one-third of the population.[53] Today, 2 million seems a more likely figure, but a substantial one no less. The immense labor redundancy in the North will put pressure on the border southbound, as northerners migrate in search of opportunity. We also shouldn't discount the destabilizing effects of southerners pressing northward for lands occupied by northerners, based on genealogical claims. Therefore, as unappetizing as it may sound, there would likely have to be immigration-type checkpoints for north-south travel, and perhaps a visa system akin to what Hong Kong and China currently have in place. In the North, the groups hardest hit would likely be the military and the chemical and steel industries. North Korea currently has a standing military of 1.2 million, the fourth-largest in the world.[54] With the loss of the military's raison d'être, its southern rival, much of the northern military will no longer be necessary. And they can't simply be incorporated into the armed forces of the South, itself numbering 655,000 (for a potential combined total of 1.85 million), for such a large military would hardly be necessary nor sustainable in the absence of a North Korean threat.[55] But recent demographic research carried out by Dr. Elizabeth Stephen at Georgetown finds that the ROK military will likely face a shortfall of as much as 200,000 in its projected military force level, due to declining birth rates and the aging South Korean population. Therefore, it is possible that at least some of the North's military could be incorporated into that of a unified Korean state.

Another reason for hanging on to as much of the North's military as possible is the lessons learned in Iraq. In 2003, the Coalition Provisional Authority in the country instituted a policy of "de-Ba'athification," an effort to root out the old elements of Saddam's Ba'ath Party from the Iraqi state. And yet, while it was well-meaning in its intent, the policy dissolved Iraq's 500,000-member military. And the result was half a million of armed, angry, unemployed, and increasingly disillusioned young Iraqi men, contributing, at least in part, to the multiyear, bloody civil war, which has taken hundreds of thousands of lives and simmers on to this day. And so, a quick incorporation of North Korea's military and its likely-to-be-defunct steel and chemical industries into the working force of a unified Korea will be a high priority for stabilization. One possibility for a great many of these individuals may be in the reconstruction of North Korean infrastructure outlined above. History (including that of the United States) has shown that large-scale public works projects are almost a requirement for dealing with unemployment and social security problems in transitional societies, and northern Korea would likely not be an exception to this rule.

But the majority of the northern populace won't be able to be simply and easily incorporated into a unified Korean society and government. Massive educational reform and retraining will be needed to make this transition happen. In spite of the fact that North Korea currently claims a 99 percent literacy rate and enrollment ratios of 96 percent for primary and secondary schooling (notably, 1 percent greater than the South's 95), the content and quality of North Korean education is suspect. Comparatively, when East and West Germany reunified, some 80 percent of easterners had to undergo retraining to be able to function competitively in the unified German economy,[56] and, as noted earlier, the gaps between East and West were not nearly as great as those of the two Koreas. Much like the education system, the health sector of northern Korea will have to be basically rebuilt from the ground up as well. Past cases of broken state-run health systems in Africa and Asia have shown that key priorities in reconstitution are targeted revitalization of hospitals and clinics, upgrading of skilled health-care professionals, detailed surveys of existing health assets, and costing exercises with concrete targets for training. Therefore, the unified Korean government will, at least for a time, have to deal with a greatly stressed social services system, providing high levels of educational, unemployment, and health-care subsidies, and will have to watch out for potential social disorder such as increased rates of alcoholism, drug addiction, gambling, or crime.

A third potentially problematic issue will be the monetary union of North and South. While unification will almost certainly bring a unified economy monetized by the South Korean won, the unified Korean government will need to avoid some of the dislocating effects of the German experience of monetary union. On unification, Germany decided to convert East German marks at parity with those of the West, producing an artificial increase in East German incomes and leading to high inflation rates and about 40 percent unemployment in the initial transitional stages.[57] The monetary union will, therefore, need to occur in a way that accomplishes multiple, competing objectives simultaneously. The exchange rate must be set so as to avoid the inflation and unemployment of the German experience. Yet it must also be close enough to parity to allow northerners sufficient wealth to forestall a massive influx to the south. And yet the northern Korean won must additionally be kept low enough so that northern wages are still competitively low to attract foreign investment and to take advantage of the combination of southern capital and technology and abundant, low-cost northern labor. This will most certainly be a hotly debated issue in a unified Korean government and will require policymakers to strike multiple, simultaneous fine balances between competing interests.

A final set of issues have to do with the social aspects of unifying the Korean Peninsula. One problem is that of transitional justice. How should a unified Korean government deal with the elites from the former North Korean regime? Should there be international tribunals, such as for the former Yugoslavia, or truth and reconciliation commissions, as were undertaken in South Africa at the end of apartheid? And how many of the former ruling elite should be tried and persecuted and how many should be given a "golden parachute"? As controversial as it may seem, past cases show that stabilization requires consensus, and therefore that stakeholders and preexisting elements of the former regime will need to be included. One of the recommendations of the ongoing Korea Project is that transitional justice might be administered to top political figures, but might grant amnesty to lower-level workers in exchange for information. For example, the political head of the nuclear program might be put on trial, but the scientists would be granted immunity in return for information on the location and disposition of the facilities and weapons. Similarly, the political head of the gulags might be tried, but the guards might not, in order to gain maximum information about the situation on the ground. These issues could prove to be explosive in the context of a unified Korea.

A second social hurdle will be the problem of large-scale, inter-

Korean, regional political divisions. While most Koreans will welcome the marriage of northern labor and southern capital as beneficial to the united Korean economy as a whole, South Korean labor groups may be less enthusiastic. The downward pressure on South Korean wages that results from the incorporation with the North could cause the working class in South Korea to look north with contempt. The wider southern population, too, while initially welcoming unification, may grow increasingly resentful at the costs they must bear in the form of taxes and social welfare burdens to assimilate the North. And in spite of Korea's vibrant nationalism, the more educated and affluent southerners could even come to hold superiority complexes over their northern brethren. And the northerners, in turn, may see their southern counterparts as immoral, materialistic, money-crazed, and radically individualistic. The democratically elected politicians who will be tasked with bridging these divisions and catering to their various interests will certainly have their hands full.

The third and perhaps most important and deep-seated social obstacle to overcome has to do with the North Korean people themselves. North Korea is *the* most isolated country on earth, and has been for most of the past six decades. When unification happens, the northerners will undoubtedly face a period of psychological dislocation as decades of indoctrination and brainwashing under the Great Leader lose all meaning. Many of the 21,000 North Koreans residing in the South are living proof of this. The latest figures show that the middle and high school dropout rates are six times higher among North Koreans than for the South Korean population as a whole. The unemployment rate among North Koreans in the South (14 percent) is four times higher than the South Korean national average, and their monthly wages ($1,134) are less than half of wages among average Seoulites.[58] But the unemployment rate only includes those actively seeking employment, and an even more disheartening figure is that just 41.9 percent are "employed."[59] Nearly one-third of North Korean defectors continue to identify themselves as "North Korean" as opposed to "Korean" or "South Korean," even after years of living in the South. Because of these integration challenges, the suicide rate among North Korean defectors is over 16 percent; nearly three times that of the South Korean populace.[60]

In the end, the challenges of unification are great. Some would say they are insurmountable. But pessimism of that nature truly underestimates the determination and sheer grit of the Korean people. This is a country that has thrived on adversity and turned challenge into opportunity time and time again. Undeniably, the Koreans will need help with this project from allies like the United States, and from Japan and others, and they will need to approach the unification project with an unswerving determination to succeed. And I believe they will.

CHAPTER TEN

THE END IS NEAR

DINNER AT THE 21 CLUB IN MANHATTAN IS AN EXPERIENCE. HOWEVER, IT IS EVEN more extraordinary when it is with the North Koreans. We pulled up to the New York City landmark on East 52nd Street for dinner after an afternoon of quiet bilateral talks with the visiting North Korean delegation under the auspices of the National Committee on American Foreign Policy (NCAFP). Donald Zagoria, a good friend and a professor at Hunter College, who wrote the seminal book on the Sino-Soviet split, ran these NCAFP track II dialogues, which brought together scholars and practitioners to discuss U.S.–East Asia relations, but in this instance, in April 2005, also provided an unofficial venue in which we could talk with the DPRK about how to put negotiations back on track.[1] Pyongyang had boycotted the Six-Party Talks since June 2004, claiming that then–secretary of state Condoleezza Rice's designation of it as an "outpost of tyranny" in her Senate confirmation testimony confirmed U.S. hostile intent in the second term of the Bush administration. Our team—Joe DeTrani, then–special envoy for North Korea and a former experienced CIA veteran, and Jim Foster, director of the State Department's Korea Office, was to use the NCAFP meeting as an opportunity to chart a path back to the Six-Party Talks. During the lunch break, we retired to an adjacent room from the conference. It was the first direct talks between the two sides after Bush's reelection. The North Koreans complained about Rice's statement and demanded an apology. We said that we could not give one. They maintained that without an apology, there was no chance of negotiations. They then asked what the secretary meant by her "outpost of tyranny" statement. I responded, "What do you think she meant?" This repartee continued throughout the two-hour meeting until we said that the DPRK delegation would not have been given visas by our State Department and would not be in New York if the Bush administration were not serious about negotiations. They then asked, almost rhetorically, "Can we take Rice's remarks to be her own opinion?" DeTrani, a Brooklyn Italian, responded that remarks given by an administration official in testimony to the U.S. Senate represented official policy, but that they could interpret them however the hell they wanted, as far as he was concerned. At that point, as if on cue, the new assistant secretary of state, Chris Hill, called DeTrani on his cell phone to ask how things were going. DeTrani handed the phone over to the North Korean delegate, who was visibly pleased at Hill's expressed commitment to restarting negotiations on denuclearization.

We retired for the dinner that evening, at which Zagoria brought together some foreign policy luminaries, including a former world-famous secretary of state, to try to convince the North that nuclear weapons were not the right path. The Japanese and Korean press, having gotten wind of "official" U.S.-DPRK talks taking place in New York, swarmed the 21 Club entrance like paparazzi after Lady Gaga. As we disembarked our cab on the rainy street, we were accosted by a phalanx of reporters creating a scene of flashing cameras and car horns blaring as curious passersby wondered who these unrecognizable gentlemen might be. We fought our way through the press scrum down the wet steps of the New York brownstone into the club, where we were escorted to a VIP room. There, the North Koreans sat opposite a dining table's worth of Who's Who of U.S. foreign policy stars who had worked on issues ranging from Ireland to China. The DPRK delegation was clearly pleased at the audience they were given and treatment befitting Wall Street CEOs. After the afternoon's hopeful negotiations put things back on track, I found myself suddenly despondent, not over the food or company, but over the entire evening's scene. I looked at our surroundings in this elite New York City establishment, paparazzi standing in the rain outside, and thought to myself, "Would the North Koreans ever see the inside of the 21 Club if they did not have nuclear weapons? Would they be sharing toasts with these icons of U.S. foreign policy if they were just from a poor country without nukes? Jeez, why would they ever give up their nuclear weapons?"

*   *   *

HOW DID WE get to this point? Why have the North Koreans been able to get away with the international relations equivalent of murder? Studying North Korea's odyssey as both a policymaker in the U.S. government and academic, I find myself still marveling at how this state has managed to survive. Despite making all of the wrong economic decisions throughout its history, the country eked out an existence. Despite propagating an ideology that provides luxury to the Kim family and very little to the rest of the population, the people, even defectors, retain affection for the dynasty. Despite engaging in the most threatening behavior in East Asia, including military attacks and building nuclear weapons, the regime has yet to suffer punishment in the form of retaliation or a preemptive strike. In each case, the regime has survived, though not through extraordinarily shrewd statecraft or policymaking. On the contrary, historians will remember North Korea for all the ways *not* to run a country. But it has survived through extraordinary circumstances of history and geopolitics. Fate gave North Korea a border with China, and this border has, over the years, compelled Beijing to backstop the regime to keep its northeast flank stable. This border has also prevented other powers, like the United States and South Korea, from seriously contemplating military punishment of the regime to liberate its people. The last time the United States tried this in 1950, it led to a wider war with China, which no one wants today. Kim Il-sung's sudden death in July 1994 and Kim Jong-il's death in December 2011 did not provide opportunities to overthrow the system at a vulnerable moment, because the norms of sovereignty just don't allow outsiders to do this. (The notable and controversial exception of Iraq proves the norm's validity.) Finally, the world has watched North Korea slowly build a ballistic missile and nuclear weapons program over the past twenty-five years in no small part because the world can't be bothered with North Korea. The weapons are undeniably dangerous to the United States and its allies, but ultimately, an Israeli-type attack—whether in 1981 in Iraq or in 2007 in Al-Kibar, Syria—is not likely in North Korea because the issue simply does not rank highly enough in terms of U.S. priorities. It is sad to say, but for the American people (and, therefore, the U.S. government), the North Korea issue is not like the Middle East or Afghanistan. It requires attention but not of the highest order like rooting out Al Qaeda's leaders or tending to the Arab-Israeli conflict. Thus, when North Korea threatens, the pat response is to "park" the issue: avoid a military conflagration (because it is just not worth fighting over) by diverting attention to other important issues, and put it back on a negotiation track to prevent another crisis. This "relative crisis indifference" syndrome in Washington has saved North Korea countless times and given it benefits through negotiation rather than punishment for its misdeeds. North Korea's survival is not due to its exceptionally skilled government. A concatenation of forces—sovereignty (protection from external intervention), a border with China, and relative U.S. indifference—has made North Korea's survival an accident of history. It is, truly, the impossible nation-state.

NORTH KOREA'S ARAB SPRING?

For how long can this continue? As I stated at the outset of this book, not for very much longer. I believe the next U.S. president (and South Korean president) will have to deal with a major crisis of the state in North Korea, and potentially unification, before he or she leaves office. Just as a confluence of circumstances has enabled the regime to survive against all odds, a new and unique constellation of forces—Kim Jong-il's death, his young son's inexperience, the society's growing marketization, and cracks in the information vacuum—is emerging that bodes ill for the regime. Skeptics would disparage such an assessment. In May 2010, I participated in a conference (unclassified) hosted by the intelligence community, focused on this very question, and longtime analysts of North Korea predicted no change to the DPRK's stability. They pointed to past history as their evidence. North Korea was abandoned by its patrons at the end of the Cold War, suffered a famine, and then saw its leader Kim Il-sung's death, and yet the regime remained intact. Control today in Pyongyang remains intact, it was argued, and regime succession to Kim Jong-un is well established. The final verdict was that revolution in North Korea was unlikely. This is true, but the phenomenal events that have taken place in the Middle East and North Africa have shown us two things. First, in spite of all the reasons for thinking that things won't change, they could, and quite suddenly. And second, the mere existence of variables that could spell the collapse of an authoritarian regime tells us nothing about when or if that collapse could happen. Among the ruins of collapsed dictatorships in Libya, Egypt, and Tunisia, experts have picked out causes that have long been in existence, yet they cannot explain why they led to collapse in 2011 as opposed to decades earlier. Dictators who have fallen in the tumultuous protests of the Arab Spring—Saleh of Yemen, Ben Ali of Tunisia, Mubarak of Egypt, and Qaddafi of Libya—had each been in power longer than Kim Jong-il in North Korea. Can we simply assume that events in the Middle East have no bearing on the North Korean regime?

THE CAUSES[2]

Answering this question necessitates getting down to the root causes of popular revolutions and uprisings. The events that took place and continue to take place across the Middle East and North Africa since late 2010 are historic in their scope and scale. The dramatic self-immolation of Mohamed Bouazizi, a frustrated and humiliated twenty-six-year-old vegetable vendor in Tunisia, set off the greatest movements for political change the region has seen since the fall of the Ottoman Empire some ninety years earlier. In the months that followed, men, women, and children—individuals, young and old—rose up to challenge their governments in the face of violence and even death. From Tunisia it spread to Algeria. And then to Libya. And from Libya, on to Egypt. Within a few months, nearly every single state in the region, in one way or another, had to deal with popular uprisings of some sort. The reverberations didn't end at the edge of the desert. The Chinese government reportedly firewalled their Internet against searches of "Egypt," "Jasmine Revolution," and "Arab Spring." And in North Korea, orders were given to ban all public gatherings, and in July 2011 the government decreed the shutdown of all universities to put students under the thumb of the regime's work program.

On the surface, Bouazizi's dramatic suicide was the immediate cause, but there were obviously much larger forces at work that turned this single event into a mass movement. The causes for the Arab Spring can be divided five ways: modernization theories, development-gap theories, demographic theories, contagion theories, and regime-type theories. One collection of possible explanations falls under what political scientists refer to as the "modernization theory."[3] What this body of work argues is that the process of human development brought about by socioeconomic modernization in society leads to increased levels of desire for, and eventual sustenance of, democratic forms of government. What is generally seen across societies, whether they are Arab, Asian, or American, is that the process of modernization brings with it similar traits. Things such as urbanization, the rise of literacy rates and education levels, civic organizations, a more secular public sphere, market-type economies, the emergence of a property-owning middle class, and the temperance of class divisions, tend to accompany societal modernization. With these developments, individuals tend to think less about where they are getting their next meal and more about how their government is performing. Put simply, when wealth increases and individuals begin to develop, they are implicitly given a stake in the system. Once citizens get a taste of a better life, their expectations and demands grow exponentially faster. Thus, it was not dire poverty and other such grievances that set the Arab Spring in motion. Rather, it was, at least in part, minimal levels of individual development.[4]

Modernization is measured by looking at levels of wealth in societies. Societies with higher levels of individual wealth, unless they are primarily oil-exporting petro-states, will be more prone to movements toward democracy. It is not the wealth per se that will lead to mass movements, but the factors listed above, such as health and education, which tend to accompany this wealth.

Tunisia, for example, is, in fact, a surprisingly modern society, with the average Tunisian making nearly $3,800 in 2010. While this may not seem like a lot to developed-world audiences, it is significantly more money than was made by the average Chinese, Indian, or Indonesian, as well as by people in eighty or so other countries in the world. The U.N. Human Development Index, which combines measures of health, education, and income, puts Tunisia in the 68th percentile in the world, a full ten points above the regional average. Egypt displayed similar characteristics, though less starkly than Tunisia. In Egypt, the average individual made $2,270 in 2010, and while that doesn't put it in the class of Luxemborg ($105,044), it is also not with Burundi ($160). With regards to its human development, Egypt sits at the 62nd percentile, which is still well above the regional average. In Libya, too, we see a relatively modern society. Its per capita GDP of $9,714 is artificially in-flated by the fact that the country derives nearly 60 percent of its GDP in oil exports, but a fair amount of this does seem to trickle downward. Its human development rating is in the 75th percentile, significantly higher than Tunisia, Egypt, and most other regional states, and its life expectancy is seventy-five years. Syrian society exhibits similar tenden-cies, with a per capita level of wealth at about $2,500 and a human de-velopment ranking at just below the 60th percentile. But in some of the cases, modernization theory seems to reach its limits. For instance, in 2010, the average Yemeni made just over $1,000, and Yemen's Human Development Index rating is at about the 40th percentile, nearly twenty points below the regional average.[5] So, it seems, there must be more at play here.

Rather than focusing on the individual, some look at broad socio-economic development as a possible catalyst of unrest.[6] If growth in the overall economy occurs in a rapid fashion, it often outpaces the political institutions that make up the society and can lead to instabil-ity. This phenomenon is akin to what the late Harvard political scientist Samuel Huntington referred to as a "development gap": people's aspira-tions increase at a faster rate than the government is able to meet them.[7] Their "wants" begin to form faster than they can be satisfied. There is some evidence of this in a number of the Arab Spring countries, as the past decade has been marked by steady economic growth but stagnant authoritarianism. In Libya, for instance, the economy has grown at an average of just over 4 percent per year, peaking at 13 percent in 2003, with only modest increases in its population. Tunisia, too, has grown at an average of 4.5 percent per year over the past ten years, adding only about 10 percent to its total population during that time. Yemen as well, believe it or not, has averaged just under 4.5 percent growth per year since 2000, but has seen more substantial population growth numbers. Syria and Egypt also have had growth rates averaging con-sistently above 4 percent, but their more-rapid population growth has taken some of the force from this increased economic power.[8] GDP per capita growth mirrors these developments. Since the year 2000, Egypt experienced a 31 percent increase in its real GDP per capita.[9] Over the same period, Libya's was just under 20 percent and Syria's just shy of 23 percent. Tunisia, over the past decade, has seen its GDP per capita increase by a full 41 percent, with Yemen trailing quite well behind the rest with just 12 percent growth.[10] And yet, while there may be some variation in growth levels among these countries, what they all share in common is political stagnation at the highest levels, something political scientists refer to as "authoritarian entrenchment."[11] Saleh of Yemen has been in power since 1990, Ben Ali of Tunisia since 1987, Mubarak of Egypt since 1981, and Qaddafi since 1979. Bashar al-Assad in Syria took power in 2000, but he inherited the throne from his father, Hafez, who ruled the country for twenty-nine years. In 2010, these five states had either a six or a seven out of seven (seven is the least freedom; one is the most), according to Freedom House's Freedom in the World index, and were all labeled "not free."[12] The steady growth of their economies during the 2000s essentially meant that the people began to outgrow their governments.

Another group of theories looks at the demographic makeup of a society.[13] The younger a population is and the less it is employed, the higher are the chances for civil unrest. It is easy to imagine how hundreds of thousands, or even millions of underemployed, disaffected youth can lead to trouble for a government in relatively short order. And in many cases this is what was seen in the Arab Spring, with some referring to what happened in the region as a "youthquake."[14] Yemen is, perhaps, the quintessential example of this theory at work. Its median age is just 18 years old,[15] and its unemployment rate, the last time it was officially measured (which was 2003), was 35 percent. Libya also seems to fit the bill. Half of the population in the country is under 24.5 years, with an unemployment rate of a whopping 30 percent. Tunisia, too, had a fairly high unemployment rate of 14 percent in 2010, and a median age of 30 years; still significantly lower than developed countries like the United States (37 years), Canada (41 years), and Japan (44 years). Egypt, as well, has a fairly young population; half being under 24.3 years. Yet its unemployment rate is surprisingly low, at just under 10 percent. And Syria, which also has a relatively young population, has a median age of 21.9 years, but a surprisingly low unemployment rate of its own, floating just over 8 percent.[16] And so, the sort of hit-and-miss nature of the "youthquake" hypothesis points to the possibility of still more factors making their presence felt.

Getting beyond the internal, structural factors in these societies, there are powerful arguments for external factors as having contributed to the Middle East and North African uprisings. One such example is what commentators have referred to as "contagion" effects. A man in Egypt was said to have set himself alight after the inspiration of his Tunisian comrade. Then Facebook groups started popping up all over the region and the world, claiming "We are all Egyptians now!" The inspiration effect of one country's struggle on another is unquestionable. But how does this happen? In the modern era, the rise of rapid communications technology and the twenty-four-hour news cycle ensures that in all but the most repressive regimes, information is ubiquitous. Although the press in individual countries may be harshly repressed, social media such as Facebook, Twitter, YouTube, and SMS ensures that dictators can no longer plug every leak. In Tunisia, for instance, 91.8 percent of its 10.6 million people have mobile phones, and 33 percent have Internet access, the highest in North Africa. Similarly, in Egypt, 64.7 percent have cell phones, and about 25 percent are Internet users. In Libya, 76 percent have cell phones, and in Yemen, 34 percent. In Syria, too, 37 percent have mobile phones and just under 20 percent use the Internet regularly.[17] Though some of these numbers may seem small compared to the developed West, they were certainly enough for all of us to see personal footage from inside these movements on the news on a nightly basis. The relatively high literacy rates in these countries, moreover, act as a force multiplier for these types of media. In Libya, it is 89 percent, in Syria 84, in Tunisia 78, in Egypt 66, and even in Yemen, 62. This means that the potential for spread is all the greater. While a literacy rate of 62 percent may not seem all that impressive, it must be remembered that a number of sub-Saharan African states have rates that are less than half that.[18] Through these media, individuals can share information, organize protests, and post pictures and videos online for all to see. But perhaps more important than these new, Internet- and handheld-based social media, is the good old television. In the Arab Spring, this is what some commentators referred to as the "Al Jazeera effect."[19] Libyans saw coverage of the Tunisian revolt on Al Jazeera, which, in part, encouraged them to rise up. Followed similarly by Egypt, then by Yemen, and so on. And the relative ubiquity of televisions in society facilitated this effect. In Yemen, for instance, there are at least 34 televisions for every 100 inhabitants. In Egypt, there are 24. Syria boasts 19, and Libya 14.[20] Again, while these numbers may not seem all that impressive for the average American (where there are 74 TVs for every 100 people), it is worth remembering that in the world's most impoverished societies, such as Eritrea (0.02/100), Chad (0.1/100), and Tanzania (0.28/100), television is basically nonexistent for the vast majority of the population.[21] And rather than literacy, in the case of the Al Jazeera effect, the force multiplier was the fact that Arabic (the language of Al Jazeera) is widely spoken in at least twenty-eight countries worldwide, basically all situated in the Middle East and North Africa. In this way, protest among Arab states was "contagious," in that it went from one to the other to the other, until even the Chinese and the North Koreans began to get nervous.

A final important causal factor has to do with the type of regime in charge of the country.[22] It can be argued that regime types that allow some freedoms in the name of economic growth or as a steam valve for popular dissatisfaction are more liable to face upheaval among their people. It is this type of "soft authoritarianism" that opens up the classic dictator's dilemma: a snowball effect where leaders may allow some freedoms to keep growth rates up, but in doing so they sow the seeds of their own destruction as they lose control of the population. In Tunisia, this was most certainly the case. According to the Economist Intelligence Unit (EIU) Democracy Index, its civil liberties are rated 3.2 out of 10, and its political culture 5.6, but its electoral process is given a 0. Freedom House echoes these figures, giving Tunisia a 5 out of 7 (higher) for civil liberties but a 7 (lower) for political rights. We see similar trends in Egypt. The EIU gives it 5 out of 10 for political culture and 3.5 for civil liberties, but only 0.8 for its electoral process. Similarly, Egypt is given a 5 (higher) for civil liberties, but a 6 (lower) for its political rights by Freedom House. According to the EIU, Libya scores 5 out of 10 for political culture and just 1.5 for its civil liberties, but 0 for its electoral process.

According to Freedom House, Yemen as well has greater civil liberties (5) than its political rights (6). Finally, Syria: though its political culture is ranked by the EIU 5.6 out of 10 and its civil liberties 1.8, its electoral process rating is also 0. Freedom House again agrees here, giving Syria a lower political rights ranking (7) than its civil liberties (6).[23] And, according to the World Bank, not one of these countries has had a "voice and accountability" ranking greater than the 15th percentile in the past three years, with some (Libya, Syria) barely breaking the 5th percentile.[24] The difference of one or two points on a 0-to-10 or 7-to-1 scale may not seem like much, but it likely proved just enough to set the process of revolt in motion. So, in sum, there appears to be an inherent contradiction in the sort of soft authoritarianism seen in many of these Middle Eastern states. In many cases, the people were free to choose their own jobs, their own religions, even their own civil society organizations, but not their own leaders. And this taste of freedom they have been given seems to have set off a ravenous hunger, which may not be satiated until all of the dictators are gone.

ARAB SPRING IN PYONGYANG?

There are five potential variables—wealth accumulation, rates of growth, demography, contagion effect, or regime type—that could bring the Arab Spring to North Korea's doorstep. Do we see the possibility for change in the DPRK from any of these? Not really. There is no development gap in North Korea. Wealth accumulation and economic growth have not been apparent. Rather than modernizing and growing, the society has seen little development. Traversing the streets of Pyongyang, one is struck by how the city skyline and streets, though neatly maintained, have not really seen any development since the 1960s. Not just the architecture, but the public phone booths, trolley cars, streetlamps, and other fixtures all look over forty years old. The economy has been contracting. GDP growth, when it was not contracting in the 1990s, has trudged along at unimpressive rates. Per capita gross national income, moreover, has been decreasing over the past two decades from $1,146 in 1990 to as low as $573 in 1998, and reaching $960 in 2009, which is still a net decrease from two decades earlier.

ECONOMIC GROWTH IN THE DPRK, 1990–2009		
	PER CAPITA GNI (SUS)	GDP GROWTH (% CHANGE)
1990	1146	-4.3
1991	1115	-4.4
1992	1013	-7.1
1993	969	-4.5
1994	992	-2.1
1995	1034	-4.4
1996	989	-3.4
1997	811	-6.5
1998	573	-0.9
1999	714	6.1
2000	757	0.4
2001	706	3.8
2002	762	1.2
2003	818	1.8
2004	914	2.1
2005	1056	3.8
2006	1108	-1.0
2007	1152	-1.2
2008	1056	3.1
2009	960	-0.9

Source: Bank of Korea (2011).

Other signs of a modernizing consumer-oriented society are just not present. Life expectancy is 67.4 years, down from 70.2 years in 1990.[25] One-third of the population is undernourished.[26] Given this state, the people of North Korea do not entertain notions of demanding a new political leadership that can improve their lifestyles. Rising expectations only come with a degree of hope, which is nonexistent. Instead, the people are preoccupied with survival, finding their next meal, and staying warm in the depths of winter.

North Korea does have a relatively young and literate population, two important variables for the Arab Spring. The median age is 32.9 years

GDP Growth in Arab Countries and the DPRK

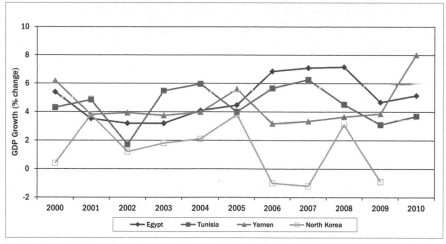

Sources: Arab country data (GDP) from IMF.org (2011); DPRK (GNI) data from Bank of Korea (2011).

GDP/Capita Growth in Arab Countries and the DPRK

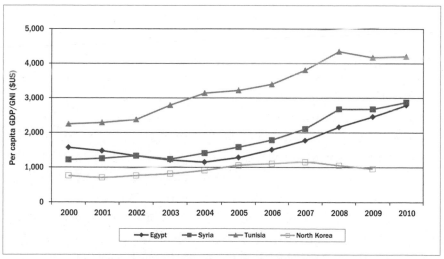

Sources: Arab country data (GDP) from IMF.org (2011); DPRK (GNI) data from Bank of Korea (2011).

and literacy rates are near 100 percent. But the likelihood of a "youth-quake" is remote. Contrary to what many may think, the North's poor economic performance does not translate into widespread idle and un-employed youth susceptible to lashing out at the government. First of all, as a Communist economy, North Korea technically has no unemployment rate, as everyone works for the state. Of course, given that the state cannot pay the workers for months at a time, this population would by any other definition be considered unemployed. But this does not lead to idleness, because most workdays are spent devising coping mechanisms to subsist. The average factory worker at a state-owned enterprise might choose not to continue to work at the factory because he is not getting paid, but he will not quit his job. Instead, he will report to work in the morning, punch the time clock, and then bribe the foreman to allow him to spend the day trying to catch fish or forage for scrap metal that he can sell on the black market. Aside from these coping mechanisms to occupy their time, all young males are gainfully employed for up to twelve years in the military. The DPRK has a military conscription system where service in the army is between five and twelve years, service in the navy five to ten, and in the air force three to four years; by a very wide margin, the longest service terms in the entire world.[27] Thereafter, all are obligated to serve part-time until forty and must serve in the Worker/Peasant Red Guard until sixty.[28] This system is set up ostensibly to keep the military strong, but it also serves the purpose of keeping young men harnessed and off the streets. Finally, leisure time in North Korean society, to the extent that it exists, is largely spent in ideological indoctrination. There is no idle time when one is serving the Dear Leader. After school, for example, students will march with their work units to the square in front of Kim Il-sung's mausoleum to practice performances for the spring festival, or they will be in sessions reading about the greatness of Kim Il-sung's thought. There do not appear to be objective indicators of an impending youthquake in North Korea any time soon.

What about a contagion effect? Can news of what happened in the Middle East and North Africa spread to the DPRK? Could a demonstration effect occur where North Koreans do not necessarily identify with the frustrations of a Tunisian street merchant, but where they simply learn of the fact that popular protest is a mode of expressing needs and effecting change? One of the major priorities of human rights NGOs on North Korea in the aftermath of the Arab Spring was to try to get as much information as possible into the country about the unprecedented events. After the 2010 artillery shelling of Yeonpyeong Island, the ROK military sent nearly three million leaflets into North Korea, describing the Arab Spring. Another method entailed flying hot-air balloons from islets off the west coast of the peninsula into North Korea. Packages attached to these balloons carried money, food, and newspaper reports about events in the Middle East. If the winds blew in the desired direction, these balloons would land in the North and disseminate the kind of information that bursts the bubble of tightly controlled information the regime seeks to maintain. But these launches are small-scale when it comes to educating an entire population; moreover, they put North Koreans at great risk if they are caught by state authorities with these materials. Human rights–based and reform-advocacy radio broadcasting NGOs, such as Radio Free Asia, Radio Free Chosun, and NK Reform Radio, also broadcast news of the events in the Middle East into North Korea on a daily basis. But the signals for these broadcasts are often well jammed by the DPRK authorities, and most North Koreans don't have access to the kinds of radios that can pick them up anyway.

In order to create a contagion effect, you need high literacy rates and social media, or a somewhat-free press. In North Korea's case, you clearly have the former but neither of the latter. There is no access to the World Wide Web from within the country, and the only Internet that exists is an "intranet" that connects to tightly controlled government Web sites. There is only one Twitter and Facebook account in the whole country (set up by the government). All of North Korea's television stations are state-run, with no regional or even inter-Korean Al Jazeera–type networks. And, based on the latest statistics, there are only about five TVs for every hundred North Koreans.[29] There is no foreign travel, and domestic travel is severely restricted. And it is safe to say that the average North Korean is oblivious to the plethora of personal media and entertainment devices that have become staples in our lives. When I traveled to Pyongyang in 2007, I was allowed to keep my iPod, largely because the airport security personnel did not know what the device was. I assured them it could not be used as a communications device within the country (there is no wireless Internet), and had only music and videos on it.

The two most interesting recent developments in this regard have been the introduction of cell phones into the country and the opening of a new computer lab at the Pyongyang University of Science and Technology (PUST). The North Koreans introduced cell phones into the country only for the elites in Pyongyang, but in 2004, it banned them after an explosion at a local train station looked uncomfortably close to an assassination attempt on Kim Jong-il. In the rubble of the blast, officials found what looked to be evidence of a cell phone–detonated bomb. In 2008, the Egyptian company Orascom won the exclusive contract worth $400 million to provide cell phones in North Korea.[30] The first year of operation in 2009 started with 70,000 units. There are nearly one million units now in Pyongyang, but this only represents about 3.5 percent of the population, and the phones do not have the capacity to dial outside of the country. PUST was opened in October 2010 through the efforts of evangelical Americans and a combination of academic, Christian, and corporate-world funders in South Korea.[31] The facility features 160 computers, for which a select group of university students are being trained. The use of these computers, however, is heavily restricted to these select students, whose job is to glean from the Internet information useful to the state. By comparison, Tunisia had 40 percent of its population conversant with the Internet. This level of exposure to outside information in North Korea is miniscule when compared with that of the Arab countries.

North Korea remains the hardest of hard authoritarian regimes in the world. Unlike South Korea in the 1980s, which shifted to a soft authoritarian model with a burgeoning middle class that eventually demanded its political freedoms in 1987, the North has resisted all change. Those who visit Pyongyang come out claiming life does not look so bad. People walk freely in the streets without omnipresent military patrols. Society seems very orderly. There are no urban homeless visible. CNN broadcasts from Pyongyang showed city dwellers attending a street carnival, eating cotton candy, and texting on their cell phones. These episodic reports, however, mis-portray a terribly restricted society with draconian controls on all liberties. North Korea still ranks seven out of seven (lowest possible score) on Freedom House's Freedom in the World index, and it has thereby earned the odious title of "the Worst of the Worst," for its political rights and civil liberties record.[32] It sits dead-last of 167 countries on the EIU's democracy index.[33] It is in the 0th percentile for the World Bank's Voice and Accountability index and is ranked 196 out of 196 countries in the Freedom of the Press index.[34] What is astonishing about these rankings is not the absence of movement to a softer form of authoritarianism, necessitated by the need for economic reform, but that the regime has consistently maintained such controls decade after decade with no letting up whatsoever. This persistence stems not from a lack of understanding that some liberalization is necessary for economic reform, but from the Kim regime's conscious choice to prize political control over anything else. This puts the Kim regime in a class of authoritarianism of its own.

According to respected scholars of political diasporas, creating political change at home often requires outside resources and a vibrant expatriate community with a political agenda to push for change.[35] But there is no real dissident exile community for North Korea like the ones we see with Egypt, Iran, and other cases. Defectors from North Korea show anger toward their former prison guards or toward corrupt bureaucrats, but this, surprisingly, does not aggregate into an anger to expel the Kim leadership. A July 2008 survey of refugees in Seoul, for example, found that 75 percent had no negative sentiment for Kim Jong-il.[36] Kang Ch'ŏl-hwan, the defector who wrote the famous book *Aquariums of Pyongyang*, displayed anger in his writing toward the guards in his prison camp but not to Kim Il-sung. A National Geographic documentary, *Inside North Korea*, followed around the country an eye doctor who performed cataract surgeries for ailing citizens.[37] After thousands of surgeries, upon having their bandages removed, every single patient immediately and joyously thanked for their renewed eyesight Kim Il-sung and Kim Jong-il, not the doctor. Even news of Kim Jong-il's stroke elicits from a defector empathy rather than anger:

> *[I don't know] whether I should reveal my sadness over Kim Jong-il's health . . . He is still our Dear Leader. It is the people who work with him and give him false reports who are bad. When I hear about his on-the-spot guidance and eating humble meals, I believe he cares for the people.*[38]

This is not to say that dissident movements started by North Korean defectors are wholly absent. The Committee for the Democratization of North Korea (CDNK), Fighters for a Free North Korea (FFNK), and the Citizens' Alliance for North Korean Human Rights are examples of

NGOs devoted to creating political change in the North, but relative to other cases, these movements are small and do not pose a direct threat to the regime.

There are several reasons for the lack of a politically active exile community. First, the recent migrants out of North Korea are almost all female and are leaving the country purely for economic reasons. Some 75 percent of recent defectors are from the northern Hamgyŏng provinces, which is the worst economically hit area of North Korea. Women, therefore, leave the country purely as an economic coping mechanism to survive rather than to act out political ambitions against the regime. Prior to the 1990s, the flow of refugees might have been more liable to protest as it was constituted of male political elites and military officers, who left for ideological reasons or because they were accused of committing state crimes. The numbers of these, however, were fairly small (607 total between 1949 and 1989), compared with the recent wave (nearing 22,000 currently resettled in South Korea).[39]

DPRK Defectors Entering the ROK

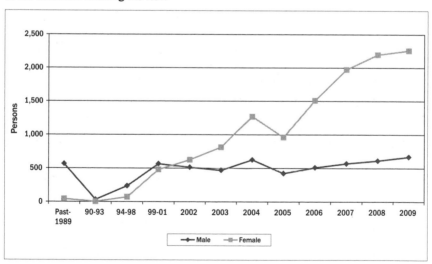

Source: Republic of Korea Ministry of Unification (2011).

Second, as noted in previous chapters, defectors from North Korea have significant enough difficulties adjusting to life outside of the North, which preclude the luxury to entertain ideas about promoting political change in their former home country. Life in South Korea, where many of these defectors resettle, is fast-paced and often filled with social challenges, including disadvantages due to a lack of education, physical diminutiveness compared to well-fed southerners, and social discrimination in terms of jobs and marriage. Many northerners are preoccupied with meeting these challenges, as well as with paying off brokers' charges as high as $6,000 for their successful escape to a life that is different, undoubtedly free, but challenging nonetheless. For this reason, many northerners still feel a sense of pride about their former homeland, and though they are fully cognizant of its shortfalls, most said that if they had to do it all over again, they would still be happy to have been born in the North.

CEAUSESCU'S MOMENT

By all of our political science metrics, the DPRK shows no potential to have an Arab Spring. But then why has the North Korean regime seemed so worried? Why did it stifle the inflow of all news regarding events in Libya, Egypt, Tunisia, and Syria? Why did it amass tanks and troops in urban centers as a precaution against public gatherings? Why did Kim Jong-il issue a personal directive in February 2011 to organize a special mobile riot squad a hundred-strong in each provincial office of the Ministry for People's Security? Why did it bolster surveillance of all organizations on university campuses and then issue a decree in 2011 closing all universities for months and sending all students to work units? Why did the government order a countrywide inventorying of all computers, cell phones, flash drives, and MP3 players among the elite population? Why did it crack down on all public assembly, even to the extent of removing dividers in restaurants to prevent private gatherings? Why did they threaten to fire artillery on NGO balloons from offshore South Korean islets carrying news of the Arab Spring into North Korea?[40]

Indeed, there seems to be a significant gap between what theories of revolution tell us and what the gut instincts of the DPRK leadership tell. The regime's actions reflect a sense of vulnerability. For Kim Jong-un, the stark fact is that dictators who held power much longer than his late father—like Qaddafi of Libya, Mubarak of Egypt, and Ben Ali of Tunisia—all have fallen from power, or have been hanging on by their fingernails. This must have sent a chilling message. The fact that all of the political science indicators for revolution were in existence but dormant in the Middle East and North Africa till now must give junior Kim little comfort about the absence of any such indicators in his own country.

The main lesson of the Arab Spring is that authoritarian regimes, no matter how sturdy they look, are all inherently unstable. They maintain control through the silence of people's fears, but they also cultivate deep anger beneath the surface. Once the fear dissipates, the anger boils to the surface and can be sparked by any event akin to a Tunisian police officer slapping the face of a street merchant. The late North Korean leader Kim Jong-il once admitted to Hyundai founder Chŏng Chu-yŏng to having dreams where he was stoned to death in the public square by his people.[41] What the Dear Leader and the Great Successor fear is their "Ceausescu moment." Condoleezza Rice explained this at a 2011 meeting at the Bush Presidential Center in Dallas, Texas, as the moment where the Romanian dictator went out into the streets to quell protests by declaring all the positive things his rule had done for the people. A quieted crowd, once fearful of the leader, listened. Then, after a pause, one elderly woman in the crowd yelled out, "Liar!" and others joined in the chant, replacing their fear of the dictator with anger against him. Ceausescu was subsequently executed in the streets of Trâgovişte, Romania. Kim Jong-un thus must feel like he is living on borrowed time. A collapsing domino row of dictators, many of whom were personal friends of his father and grandfather, becomes the larger context in which the junior Kim is trying to take over for his dead father. Blocking information about the Arab Spring and taking precautions to stifle all public assembly becomes paramount.

The post–Kim Jong-il leadership must be paranoid about the Arab Spring, because it is watching fellow dictators lose control in the context of dramatic changes in their own societies, and Kim Jong-un has his own challenges stemming from a changing North Korean society. There are two forces at work here in diametrically opposed ways: marketization and ideological reification. After the 2002 economic reforms allowed some markets to spring up in the North, the society changed permanently. Recall from chapter 4 that Pyongyang undertook these reforms, which lifted price controls and introduced market mechanisms, not because of a newfound love for liberalization but because the PDS had broken down and the government was essentially telling the citizens to fend for themselves. Markets opened everywhere and society permanently changed after that. Even with the government's reinstitution of the ration system and crackdown on market activity, citizens refused to rely solely on the government, and, according to defectors, the majority of North Korean citizens today rely on the markets for some significant portion of their weekly food, goods, and a wide range of other products. Farmers meet their production quotas and then sell their best produce in the market. Or factory workers at the Kaesŏng Industrial Complex save their Choco Pies from the cafeteria lunch and sell them on the black market. A 2008 study by Stephan Haggard and Marcus Noland found that more than two-thirds of defectors admitted that half or more of their income came from private business practices. More than 50 percent of former urban residents in the DPRK reported that they purchased as much as 75 percent of their food from the market. These numbers were reported, moreover, when the government was in the midst of a crackdown on markets and aiming to reinstitute the PDS. These markets in North Korea have become a fixture of life that now is virtually impossible to uproot.

Markets create entrepreneurship. And entrepreneurship creates an individualist way of thinking that is alien to the government. This change is slow, and incremental, but it affects a good part of the population and is growing every day in a quiet but potent way. The change was evident in the way in which the people responded to the government's effort to crack down definitively on marketization by instituting a currency redenomination in 2009. This redenomination wiped out the hard work of many families who could exchange only a fraction of their household savings for the new currency. People reacted not with typical obedience out of fear, but with anger and despair. Some committed suicide. Others fought with police who tried to close down the local market. Still others scrawled antigovernment graffiti on university walls. The greatest vulnerability for a regime like North Korea is when a population loses its fear of the government. Once the fear is gone, all that is left is the anger.

NEOJUCHE'S IDEOLOGICAL RIGIDITY

The inescapable dilemma for Pyongyang is that its political institutions cannot adjust to the changing realities in North Korean society. It can take short-term measures to dampen the anger. After the botched currency redenomination measure, for example, Pyongyang tried to adjust by raising the ceiling on the amount of old currency that citizens could exchange. They also shot in public the seventy-six-year-old director of Planning and Finance Department, as the scapegoat for the policy mistake. But in the longer term, North Korean political institutions and ideology are growing more rigid, not more flexible, as the leadership implements the third dynastic passing of power within the Kim family. *Neojuche* revivalism is in many ways the worst possible ideology that the regime could follow in parallel with the society's marketization. The ideology's emphasis on reliving the Cold War glory days through mass mobilization and collectivist thought is, in fact, the complete opposite direction from that in which society is moving. And yet, the government cannot adjust its course because: (1) it needs a new ideology that has a positive vision for a new leader (and the only positive vision the state ever experienced was early Cold War *juche*); and (2) it attributes the past poor performance of the state over the last two decades not to Kim Jong-il but to the "mistakes" of allowing experimentation with reform, which "polluted" the ideology. Another lesson that Pyongyang learned from the Arab Spring was that this new neoconservative *juche* ideology must be implemented without giving up their nuclear weapons. The example of Libya made clear to North Koreans that Qaddafi's decision to give up his nuclear programs to the United States was an utter mistake: precisely because he no longer had these capabilities, NATO and the United States were at liberty to take military actions against him.

This confluence of forces gives rise to a ticking time bomb—or a train wreck in slow motion, whatever metaphor you prefer. A dead dictator compels a rushed power succession to his son, and the regime pushes an ideology that moves the country backward, not forward. Meanwhile, society is incrementally moving in a different direction from North Korea's past—in large part, sparked by the economic failures of the government. One might call this a North Korean version of

Samuel Huntington's development gap. Rather than economic growth outpacing static political institutions in an unstable, democratizing society, you have a growing gap between a rigidifying ideology and slowly changing society in North Korea. A single event—akin to a botched government measure or a severe nationwide crackdown on markets—could spark a process that could topple an already brittle dictatorship. A young and inexperienced dictator will in all likelihood fail spectacularly to cope with this ideology-society gap. In the end, the new regional leaders, including the United States, Russia, China, and South Korea, who take the reins of power in 2012, will be faced with fundamental discontinuities in North Korea before they leave office.

Pyongyang's fears about the Arab Spring also presumably derive from an understanding of the role social media played in those countries, and the realization that the recent baby steps by the DPRK into acquiring cell phones and accessing the Internet have the potential to puncture the hermetically sealed information bubble around the country. As I noted earlier, recent North Korean ventures are modest by comparison with the Middle East states, so there is little chance of a technology-driven contagion effect today. Indeed, the regime sees these technology instruments as enhancing the state's power, not weakening it. But their introduction creates a slippery slope for the regime with regard to information penetration. The Internet, for example, is like marketization. Once a society is exposed to it even a little, the conveniences associated with it become a fixture of life that is very difficult to uproot. North Korea is, ironically, a country that desperately needs the Internet—its citizens are not allowed to travel overseas, and yet the country wants information from the outside world cheaply and without a lot of interaction. Access to the Web handsomely meets these needs. In 2003, the DPRK set up their official Web site, *uriminzokkiri.com,* hosted on a server in Shanghai, and in 2010 the government joined Twitter and Facebook. The government wanted to carefully restrict all use of the Web, but then they realized that the Internet allowed access to information instantaneously and costlessly, without having to send anyone abroad to get it. Moreover, the government realized that greatly restricting international access to their Web sites undercut the purposes of trying to attract foreign direct investment. In meeting these needs, the government started walking down the slippery slope, gradually relaxing restrictions. Now, there are twelve Web domains in North Korea, and about a thousand government and non-government users of the Internet, albeit greatly censored.[42] Some users must be fairly sophisticated, given reports about hacking attempts on ROK and U.S. government sites originating from within North Korea. The PUST project is another step down the slippery slope, as it teaches some of Pyongyang's best and brightest youth how to use the Internet. While this is limited to only a handful of carefully selected students who are monitored at all times as they download information useful to the state, the basic fact remains that there are youth in North Korea who know how to surf the Web and will someday gain access to a South Korean or Chinese computer that is not monitored. Cell phones followed a similar trajectory. The government eventually reintroduced them to the country after the 2004 Ryongch'ŏn train blast and the number of phones continues to grow every year.

The purpose of phasing in these devices was to serve the state. Phones would enable better communication among the elite and another means of coordination and control among security services. Seventy thousand units were introduced for the elite in 2009, but this turned into nearly half a million phones by April 2011, and predictions are they could go as high as 2 million units by the end of 2012. These phones cannot call outside of the country, but they do give a broader portion of the population familiarity with phones, texting features, and Web access. Moreover, there are an estimated thousand phones smuggled in from China with prepaid SIM cards. With these phones, North Koreans near the Chinese border can call within the DPRK and to China, and, reportedly, as far as Seoul. Again, these are small steps, carefully controlled by the government, and do not come near replicating the use of social media in other parts of the world. But the Internet and cell phones are truly a slippery slope for the regime. They quickly become fixtures of life, and a new generation of North Koreans will be literate in these technologies.

Finally, the North Korean leadership evinces a growing discomfort with the way the fight for freedom in distant Arab states reverberates internationally. Analysts talk about a new wave of democratization and hypothesize whether it will move to Asia. This raises concerns about international recognition of human rights abuses in the DPRK. As late as 2004, it was fair to say that outside of the human rights movement, the global community did not acknowledge the plight of the North Korean people. Among the many other causes around which the world organized, North Korea was notably absent.

But, thanks in large part to efforts by the United States, this is no longer the case. Both Presidents Bush and Obama have succeeded in connecting the cause of the North Korean people with the global American agenda of promoting freedom and human dignity. Bush, in particular, was the first U.S. president to appoint a congressionally mandated special envoy for human rights abuses in North Korea. He was the first U.S. president to make a statement protesting China's *refoulement* of North Korean refugees, and to allow for a refugee resettlement program for North Koreans in the United States. Bush also invited the first North Korean defector into the Oval Office, Kang Ch'ŏl-hwan. The meeting was a private one, not listed on the president's official schedule. But afterward, the decision was made to release only one picture of the meeting to the Associated Press with a simple caption saying the president welcomes Mr. Kang to the Oval Office. The picture spread like wildfire around the world. It did not spur human rights protests within North Korea, because the government did not allow the picture into the country, but it did create an international contagion effect. The world suddenly was awakened to the abuses inside North Korea. Newspaper editorials in Asia questioned why their governments did not have a North Korean human rights envoy, or why their leaders had not read *Aquariums of Pyongyang* like Bush had done. G8 countries put the issue on their agenda and released statements condemning the government's atrocities against its people. Obama maintained U.S. focus on this issue under his administration, so that in May 2011, the DPRK for the first time allowed a visit by the U.S. human rights envoy, Ambassador Robert King. In short, how the DPRK runs its country is now under the magnifying glass more than ever before. And the Arab Spring only highlights how tenuous an authoritarian regime's control can be, and how the breakdown of this control can capture the imagination and support of the free world.

Skeptics might argue that my speculation about the regime's limited days is not borne out by the history of the regime's stability. The fact is, skeptics would argue, that there have been no instances of coups or domestic instability in the North over the past fifty years, like we have seen in South Korea, for example, with two military coups—in 1961 and in 1979—that overthrew standing governments. The people are too weak and the military and state controls are simply too strong for anything untoward to happen to the leadership. However, if we quickly peruse the history, domestic disturbances are not exactly an unknown occurrence in the North. These have taken place within the military, between the military and the citizens, and even against the leadership.

In 1981, there were reports of armed clashes between soldiers and workers in the industrial center of Ch'ŏngjin, on the eastern coast of the country, that left as many as five hundred dead. In 1983, there were Soviet-based reports of similar clashes in Sinŭiju. In 1985, there were reports of a massacre of hundreds of civilians in Hamhŭng over food. In 1990, a small group of students at the elite Kim Il-sung University reportedly were arrested and tortured for organizing protests. In January 1992, there were reports of a failed attempt by officers in the State Security Department's bodyguard bureau to stage a coup preventing Kim Jong-il from assuming the position as commander of the KPA. In April 1992, rumors surfaced that thirty officers were executed for a failed plot to assassinate Kim Jong-il. In March 1993, thirty officers of the VII Corps headquarters stationed in Hamhŭng tried unsuccessfully to stage a rebellion against their superiors. In 1995, upset with Pyongyang's decision not to ship food to the Hamgyŏng provinces, senior officers of the VI Corps stationed in Ch'ŏngjin sought to take control of a university, communications center, Ch'ŏngjin port, and missile installations, and, reportedly, planned to team up with VII Corps in Hamhŭng to oppose the government. In December 1996, leaflets were found in front of Kim Il-sung mausoleum, criticizing the costs of the mausoleum when citizens were starving. In 1997, a statue of Kim Il-sung was found vandalized and reports of anti-regime graffiti were found. In March 1998, there was a report of a failed assassination attempt by one of Kim's bodyguards. In late 2001–early 2002, there were reports of another failed assassination attempt on Kim by one of his bodyguards. In 2004, a terrorist bombing at Ryongch'ŏn station killed 170 people, narrowly missing Kim Jong-il's train as it passed through the station returning from a trip to China. In 2005, a video surfaced online that showed a nervous youth under a bridge in rural North Korea, hanging a banner that denounced Kim Jong-il in bright red letters and was signed by the "Freedom Youth League." In December of 2007, when the government decided to ban market activity for women under the age of fifty (by far the most important group in the markets), protests sprang up in Ch'ŏngjin within months, with female participants reportedly calling out, "If you do not let us trade, give us rations!" and "If you have no rice to give us, let us trade!"[43] In 2009, whole families committed suicide over the government's surprise currency redenomination measure that wiped out their life savings. In Hamhŭng, fights broke out in markets that police officers unsuccessfully tried to close down. Anti–Kim Jong-il graffiti was found in alleyways. In 2011, "Down with Kim Jong-un" messages were found scrawled on university walls and in markets. And the list goes on. It is hard to confirm the severity of these incidents, because no one inside the country can report on them. It is also impossible to know whether these reports represent the entirety of dissent within the North or only the tip of the iceberg. Most of the reports of dissent occurred in the 1990s, after Kim Il-sung's death and during the famine years. But we do not know if the dissent has disappeared or if the government has just gotten better at stifling news of it. It is clear, however, that internal dissent is not unheard of, despite the draconian controls of the DPRK system. It has emerged in the past. It can emerge again.

But who would be North Korea's Bouazizi? Two possible sources of discontent might be the "selectorate" and the urban poor. The "selectorate" refers to the elite in North Korean society—party members, military officers, and government bureaucrats who have benefited from the regime's rule.[44] Their support is co-opted by the state through the promise of benefits doled out by the leadership. They are the most loyal, ranging in number from two hundred to five thousand, according to different estimates. And to retain their loyalty, they are showered with benefits, such as highly coveted employment positions, desirable residences, plentiful and high-quality foods, and access to luxury items such as red meat, liquor, and other imported goods. In many cases, elites are even given lavish gifts, such as luxury cars, jewelry, electronics—even wives.[45] In 2005, after we had achieved the Six-Party Joint Statement, we heard that Kim Kye-gwan, the DPRK lead negotiator, was given a new Mercedes-Benz sedan. (I, on the other hand, got to watch a preview of *James Bond: Casino Royale* in the White House Family Theater, with the president and about fifty NSC and domestic staff whom President Bush thanked for their hard work.)

Some scholars claim that Kim Jong-il has "coup-proofed" himself by prioritizing the bribing of these officials over any broader economic performance metrics for the state. But this loyalty lasts only as long as the regime can continue the handouts, and the government's capacity in this regard is increasingly shrinking. The cumulative effect of years of U.N. sanctions on luxury goods, the continued decline in the economy, and the inability of China to backstop the regime forever will take its toll, making the circle of the selectorate smaller and smaller. Favorites will have to be chosen to receive the shrinking handouts, leaving some disaffected. The rushed leadership transition from Kim Jong-il to Kim Jong-un, moreover, promises even more disaffection in the party and military, as the new Kim will have to choose his inner circle as his basis of leadership, which will send ripples throughout the selectorate, giving opportunities to some but, more ominously, taking opportunities away from others.

Moreover, as *neojuche* ideology puts more strain on the economy, the segment of society that will feel the most pain are the urban poor. In 2002, when the DPRK undertook economic reforms that lifted price controls, the resulting inflation badly hurt salaried urban populations, who suffered increases in their cost of living. While farmers could off-set this with the higher prices they enjoyed from the sale of their own produce in the black market, urban workers faced a double whammy—higher prices and delayed salary disbursements from the government. The result is a potentially unhappy urban population that is literate, educated, and may have more knowledge of the outside world than most others in the country. Moreover, they identify with the system because they once benefited from it, which may give them cause to regain those advantages. And they probably have cell phones.

FIVE POLICY PRINCIPLES

So what should the United States and its allies do until the fateful day comes? Fashioning a comprehensive policy to deal with North Korea's nuclear programs, its human rights abuses, and its failed economy is hardly child's play. No administration thus far has been successful at addressing one, let alone all three. The specifics of a policy will depend on the circumstances at any given moment in time. Policy operates on tactics as much as it does on strategy. Often the tactics overcome the strategy, as governments are forced to react piecemeal to DPRK provocations. But there are some core principles in which any administration must embed its thinking about North Korea.

First, any administration must understand that patience is part of a policy to wait out the regime. Thirty-plus years of U.S. diplomacy, practiced by some of our best diplomats and statesmen, have proven this point. As frustrating as need for patience can sometimes be, the alternative policy of pushing the regime toward collapse only triggers counterbalancing forces in the region (i.e., China) that keep the regime afloat with more assistance and backdoor support. The military option has the potential to be extremely costly if it escalates to all-out war; moreover, it may not be successful. A surgical strike on the Yongbyon nuclear complex still would not guarantee that all weapons and programs, which may be hidden throughout the country's caves, had been eliminated. An operation to take out the leadership of North Korea is probably within the realm of U.S. capabilities, given the successful operations against Saddam Hussein and, more recently, Osama Bin Laden. But any future president is unlikely to take this route. A Presidential Finding for a covert operation of this magnitude would mean that the United States had made elimination of the North Korean leadership a top priority just like in the case of Iraq and Al Qaeda. No administration thus far has prioritized the problem to this extent. It remains a second-tier problem at best, and when it periodically erupts into a crisis, then the modus operandi is to stabilize the situation, not to end the problem. United States' relative indifference is probably the North Korean regime's greatest blessing. The only circumstance in which North Korea might appear in our crosshairs is if a terrorist attack on the homeland was traced to weapons that originated in North Korea. Should that day come, the regime's days would be numbered.

Second, any administration must consider as the baseline of its policy a robust set of counterproliferation and financial sanctions. The Obama administration oversaw the creation of a U.N.-backed international regime of sanctions against the North based on Security Council Resolution 1874. These sanctions must continue with an emphasis on closing loopholes that allow the DPRK to receive intermediate goods for production of more missiles or development of their plutonium- and uranium-based nuclear weapons. Vigilant efforts like the Proliferation Security Initiative—a ninety-plus-country multilateral institution dedicated to stopping, at ports or in transit, the movement of WMD and component parts—must continue to focus on North Korea as one of its main targets. Two major areas of improvement in the PSI are better cooperation from China on land crossings with the DPRK and the closing off of Chinese and Russian airspace to suspect DPRK cargo and passenger flights. An equally important piece is to engage with potential customers and secondary facilitators of North Korean military wares, and persuade them that any transactions with the North would be ill-advised and subject to secondary sanctions. Financial sanctions that target the activities of DPRK front companies engaged in proliferation financing, and that also target the personal finances of the leadership, have proven to be effective. All of these measures force the leadership in Pyongyang to focus their energies on finding different ways to circumvent the sanctions. This conveys the message to the leadership that the costs of their nuclear program carry long-lasting penalties that outweigh the benefits. Ideally, all or any one component of this battery of sanctions should not be up for negotiation with the North. These sanctions are designed for counterproliferation; therefore, as long as the North maintains a single nuclear weapon, the sanctions should remain in place. They should end only when the last nuclear weapon is taken out of North Korea. No sooner.

Sanctions have been and will continue to be the primary means of addressing the North's vertical (development of own programs) and horizontal (selling to others) proliferation potential. However, these sanctions contain North Korea; they do not denuclearize North Korea.

That is, a thirty-year campaign of sanctions may help to stop proliferation, but they do not force the government to give up their nuclear
weapons. Thus, the third principle is negotiation. Any administration
will, at some point in its dealings, be compelled to negotiate with North
Korea. Indeed, every administration for the past twenty-eight years—
some with the toughest stances on North Korea has sooner or later
entered into a dialogue in order to freeze Kim's programs and ultimately
dismantle pieces of it. Given all the past violations of agreements, the
North's ludicrous rhetoric, and their flagrant nuclear and missile tests,
the thought of sitting down with them and hammering out painstaking new agreements may seem entirely distasteful. Washington, D.C.,
inside-the-Beltway pundits would point to three decades of U.S. negotiations that have provided the North with over $1.28 billion in benefits,
and in return received two nuclear tests and thirty-three ballistic and
cruise missile tests (since 2006 alone), and scoff at any future administration that got fooled into negotiations again.

But for a pundit, it is easy to say there should be no talks whatsoever with North Korea. From the perspective of policy, however, lack of
negotiations has its costs, because you are left with a runaway nuclear
program with no insight into where it is headed and with whom it is
interacting. The term of art, therefore, is "you must hold your nose and
negotiate." Negotiations have three objectives. First, they aim for denuclearization, however distant that goal may appear. One can never
abandon this as the objective of negotiation, because it would imply that
the United States and allies have resigned to accepting the DPRK as a
nuclear weapons state, in which case negotiations would be about reductions in their arsenal—i.e., an arms control negotiation, not a denuclearization negotiation. Second, these negotiations help to manage
escalation and prevent crises. A study conducted at CSIS charted all
North Korean major provocations on a weekly basis, dating from March
1984 through the present. It then superimposed on this chart a graph of
all periods of major negotiations between the United States and DPRK
in bilateral or multilateral formats (e.g., Four-Party, Six-Party Talks).
Over three decades, there has only been one instance in which DPRK
provocations took place during ongoing negotiations (August 31, 1998,
missile test). Thus, dialogue does appear to help prevent crisis and esca-

lation, which some administrations may see as an important goal (although the end of that dialogue will be met almost certainly with more DPRK provocations, according to the CSIS study).

Third, negotiations, if successfully concluded, will result in agreements that get incrementally at pieces of the nuclear program. The DPRK will continue to keep their actual nuclear weapons as the last bargaining chip in any negotiation. Thus, any attempts at a single "mega-deal" that offers more incentives to get more in return may sound great, but these are all eventually whittled down by the North to smaller steps. It was maddening to hear pundits criticize the deals we concluded with the North as misconceived, because we were not successful at bringing home their nuclear weapons. Every negotiator in any administration wants to get the weapons first, but if the North won't give them up, you are left with walking away from the talks and sparking a crisis. You, therefore, have to make do with hard-nosed negotiations to reach as far into the program as you can get. The negotiations and implementation of the first nuclear agreement in 1994 were able to achieve a freeze of the North's nuclear operations. The Six-Party Talks agreements of 2005 and 2007 were able to get beyond a freeze to partial dismantlement of its nuclear programs. To borrow a football analogy, negotiating with North Korea is not done with the eighty-yard-long pass. It is a ground game, where you are fighting to get one yard at a time.

The fourth principle of dealing with the North has less to do with Pyongyang and more to do with the surrounding countries. The subtext of any multilateral negotiations over North Korea's nuclear program must be preparation for unification. It is one of the two contingencies in Asia that could plunge the region into crisis (the other is the Taiwan Straits), and yet the region is incredibly poorly prepared for it. After Kim Jong-il's stroke in 2008, the United States and ROK made substantial progress in planning for how to respond to a collapse of the DPRK, but outside of these two countries, there is no regionwide plan. China is a key player, and yet it is remarkably unwilling to have conversations, even on a secret basis, regarding how to coordinate responses, even after Kim Jong-il's death in 2011. Beijing is reluctant to do so for fear of leaks and because it does not want to give the impression that it is a willing accomplice in a plan to collapse the North. Yet some discussion

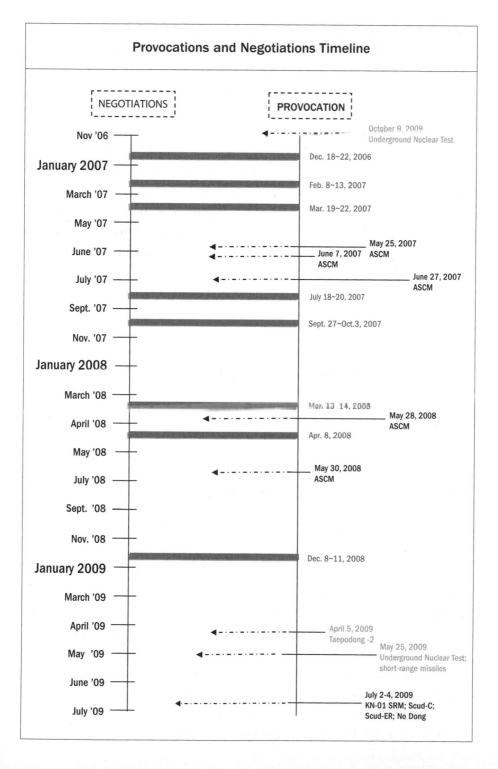

Provocations and Negotiations Timeline

is absolutely necessary. If the North collapses and the United States, ROK, and China have mutual suspicions of each other's actions and no benefit of transparency based on prior consultations, then the margin for miscalculation and conflict is large. However, if we all have a prior understanding of what each country sees as its key vulnerabilities in a DPRK collapse scenario, there is less margin for error.

In recent years, former cabinet-level and NSC officials from the Bush administration (including the author) engaged in a Track 1.5 dialogue with Chinese counterparts, which was modestly successful in making first steps. The Obama administration has pressed this issue with the Chinese in their annual Strategic and Economic Dialogue, and the ROK government has undertaken its own back-channel discussion with Beijing led by Blue House officials, which has, reportedly, made progress. It is clear, for example, that the Chinese worry about refugee flows into their country if order broke down in the North. Beijing is also worried about a possible nuclear accident in North Korea (especially after the nuclear disaster in Fukushima, Japan, in 2011) and the need for humanitarian relief in the event of another famine in Hamgyŏng provinces. They are also uncertain about the disposition of the rash of mining and business contracts signed with the North in recent years if order breaks down in Pyongyang. The ROK's top priority is to prevent migration into the South and to stabilize the humanitarian situation. Seoul also does not want any external power intervening without its consent. The U.S. top priority would be to secure the nuclear weapons and missile sites. Even these little kernels of information can constitute the start of mutually useful dialogue among Washington, Seoul, and Beijing.

Such preparations sound so commonsensical that to advocate them with urgency might appear comical. When I explain to long-term institutional investors in Asia, for example, that such preparations are not nearly as developed as one might think, many react with surprise that such a rational concern should not be addressed among even distrustful governments. But the fact of the matter is that it is hard to get governments to prepare for things that may happen tomorrow, because they are too busy reacting to things that happened yesterday.

The fifth principle for any future administration's policy toward

North Korea is not to forget about the people. The top-line issue for any administration is the threats posed by the North's nuclear programs and other weapons. Yet when the regime eventually collapses, what is likely to be revealed is one of the worst human rights disasters in modern times. In this regard, among any administration's policy objectives must be promoting measurable improvements in the lives of North Korean citizens and letting the North Korean people know that the United States wants to help them even as it opposes the DPRK government. Past administrations have laid out a template already, which future administrations can seek to improve on: a human rights envoy, a DPRK refugee resettlement program in the United States, food aid, advocacy to allow the UNHCR to interview North Korean defectors in China, and raising general international awareness of the human rights situation in the North.

Given the events of the Arab Spring, one of the key objectives of such a policy should be to use all means possible to increase the flow of information from the outside world into North Korea. Though the North Korean regime has done physical damage to its people through famine, imprisonment, and other draconian controls, perhaps the greatest human rights violation has been the effort to control the minds of its citizens by disallowing basic access to ideas. The DPRK regime is only as strong as its ability to control knowledge. This control enables the regime to stand on its ideology. *Neojuche*-ism and service to the Kim family is both the regime's strength and its weakness. Without control of information, there is no ideology. Without ideology, there is no North Korea as we know it. The Kim regime knows that its biggest threat comes from within rather than from without, and therefore would oppose an information campaign. Thus the data or message does not have to be of a blatantly political nature, explaining the virtues of American-style democracy over *juche* ideology. Given the efforts to hardwire the brains of North Koreans, this message may be more than the wavelengths can bear. But one could increase radio broadcasting into North Korea to puncture the bubble of propaganda that suffocates the people every day. A related effort would promote a "skills campaign" designed to inject more basic know-how into the country. With enhanced knowledge of practical things such as medicine, agriculture, engineering, computers, and foreign language, the North Korean people can do better for themselves and in the process become empowered with understanding of the outside world. Rather than give only heavy fuel oil in exchange for the next freeze on their operating nuclear programs, for example, future administrations might consider offering vocational training, medical supplies, vaccinations, and basic computers as part of a denuclearization package. Other nations not part of the U.S.-DPRK confrontation might also be called upon, because they might have better success at providing needed skills to the people. Many countries now have diplomatic relations with the DPRK, including Australia, Canada, New Zealand, and Indonesia, and they could be more effective than the United States or ROK in proposing such programs. Given the panoply of sanctions against the DPRK, some coordination would be necessary to ensure skills could be offered in a way that is compliant with the sanctions. But a wholesale importation of such skills might in the end be more potent than any sanction. Outside information would strike at the core of the ideology. Improving people's lives empowers them.

FINAL THOUGHTS

To paraphrase New York Yankees great Yogi Berra, making predictions about North Korea is difficult, especially those about their future. Many pundits speak with authority on a country about which we know less than almost any other in modern international relations. I have not claimed in this book to have any special knowledge about the regime. What I have offered in these pages is based on my study of the country as a scholar and my interaction with the regime during my period of service in the U.S. government. Even then, I cannot tell you with any degree of certainty what will happen tomorrow in this country. If you were to open your paper at your doorstep tomorrow morning, or turn on your computer with your morning coffee, and find a headline that informed you the DPRK had collapsed, I would have to admit that I would not be surprised. But if ten years from now the regime has outlived my predictions of serious crisis, I would also tell you that I am not surprised. The range of probability regarding the DPRK's ultimate fate is that wide. In this sense, it is truly the impossible state.

But one thing I am fairly certain of is that when the fateful day comes, the source of this battered country's renewal will be its people. Of the many memories seared into my mind from my short stint at the White House was the helicopter ride from the DMZ back to Seoul. I had just crossed over from the North, having spent four days there. As I was talking through the headsets with my control officer about the next part of my itinerary, my mind could not leave behind what I had seen in the North. Then the chopper banked to the left and the skyline of Seoul came into view. At that moment, I stopped to think about what I was seeing. I had seen this skyline at least one thousand times already, but it had a different meaning after my days in Pyongyang. While my control officer's voice was a distant mumble coming through my headset, I gazed at these ultramodern spires, the bustling traffic, and the energy of Seoul, and could not help but think as a political scientist that the only reason, the only possible explanation, for why this scene did not replicate in the North was because of politics. The North Korean people did not choose to be poor. They did not choose to have scores of windowless buildings and miles of barren farmland through which I had just been driven earlier that morning. North Koreans, I thought, are genetically as capable of producing what I saw from that helicopter over Seoul. Politics prevented them from doing so.

It was a moment I will never forget. It made me angry and sad, but it also made me hopeful. Because when the politics are gone, the North Korean people will have their chance. And just like the South, they will make the most of that opportunity in ways that will defy all the naysayers' low expectations. This is a day I hope to see in my lifetime.

ACKNOWLEDGMENTS

"THANK YOU FOR YOUR SERVICE TO THE NATION. YOU LEFT IT IN A BETTER PLACE than when you got here."

Those were the words of the president, referring to the vexing problem of North Korea, when we last spoke in the Oval Office. When you leave the National Security Council staff, you and your family are invited for a brief visit with the president to say good-bye and to take some pictures. It is a very nice practice and one that the president was extraordinarily genuine about. He felt his staff worked hard for him, and he never wanted any of them to leave without personally thanking them for their efforts.

When I departed the White House in 2007, I had no plan to write a book about North Korea. Although the Korean Peninsula was only one aspect of my Asia portfolio, it constituted such a time-suck that I was more than happy to be liberated from it. My NSC responsibilities were much broader, including relations with allies and partners like South Korea, Japan, Australia, New Zealand, and the Pacific Island nations; yet they were not the ones shooting ballistic missiles into the Pacific, or conducting nuclear tests in the middle of the night. The thought of trying to write about North Korea after having experienced everything from the euphoria of reaching unimagined denuclearization agreements to the nadir of a nuclear weapons test was both daunting and exhausting. It would have been like a runner, having just finished a marathon, writing about every exhausting step in excruciating detail. Instead, when I returned to campus as a professor at Georgetown University, I pulled out of my drawer a file full of articles and clippings I had collected about a topic I found terribly interesting—sports and politics—and ended up writing a book about the topic in the aftermath of the Beijing Olympics. That book was my way of decompressing after three years on the NSC.

I continued to consult for various branches of the U.S. government, and wrote some articles about U.S. policy in Asia, but there was always a nagging feeling inside of me that there was more to be said on North Korea than what I was reading in print. Some of this work was by authors who studied North Korea and who had forceful policy prescriptions about how to deal with their nuclear threats, but who had never had direct policy experience dealing with Pyongyang. Other works were by former policymakers who had visited North Korea but did not understand the country beyond their personal experiences and anecdotes. Having studied the place as a scholar, visited it as a White House official, and having negotiated with them for countless hours in denuclearization talks, I felt that I had a unique perspective to offer.

This book is meant to help you understand what you might hear on the news on any given day about North Korea. Undoubtedly, the news will usually be about a brash action or threat undertaken by the regime. To most, the country seems a little isolated. It was once led by a kooky leader, Kim Jong-il, who did unpredictable things. His death put power in the hands of a twentysomething who is even more unpredictable. But that is only half of the story. I hope to have educated you about the history of this country, how their leadership may view the world, why they are dead-set on pursuing nuclear weapons, and how the regime may be closer to its end than many think. Yet if the latter is true, the United States and the world are terribly unprepared and spectacularly misinformed if something goes really wrong there.

I owe a debt of gratitude to a stable of young and eager researchers: Alex Bartlett, Marie Dumond, Jeonghoon Ha, Kat Harrington, Andrea Hong, Jenny Jun, Barbra Kim, Ellen Kim, Sang Jun Lee, Sookook Kim, Hanseok Ko, Anna Park, Yuri Park, and Daniel Yoon. Special thanks go to Nick Anderson. As a graduate student, Nick came to Georgetown, where he also worked as an intern at CSIS before I took him on as a full-time research assistant. He has been tremendously helpful in filling in what needed to be filled in, both in terms of the book's substantive arguments and its facts. This book was written under severe time constraints and it could not have happened without Nick's consistently excellent research support. I feel fortunate to have worked with him, because his future as a scholar of Asian studies is bright.

I would like to thank the following individuals, all close colleagues in academia and policy, for reading portions of the manuscript: Kurt

Campbell, Bob Gallucci, Brad Glosserman, Mike Green, David Kang, Sung Kim, and Jennifer Maher. Special thanks to Bob Gallucci for providing helpful comments on chapter 7. I have benefited greatly from ongoing conversations about Korea with John Hamre at CSIS and Chong Moon Lee, Jungwook Kim, Jeff Bader, Danny Russel, Dennis Wilder, Kurt Tong, Edgard Kagan, Christopher Hill, and Syd Seiler.

I am grateful to Daniel Sanborn and Mary Ronan at the National Security Council for having the manuscript vetted in such a timely fashion.

I am indebted to my friend and former NSC colleague Paul Haenle for permission to use his pictures. I also thank Paul Morse and Eric Draper for the use of pictures from my time at the White House. An earlier version of pages 300–310 in chapter 7 and pages 449–56 in chapter 10 appeared in the *Washington Quarterly* (October 2009); as well as pages 416–22 of chapter 9, which appeared in *Orbis* (Spring 2011).

This book would not have happened without Dan Halpern, my editor at Ecco, who patiently pursued me to become one of his authors, then gently urged me to write the book quickly, and then offered sage advice along the way. I am grateful to Shanna Milkey for her shepherding of the work to completion. Kudos to Andrew Schwartz, Heather Drucker, and Joanna Pinsker for publicizing the work. Thanks to Anne Routon and Chuck Myers for their patience in allowing me to take on this project while I owe each of them something else.

I thank the Academy of Korean Studies and Korea Global Lab for their generous support.

This book is dedicated to my mother, Soon Ock, and my wife, Hyun Jung. The two women in my life who constitute my moral compass, always encouraging me to undertake every task with responsibility and never let down those who count on me.

Dad, I miss you every day and know you are smiling down on us.

Thanks to my sons, Patrick and Andrew, who tolerated my habitual tardiness in picking them up from baseball, tennis, and basketball practices because I tried to steal an extra ten minutes to finish writing just one more page of the book at the local Panera Bread.

NOTES

CHAPTER ONE: CONTRADICTIONS

1. Helen-Louise Hunter, "The Society and Its Values," in Robert L. Worden, ed., *North Korea: A Country Study* (Washington, D.C.: Library of Congress, 2009), pp. 76–77.
2. Goohoon Kwon, "A Unified Korea? Reassessing North Korea Risks," *Goldman Sachs Global Economics Paper 188* (September 21, 2009), p. 10.
3. The eight other states are Burma, Equatorial Guinea, Eritrea, Libya, Somalia, Sudan, Turkmenistan, and Uzbekistan, having both political rights and civil liberties scores as low as is possible (7). See "Worst of the Worst 2011: The World's Most Repressive Societies," Freedom House (2011), http://www.freedomhouse.org/uploads/special_report/101.pdf (accessed June 3, 2011).
4. *Shuang Long Hui (Twin Dragons),* directed by Ringo Lam and Hark Tsui (Hong Kong: Golden Harvest and Media Asia Distribution, 1992).
5. According to the Unification Ministry, as of April 17, 2011, the total number of North Korean defectors residing in South Korea is 21,165. See "Number of N. Korean Defectors in S. Korea Tops 21,000," *Yonhap News,* May 14, 2011, http://english .yonhapnews.co.kr/ (accessed June 4, 2011).
6. *Survey of 297 North Korean Defectors* (Seoul National University: Institute for Peace and Unification Studies, July 24, 2008).
7. Michael Breen, *Kim Jong-Il: North Korea's Dear Leader* (Singapore: John Wiley & Sons, 2004), p. 5.
8. *Gone with the Wind,* directed by Victor Fleming (USA: Warner Bros., 1940).
9. *Team America: World Police,* directed by Trey Parker (USA: Paramount Pictures, 2004).
10. *The Economist* (June 17–23, 2000).
11. Chico Harlan, "North Korean Ruler and Heir Attend Parade," *Washington Post,* October 11, 2010.
12. Andrew Higgins, "Who Will Succeed Kim Jong-il?" *Washington Post,* July 16, 2009.

CHAPTER TWO: THE BEST DAYS

1. "Chapter 25: The Korean War, 1950–1953," in *American Military History* (Washington, D.C.: Center for Military History, U.S. Army, 2001), p. 570.
2. Kongdan Oh and Ralph C. Hassig, *North Korea: Through the Looking Glass* (Washington, D.C.: Brookings Institution Press, 2000), p. 48.
3. Energy consumption is measured as primary energy use (before transformation to other end-use fuels) in kilograms of oil equivalent, per capita. "World Development Indicators," Worldbank.org (2011), http://data.worldbank.org/data-catalog/world-development-indicators (accessed January 31, 2011).
4. See Joseph S. Chung, "The Economy," in Andrea Matles Savada, ed., *North Korea: A Country Study* (Washington, D.C.: Library of Congress, 1994).

5. Ibid.
6. Ibid.
7. Ibid.
8. Jon Halliday, "The North Korean Enigma," *New Left Review*, no. 127 (May–June 1981), p. 39.
9. Harrison E. Salisbury, *To Peking and Beyond—A Report on the New Asia* (New York: Pedigree, 1973), p. 175.
10. Tim Kane, "Global U.S. Troop Deployment, 1950–2003," Heritage.org (October 27, 2004), http://www.heritage.org/research/reports/2004/10/global-us-troop-deployment-1950–2003 (accessed February 24, 2011).
11. Andrew Scobell and John M. Sanford, *North Korea's Military Threat: Pyongyang's Conventional Forces, Weapons of Mass Destruction, and Ballistic Missiles* (Carlyle, Pa.: Strategic Studies Institute, 2007), p. 21.
12. Homer T. Hodge, "North Korea's Military Strategy," *Parameters* (Spring 2003), pp. 68–81.
13. Scobell and Sanford, *North Korea's Military Threat*, p. 34.
14. See Chung "The Economy," in Savada, *North Korea*.
15. Ibid.
16. Nikita S. Khrushchev, "The Secret Speech—On the Cult of Personality, 1956," Fordham.edu (1956), http://www.fordham.edu/halsall/mod/1956khrushchev-secret1.html (accessed February 2, 2011).
17. Philip Short, *Mao: A Life* (New York: Henry Holt and Company, 2001), pp. 503–4.
18. Thomas P. Bernstein and Andrew J. Nathan, "The Soviet Union, China, and Korea," in Gerald L. Curtis and Sung-joo Han, eds., *The U.S.–South Korea Alliance: Evolving Patterns and Security Relations* (Lexington, Mass.: LexingtonBooks, 1983), p. 99.
19. Ibid., p. 99.
20. Victor Cha, "Powerplay: Origins of the U.S. Alliance System in Asia," *International Security*, vol. 34, no. 3 (Winter 2010).
21. "President Nixon's Speech on 'Vietnamization,'" Vassar.edu (November 3, 1969), http://vietnam.vassar.edu/overview/doc14.html (accessed June 17, 2011).
22. Chen Jian, *Mao's China and the Cold War* (Chapel Hill: University of North Carolina Press, 2000), p. 269.
23. Jimmy Carter quoted in Victor D. Cha, *Alignment Despite Antagonism: The United States-Korea-Japan Security Triangle* (Stanford, Calif.: Stanford University Press, 1999), p. 145.
24. Syngman Rhee was ousted by widespread demonstrations in 1960. His successor, Yoon Bo-seon (1960–1962), was overthrown in a military coup by Park Chung-hee in 1961. Park remained in power until 1979, when he was assassinated by his director of intelligence. Park's successor, Choi Kyu-ha (1979–1980), was overthrown in a military coup in December 1979.
25. Han S. Park, *North Korea: The Politics of Unconventional Wisdom* (Boulder, Colo.: Lynne-Reiner, 2002).
26. B. R. Myers, *The Cleanest Race: How North Koreans See Themselves and Why It Matters* (New York: Melville House, 2010).
27. Sin Sang-ok and Ch'oe Ŭn-hŭi, *Sugi: Nere Kim Jong il Ipnida* (Diary: I Am Kim Jong-il) (Seoul: Haenglim Publisher, 1994), p. 19.

28. C. Kenneth Quinones and Joseph Tragert, *The Complete Idiot's Guide to Understanding North Korea* (New York: Alpha Books, 2003).

29. Hy-Sang Lee, *North Korea: A Strange Socialist Fortress* (Westport, Conn.: Praeger Publishers, 2001), p. 27.

30. Ibid., p. 103.

31. Ermanno Furlanis, "I Made Pizza for Kim Jong-il," *Asia Times,* August 4, 2001, http://www.atimes.com/koreas/CH04Dg01.html (accessed May 18, 2010).

32. Kim Il-sung, "The Results of the Agrarian Reforms and Future Tasks," report to the sixth enlarged executive committee meeting of the North Korean Organizing Committee of the Communist Party of Korea, April 10, 1946, *Selected Works,* vol. 1 (1971), p. 37.

33. Donald Oberdorfer, *The Two Koreas: A Contemporary History* (New York: Basic Books, 2001), p. 10.

34. At this time, Kim's confidence was also manifest in his wholesale rejection of the Cultural Revolution in China. When Kim secretly met CPSU general secretary Leonid Brezhnev in Vladivostok in December 1966, he described the Cultural Revolution as "massive idiocy" and declared that the DPRK would follow a self-reliant and independent path from China. Similarly, North Koreans talked disparagingly to the Cubans about Mao's senility. GDR archives cited in Bernd Schaefer, "North Korean 'Adventurism' and China's Long Shadow, 1966–1972," Woodrow Wilson Center Cold War Archives Project, Working Paper 44 (October 2004), http://www.wilsoncen ter.org/topics/pubs/swp44.pdf (accessed December 19, 2010), pp. 9–13.

35. Bui Tin, "Fight for the Long Haul: The War as Seen by a Soldier in the People's Army of Vietnam," in Andrew Wiest, ed., *Rolling Thunder in a Gentle Land: The Vietnam War Revisited* (Oxford, UK: Osprey Publishing, 2006), p. 64.

36. "Embassy of the GDR in the PRC. October 22, 1971. The Position of the DPRK on the Forthcoming Nixon Visit in the PRC," cited in Schaefer, "North Korean 'Adventurism,'" http://www.wilsoncenter.org/topics/pubs/swp44.pdf (accessed December 19, 2010), pp. 34–35.

37. "Excerpts from Speech Delivered at a Banquet Given at the Great Hall of the People in Peking by the Central Committee of the Communist Party of China and the State Council of the People's Republic of China in Honor of the Party and Government Delegation of the Democratic People's Republic of Korea," Songun politicsstudygroup.org (April 18, 1975), http://www.songunpoliticsstudygroup .org/kimilsungspeechapril181975.html (accessed December 19, 2010).

38. "Report on the Official Friendship Visit to the DPRK by the Party and State Delegation of the GDR, led by Com. Erich Honecker, December 8, 1977, SAPMO-BA, DY 30, J IV 2/2A/2123," in North Korea in the Cold War Collection, Woodrow Wilson Center Cold War International History Project, http://www.wilsoncenter .org/index.cfm?topic_id=1409&fuseaction=va2.document&identifier=F26BC540-0F93-4A9A-FC10ADDBD95F582B&sort=Collection&item=North%20Korea%20 in%20the%20Cold%20War (accessed December 29, 2010).

39. Stenographic record of conversation between Erich Honecker and Kim Il-sung, May 30, 1984, SAPMO-BA, DY 30, 2460, in North Korea in the Cold War Collection, Woodrow Wilson Center Cold War International History Project, http://www.wilsoncenter.org/index.cfm?topic_id=1409&fuseaction=va2.document

&identifier=011D0BD8-C4D3-4C59-CCF31FC248028B81&sort=Collection&item=North%20Korea%20in%20the%20Cold%20War (accessed December 29, 2010).

40. Taik-young Hamm, *Arming the Two Koreas: State, Capital and Military Power* (London: Routledge, 1999), pp. 106–7.

41. "World Development Indicators," Worldbank.org.

42. RAND Corporation study cited in Hamm, *Arming the Two Koreas,* p. 56.

43. Ibid., p. 131.

44. "The Bank of Korea Economic Statistics System," BOK.or.kr (2011), http://ecos.bok.or.kr/ (accessed March 2011).

45. Joseph S. Bermudez, *The Armed Forces of North Korea* (New York: St. Martin's Press, 2001), pp. 38–39.

46. *2010 Defense White Paper* (Seoul: Republic of Korea Ministry of National Defense, 2010), p. 24.

47. Bruce E. Bechtol, *Defiant Failed State: The North Korean Threat to International Security* (Dulles, Va.: Potomac Books, 2010), p. 24.

48. Stu Russell, "The Digit Affair," USSPueblo.org (2010), http://www.uss pueblo.org/Prisoners/The_Digit_Affair.html (accessed February 23, 2011).

49. Michael Breen, *Kim Jong-il: North Korea's Dear Leader* (Hoboken, N.J.: John Wiley & Sons, 2004), p. 28.

50. John Glionna, "The Face of South Korea's Boogeyman," *Los Angeles Times,* July 18, 2010.

51. David E. Pearson, *The World-Wide Military Command and Control System: Evolution and Effectiveness* (Maxwell AFB, Ala.: Air University Press, 2000), pp. 84–91.

52. Oberdorfer, *The Two Koreas,* p. 59.

53. "DMZ—DPRK Tunnels," Globalsecurity.org (2011), http://www.globalsecu rity.org/military/world/dprk/kpa-tunnels.htm (accessed January 31, 2011).

54. Oberdorfer, *The Two Koreas,* p. 142.

55. Video of the assassination attempt is available at "Burma, Myanmar: South Korean President Chun Doo Hwan Assassination Attempt," Ash inmettacara.org (July 3, 2009), http://www.ashinmettacara.org/2009/07/burma-myanmarsouth-korean-president.html (accessed January 5, 2011).

56. As University of Georgia professor and acclaimed *juche* expert Park Hanshik states, "The notion that nuclear weaponry is the only 'guarantor' for national security and a reliable means of deterrence against military provocation from hostile governments is a direct product of *sŏn'gun* politics." Han S. Park, "Military-First (*Sŏn'gun*) Politics: Implications for External Policies," in Kyung-Ae Park, ed., *New Challenges of North Korean Foreign Policy* (New York: Palgrave, 2010), p. 103.

57. Han S. Park, "Military-First (*Sŏn'gun*) Politics," in Kyung-Ae Park, ed., *New Challenges of North Korean Foreign Policy,* p. 91.

58. Rüdiger Frank, "Socialist Neoconservatism and North Korean Foreign Policy," in Kyung-Ae Park, ed., *New Challenges of North Korean Foreign Policy,* pp. 15–16.

59. Ibid., p. 10.

60. "Joint New Year Editorial Issued," KCNA (January 1, 2009 [*Juche* 98]), http://www.kcna.co.jp/index-e.htm (accessed January 18, 2011).

61. The typically verbose title of the 2011 editorial is "Bring About a Decisive Turn in the Improvement of the People's Standard of Living and the Building of a Great, Prosperous and Powerful Country by Accelerating the Development of Light Industry Once Again This Year." See "Joint New Year Editorial," KCNA (January 1, 2011 [*Juche* 99]), http://www.kcna.co.jp/index-e.htm (accessed January 18, 2011).

62. "Joint New Year Editorial of Leading Newspapers in DPRK," KCNA (January 1, 2008 [*Juche* 97]), http://www.kcna.co.jp/index-e.htm (accessed January 18, 2011).

63. KCNA (January 1, 2009).

CHAPTER THREE: ALL IN THE FAMILY

1. Kenji Fujimoto, "I Was Kim Jong Il's Cook," reprinted in *The Atlantic* (January/February 2004), http://www.theatlantic.com/issues/2004/01/fuji moto.htm (accessed June 19, 2011).

2. Sydney A. Seiler, *Kim Il-sŏng 1941–1948: The Creation of a Legend, the Building of a Regime* (Lanham, Md.: University Press of America, 1994), pp. 55–56.

3. Dae-Sook Suh, *Kim Il Sung: The North Korean Leader* (New York: Columbia University Press, 1988), p. 5; Don Oberdorfer, *The Two Koreas: A Contemporary History*, rev. ed. (New York: Basic Books, 2001), p. 12; Sung Chul Yang, *Korea and the Two Regimes: Kim Il Sung and Park Chung Hee* (Cambridge, Mass.: Schenkman Publishing Company, 1981), p. 32.

4. Andrei Lankov, *From Stalin to Kim Il Sung: The Formation of North Korea 1945–1960* (New Brunswick, N.J.: Rutgers University Press, 2002), p. 59.

5. Seiler, *Kim Il-sŏng 1941–1948*, pp. 31–38.

6. "Report Describes Soviet Abuses in N. Korea," *Dong-A Ilbo*, March 10, 2010, http://english.donga.com/srv/service.php3?bicode=050000&biid=2010031031168 (accessed October 14, 2010).

7. "Stalin's Meeting with Kim Il Sung," March 5, 1949, Archive of the Foreign Policy of the Russian Federation, *fond* 059a, *opis* 5a, *delo* 3, *papka* 11, *listy* 10–20. Cold War International History Project, Woodrow Wilson Center.

8. Jasper Becker, *Rogue Regime: Kim Jong Il and the Looming Threat of North Korea* (New York: Oxford University Press, 2005), p. 127.

9. Ibid., p. 69.

10. Hahn Jae Duk, quoted in Yang, *Korea and the Two Regimes*, p. 82.

11. *Kim Il Sung: The Great Man of the Century, Volume II* (Pyongyang, Korea: Foreign Languages Publishing House, 1994), p. 93.

12. B. R. Myers, "North Korea's Race Problem: What I Learned in Eight Years Reading Propaganda from Inside the Hermit Kingdom," *Foreign Policy Magazine* (March/April 2010), pp. 100–101.

13. Andrei Lankov, "Why the United States Will Have to Accept a Nuclear North Korea," *Korean Journal of Defense Analysis*, vol. 21, no. 3 (September 2009), pp. 253–54.

14. Kyung-Ae Park, "People's Exit, Regime Stability and North Korean Diplomacy," in Kyung-Ae Park, ed., *New Challenges of North Korean Foreign Policy* (New York: Palgrave, 2010), pp. 49–52.

15. Bruce Cumings, *The Korean War: A History* (New York: Modern Library, 2010), p. 35; Oberdorfer, *The Two Koreas*, p. 9.

16. *James Bond: Die Another Day,* directed by Lee Tamahori (USA: MGM Studios, 2002).
17. Seiler, *Kim Il-sŏng 1941–1948,* pp. 196–97.
18. Michael Breen, *Kim Jong-Il: North Korea's Dear Leader* (Singapore: John Wiley & Sons, 2004), pp. 64–65.
19. Breen, *Kim Jong-Il,* p. 6; Becker, *Rogue Regime,* p. 127.
20. Mark Ziegler, "While the Rest of the World Watches Kim Jong Il, Fearful of North Korea's Nuclear Threat, the Dictator Often Can't Take His Eyes Off . . . the NBA," *San Diego Union-Tribune,* October 29, 2006, http://legacy .signonsandiego.com/news/world/20061029-9999-1n29kim.html (accessed October 7, 2010).
21. Fujimoto, "I Was Kim Jong Il's Cook."
22. Becker, *Rogue Regime,* pp. 43–44.
23. Ermanno Furlanis, "I Made Pizza for Kim Jong-il. Part 2: Hot Ovens at the Seaside," *Asia Times,* August 11, 2001, http://www.atimes.com/koreas/CH11Dg02.html (accessed October 15, 2010). For complete story, see also part 1 (http://www.atimes.com/koreas/CH04Dg01.html) and part 3 (http://www.atimes.com/koreas/CH17Dg03.html).
24. Jasper Becker, "A Gulag with Nukes," Opendemocracy.net (July 18, 2005), http://www.opendemocracy.net/globalization-institutions_government/north_korea_2686.jsp (accessed October 18, 2010).
25. *Joongang Ilbo,* October 4, 1991.
26. Yuriko Koike, "A Ruthless Sister Becomes North Korea's Next Ruler," *Daily Star* (September 16, 2010), http://www.dailystar.com.lb/article.asp?edition_id=10&categ_id=5&article_id=119330#axzz0zwdV6uYa (accessed October 9, 2010); and Michael Madsen, "Biographical Sketch of Kim Kyong-hui" (2010), http://nkleadershipwatch.files.wordpress.com/2010/04/kim-kyong-hui-basic (accessed October 9, 2010).
27. "Kim Ok at Dear Leader's Sickbed," *Korea Times,* September 13, 2008, http://www.koreatimes.co.kr/www/news/nation/2010/05/113_31010.html (accessed October 9, 2010).
28. Yang Jung A, "Kim Jong Il's Wife Kim Ok Pursues Kim Jong Woon as Successor" (June 2, 2008), http://www.dailynk.com/english/read.php?cataId=nk02300&num=3672 (accessed October 9, 2010).
29. Sin Sang-ok and Ch'oe Ŭn-hŭi, *Sugi: Nere kim jong il ipnida* (Diary: I Am Kim Jong-il) (Seoul: Haenglim Publisher, 1994), p. 19. Also see Helen-Louise Hunter, *Kim Il-song's North Korea* (New York: Praeger, 1999).
30. "KPA Warning on U.S.–S. Korea War Manuevers," KCNA (August 15, 2010), http://www.kcna.co.jp/index-e.htm (accessed November 9, 2010).
31. "Japanese Reactionaries' Visits to 'Yasukuni Shrine' Blasted," KCNA (August 25, 2008), http://www.kcna.co.jp/index-e.htm (accessed November 9, 2010).
32. "KCNA Blasts S. Korea's Anti-DPRK 'Human Rights' Racket," KCNA (December 5, 2009), http://www.kcna.co.jp/index-e.htm (accessed November 9, 2010).
33. "North Korea Bans Bolton from Talks," Washingtontimes.com (August 4, 2003), http://www.washingtontimes.com/news/2003/aug/4/20030804-121425-6611r/ (accessed November 9, 2010).
34. "U.S. VP's Vituperation Against DPRK's Headquarters Rebuked," KCNA (June 3, 2005), http://www.kcna.co.jp/index-e.htm (accessed November 9, 2010).

35. "KCNA Blasts Rumsfeld's Vituperation," KCNA (November 25, 2003), http://www .kcna.co.jp/index-e.htm (accessed November 9, 2010).

36. U.S. State Department, "Patterns of Global Terrorism, 2000—Overview of State Sponsored Terrorism" (April 30, 2001), http://www.state.gov/s/ct/rls/crt/2000/2441 .htm (accessed November 10, 2010).

37. Mark E. Manyin, "North Korea: Back on the Terrorism List?" Congressional Research Service Report for Congress, RL30613 (June 29, 2010), pp. 20–25; Bruce E. Bechtol Jr., *Defiant Failed State: The North Korean Threat to International Security* (Dulles, Va.: Potomac Books, 2010), pp. 63–66.

38. The nuclear tests took place in 1991, according to North Korean defector Hwang Chang-yŏp. See Bradley Martin, *Under the Loving Care of the Fatherly Leader: North Korea and the Kim Dynasty* (New York: St. Martin's Press, 2004), p. 436.

39. Paul French, *North Korea: The Paranoid Peninsula—A Modern History,* 2nd ed. (New York: Zed Books, 2007), p. 59.

40. Martin, *Under the Loving Care,* pp. 282–86, 317.

41. French, *North Korea,* p. 59; Martin, *Under the Loving Care,* p. 244; Oberdorfer, *The Two Koreas,* p. 346.

42. Martin, *Under the Loving Care,* p. 507; Richard Worth, *Kim Jong Il* (New York: Chelsea House, 2008), p. 84.

43. Han S. Park, "Military-First (*Sŏn'gun*) Politics: Implications for External Policies," in Kyung-Ae Park, ed., *New Challenges of North Korean Foreign Policy* (New York: Palgrave, 2010), p. 103.

44. "The Crumbling State of Healthcare in North Korea," Amnesty.org (July 2010), http://www.amnesty.org/en/library/info/ASA24/001/2010/en (accessed November 15, 2010).

45. Stephan Haggard and Marcus Noland, *Famine in North Korea: Markets, Aid, and Reform* (New York: Columbia University Press, 2007), p. 1.

46. Becker, *Rogue Regime,* p. 145.

47. Martin, *Under the Loving Care,* p. 642.

48. Madeleine Albright, *Madam Secretary* (New York: Miramax Books, 2003), p. 467.

49. "Interview: Charles Kartman," PBS.org (February 20, 2003), http://www .pbs.org/ wgbh/pages/frontline/shows/kim/interviews/kartman.html (accessed December 11, 2010).

50. There remain questions over whether Kim Jong-il's second son, Kim Jong-chol, attended the International School of Berne while Kim Jong-un attended Liebefeld. Stories that are associated with Kim Jong-un at the International School may be mistakenly referring to his older brother, Jong-chol.

51. Personal interview, January 4, 2010, Washington, D.C.

52. Andrew Higgins, "Who Will Succeed Kim Jong Il?" *Washington Post,* July 16, 2009.

53. Cited in ibid.

54. "N. Propaganda Describes Kim Jong-eun as 'Genius,'" *Chosun Ilbo,* October 20, 2010.

55. "Data and Statistics," International Monetary Fund (2010), http://www.imf.org/ex ternal/data.htm (accessed December 8, 2010).

56. "Freedom of the Press 2010," Freedom House (2010), http://www.freedom house.org/

template.cfm?page=16 (accessed December 8, 2010); "The 2009 Corruption Perceptions Index," Transparency International (2010), http://www.transparency.org/policy _research/surveys_indices/cpi/2009 (accessed December 8, 2010).

57. Victor D. Cha, "Korea's Place in the Axis," *Foreign Affairs,* vol. 81, no. 3 (May/June 2002), pp. 79–92.

58. "North Korea Reverts to Hard-line State Control," *Chosun Ilbo,* January 3, 2011.

CHAPTER FOUR: FIVE BAD DECISIONS

1. North Korean GNI per capita for 2009 is estimated at $960 while South Korea's latest GNI per capita figure is $20,759 (for 2010). "Bank of Korea Economic Statistics System," BOK.or.kr (2011), http://ecos.bok.or.kr/EIn dex_en.isp (accessed April 15, 2011).

2. John Wu, "The Mineral Industry of North Korea," 2005 Minerals Yearbook: North Korea (U.S. Geological Survey, June 2007), p. 151.

3. Goohoon Kwon, "A Unified Korea? Reassessing North Korea Risks," *Goldman Sachs Global Economics Paper 188* (September 21, 2009), p. 10.

4. "Soviet Economic Assistance to Its Sino-Soviet Bloc Countries," CIA Declassified Document (June 13, 1955), http://www.foia.cia.gov/ (accessed April 7, 2011).

5. Samuel S. Kim, "Sino–North Korean Relations in the Post–Cold War World," in Yong Hwan Kihl and Hong Nak Kim, eds., *North Korea: The Politics of Regime Survival* (Armonk, N.Y.: M. E. Sharpe, 2006), p. 195.

6. Eui Gak Hwang, *The Korean Economies: A Comparison of North and South* (New York: Oxford University Press, 1993), p. 204.

7. Ibid.

8. Kim Il-sung, "On Accelerating the Construction of the Taedonggang Power Station," May 8, 1974, *Chojakchip* (Works), vol. 29, 1987, pp. 192–93 cited, in Hy-Sang Lee, *North Korea,* p. 110.

9. Kim Il-sung, "On the Immediate Tasks of the Government of the Democratic People's Republic of Korea," speech at the First Session of the Third Supreme People's Assembly, October 23, 1962, *Selected Works,* vol. 3 (Pyongyang: Foreign Languages Publishing House, 1971), p. 392.

10. Andrew Scobell and John M. Sanford, *North Korea's Military Threat: Pyongyang's Conventional Forces, Weapons of Mass Destruction, and Ballistic Missiles* (Washington, D.C.: Strategic Studies Institute, 2007), pp. 21–23.

11. Hy-Sang Lee, *North Korea,* p. 3.

12. Robert Marquand, "North Korea Offers to Pay Off Czech Debt," *Christian Science Monitor* (August 11, 2010), http://www.csmonitor.com/World/Eu rope/2010/0811/North-Korea-offers-to-pay-off-Czech-debt-with-Korean-ginseng (accessed February 8, 2011).

13. See Victor Cha, *Beyond the Final Score: The Politics of Sport in Asia* (New York: Columbia University Press, 2009), chapter 4.

14. "Vinalon, the North's Proud Invention," FAS, http://www.fas.org/nuke/guide/dprk/facility/industry38.htm (accessed April 15, 2011).

15. One ri is equal to 500 meters or 1,640 feet. "Treasure House of Literature and Arts Enriched," KCNA (December 9, 2010), http://www.kcna.co.jp/item/2010/201012/news09/20101209-08ee.html (accessed April 14, 2011); "Kim Jong Il Enjoys 'Octo-

ber Concert,'" KCNA (November 1, 2010), http://www.kcna.co.jp/item/2010/201011/news01/20101101-17ee.html (accessed April 14, 2011); "Art Performance Goes on in Hamhung," KCNA (March 13, 2010), http://www.kcna.co.jp/item/2010/201003/news13/20100313-03ee.html (accessed April 14, 2011).

16. Eva Hagberg, "The Worst Building in the History of Mankind," *Esquire* (January 28, 2008), http://www.esquire.com/the-side/DESIGN/hotel-of-doom-012808 (accessed February 13, 2011).

17. Donald Kirk, "Orascom Gets into Pyramid Business," *Asia Times,* December 23, 2008, http://www.atimes.com/atimes/Korea/JL23Dg01.html (accessed February 13, 2011).

18. Stephan Haggard and Marcus Noland, *Famine in North Korea: Markets, Aid, and Reform* (New York: Columbia University Press, 2007), p. 28.

19. Nicholas Eberstadt, *The North Korean Economy: Between Crisis and Catastrophe* (New Brunswick, N.J.: Transaction Publishers, 2007), pp. 75–76.

20. Ibid., p. 106.

21. Joseph S. Chung, "The Economy," in Andrea Matles Savada, ed., *North Korea: A Country Study* (Washington, D.C.: Library of Congress, 1994).

22. Philip H. Park, *Self-Reliance or Self-Destruction: Success and Failure of the Democratic People's Republic of Korea's Development Strategy of Self-Reliance "Juche"* (New York: Routledge, 2002), p. 114.

23. Jaewoo Choo, "Mirroring North Korea's Growing Economic Dependence on China: Political Ratification," *Asian Survey,* vol. 48, no. 2 (March/April 2008), p. 359.

24. Ibid., pp. 347–48.

25. Stephan Haggard and Marcus Noland, "North Korea's External Economic Relations," *PIIE Working Paper Series,* WP 07-7 (August 2007), p. 28.

26. "World Food Programme Food Aid Information System," World Food Programme (2011), http://www.wfp.org/fais/ (accessed April 4, 2011).

27. Haggard and Noland, *Famine in North Korea,* pp. 30–31.

28. Food made up 50 percent of total South Korean outlays to the DPRK and more than 50 percent of all U.S. assistance. It constituted almost all of Japanese assistance until Tokyo ceased all food shipments in 2002 over revelations about North Korean abductions of Japanese citizens.

29. "North Korea Probes Corruption in Investment Agencies," RFA.org (January 30, 2008), http://www.rfa.org/english/news/nkorea_corruption-20080130.html (accessed April 11, 2011).

30. Andrei Lankov, quoted in "Investing in the Fatherland: Corruption in North Korea," RFAUnplugged.org (January 30, 2008), http://www.rfaun plugged.org/ (accessed April 11, 2011).

31. Hazel Smith, *Hungry for Peace: International Security, Humanitarian Assistance, and Social Change in North Korea* (Washington, D.C.: United States Institute of Peace Press, 2005), p. 67.

32. U.N. report quoted in Smith, *Hungry for Peace,* p. 67.

33. The North Korean economy was approximately US$23.2 billion in 1990 and contracted to $12.6 billion by 1998.

34. The Staff of U.S. Representative Ed Royce (R-CA), "Gangster Regime: How North Korea Counterfeits U.S. Currency," House.gov (March 14, 2007), http://www.royce

.house.gov/uploadedfiles/report.3.12.07.FINAL.Ganster Regime.pdf (accessed March 14, 2011).

35. David E. Kaplan, "The Wiseguy Regime," USNews.com (February 7, 1999), http://www.usnews.com/usnews/news/articles/990215/archive_000266.htm (accessed March 14, 2011).

36. "Narco Korea," *TIMEasia* (June 2, 2003), http://www.time.com/time/asia/covers/501030609/index.html (accessed March 14, 2011).

37. Bill Powell and Adam Zagorin, "The Tony Soprano of North Korea," Time.com (July 12, 2007), http://www.time.com/time/magazine/article/0,9171,1642898,00.html (accessed March 14, 2011).

38. See Paul Rexon Kan, et al., "Criminal Sovereignty: Understanding North Korea's Illicit International Activities," *Strategic Studies Institute Letort Paper* (April 12, 2010), http://www.strategicstudiesinstitute.army.mil/pubs/display.cfm?pubID=975 (accessed March 14, 2011).

39. Sheena Chestnut, "Illicit Activity and Proliferation: North Korean Smuggling Networks," *International Security*, vol. 32, no. 1 (Summer 2007), pp. 85–86; Andrew J. Coe, "North Korea's New Cash Crop," *Washington Quarterly*, vol. 28, no. 3 (Summer 2005), p. 75.

40. Balbina Y. Hwang, "Curtailing North Korea's Illicit Activities," *Heritage Foundation Backgrounder*, no. 1679 (August 25, 2003), p. 3.

41. Chestnut, "Illicit Activity and Proliferation," p. 92; Hwang, "Curtailing North Korea's Illicit Activities," p. 2; Raphael F. Perl, "Drug Trafficking and North Korea: Issues for U.S. Policy," Congressional Research Service Report for Congress, RL32167 (January 25, 2007), p. 15; Liana Sun Wyler and Dick K. Nanto, "North Korean Crime-for-Profit Activities," Congressional Research Service Report for Congress, RL33885 (August 25, 2008), p. 3.

42. Chestnut, "Illicit Activity and Proliferation," pp. 89–90; Hwang, "Curtailing North Korea's Illicit Activities," p. 3; Kan, et al., "Criminal Sovereignty," p. 5.

43. Hwang, "Curtailing North Korea's Illicit Activities," p. 3.

44. Kan, et al., "Criminal Sovereignty," p. 24.

45. Chestnut, "Illicit Activity and Proliferation," p. 89; Hwang, "Curtailing North Korea's Illicit Activities," p. 3.

46. Chestnut, "Illicit Activity and Proliferation," p. 90.

47. Kim Young-il, "North Korean Narcotics Trafficking: A View from the Inside," *North Korea Review*, vol. 1, no. 1 (February 29, 2004), http://www.jamestown.org/single/?no_cache=1&tx_ttnews[tt_news]=26320 (accessed March 17, 2011).

48. On the Burmese, see Chestnut, "Illicit Activity and Proliferation," p. 98; on the Taiwanese delegations, see Kan, et al., "Criminal Sovereignty," p. 12; on the Chinese and Taiwanese counterfeiters, see Chestnut, "Illicit Activity and Proliferation," p. 91.

49. See Chestnut, "Illicit Activity and Proliferation," p. 95; Kan, et al., "Criminal Sovereignty," p. 11.

50. It is important to note that the Australian government acquitted all of the North Korean crew members due to insufficient evidence. Stephan Haggard and Marcus Noland, "North Korea's External Economic Relations," *Peterson Institute for International Economics Working Paper Series*, WP 07-7 (August 2007), pp. 6–7; Perl, "Drug

Trafficking and North Korea," pp. 6–7n23, p. 13; Wyler and Nanto, "North Korean Crime-for-Profit Activities," pp. 4–5.

51. Wyler and Nanto, "North Korean Crime-for-Profit Activities," p. 4.

52. Jasper Becker, *Rogue Regime: Kim Jong Il and the Looming Threat of North Korea* (New York: Oxford University Press, 2005), p. 162.

53. Methamphetamines are produced in lab-like environments, using all chemical components. Perl, "Drug Trafficking and North Korea," p. 11.

54. Hwang, "Curtailing North Korea's Illicit Activities," p. 3; Perl, "Drug Trafficking and North Korea," p. 9.

55. Wyler and Nanto, "North Korean Crime-for-Profit Activities," p. 6.

56. Haggard and Noland, *Famine in North Korea*, p. 8; Perl, "Drug Trafficking and North Korea," pp. 9–10; Benjamin K. Sovacool, "North Korea and Illegal Narcotics: Smoke but no Fire?" *Asia Policy* (January 2009), p. 108.

57. Defector testimony quoted in Kan, et al., "Criminal Sovereignty," p. 8.

58. 2007 World Drug Report, UNODC.org (2007), http://www.unodc.org/pdf/research/wdr07/WDR_2007.pdf (accessed March 17, 2011), pp. 128, 138, 157.

59. 2010 International Narcotics Control Strategy Report, vol. 1, State.gov (March 2011), http://www.state.gov/p/inl/rls/nrcrpt/2010/index.htm (accessed March 17, 2011), p. 432.

60. Chestnut, "Illicit Activity and Proliferation," p. 92; Dick K. Nanto, "North Korean Counterfeiting of U.S. Currency," Congressional Research Service Report for Congress, RL33324 (12 June 2009), p. 1.

61. Hwang, "Curtailing North Korea's Illicit Activities," p. 4.

62. Ibid.; Kan, et al., "Criminal Sovereignty," p. 13.

63. Bertil Lintner, "North Korea's Burden of Crime and Terror," *Asia Times Online* (April 20, 2007), http://www.atimes.com/atimes/Korea/ID20Dg02.html (accessed March 17, 2011).

64. Kan, et al., "Criminal Sovereignty," p. 18.

65. Wyler and Nanto, "North Korean Crime-for-Profit Activities," p. 1.

66. U.S. government official quoted in Royce, "Gangster Regime," p. 10.

67. Chestnut, "Illicit Activity and Proliferation," p. 91.

68. Ibid., p. 92; Haggard and Noland, *Famine in North Korea*, p. 10; Wyler and Nanto, "North Korean Crime-for-Profit Activities," p. 12.

69. Kan, et al., "Criminal Sovereignty," p. 16.

70. Wyler and Nanto, "North Korean Crime-for-Profit Activities," pp. 12–13, 16.

71. Kan, et al., "Criminal Sovereignty," pp. 15–16.

72. Chestnut, "Illicit Activity and Proliferation," p. 91; Wyler and Nanto, "North Korean Crime-for-Profit Activities," p. 6.

73. Wyler and Nanto, "North Korean Crime-for-Profit Activities," p. 14.

74. Perl, "Drug Trafficking and North Korea," p. 5.

75. Wyler and Nanto, "North Korean Crime-for-Profit Activities," p. 13.

76. The ten others are: Burma, the Democratic Republic of the Congo, Cuba, the Dominican Republic, Eritrea, Iran, Mauritania, Papua New Guinea, Saudi Arabia, Sudan, and Zimbabwe. See the Trafficking in Persons Report, 10th ed., State.gov (June 2010), http://www.state.gov/documents/organiza tion/142979.pdf (accessed March 21, 2011).

77. Perl, "Drug Trafficking and North Korea," pp. 15–16; Wyler and Nanto, "North Korean Crime-for-Profit Activities," p. 17.

78. Peter M. Beck and Nicholas Reader, "Facilitating Reform in North Korea: The Role of Regional Actors and NGOs," *Asian Perspective,* vol. 29, no. 3 (2005), pp. 36–37.

79. Michael Rank, "North Korea: Beyond the Capital Lies a Different World," *Guardian* (September 26, 2010), http://www.guardian.co.uk/world/2010/sep/26/north-korea-rason-beyond-capital (accessed April 13, 2011).

80. Toru Makinoda, "N. Korea Plans Free Trade Zone on Island," *Daily Yomiuri* (January 23, 2009).

81. "Editorial Comment," *Rodong Sinmun* (November 21, 2001).

82. Marcus Noland, "West-Bound Train Leaving the Station: Pyongyang on the Reform Track," IIE.com (October 14–15, 2002), http://www.iie.com/publications/papers/noland1002.htm (accessed February 25, 2004).

83. "NK Embarks on Initial Phase of Market Economy," *Korea Update,* vol. 14, no. 10 (September 30, 2003).

84. Jonathan Watts, "How North Korea Is Embracing Capitalism by Any Other Name," *Guardian* (December 3, 2003), http://www.guardian.co.uk/world/2003/dec/03/north korea (accessed February 20, 2011).

85. Selig S. Harrison, *Korean Endgame: A Strategy for Reunification and U.S. Disengagement* (Princeton, N.J.: Princeton University Press, 2002), p. 27. Kim Dae-jung quote is from Becker, *Rogue Regime,* p. 196. Peter Maas, "The Last Emperor," *New York Times Magazine* (October 19, 2003); Don Gregg, "Kim Jong-il: The Truth Behind the Caricature," *Newsweek* (February 3, 2003).

86. Oh Seung-yul, "Changes in the North Korean Economy: New Policies and Limitations," in *Korea's Economy 2003* (Washington, D.C.: Korea Economic Institute, 2003), pp. 74–76; Transition Newsletter World Bank at www.world bank.org/transition newsletter/janfebmar03/pgs1-6htm (accessed February 25, 2004). For more extreme estimates, as high as 50,000 won to US$1, see Jamie Miyazaki, "Adam Smith Comes to North Korea," *Asia Times,* October 22, 2003, http://www.atimes.com/atimes/Korea/EJ22Dg01.html (accessed February 25, 2004).

87. Nicholas Eberstadt, "North Korea's Survival Game," unpublished paper, presented at the AEI–*Chosun Ilbo* meeting, February 12–13, 2004, Washington, D.C.

88. Philip P. Pan, "China Treads Carefully Around North Korea," *Washington Post,* January 10, 2003, p. A14.

89. "China to Provide Grant-in-Aid to DPRK," KCNA (October 31, 2003), http://www.kcna.co.jp/item/2003/200310/news10/31.htm (accessed April 4, 2011).

90. Michael Chambers, "Managing a Truculent Ally: China and North Korea, 2003," unpublished manuscript, Fairbank Institute, Harvard University, February 23, 2004; "China's Top Legislator Meets DPRK Premier," *Beijing Xinhua,* October 30, 2003; "China to Provide Grant-in-Aid to DPRK," *Pyongyang KCNA,* October 30, 2003; *International Herald Tribune,* January 12, 2004.

91. World Food Programme (2011).

92. Mark Manyin, "Food Crisis and North Korea's Aid Diplomacy: Seeking the Path of Least Resistance," in Kyung-Ae Park, ed., *New Challenges of North Korean Foreign Policy* (New York: Palgrave Macmillan, 2010), pp. 78–83.

93. Choo, "Mirroring North Korea's Growing Economic Dependence," p. 347.

94. Dick K. Nanto and Mark E. Manyin, "China–North Korea Relations," Congressional Research Service Report for Congress, 7-5700 (December 28, 2010), p. 15.

95. Manyin, "Food Crisis and North Korea's Aid Diplomacy," in Park, ed., *New Challenges,* p. 86.

96. World Food Programme (2011).

97. Haggard and Noland, "North Korea's External Economic Relations," p. 37.

98. Off-the-record comments by international relief worker, August 7, 2010, Los Angeles, California.

99. Manyin, "Food Crisis and North Korea's Aid Diplomacy," in Park, ed., *New Challenges,* pp. 75–76.

100. The minimum wage for workers in the complex is supposed to be $68.71 per month, with an average of $20–$30 of overtime pay. But after the North Korean authorities deduct "social insurance" (15 percent) and "socio-cultural fees" (30 percent), most workers are left with about $45.

101. For a detailed description of the complex, see Dick K. Nanto and Mark E. Manyin, "The Kaesong North–South Korean Industrial Complex," Congressional Research Service Report for Congress, RL34093 (March 17, 2011).

102. Nanto and Manyin, "China–North Korea Relations," p. 7.

103. Dick K. Nanto and Emma Chanlett-Avery, "North Korea: Economic Leverage and Policy Analysis," Congressional Research Service Report for Congress, RL32493 (January 22, 2010), p. 32.

104. See, "Rates," Mt. Kumgang Tour Reservation Guide, http://www.mtkum gang.com/eng/reservation/price/price_list.jsp (accessed March 31, 2011).

105. Haggard and Noland, "North Korea's External Economic Relations," pp. 40–41.

106. See Nanto and Manyin, "The Kaesong North–South Korean Industrial Complex," summary; and "Closing Kaesong would hit North Korea hard," *Chosun Ilbo,* March 18, 2009, http://english.chosun.com/site/data/html_dir/2009/05/18/2009051800226.html (accessed April 12, 2011).

107. Nanto and Chanlett-Avery, "North Korea," p. 47.

108. "The World Factbook—Korea, North," CIA.gov (2011), https://www.cia.gov/library/publications/the-world-factbook/ (accessed April 13, 2011).

109. Norimitsu Onishi, "South Brings Capitalism, Well Isolated, to North Korea," *New York Times,* July 18, 2006, http://www.nytimes.com/2006/07/18/world/asia/18korea.html (accessed April 13, 2011).

110. Barbara Demick, "A One-Hour Commute to Another World," *L.A. Times,* February 28, 2006, http://articles.latimes.com/2006/feb/28/world/fg-commute28/2 (accessed April 13, 2011).

111. "N. Korea Mountain Tours Popular in South Korea," UPI (September 30, 2005), http://www.spacewar.com/reports/NKorea_Mountain_Tour_Popu lar_In_SKorea.html (accessed April 4, 2011).

112. "N. Korea Covered by Slogans," UPI (October 3, 2005), http://www.spacewar.com/reports/NKorea_Covered_By_Slogans.html (accessed April 4, 2011).

113. Haggard and Noland, "North Korea's External Economic Relations," p. 11.

114. "Choco Pies Rule Black Market in North Korea," *Chosun Ilbo,* January 12, 2010;

and John Feffer, "Choco Pies vs. Cold Noodles," *Huffington Post* (March 3, 2010) http://www.huffingtonpost.com/john-feffer/choco-pies-vs-cold-noodle_b_482697 .html (accessed February 22, 2011).

115. Rüdiger Frank, "Socialist Neoconservatism and North Korean Foreign Policy," in Kyung-Ae Park, ed., *New Challenges of North Korean Foreign Policy* (New York: Palgrave, 2010), p. 18.

116. Sharon LeFraniere, "Views Show How North Korean Policy Spread Misery," *New York Times,* June 9, 2010, http://www.nytimes.com/2010/06/10/world/asia/10 koreans.html?pagewanted=all (accessed February 21, 2011).

117. Marcus Noland, "North Korea's Failed Currency Reform," *BBC Online* (February 5, 2010) http://www.iie.com/publications/opeds/print.cfm?researchid=1487&doc=pub (accessed February 21, 2011).

118. Park Hyeong Jung, "How to Move North Korea," unpublished paper, KINU, March 10, 2011, p. 1.

119. "N. Korea 'Importing Animal Feed for Human Consumption,'" *Chosun Ilbo,* February 10, 2011, http://english.chosun.com/site/data/html_dir/2011/02/10/2011 021000980.html (accessed March 30, 2011).

120. The 2008 figures are from the "World Bank World Development Indicators," Worldbank.org (2011), http://data.worldbank.org/data-catalog (accessed April 15, 2011).

121. "North Korea Halves Pyongyang in Size in Apparent Economic Bid: Source," *Yonhap News,* February 14, 2011, http://english.yonhapnews.co.kr (accessed March 30, 2011).

122. "N. Korean Protesters Demand Food and Electricity," *Chosun Ilbo,* February 23, 2011, http://english.chosun.com/site/data/html_dir/2011/02/23/2011022300383 .html (accessed March 29, 2011).

123. Park Hyeong Jung, "North Korea's Foreign and Domestic Policy and Its Relations with China," unpublished paper, KINU (June 15, 2010).

CHAPTER FIVE: THE WORST PLACE ON EARTH

1. Andrei Lankov, "Something Special About Kaesong Tour," *DailyNK* (February 19, 2009), http://www.dailynk.com/english/read.php?cataId=nk00300&num=3276 (accessed February 18, 2011).

2. Ermanno Furlanis, "I Made Pizza for Kim Jong-il," *Asia Times Online* (August 4, 2001), http://www.atimes.com/koreas/CH04Dg01.html (accessed May 18, 2010).

3. Again, there is less to the medical system than meets the eye. North Korea has a ministry of public health, and, by most international metrics, it appears to be within the norm. According to statistics, there is one family doctor per 120 to 140 families and about 800 hospitals total in the country, employing over 300,000 medical professionals. These all constitute metrics of a functioning health system in the North, but the truth is much more grim. See Dr. Margaret Chan, "Transcript of Press Briefing at WHO Headquarters, Geneva," WHO.int (April 30, 2010), http://www.who .int/media centre/news/releases/2010/20100430_chan_press_transcript.pdf (accessed February 14, 2011). See also, "WHO Country Cooperation Strategy, Democratic People's Republic of Korea," WHO.int (August 2009), http://www.who.int/ countryfocus/cooperation_strategy/ccs_prk_en.pdf (accessed February 14, 2011).

4. "President Meets with North Korean Defectors and Family Members of Japanese Abducted by North Korea," April 28, 2006. Available at http://georgewbush-whitehouse.archives.gov/news/releases/2006/04/20060428-1.html (accessed January 13, 2011).

5. This information is taken from Peter Baker and Glenn Kessler, "Bush Meets Dissidents in Campaign for Rights," *Washington Post,* June 15, 2005.

6. George W. Bush, *Decision Points* (New York: Crown, 2010), p. 422.

7. "The Invisible Exodus: North Koreans in the People's Republic of China," *Human Rights Watch,* vol. 14, no. 8 (November 2002), pp. 24–25.

8. Sharon LeFraniere, "Views Show How North Korea Policy Spread Misery," *New York Times,* June 9, 2010, http://www.nytimes.com/2010/06/10/world/asia/10koreans.html?pagewanted=all (accessed February 21, 2011).

9. Stephan Haggard and Marcus Noland, "Repression and Punishment in North Korea: Survey Evidence of Prison Camp Experiences," *East-West Center Working Papers,* no. 20 (October 2009), p. 7.

10. David Hawk, "Exposing North Korea's Prison Camps," U.S. Committee for Human Rights in North Korea (2003), p. 35.

11. "Starved for Rights: Human Rights and the Food Crisis in the Democratic People's Republic of Korea (North Korea)," Amnesty International (January 2004), p. 35.

12. Hawk, "Exposing North Korea's Prison Camps," p. 24.

13. Ibid., p. 55.

14. Ibid., p. 37.

15. Ibid., p. 45.

16. *Children of the Secret State,* directed by Carla Garapedian (London: Hardcash Productions, 2000).

17. Human Rights Watch, "The Invisible Exodus," pp. 24–25.

18. Amnesty International, "Starved for Rights," p. 29.

19. Human Rights Watch, "The Invisible Exodus," pp. 23–24.

20. Hawk, "Exposing North Korea's Prison Camps," p. 67.

21. Ibid., p. 61.

22. Ibid., p. 62.

23. Text of the 1951 United Nations Convention Relating to the Status of Refugees, Chapter 1, Article 33.1.

24. DPRK Population Center, *Analysis of 1993 Population Census Data, DPR of Korea* (Pyongyang: Population Center, 1996), as cited in Courtland Robinson, "North Korea: Migration Patterns and Prospects," unpublished working paper for the CSIS-USC Korea Project (August 21, 2010), http://csis.org/files/publication/101215_North_Korea_Migration_Patterns.pdf (accessed January 12, 2011).

25. Rhoda Margesson, Emma Chanlett-Avery, and Andorra Bruno, *North Korean Refugees in China and Human Rights Issues: International Response and U.S. Policy Options,* Congressional Research Service Report to Congress, RL 34189, September 26, 2007, p. 4; http://www.fas.org/sgp/crs/row/RL34189.pdf (accessed January 3, 2011).

26. Courtland Robinson, "Famine in Slow Motion: A Case Study of Internal Displacement in the Democratic People's Republic of Korea," *Refugee Survey Quarterly,* vol. 19, no. 2 (2000).

27. Some refugees use their resettlement funds given by the ROK government to bring

additional family members out of the North. This practice is known as "chain refugees." Kyung-Ae Park, "People's Exit, Regime Stability, and North Korean Diplomacy," in Kyung-Ae Park, ed., *New Challenges of North Korean Foreign Policy* (New York: Palgrave Macmillan, 2010), p. 46.

28. A new facility was created in 2006, specifically for children. Located outside of Seoul, it caters to refugees 13–24 years old. Many of these children do not have parents. Justin McCurry, "North Korean Refugees Adapt to Life, School, and Prejudice in South Korea," *Christian Science Monitor* (August 4, 2010).

29. "Humanitarian Assistance: Status of North Korean Refugee Resettlement and Asylum in the United States," United States Government Accountability Office Report to Congressional Requesters (June 2010), http://www.gao .gov/new.items/d10691. pdf (accessed February 14, 2011).

30. "China and North Korea: Comrades Forever?" *International Crisis Group—Asia Report,* no. 112 (February 2006), p. 9.

31. John Pomfret, "North Koreans Export Girls for Marriage," *Washington Post,* February 12, 1999.

32. Human Rights Watch, "The Invisible Exodus."

33. For this entire story, see ibid., pp. 13–14.

34. Park, "People's Exit," p. 59.

35. Courtland Robinson, "North Korea: Migration Patterns and Prospects," unpublished working paper for the CSIS-USC Korea Project (August 21, 2010), http://csis .org/files/publication/101215_North_Korea_Migration_Patterns.pdf (accessed January 12, 2011).

36. Jasper Becker, *Rogue Regime: Kim Jong Il and the Looming Threat of North Korea* (New York: Oxford University Press, 2005), p. 94.

37. Hawk, "Exposing North Korea's Prison Camps," p. 63.

38. Peter Baker, "White House Puts Face on North Korean Human Rights Abuses," *Washington Post,* April 16, 2006.

39. Yoshi Yamamoto, *Taken!: North Korea's Criminal Abduction of Citizens of Other Countries* (Washington, D.C.: Committee for Human Rights in North Korea, 2011).

40. For excellent yet heartbreaking footage of these children from inside North Korea, see *Children of the Secret State.*

41. Briefing by representatives of USNGOs, a consortium of American NGOs operating in North Korea, March 2, 2011, Center for Strategic and International Studies, Washington, D.C.

42. Park, "People's Exit," p. 50.

43. Stephan Haggard and Marcus Noland, *Famine in North Korea: Markets, Aid, and Reform* (New York: Columbia University Press, 2007), pp. 73–76.

44. "The Universal Declaration of Human Rights," United Nations (December 10, 1948), http://www.un.org/en/documents/udhr/index.shtml (accessed January 3, 2010).

45. "The International Covenant on Economic, Social and Cultural Rights," United Nations (December 16, 1966), http://www2.ohchr.org/english/law/cescr.htm (accessed January 3, 2010).

46. Stephan Haggard and Marcus Noland, "Hunger and Human Rights: The Politics

of Famine in North Korea," U.S. Committee for Human Rights in North Korea (2005), p. 9.

47. Nicholas Eberstadt, *The End of North Korea* (Washington, D.C.: AEI Press, 1999), p. 61.

48. For a complete list of the famines of the twentieth century, see Haggard and Noland, *Famine in North Korea*, p. 7.

49. Eberstadt, *The End of North Korea*, p. 61.

50. Amartya Sen, *Development as Freedom* (New York: Anchor Books, 2000), p. 16.

51. Documents containing the text of an unusually candid speech by Kim Jong-il at Kim Il-sung University were subsequently smuggled out of the country. See Don Oberdorfer, *The Two Koreas: A Contemporary History*, revised ed. (New York: Basic Books, 2001), p. 395.

52. Eberstadt, *The End of North Korea*, p. 47.

53. Haggard and Noland, "Hunger and Human Rights," p. 16.

54. Ibid.

55. Haggard and Noland, *Famine in North Korea*, p. 27.

56. The other 30 to 40 percent live and work on the cooperative farms that fuel the PDS, and so they are allocated an annual stock of food directly from the farm.

57. Haggard and Noland, *Famine in North Korea*, p. 55.

58. Ibid., p. 54.

59. "A Matter of Survival: The North Korean Government's Control of Food and the Risk of Hunger," *Human Rights Watch*, vol. 18, no. 3 (May 2006), p. 10.

60. Human Rights Watch, "The Invisible Exodus," p. 8.

61. Hazel Smith, *Hungry for Peace: International Security, Humanitarian Assistance, and Social Change in North Korea* (Washington, D.C.: United States Institute of Peace Press, 2005), p. 87; Paul French, *North Korea: The Paranoid Peninsula* (New York: Zed Books, 2007), p. 129.

62. Haggard and Noland, *Famine in North Korea*, p. 56.

63. Eberstadt, *The End of North Korea*, p. 46.

64. Amnesty International, "Starved for Rights," pp. 8–9.

65. Smith, *Hungry for Peace*, p. 67.

66. Ibid., p. 70.

67. Haggard and Noland, *Famine in North Korea*, p. 25.

68. World Food Programme, "Full Report of the Evaluation of DPRK EMOPs 5959.00 and 5959.01—'Emergency Assistance to Vulnerable Groups'—20 March-10 April 2000" (September 2000), p. 6.

69. Haggard and Noland, "Hunger and Human Rights," p. 15.

70. Human Rights Watch, "The Invisible Exodus," p. 10.

71. Haggard and Noland, *Famine in North Korea*, pp. 72–73.

72. Amnesty International, "Starved for Rights," p. 25.

73. World Food Programme, "Full Report of the Evaluation of DPRK EMOPs," (2000), p. 18.

74. Human Rights Watch, "The Invisible Exodus," p. 11.

75. Ibid., p. 27.

76. Smith, *Hungry for Peace*, p. 71; Eberstadt, *The End of North Korea*, p. 46.

77. Smith, *Hungry for Peace*, p. 92.
78. Amnesty International, "The Crumbling State of Healthcare in North Korea," (2010), ASA 24/001/2010, p. 22, www.amnesty.org/en/library/info/ASA24/001/2010 (accessed January 16, 2012).
79. Ibid.
80. Ibid., p. 23.
81. Ibid., pp. 11–12.
82. Ibid., pp. 5–6.
83. Ibid., p. 12.
84. Ibid., p. 12.
85. Smith, *Hungry for Peace*, p. 84.
86. Becker, *Rogue Regime*, p. 29.
87. French, *North Korea*, p. 130.
88. *Children of the Secret State*.
89. Amnesty International, "Starved for Rights," p. 23.
90. Ibid.
91. Becker, *Rogue Regime*, p. 37.
92. *Children of the Secret State*.
93. "Special Report: FAO/WFP Crop and Food Supply Assessment—Mission to the Democratic People's Republic of Korea," United Nations Food and Agricultural Organization (October 30, 2003), p. 19.
94. "Special Report: FAO/WFP Crop and Food Supply Assessment—Mission to the Democratic People's Republic of Korea," United Nations Food and Agricultural Organization (November 22, 2004), p. 22.
95. "Tracking Progress on Child and Maternal Nutrition: A Survival and Development Priority," UNICEF (November 2009), pp. 11, 104.
96. Haggard and Noland, "Hunger and Human Rights," p. 14.
97. Amnesty International, "Starved for Rights," p. 26.
98. All food aid statistics from "Food Aid Information System," World Food Programme (2011), http://www.wfp.org/fais/ (accessed January 7, 2011).
99. Haggard and Noland, *Famine in North Korea*, pp. 93–95.
100. Haggard and Noland, "Hunger and Human Rights," pp. 12, 96–97.
101. Mark E. Manyin and Mary-Beth Nikitin, "Foreign Assistance to North Korea," Congressional Research Service Report for Congress, R40095 (March 2010), p. 2.
102. Ibid., pp. 15–18.
103. Ibid., pp. 20–22.
104. "World Food Programme International Food Information System," World Food Programme (2011), http://www.wfp.org/fais/ (accessed February 14, 2011).
105. Mark E. Manyin, "Food Crisis and North Korea's Aid Diplomacy: Seeking the Path of Least Resistance," in Kyung-Ae Park, ed., *New Challenges of North Korean Foreign Policy* (New York: Palgrave Macmillan, 2010), p. 80.
106. Bob Woodward, *Bush at War* (New York: Simon and Schuster, 2002), p. 340.
107. "Humanitarian Assistance: Status of North Korean Refugee Resettlement and Asylum in the United States," United States Government Accountability Office Report to Congressional Requesters (June 2010), http://www.gao.gov/new.items/d10691.pdf (accessed February 14, 2011).

108. "Joint Statement of the Fourth Round of the Six-Party Talks," http://www.state.gov/p/eap/regional/c15455.htm (accessed January 31, 2011).

109. Woodward, *Bush at War*, p. 340.

110. Park, "People's Exit," p. 56.

111. "Half of North Korean Defectors' Households Income Less than One Million Won a Month: Poll," *Yonhap News*, February 16, 2011.

CHAPTER SIX: THE LOGIC OF DETERRENCE

1. Michael E. O'Hanlon and Mike M. Mochizuki, *Crisis on the Korean Peninsula: How to Deal with a Nuclear North Korea* (Blacklick, Ohio: McGraw-Hill Professional Publishing, 2003), p. 59.

2. "Chapter 8: The Korean War, 1950–1953," in Richard W. Stewart, ed., *American Military History Volume II: The United States Army in a Global Era, 1917–2003* (Washington, D.C.: Center for Military History, 2005), p. 246. Available online at: http://www.history.army.mil/books/AMH-V2/AMH%20V2/chapter8.htm (accessed May 14, 2011). For the Koreans, it is: ROK soldiers—187,000 dead and 30,000 missing; ROK civilians—500,000 to 1 million dead; DPRK soldiers and civilians—1.5 million dead.

3. International Institute for Strategic Studies, *The Military Balance 2011* (London: IISS, 2011), pp. 205–6.

4. Bruce E. Bechtol Jr., *Defiant Failed State: The North Korean Threat to International Security* (Washington, D.C.: Potomac Books, 2010), p. 21.

5. In 1954, U.S. Forces Korea (USFK) consisted of 225,590 personnel. Today (2011) that number has fallen to 28,500. See, Tim Kane, "Global U.S. Troop Deployment, 1950–2003," Heritage Foundation (October 27, 2004), http://www.heritage.org/research/reports/2004/10/global-us-troop-deployment-1950-2003 (accessed April 21, 2011).

6. International Institute for Strategic Studies, *The Military Balance*, pp. 249–54.

7. Dennis C. Blair, Annual Threat Assessment of the U.S. Intelligence Community (February 2, 2010), http://www.dni.gov/testimonies/20100202_tes timony.pdf (accessed April 21, 2011), pp. 13–14.

8. Bruce Cumings, *North Korea: Another Country* (New York: New Press, 2004), p. 53.

9. O'Hanlon and Mochizuki, *Crisis on the Korean Peninsula*, p. 174.

10. Don Oberdorfer, *The Two Koreas: A Contemporary History*, revised and updated ed. (New York: Basic Books, 2001), pp. 312, 325; Ashton B. Carter and William J. Perry, *Preventive Defense: A New Security Strategy for America* (Washington, D.C.: Brookings Institution Press, 1999), pp. 128–30, 217–18.

11. Cited in Oberdorfer, *The Two Koreas*, p. 288.

12. Personal interview, USFK officer, Washington, D.C., March 14, 2011.

13. Narushige Michishita, "The Future of North Korean Strategy," *Korean Journal of Defense Analysis*, vol. 21, no. 1 (2009), p. 107; Koo Sub Kim, "Substance of North Korea's Military Threats and the Security Environment in Northeast Asia," *Korean Journal of Defense Analysis*, vol. 21, no. 3 (2009), p. 243.

14. Joseph Bermudez Jr., *North Korean Special Forces* (Surrey, UK: Jane's Publishing Company, 1988), p. 62; Bechtol, *Defiant Failed State*, pp. 22–23.

15. Bermudez, *North Korean Special Forces*, p. 64.

16. Ibid., p. 62.

17. O'Hanlon and Mochizuki, *Crisis on the Korean Peninsula*, p. 62.

18. "Kim Jong-Il Using Body Doubles in Appearances, Even Photos," Worldtri bune. com (October 4, 2006), http://www.worldtribune.com/worldtribune/ (accessed April 27, 2011).

19. C. Kenneth Quinones and Joseph Traggart, *The Complete Idiot's Guide to Understanding North Korea* (New York: Alpha Books, 2003), p. 278.

20. Personal conversation with Hwang Jhang-yŏp, March 31, 2010, Washington, D.C.

21. Jasper Becker, *Rogue Regime: Kim Jong Il and the Looming Threat of North Korea* (New York: Oxford University Press, 2005), pp. 144–45.

22. Robert M. Gates, "Media Roundtable with Secretary Gates from Beijing, China," Defense.gov (January 11, 2011), http://www.defense.gov/tran scripts/transcript .aspx?transcriptid=4751 (accessed April 18, 2011).

23. Cumings, *North Korea*, p. 89.

24. A heat shield for the Nodong missile is in operation, but this would not work on a longer-range ballistic missile. David Wright, "North Korea's Missile Program" UCSUSA.org (2009), http://www.ucsusa.org/assets/documents/nwgs/north-koreas-missile-program.pdf (accessed April 25, 2011), pp. 6–7.

25. Daniel A. Pinkston, *North Korea's Ballistic Missile Program* (Carlyle, Pa.: Strategic Studies Institute, 2008), pp. 14–15.

26. Ibid., p. 15.

27. Becker, *Rogue Regime*, p. 160.

28. Nodong missiles have a range of up to 13,000 kilometers (8,080 mi) with a payload of 700–1,000 kilogram (1,543–2,204 lb). Wright, "North Korea's Missile Program," p. 4.

29. D. Wright and T. Postol, "A Post-Launch Examination of the Unha-2," *Bulletin of the Atomic Scientists* (June 29, 2009), http://thebulletin.org/web-edition/features/post-launch-examination-of-the-unha-2 (accessed May 14, 2011).

30. "Kim Jong Il Observes Launch of Satellite Kwangmyongsong-2," KCNA (April 5, 2009), http://www.kcna.co.jp/item/2009/200904/news05/20090405-12ee.html (accessed May 14, 2011).

31. "NORAD and USNORTHCOM Monitor North Korean Launch," North American Aerospace Defense Command (April 5, 2009), http://www .norad.mil/News/2009/040509.html (accessed May 14, 2011).

32. Sharon A. Squassoni, "Weapons of Mass Destruction: Trade Between North Korea and Pakistan," Congressional Research Service Report for Congress, RL31900 (November 28, 2006), pp. 1–17; Gaurav Kampani, "Second-Tier Proliferation: The Case of Pakistan and North Korea," *The Non-proliferation Review* (Fall/Winter 2002), pp. 107–16.

33. Bechtol, *Defiant Failed State*, pp. 49–69.

34. Dinshaw Mistry, *Containing Missile Proliferation: Strategic Technology, Security Regimes, and International Cooperation in Arms Control* (Seattle: University of Washington Press, 2003), pp. 134–35.

35. Becker, *Rogue Regime*, p. 149; Bruce E. Bechtol Jr., "North Korea and Support to Terrorism," *Journal of Strategic Security*, vol. 3 (2010), pp. 45–54; Mark E. Manyin,

"North Korea: Back on the Terrorism List?" Congressional Research Service Report for Congress, RL30613 (June 29, 2010), pp. 22–25.

36. U.S. Department of State, "Patterns of Global Terrorism, 2000—Overview of State Sponsored Terrorism" (April 30, 2001), http://www.state.gov/g/ct/rls/crt/2000/2441 .htm (accessed November 10, 2010).

37. Jeff Stein, "Wikileaks Documents: N. Korea Sold Missiles to Al-Qaeda, Taliban," *Washington Post,* July 26, 2010, http://voices.washingtonpost.com/spy-talk/2010/07/ wiki_n_korea_sold_rockets_to_a.html (accessed January 16, 2012).

38. The other four are Angola, Egypt, Somalia, and Syria. See "Non-Member States," OPCW (2011), http://www.opcw.org/about-opcw/non-member-states/ (accessed May 3, 2011).

39. "North Korea's Chemical and Biological Weapons Programs," *International Crisis Group Asia Report,* no. 167 (June 18, 2009), p. 7.

40. Bechtol, *Defiant Failed State,* p. 53.

41. Ibid., p. 149.

42. See Daniel Kahneman and Amos Tversky, "Prospect Theory: An Analysis of Decision Under Risk," *Econometrica,* vol. 47, no. 2 (March 1979), pp. 263–92.

43. "Servicepersons and Pyongyangites Hail Successful Nuclear Test," KCNA (October 20, 2006), http://www.kcna.co.jp/item/2006/200610/news10/21 .htm#1 (accessed May 2, 2011).

44. "DPRK Regards S. Korea's Full Participation in PSI as Declaration of War against DPRK," KCNA (May 27, 2009), http://www.kcna.co.jp/item/2009/200905/news27/ 20090527-17ee.html (accessed May 2, 2011).

45. "Meeting Marked Anniversary of Assumption of Supreme Commander," KCNA (December 23, 2009), http://www.kcna.co.jp/item/2009/200912/news23/20091223- 14ee.html (accessed May 2, 2011).

46. "DPRK Will Develop Friendly Relations with UN Member," KCNA (October 2, 2010), http://www.kcna.co.jp/item/2010/201010/news02/20101002-04ee.html (accessed May 2, 2011).

47. Rüdiger Frank, "Socialist Neoconservatism and North Korean Foreign Policy," in Kyung-Ae Park, ed., *New Challenges of North Korean Foreign Policy* (New York: Palgrave Macmillan, 2010), pp. 34–35.

48. Cited in Chico Harlan, "North Korean Ruler and Heir Attend Parade" *Washington Post,* October 11, 2010.

49. "Meeting Marks Anniversary of KPA Supreme Commander," KCNA (December 23, 2010), http://www.kcna.co.jp/item/2010/201012/news23/20101223 -13ee.html (accessed May 2, 2011).

50. "Foreign Ministry Spokesman Denounces U.S. Military Attack on Libya," KCNA (March 22, 2011), http://www.kcna.co.jp/index-e.htm (accessed April 18, 2011).

51. Lee Myung-bak, "Address to the Nation by President Lee Myung-bak on the Shelling of Yeonpyeongdo," *Yonhap News,* November 24, 2010, english.yonhapnews .co.kr/northkorea/2010/11/29/32/0401000000AEN20101129006400315F.html (accessed January 16, 2012) .

52. Admiral Mike Mullen, chairman of the Joint Chiefs of Staff, made a special trip to the ROK in the aftermath of the *Cheonan* sinking and Yeonpyeong shelling (De-

cember 7, 2010). Ostensibly, this visit was for the purpose of showing alliance solidarity, since rarely does the top military official in the U.S. government make a trip solely to Korea and Japan. But Mullen's trip was also out of concern that the new ROK rules of engagement were too overzealous.

53. Victor D. Cha, "Testimony of Dr. Victor D. Cha Before the United States House of Representatives, Committee on Foreign Affairs," House.gov (March 10, 2011), http://foreignaffairs.house.gov/112/cha031011.pdf (accessed April 18, 2011).

54. Personal interviews, ROK official and U.S. official, December 21, 2010, and December 30, 2010, Washington, D.C.

55. Oberdorfer, *The Two Koreas,* pp. 312, 325; Carter and Perry, *Preventive Defense,* pp. 128–30, 217–18.

56. Ibid.

CHAPTER SEVEN: COMPLETE, VERIFIABLE, AND IRREVERSIBLE DISMANTLEMENT (CVID)

1. Uzi Mahnaimi, "Israelis 'Blew Apart Syrian Nuclear Cache,'" *Sunday Times,* September 16, 2007, http://www.timesonline.co.uk/tol/news/world/middle_east/arti cle2461421.ece (accessed October 1, 2007).

2. The information in the section above is based on briefings by U.S. intelligence officials as cited in the video "Syria's Covert Nuclear Reactor at Al-Kibar," available at http://www.armscontrolwonk.com/1864/why-now. Also see *Der Spiegel*'s exposé: Erich Follath and Holger Stark, "The Story of 'Operation Orchard': How Israel Destroyed Syria's Al Kibar Reactor," *Der Spiegel* (February 11, 2009), http://www.spie gel.de/international/world/0,1518,658663,00.html (accessed April 18, 2011); and Seymour Hersh, "A Strike in the Dark—Why Did Israel Bomb Syria?" *New Yorker* (February 11, 2008), http://www.newyorker.com/reporting/2008/02/11/080211fa_ fact_hersh/?printable=true (accessed April 18, 2011); and Laura Rozen, "Operation Orchard," *Mother Jones* (April 28, 2008), http://motherjones .com/mojo/2008/04/ operation-orchard (accessed April 18, 2011).

3. Mary-Beth Nikitin, "North Korea's Nuclear Weapons: Technical Issues," Congressional Research Service Report for Congress, R40095 (January 20, 2011), p. 1.

4. "North Korea: Nuclear Weapons Program," FAS (2006), http://www.fas .org/nuke/ guide/dprk/nuke/index.html (accessed April 18, 2011); Larry A. Niksch, "North Korea's Nuclear Weapons Development and Diplomacy," Congressional Research Service Report for Congress, RL33590 (January 5, 2010); Mark E. Manyin and Mary-Beth Nikitin, "Foreign Assistance to North Korea," Congressional Research Service Report for Congress, R40095 (March 12, 2010); Don Oberdorfer, *The Two Koreas: A Contemporary History,* revised and updated ed. (New York: Basic Books, 2001), pp. 249–80; Michael J. Mazaar, *North Korea and the Bomb: A Case Study in Nonproliferation* (London: Macmillan Press, 1997), pp. 15–34; Charles L. Pritchard, *Failed Diplomacy: The Tragic Story of How North Korea Got the Bomb* (Washington, D.C.: Brookings Institution Press, 2007); Jasper Becker, *Rogue Regime: Kim Jong Il and the Looming Threat of North Korea* (New York: Oxford University Press, 2005), pp. 165–89.

5. Leslie Gelb, "The Next Renegade State," *New York Times,* April 10, 1991, http:// www.nytimes.com/1991/04/10/opinion/foreign-affairs-the-next-renegade-state .html (accessed February 27, 2011).

6. Mary-Beth Nikitin, "North Korea's Nuclear Weapons: Technical Issues," Congressional Research Service Report for Congress, RL34256 (January 20, 2011), p. 5.

7. Joel S. Wit, Daniel B. Poneman, and Robert L. Gallucci, *Going Critical: The First North Korea Nuclear Crisis* (Washington, D.C.: Brookings Institution Press, 2004), pp. 331–32.

8. The other member countries/entities were: Australia, Argentina, Canada, Chile, the Czech Republic, the European Union, Indonesia, New Zealand, Poland, and Uzbekistan.

9. Zachary S. Davis, "Leading or Following?: The Role of KEDO and the Agreed Framework in Korea Policy," Nautilus Institute (June 2000) http://www.nautilus .org/publications/books/dprkbb/agreedFramework/ (accessed April 20, 2011), p. 62.

10. Morton Abramowitz and Stephen Bosworth, "Adjusting to the New Asia," *Foreign Affairs* (July/August 2003), pp. 119–31; Kent Calder, "The New Face of Northeast Asia," *Foreign Affairs* (January/February 2001), pp. 106–22.

11. Glenn Kessler, "North Korea May Have Sent Libya Nuclear Material, U.S. Tells Allies," *Washington Post,* February 2, 2005; David E. Sanger and William J. Broad, "Tests Said to Tie Deal on Uranium to North Korea," *New York Times,* February 2, 2005, http://www.nytimes.com/2005/02/02/politics/02nukes.html (accessed April 18, 2011).

12. Nikitin, "North Korea's Nuclear Weapons," p. 5.

13. U.S. Department of State, "Joint Statement of the Fourth Round of the Six-Party Talks" (September 19, 2005), http://www.state.gov/p/eap/regional/c15455.htm (accessed April 18, 2011).

14. Christopher R. Hill, "North Korea—U.S. Statement," National Defense University (September 19, 2005), http://merln.ndu.edu/archivepdf/north korea/state/53499 .pdf (accessed April 18, 2011).

15. "Spokesman for DPRK Foreign Ministry on Six-Party Talks," KCNA (September 21, 2005), http://www.kcna.co.jp/index-e.htm (accessed April 18, 2011).

16. A pedantic issue I flag here is that almost all analyses have referred to BDA as a U.S. "financial sanction" that froze North Korean money. As my narrative shows, this is an incorrect characterization. The United States never froze any North Korean accounts. It issued a financial advisory to U.S. institutions to beware of business with BDA because of money-laundering concerns. The Macau monetary authorities then seized the North Korean accounts, and other banks around the world started to hold DPRK accounts suspect.

17. J. Michael McConnell, "Annual Threat Assessment of the Director of National Intelligence for the Senate Select Committee on Intelligence," Senate.gov (February 5, 2008), http://intelligence.senate.gov/080205/mcconnell .pdf (accessed April 18, 2011).

18. ODNI News Release No. 19-06 at http://www.dni.gov/announcements/20061016_ release.pdf; and Mark Mazzetti, "Preliminary Samples Hint at North Korean Nuclear Test," *New York Times,* October 14, 2006, http://www.nytimes.com/2006/10/14/ world/asia/14nuke.html (accessed October 27, 2006).

19. Siegfried Hecker, "Report on North Korean Nuclear Program," Center for International Security and Cooperation, Stanford University (November 15, 2006);

Thom Shanker and David Sanger, "North Korean Fuel Identified as Plutonium," *New York Times,* October 17, 2006, at http://www .nytimes.com/2006/10/17/world /asia/17diplo.html (accessed October 27, 2006).

20. The process of returning the money took much longer than anticipated and was hotly contested within the U.S. government as Treasury and State Department officials nearly came to blows in the St. Regis hotel in Beijing over the decision. The BDA funds were considered so tainted by the financial community that the only institution that could return the money to North Korea without fear of losing its reputation was the U.S. Federal Reserve.

21. Nikitin, "North Korea's Nuclear Weapons," p. 5.

22. "Five Years Later in North Korea," *New York Times,* July 17, 2007.

23. "President Barack Obama's Inaugural Address," Whitehouse.gov (January 21, 2009), http://www.whitehouse.gov/blog/inaugural-address/ (accessed March 29, 2011).

24. "DPRK Foreign Ministry Vehemently Refutes UNSC's 'Presidential Statement,'" KCNA, April 14, 2009.

25. Statement by the Office of the Director of National Intelligence on North Korea's Declared Nuclear Test on May 25, 2009, http://www/dni/gov/press_releases /20090615_release.pdf (accessed January 16, 2012).

26. "UNSC Urged to Retract Anti-DPRK Steps," KCNA (April 29, 2009), http://www .kcna.co.jp/item/2009/200904/news29/20090429-14ee.html (accessed April 18, 2011).

27. Niksch, "North Korea's Nuclear Weapons," p. 17.

28. "Five Years Later on North Korea," *New York Times,* July 17, 2007.

29. Leon Sigal, "N. Korea: Fibs v. Facts," *Baltimore Sun,* August 5, 2003.

30. "The North Korea Deal," *New York Times,* June 27, 2008.

31. "Korean Paralysis," *New York Times,* March 4, 2003; "The North Korean Challenge," *New York Times,* February 11, 2005; "Going Nowhere on North Korea," *New York Times,* July 16, 2005; "The U.N. Sideshow on North Korea," *New York Times,* July 16, 2006; "Testing North Korea," *New York Times,* November 5, 2006; "The Lesson of North Korea," *New York Times,* February 14, 2007; "Five Years Later in North Korea," *New York Times,* July 17, 2007; "Now He's Ready to Deal," *New York Times,* April 19, 2008; "The North Korea Deal," *New York Times,* June 27, 2008.

32. "Next Steps with North Korea," *New York Times,* August 5, 2009.

33. Leon Sigal, "A Bombshell That's Actually an Olive Branch," *Los Angeles Times,* October 18, 2002; and "N. Korea: Fibs v. Facts," *Baltimore Sun,* August 5, 2003.

34. Georgy Toloraya, "Yadernyi poker v. Koree [Nuclear Poker in Korea]," Center for the Study of Contemporary Korea, Far Eastern Institute, Moscow, December 9, 2004, http://world.lib.ru/k/kim_o_i/a9628.shtml, cited in Leszek Buszynski, "Russia and North Korea," *Asian Survey,* vol. 49, no. 5 (September/October 2009), pp. 809–30.

35. "Now He's Ready to Deal," *New York Times,* April 19, 2008.

36. Selig Harrison, Testimony Before the House Committee of Foreign Affairs (June 17, 2009), http://ciponline.org/asia/Jun17-Korea-Testimony.html (accessed January 16, 2012).

37. "U.S. Policy Toward the Korean Peninsula," Testimony of Assistant Secretary of State for East Asian and Pacific Affairs Winston Lord, House Committee on International Relations, Subcommittee on Asia and the Pacific (March 19, 1996), http://

dosfan.lib.uic.edu/ERC/bureaus/eap/960319LordKorea.html (accessed July 18, 2010); Joel Wit, "United States and North Korea," Policy Brief No. 74, Brookings Institution, 2001; and U.S. Department of State, "Background Notes: North Korea," Bureau of Public Affairs, June 1996.

38. Erik Eckholm, "Where Most See Ramparts, North Korea Imagines a Wall," *New York Times,* December 8, 1999.

39. "Korean War Accounting," DTIC (2011), http://www.dtic.mil/dpmo/korea/ (accessed April 19, 2011).

40. Mark E. Manyin, "Foreign Assistance to North Korea," Congressional Research Service Report for Congress, RL31785 (May 26, 2005), pp. 28–29.

41. Robert L. Goldich, "POWs and MIAs: Status and Accounting Issues," Congressional Research Service Report for Congress, IB92101 (April 14, 2003), p. 15.

42. Details based on discussions with Arnold Kanter, July 13, 2009, Washington, D.C. Also see Oberdorfer, *Two Koreas,* pp. 265–67; Wit, et al., *Going Critical,* pp. 11–13; Mazaar, *North Korea and the Bomb,* pp. 70–71; Chae-jin Lee, *A Troubled Peace: U.S. Policy and the Two Koreas* (Baltimore, Md.: Johns Hopkins University Press, 2006), pp. 135–36; Rinn-Sup Shinn, "The United States and the Two Koreas: An Uncertain Triangle," in Young Jeh Kim, ed., *The New Pacific Community in the 1990s* (Armonk, N.Y.: M. E. Sharpe, 1996), p. 91.

43. Winston Lord, "U.S. Policy Toward the Korean Peninsula," *U.S. Department of State Dispatch,* April 1, 1996, pp. 165–70; and Kelly Smith Tunney, "U.S. Reportedly Gives North Korea Deadline for Opening Nuclear Facilities," Associated Press, January 23, 1992.

44. For example, see Snyder, "North Korea's Nuclear Program," pp. 59–61; and Oberdorfer, *Two Koreas,* pp. 266–67.

45. Brent Scowcroft and Arnold Kanter, "The Time for Temporizing Is Over," *Washington Post,* June 15, 1994.

46. Marion V. Creekmore Jr., *A Moment of Crisis: Jimmy Carter, the Power of a Peacemaker, and North Korea's Nuclear Ambitions* (New York: Public Affairs, 2006), p. 176.

47. "U.S.-DPRK Joint Communique," Nautilus Institute (October 12, 2000), http://www.nautilus.org/publications/books/dprkbb/agreements/ (accessed April 18, 2011).

48. Madeleine K. Albright, "Press Conference, Koryo Hotel" (October 24, 2000), usinfo.org/wf-archive/2000/001024/epf204.htm (accessed January 16, 2012).

49. Mike Chinoy, *Meltdown: The Inside Story of North Korean Nuclear Crisis* (New York: St. Martin's Press, 2008), pp. 53–55.

50. George W. Bush, *Decision Points* (New York: Crown Publishers, 2010), p. 424.

51. Pritchard, *Failed Diplomacy.*

52. Bush, *Decision Points,* p. 423.

53. Quote by Derek Mitchell in "Bush Letter to Kim Jong-il Shows Policy Change," *USA Today* (December 6, 2007), http://www.usatoday.com/news/washington/2007-12-06-bush-letter_N.htm (accessed March 18, 2011).

54. "Transcript: Fourth Democratic Debate," *New York Times,* July 24, 2007, http://www.nytimes.com/2007/07/24/us/politics/24transcript.html?pagewanted=all (accessed April 20, 2011).

55. "Transcript: First Presidential Debate," CBS News (September 26, 2008), http://www.cbsnews.com/stories/2008/10/06/politics/2008debates/main4504409.shtml (accessed April 20, 2011).

56. See U.S. Department of State, Bureau of Public Affairs: Office of Electronic Information and Publications, "U.S.-Asia Relations: Indispensable to Our Future," Secretary Clinton's remarks (February 13, 2009), http://www.state .gov/secretary/rm/2009a/02/117333.htm; U.S. Department of State, Bureau of Public Affairs: Office of Electronic Information and Publications, "Putting the Elements of Smart Power into Practice," Secretary Clinton's remarks (February 19, 2009), http://www.state .gov/secretary/rm/2009a/02/119 411.htm.

57. Adam Gabbatt, "Obama Sends Letter to Kim Jong-il," *Guardian* (December 16, 2009), http://www.guardian.co.uk/world/2009/dec/16/obama-letter-kim-jong-il (accessed March 17, 2011); "Obama Wrote Personal Letter to Kim Jong-il," CBS News (December 16, 2009), http://www.cbsnews.com/stories/2009/12/16/politics/washingtonpost/main5986078.shtml (accessed March 17, 2011).

58. Ian Rinehart, "The Value of Strategic Patience," unpublished paper, Georgetown University, March 3, 2011.

59. U.S. Department of State, "Joint Statement of the Fourth Round of the Six-Party Talks" (September 19, 2005), http://www.state.gov/p/eap/regional/c15455.htm (accessed June 20, 2011).

60. Senate, Foreign Relations Committee hearing, "North Korea: Back at the Brink?" June 11, 2009.

61. An earlier version of this argument appeared in the "What Do They Really Want: Obama's North Korea Conundrum," *Washington Quarterly,* vol. 32, no. 4 (2009), pp. 119–38.

62. For seismic activity, see U.S. Geological Survey, ov/eqcenter/recenteqsww/Quakes /us2009hbaf.php#summary. For assessments of the October 2006 and May 2009 tests, see M. B. Kalinowski, O. Ross, "Data Analysis and Interpretation of the North Korean Nuclear Test Explosion of 9 October 2006." *INESAP Information Bulletin,* no. 27, pp. 39–43 (http://www.ine sap.org/bulletin27/art12.htm); Martin Kalinowski, "Second Nuclear Test Conducted by North Korea on 25 May 2009 Fact Sheet," Carl Friedrich von Weizsäcker Centre for Science and Peace Research (ZNF), University of Hamburg (www.armscontrolwonk.com/file_download/177/ Kalin owski.pdf).

63. For examples of the "up the ante" argument, see John Glionna, "North Korea's Nuclear Test May Be for Kim's Legacy," *Los Angeles Times,* May 26, 2009.

64. It is worth noting that while the North Koreans learn from their tests, the United States learns a great deal more about the state of their programs and their level of development. See Richard Halloran, "How U.S. Exploited N. Korea Missile Tests," *Honolulu Advertiser,* July 12, 2009.

65. "Agreed Framework Between the United States and the Democratic People's Republic of Korea," October 21, 1994, http://www.kedo.org/pdfs/AgreedFramework .pdf.

66. See statement by Evans Revere before the Senate Foreign Relations Committee (June 11, 2009), http://foreign.senate.gov/testimony/2009/Rever eTestimony09 0611p.pdf.

67. "U.S.-DPRK Joint Communique," October 12, 2000, Washington, D.C., available at http://www.fas.org/news/dprk/2000/dprk-001012a.htm.

68. Victor Cha, "Korea's Place in the Axis," *Foreign Affairs* (May/June 2002).

CHAPTER EIGHT: NEIGHBORS

1. Xiaobing Li, *A History of the Modern Chinese Army* (Lexington: University of Kentucky Press, 2007), p. 105.

2. S. B. Thomas, "The Chinese Communists' Economic and Cultural Agreement with North Korea," *Pacific Affairs*, vol. 27, no. 1 (March 1954), p. 63.

3. Thomas P. Bernstein and Andrew J. Nathan, "The Soviet Union, China, and Korea," in Gerald L. Curtis and Sung-joo Han, eds., *The U.S.–South Korea Alliance: Evolving Patterns and Security Relations* (Lexington, Mass.: Lexington Books, 1983), p. 99.

4. Bernstein and Nathan, "The Soviet Union," p. 99.

5. Joseph S. Chung, "The Economy," in Andrea Matles Savada, ed., *North Korea: A Country Study* (Washington, D.C.: Library of Congress, 1994).

6. Chen Jian, "Limits of the 'Lips and Teeth' Alliance: An Historical Review of Chinese–North Korean Relations," Woodrow Wilson Center Asia Program Special Report, no. 115 (September 2003), p. 6.

7. Dae-Sook Suh, *Kim Il Sung: The North Korean Leader* (New York: Columbia University Press, 1988), p. 192.

8. Chin O. Chung, *Pyongyang Between Peking and Moscow: North Korea's Involvement in the Sino-Soviet Dispute, 1958–1975* (Tuscaloosa: University of Alabama Press, 1978), p. 129.

9. Bernd Schaefer, "North Korean 'Adventurism' and China's Long Shadow, 1966–1972," Woodrow Wilson Center Cold War Archives Project, Working Paper 44 (October 2004), http://www.wilsoncenter.org/topics/pubs/swp44.pdf (accessed December 19, 2010), pp. 9–13.

10. Suh, *Kim Il Sung*, pp. 192–93.

11. Jasper Becker, *Rogue Regime: Kim Jong Il and the Looming Threat of North Korea* (New York: Oxford University Press, 2005), p. 150.

12. Victor Cha, *Beyond the Final Score: The Politics of Sport in Asia* (New York: Columbia, 2009), pp. 94–95.

13. The 2000 bid was ultimately unsuccessful for China. While the ROK may have been able to forget about Tiananmen, the IOC could not, and eventually awarded the 2000 games to Sydney, Australia.

14. Joint Communiqué cited in Chae-jin Lee, "South Korean Foreign Relations Face the Globalization Challenge," in Samuel S. Kim, ed., *Korea's Globalization* (Cambridge, UK: Cambridge University Press, 2000), p. 174.

15. Nicholas D. Kristof, "Chinese and South Koreans Formally Establish Relations," *New York Times*, August 24, 1992.

16. "Growing Ties Herald Fresh Era for Asia," *South China Morning Post*, September 29, 1992.

17. Victor D. Cha, "South Korea: Anchored or Adrift?" in Richard J. Ellings, Aaron L. Friedberg, and Michael Wills, eds., *Strategic Asia 2003–04: Fragility and Crisis* (Seattle: The National Bureau of Asian Research, 2004); David C. Kang, "Hierarchy, Balancing, and Empirical Puzzles in Asian International Relations," *International*

Security, vol. 27, no. 3 (Winter 2003/2004), pp. 178–79; G. John Ikenberry, "American Hegemony and East Asian Order," *Australian Journal of International Affairs,* vol. 58, no. 3 (September 2004), p. 362; Morton Abramowitz and Stephen Bosworth, "Adjusting to the New Asia," *Foreign Affairs* (July/August 2003), pp. 119–31; Patrick M. Morgan, "The U.S.-ROK Alliance: An American View," *International Journal of Korean Studies,* vol. 11, no. 1 (Spring/Summer 2007), pp. 17–18.

18. Scott Snyder, *China's Rise and the Two Koreas* (Boulder, Colo.: Lynne Reinner Publishers, 2009), p. 11.

19. Mark E. Manyin, "Food Crisis and North Korea's Aid Diplomacy: Seeking the Path of Least Resistance," in Kyung-Ae Park, ed., *New Challenges of North Korean Foreign Policy* (New York: Palgrave Macmillan, 2010), p. 76.

20. Mike Chinoy, *Meltdown: The Inside Story of the North Korean Nuclear Crisis* (New York: St. Martin's Press, 2008), pp. 292–93.

21. Ibid., p. 295.

22. Ibid., p. 296.

23. The Article 41 designation meant mandatory implementation of the sanctions, but not with U.N. authorization to use force.

24. Chinoy, *Meltdown,* p. 302.

25. Ibid., p. 303.

26. Marcus Noland, "The (Non)-Impact of U.N. Sanctions on North Korea," *Asia Policy,* vol. 7 (January 2009), pp. 61–88.

27. "N. Korean Submarine 'Left Base Before the *Cheonan* Sunk,'" *Chosun Ilbo,* March 31, 2010, http://english.chosun.com/site/data/html_dir/2010/03/31/2010033101024 .html (accessed May 24, 2011); "N. Korean Top Leadership 'Closely Involved in *Cheonan* Sinking,'" *Chosun Ilbo,* May 27, 2010, http://english.chosun.com/site/ data/html_dir/2010/05/27/2010052701465.html (accessed May 24, 2011).

28. Personal conversation, Blue House official, May 14, 2010. This account of the meeting was told to me by a Blue House official who was present at the meeting.

29. Unpublished survey by the ASAN Institute for Policy Studies, November 27, 2010.

30. Drew Thompson, *Silent Partners: Chinese Joint Ventures in North Korea,* U.S. Korea Institute at SAIS, February 2011; and John S. Park, "North Korea Inc.: Gaining Insights into North Korean Regime Stability from Recent Commercial Activities," United States Institute of Peace Working Paper, April 22, 2009.

31. John C. Wu, "The Mineral Industry of North Korea," *2005 Minerals Yearbook,* North Korea, U.S. Geological Survey (June 2007), p. 151.

32. Goohoon Kwon, "A Unified Korea? Reassessing North Korea Risks," Goldman Sachs Global Economics Paper 188, September 21, 2009, p. 10.

33. Thompson, *Silent Partners,* p. 53.

34. Scott Snyder and See-won Byun, "China-Korea Relations: China Embraces South and North, but Differently," *Comparative Connections,* vol. 11, no. 4 (January 2010).

35. Desiree Polyak, "Molybdenum," *2008 Minerals Yearbook,* U.S. Geological Survey (January 2010), pp. 106–7.

36. Thompson, *Silent Partners,* p. 58

37. Ibid., pp. 50–51.

38. Leo Lewis and Tim Reid, "Kim Jong-Il's Son 'Made Secret Visit to China,'" *Times,* June 17, 2009, http://www.timesonline.co.uk/tol/news/world/asia/article6508436

.ece (accessed May 21, 2011); Justin McCurry and Jonathan Watts, "North Korean Leader Kim Jong-il 'Visiting China with His Son,'" *Guardian*, August 26, 2010, http://www.guardian.co.uk/world/2010/aug/26/north-korean-leader-china (accessed May 21, 2011).

39. Park Hyeong-jung, "North Korea's Foreign and Domestic Policy and Its Relations with China," KINU, June 15, 2010 (unpublished paper).

40. Thompson, *Silent Partners*, pp. 33–34

41. Manyin, "Food Crisis," in Kyung-Ae Park, ed., *New Challenges*, p. 81.

42. Thompson, *Silent Partners*, p. 28.

43. David C. Kang, "'China Rising' and Its Implications for North Korea's China Policy," in Kyung-Ae Park, ed., *New Challenges*, p. 121.

44. Up until the time of writing (June 2011), Bosworth's sole trip to Moscow was December 14, 2009.

45. Seung-Ho Joo, "Russia and the Korean Peace Process," in Tae-Hwan Kwak and Seung-Ho Joo, eds., *The Korean Peace Process and the Four Powers* (Hampshire, UK: Ashgate Publishing, 2003), pp. 142–44.

46. Jacob Neufeld and George M. Watson Jr., eds., *Coalition Air Warfare in the Korean War, 1950–1953* (Washington, D.C.: U.S. Air Force Historical Foundation, 2005), p. 61; Zhang Xiaoming, *Red Wings Over the Yalu: China, the Soviet Union, and the Air War in Korea* (College Station: Texas A&M University Press, 2002), pp. 138–39.

47. Joseph P. Ferguson, "Russia's Role on the Korean Peninsula and Great Power Relations in Northeast Asia," *NBR Analysis*, vol. 4, no. 1 (June 2003), p. 35.

48. Byung-joon Ahn, "South Korean–Soviet Relations: Contemporary Issues and Prospects," *Asian Survey*, vol. 31, no. 9 (September 1991), p. 816; Coit D. Blacker, "The USSR and Asia in 1989: Recasting Relationships," *Asian Survey*, vol. 30, no. 1 (January 1990), p. 2.

49. Roy Kim, "Gorbachev and the Korean Peninsula," *Third World Quarterly*, vol. 10, no. 3 (July 1988).

50. Gary Lee, "Gorbachev Announces Reduction of 6,000 in Afghanistan Force," *Washington Post*, July 29, 1986.

51. Kim, "Gorbachev and the Korean Peninsula."

52. Gorbachev's February 1988 announcement that all troops would be withdrawn from Afghanistan within a year took care of that obstacle, and a visit by Foreign Minister Qian to Moscow in December 1988 settled the Cambodia problem, leaving just the Sino-Soviet border "obstacle" to be surmounted. See John Garver, "The 'New Type' of Sino-Soviet Relations," *Asian Survey*, vol. 29, no. 12 (December 1989), pp. 1136–52.

53. Yasuhiro Izumikawa, "South Korea's *Nordpolitik* and the Efficacy of Asymmetric Positive Sanctions," *Korea Observer*, vol. 37, no. 4 (2006), pp. 605–42.

54. Viktor Levin, "Shevardnadze Arrives in DPRK, Talks 'Unlikely to Be Simple,'" *Moscow Home Service*, September 2, 1990.

55. *Asahi Shimbun*, January 1, 1991, cited in Wada Haruki, "The North Korean Nuclear Problem, Japan, and the Peace of Northeast Asia," *Japan Focus* (March 10, 2006), http://www.japanfocus.org/-Haruki-Wada/2376 (accessed May 23, 2011).

56. Don Oberdorfer, *The Two Koreas: A Contemporary History*, revised and updated ed. (New York: Basic Books, 2003), p. 213.

57. Lee Young-Hoon, "An Analysis of the Effect of North Korea's International Trade and Inter-Korean Trade on Its Economic Growth," *Bank of Korea Economic Papers,* vol. 8, no. 1 (2005), pp. 175–211; UNSTAT; KOTRA.

58. Stephan Haggard and Marcus Noland, *Famine in North Korea: Markets, Aid, and Reform* (New York: Columbia University Press, 2007), p. 28.

59. Nicholas Eberstadt, *The North Korean Economy: Between Crisis and Catastrophe* (New Brunswick, N.J.: Transaction Publishers, 2007), pp. 75–76.

60. Joseph S. Chung, "The Economy," in Andrea Matles Savada, ed., *North Korea: A Country Study* (Washington, D.C.: Library of Congress, 1994).

61. Stephen Handelman, "Gorbachev Wins More Leverage in Asia," *Toronto Star,* June 8, 1990.

62. Joseph E. Yang and Eleanor Randolph, "Gorbachev, Roh to Seek Full Ties; Moscow-Seoul Accord Could Realign Asia," *Washington Post,* June 5, 1990.

63. "Gorbachev Report on Far East Trip," *BBC Summary of World Politics,* April 29, 1991.

64. Seung-Ho Joo, "Russia and the Korean Peace Process," in Kwak and Joo, eds., *The Korean Peace Process and the Four Powers,* p. 147.

65. "The Bank of Korea Economic Statistics System," Bank of Korea (2011), http://ecos .bok.or.kr/EIndex_en.jsp (accessed May 23, 2011).

66. Ronald Reagan, "Address to the Nation on a Korean Airliner (KAL 007)," *Rescue007 .org* (September 5, 1983), http://www.rescue007.org/speech.htm (accessed May 29, 2011).

67. In fact, in a diplomatic gaffe, it turned out the boxes that Yeltsin handed over were missing the crucial flight data recorder (FDR) tape that stored all of the necessary information. This tape would be handed over to the International Civil Aviation Organization (ICAO) in January of 1993.

68. Jung Sung-ki, "Seoul, Moscow Discuss Swapping Arms for Debts," *Korea Times,* September 12, 2007.

69. Woo Pyung-kyun, "NK-Russia Ties Under Medvedev's Government," *Vantage Point,* vol. 31, no. 8 (August 2008), pp. 20–23.

70. "DPRK-Russia Joint Declaration Released," KCNA (July 20, 2000), http://www .kcna.co.jp/index-e.htm (accessed May 23, 2011).

71. Yoshinori Takeda, "Putin's Foreign Policy Towards North Korea," *International Relations of the Asia-Pacific,* vol. 6, no. 2 (2006), pp. 192.

72. "Chronology of U.S.-DPRK Nuclear and Missile Diplomacy: December 1985–June 2003," Armscontrol.org (June 2003), http://www.armscontrol .org/pdf/dprkchron .pdf (accessed May 23, 2011), p. 4.

73. Seung-Ho Joo, "Moscow-Pyongyang Relations Under Kim Jong-il: High Hopes and Sober Reality," *Pacific Focus,* vol. 24, no. 1 (April 2009), p. 118.

74. One of Putin's priorities was to organize a major debt resettlement campaign for Russia. The ministry of finance reached a debt restructuring agreement with the ROK in 2003 ($660 million in interest written off by Seoul, $300 million paid in armaments, and $1.4 billion restructured and extended to 2025). In 2005 it reached agreement with China on Soviet-era debts, and in 2006 it paid off $3.59 billion to Japan. See Alexandre Mansourov, "Russia's Advances and Setbacks in Northeast

Asia Under President Putin (1999–2007)," in Hans J. Geissmann, ed., *Security Handbook 2008: Emerging Powers in East Asia: China, Russia and India: Local Conflicts and Regional Security Building in Asia's Northeast* (Baden-Baden, Germany: Nomos, 2008), p. 117.

75. Michael J. Mazaar, "Kim Jong-il: Strategy and Psychology," *Korea Economic Institute Academic Paper Series, On Korea,* no. 1 (2006), p. 8.

76. "Kim Jong Il: Bow When You Don't Say That Name," *Christian Science Monitor,* March 14, 2003, http://www.csmonitor.com/2003/0314/p11s01-cogn.html (accessed May 26, 2011).

77. Tadashi Ito, "PRC Source Cited on Putin Rejecting Kim Chŏng-il Request to Host Talks in Russia," *Sankei Shimbun,* September 9, 2003.

78. Andrew E. Kramer, "Dmitry A. Medvedev: Young Technocrat of the Post-Communist Era," *New York Times,* December 11, 2007, http://www.ny times.com/2007/12/11/world/europe/11medvedev.html (accessed May 27, 2011).

79. Yong-Chool Ha and Beon-Shik Shin, *Russian Nonproliferation Policy and the Korean Peninsula* (Washington, D.C.: Strategic Studies Institute, 2006), p. 10. Available online at: http://www.strategicstudiesinstitute.army.mil/pdffiles/pub747.pdf (accessed May 26, 2011).

80. Georgy Toloraya, "The Six-Party Talks: A Russian Perspective," *Asian Perspective,* vol. 32, no. 4 (2008), pp. 45–69.

81. Ibid.

82. Ibid., p. 47.

83. "No Plans for N. Korea to Give Up Six-Nation Talks—Deputy Russian FM," RIA Novosti (October 15, 2006), http://en.rian.ru/world/20061015/54822806.html (accessed May 23, 2011).

84. U.S. Department of State, "Joint Statement of the Fourth Round of the Six-Party Talks, Beijing, September 19, 2005," http://www.state.gov/p/eap/re gional/c15455.htm (accessed May 23, 2011), Clause 1, Paragraph 3.

85. Mark Manyin, "Japan–North Korea Relations: Selected Issues," Congressional Research Service Report for Congress, RL 32161(November 26, 2003).

86. International Institute for Strategic Studies, *The Military Balance, 2011* (London: IISS, 2011), p. 250.

87. "Japan and North Korea: Bones of Contention," *International Crisis Group (ICG) Asia Report,* no. 100 (June 27, 2005), p. 2.

88. *"Chaeoe Tongp'o Hyŏnhwang"* [Current Status of Overseas Compatriots], MOFAT. go.kr (2011), http://www.mofat.go.kr/consul/overseascitizen/com patriotcondition/index.jsp (accessed June 2, 2011).

89. "Japan and North Korea: Bones of Contention," p. 3.

90. Oberdorfer, *The Two Koreas,* p. 221.

91. Marcus Noland, *Avoiding the Apocalypse: The Future of the Two Koreas* (Washington, D.C.: Institute for International Economics, 2000), p. 105.

92. There were about 6,500 Japanese spouses of Korean nationals who had been placed in Japan during the occupation period as part of labor conscription policies during the Pacific War. At the end of the war, many of these Koreans in Japan chose to return to their homeland, bringing their Japanese brides with them.

93. To National Security Adviser Steve Hadley's credit, a number of these ideas did come to fruition, including not only Graceland but later trips by President Bush for summits in historic ancient cities of Kyŏng-ju, Korea, and Kyoto, Japan.

94. *Kidnapped!: The Japan–North Korea Abduction Cases,* directed by Melissa Kyung-ju Lee (Australia: The Australian Film Commission, 2005).

95. Yoshi Yamamoto, *Taken!: North Korea's Criminal Abduction of Citizens of Other Countries* (Washington, D.C.: Committee for Human Rights in North Korea, 2011), p. 66.

96. "Woman May Be No. 17 on Abductee List," *Japan Times,* November 11, 2006.

97. Unmesh Kher, "Accounted for at Last," *Time* (October 3, 2002), http://www.time .com/time/magazine/article/0,9171,354086,00.html (accessed June 2, 2011).

98. *Kidnapped!,* directed by Melissa Kyung-ju Lee.

99. "Terrorism by the Democratic People's Republic of Korea," NPA.go.jp (2005), http://www.npa.go.jp/keibi/kokutero1/english/0401.html (accessed June 2, 2011).

100. "Chapter 6: Just Cry When You Feel Like It," in *The Families* (Washington, D.C.: Reach, 2005), pp. 11–12.

101. "Terrorism by the Democratic People's Republic of Korea."

102. "Chapter 8: A Letter from Ms. Soga," in *The Families,* p. 6.

103. "Chapter 4: She Is Our Strong Ally," in *The Families,* p. 8.

104. "Chapter 5: A Fight to Protect Children," in *The Families,* p. 13.

105. *Kidnapped!,* directed by Melissa Kyung-ju Lee.

106. See "Abductions of Japanese Citizens by North Korea," MOFA.go.jp (2011), http://www.mofa.go.jp/region/asia-paci/n_korea/abduction/pdfs/abduc tions_en.pdf (accessed June 2, 2011).

107. From about March 2003 until its decision in December 2003, Britain had been in secret talks with Muammar Qaddafi's regime to give up Libya's WMD programs to the United States.

108. "G8 Foreign Minister's Meeting, Summary of the G8 Presidency," *G8 Information Centre* (May 23, 2003), http://www.g8.utoronto.ca/foreign/fm230503.htm (accessed May 23, 2011).

109. In 2008, Bush took North Korea off the terrorism list in the course of DPRK nuclear dismantlement, even though the abductions issue had not been resolved, on the legal grounds that there was no evidence of recent DPRK terrorist-related activities or support for terrorist organizations.

CHAPTER NINE: APPROACHING UNIFICATION

1. Hong Soon-young, "Thawing Korea's Cold War: The Path to Peace on the Korean Peninsula," *Foreign Affairs,* vol. 78, no. 3 (May/June 1999), p. 10.

2. For a well-informed critical treatment of the Sunshine Policy, see Donald Kirk, *Korea Betrayed: Kim Dae Jung and Sunshine* (New York: Palgrave Macmillan, 2009).

3. Figure is from government sources quoted in "South Korea Paid Astronomical Sums to North Korea," *Chosun Ilbo,* December 3, 2010.

4. Don Kirk, "South Korean Leader Says Move Was Meant to Aid 'Sunshine' Policy: Payment to North Puts Seoul on the Defensive," *New York Times,* January 31, 2003,

http://www.nytimes.com/2003/01/31/news/31iht-a1_43 .html (accessed May 29, 2011); Kirk, *Korea Betrayed*, pp. 157–58.

5. "N. Korea to Extort New Demands for Kaesong Complex," *Chosun Ilbo*, June 12, 2009.

6. Jay Lefkowitz, "Freedom for All Koreans," *Wall Street Journal*, April 28, 2006.

7. "North Korea: Workers' Rights at the Kaesong Industrial Complex," Human Rights Watch Background Briefing Paper, no. 1 (October 2006).

8. Shin Hye-son, "Mt. Kumgang Tour Gains Popularity Among Honeymooners, Group Tourists," *Korea Herald*, December 1, 1998.

9. Dick K. Nanto and Emma Chanlett-Avery, "North Korea: Economic Leverage and Policy Analysis," Congressional Research Service Report for Congress, RL32493 (January 22, 2010), p. 32.

10. See Dick K. Nanto and Mark E. Manyin, "The Kaesong North-South Korean Industrial Complex," Congressional Research Service Report for Congress, RL34093 (March 11, 2011), summary; Nanto and Chanlett-Avery, "North Korea: Economic Leverage and Policy Analysis," p. 47.

11. Stephan Haggard and Marcus Noland, "North Korea's External Economic Relations," *PIIE Working Paper Series*, WP 07-7 (August 2007), pp. 40–41.

12. Bill Powell, "A Korean Killing with Terrible Timing," *Time* (July 13, 2008), http://www.time.com/time/world/article/0,8599,1822310,00.html (accessed June 1, 2011).

13. Roh Moo-hyun quoted in Kang In-duk, "Toward Peace and Prosperity: The New Government's North Korea Policy," *East Asian Review*, vol. 15, no. 1 (Spring 2003), p. 3.

14. "South-North Joint Declaration, June 15, 2000," USIP (June 15, 2000), http://www.usip.org/publications/peace-agreements-north-korea-south-korea (accessed May 29, 2011).

15. "2 Korean Leaders Enjoy Soaring Popularity After Summit," *Korea Times*, June 19, 2000.

16. For examples, see Morton Abramowitz and Stephen Bosworth, "Adjusting to the New Asia," *Foreign Affairs* (July/August 2003), pp. 119–31; Kent Calder, "The New Face of Northeast Asia," *Foreign Affairs* (January/February 2001), pp. 106–22.

17. Germany data from Holger Wolf, "Korean Unification: Lessons from Germany," in Marcus Noland, ed., *Economic Integration of the Korean Peninsula*, Special Report 10 (Washington, D.C.: Institute for International Economics, 1998), pp. 168–69; Korean data from "Bank of Korea Economic Statistics System," BOK.or.kr (2011), http://ecos.bok.or.kr/EIndex_en.jsp (accessed May 30, 2011).

18. South Korea went from an "A1" rating down to a "Ba1" rating for its long-term sovereign credit rating. See Suduk Kim, "Currency Crisis in Korea—When and Why It Happened," *Asia-Pacific Financial Markets*, vol. 7, p. 13.

19. Deok Ryung Yoon, "The Economic Impacts of a North Korean Collapse," *IIRI Working Paper Series*, no. 7 (October 2010).

20. Kim Dae Jung, "Nobel Lecture," Nobelprize.org (December 10, 2000), http://nobelprize.org/nobel_prizes/peace/laureates/2000/dae-jung-lecture .html (accessed May 31, 2011).

21. Samuel S. Kim, "North Korea in 1999: Bringing the *Grand Chollima* March Back

In," *Asian Survey,* vol. 40, no. 1 (January/February 2000), pp. 151–63; Samuel S. Kim, "North Korean Informal Politics," in Lowell Dittmer, et al., eds., *Informal Politics in East Asia* (New York: Cambridge University Press, 2000), pp. 237–68.

22. Don Oberdorfer, *The Two Koreas: A Contemporary History,* revised and updated ed. (New York: Basic Books, 2001), pp. 15–16, 23–24.

23. Ibid., p. 25.

24. On tethering adversaries in international relations, see Patricia A. Weitsman, *Dangerous Alliances: Proponents of Peace, Weapons of War* (Stanford, Calif.: Stanford University Press, 2004), pp. 21–24.

25. Entire document can be seen at "Agreement on Reconciliation, Nonaggression, and Exchanges and Cooperation Between South and North Korea," UCLA (February 19, 1992), http://www.international.ucla.edu/eas/docu ments/korea-agreement .htm#CHAPTER%203 (accessed May 30, 2011).

26. Entire document can be seen at "Joint Declaration on the Denuclearization of the Korean Peninsula," FAS (February 19, 1992), http://www.fas.org/news/dprk/1992 /920219-D4129.htm (accessed May 30, 2011).

27. The per capita GDP for the West was $20,887, while for the East it was $7,300. See Wolf, "Korean Unification: Lessons from Germany," pp. 168–69.

28. Becky A. Gates, "The Economy," in Stephen R. Burant, ed., *East Germany: A Country Study* (Washington, D.C.: Library of Congress, 1987). Can be viewed online at: http://lcweb2.loc.gov/frd/cs/gxtoc.html (accessed May 31, 2011).

29. Susan Larson, "Foreign Policy" in "Government and Politics," in Burant, *East Germany.*

30. Wolf, "Korean Unification: Lessons from Germany," p. 170.

31. Population statistics from "World Development Indicators," World Bank (2011), http://data.worldbank.org/data-catalog/world-development-indicators (accessed May 30, 2011); GDP statistics from BOK.or.kr (2011).

32. For comprehensive lists of a number of the studies on costs of unification see Marcus Noland, Sherman Robinson, Li-Gang Liu, "The Costs and Benefits of Korean Unification: Alternate Scenarios," *Asian Survey,* vol. 38, no. 8 (August 1998), p. 802; and Yoon, "The Economic Impacts of a North Korean Collapse," pp. 13–15.

33. Charles Wolf Jr. and Kamil Akramov, *North Korean Paradoxes: Circumstances, Costs, and Consequences of Unification* (Santa Monica, Calif.: RAND, 2005).

34. "Korean Unification to Cost Over $3 Trillion," *Korea Herald,* September 14, 2010.

35. Hong, "Thawing Korea's Cold War," p. 10.

36. "N. Korean Envoys Visit South to Pay Respect for Former President," *Chosun Ilbo,* August 22, 2009.

37. James Atlas, "What Is Fukuyama Saying? And to Whom Is He Saying It?" *New York Times Magazine* (October 22, 1989); Francis Fukuyama, "The End of History?" *National Interest* (Summer 1989).

38. This section is adapted from an earlier version published in *Orbis:* Victor D. Cha, "The End of History: 'Neojuche Revivalism' and Korean Unification," *Orbis,* vol. 55, no. 2 (Spring 2011), pp. 290–97.

39. I do not deny that there are economic risks that affect the discount, including a

highly leveraged country both in terms of household and corporate debt. Korea also has active labor unions that strike six times more, on average, than in Japan. But the North Korea threat is undeniably a significant factor.

40. "Seoul Stocks End 0.34 Percent Lower on Geopolitical Fears," *Yonhap News,* March 29, 2010, http://english.yonhapnews.co.kr (accessed May 31, 2011).

41. "Stocks, Currency Cut Losses After N. Korean Attack," *Yonhap News,* November 24, 2010, http://english.yonhapnews.co.kr (accessed May 31, 2011).

42. Nicholas Eberstadt, "Hastening Korean Unification," *Foreign Affairs,* vol. 76, no. 2 (March/April 1997), pp. 82–83.

43. Ibid., p. 83.

44. "Joint Vision for the Alliance of the United States of America and the Republic of Korea," Whitehouse.gov (June 16, 2009), http://www.whitehouse .gov/ (accessed May 31, 2011).

45. Victor Cha and David Kang, *Approaching Korean Unification: What We Learn from Other Cases* (Washington, D.C.: CSIS, 2011); Report available online at: http://csis .org/files/publication/101217_Cha_ApproachingUnifi cation_WEB.pdf (accessed June 6, 2011).

46. Yoon, "The Economic Impacts of a North Korean Collapse," pp. 13–14.

47. North Korea's territory is 120,538 square kilometers (46,539 sq mi) while that of the South is 99,720 square kilometers (38,502 sq mi).

48. The length of North Korea's roadways totals 25,554 kilometers (15,870 mi), whereas South Korea's total sits at 103,029 kilometers (64,020 mi). *The CIA World Factbook,* CIA (2011), https://www.cia.gov/library/publications/the-world-factbook/ (accessed June 6, 2011).

49. Ibid.

50. Ibid.

51. South Korea is estimated to have 19.289 million landlines plus 47.944 million cell phones. North Korea is believed to have 1.18 million landlines plus an additional 450,000 cell phones. CIA (2011); "Mobile Phone Use Growing in North Korea," *Chosun Ilbo.* April 9, 2011, http://english.cho sun.com/site/data/html_dir/2011/04/09/2011040900314.html (accessed June 7, 2011).

52. In 2010, South Korea's oil and gas pipeline length was 3,003 kilometers (1,865 mi). North Korea's total was just 154 kilometers (95 mi). CIA (2011).

53. *Economist Intelligence Unit Special Report,* no. M212 (London: The Economist Intelligence Unit, April 1992), p. 102.

54. International Institute for Strategic Studies, *The Military Balance, 2011* (London: IISS, 2011), p. 249.

55. ROK military figure from ibid., p. 251.

56. Nicholas Eberstadt, *Korea Approaches Reunification* (Armonk, N.Y.: M. E. Sharpe, 1995), pp. 112, 122.

57. Kang-suk Rhee, "Korea's Unification: The Applicability of the German Experience," *Asian Survey,* vol. 33, no. 4 (April 1993), p. 371.

58. "Defector Among Us: What Does She Look Like?" *Joongang Ilbo,* October 19, 2011, http://joongangdaily.joins.com/article/view.asp?aid=2927327 (accessed June 6, 2011).

59. Hwang-ju Lee, "Inadequate Training, Unrealistic Expectations," *DailyNK,* August 21, 2010, http://www.dailynk.com/english/read.php?cataId=nk00400&num=6713 (accessed June 6, 2011).

60. "Defector Among Us," *Joongang Ilbo,* October 19, 2011.

CHAPTER TEN: THE END IS NEAR

1. Donald S. Zagoria, *The Sino-Soviet Conflict: 1956–1961* (Princeton, N.J.: Princeton University Press, 1962).

2. I am grateful to Nick Anderson for his research support on this section.

3. Seymour Martin Lipset, "Some Social Requisites of Democracy: Economic Development and Political Legitimacy," *American Political Science Review,* vol. 53, no. 1 (March 1959), pp. 69–105; Ronald Inglehart and Christian Welzel, "How Development Leads to Democracy: What We Know About Modernization," *Foreign Affairs,* vol. 88, no. 2 (March/April 2009), pp. 33–41.

4. Eric Goldstein, "A Middle-Class Revolution," *Foreign Policy* (January 18, 2011), http://www.foreignpolicy.com/articles/2011/01/18/a_middle_class_revolution?page=full (accessed May 10, 2011); David Brooks, "The Forty Percent Nation," *New York Times,* February 5, 2011, http://www.nytimes .com/2011/02/06/opinion/06brooks .html (accessed May 10, 2011).

5. GDP per capita figures and life expectancy from "World Bank Open Data," World Bank (2011), http://data.worldbank.org/ (accessed May 10, 2011); Human Development ratings from "UN Human Development Reports," UNDP (2011), http://hdr .undp.org/en/ (accessed May 10, 2011).

6. Francis Fukuyama, "Is China Next?" *Wall Street Journal,* March 12, 2011, http://online.wsj.com (accessed May 10, 2011).

7. Samuel Huntington, *Political Order in Changing Societies,* 2nd ed. (New Haven, Conn.: Yale University Press, 2006), pp. 53–56.

8. "World Economic Outlook Database," IMF (2011), http://www.imf.org/ex ternal/pubs/ft/weo/2011/01/weodata/index.aspx (accessed May 10, 2011).

9. Real GDP per capita is a measure of the average income per individual in society adjusted for inflation.

10. All Real GDP per capita figures from IMF.org (2011).

11. Steven Levitsky and Lucan A. Way, "Elections Without Democracy: The Rise of Competitive Authoritarianism," *Journal of Democracy,* vol. 13, no. 2 (April 2002), pp. 51–65.

12. "Freedom in the World 2011," Freedom House (2011), http://www.freedomhouse .org/template.cfm?page=594 (accessed May 10, 2011).

13. Ellen Knickmeyer, "The Arab World's Youth Army," *Foreign Policy* (January 27, 2011), http://www.foreignpolicy.com/articles/2011/01/27/the_arab_world_s_youth_army (accessed May 10, 2011).

14. Bobby Ghosh, "Rap, Rage, and Revolution: Inside the Arab Youth Quake," *Time* (February 17, 2011), http://www.time.com/time/world/article/0,8599,2049808,00 .html (accessed May 10, 2011).

15. Median age shows the distribution of age in a population. It essentially divides a population into two equal halves; half being older than the given age and half being

younger. And so, in the case of Yemen, half of its population is eighteen or younger, the other half being eighteen and older.

16. All demographic and employment figures from *The World Factbook,* CIA (2011), https://www.cia.gov/library/publications/the-world-factbook/ (accessed May 10, 2011).

17. Cell phone and Internet penetration data from *The World Factbook* (2011).

18. All literacy data from "World Bank Open Data," World Bank (2011).

19. Hugh Miles, "The Al Jazeera Effect," *Foreign Policy* (February 8, 2011), http://www.foreignpolicy.com/articles/2011/02/08/the_al_jazeera_effect (accessed June 8, 2011).

20. "ICT Indicators," *Arab Information and Communications Technology Organization* (2008), http://www.aicto.org/index.php?id=432&L=0 (accessed June 8, 2011).

21. "Televisions Per Capita by Country," *Nationmaster.com* (2011), http://www.nationmaster.com/graph/med_tel_percap-media-televisions-per-capita (accessed June 8, 2011).

22. Paul R. Pillar, "How Does a Ruler Stay in Power?" *National Interest* (April 7, 2011), http://nationalinterest.org/blog/autocracy/how-does-ruler-stay-power-5133 (accessed May 10, 2011).

23. All EIU data from "Economist Intelligence Unit Democracy Index 2010: Democracy in Retreat," EIU (2011), http://graphics.eiu.com/PDF/Democracy_Index_2010_web.pdf (accessed May 10, 2011).

24. "World Bank World Governance Indicators," World Bank (2011), http://info.worldbank.org/governance/wgi/index.asp (accessed May 10, 2011).

25. "World Bank Open Data," World Bank (2011).

26. UNDP, "U.N. Human Development."

27. The next-closest military service terms are in Vietnam (24–48 months), Chad (36 months), Egypt (12–36 months), and Venezuela (30 months). See *The World Factbook* (2011); International Insititute for Strategic Studies, *The Military Balance, 2011* (London: IISS, 2011).

28. *The Military Balance*, p. 249.

29. "Televisions per Capita," *Nationmaster.com.*

30. "Orascom Signs Mobile Phone Deal with North Korea," *New York Times,* November 15, 2008, http://www.nytimes.com/2008/12/15/technology/15iht-orascom.4.18698081.html (accessed June 7, 2011).

31. Bill Powell, "The Capitalist Who Loves North Korea," *Fortune* (September 15, 2009), http://money.cnn.com (accessed June 7, 2011).

32. "Freedom in the World 2011," Freedomhouse.org.

33. "Economist Intelligence Unit Democracy Index 2010," EIU.com.

34. "World Governance Indicators," World Bank (2011); "Freedom of the Press 2011," Freedom House (2011), http://freedomhouse.org/template.cfm?page=668 (accessed June 7, 2011).

35. Yossi Shain, "Mexican-American Diaspora's Impact on Mexico," *Political Science Quarterly,* vol. 114, no. 4 (Winter 1999–2000), pp. 661–91.

36. *Survey of 297 NK defectors* (Seoul: Institute for Peace and Unification Studies, Seoul National University, July 24, 2008).

37. *Inside North Korea*, directed by Peter Yost (USA: National Geographic Television, 2007).

38. Andrew Salmon, "North Koreans Escape Freedom but Still Hold Kim Jong Il Dear," *The Times*, May 29, 2009.

39. "Number of N. Korean Defectors in S. Korea Tops 21,000," *Yonhap News*, May 14, 2011, http://english.yonhapnews.co.kr/ (accessed June 4, 2011); "Settlement Support for Dislocated North Koreans," Republic of Korea Ministry of Unification (2011), http://eng.unikorea.go.kr/eng/default .jsp?pgname=AFFhumanitarian_settlement (accessed June 7, 2011).

40. Park Hyeong Jung, "How Can We Move North Korea?" unpublished paper for the Fourth Korea Institute for National Unification–U.S. Institute of Peace Washington Workshop, March 10, 2011; and "NK Tightens IT Gadget Control to Block Outside Info," *Korea Herald*, April 1, 2011.

41. "Kim Jong-il 'Has Nightmares of Being Stoned by His People,'" *Chosun Ilbo*, March 28, 2011, http://english.chosun.com/site/data/html_dir/2011/03/28/2011032801124 .html (accessed June 7, 2011).

42. Nina Hachigian, "The Internet and Power in One-Party East Asian States," *Washington Quarterly*, vol. 25, no. 3 (2002), pp. 41–58; Ko Kyungmin, Heejin Lee, and Seungkwon Jang, "The Internet Dilemma and Control Policy," *Korean Journal of Defense Analyses*, vol. 21, no. 3 (2009), pp. 279–95; and "North Korea Takes to Twitter and YouTube," *New York Times*, August 16, 2010.

43. Andrei Lankov, "Pyongyang Strikes Back: North Korean Policies of 2002–08 and Attempts to Reverse 'De-Stalinization from Below,'" *Asia Policy*, no. 8 (July 2009), pp. 61–62.

44. Daniel Byman and Jennifer Lind, "Pyongyang's Survival Strategy: Tools of Authoritarian Control in North Korea," *International Security*, vol. 35, no. 1 (Summer 2010), pp. 44–74.

45. Ibid., pp. 60–64.

INDEX

Abe Shinzo, 345–46, 370–71

Afghanistan, 20, 54, 130, 218, 239, 352, 377, 429–30

Agreed Framework (1994), U.S.-DPRK, 22, 89, 125, 139, 146, 252–55, 256, 257, 260, 261, 270, 276–77, 288, 290, 291, 293, 300, 309, 364, 365, 375, 458

agriculture, DPRK, 24–25, 26, 43, 44, 103, 107, 112, 113, 115, 116, 123–24, 142–48, 190, 192–93

Al-Kibar (Syria), 247–49, 429

Albright, Madeleine, 80, 84, 89, 94, 96, 289–90, 309

all-out war option, 58, 223, 235, 236, 243–46, 253, 285, 286, 291, 455

Arab Spring, 7, 14, 18, 106, 410, 415, 430–55, 461

Asian Games, 324–25, 326–30

Assad-Bashar al-, 248, 434

assistance, foreign: bad decisions and, 122–28, 129, 144, 145, 146–47, 156, 160; deterrence and, 246; donor fatigue and, 127, 411; DPRK reform and, 144, 145, 146–47, 155; DPRK survival and, 13; DPRK violation of norms of, 201; monsoons and, 129; preparation for collapse of DPRK and, 462; real desires of DPRK and, 301, 302; U.S. security assurances to DPRK and, 312, 314. *See also specific nation, organization, or type of aid*

Australia, 138, 246, 334, 462

authentic Korean, 34–37, 38, 45–46, 59, 73–74, 177

bad decisions: cause for, 138–39; Ch'ŏllima movement and, 113–16, 154; corruption and, 127; debt and, 116–18,

125, 129, 130; foreign assistance and, 122–28, 129, 144, 145, 146–47, 156, 160; illicit activities and, 129–37; *juche* ideology and, 112, 114, 154; Moonshine policy and, 147–53, 160; neojuche revivalism and, 153–61; Olympic games and, 118–22; overview about, 110–13; political control and, 138–39, 141, 143, 154, 159, 161; reform and, 137–53, 154–61; Soviet abandonment and, 121–24

Banco Delta Asia (BDA) incident, 264–67, 268, 294, 333, 367

banks, DPRK, 157–59

Basic Agreement on Reconciliation (1992), ROK-DPRK, 139, 260, 283, 399–400

Battle of Dongning (1933), 67–68

Beijing Channel, 280, 281, 284

belligerence, DPRK, 52–58, 235, 236–39, 279, 387, 392

Bin Laden, Osama, 17, 108, 222, 455

biochemical weapons, 218, 219, 233–34, 237, 263, 372, 411

black market, 14, 132, 136, 144, 155, 157, 172, 186, 440, 447, 454

Blitzer, Wolf, 8, 311

Blix, Hans, 251, 252

Blue House: DPRK commando raid on (1968), 54, 56, 58, 235; U.S.-ROK discussions about unification at, 403–4, 407–8

Bolton, John, 85, 370

Bosworth, Stephen, 10, 272, 296, 305, 347

Bouazizi, Mohamed, 14, 431

Bryant, Kobe, 16, 102

Buddhism, 73, 164

Bureau 39 (Korean Workers' Party), 84, 131–32

Burma, 57, 86, 132–33, 166, 205, 232, 233, 279, 305, 323, 373

Bush, George H.W., 281–85, 288, 304, 307–8, 368

Bush, George W.: aid to DPRK and, 294; all-out war option and, 291; axis of evil comment of, 255, 303; BDA incident and, 266–67, 293; blame on U.S. for DPRK nuclear program and, 290–94; Cha as speech writer for, 19; China-U.S. relations and, 291–92, 331, 460; Chinese ambassador Cha discussion about, 137–38; Chinese reaction to DPRK nuclear tests and, 330, 331; conundrum facing, 305–6; deterrence and, 230; DPRK admission to U.N. and, 283; DPRK defectors meetings with, 166–70, 204, 451; DPRK illicit activities and, 266–67; DPRK missile program and, 104, 226–27, 267; DPRK nuclear program and, 2, 22–23, 256, 257–58, 262, 268, 274, 290–94, 330, 331, 367, 408; DPRK as state sponsor of terrorism and, 270, 312; DPRK terrorist links and, 232; DPRK-U.S. bilateral meetings in New York and, 428; flexibility of, 293–94, 302; form for addressing DPRK leader by, 288; goals for DPRK-U.S. relations of, 291; human rights and, 166–70, 183, 184–85, 203, 204–5, 206, 211, 292–93, 383–84, 451; Japan-DPRK relations and, 378, 382; Jenkins case and, 382; Jiang Zemin meeting with, 331; Kim Jong-il and, 203–4, 205, 292, 293–94, 296, 302, 356; Koizumi visit with, 376–78; Libya and, 240; Megumi kidnapping and, 383–84; *New York Times* criticisms of, 270, 274, 275, 277, 290; NSC thank you from, 454; real desires of DPRK and, 302; Richardson visit to DPRK and, 2; Roh Moo-hyun conversation with, 268; ROK-U.S. relations and, 20, 292; Russia-U.S. relations and, 363; security assurances to DPRK by, 11, 310–15; Six-Party Talks and, 11, 257–58, 262, 266–67, 272, 275, 291, 293–94, 298, 301, 311, 312; unification of Korea and, 408, 460; views about ROK of, 20; withdrawal of nuclear weapons around the world and, 283; Woodward book about, 203–5

Cambodia, 50, 136, 189, 351

cars; in DPRK, 9, 164–65

Carter, Jimmy, 6, 33, 65, 89, 90, 143, 253, 282–83, 287

Catholics, 51–52, 164

"Ceausescu moment," 445–48

Ceausescu, Nicolae, 30, 40, 105–6, 410, 446

Center for Strategic and International Studies (CSIS), 38, 78, 237, 418, 457, 458

Central Intelligence Agency, Korea (KCIA), 34, 45, 78, 96, 397, 399

Central Intelligence Agency, U.S.. (CIA), 24, 112, 252

Central Military Committee, DPRK, 98, 100

Chang Sŏng-t'aek (brother-in-law of Kim Jong-il), 83, 100

Channing Liem, 398–99

Cheney, Dick, 85, 275, 278

Cheonan (ROK ship): DPRK attack on, 10, 103, 159, 236, 238, 241, 242, 245, 296, 334–35, 336, 362, 407, 416, 419

China: aid to DPRK from, 11, 15, 21, 23–24, 27–28, 32, 41, 63, 111, 112, 113, 117, 119, 122, 123–28, 145–46, 153, 154, 160, 201, 202, 257, 258, 319–20, 321, 323, 327, 340–42, 388, 411, 454, 460; Arab Spring and, 431, 449; Beijing Channel and, 280, 281, 284; border between DPRK and, 343, 429, 430; Bush (George W.) administration and, 291–92; Ceausescu execution and, 105–6; changes in support of DPRK by, 317, 323–34; *Cheonan* incident and, 334–35, 419; Choco Pies in, 154; civil war in, 70; Cold War and, 20, 27–28, 316, 319; counterfeiting in, 43, 133; Cultural Revolution in, 29, 39, 48, 49, 320, 322; currency in, 144; dissidents in U.S.

from, 206; domestic issues in, 339–42, 346; DPRK agreement (1953) with, 319; DPRK agreement (1962) with, 343; DPRK agreement (1971) with, 225; DPRK agreement (1986) with, 178, 181; DPRK agreement (2010) with, 336; and DPRK and China as mutual hostages, 17, 315–46; and DPRK distrust/anti-Chinese sentiment, 161, 316, 338–39; DPRK famine and, 123, 192, 201, 202, 328, 460; DPRK illicit activities and, 132, 133, 134, 136; DPRK image in, 48; DPRK joint projects with, 335, 337–38, 340; DPRK military ties with, 31–32, 268; DPRK missile program and, 225–27; DPRK Moonshine policy and, 151–53; DPRK nuclear program and, 11, 257, 258, 259, 262, 267–68, 269–70, 317, 329–34, 336, 344, 345–46, 366, 383, 411, 419, 460; DPRK refugees/ defectors in, 9, 172, 177, 178–86, 187, 307, 322, 328, 339, 340, 342, 416, 451, 460, 461; DPRK resentment of, 315; DPRK special relationship with, 316; DPRK support by, 3, 13, 15; DPRK survival and, 17, 429, 430; DPRK terrorist attacks on ROK and, 323; DPRK trade with, 112, 123–25, 145–46, 316, 318, 319–20, 324, 327–28, 334, 335, 337–38, 339, 340; DPRK value to, 318, 321, 326, 339–46; economy of, 7; famine in, 25; food production in DPRK and, 25; Great Leap Forward in, 189, 323; human rights and, 292; human trafficking and, 136; Japan-DPRK relations and, 377, 383; Japanese relations with, 343, 345–46, 373, 377; *juche* ideology and, 39, 41, 62–63; Kim Il-sung and, 48, 49–50, 67–68, 69, 76–77, 79, 108, 112, 249, 315, 319, 320–22, 326; Kim Jong-il and, 83, 96, 151–53, 160, 315–16, 327, 328, 330, 333, 336, 345, 362, 409; Kim Jong-il death and, 419; Kim Jong-un and, 103, 104, 107, 160, 338, 344; Korean War and, 66, 76, 213, 303, 317–19, 321, 323, 326, 334; Korean Workers' Party delegation in, 32; as model for DPRK, 14, 93, 153–54, 321; modernization/reform in, 30, 60, 93, 139, 144, 145, 321, 326, 339; Nixon trip to, 31–32, 48–49, 397; nuclear program of, 246, 249; Olympic and Asian Games and, 118–19, 324–28; plans for collapse of Kim family and, 307; predatory economic policy of, 315, 334–46; PSI and, 456; Reagan's modest initiative policy and, 280; real desires of DPRK and, 298–99; rebuilding of DPRK and, 23–24; recognition of DPRK by, 318; repatriation (*refoulement*) of North Koreans from, 177, 178–86, 204, 210, 328, 451; ROK-DPRK relations and, 243, 244; ROK relations with, 20, 27–28, 304, 317, 324–28, 331, 334–35, 399, 460; Russia-DPRK relations and, 365; Russian relations with, 28–30, 39, 76–77, 315, 320–21, 326, 351, 352, 359; sanctions on DPRK and, 306; Six-Party Talks and, 11, 256, 258, 259, 262, 265, 266, 269, 295, 298–99, 304–5, 316, 317, 347, 362, 368–69; smuggling of cell phones from, 450; special economic zones and, 139–40; student demonstrations in, 106; Tiananmen Square demonstrations in, 106, 139, 324, 410; triads in, 132, 135; troops in DPRK of, 26, 319, 322; unification and, 410, 413, 416, 419, 458, 460; U.S. relations with, 32, 117, 246, 262, 306, 318, 330–35, 339, 416, 429, 460; U.S. security assurances to DPRK and, 304–5, 368–69; U.S. trade embargoes and sanctions on, 318–22; in World War II, 343. *See also specific agreement or treaty*

Chinese Communist Party (CCP), 28, 316, 335, 337, 410

Choco Pies, 154–55, 443

Ch'ŏllima movement, 44–45, 61, 62, 106, 113–16, 154

Chŏng Chu-yŏng, 386, 389, 390, 391, 407, 446

Chŏng Mong-hŏn, 388–89
Chosen Soren (Japanese organization), 372, 374, 376
Christians, 66, 67, 68, 73, 76, 164, 201
Chun Doo-hwan (ROK president), 51–52, 57, 86, 232, 279, 323, 398–99
civil unrest, DPRK, 158–59, 161, 189, 191, 209–11, 452–55
Clinton, Bill: blame for DPRK nuclear program and, 276–77, 285–90; Bush (George W.)–DPRK relations and, 290, 291; deterrence and, 213, 218, 229–30, 237; DPRK missile program and, 229–30, 237, 288–89; DPRK nuclear program and, 22, 124, 203, 254–55, 276–77, 285–90, 308–12; Japan-DPRK relations and, 375; Jo Myong-rok meeting with, 289; journalists detainment incident and, 296; Kim Il-sung–Carter meeting and, 89, 287; Kim Jong-il and, 95–96, 230, 288, 289, 290, 294; non-hostile intent of, 285–90, 304, 308–12; real desires of DPRK and, 300; sanctions against DPRK and, 125. *See also* Agreed Framework (1994), U.S.-DPRK; Joint Communique (2000), U.S.-DPRK
Club Med, 93–94
CNN, 4, 8, 21, 74, 80, 163, 216, 269, 442
Cold War: aid for DPRK during, 28; Arab Spring in DPRK and, 430; authentic Korea during, 34–37, 45–46, 58; bad decisions and, 115; China-DPRK relations and, 316, 317, 319; division of Korean Peninsula and, 7; DPRK belligerence during, 53–58; DPRK confidence during, 46–52; DPRK ideology during, 14, 21, 30, 37–46, 58–63, 106; DPRK nuclear program during, 246; DPRK trade during, 25; end of, 417; impact on DPRK of, 20–21, 24–25, 27–28, 30, 62–63, 105, 111, 121; impact on ROK of, 20–21, 30; Japan-DPRK relations during, 373; Korean independence and, 70; *neojuche revivalism* and, 448; ROK-DPRK

relations and, 395, 396–97, 400; ROK-U.S. relations during, 19, 20, 27, 30–32; Russia-DPRK relations during, 76, 315, 348; Russia-U.S. relations during, 246, 298, 301, 369; Sino-Soviet relations during, 28–30; unification of Korea and, 395, 396–97, 400. *See also specific person, nation, or topic*
communications technology, 12, 421, 435–36, 449–50. *See also* Internet; mobile/cell phones
communism/communists: DPRK as model for, 22; "the end of history" and, 408; *juche* ideology and, 37–39; Khrushchev's "Secret Speech" and, 28–30; Kim Il-sung and, 47–49, 66, 67, 68, 69; Kim Jong-il and, 78; in ROK, 26; in ROK police/military force, 47; Sino-Soviet relations and, 29–30. *See also* Marxist-Leninism; *specific person*
confidence, DPRK, 46–52, 54, 58, 241
Confucianism, 40–41, 75
Congress, U.S., 33, 52, 141, 203, 206, 243, 256, 299, 396
Congressional Research Service, U.S., 133, 341–42
contagion effect, 432, 435–36, 437, 440–41, 449, 451
corruption, 127, 147, 211
counterfeiting, 8, 43, 129, 131, 132, 133, 134–36, 264, 265–67, 367
cows: unification of Korea and, 386, 391
crime, 170–71, 197, 444. *See also* illicit activities
Cuba, 48, 205, 322
Cui Tankei, 368–69
currency issues, 9, 93, 141–42, 156–58, 264, 265–67, 367, 423–24, 447–48, 453
CVID (complete, verifiable, and irreversible dismantlement): crises and, 252–74; and DPRK blame on U.S., 275–98; DPRK as "horizontal proliferation threat" and, 249; Israeli bombing of Al-Kibar facility and, 247–49; origins of DPRK nuclear program and, 249–52; real desires of DPRK and, 298–305;

U.S. conundrum concerning, 305–10;
U.S. security assurances to DPRK and,
298–314
Czechoslovakia/Czech Republic, 81, 117,
356

debt, DPRK, 116–18, 125, 130, 359–60, 362
decapitation strikes, 221–22, 455
Defense Department, U.S., 2, 3, 52
Demilitarized Zone (DMZ): Bush (George
W.) security assurances to DPRK and,
310; *chaju* (self-reliance) carving at, 45;
Chong cows and, 386, 391; description
of, 214; deterrence and, 213–14, 219,
220, 234, 241–42; DPRK biochemical
weapons and, 234; DPRK forces at, 12,
53, 116, 213, 219, 220; establishment of,
213; KPA "Two-Front War" doctrine
and, 27; standoff between DPRK and
ROK and, 213–14; unification of Korea
and, 386, 391, 395
demographic effect, 432, 434–35, 437
Deng Xiaoping, 14, 30, 49, 60, 79, 93, 107,
139, 225, 321, 323, 326, 352
deterrence: all-out war option and, 236,
243–46; biochemical weapons and,
218, 219, 233–34, 237; change in ROK
attitudes and, 242, 243; conventional
military balance and, 215–22;
dangerous and misinformed strategic
thinking and, 223–31; decapitation
strikes and, 221–22; Defense Reform
304 and, 245; definition of, 244;
desperation of DPRK and, 234–46;
DMZ and, 213–14, 219, 220, 234,
241–42; double or nothing mind-set
and, 234–38, 245; DPRK "invasion" of
ROK and, 212–13, 219; DPRK second-
strike capability and, 241, 246; foreign
investments and, 223, 229; geography
and, 217–18, 220–21; international
assistance and, 246; invulnerability of
DPRK and, 240, 241; miscalculations
and, 234–46; missiles and, 220, 223–31,
234, 237, 238, 241, 245; nuclear program
and, 215, 218, 219, 223, 224, 228, 230,

234, 237, 238–43, 245, 246; passive vs.
proactive, 242; provocations by DPRK
and, 236–38, 241, 245; readiness and,
245; ROK-U.S. "invasion" of DPRK and,
219–22; terrorism and, 231–33, 237; U.S.
role in, 212, 213, 215, 217, 218–19, 221,
223, 224–25, 227, 228, 229–32, 237–38,
239–40, 241, 242–46; as way to employ
force, 244. *See also specific nation*
DeTrani, Joe, 427, 428
development-gap theories, 13, 432, 433–
34, 437, 449
diplomats, DPRK: illicit activities and,
130, 134, 136
Director of National Intelligence, U.S.,
267, 273
double or nothing mind-set, 234–38, 245
drugs: illicit activities and, 8, 131, 132–34,
135–36

East Germany, 30, 40, 50–51, 105, 156,
303, 398, 423–24
Eastern Europe, 122, 139, 209, 282
Eberstadt, Nicholas, 145, 189, 417
Economist Intelligence Unit (EIU)
Democracy Index, 436, 437, 442
Economist magazine, 16, 402
economy, DPRK: Arab Spring and, 437,
438, 443, 447, 449, 454; bad decisions
concerning, 13, 110–61; China-DPRK
relations and, 334–46; Cold War and,
25, 40, 111; decentralization of decision
making and, 142–48; decline/failure in,
12, 14, 111, 454; dependency on foreign
aid of, 126; DPRK as impossible state
and, 7–8; DPRK survival and, 12, 429;
growth in, 438, 439; gulag prisoners
and, 172; ideology and, 40, 59, 61,
113–16, 154–61, 454; illicit activities
and, 129–37; impact on Korean people
of, 154–61; inflation and, 144, 159, 424,
454; Japan-DPRK relations and, 370,
371, 374, 376, 378, 380; Kim Il-sung
and, 90, 112–13, 114–15; Kim Jong-il
and, 87, 90, 93; "Korea discount" and,
416–17; Moonshine policy and, 147–53;

economy, DPRK (*continued*)
nuclear program and, 365–66; political control and, 138–39, 141, 143, 154, 159, 161; reform/modernization of, 139–61, 417, 443, 447, 454; refugees/defectors and, 10, 444; ROK compared with, 12, 87, 400, 401; ROK-DPRK relations and, 208, 388, 393–94, 400, 401, 405, 412; Russia-DPRK relations and, 122–24, 348, 350–51, 365–66; unification and, 388, 393–94, 400, 401, 405, 416–17, 419, 421, 423–24, 425. *See also* agriculture; Ch'ŏllima movement; energy; food/famine; industry; Seven-Year Plan (1961–67); Three-Year Plan (1954–56)
education, 7, 165, 191, 211, 423, 425, 432, 435, 445. *See also* reeducation
Egypt, 18, 26, 106, 161, 226, 229, 431, 432–34, 435, 436, 443, 445
Eighty-eighth Special Independent Sniper Brigade, Russian, 69–70, 82
elites/"selectorate": as source of discontent, 453–54
energy, DPRK: bad decisions about, 114–15, 117, 122–24, 128, 141, 146; China-DPRK relations and, 321, 328, 340, 341; Ch'ŏllima movement and, 45; Cold War aid to DPRK and, 28; division of Korean peninsula and, 23; famine and, 192; goat-breeding campaign and, 110; ideology and, 60; international assistance, 24, 28, 122–24, 293, 297, 301, 312; Japan-DPRK relations and, 383; monsoons and, 128; *neojuche revivalism* and, 58–59; real desires of DPRK and, 302, 303; reform/modernization and, 25, 141, 146; Russia-DPRK relations and, 24, 28, 122–24, 355–56, 359, 361, 367; Six-Party Talks and, 382; South Korea and, 23, 24, 25, 87; unification of Korea and, 411, 421–22. *See also* nuclear program, DPRK
entitlements, DPRK, 190–91
entrepreneurship, 13, 93, 107, 139, 142, 144, 155, 157, 443
European Union, 146, 159, 313, 413

executions, 8, 107, 158, 166, 173, 174, 191, 197, 209, 448, 452

Facebook, 435, 441, 449
farms/farmers, 46–47, 134, 144, 155, 165, 190, 192, 447, 454. *See also* agriculture; marketization
Federal Bureau of Investigation (FBI), 78, 134
filial piety, 41, 74–75, 78
fisherman, ROK: DPRK capture of, 374, 405
Five Policy Principles, 455–62
food/famine: alternative, 187, 196; Arab Spring and, 430; and average diet in DPRK, 9; bad decisions and, 110, 111, 112, 113, 122, 124, 125–26, 127, 128, 129, 133, 141, 144, 146, 147, 158–59; and causes of famine, 190–93; China-DPRK relations and, 124, 192, 201, 202, 328, 460; civil unrest and, 158, 188, 191, 210, 452, 453; collectivization and, 47; comparison between ROK and, 87; corruption and, 127; deaths during, 9, 188, 193, 194, 393; disease and, 194–95; DPRK collapse scenario and, 461; future of DPRK and, 203; geography and, 192–93; goat-breeding campaign and, 110; in gulags, 172, 173, 175, 182, 191; human rights and, 188; ideology and, 60; illicit activities and, 130, 133; impact of, 186–90, 193–99; instability of DPRK leadership and, 412; international assistance and, 9, 11, 15, 23, 28, 113, 122–27, 129, 144, 146, 147, 155, 159, 190, 199–202, 205, 211, 289, 294, 297, 301, 312, 327, 328, 340, 342, 375–76, 405, 460; Japan-DPRK relations and, 375, 376; Kim Jong-il and, 81, 91, 92–93, 108, 188; Kim Jong-un and, 103, 107; Marxist-Leninist approach to government and, 189; migrations out of DPRK and, 178, 182, 187–88, 191, 199, 328; monsoons and, 128, 129; *neojuche* revivalism and, 58–59; NGO assessment of food needs during,

187; rationing of, 87, 187; reform and, 141, 144, 146; ROK-DPRK relations and, 201, 202, 393; social stratification and, 186, 190–91, 193, 194; survival of DPRK and, 12; unification and, 412; U.S.-DPRK relations and, 204; youth and, 199. *See also* agriculture, DPRK; marketization; public distribution system

Ford (Gerald) administration, 57, 58

foreign investments: Arab Spring and, 450; deterrence and, 223, 229; Japan-DPRK relations and, 372, 373; "Korea discount" and, 416–17; reform and, 139, 140, 142–48; special economic zones and, 139, 140; unification and, 412, 416–17, 424; U.S. security assurances to DPRK and, 313

Foyer, Mats, 2–3, 137

France, 33, 81, 117, 135, 185, 199, 364

Frank, Rüdiger, 61, 156

Freedom House, 200, 434, 436, 437, 442

Freedom of the Press Index, 8, 442

Freedom in the World index, 8, 434, 442

Friendship, Cooperation, and Mutual Assistance Treaty (1961, 2000), Russia-DPRK, 27–28, 319, 348, 356, 359

Friendship, Cooperation, and Mutual Assistance Treaty (1961), China-DPRK, 28, 319, 328

G8 Summits, 358, 360, 382, 384

Gallucci, Robert, 253, 286, 287

gas pipelines, Russian, 359, 411

Gates, Robert, 223, 224

geography, DPRK, 13, 192–93, 217–18, 220–21

Germany: unification of, 400–401, 423–24

Gimpo International Airport (Seoul): bombing of (1986), 86, 232

Goldman Sachs: reports about DPRK by, 7–8, 111, 337

Gorbachev, Mikhail, 107, 326, 351, 353, 355

Gore, Al, 285, 286, 293–94, 295

Graceland: Koizumi-Bush visit to, 376–77

Green, Michael, 5, 19, 184, 256, 376, 404

gulags, DPRK, 8, 107, 124, 166, 169, 170–78, 191, 198–200, 211, 424

Hadley, Steve, 5, 262, 329, 330

Haggard, Stephan, 125, 190, 342, 447

Hallstein Doctrine, 395, 398

health care, 166, 191, 195, 205, 423, 432

Hill, Christopher, 260, 261, 263, 270, 301, 304, 335, 370, 371, 428

Honecker, Erich, 30, 40, 50, 105, 410

Hu Jintao, 184, 330, 333, 334, 336

human rights: Arab Spring and, 440; bad decisions and, 115; Bush (George H.W.) administration and, 281; Bush (George W.) and, 166–70, 183, 184–85, 203, 204–5, 206, 211, 292–93, 383–84, 451; China-U.S. relations and, 292; definition of, 163; DPRK kidnappings and, 383–84; DPRK nuclear program and, 205, 212, 293; famine and, 188; human trafficking and, 137; importance of DPRK rectification of problems concerning, 211; international recognition of DPRK abuses of, 451, 461; interracial births and, 177; Kaesŏng Industrial Complex and, 389–90; as key barometer of reform, 207; major issues concerning, 211; of North Korean people, 8, 13, 451, 461; Obama and, 297, 451; and reactions of DPRK people, 207–11; *refoulement* and, 178–86; in ROK, 20; ROK-DPRK relations and, 207, 211, 272, 389–90, 404, 405, 406, 408; Six-Party Talks and, 170, 205, 261, 263; unification and, 389–90, 404, 405, 406, 408, 412; U.S. conundrum and, 305; U.S.-DPRK relations and, 166–70, 183, 184–85, 203–7, 211, 212, 281, 292–93, 297, 305, 383–84, 451. *See also* gulags

human trafficking, 136–37, 179, 197

Hungnam Chemical Fertilizer Plant, 24, 154

Huntington, Samuel, 433, 449

Hussein, Saddam, 17, 222, 229, 233, 455

Hwang Jang-yŏp, 78, 83, 86, 89–90, 209–10, 402

Hwasŏng missile, 226–27, 228

Hyundai, 148, 149, 325, 386, 389, 390, 391–92, 404, 407

ideology, DPRK: Arab Spring and, 440, 447, 448–55; and "back-to-the-future" thinking, 21, 59–63, 106, 109; Cold War and, 21, 30, 37–46, 106; collapse of DPRK scenario and, 461; control of outside information and, 462; as core of state, 60; crisis of governance and, 13–14; economy and, 40, 59, 61, 113–16, 154–61, 454; Kimilsungism, 88; KPA and, 116–17, 147, 154; material well-being and, 26; reform and, 60–63, 141, 144; survival of DPRK and, 13, 429; unification and, 40, 45, 410, 411, 412. *See also specific leader or ideology*

illicit activities, 8, 129–37, 197, 263, 264, 266–67, 269. *See also* BDA incident; crime; *type of activity*

"in my lifetime" concept, 417–19

Incheon International Airport (Seoul), 233, 235

India, 301–3, 305

industry, DPRK: aid for building, 112; bad decisions about, 112–13, 114, 115, 116–17, 142–48; China-DPRK relations and, 321, 337–38; Ch'ŏllima movement and, 44–45, 114, 115; Cold War and, 25–26, 28; expansion of, 111, 112–13; geography of DPRK and, 192; GNP and, 24; Japan-DPRK relations and, 372; Japanese occupation and post–World War II, 12, 22, 23; Kim Il-sung and, 112–13; reform and, 142–48; Russia-DPRK relations and, 359; Three-Year Plan and, 23; unification and, 417, 422, 423. *See also specific industry or company*

infanticide, 176–77

inflation, 144, 159, 424, 454

information: Arab Spring and, 435–36, 449–50; control of, 4–5, 18, 204, 205,

430, 441–42, 445, 446, 449–50, 461–62; and lack of knowledge about DPRK, 65, 99–100, 102, 221–22; as seeping into DPRK, 415. *See also* communications technology; Internet; mobile/cell phones

intelligence community, 16, 65, 221–22, 250, 251, 270, 281, 430

International Atomic Energy Agency (IAEA): Bush (George H.W.) administration concerns about DPRK compliance with safeguards of, 281; DPRK agreement (1977) with, 250; DPRK nuclear declarations and, 285; DPRK safeguards agreement with, 281, 285; DPRK uranium-based nuclear program and, 256; DPRK withdrawal from NPT and, 253, 285, 343; inspection of DPRK nuclear facilities and, 271, 285; Kim-Kanter meeting and, 284; origins of DPRK nuclear program and, 251–52; real desires of DPRK and, 302; Russian proposals for multilateral talks and, 363; Six-Party Talks and, 260, 261; Team Spirit exercises and, 281; Yongbyon reactor and, 343

International Convention on Economic, Social, and Cultural Rights (ICESR), 188, 206

International Criminal Court (ICC), 163, 208

International Olympic Committee (IOC), 118, 279, 325

Internet, 421, 435, 441, 442, 449–50

interracial marriage, 38, 179–80

Iran, 17, 81, 226, 228–29, 232–33, 239, 255, 295, 311, 443

Iran-Iraq War, 134, 228, 232–33

Iraq, 17, 20, 54, 229, 233, 239, 251, 255, 422–23, 429

Iraq War, 218, 221, 222, 377, 455

Irish mobsters, 132, 135

Israel, 86, 229, 230, 247–49, 429

Japan: anti-DPRK emotions in, 372–73, 380–81, 382, 384; assistance to DPRK from, 125, 126, 146, 200, 236, 255, 258,

315, 375, 382, 384, 390, 412; biochemical weapons and, 233; China-DPRK relations and, 320, 344–46; Chinese relations with, 343, 344–46, 373, 377; Choco Pies in, 154; deterrence and, 212, 218, 223, 226, 227, 228, 231, 246; DPRK borrowing from, 117; DPRK economy and, 370, 371, 374, 376; DPRK hatred of, 372–73, 382–83; DPRK illicit activities and, 132, 133, 134, 135; DPRK "invasion" of ROK and, 212; DPRK kidnappings in, 86, 185, 200, 231, 261, 270, 315, 370–71, 373, 375, 376, 378–85; DPRK missile program and, 290, 348, 363, 372, 378, 418; DPRK nuclear program and, 246, 254, 255, 257, 258–63, 269, 331–35, 344–46, 366, 374, 375, 378, 382, 411, 418; DPRK peace settlement with, 20; DPRK refugees in, 372, 375; DPRK relations with, 369–85, 406; DPRK trade with, 25, 372; DPRK-U.S. relations and, 284, 428; economy of, 7; ideology and, 59, 161; Kim Chŏng-nam Disneyland incident in, 97–98; Kim family fall and, 307; Kim Jong-il and, 85, 94, 344, 371, 373; Korean Air Lines Flight 858 and, 231; Korean nationalism and, 46; nuclear program of, 249; nuclear and tsunami disasters in, 218; occupation of Korea by, 12, 22, 23, 35, 36, 47, 66, 67, 168, 233, 249, 372; planning for collapse of Kim family and, 307; Pyongyang Declaration (2002) with, 255; remilitarization of, 284, 383; ROK-China trade and, 324; ROK relations with, 31, 371, 375, 376, 382, 383; ROK-U.S. relations and, 20; Russia-DPRK relations and, 359, 364, 366; Russia relations with, 348; Six-Party Talks and, 256, 258–63, 265, 295, 304–5, 346, 348, 368, 370–71, 382–83, 384–85; unification of Korea and, 406, 411, 412, 413, 415–16, 418, 426; U.S.-DPRK relations and, 284, 296, 370–71; U.S. relations with, 346–48, 363, 373, 375, 376–77; U.S. security assurances

for DPNK and, 304–5, 368; World War II and, 68, 69, 70, 111, 233, 343; youth in, 434
Japanese Red Army (JRA), 86, 232
Jenkins, Charles Robert, 381–82
Jiang Zemin, 95, 291, 328, 331
Jilin Province (China), 36, 67, 83, 153, 179, 181, 316, 338–39
Johnson (Lyndon) administration, 34, 55, 58
Joint Communiqué (1972), ROK-DPRK, 26, 34, 46, 396–97, 398
Joint Communiqué (1992), China-ROK, 325–29
Joint Communiqué (2000), U.S.-DPRK, 289, 290, 304, 309
Joint Denuclearization Declaration (1992), ROK-DPRK, 251, 399, 400
Joint New Year's Editorial, 61–62
Joint Statement (1993), U.S.-DPRK, 290, 308
joint ventures, 148–49, 160, 373, 389–93. See also special economic zones
Jordan, Michael, 15, 16, 80, 102
journalists, U.S.: DPRK detaining of, 95–96, 238, 277, 296
juche ideology, 13, 37–46, 60, 62–63, 72, 78, 88, 106, 112, 114, 154, 185, 192, 210, 410, 448
justice system: unification and, 424–25

Kaesŏng Industrial Complex, 142, 148–49, 150, 154–55, 156, 165, 389–90, 391, 392, 403, 407, 447
Kanemaru Shin, 373–76
Kang Ch'ŏl-hwan, 168–70, 172, 178, 197, 199, 204, 443, 451
Kang, David, 342, 419–20
Kangnam (DPRK ship), 233, 305
Kangsŏn Steel Plant, 24, 44–45, 61, 62, 114
Kanter, Arnold, 283–85, 287
Kartman, Charles, 94–95
Kelly, James, 255–56, 259
Kennedy (John F.) administration, 31, 47
Khrushchev, Nikita, 27, 28–30, 39, 321, 322, 326

Kim Chŏng-ch'ŏl (son of Kim Jong-il), 84, 98
Kim Chŏng-nam (son of Kim Jong-il), 84, 97–98
Kim Chŏng-suk (wife of Kim Il-sung), 68, 82–83
Kim Chun-Hee (Ch'ŏn-hŭi), 183–85, 193
Kim Dae-jung (ROK president): DPRK economy and, 147, 161; DPRK food aid and, 202; DPRK nuclear program and, 258; DPRK reform and, 143, 146, 148, 161; funeral of, 405–10; Gregg relationship with, 143; human rights and, 166; Japan-DPRK relations and, 375, 378, 382; Kim Jong-il summit with (2000), 149, 388, 393; Kim Jong-il summit with, 94; Nobel Prize for, 393, 394, 403; Sunshine Policy and, 147, 161, 258, 375, 387, 388, 390, 391, 402–3; Trans-Siberian Railway and, 360; unification and, 147, 387, 388, 390, 391, 394, 402–3; U.S. security assurance to DPRK and, 310
Kim Han-mi, 167–68, 169, 204
Kim Il-sung (Great Leader): accomplishments of, 66, 75–76; assassination attempts on, 71; authentic Korean and, 34–35, 36, 46; bad choices of, 112, 114–15, 117–18; badge of, 6, 43; biographical information about, 35, 39, 65–77; Carter meeting with, 65, 89, 90, 253, 282–83, 287; China-DPRK relations and, 28, 32; China relations with, 49–50, 76–77, 108, 112, 249, 315, 319, 320–21, 322–23, 326; Ch'ŏllima movement and, 44–45, 61, 62, 114–15; as Christian, 66, 67, 68, 73, 76; Clinton communications with, 308; communism and, 47–49, 66, 67, 68, 69, 232; confidence of, 47–51; consolidation of power by, 71–72, 76; death of, 4, 39, 42, 66, 75, 83, 89, 90–91, 107, 119, 328, 429, 430, 453; debt and, 116–18; economy and, 90, 112–13, 114–15; as Eternal President, 66, 91; filial piety and, 74–75, 78; Great Leader reference of, 72; greatness of

DPRK and, 108; industry and, 112–13; Japan-DPRK relations and, 372, 374; Japanese occupation of Korea and, 35, 66; joint projects and, 390; *juche* ideology and, 37, 38–40, 42–44, 45, 61, 62, 88; Kanemaru meeting with, 374; Kim Jong-il relationship with, 78–79, 83, 85, 86–87, 90, 91, 108; Kim Jong-un resemblance to, 100; Kim Jong-un as successor and, 109; Kim Young-sam summit meeting with, 34, 89–90; Korean War and, 23, 66, 73, 76, 317, 323; Korean Workers' Party and, 42, 72; as KPA founder, 67; Liem meeting with, 399; as loving mother, 74–75; loyalty/affection for, 10, 13, 16, 34, 37, 38, 39, 42, 44–45, 74, 75, 78, 86–87, 149, 164, 165, 210, 443; military/guerrilla background of, 5, 35, 36–37, 66, 67–70, 82, 373; monuments/statues of, 11, 21, 53, 72–73, 79, 121, 323, 452; Mun Sŏn-myŏng meeting with, 390; named leader of DPRK, 71; "New Epochal Save-the-Nation" plan of, 282; nuclear program and, 10, 88, 249, 250, 253; official residence of, 4; official state history about, 66, 67, 69–70, 72; personality cult for, 39, 66, 72–75, 76, 85, 90–91, 100, 108, 321, 323; physical appearance of, 34, 84; post–World War II return to DPRK of, 70; posters/paintings of, 1, 8, 30, 41, 43, 74–75, 87, 172; promises of 1960s of, 187; rebuilding of DPRK and, 23; ROK-DPRK relations and, 34, 89–90, 282, 390; Russia and, 27–28, 66, 68, 69–72, 76–77, 105, 108, 112, 315, 321, 348, 354; Russia-ROK relations and, 354; Sino-Soviet relations and, 29, 30, 39, 76–77, 315, 320–21, 351; Tan'gun myth and, 35–36; terrorism and, 232; translation of works by, 199; unification and, 40, 45, 47, 51–52, 390, 397, 398; U.S. security assurances and, 308; USS *Pueblo* incident and, 54–55; workers and, 114, 149; worldliness of, 105–6, 411; Yi Hu-rak meeting with, 397

Kim Il-sung Mausoleum (Pyongyang), 66, 79, 91, 440, 452

Kim Il-Sung University, 4, 83, 162, 249, 452

Kim Jong-il (Dear Leader): Abe Shinzo summit with, 371; accomplishments of, 93–95, 108–9, 410; Albright meeting with, 289–90; American favorites of, 15; Arab Spring and, 18; assassination attempts against, 93, 96, 442, 452–53; biographical information about, 77–91; Bush (George W.) and, 184, 203–4, 205, 292, 293–94, 296, 302, 356; and calls for bringing Kim before International Criminal Court, 208; caricatures of, 16, 64–65, 234; Carter meeting with, 65; China and, 11, 83, 151–53, 160, 315–16, 327, 328, 330, 333, 336, 345, 362, 409; Chinese gift to, 11, 80; Ch'ŏllima movement and, 106; cinematic interests of, 77–78, 85; civil unrest and, 158, 161, 189; Clinton and, 95–96, 230, 288, 289, 290, 294; communism and, 78; crisis of governance in DPRK and, 13; criticisms of, 158, 453; as Dear Leader, 79; death of, 7, 9, 13, 15, 58, 91, 98, 103, 107–8, 297, 303, 305, 317, 338, 345, 408–9, 412, 419, 429, 430, 458; decapitation strikes and, 222, 455; decline of DPRK and, 108–9; deterrence and, 222, 234; dreams of, 446; education of, 82, 83; election as leader of, 91; elites and, 454; as failed ruler, 60, 93–94; famine/food issues and, 91, 92–93, 108, 189; "4-15 Creation Group" and, 79; as golfer, 16; hatred of U.S. by, 83; health/stroke of, 94–95, 98, 271, 413, 443, 458; ideology and, 13, 39, 41, 42, 61–62, 88, 161, 448; illicit activities and, 130, 131, 134; Japan and, 371, 373, 377–78, 380, 381; Kangsŏn steel visit by, 61; kidnappings and, 380, 381; Kim Dae-jung summit with (2000), 94, 150, 388, 393; Kim Il-sung and Kim Young-sam summit and, 89–90; Kim Il-sung relationship with, 78–79, 83, 85, 86–87, 90, 91, 108; Koizumi meetings with, 255, 377–78, 381, 382,

406; Korean War and, 83; Lee Myung-bak and, 406–7; legacy of, 91–97, 303–4; lifestyle of, 64, 79–82, 87, 95, 98, 292; look-alikes of, 222; loyalty to, 9, 10, 13, 16, 42, 149, 161, 222, 393, 443; military and, 88–89, 91–92, 452; "military-first" politics of, 60, 91–92, 106, 109; missile program and, 104; monuments for, 11, 79; Moonshine policy and, 151–53; and mother's death, 82–83; Mubarak relationship with, 18, 106; NDC and, 42; nuclear program and, 11, 60, 61, 88, 106, 108, 252, 271, 303–4, 330, 333, 382, 410; Obama letter to, 296; personality cult for, 86, 87, 100, 108, 165; personality of, 89; physical appearance of, 84; pictures of, 8, 44, 79, 87, 104, 172; post–World War II return to Korea of, 83; preparation for succession of, 108; professional activities of, 84–85; public image of, 94–95; purges by, 88; Putin and, 358, 359–61; real desires of DPRK and, 299, 300, 304; as recluse, 87, 94; reform and, 139, 143, 144, 147, 304; reputation of, 64–65, 84, 91; rich nation, strong army (kangsŏng) and, 147, 302–3; rise of, 77; Roh Moo-hyun summit with, 392, 406; ROK-DPRK relations and, 146, 148, 150, 388, 392, 393, 406–7; ROK views about, 393; Russia and, 82, 354, 356, 359–61, 363; security detail for, 222; Six-Party Talks and, 362, 364; as successor to Kim Il-sung, 78, 79, 87, 105; successor to, 96–98, 99–100; terrorist activities of, 86, 119; Thailand as model admired by, 96; unification and, 388, 392, 393, 406–7, 408–9, 416; U.S.-DPRK relations and, 15; U.S. views of, 85–86; wives/mistresses and children of, 83–84; workers and, 106, 150; worries of, 445; Yeltsin and, 356

Kim Jong-un (Great Successor): agriculture and, 103, 107; American popular culture/basketball and, 16, 409; Arab Spring and, 430, 445, 449; belligerent acts of, 103–4; birth of, 84;

Kim Jong-un (*continued*)
challenges/obstacles facing, 105–8,
109, 445; China and, 103, 104, 107, 159,
317, 338, 344; crisis of governance in
DPRK and, 13; decapitation strikes
and, 221–22; deterrence and, 221–22,
234, 236; documentary about, 103, 104;
education of, 13, 100–103, 104–5, 409;
as enigma, 16, 17; as enlightened leader,
104–8; food supply and, 103, 107; as
heir apparent, 98–104, 107–8, 109;
ideology and, 7, 59, 106–7, 108, 109, 159,
409; Korean Workers' Party and, 99;
lack of information about, 65, 99–100,
102, 221–22; loyalty to, 10, 13, 16, 59,
99, 107, 160; military and, 98, 103, 454;
missile program and, 229; nuclear
program and, 103, 109, 239; physical
appearance of, 99–100; pictures of,
99; preparation and transition to
leadership of, 18, 88, 99–100, 107–8,
236, 303, 304, 409, 430, 454; real desires
of DPRK and, 300, 304, 305; reform
and, 159, 304, 305, 409–10; resemblance
to Kim Il-sung of, 100; ROK-DPRK
relations and, 103–4; in Switzerland, 16,
100–103, 104–5; unification and, 409,
409–10; U.S. conundrum and, 306, 307;
war aims of, 229
Kim Kye-gwan (DPRK Vice Minister),
263–64, 370–71, 454
Kim Kyŏng-hŭi (sister of Kim Jong-il),
82–83, 84, 100, 409
Kim P'yŏng-il (step-brother of Kim
Jong-il), 78, 82
Kim Shin-jo, 55–56
Kim Sŏl-song (daughter of Kim Jong-il),
83–84
Kim, Sung, 269, 272, 305
Kim Yŏng, 194–95
Kim Yŏng-il (step-brother of Kim Jong-il),
82, 132
Kim Yŏng-ju (brother of Kim Il-sung), 45,
78, 396–97, 409
Kim Yŏng-nam (DPRK Foreign Minister),
145, 280, 281, 354

Kim Yŏng-sun, 283–85
Kim Young-sam (ROK president), 89–90,
287, 309, 400, 402
Kim family: affection/personality cult
for, 13, 429; as enigma, 65, 108; gulag
prisoners as threat to, 172; history of,
13; ideology and, 41, 60; illicit activities
and, 131; and politics of family
succession, 78; real desires of DPRK
and, 301, 302, 304–6; reform and, 139;
rivalry within, 78–79; U.S. conundrum
and, 307
King, Robert, 206, 207, 451
Kissinger, Henry, 32, 58, 138, 169
Koizumi Junichiro, 86, 255, 371, 376–78,
380, 381, 382, 406
Korea: division of, 70, 349, 386, 388;
Japanese occupation of, 12, 22, 23,
35, 36, 46, 66, 67, 168, 233, 249, 372;
post–World War II division of, 23;
reunification of, 308; Soviet withdrawal
from, 26; unification of, 386–426; U.S.-
Soviet liberation of, 22; victimization
of, 388
"Korea discount," 416–17
Korea Project, 419, 424
Korean Airlines Flight 007: Russian attack
on, 353, 357
Korean Airlines Flight 858: bombing of,
86, 118, 231, 279
Korean Central News Agency (KCNA), 61,
75, 85–86, 96, 239, 240, 273
Korean People's Army (KPA) (DPRK):
anniversaries of, 55; Arab Spring and,
440, 452; buildup/modernization of,
26–27, 112, 115–16, 126, 216–17; China
ties with, 268; Chinese withdrawal
from DPRK and, 26; civil unrest and,
209; Cold War and, 26–27, 31–32,
53–58; conscription for, 92, 116, 440;
at DMZ, 12, 53, 116, 213, 219, 220;
executions and, 107, 452; food/famine
and, 158, 190, 191, 194, 199; founding
of, 67, 72; function of, 92; ideology and,
116–17, 147, 154; illicit activities and,
131; inflation and, 159; influence of, 92;

Kim Jong-il and, 60, 88–89, 91–92, 452;
Kim Jong-un and, 98, 103, 454; Korean
War and, 73; Kumgang Mountain
tourism project and, 390; Moonshine
policy and, 151; politicalization of, 217;
POWs and, 2; reform and, 145; ROK
forces compared with, 53–54, 116,
215–22; Russia-DPRK relations and,
28, 31–32, 122, 360; Russia withdrawal
from Korea and, 26; size of, 27, 53,
116, 215, 221; social stratification and,
166, 169, 186; special forces unit of, 27,
53–54, 116, 191, 212, 220, 222; spending
for, 53–54, 190, 215; "Two-Front War"
doctrine of, 27; unification and, 422,
423; West Sea barrage project and,
119; *Wolmido* movie about, 85. *See also*
deterrence; "military-first" ideology
Korean War: armistice (1953) in, 23, 31,
49, 53, 112, 213, 214, 235, 274, 334,
396; bad decisions following, 112;
beginning of, 47, 66, 76; casualties in,
19, 213; cease-fire in, 3; ceremonies in
remembrance of, 56; China and, 66, 76–
77, 303, 317–19, 321, 323, 326, 343, 429;
DPRK debt from, 112; establishment
of DMZ and, 213, 214; family divisions
during, 208; gulags and, 172; impact on
DPRK of, 23, 111; *juche* ideology and,
40; Kim Il-sung and, 49–50, 52, 66, 73,
76; Kim Jong-il and, 83; peace treaty
for, 15, 20, 52, 281, 289, 302, 309, 396,
411; POWs/MIAs from, 2; recovery of
remains of U.S. soldiers in, 281, 282–83;
and ROK release of DPRK prisoners, 31;
ROK-U.S. relations and, 31; Russia and,
28–29, 76–77, 317, 348; Six-Party Talks
and, 2; survival of DPRK and, 429;
unification and, 396, 411; U.S. bombing
of DPRK during, 23, 111, 222; U.S. role
in, 15, 318; U.S. trade sanctions and,
124; *Wolmido* movie about, 85
Kumchangri facility (DPRK), 254, 289
Kumgang Mountain tourism project,
142, 148, 149, 150, 156, 389, 390–92,
403, 407

land, 46–47, 113, 119, 123, 192–93
Lebanon, 20, 86, 185
Lee, Euna, 275, 277, 295–96
Lee Hy-Sang, 116, 124
Lee Myung-bak (ROK president):
China-DPRK relations and, 334, 336;
China-ROK relations and, 334, 336;
deterrence and, 236, 242, 243; DPRK
missile program and, 273; DPRK
nuclear program and, 272; Hu Jintao
meeting with, 334; human rights and,
207, 272; Japan-DPRK relations and,
383; Sunshine Policy and, 272, 340, 404,
405; unification and, 392, 404–7, 413,
415, 418; U.S. security assurances to
DPRK and, 313, 314
Lefkowitz, Jay, 204, 205, 206, 207, 389
Liaoning Province (China), 152, 316, 335,
338, 339
Liberal Democratic Party, Japan, 373–74,
384
Libya, 161, 229, 240, 256, 343, 382, 431,
433, 434, 435, 436, 437, 445, 448
Liem, Channing, 398, 399
light water reactor (LWR) technology, 22,
23, 254–55, 260, 261, 264, 288, 301, 302,
367, 411
Ling, Laura, 275, 277, 295
luck, 13, 418
Luck, Gary, 213, 285

manufacturing, DPRK, 112, 140, 173, 175
Manyin, Mark, 341–42
Mao Zedong, 29, 32, 43, 48, 49, 76, 77, 249,
318, 321, 322, 323
marketization system, 13, 14, 139, 141–48,
157, 158, 159, 160, 161, 191, 197, 430,
447, 448, 449, 453
Marx, Karl, 38, 40–41
Marxist-Leninism, 26, 37–38, 40–41, 189,
322. *See also* communism
media, 14–15, 16, 21–22, 346–47, 428,
435, 451. *See also specific person or
organization*
Megumi, Yokota: kidnapping of, 378–79,
380, 383–85

Meng Jainzhu, 315–19
Middle East, 18, 226, 386, 411, 429, 430, 431, 435, 436, 437, 441, 446, 449. *See also* Arab Spring; *specific nation*
Military Armistice Commission (MAC), 87, 88, 395
"military-first" ideology, 60, 61, 62, 91–92, 100, 106, 109, 126, 154, 410
missile program, DPRK: blame on U.S. for, 277, 298; China-DPRK relations and, 225–27, 244; Clinton administration and, 288–89, 290; deterrence and, 220, 223–31, 234, 237, 238, 241, 244, 245; DPRK "invasion" of ROK and, 212; and DPRK sales of missiles, 226–27, 228–29, 232–33; end of threat of, 417; Five Policy Principles and, 456, 457, 458; illicit activities and, 130; Japan-DPRK relations and, 348, 372, 373, 375, 378, 383; Kim Jong-un and, 104; Obama administration and, 409; real desires of DPRK and, 300–301; ROK-DPRK relations and, 226–27, 290, 363, 406; Russia-DPRK relations and, 347, 359, 363; Russian technology and, 225, 226, 230; sanctions and, 456; satellite launch and, 273; Six-Party Talks and, 261, 263; survival of DPRK and, 429; testing of, 2, 10, 11, 15, 104, 223–24, 226–27, 230, 238, 241, 245, 256, 263–68, 273, 277, 288–89, 296, 300–301, 303, 363, 372, 375, 406, 409, 416, 457, 458; U.N. and, 383; unification and, 406, 409, 411, 417, 418, 460
missionaries, 73, 182
mobile/cell phones, 8, 9, 12, 19, 106, 107, 121, 164, 421, 435, 441–42, 445, 449, 450, 454
modernization theories: Arab Spring and, 432–33
modest initiative policy, Reagan's, 278–81, 282
Mongolia, 136, 179, 189, 351
monsoons, 110, 128–29
Moonshine policy, DPRK: bad decisions

and, 147–53, 160; China and, 151–53; Kim Jong-il and, 150–53; nuclear program and, 403; reform and, 147–53; ROK and, 148, 150, 153, 160, 161; unification of Korea and, 403
Mubarak, Gamal, 18, 106
Mubarak, Hosni, 18, 106, 431, 434, 445
Myers, B. R., 38, 73

National Basketball Association, 16, 75, 80, 102
National Committee On American Foreign Policy (NCAFP); DPRK-U.S. discussions and, 427–28
National Defense Commission, DPRK, 42, 91–92, 98–99, 100
national liberation movements, 48, 50
National Security Agency, DPRK, 132, 171
National Security Council (NSC), 2, 5–6, 19, 328–29, 376, 454, 460
nationalism, 34–37, 38, 41, 45–46, 372, 425
NATO forces, 240, 448
natural disasters, 112, 192, 398
natural resources, DPRK, 7–8, 22, 24, 25, 111–12, 117, 315, 335–39, 372
negotiations: Five Policy Principles and, 457–58, 459. *See also specific person, nation, or treaty/agreement*
neojuche revivalism, 13–14, 58–63, 106, 108, 109, 153–61, 410, 411, 448–55, 461
New York City: DPRK motorcade in, 369–70; DPRK-U.S. dinner at 21 Club in, 427, 428
New York Times, 143, 251, 270, 274, 275, 276, 277, 290
Nixon, Richard M., 31–32, 48–49, 397
Nodong missiles, 227, 228, 229, 263, 290, 372, 373
Noland, Marcus, 125, 190, 334, 342, 402, 447
Non-Aligned Movement (NAM), 30, 396
nonproliferation agreements, 16, 329, 378, 457. *See also specific agreement*
North Africa, 18, 431, 435, 436, 446. *See also* Arab Spring; *specific nation*

North Korea (DPRK): American public opinion about U.S. involvement in, 32–33; axis of evil and, 304; belligerence of, 52–58, 235, 236–39, 279, 387, 392; centralization of control in, 107; Chinese recognition of, 318; as closed society, 208–11; CNN documentary about, 8, 80, 164, 216, 269, 442; collapse scenario for, 306–7, 394, 409, 458, 460–61; collectivization in, 47; confidence of, 46–52, 54, 58, 241; crisis of governance in, 13–18; desperation of, 234–46; as enigma, 8–9, 15–16; fears/insecurity of, 11–12, 13, 387, 392, 399, 400; founding of, 7, 95; freezing of assets of, 264–65, 333; as "full-fledged nuclear weapons state," 239, 246, 299, 302, 303, 304, 457; future of, 203, 208–11; geography of, 192–93, 217–18, 220–21; images of, 21–22, 393; as Impossible State, 7, 12–13, 430, 463; instability of leadership in, 14, 412–13, 416, 430–55; isolation of, 7, 60, 105–6; as model of communism/socialism, 22, 30, 33; official Web site of, 449–50; options/alternatives for, 315; predictions about, 462–63; provocations, 10–11, 236–40, 241, 245, 274, 297, 303, 306, 387, 392, 406, 407, 408, 416–17, 457–58, 459; rationality of, 234–38; real desires of, 298–305; as second-tier problem for U.S., 455–56; security for Americans in, 1–2, 3–4; self-image of, 9–10, 12, 13; as socialist paradise, 162–66, 186; stability of, 452; as state sponsor of terrorism, 233, 269, 270, 293, 312; survival of, 7, 12–15, 429–30; as terrorist state, 384; U.S. security assurances for, 11, 298–314, 367–69; world can't be bothered with, 429–30. *See also specific person or topic*

North Korea Human Rights Act (2004, 2008), U.S., 203, 205

North Korean people: anger of, 448; authentic Korea and, 34–37, 38, 45–46, 59, 73–74, 177; control of information for, 4–5, 8, 18, 204, 205, 430, 441–42, 445, 446, 449–50, 461–62; diet of, 9; Five Policy Principles and, 461–62; future of DPRK and, 463; human rights abuses of, 8, 13, 207–11, 451, 461; as learning about outside world, 411; psychological dislocation of, 425; unification and, 411, 425

North Korean Workers' Party (KWP): China-DPRK relations and, 335, 337; civil unrest and, 158; Cold War and, 41; conference of (2010), 16; corruption and, 127; as defectors in China, 322; founding of, 72, 95; illicit activities and, 131–32; *juche* ideology and, 41–42, 43; Kim Dae-jung funeral delegation and, 405–10; Kim Il-sung comments about China to, 322; Kim Jong-un and, 99, 239; as loyalists, 186; "military-first" politics and, 100; purging of, 322; reform and, 158; social stratification and, 186

Northeast Asian Peace and Security Regime, 269, 293

Northern Command, U.S., 227–28

Northern Policy (*Nordpolitik*), ROK, 121, 139, 282, 326, 352–53, 399, 400

Nuclear Non-Proliferation Treaty (NPT) (1985), 88, 229, 238, 246, 250–51, 252, 253, 255, 256, 260, 261, 288, 343, 364

nuclear program, DPRK: all-out war option and, 253; Arab Spring and, 448; blame on U.S. for, 275–98, 299–300, 333–34, 367, 409; Bush (George H.W.) administration and, 281, 282; Bush (George W.) administration and, 2, 22–23, 367, 408; China and, 11, 291–92, 317, 329–34, 336, 339, 344, 345, 419, 460; Clinton administration and, 22; crises concerning, 252–74; deterrence and, 215, 218, 219, 223, 224, 228, 230, 234, 237, 238–43, 245, 246; dismantling of, 294, 458; DPRK declaration of nuclear holdings and, 270–71, 285, 294; DPRK economy and, 365–66;

nuclear program, DPRK (*continued*)
and DPRK as "full-fledged nuclear
weapons state," 239, 246, 299, 302, 303,
304, 457; and DPRK as "horizonal
proliferation threat," 249, 457; and
end of DPRK threat, 417; Five Policy
Principles and, 456, 457, 461; game
changers in, 268–70; "Grand Bargain"
proposal concerning, 404; human rights
and, 205, 212, 293; ideology and, 13,
60; illicit activities and, 130; insecurity
of regime and, 304; inspections of,
251–52, 253, 284, 285–86, 287, 289,
294, 302, 305, 307, 367; Japan-DPRK
relations and, 374, 375, 378, 382, 383;
Kim Il-sung and, 88, 249, 250, 253;
Kim Jong-il and, 60, 61, 88, 106, 109,
252, 271, 330, 410; Kim Jong-un and,
103, 109, 239; light-water reactors
(LWRs) and, 22, 23, 254–55, 260, 261,
264, 288, 301, 302, 367, 411; media
images of DPRK and, 22; "mega-deal"
concerning, 458; military-first ideology
and, 106; Moonshine policy and, 403;
mutual nuclear arms reduction and,
302; Obama administration and, 408;
origins of, 249–52; plutonium-based, 89,
250, 251–53, 255, 256, 260, 267, 270, 271,
277, 281, 285, 293, 298, 301, 344, 400,
456; provocations by DPRK, 10–11, 274,
297, 303, 306, 387, 392, 457–58, 459; real
desires of DPRK and, 298–305; reform
and, 146, 147–48, 403; Richardson trip
and, 2, 6; ROK-DPRK relations and,
22–23, 161, 240–41, 246, 251, 254–60,
262, 268, 269, 272–73, 274, 333, 358,
366, 383, 387, 392, 400, 403–6, 408,
411; Russia-DPRK relations and, 249,
250, 335, 355, 358, 359, 363–66; Russian
proposals for multilateral conferences
concerning, 363–66; sanctions and,
252, 254, 257, 258, 263–68, 273–74,
344, 456–57; self-defense justification
for, 11–12; self-sufficiency and, 103;
Six-Party Talks and, 22–23, 239–40,
255–64, 269, 291, 292, 293, 333, 363,
364, 366, 367–69, 382, 408; survival of
DPRK and, 13, 429; terrorism and, 233;
as threat to North Korean people, 461;
U.N. and, 383, 404; unification and, 387,
392, 400, 403, 404, 405, 406, 408, 409,
411, 412, 416, 417, 418, 419, 424, 460;
uranium-based, 10, 228, 238, 249, 255,
256, 260, 261, 269, 271, 274, 275, 291,
293, 296, 363, 378, 400, 456; U.S.-DPRK
bilateral meetings about, 428; U.S.-
DPRK relations and, 10, 15, 89, 125, 139,
146, 170, 203, 205, 206, 212, 291–92,
305–10; U.S. security assurances to
DPRK and, 11, 307–17; violations
of nuclear agreements, 365. *See also*
Agreed Framework; energy: nuclear;
International Atomic Energy Agency;
Joint Denuclearization Declaration
(1992), ROK-DPRK; Nuclear Non-
proliferation Treaty (1985); nuclear
program, DPRK—testing for; Yongbyon
nuclear complex
nuclear program, DPRK—testing for: Bush
administration and, 293; China-DPRK
relations and, 11, 317, 329–34, 336,
344, 345, 419; deterrence and, 239, 245;
DPRK as full-fledged nuclear state and,
239; DPRK provocations and, 10, 15,
245, 267; DPRK underground, 88, 267;
as game changer, 268–70; Japan-DPRK
relations and, 383; "Korea discount"
and, 416; Obama administration and,
10, 270–74, 296, 297, 409; origins of
DPRK nuclear program and, 250; real
desires of DPRK and, 299, 300–301, 303,
305; ROK-DPRK relations and, 161, 392,
400, 406; ROK-Russia relations and,
358; Russia-DPRK relations and, 363,
366–67; sanctions and, 125, 267, 268,
457; U.N. resolutions, 267–68, 362, 383;
unification and, 416; U.S. conundrum
and, 306

Obama, Barack: appointment of special
envoy to DPRK by, 10, 206–7; China-
U.S. relations and, 460; Clinton–Kim

Jong-il meeting and, 296; conundrum facing, 305–10; deterrence and, 230; DPRK missile program and, 104, 277; DPRK nuclear program and, 10, 270–74, 277, 408; human rights and, 297, 451; Iran and, 295; journalists detainment and, 296; letter to Kim Jong-il from, 10, 296; Ling and Lee abduction case and, 277; *New York Times* support for, 275; sanctions and, 303, 305, 456; Six-Party Talks and, 294–95, 296, 312, 408; "strategic patience" policy of, 274, 275, 294–98, 306; unification and, 408, 409; and U.S. as the problem, 275–76; U.S. security assurances to DPRK and, 312–17; views about ROK of, 20

Olympic games (1988), 86, 87, 118–22, 279–80, 324, 353, 400

Operation Orchard, Israeli, 247–49

Operational Plan 5027 (OPLAN) (U.S.-ROK), 218, 244

opium, 132, 133

Orascom Group, 106, 121, 442

Pak Chŏng-il, 182–83

Pakistan, 17, 52, 226, 228, 302, 303

Park Chung-hee (ROK president), 26, 31, 32–34, 35, 45, 46, 47, 51, 55, 56, 58, 143, 398, 399

Park Han-shik, 38, 60, 92

patience: Five Policy Principles and, 455–56

Peng Dehuai, 76, 323

People's Liberation Army, 268, 316, 330–31, 335

Perry, William, 89, 285, 286, 289, 375

Politburo, DPRK, 41, 86, 87, 89, 100, 131

politics/political institutions: Arab Spring and, 14, 449; crisis of governance in DPRK and, 13; future of DPRK and, 463

poplar tree ax murders (1976), 57, 58, 86, 213

population control: unification and, 422–23

Powell, Colin, 290, 310, 311, 414

"powerful and prosperous nation" (*kangsŏng tae'guk*), 7, 13, 59, 62, 63

Presley, Elvis, 15, 376–77

prison camps, 9, 136, 443. *See also* gulags

prisoners of war, 2, 57, 208, 233, 405

Proliferation Security Initiative (PSI), 229, 273, 274, 306, 456

public distribution system (PDS), DPRK, 9, 14, 93, 127, 141–48, 155, 159, 190–91, 192, 196, 447

Putin, Vladimir, 80, 259, 357, 358, 359–62, 367

Pyongyang Declaration (2002), Japan-DPRK, 255, 377–78

Pyongyang (North Korea): Albright description of, 289–90; cars in, 164–65; Cha trips to, 2–7, 441, 463; city-dwellers as privileged in, 163; description of, 162; deterrence and, 222; Richardson group visit to, 1–7; underground facilities in, 222

Pyongyang University of Science and Technology (PUST), 441, 442, 450

Qaddafi, Muammar, 17, 240, 431, 434, 445, 448

Qian Qichen, 281, 325

Radio Free Asia, 204, 415, 441

railroads, 12, 359, 361, 392, 420–21

RAND Corporation, 53, 402

Reagan, Ronald, 15, 124, 278–81, 282, 323, 357

Red Cross, International, 128, 397, 398

reeducation, 171–72, 175, 182

reform, DPRK: bad decisions and, 137–54, 155–61; China-DPRK relations and, 338; China as model for, 60, 153–54; Cold War and, 24–25; Defense Reform 304 and, 245; dilemma concerning, 304–5; and DPRK as closed society, 208–11; DPRK economy and, 139–61, 417, 443, 447, 454; as failure, 154; foreign assistance and, 144, 145, 146–47, 156; future of, 137–39, 161; government backtracking and, 158–59;

reform, DPRK (*continued*)
  halfhearted, 139–41; human rights
  as key barometer of, 207; impact on
  society of, 155–61; of July 2002, 141–48;
  Kim Jong-il and, 139, 143, 144, 147;
  Kim Jong-un and, 105–8, 109, 160,
  409–10; Moonshine policy and, 147–53;
  motivation for, 144; *neojuche* revivalism
  and, 59–63; nuclear program and, 403;
  obstacles to, 105–8, 109; optimism
  about, 147, 160; political control and,
  138–39, 140, 141, 143, 154, 159, 161;
  ROK-DPRK relations and, 139, 155, 160,
  161, 387, 394, 403; unification and, 387,
  394, 403, 410–11; U.S.-DPRK relations,
  146, 147, 154
refoulement, 178–86, 204, 210, 328, 451
refugees/defectors, DPRK, 9–10, 14, 75,
  95, 134; adjustment to new life for,
  444–45; affection for Kim family
  by, 9–10, 210, 429, 443; anti-DPRK
  sentiment among, 210; Arab Spring
  and, 443–45; Bush meetings with,
  166–70; in China, 172, 177, 178–86,
  187, 191, 307, 322, 328, 339, 340, 342,
  393–94, 416, 451, 460, 461; dissident
  movements and, 443–45; families of,
  186, 211; during famine, 187–88, 191,
  199; foreign embassies and, 181; human
  rights abuses and, 170, 173–74, 177,
  178–86, 199–200, 211; income of, 447;
  refoulement of, 178–86, 203, 211, 328,
  451; in ROK, 179, 182, 200, 204, 208,
  210, 425, 439, 443, 444–45; ROK-DPRK
  relations and, 393–94; in Russia, 359;
  unification and, 393–94, 415, 416, 422,
  425, 460; in U.S., 166–70, 179, 203–4,
  206, 210, 451, 461; women as, 444. *See
  also specific person*
regime-type theories, 432, 436–37, 442–
  43, 446, 451–52
"relative crisis indifference" syndrome,
  U.S., 430, 455–56
Rhee, Syngman, 27, 30–31, 34, 35, 47, 70,
  71, 395
Ri Yŏng-ho, 100, 239

Rice, Condoleezza, 5, 262, 268, 310, 311,
  329, 333, 414, 427, 428, 446
rich nation, strong army (*kangsŏng*), 60,
  61, 147, 302–3
Richardson, Bill, 2, 3, 53
Rodong Sinmun newspaper, 48, 61, 96
Roh Moo-hyun (ROK president), 146, 147,
  160, 201, 258, 259, 268, 307, 311, 333,
  355, 357, 387, 392–93, 406
Roh Tae-woo, 276, 282, 325, 333, 352, 353,
  356, 374, 399
Romania, 30, 40, 105, 134, 185, 356
Rumsfeld, Donald, 34, 85–86
Russia: abandonment of DPRK by, 122–
  24, 351–59; aid for DPRK from, 21, 23,
  27–28, 41, 44, 63, 72, 111, 112, 113–14,
  119, 120, 122–24, 172, 190, 193, 326,
  348, 354–55, 400; Arab Spring in DPRK
  and, 449; border of, 347; China-DPRK
  relations and, 345, 365; China relations
  with, 28–30, 39, 76–77, 315, 320–21,
  326, 351, 352, 359; Cold War and, 315,
  348; collapse of, 30, 139, 190, 303,
  356, 408; dilemmas facing, 347, 363;
  dissidents in U.S. from, 205; division of
  Korean Peninsula and, 7; DPRK debt
  and, 117; DPRK economy and, 122–24,
  348, 350–51, 365–66; DPRK illicit
  activities and, 132, 133, 135, 136; DPRK
  military ties with, 31–32, 360; DPRK
  missile program and, 225, 226, 230,
  359, 363; DPRK nuclear program and,
  246, 258–59, 263–68, 269, 335, 355, 358,
  359, 363–67, 383, 411; DPRK refugees
  in, 359; DPRK relations with, 249, 250,
  304, 320–21, 326, 345–69; DPRK trade
  with, 25, 112, 122–23, 124, 128, 190,
  348, 355, 400; DPRK value to, 348, 351,
  358–59; famine in DPRK and, 190, 193;
  famine in, 189; gas pipelines of, 359,
  411; Japan-DPRK relations and, 383;
  Japan relations with, 348, 359; *juche*
  ideology and, 39, 41, 62–63; Kim Il-
  sung and, 66, 68, 69–72, 76–77, 79, 105,
  108, 112, 315, 321, 348; Kim Jong-il and,
  82, 344, 356, 359, 359–61, 363; Korean

nationalist narrative and, 37; Korean War and, 28–29, 76–77, 317; liberation of Korea and, 22; mafia in, 132; marginalization of, 363–66; nuclear program of, 88, 249, 250; occupation of DPRK by, 71, 348; Olympic games and, 118–19, 279, 353; *perestroika* in, 351–59; PSI and, 456; real desires of DPRK and, 298; rebuilding of DPRK and, 23–24; recognition of DPRK by, 348; ROK-DPRK relations and, 243; ROK relations with, 20, 87, 122, 282, 315, 326, 352–54, 355, 356–57, 366, 399, 400; role in international negotiations with DPRK of, 346–69; Six-Party Talks and, 258–59, 295, 298, 304–5, 346–47, 359, 361, 363, 364, 365, 366, 367–69; special economic zones and, 139, 359; troops in DPRK, 40, 348; U.N. role of, 347; unification and, 399, 400, 411; U.S. relations with, 117, 246, 298, 302, 359, 359, 360, 363; U.S. security assurances for DPRK and, 304–5, 367–69; USS *Pueblo* incident and, 54–55; as victim of DPRK collateral damage, 363–66. *See also* Cold War; *specific person or topic*

Ryongch'ŏn rail station: explosion at (2004), 96, 442, 450, 453

Ryugyŏng Hotel, 120–21

Salisbury, Harrison, 25–26
Samsung Electronics, 19–20, 80, 390
sanctions on DPRK: circumvention of, 456; Clinton and, 124, 289; DPRK survival and, 7; financial, 244, 267, 297, 408, 456; Five Policy Principles and, 456–57, 462; foreign assistance and, 462; on luxury goods, 454; as means of containment not denuclearization, 456; nuclear program and, 252, 254, 257, 258, 267–68, 273–74, 344, 456–57; Obama administration and, 303, 305, 456; Six-Party Talks and, 293; U.N., 3, 6, 229, 236, 237, 244, 252, 267–68, 273–74, 275, 286, 296, 303, 306, 335, 343,

454, 456; unification and, 415; U.S., 15, 124–25, 408
satellites, 230–31, 273, 359, 361
Scud missiles, 26, 116, 212, 226, 227, 228, 229, 232, 267, 372
second-strike capability, DPRK, 241, 246
"Secret Speech," Khrushchev's, 28–30
security assurances, U.S.-DPRK, 298–314, 367–69
self-reliance/sufficiency (*chaju*), 30, 45, 46, 72, 103, 112, 113, 116–17, 192–93. *See also juche* ideology
Senate Foreign Relations Committee, U.S.: Lugar comments at, 299–300; Powell testimony before, 310
Senate, U.S.: Rice confirmation comments about DPRK to, 427, 428
Seoul (South Korea): deterrence and, 219–20, 233
September 11, 2001, 255, 278
Seven-Year Plan (1961–67), 115
Shevardnadze, Eduard, 352, 354
Shinzo, Abe, 83, 345–46, 370–71, 380, 382
Sigal, Leon, 274, 276–77
Sihanouk, Samdech Norodom, 48, 50
Six-Party Talks: BDA incident and, 264–66; bilateral meetings at, 347; Bush (George W.) and, 291, 293–94, 298, 301, 311, 312; China and, 11, 316, 317, 347, 362, 368–69; China-DPRK relations and, 316, 317; China-U.S. meetings at, 347; closing statements in, 263–64; criticism of U.S. and, 275; DPRK fear of U.S. invasion and, 11–12; DPRK missiles and, 261, 263; DPRK nuclear program and, 22–23, 239–40, 255–64, 269–71, 291, 292, 293, 333, 359, 363, 364, 366, 367–69, 382, 408; DPRK reform policies and, 153–54; DPRK terrorist links and, 232; DPRK withdrawal from, 273, 302, 427; first (July 2005) round of, 255–64, 275; gas pipelines and Trans-Siberian Railway issues at, 359; goal of, 260, 293–94; human rights and, 170, 204, 261, 263;

Six-Party Talks (*continued*)
Japan-DPRK relations and, 382–83, 384–85; Joint Statement (2005) of, 260, 261–62, 263–64, 266, 268, 269, 272, 293, 295–96, 298, 301, 311, 457; Joint Statement (2007), 260, 293, 297; Kim Jong-il and, 65, 362, 364; Korean War and, 2; media and, 345–47; members of, 258–59, 362; New York City motorcade for DPRK delegation and, 369–70; Obama administration and, 274, 295, 296, 312, 408; POWs/MIA issues and, 2; real desires of DPRK and, 301, 302; results of, 259–60; Richardson trip to DPRK and, 2; Russia and, 346–47, 359, 361, 363, 364, 365, 366, 367–69; Russia-DPRK relations and, 361, 363, 364, 365, 366, 367–69; Team Spirit exercises and, 281; U.S. conundrum and, 305, 306; U.S.-DPRK meetings at, 347–48, 369–70; U.S. flexibility and, 294, 306; U.S. security assurances to DPRK and, 304–5, 310, 311, 312, 367–69
slavery, 186, 211
social media: Arab Spring and, 441, 449–50
social stratification, 185–86, 190–91, 193, 194
"socialization" of globe, 413–15, 418
"soft authoritarianism," 436, 437, 442
Somali pirates: attack on DPRK vessel by, 14–15
Song Hye-rim, 84, 97
South Korea (ROK): anti-Americanism in, 51; assistance to DPRK from, 13, 125, 126, 127, 145, 147, 148, 161, 201, 202, 208, 211, 236, 240–41, 272, 292, 314, 340, 388, 389–93, 403, 404, 405; Bush (George H.W.) administration and, 281, 282, 285; Bush (George W.) administration and, 19, 20, 292; Carter proposals concerning, 33; change in ROK attitudes and, 242, 243; China-DPRK relations and, 317, 320, 324–25, 345, 429; China relations with, 243, 244, 304, 317, 324–28, 330, 331, 334–35, 399, 460; civil defense exercises in, 287; civil

rights in, 33; criminal organizations in, 132; as democracy, 20, 60–61, 356; deterrence and, 215, 227, 231–32, 234, 235, 236, 240–41, 242, 243, 244, 246; DPRK assistance to, 398, 399; DPRK compared with, 463; DPRK confidence and, 47, 48; DPRK criticisms of, 45, 46; DPRK ideology and, 40, 59; DPRK kidnappings in, 185, 208, 232; DPRK peace settlement with, 20; DPRK provocations against, 274, 387, 392, 406, 407, 408; DPRK refugees in, 10, 179, 182, 200, 204, 208, 210, 425, 439, 443, 444–45, 460; DPRK survival and, 429; DPRK tunnels infiltrating, 56; DPRK views about, 34, 74, 161, 209; DPRK's threats against, 6, 12; economy of, 7, 12, 19–20, 31, 53, 87, 208, 388, 393–94, 400, 401, 405; financial crisis in, 394, 402; German unification as model for, 400–401; growth and development in, 117; hacking into DPRK Web site by, 450; industry in, 19–20, 22, 24, 31, 117; Japan and, 20, 371, 375, 376, 382, 383; Japan-DPRK relations and, 373; joint ventures between DPRK and, 148–49, 160, 389–93; Kennedy administration and, 31, 47; Kim family fall and, 307; Kim Il-sung and, 51–52; Kim Jong-il and, 85, 87–88, 345; Kim Jong-un and, 103–4; lack of criticism of DPRK by, 208; land reform and, 46–47; military coups in, 452; nationalism and, 34–37; natural disasters in, 398; Nixon administration and, 31–32; nuclear program of, 33–34; plans for collapse of Kim family and, 307; political upset/corruption in, 33, 40, 47, 51; prisoners of war and, 208; Reagan's modest initiative policy and, 279; rivalry in, 86–88; and ROK release of DPRK prisoners, 31; Russia and, 20, 87, 243, 282, 315, 326, 352–54, 355, 356, 357–58, 366, 399, 400; Russia-DPRK relations and, 267, 326, 365, 366; security commitments and, 30–31; Six-Party Talks and, 256, 257,

258, 259, 260, 262, 265–66, 292, 295,
304–5, 347, 368; as soft authoritarian
model, 442; terrorism and, 231–32;
trade and, 141, 146–47; true historic
seat of Korean ethnicity and, 35–36;
U.N. membership of, 283, 325, 352,
396; underground radicalism in, 40,
unification and, 40, 45, 47, 51–52, 147,
161, 386–426, 458, 460; U.S.-DPRK 1994
nuclear agreement and, 139; U.S.-DPRK
relations and, 89, 297; U.S. occupation
of, 37; U.S. relations with, 19, 20, 27,
30–32, 37, 44, 45, 46, 47, 58, 307, 358,
395, 418, 458; U.S. security assurances
to DPRK and, 304–5, 368; U.S. takeover
of, 71; U.S. troops in, 30, 32, 33, 52,
215, 281, 283, 284, 286, 287, 396; U.S.
unification discussions with, 403–5,
407–8; U.S. views about, 20; "Yusin"
system in, 33. See also specific person,
nation, or topic
South Korean police/military force: in
Afghanistan and Iraq, 20; Arab Spring
and, 440–41; communists in, 47;
creation of, 37; deterrence and, 215–22,
242; Korean nationalist narrative
and, 37; KPA compared with, 27,
53–54, 116, 215–22; on peacekeeping
missions, 20; reorientation of, 242,
243; ROK-DPRK relations and, 393;
Russian joint operations with, 358;
size of, 116, 215; spending for, 53,
215; unification and, 422, 423; U.S.-
ROK relations and, 27; weakness of,
27; Yeonpyeong Island shelling and,
440–41; Yŏsu rebellion and, 47. See
also deterrence
Southeast Asia, 48, 132, 134
special administrative and industrial
zones, 142–48
special economic zones (SEZs), 139–41,
359
special envoys, U.S., 10, 204, 206–7, 272,
451, 461
Stalin, Josef, 29, 39, 70, 72, 76, 77, 79, 105,
318, 321, 372

State Department, U.S.: DPRK illicit drug
activities report by, 134; DPRK nuclear
program and, 253, 261, 262, 269; DPRK
refugees in U.S. and, 203; DPRK-U.S.
bilateral meetings in New York and,
428; human rights in DPRK and, 204;
human trafficking report of, 136–37,
179; Kim Il-sung–Carter meeting and,
287; Kim Jong-il–Bush (George W.)
relations and, 292; Kim-Kanter
meeting and, 284–85; Obama "strategic
patience" strategy and, 294; Reagan's
modest initiative policy and, 278, 280;
Russian role in talks and, 346–47; and
sanctions against DPRK, 124; and
Somali pirate attack on DPRK vessel,
14–15. See also specific person
State Security Department, DPRK, 100,
452
"strategic patience" policy, Obama's, 274,
275, 294–98
students: Arab Spring and, 440, 442, 445,
450, 452; Chinese, 106; communications
technology and, 442, 450; domestic
disturbances by, 209, 452; DPRK, 172,
431, 440, 442, 445, 450, 452; as gulag
prisoners, 172; Marxist-Leninism
among, 26; ROK, 26, 40, 51, 74, 209,
414–15; underground radicalism of, 40;
unification and, 414–15
Suh Dae-sook, 67, 68
suicides, 157, 197, 425, 447, 453
Sunch'ŏn Vinylon Complex, 119–20, 154
Sunshine Policy, ROK: accomplishments
of, 388, 389–93, 407; assistance to
DPRK and, 201, 340, 388; controversy
about, 387–88; DPRK corruption and,
127; DPRK economy and, 412; DPRK
nuclear program and, 258, 272, 387,
392, 403; DPRK reform and, 59, 146,
156, 387, 394, 403; duration of, 387;
end of, 272, 340; failure of, 59; focus/
purpose of, 59, 387, 394, 412; Japan-
DPRK relations and, 375, 378; Kim
Dae-jung as father of, 161; Kim Dae-
jung and Kim Jong-il summit and, 388;

Sunshine Policy, ROK (*continued*)
Lee Myung-bak and, 404, 405;
Moonshine policy and, 147, 148, 149,
151, 153; naming of, 387; Roh Moo-
hyun and, 387; Samsung and, 80;
unification and, 161, 386–94, 396,
401–3, 408, 414, 417; U.S.-ROK
relations and, 292
"supernotes," DPRK, 8, 134–35, 136, 264
Supreme People's Assembly, DPRK, 5, 42,
44, 83, 91, 114–15, 285
Sweden, 2–3, 137, 334
Switzerland: Kim Jong-un in, 16, 100–103,
104–5
Syria, 17, 205, 226, 229, 233, 234, 247–49,
429, 433–35, 436, 437, 445

T'aech'ŏn power station, 119, 253
Taep'odong missiles, 227, 228, 237, 267,
273, 289, 300, 372, 375
Taiwan, 48, 76, 132, 134, 135, 292, 318,
320, 323
Tamil Tigers, 86, 232
Tangshan Iron and Steel, 337–38
Tan'gun, myth of, 35–36
Taro, Aso, 345, 382
Team America (movie), 16, 64–65
Team Spirit (ROK-U.S. military exercises),
281, 283, 307, 399
television, 4–5, 436, 441
terrorism: Bush (George H.W.)
administration and, 281; Bush
(George W.) "axis of evil" comment
and, 255; deterrence and, 231–33, 237;
DPRK illicit activities and, 132; DPRK
nuclear program and, 233; and DPRK
sales to terrorists, 256; DPRK as state
sponsor of, 269, 293, 312, 384; and
DPRK as U.S. priority, 456; Reagan
administration and, 279; ROK-DPRK
relations and, 231–32; Six-Party Talks
and, 263. *See also specific incident*
Thailand, 81, 96, 132, 179, 185
Three-Year Plan (1954–56), 23, 44,
113–14
Time magazine: Kim Jong-il as "Asian

of the Year" in, 94; USS *Pueblo* article
in, 54
Tobey, William, 256, 347
Toloraya, Georgy, 277, 356, 364
tourist, Kumgang Mountain: shooting of,
392, 407
trade, DPRK: bad decisions and, 112,
113, 122–23, 124–25, 141, 145–47; with
China, 112, 124–25, 145–46, 316, 318,
319–20, 324, 327–28, 334, 335, 337–38,
339, 340; Cold War and, 25, 112; famine
and, 190, 193; with Japan, 372, 383;
neojuche revivalism and, 61; Reagan's
modest initiative policy and, 280–81;
reform and, 140, 141; ROK-DPRK
relations and, 87, 140–41, 146–47; with
Russia, 112, 122–23, 124, 128, 190,
348, 350–51, 355, 357, 400; sanctions
concerning, 124–25, 244, 335; U.N.
resolutions concerning, 335; U.S.-
DPRK nuclear agreement and, 125;
U.S. security assurances to DPRK and,
312, 313
transportation: unification and, 420–21.
See also railroads
Treasury Department, U.S., 264, 265–66,
333
Tunisia, 14, 431, 432, 433, 434, 435, 436,
440, 442, 445
21 Club (New York City), 427, 428

UNICEF, 127, 128, 198–99
unification: Arab Spring in DPRK and,
430; avoiding, 393–94; cost of, 402,
415, 417, 420, 425; cows and, 386, 391;
current discussions about, 403–12;
discourses about, 395–403; DPRK
missiles and, 406, 409, 411, 417, 418;
DPRK nuclear program and, 387,
392, 400, 403, 404, 405, 406, 408, 409,
411, 412, 416, 417, 419, 424; DPRK
provocations and, 387, 392, 406, 407,
408, 416–17; DPRK reform and, 387,
394, 403, 410–11; "the end of history"
and, 408; Five Policy Principles and,
458, 460–61; German unification as

model for, 400–401, 423–24; as "hard
landing" or "soft landing," 419–26;
human rights and, 389–90, 404, 405,
406, 408, 412; ideas not power and,
415; ideology and, 40, 46, 410, 411, 412;
"in my lifetime" concept and, 417–19;
instability of DPRK leadership and,
394, 409, 412–13, 416; international
conferences about, 414–15, 418;
international role in, 413–15, 426; Kim
Il-sung and, 47, 51–52; Kim Jong-il's
death and, 408–9; Kim Jong-un and,
409–10; "Korea discount" and, 416–17;
Korean War and, 396; land reform and,
46–47; Moonshine policy and, 403;
new paradigm for, 412–17; openness
of discussions about, 408–12, 413;
opportunities and, 415–16; population
control and, 422–23; as pragmatic, 412–
13; preparation for, 458, 460–62; ROK-
DPRK joint projects and, 389–93, 403;
social aspects of, 424–25; "socialization"
of globe and, 413–15, 418; Sunshine
Policy and, 161, 386–94, 396, 401–3,
408, 414, 417; tasks of, 418, 419–26; tax
for, 413, 418, 425; uncertainties of, 416;
U.S.-ROK discussions about, 403–5,
407–8; zero-sum mentality and, 395–96,
397–98, 399, 413, 415
Unification Church, 147, 390, 391
United Nations High Commissioner for
    Refugees (UNHCR), 178, 180–81, 183,
    184, 203, 210, 461
United Nations (U.N.): assistance to
    DPRK from, 125, 126, 146, 159, 340;
    Bush-Megumi issue and, 384; *Cheonan*
    incident and, 334–35; Department
    of Human Affairs of, 128; DPRK
    collapse scenario and, 307; DPRK
    membership in, 283, 396; DPRK
    missile program and, 273, 383; DPRK
    nuclear program and, 252, 258, 259,
    261, 267–68, 273–74, 305, 335, 343,
    362, 364, 366–67, 383; and elections
    in Korea, 71; EVERREADY Plan and,
    31; famine in DPRK and, 196; "Grand
Bargain" proposal of, 404; human
    rights resolutions in, 207; Japan-
    DPRK relations and, 383; Korean
    independence and, 70; and migrations
    out of DPRK, 178; PSI and, 306–7;
    Refugee Convention (1967) of, 178, 183,
    184; ROK-DPRK relations and, 243–44;
    ROK as member of, 283, 325, 352, 396;
    Russian role in, 347; and sanctions
    against DPRK, 3, 6, 229, 236, 237, 244,
    252, 267–68, 273–74, 275, 286, 296,
    303, 306, 335, 343, 454, 456; unification
    and, 413
United States: assistance for DPRK
    from, 126, 147, 160, 201, 204, 205,
    207, 236, 256, 264, 270, 289, 293, 294;
    blame for DPRK nuclear program
    on, 275–98, 333–34, 367, 409; China-
    DPRK relations and, 429; Chinese
    ambassador Cha discussion about U.S.-
    DPRK relations, 137–38; conundrum
    concerning, 305–10; deterrence
    and, 212, 213, 215, 217, 218–19, 221,
    223–25, 227, 228, 229–30, 237–38,
    239–40, 241, 242–46; DPRK bilaterial
    negotiations with, 10, 294, 295, 302,
    369–70, 427–28; and DPRK fear of
    U.S. invasion, 11–12; DPRK hatred
    of, 161; DPRK as second-tier problem
    for, 429–30, 455–56; elections of 2000
    in, 290; form for addressing DPRK
    leaders by, 288; human rights policies
    of, 203–7; image in DPRK of, 74; Kim
    Il-sung comments about imperialism
    of, 49–51; Kim Jong-il views about,
    85–86; Korean nationalist narrative
    and, 37; and "obstacles" to DPRK-
    U.S. relations, 284; PLA delegation
    in, 330–31; real desires of DPRK and,
    298–305; "relative crisis indifference"
    syndrome of, 430, 455–56; security
    guarantees for DPRK of, 11, 298–314,
    367–69; survival of DPRK and, 429–30;
    withdrawal of nuclear weapons by, 283.
    *See also specific person, organization,
    nation, or topic*

United States Agency for International Development (USAID), 19, 201, 205
United States Forces Korea (USFK), 219
urban poor, DPRK: as source of discontent, 453, 454–55
USS *James E. Williams*, 14–15
USS *Pueblo*, 52–53, 54–55

Vietnam, 48, 49, 50, 143, 153, 179, 180, 189, 230, 351, 382, 386
Vietnam War, 21, 27, 31, 32
Voice of America, 205, 415

wages, 149, 154, 155, 156, 158, 389–90, 417, 424, 425
wealth: causes of Arab Spring and, 432–33, 437
weapons: DPRK as trafficker in, 16–17, 86, 232, 273, 335, 456, 457
Wen Jiabao, 333, 335
Woodrow Wilson Center, 30, 71
Woodward, Bob, 203, 205
workers, DPRK: Arab Spring and, 438–39, 447; bad decisions and, 114, 126–27, 145, 149, 155–56; Ch'ŏllima movement and, 44, 106, 114; famine and, 191; Kim Il-sung and, 75, 114; Kim Jong-il and, 106; Moonshine policy and, 149; reform and, 145, 155–56, 411; ROK-DPRK joint projects and, 389–90; social stratification and, 186, 191; unification and, 389–90, 424, 425. *See also* North Korean Workers' Party; wages
World Bank, 8, 233, 386, 437, 442
World Festival of Youth and Students, 120–21
World Food Programme (WFP), 93, 125–26, 128, 159, 194, 197, 198, 200–203, 205, 293, 328, 339, 340, 375
World Health Organization (WHO), 128, 166

World War II: impact on Korea of, 22, 23, 26, 110–11; Japan-DPRK unfinished business from, 372; Japan in, 22, 23, 68, 69, 70, 111, 233, 343; Kim Il-sung role in, 66; nationalism and, 36; prisoners of war during, 233; Russia-Japan relations during, 348
Wuhan Iron and Steel, 337–38

Yeltsin, Boris, 356, 358, 359, 360, 362
Yemen, 229, 431, 433, 434, 435, 436, 437
Yeonpyeong Island: DPRK shelling of, 103–4, 159, 235–36, 237, 238, 240, 241, 242, 243–44, 245, 296, 335, 362, 406, 407, 416, 440; ROK exercises on, 243–44
Yi Hu-rak, 26, 34, 396–97
Yi Tong-hwi, 69, 72
Yi Yŏng-guk, 81–82
Yodŏk concentration camp, 174–75, 177
Yongbyon Nuclear Facility: Bush (George H.W.) administration concerns about, 281; Clinton administration concerns about, 89, 285–86, 300; defueling/dismantlement of, 269, 270, 271, 343; Kim Jong-il statue at, 11, 79; monitoring of, 273; nuclear crises and, 89, 252, 253, 254, 255, 256, 260, 269, 270, 271; origins of nuclear program and, 249, 250, 251; real desires of DPRK and, 301; ROK-DPRK relations and, 272; Russia-DPRK relations and, 363; as urananium-based facility, 274; U.S. contingency plans concerning, 6, 89, 286, 287, 291, 363, 455
youth, 199, 434–35, 438–39, 440
Yuk Yŏng-su, 56, 398

Zagoria, Donald, 427, 428
zero-sum mentality, 395–96, 397–98, 399, 413, 415
Zhou Enlai, 32, 49, 321